THE COUNTERREVOLUTION

OF SLAVERY

Copy of the secession banner that hung at the South Carolina secession
convention. (Reprinted from John Amasa May and Joan Reynolds,
South Carolina Secedes [Columbia, S.C., 1960], 80)

The Counterrevolution of

Slavery

Politics and Ideology in
Antebellum South Carolina

MANISHA SINHA

The University of North Carolina Press | Chapel Hill and London

© 2000 The University of North Carolina Press
All rights reserved

Designed by April Leidig-Higgins
Set in New Baskerville by Keystone Typesetting, Inc.
Manufactured in the United States of America

The paper in this book meets the guidelines for permanence
and durability of the Committee on Production Guidelines
for Book Longevity of the Council on Library Resources.

Parts of Chapters 5 and 6 have appeared earlier in "Judicial
Nullification: The South Carolinian Movement to Reopen
the African Slave Trade in the 1850s," in Maria Diedrich,
Henry Louis Gates Jr., and Carl Pederson, eds., *Black
Imagination and the Middle Passage* (New York: Oxford
University Press, 1999), 127–43.

Library of Congress Cataloging-in-Publication Data
Sinha, Manisha.
The counterrevolution of slavery: politics and ideology in
antebellum South Carolina / Manisha Sinha.
p. cm.
Includes bibliographical references (p.   ) and index.
ISBN 0-8078-2571-9 (cloth: alk. paper) —
ISBN 0-8078-4884-0 (pbk.: alk. paper)
1. South Carolina — Politics and government — 1775–1865.
2. Slavery — Political aspects — South Carolina — History —
19th century. 3. Slaveholders — South Carolina — Political
activity. 4. Secession — South Carolina. 5. Political culture —
South Carolina — History — 19th century. I. Title.
F273.S64   2000
975.7′03 — dc21   00-032590

04 03 02 01 00   5 4 3 2 1

FOR MY PARENTS,

Srinivas Kumar Sinha and Premini Sinha

CONTENTS

Acknowledgments xi

INTRODUCTION

The Problem of South Carolina Revisited 1

ONE

The Genesis of the Political Ideology of Slavery 9

TWO

Nullification 33

THREE

The Discourse of Southern Nationalism 63

FOUR

South Carolina and the First Secession Crisis 95

FIVE

The Carolinian Movement to
Reopen the African Slave Trade 125

SIX

Judicial Nullification 153

SEVEN

The Coming of Secession 187

EIGHT

Secession 221

EPILOGUE

The Counterrevolution of Slavery 255

Notes 259

Bibliography of Primary Sources 323

Index 343

CONTENTS

MAPS AND TABLES

MAPS

1. South Carolina Districts and Parishes in 1860   11
2. South Carolina Black Belt, 1830   46
3. South Carolina Black Belt, 1850   118

TABLES

1. South Carolina Population, 1820–1860   12
2. Election for the State Legislature, 1832   45
3. Election for the Southern Congress, 1851   119

ACKNOWLEDGMENTS

As anyone who has written a book knows, the people who help alleviate a lonely and usually arduous task deserve special gratitude. I would like to thank the librarians and staff of Columbia University, the University of South Carolina, the South Carolina Department of Archives and History, the South Carolina Historical Society, the Charleston Library Society, Duke University, the University of North Carolina, Chapel Hill, the Library of Congress, the American Antiquarian Society, the College of the Holy Cross, Harvard University, and the University of Massachusetts, Amherst, for their invaluable help and assistance. I would like to thank Dr. Allen Stokes and his staff at the South Caroliniana Library for putting up with the Indian woman who virtually set up camp in their premises. I must single out Mrs. Thelma Hayes for her cheerfulness and patience. Bob Henry from the computer laboratory at Holy Cross deserves special thanks for helping me to design the maps.

The Institute of Southern Studies, University of South Carolina, provided me with much needed institutional support and with luxurious accommodations at Gibbes Court while I was doing research. For that I would like to thank its erstwhile director, Dr. Walter Edgar, and secretary, Ms. Tibby Dozier. I would also like to thank Mark Malvasi and Professor Clyde Wilson for allowing me to go through the unpublished Calhoun papers. It gives me great pleasure to thank Omi and Binu Hasija of Charleston and Indu and Nikki Singh of Fairfax, Virginia, for keeping up the traditions of Indian hospitality in their adopted country. And I would like to thank my aunt and her husband, Abha and Amit Sawhney, for always welcoming me into their home in New York City.

Several sources of financial support helped me to research and write the book and the dissertation on which it is based. A year-long writing grant from the Mrs. Giles Whiting Foundation for the Humanities, administered by Columbia University, helped me to write the dissertation. A fellowship from the W. E. B. Du Bois Institute for Afro-American Research at Harvard University, a Rockefeller Post-Doctoral Fellowship in the Humanities from the Institute for the Arts and Humanities at the University of North Carolina at Chapel Hill, and a research fellowship from the American Philosophical Society in Philadelphia helped me to convert an unwieldy dissertation into a book manuscript. I would particularly like to express my gratitude to Henry Louis Gates Jr. of Harvard University and James Peacock of the University of North Carolina at Chapel Hill for their support and generosity. I would also like to thank my research assistants at the Du Bois Institute, Greg Supriano and Susan Wyly.

Several people have commented on this manuscript and its earlier incarnations. I would like to thank Elizabeth Blackmar and the history dissertation seminar at Columbia University for going through a rather large draft of my first two chapters. Patrick Williams and Nancy Cohen provided especially useful comments. Drew Faust, Elizabeth Fox-Genovese, and Eric Walther raised good questions on the introduction and certain sections of the book. Bertram Wyatt-Brown wrote a lengthy criticism of the manuscript for which I am grateful. Michael P. Johnson and Peter Coclanis commented perceptively on the manuscript for the University of North Carolina Press and forced me to clarify my arguments and learn the virtues of brevity. It has been a pleasure to work with Lewis Bateman at the University of North Carolina Press. His vast experience with the publishing business and adept handling of the manuscript have made this a considerably better book.

I owe my greatest intellectual debt to two of my former teachers at Columbia. A very special acknowledgment goes out to Barbara Fields James, whose understanding of southern history I can only hope to acquire some day. Barbara has been a great source of intellectual inspiration and friendship from the start. Her wonderfully crafted criticism of the dissertation was my template for working on the book manuscript. Above all, I would like to thank my adviser and mentor, Eric Foner. It has been my enormous privilege to study with a historian whose works I so admire and respect. Eric read through countless versions of the manuscript, provided detailed and brilliant criticisms, and has supported this project from start to finish. I am sure he will be amused to learn that he is the embodiment of the original Indian concept of a "guru": a scholar, a teacher, and a humanist par excellence.

I would like to thank my colleagues at the University of Massachusetts, Amherst, for their support: John Bracey, Esther Terry, Ernie Allen, Robert Wolff, Femi Richards, Mike Thelwell, Bill Strickland, and Steve Tracy of Afro-American studies and Bruce Laurie, Kathy Peiss, John Higginson, Joye Bowman, and Leo Richards of the history department. Members of the Five College Social History Seminar, especially David Blight of Amherst College, provided thoughtful comments and encouragement. Several current and former graduate students have helped me to write a better book, especially those who read and commented on the manuscript in my Politics of Slavery seminar. They are: Shawn Alexander, Patrick Crim, Germaine Etienne, Julie Gallagher, Richard Gassan, Peter Lau, Chris Lehman, Dinah Mayo, Tanya Mears, Ken Miller, Carolyn Powell, Andrew Rosa, James Ross, and R. Paul Spring.

Finally, I would like to thank my family. My parents, to whom this book is lovingly dedicated and whose passion for history we all share, for everything. My brother, Yash Sinha; my sister-in-law, Girija Sinha; my brother-in-law, Eulogio Oset; and my niece and nephews, Anjali and Raul Oset Sinha, Ambuj and Vinayak Sinha, for their love and support. My sister, Meena Sinha, for giving me timely stylistic pointers on an early draft of the manuscript. My brother-in-law, Clement Hawes, for teaching me to appreciate American English and for reading a final version of the manuscript on his research trip to Ireland. My sister, Mrinalini Sinha, for taking time off her work in South Asian history to read through the entire manuscript, for making astute suggestions on authorship and the production of historical knowledge, and for being an unfailing source of encouragement. My husband, Karsten Stueber, for detecting all the logical fallacies in my arguments with the keen eye of a philosopher, for his computer skills, for helping me at every stage of the manuscript, and for all that life has been since I met him in graduate school. I cannot imagine having accomplished anything, including this book, without him. Our darling son, Sheel, whose birth definitely delayed the completion of our books but who has made our lives wonderful and fulfilling in countless ways. At the tender age of two he is already determined to "write books," and I can only hope that this book inspires others to do the same.

THE COUNTERREVOLUTION

OF SLAVERY

The Problem of
South Carolina Revisited

Antebellum Carolinian political history can perhaps tell us more about the creation of the Confederacy than the history of any other southern state. South Carolina's slaveholding politicians not only pioneered in elaborating an ideological defense of racial slavery but also developed the political theories that justified disunion: nullification, state sovereignty, state ownership of national territories, and the constitutional right to secession. Given the crucial role Carolinian slaveholders played in the rise of southern separatism and proslavery thought, it is surprising that we still lack a comprehensive and unified historical account of their political brinkmanship. Some of the best political histories of pre–Civil War South Carolina focus mainly on individual events. Recent works in Carolinian history look at only certain sections of the state and either undermine or ignore the state's exceptionality. As one historian has observed, "the need for a monograph which persuasively bridges the generational distance between nullifiers and secessionists remains clear."[1] An analysis of politics and ideology in antebellum South Carolina would not only fill a historical void but also answer important questions on the origins and nature of southern nationalism and the coming of the Civil War.

This book examines the political history of South Carolina from 1828 to 1860, or from nullification to secession. It focuses on four events: the Nullification Crisis of 1828–1834; the first secession crisis over the Compromise of 1850; the movement to reopen the African slave trade in the 1850s; and lastly, South Carolina's secession in 1860. Each of these historical events is indicative of Carolinian planter politicians' leading role in the formulation of the ideological and political discourse of slavery that precipitated secession. It is perhaps proper to focus on the sectional crises to understand secession and the coming of the Civil War rather than mundane local politics that had little to do with the growth of southern separatism. The conservative and novel substance of the political ideology of slavery must be distinguished from the everyday rhetoric of representative politics that has so caught historians' fancy. This book, therefore, does not deal with issues in state politics whose connection to secession was remote. Instead, it focuses on moments of crisis when Carolinian planter politicians articulated the rationale for southern independence. Secession was a departure from politics as usual, and South Carolina was known for its exceptional commitment to the politics of slavery and secession.

The book also restates the problem of Carolinian exceptionalism. South Carolina was not representative of the South. Its peculiarly anti-democratic political structure, statewide plantation belt, and lack of a two-party system set it apart from most other southern states. At the same time, these very features put the state's slaveholding aristocracy at the cutting edge of southern separatism. This book explores the special role that Carolinian planter politicians carved out for themselves, as the leading proponents of a slavery-based southern identity. They were preeminent propagandists for secession and initiated the breakup of the Union in 1860. The state's slaveholding elite could lead the secession movement precisely because they were exceptional in their early and firm adherence to the cause of slavery. South Carolina's so-called political extremism did not make it irrelevant and cannot be explained away as simply another variant of national politics.[2] Carolinian planter politicians were not in the political mainstream, but as separatist agitators they defined the issues of the sectional crisis. They lost many political battles but they ultimately won the more significant ideological war in much of the South.

South Carolina was exceptional not because it was different from, but because it was ahead of, its sister states. Since nullification, the Carolina doctrine of slavery and separatism acted as an alternative to the ideals of Jacksonian democracy and the Second Party System. By the 1850s, most lower south states started resembling South Carolina in more ways than one. The disintegration of the party system, the ideological dominance of the politics of slavery, and the secession of a majority of the southern states represented the victory of Carolina-style politics. Secession represented the overthrow rather than the fulfillment of Jacksonian democracy and the Second Party System in the Old South.[3] To recognize the leadership position of South Carolina in the secession movement is thus also to reckon with the nature of southern nationalism.

Contrary to recent works on southern history, this book illustrates that the growth of a distinct, separatist ideology based on the values of slavery and a rigorous critique of democracy, rather than democratic and republican principles, animated Carolinian politics and the movement for an independent southern nation. According to the republican school of southern political historians, secession was an allegedly democratic movement and the outcome of a widespread republican fear of enslavement rather than a bid to save slavery. The presence of racial slavery not only left untouched the supposedly democratic nature of southern society and polity but actually furthered southern white men's republican love of liberty and independence. The relevance of racial slavery is confined to a republican cosmology in which it apparently merely fortified fears of political slavery among southern white men. The republican thesis deflects attention from racial slavery to fears of political slavery among white men and minimizes class differences within slave society by ignoring slaveholders' special stake in the institution of slavery and planters' political power. This interpretation has been extended to upcountry South Carolina. According to Lacy Ford white South Carolinians fought to preserve "slave-labor republicanism" and the state seceded "because the dominant ideal in her society was not the planter ideal or the slaveholding ideal, but the old 'country republican' ideal of personal independence, given peculiar fortification by the use of black slaves as a mud-sill class."[4]

Surely slavery had a far greater political significance than its rather benign place in the republican framework would imply. If southern slaveholders dreaded the very idea of slavery, how could they defend it as the basis of all good society and government? In the republican view of slave society, southern white men, especially slaveholders, literally and figuratively lived in a black-and-white world. In this Manichean world, they were despots as far as black people were concerned, and republicans in a white world of politics. The republican thesis posits an unnatural dichotomy between the material and political history of the slave South. We cannot write off the effects of racial slavery on the nature of southern politics by maintaining that it was confined to African Americans who were excluded from the formal political arena. Scholars of the sectional conflict have studied the rise of slavery as the main topic of contention between the North and South,[5] but few have discussed the impact of racial slavery on the nature of southern politics.

Some historians have argued that southern slaveholders and planters developed an extremely conservative and elitist version of republicanism that rested on the justification of slavery and an antidemocratic sensibility. Not surprisingly, much of the work on the southern variant of conservative republicanism has been done in the context of Carolinian history.[6] Indeed, as discussed by scholars like J. G. A. Pocock, republican thought cuts a broad swath across western history from Plato and Aristotle to the rise of American republicanism, and could probably include any number of ideological positions. Republicanism contained enough conservative features to allow for such a development: a belief in mixed government and an aversion to an unmixed democracy, exclusion of the nonpropertied and dependent from the body politic, and the idea that representation must be based on property. However, republicanism has also been seen as the distinct class ideology of nonplantation-belt yeoman farmers rooted in the political economy of independent petty producers and not in slavery. Steven Hahn effectively grounds this yeomanry's political accommodation to, and differences from, the regime of planters and the roots of the post–Civil War populist revolt against the incursion of the market within this worldview.[7] Drew Faust has suggested that perhaps a common ideology of republicanism and southern evangelicalism mediated between the democratic sensibilities and the more hierarchical and conservative worldview of different classes in southern society. Stephanie McCurry's recent work on lowcountry South Carolinian yeomen attempts to reconcile the conservative and democratic aspects of republican ideology. She examines the underside of republicanism, the dependence of women and slaves that made the independence of white men possible. But when it comes to explaining secession, McCurry also uses the conventional republican thesis in southern political history and makes it out to be primarily a yeomen's fight for white liberty and independence, with black slavery as merely the inconsequential ideological addendum.[8]

The extension of the republican paradigm to antebellum southern history is part of the virtually hegemonic interpretive status of republicanism in contemporary American historiography.[9] Historians have constructed republicanism on the one hand as a sort of neoconsensus framework and on the other hand, more fruitfully, as an alternative tradition of radicalism that allowed small farmers, artisans, and workers to develop a coherent critique of an emerging capitalist society. For reasons of chronology, evidence, interpretation, and semantics, I have purposely avoided using the currently fashionable republican framework. This book explores antebellum Carolinian planter politicians' formulation of a political ideology of slavery and separatism, which must be distinguished from revolutionary thought, Jeffersonian republicanism, and a petty producer worldview. We must also differentiate between the republican rhetoric employed routinely by almost all antebellum Americans and the conservative proslavery ideology that gave meaning and purpose to southern nationalism. My refusal to use the republican framework is based on what I see as a burgeoning republican neoconsensus view of American history, which subsumes conflicting and widely differing political positions and ideologies under the rubric of republicanism. Such a framework has particularly unfortunate repercussions for the history of the slave South and the Civil War, which some scholars now view as the result of a mere bifurcation of republican ideology.[10]

The distinctiveness of southern nationalist discourse in South Carolina lay in the fact that the vindication of racial slavery led to the questioning of the ideals of universal liberty, equality, and democracy that lay at the heart of the antebellum American republic and, in the end, of the republic itself. In exploring this new slavery-centered conservative and antidemocratic discourse, I have avoided some of the old debates on the nature of southern polity and society. I would hesitate using the terms capitalist, noncapitalist, or precapitalist to describe a hybrid conservative ideology that defended bound labor with as much vigor as the notion of property. However, I do insist that the political ideology of slavery be seen as developing in opposition to rather than as a variant of political liberalism.[11] Nor would I characterize this ideology as simply race or class based. Scholars who posit a dualism between a race-based versus a class-based interpretation of the slave South or who argue that race acted as a substitute for class divisions quite simply miss the point. It should come as no surprise that the defense of racial slavery gave rise to a profoundly reactionary worldview.[12] Racial and, one might add, gender inequality were glaring exceptions to the alleged norm of equality for many Americans, but they were part of the norm of inequality for most antebellum Carolinian planters and slaveholders.

My study of Carolinian politics concentrates on the men who formulated this conservative and antidemocratic political ideology, prominent politicians and propagandists of slavery and secession. The nature of southern nationalism can be understood through the words and actions of those who initiated and defined the secession movement. To argue that secession was a yeomen's movement, when a majority of the men who held political office and led the movement for a separate southern nation were planters or substantial slaveholders, seems both analytically faulty and factually incorrect. Slaveholding farmers and the plantation-belt yeomanry in general were certainly avid followers of the planter elite, as South Carolina's and the Lower South's pre–Civil War political history so amply demonstrates, but they were neither the primary instigators of secession nor the formulators of its political ideology. Carolinian planter politicians were successful in leading their state and, one might argue, the rest of the Lower South to secession because slavery and slaveholding were widespread in these areas.[13]

In antebellum South Carolina, the political was preeminently the sphere of the powerful and the articulate, and I have chosen to explore this world. Only by understanding how ruling classes maintain and reproduce political power can we comprehend how issues of national import reverberate in the lives of all classes and groups in society and also how the actions and position of these classes were relevant to the political events of the day. This perspective on Carolinian political history would take into account not only the political ascendancy of its slaveowning planter class and the reasons why the plantation-belt yeomanry supported secession but also the enslavement and political disfranchisement of African Americans. My view of political history is thus different from the traditional top-down approach and the so-called new political history, which focuses on partisan and ethnic loyalties and tends to employ a neorevisionist perspective on the Civil War by downplaying the issue of slavery in the sectional conflict.[14]

The book is structured primarily as a narrative of events organized chronologically and thematically. My analysis of particular events and Carolinian politics is embedded in the narrative, which traces the rise and development of the discourse of slavery and separatism in antebellum South Carolina. The terms "ideology" and "discourse" are used interchangeably and in a nonjargonistic sense. They imply not only a formal set of beliefs but also, more generally, a dominant language of political meaning. The fact that Carolinian planter politicians were in a position to assign political meaning to events or to construct a specific political ideology was pivotal to their hegemony.[15] Qualitative evidence thus outweighs quantitative material, but the book also analyzes the results of crucial elections and voting patterns in the legislature. I have followed the traditional definition of a planter as an owner of over twenty slaves, and I use the term "planter politician" to refer to planters active in politics. I have usually followed contemporary usage to refer to different classes and groups of people: slaves, free people of color, yeoman farmers, mechanics, and merchants. I employ the terms "separatism," "sectionalism," and "nationalism" without entering the debate over whether the slave South developed a national identity. Instead, I argue that the politics of separatism in South Carolina was the basis of southern nationalism.[16] Finally, the bibliography includes only primary sources cited in the text. Full citations of secondary sources are available in the footnotes. I have used short titles of pamphlets, many of which have titles that would occupy half a page. The reader should have no difficulty in identifying them.

This book is about politics and ideology in antebellum South Carolina. Social or economic history is pertinent only when it illuminates its main focus. The culture of honor, I argue, cannot be understood apart from most white Carolinians' political commitment to the institution of slavery. Nor can the concept of honor be used as a substitute for slavery in understanding southern politics.[17] The economic dimension of nullification, the movement to reopen the African slave trade, and the slavery expansion issue was connected to slaveholders' overriding fears for the safety and perpetuity of slavery. Issues such as economic diversification and agricultural reform were nonstarters, especially after the cotton boom of the 1850s.[18] Railroads, internal improvements, and banks — staples of national partisan politics — had little to do with the politics of secession. I do not agree with the conclusion of some historians that angst over economic development propelled the South toward disunion.[19]

The reactionary and antidemocratic discourse of slavery and separatism, developed by antebellum Carolinian slaveholders, amply bears out W. E. B. Du Bois's argument. He had noted long ago that the presence of slavery had emasculated American democracy. The age of democratic revolutions inaugurated by the American revolution made the existence of slavery and servile labor questionable for the first time in western history.[20] Whatever revolutionary precedent some slaveholders evoked to justify and legitimize their fight for a separate southern nation, their movement was fundamentally of a different ideological cast. Their cause was a part of the tide of reaction that followed the revolutionary era in the Atlantic world. Like European conservatives who bemoaned the spread of democracy and the alleged excesses of the age of revolution, they sought to safeguard racial slavery from the onset of forces that defined modernity. In this sense, the counterrevolution inaugurated by them was long in the making and encompassed more than a reaction to the election of Abraham Lincoln.[21] One might also point out that the true inheritors of the revolutionary fervor of this era were not the slaveholders but the slaves of the New World.[22] Carolinian slaveholders were bent on counterrevolution, not revolution.

1

The Genesis of the
Political Ideology of Slavery

Domestic servitude is the policy of our country.
— BRUTUS [Robert J. Turnbull], 1827

By the dawn of the antebellum era, the southern half of the United States had given rise to a distinct slave society. More than any other southern state, South Carolina represented the coming of age of American slavery. As in Virginia, slavery had roots stretching far back to the colonial period, and as in the new southwestern states, the cotton boom of the late eighteenth and early nineteenth centuries made racial slavery an expansive rather than a declining institution. In South Carolina, slavery lay at the heart of a relatively unified plantation economy presided over by a statewide planter class. A majority of the population were slaves, and in no other state did the nonplantation-belt yeomanry lie more at the fringes of slave society.[1]

On the eve of the nullification crisis, the state's planter class was poised not only to take over the leadership of the slave South from Virginia but also to formulate a new brand of slavery-based politics that would culminate thirty years later in the creation of the southern Confederacy. They had already played a historic role in the formation of the Constitution as the most articulate and fervent champions of slavery and opponents of democratic measures. Lowcountry South Carolina had been a stronghold of proslavery Federalism in the early republic. The state had long represented a conservative alternative to the republicanism of Virginian slaveholders.[2]

It was neither periodic bouts of lunacy nor an adherence to the tenets of an archaic republicanism but, rather, the unfolding of the political ideology of slavery during the nullification crisis, that can best explain the sectional extremism of antebellum South Carolina. Despite the establishment of some important precedents during the Missouri crisis and the Hartford convention, the idea of nullification or a state veto of federal law presented the first substantive challenge to the survival of the American republic. Historians have rightly looked to South Carolina for the seeds of southern separatism. However, while they have discussed the emergence of the issue of slavery with the tariff question, they have not sufficiently shown us how slavery affected the very nature of Carolinian political discourse.[3] Indeed, some recent historians have argued that nullification had little to do with slavery and that South Carolina's repudiation of the tariff was an exercise in the defense of republican liberty.[4]

But Carolinian planter politicians' attempt to nullify federal tariff laws encompassed a rousing vindication of slavery and the interests of a slaveholding minority in a democratic republic. The Carolina doctrine of nullification was the political expression of a self-conscious and assertive slaveholding planter class that deviated significantly from the republican heritage of the country and the growing democratization of national politics. Couched in the language of states' rights and constitutionalism, the nullifiers, led by John C. Calhoun, poured new wine into old bottles. They were political innovators. In their rejection of majority rule and democracy and in their aggressive defense of slavery, nullifiers articulated a political ideology that owed its inspiration to the values of a mature slave society.

South Carolina's peculiar social geography allowed its planter politicians to emerge as the spokesmen of a new slavery-centered political discourse. Geographically divided into three broad sections — the lowcountry, the middle country, and the upcountry, which lay above the fall line — the state contained a very small mountainous region; most of its terrain formed no barrier to the spread of plantation agriculture. By the turn of the nineteenth century, with the rise of short-staple cotton cultivation, plantation slavery spread from the lowcountry to the piedmont. This development undermined internecine sectional divisions, which spurred democratic reforms in the rest of the South, and marked the emergence of a new slaveholding elite in the interior. In South Carolina, the non-plantation belt dominated by slaveless yeoman farmers was extremely small and continued to shrink throughout the antebellum era. Significantly, a majority of the Carolinian yeomanry lived in the plantation belt, and many participated in the slave economy as slave owners, slave hirers, overseers, and patrollers. By 1850, the growth of plantation slavery had converted the state into one gigantic black belt. And even though the

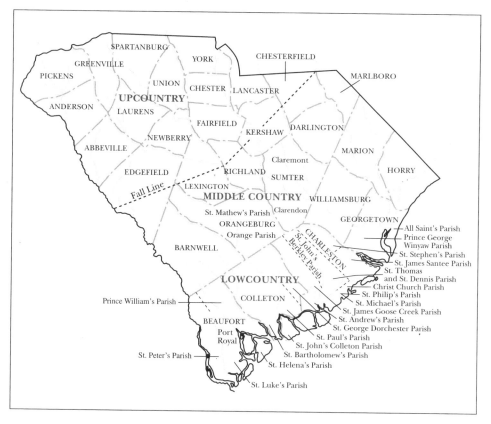

MAP 1. South Carolina Districts and Parishes in 1860
Source: William A. Schaper, "Sectionalism and Representation in South
Carolina," *Annual Report of the American Historical Association* (Washington,
1900–1901), facing p. 245.

lowcountry, with its high concentration of slaves, wealth, and large rice
and sea island cotton plantations, differed from the rest of the state,
South Carolina achieved a unified slave economy and society virtually
unique in the South.[5]

Demographically also, the expansion of slavery and slaveholding made
South Carolina a slave state par excellence. The slowing down of the
cotton economy in the 1830s and 1840s did not spell the decline of
slavery here. Throughout this period the plantation belt continued to
grow. South Carolina's average farm size was the largest in the nation in
1850, even as many small farmers were squeezed out of the state. From
1830 to 1850, the proportion of whites in the state's population fell, and
many more whites migrated out of the state than into it. The slump in the
state's economy would not be relieved until the cotton boom of the

TABLE 1. South Carolina Population, 1820–1860

Year	White		Black	
	Number	Percentage	Number	Percentage
1820	237,440	47.2	265,301	52.8
1830	257,863	44.4	323,322	55.6
1840	259,084	43.6	335,314	56.4
1850	274,563	41.1	393,944	58.9
1860	291,300	41.4	412,320	58.6

Source: Jullian J. Petty, *The Growth and Distribution of Population in South Carolina* (Columbia, S.C., 1943), 64.

1850s. By mid-century just over 50 percent of Carolinian white families owned slaves; South Carolina became the first southern state to have a slaveholding majority in its white population.[6]

The number of slaves in the state also grew. In 1810, slaves composed over 80 percent of the total population in most lowcountry parishes, half of the population of most middle districts, and nearly one-third of the population in much of the upcountry. Only the population of the mountain districts of Greenville, Spartanburg, and Pendleton contained less than 20 percent slaves. In 1820, the black population of the state would surpass the white, re-creating its slave majority of the colonial days. On the eve of nullification, black people comprised over 40 percent of the population in a majority of the state's districts. By 1850, they constituted less than 50 percent of the population in only seven of the state's twenty-eight districts and they made up around 59 percent of the total population. For every 100 whites in the state there were 140 slaves. Only during the last decade before the Civil War did the black proportion of the state's population fall slightly. In 1840, South Carolina's population consisted of 259,084 whites and 335,314 blacks, of whom 327,158 were enslaved and 454 owned slaves themselves. The state's free black population comprised only around 1 to 2 percent of its population through much of the pre–Civil War period, of whom only a few achieved economic prosperity. An overwhelming majority of black people were enslaved and labored in the swampy rice and sea island cotton plantations and the short-staple cotton fields of the piedmont.[7]

Slavery, more than any other issue, determined the state's geopolitics. Carolinian rice aristocrats and the cotton planters from the hinterland formed an intersectional ruling class, bound together by kinship, economic, political, and cultural ties. They presided over the state government and gave birth to the most undemocratic political structure in the Union. South Carolina's antebellum government was based on its archaic 1790 constitution. An all-powerful, planter-dominated state legislature lay at the heart of a highly centralized system of governance with weak local political organization. Carolinian slaveholders monopolized not only state but also local offices. Legislative apportionment was incredibly lopsided, as the small lowcountry parishes were accorded the same representative weight as the much larger and more populous interior election districts. State representatives were required to have 500 acres and 10 slaves or real estate valued at 150 pounds sterling clear of debt, while state senators had to have a minimum of estate valued at 300 pounds sterling, also clear of debt. An estate of 15,000 pounds sterling clear of debt qualified a citizen for the governorship. Property-holding qualifications for local offices also insured that in South Carolina, as Ralph Wooster notes, "county government remained thoroughly undemocratic."

The Compromise of 1808, which increased representation for the up-country, and the 1810 law granting suffrage to most adult white males were enacted after the state was made safe for slavery. The constitutional amendment of 1808 based representation in the house on taxation and population. The amendment increased representation for the interior while keeping intact the entrenched hold of the propertied slaveholding elite on the state government. The 1808 amendment was, as Rachel Klein has argued, an official though belated recognition of the rise of a planter-led slave society in the backcountry. The state senate remained a stronghold of the rotten borough lowcountry parishes. The retention of the parish system and high property qualifications for office holding still gave the lowcountry aristocracy and the planter class as a whole a decisive representative edge in the legislature. In 1810, when all resident, adult, white, male citizens, with the exception of paupers and noncommissioned officers and soldiers of the United States Army, were given the right to vote, the state government was already firmly under the control of the slaveholding planter elite. South Carolina's antebellum citizenry could exercise its right to vote only in the elections for state legislators and congressional representatives, as state and local officers, the governor, and presidential electors were appointed by the legislature. While voter turnout fluctuated widely, the rate of turnover in the legislature rarely exceeded 50 percent in the antebellum period. Most of the congressional elections were "non-competitive" and "involved no opposing candidates at all."[8]

Even those historians who have tried to weave the Old South into an overarching democratic interpretation of American politics were careful to note the exception of South Carolina. The state remained immune to the wave of constitutional reforms that inaugurated Jacksonian democracy in the country. South Carolina was the only state in the Union that did not have a two-party system or popular elections for the presidency, the governorship, and a host of state and local offices. And it retained property and slaveholding qualifications for political office as well as a severely malapportioned legislature until Reconstruction. In the 1850s, Carolinian leaders allowed only a few minor changes to the state's political system. The upcountry district of Pendleton was divided into two, Pickens and Anderson, and a few local offices were made elective. However, repeated attempts to institute popular elections for governor and for presidential electors and to reapportion the legislature failed.[9]

Antebellum Carolinian planters' local stranglehold on state politics went hand in hand with their declining national power. Recent works reveal the highest levels of slaveholding, real and personal property ownership, and planter status among South Carolina state and local officials in comparison to those in the rest of the South. Many prominent planter families such as the Butlers, Mannings, Richardsons, Middletons, Manigaults, Pinckneys, Rutledges, Rhetts, Lowndes, Calhouns, Hamptons, and Smiths retained political power through generations. At the same time, between 1832 and 1842 the state would lose two representatives in Congress, and between 1840 and 1860 its overall congressional representation would fall from nine to six.[10] South Carolina's slaveholding planter class, so potent at home but increasingly impotent in the national arena, would become the foremost spokesmen for southern separatism.

The third decade of the nineteenth century, beginning with the Missouri crisis and ending with the collision between South Carolina and the federal government over the tariffs, was a period of incubation for the politics of slavery. While Carolinian slaveholders had defended slavery since the earliest days of the republic, the emergence of a systematic body of proslavery literature and thought in the state during the 1820s marked the start of a new era. It was not just slavery itself but the tariff issue that ultimately led to the construction of the political ideology of slavery. But slavery transformed a dispute over economic policy into one of unsurpassed sectional bitterness. By the end of the decade, both slavery and the tariff had emerged as points of sectional dispute in the national political arena. It was the fatal intertwining of these two issues in the hands of Carolinian nullifiers by the end of the decade that precipitated nullification.

In the 1820s, Carolinian planter politicians were convinced that internal and external threats endangered slavery. Between the Haitian revolution and Nat Turner's uprising, the state suffered from a host of slave rebellion scares, including the famous Denmark Vesey conspiracy of 1822. The plot was discovered and put down by such future nullifiers as Robert J. Turnbull, Robert Y. Hayne, and James Hamilton Jr., then the intendant or mayor of Charleston. In response to the Vesey affair, the legislature passed the Negro Seamen's Act, which interred all black sailors visiting Charleston on the theory that all free black people should be viewed as potential security risks. Passed in defiance of federal treaties and law, this act has been claimed as the first nullification by South Carolina. Despite the disapproval of the federal government, it remained on the statute books until the 1850s and became a model for similar laws in other southern states. Governor John Wilson, a "violent nullifier" and author of a handbook on dueling, defended the act as a "law of self-preservation." Leading planters formed the South Carolina Association in 1823 to more strictly police slaves and free African Americans. As Edwin C. Holland, an early proslavery pamphleteer, bemoaned, the slaves were the "true Jacobins" and "anarchists" in his state.[11]

Proposals for emancipation and colonization in the 1820s also evoked a strong reaction in South Carolina, and the state senate warned the federal government against interfering "with the domestic regulations and preservatory measures in respect to that part of her property which forms the colored population of the State." Whitemarsh Seabrook, proslavery writer and nullifier, asked, "Did not the unreflecting zeal of the North and East, and the injudicious speeches on the Missouri question inspire Vesey in his hellish efforts?" The rise of Garrisonian abolitionism seemed to confirm Carolinian slaveholders' suspicions that northern antislavery feeling encouraged slave resistance. Judge William Harper, second only to John C. Calhoun as a nullification theorist, somberly noted, "It was the 'Amis des Noirs' who set on foot the Insurrection at St. Domingo."[12]

Slavery, according to Carolinian slaveholders' construction, was well on its way to becoming the wellspring of southern thought.[13] Long before Thomas R. Dew wrote one of the most well-known proslavery tracts in the aftermath of the Virginia slavery debates, Carolinian planters and clergymen produced a slew of proslavery pamphlets in the 1820s. They began defending slavery as the essential and defining element of southern society. Anticipating the main lines of the antebellum proslavery argument, Charles Cotesworth Pinckney argued that slavery was an institution of "Mosaic dispensation" and that it was not "a greater or more unusual evil than befalls the poor in general." Approving of the destruction of the African Methodist Episcopal Church in the wake of the Vesey conspiracy, Reverends Richard Furman and Frederick Dalcho developed the biblical defense of slavery while pleading for the proper religious instruction of the slaves.[14]

The Carolinian view of slavery became the justification of a new theory of politics with the rise of the tariff controversy. Besides being the major source of national revenue, tariffs for the protection of infant manufactures were part of an economic program resurrected after the 1812 war in Henry Clay's American system. The system included the establishment of a national bank and internal improvement projects. The only detractors, at this point, were a group of southern conservatives led by John Randolph of Virginia and younger states' rights men such as William H. Crawford of Georgia and his ally, William Smith of South Carolina. In 1825, under Smith's guidance, the South Carolina legislature passed resolutions declaring the system of internal improvements and the tariff unconstitutional. Calhoun and William Lowndes, both of whom had begun their careers as War Hawks, led the dominant nationalist group against the states' rights Smith faction. The ardent George McDuffie, whose only fault according to unionist Benjamin F. Perry was that he allowed his mentor, Calhoun, to dictate his public course, went so far as to declare states' rights the refuge of ambitious and less talented men who could not make their mark in national politics. But even as McDuffie put his view of states' rights to the test of a bullet in a series of duels with an offended Georgian, Calhoun and Lowndes reevaluated their nationalist position.[15]

Not only the Missouri crisis, which had Lowndes spouting states' rights, but also the economic downturn in the South Atlantic states made southern nationalists reverse themselves. The federal census of 1820 revealed the slower population and economic growth of the slave South. The panic of 1819 had hit the South hard, especially the older seaboard states. South Carolina, after a prolonged cotton boom between 1790 and 1820, entered into a period of economic stagnation made severe by soil erosion, unparalleled out-migration of population, overproduction of cotton in the fresher lands of the Southwest, and a precipitous decline in the price of cotton. But rather than blaming these developments, nullifiers like Hayne claimed that the federal "*system of restrictions*" imposed on the trade of southern staples was responsible for the economic downturn. While the tariff no doubt acted against the interest of the average consumer and favored industry over agriculture, Carolinian planter politicians argued that duties particularly hurt the slave South, as they might destroy its export trade in cotton if the British chose to retaliate. During the debate over the 1824 tariff bill, the opposition of Calhoun's Carolinian followers in Congress was serious enough to make the future unionist leader Joel R. Poinsett worry for the safety of the American republic.[16]

South Carolina's opposition to the tariff was marked not just because it differed in its vehemence and scope compared to some other southern states but also because Carolinian planter politicians would make their dissent a part of a broader sectionalist and proslavery outlook. A former Englishman, Dr. Thomas Cooper, and a lowcountry planter, Robert J. Turnbull, who were most responsible for linking the tariff with slavery, became the early seers of southern nationalism. The notion that the tariffs were a northern conspiracy to destroy the South became the peculiar contribution of the Cooper-led Columbia junto to the general opposition against the revenue policy of Congress. The temperamental Dr. Cooper, who inveighed regularly against northern "consolidation," was president of South Carolina College, the breeding ground of the state's planter politicians. He had earned the friendship of Jefferson and flirted with ideas of radical democracy and antislavery until his falling out with Pennsylvania democrats. He moved to South Carolina reincarnated as the reactionary spokesman of the southern slaveholding class, drilling his pupils in Columbia with the dogmas of proslavery, states' rights, and free trade. Cooper, who would be removed from the presidency of the college for being an atheist, now argued that slavery "is encouraged throughout the whole of the Scriptures from beginning to end." In his Consolidation essays, he also attacked the federalist heresy of Calhoun and McDuffie.[17]

In July 1827 Cooper made a premature disunion speech at the anti-Woollens tariff meeting in Columbia. He portrayed the tariff question as a struggle between the planter class and the manufacturing class, and, hence, between the North and the South, in a familiar analysis that conflated class and section. He warned that along with wealth, power was being transferred to the North and dramatically concluded, "we shall 'ere long be compelled to calculate the value of our union; and to enquire what use to us is this most unequal alliance? By which the south has always been the loser, the north always the gainer?" Seconding Cooper, David J. McCord illustrated the "injurious tendency" of the tariff on the cotton planter. He contended that with the program for internal improvements, the tariff was the result of an unholy bargain struck between the North and the West at the cost of the South. In a letter to a Louisiana senator, William Campbell Preston appealed for sectional unity on slavery over the advantages of a duty on sugar.[18]

Even more explicitly than Cooper and his Columbia junto, Turnbull claimed that the tariff was really an antislavery plot. Turnbull's Crisis essays first appeared in the *Charleston Mercury*, which would become the official organ of Carolinian nullifiers and secessionists, under the pseudonym Brutus. Dedicated to the people of the "Plantation States," they were republished in a pamphlet with additional numbers and became

the single most effective piece of propaganda in the hands of the nullifiers. According to Turnbull, the greatest danger facing the slave south
was the tendency of a northern-dominated federal government to interfere in slavery, the "LIFEBLOOD" of the state. He contended that the same
constitutional clauses that were used to justify economic measures such
as the tariff and internal improvements could be used for the abolition of
slavery. If the powers of the federal judiciary and Congress were not kept
in check, then the South's "colonial vassalage" to the North on the tariff
would be a prelude to "African emancipation." Carolinians must oppose
colonization and any antislavery discussion because "Domestic servitude
is the policy of our country," and because they would raise "illusory
hopes" among the slaves. To protect themselves from a hostile majority,
southern slaveholders must look to their states. If, in the future, three-
fourths of the states amended the Constitution to abolish slavery, then
the slave states would have the right to dissolve the Union.[19] The political
ideology of slavery and its path to its logical goal, the southern nation,
had already been illuminated. Here then was the finished statement of
sectionalism, slavery, and antitariff feeling in South Carolina.

Carolinian slaveholders were learning to make connections between
the tariff, antislavery, and the fear of losing political ground in a democratic republic. State leaders such as Stephen D. Miller, Seabrook, D. R.
Evans, J. R. Girardeau, J. S. Deas, and T. W. Glover organized protest
meetings against the Woollens bill that were particularly solicitous of
planter interests. Memorials from Barnwell, Kershaw, Edgefield, Fairfield, Orangeburg, Lancaster, Laurens, Marlborough, Newberry, Chesterfield, and St. Andrew's Parish to Congress in 1827 and 1828 testified
to the unjust and unconstitutional nature of protective duties and called
them a tax on planters' income. While many opposed the tariff, some
leading planter politicians were also influenced by the proslavery and
separatist logic of Cooper's and Turnbull's arguments. The Columbia
memorial argued that "the benefit of the Union to this State is becoming
more dubious and disputable," and the memorial from St. John's Colleton asked why should "the Southern Planter humbly kiss the rod which
chastens him?" The Sumter meeting, led by Miller, future governor and
nullifier, declared that neither the federal courts nor "the elective principle" could protect the rights of the slaveholding minority in this case. An
antitariff gathering of St. Paul's Agricultural Society also warned that
criticisms of slavery tended "to weaken the sacred tie which binds the
states to the union." However, the Charleston Chamber of Commerce
memorial sounded a cautionary note about "the growth of a spirit of
disaffection, that may come to regard the federal charter with alien-
ated feelings."[20]

Prominent planter politicians were able to influence public opinion at the local level as well as the official course of the state. The state senate, under the leadership of such future nullifiers as John Ramsay, Miller, and Seabrook, presented an antitariff report and resolutions that recommended that the state should approach the federal government as a "SOVEREIGN" to demand the repeal of tariff laws. Moreover, it dragged in the question of slavery, stating that there could "be no reasoning, between South Carolina and any other government" on this subject. Carolinian slaves should not be able to look to any source of authority other than the state government. The report concluded that not just the tariffs but any scheme for emancipation and colonization was unconstitutional. The importance of this first wave of sectional agitation was emphasized by an early historian of nullification, David Franklin Houston, who argued that the "principles that were fought for in the Civil War were formally enunciated in South Carolina" in the 1820s.[21] The joining of the questions of slavery and tariff in South Carolina prepared the ground for nullification.

Nullification went far beyond traditional states' rights opposition to economic nationalism because it linked broader and more important issues to the tariff. Calhoun's formulation of the novel theory of state interposition changed the character of the tariff debate. With a handful of exceptions, old states' rights men, following Smith, opposed nullification, while the erstwhile Calhoun nationalists, with all the zeal of the newly converted, emerged as its strongest champions. The political philosophy of Calhoun and his followers somersaulted from qualified nationalism to unqualified sectionalism.

Before nullification, however, Calhoun had proven himself to be more of an adroit politician than a metaphysical theorist, as many contemporaries charged. As vice president in opposition, he had distanced himself from John Quincy Adams's unpopularity and survived the administration's downfall. He soon emerged as the vice presidential nominee on the opposing Jacksonian ticket. Calhoun had also killed the 1827 Woollens bill by his deciding vote in the Senate and condemned the tariff as a sectional measure designed to impoverish the slave South. Calhoun's plan was to build a political following through a southern-based antitariff movement. Duff Green, editor of the *United States Telegraph*, was more accurate in his assessment of the fallout from such a tactic, as his urgent letters to Calhoun and his followers indicate. The sectionalist tone of the antitariff agitation, Green predicted, would hinder rather than further Calhoun's presidential prospects.[22] Calhoun linked his personal fortunes with the good of his class and, in his estimate, his state and section; it would be wrong to see him either as motivated solely by ambition or as sacrificing himself for the cause of the slave South. As Perry noted, "He is an ambitious man, but I believe is honest as most statesmen of the present age."[23]

Calhoun assumed leadership of the Carolinian antitariff movement by 1828. During the congressional debate over the tariff bill, Calhounites such as Hamilton argued that the passage of the tariff would force slaveholders to inquire whether they could "afford" to be in the Union because Congress was making them choose between the laws of God and nature and an "artificial political association." When the 1828 tariff became the law of the land, an irate South Carolina delegation, with the exception of Senator Smith, met at Hayne's Washington lodging and apparently discussed withdrawing from Congress and disunion as a possibility. Calhounites blamed their leader's Jacksonian rival, Martin Van Buren, for the passage of the tariff.[24] And Calhoun came up with the idea of a state veto of a federal law.

Calhoun's construction of the doctrine of nullification would soon make him the preeminent political spokesman of the slaveholding gentry, a position he would retain until his death. While most historians agree that the idea of nullification or a state veto of federal law was put forward publicly in 1828, they disagree as to when exactly that happened and who first conceived of it. Some have also surmised that while Calhoun perfected this doctrine, he was not its originator. The most oft-quoted instances are the Sydney letters (authored by Francis W. Pickens) and the Colleton letters that appeared in the *Charleston Mercury* in July, the Abbeville antitariff meeting in September, and Hamilton's Walterborough speech in October. Turnbull's Crisis essays, which are credited with putting forward the idea of state veto, had merely called for state action without specifying what form it should take. The logic and language of the Abbeville preamble resemble Calhoun's so closely that one suspects that if he was not its author, he was at least its inspiration. Abbeville was also his home. And both Pickens and Hamilton were part of Calhoun's coterie and influenced by his ideas. Despite the enormous concessions in the Constitution, Calhoun had become convinced that additional safeguards were needed for slaveholders in a system of representative government. His correspondence reveals that as early as 1827 he had already come up with the idea of a state "negative" as a way to "*compel the majority*" to redress the grievances of the slaveholding minority. But at this point he was uncertain of how far a state veto of federal law "would be found consistent with the general power" and the 1789 Judiciary Act, which gave federal courts appellate jurisdiction over state courts.[25]

The Carolinian politician wanted to follow in the footsteps of Jefferson

THE POLITICAL IDEOLOGY OF SLAVERY

and Madison, whose Kentucky Resolutions and Virginia Resolutions and Report against the Alien and Sedition Acts, respectively, had carried both men to the presidency. However, in this overall plan of action he followed Jefferson and Madison more closely than in his doctrine of nullification. He initially admitted as much in a letter to Preston when he noted that "the dissimilarity between the character of the encroachments of the General Government then and now, very little aid can be derived from them in drawing up a paper for the present occasion." Calhoun did end up using the resolutions. It was important for nullifiers to assume the mantle of states' rights tradition to establish the orthodoxy of nullification. T. N. Brevard argued they must "cling to States rights" and Hayne felt that by appealing to the Virginia resolutions, nullifiers could carry "the whole South."[26]

Superficially, both nullification and the 1798 resolutions sought to evoke state power against the actions of the federal government, but instead of appealing to local majorities to check an undemocratic federal government, Calhoun devised ways to secure the interests of the slave-holding minority against the voice of the majority. While Jefferson had used the word "nullification," which nullifiers seized on, there is no indication in his resolutions of the elaborate constitutional check devised by Calhoun. The wording of the Kentucky Resolutions of 1798 and 1799 and the Virginia Resolutions of 1798 and Report of 1800, which constantly refer to "states" and "sovereignties," make it apparent that beyond declaratory resolutions, action by an individual state was not visualized by either of the authors. The *Camden Journal*, for example, used the same resolutions to argue against the notion of a single state veto and its dangerous consequences.[27]

Calhoun's conception of nullification was a theoretical innovation that sought to provide an ironclad guarantee for the future safety of the southern slaveholding minority in a democratic republic. He first developed this theory anonymously in the 1828 Exposition. While the Alien and Sedition Acts had been challenged as clear violations of the letter of the Constitution and contrary to specific amendments, the exposition declared the tariff laws unconstitutional on the basis of differing interpretations of the constitutional clause that gave the federal government the power to regulate commerce. Calhoun turned this discrepancy in his own favor by arguing, "It is, in a word, *a violation of perversion*, the most dangerous of all, because the most insidious, and difficult to resist." According to him, the safe rule by which to judge the constitutionality of laws were the journals of the constitutional convention, which would reveal the intent of the framers.[28] He chose to ignore the fact that differing interpretations could result even after the application of this rule.

Without dwelling too long on the unconstitutionality of the tariff, he went on to deal with the economic oppression of the tariff on the South. The destruction of the planter class and the slave South, Calhoun felt, was the ultimate object of the protariff northern groups. In a frank declaration, he defended the use of "sectional language" while speaking of a "sectional issue." He then made the startling and unique claim that import duties equaled export duties and thus the main "burden" of the tariff fell on southerners, the nation's main exporters. By this logic, the "*South almost exclusively*" and not all the consumers in the nation paid import duties. The legitimate complaint that the tariff was against the interests of planters because it might destroy their foreign market and favored manufactures over agriculture and commerce was minimized by the fantastical theory that only planters, as the major exporters, paid import duties. In an interesting discovery of political economy that had eluded even the rabidly antitariff Dr. Cooper, Calhoun contended that in the end producers rather than consumers paid the tariff levied on foreign goods. And not all producers but producers of exported crops, i.e., mostly the slaveholding planter class. This he claimed was the cause of the South's economic woes. Calhoun reiterated another article of faith among many Carolinian slaveholders when he concluded, "Those who now make war on our gains would then make it on our labour." Furthermore, Calhoun did not entertain the faintest idea of an alliance with northern labor over the tariff, as he complained that protection created an artificial system in which the wages of American labor were 150 percent higher and the profits of American capital were 100 percent higher than their English counterparts. The antislavery labor economist Daniel Raymond, arguing from workingmen's viewpoint, thought that the tariff would keep wages high and prevent the degradation of labor. According to Raymond, it was a small price to pay to ensure that the republic was peopled by independent and virtuous citizens. In stark contrast to the supposed empathy of slaveholders for the toiling masses, Calhoun advocated "free and open competition" to lower wages and prices.[29]

Calhoun's championship of slaveholders' interests also informed his minority versus majority theory of politics. He argued "[t]hat our industry is controlled by the many, instead of one, by a majority in congress elected by a majority in the community having an opposing interest, instead of hereditary rulers, forms not the slightest mitigation of the evil. In fact, instead of mitigating, it aggravates." Against the danger of a sectional majority dominating a sectional minority, "*representation* affords not the slightest protection." The solution to majority domination lay in the concept of state sovereignty. The sovereign state, as representative of the minority interest and party to the constitutional compact, would have

THE POLITICAL IDEOLOGY OF SLAVERY

the power to veto a federal law that it considered unconstitutional. In the 1831 Fort Hill address, Calhoun would try to defend himself from the accusation that he did not believe in majority rule, claiming that no one could have higher respect for that "maxim" than he did. But he added that the right of the majority to rule was not "natural" but "conventional," and therefore it was not "absolute and unlimited." The United States, he contended, was marked by sectional interests and "state sovereignty" was the "only refuge of the weaker section." State veto of sectionally unequal laws was thus a "safe" and "constitutional" remedy. Otherwise the majority would have "all the power that could be desired to subject the labor and property of the minority" to their will. While Calhoun's notion of absolute state sovereignty justified interposition by a single state, it was contradicted by his assertion that after a state veto, the supreme power to decide the question at issue would lie with the Constitution-amending authority, three-fourths of the states. Hence three-fourths of the states could overturn the veto of a sovereign state, and a minority, a little more than one-fourth of the states, could make and break federal laws. Nullification, he argued, would elevate the "concurring majority" over the "absolute majority" or the "constitution making authority" over the "law making" power. The changes he made to his theory, however, did not go beyond the level of semantics and its basic implication remained unchanged. Even under the guise of a concurrent majority, nullification allowed a minority, the nullifying state plus one-fourth of the states, to interpret the Constitution and do as they would over a majority of the states.[30]

According to Calhoun, the nullifying state also had the option of acquiescing to the three-fourths majority or of seceding from the Union. In a public letter to Governor Hamilton justifying the need for nullification in 1832, Calhoun defended his theory from charges of disunion, explaining that nullification was not secession. Secession, he conceded, might follow nullification if the sovereign state in question chose to exercise this right. He also argued that the right to secession was constitutional, as it, like nullification, was a reserved right of the state. In the process of defending nullification based on absolute state sovereignty, Calhoun had vindicated the constitutional right to secession. Few in the nation followed the fine distinctions in his arguments and quickly condemned nullification as synonymous with disunion.[31]

Calhoun's ideas of absolute state sovereignty and the federal government as the mere agent of the states went far beyond traditional states' rights theory. States' rights was replaced by an unprecedented conception of state power that implied virtual independence, as his critics quickly discerned, giving rise to the paradox of a state being in and out of the Union at the same time. Following Blackstone's concept of sovereignty, Calhoun claimed that absolute, undivided sovereignty lay with the states. Much to his chagrin, the House committee amended his draft in a way that repeated the traditional states' rights idea that the powers of government were divided between the state and federal governments and that each was sovereign in its sphere. According to nullification theory, the long arm of the sovereign state could check the federal government. The committee compounded its error by adding a quotation from Jefferson that stated, "It is a fatal heresy . . . to suppose that either our state governments are superior to the federal, or the federal to the state." Later, in a report on federal relations, Calhoun undertook to defend nullification against the objections of other states' righters. By 1832, however, he made an extreme case for absolute state sovereignty and denied the existence of the federal government as a popular government. He argued that there was "*no direct* and *immediate* connection between the individual citizens of the state and the General Government." Southern politicians had employed states' rights to defend slavery during the Missouri debates and to attack the program of economic nationalism, but most traditional states' righters condemned nullification as an aberration rather than a fruition of states' rights theory. Nullification violated the cardinal tenet of states' righters — strict construction — as it was not mentioned in the Constitution and it circumvented the amendment process laid out in the Constitution. John Randolph, for example, opposed nullification as unrepublican and as going far beyond the written word of the Constitution.[32]

Calhoun innovatively combined the antidemocratic sensibility of the federalists with states' rights theory. His use of constitutional theories can be seen as a continuation of the conservative reaction to revolutionary republicanism that had led to the formation of the Constitution, when fears of majority domination had replaced suspicion of the "powers of kings and magistrates." But Calhoun had injected a new issue into the traditional fears of propertied minorities in majoritarian republics, and that was the specific dilemma of the slaveholding minority. As he wrote, "It is, in truth, high time for the people of the South to be roused to the sense of impending calamities, on an early and full knowledge of which their safety depends. It is time that they should see and feel that in regard to climate property and production their situation in the Union is peculiar, and that they are in a permanent and hopeless minority on the great and vital connected questions, with a powerful adverse monopolizing interest opposed[,] supported by a strong, united and preponderating [*sic*] majority." Since the "concurring assent" of "great and distinct interests" in society must be obtained for all policies, the slaveholding minority would have a veto on any act of the federal government and be secure from the will of the majority.[33]

Framing the question in terms of the problem of minorities in majoritarian republics, Calhoun was again evoking a venerable precedent, Madison's Federalist No. 10. In the Exposition, Calhoun had specifically referred to Madison's opinions in the Virginia resolutions and report. Madison, however, rejected nullification because he felt that safeguards for minorities could not overturn the fundamental principle of republican government, majority rule. According to Madison, the Constitution and plurality of interests in a large republic provided sufficient protection for minorities. Nullification, he wrote, had no basis either in the Constitution or in the 1798 resolutions. Madison was widely viewed as the father of the Constitution and his opinions would be a severe setback for the nullifiers. Congressman Warren Davis would pathetically try to distinguish between the Madison of 1828 and the Madison of 1787 in order to justify the Carolina doctrine.[34]

The ideological roots of Calhoun's concept of nullification lay more in the archfederalism of a later period than in Madisonian theory. It was profoundly conservative, designed to check what Carolinian slaveholders saw as the excesses of democracy and majoritarianism. Calhoun had studied in the federalist-dominated Litchfield Law School and at Yale University under Timothy Dwight. And he had learned law under the proslavery essayist Henry W. DeSaussure in another stronghold of federalism, lowcountry South Carolina. As Gordon Wood has pointed out, Calhoun's theory of a minority veto was anticipated by Timothy Ford, the lowcountry federalist aristocrat who had argued against democratic reforms. Legend has it that as a Jeffersonian, Calhoun sparred with Dwight. However, philosophically Calhoun was perhaps closer to conservative federalists, both in his constitutional critique of majority rule and in his espousal of the constitutional right to secession. After all, the New England federalists had first conceived of the constitutional right to secession in the Hartford convention as a check against the national Jeffersonian majority. Most states' righters argued that secession was a revolutionary right.[35]

The Carolina doctrine of nullification was a clear-headed and prescient defense of the prerogatives of the south's slaveholding gentry. Calhoun was an ideal political theoretician for the slave South because of his practical commitment to slave society. He reformulated the political traditions and verities of his time to construct a new political discourse well suited to meet the distinct interests of southern slaveholders. Nullification cannot be included within the rubric of republicanism or liberalism. Calhoun would have no qualms in dispensing with minority rights when it came to northern abolitionists or the unionists in his own state. And while he employed the language of constitutionalism, state interposition was an extraconstitutional doctrine. Calhoun's assessment of conflicting sectional and class interests displayed a strong skepticism about the virtue of a majority of the citizenry and the vision of a harmonious republic. Power's historic antagonist in nullification theory was not liberty but another countervailing power. A minority check, which he saw epitomized in South Carolina's government, would lead to a similar undemocratic, planter-dominated politics.[36]

Calhoun's determination to implement nullification after his tiff with Andrew Jackson, rather than his articulation of nullification theory, would touch off a national political crisis. Before that, Carolinian planter politicians seemed merely the most vigorous in their opposition to the tariff. The Georgia Assembly had pronounced the tariff unconstitutional and sectional in nature. In 1829, Virginia declared that the protection of manufactures was a violation of the Constitution. Professor Thomas Dew of William and Mary College, who sympathized with the nullifiers, advocated free trade and refuted mercantilist logic. Even the outgoing president, John Quincy Adams, recognized the injurious effects of the tariff in his message to Congress.[37]

Calhoun had ended the Exposition with the conviction that Jackson's election would provide succor to southern complaints against the tariff. Langdon Cheves, who along with Calhoun and Lowndes formed the triumvirate that dominated Carolina politics, noted in an atypical speech the benign nature of political parties such as the newly formed Democratic Party. The legislature passed resolutions and a Protest against the tariff in 1828, but future nullifier Andrew Pickens Butler's resolution calling for a state convention was rejected by a vote of eighty to forty-one in the state house. Ex-governor Wilson's antitariff resolution calling for resistance by the states was approved by the state senate but rejected by the house. The house also voted down Calhoun's Exposition, though its 1829 publication by the assembly surrounded it with an aura of official approval. State legislator William Elliot observed that while most Carolinians were against the tariff, there was "no unity of sentiment" regarding the action of the state. And before his break with Jackson, Calhoun showed little inclination to act on nullification.[38]

However, the spirit of Jacksonian democracy was alien to South Carolina's political culture. The notion of mass democratic party politics seemed ill-suited to the antimajoritarian and increasingly sectionalist sensibility of most Carolinian planter politicians. Hugh Swinton Legaré, the lowcountry unionist aristocrat whose heart was with the nullifiers, was appalled at the rambunctious nature of Jacksonian democracy. More-over, the emergence of Martin Van Buren as a key player in the admin-istration aroused fears that he might replace Calhoun as the general's heir. Sorely disappointed at not being offered a cabinet position, Hamil-ton was taken aback by Jackson's declaration to hang anyone who dis-obeyed federal law. Jackson criticized state interposition and argued that "in all Republics the voice of a majority must prevail."[39]

Jackson's abhorrence of nullification as antidemocratic and disunion-ist and his suspicions that Calhoun was involved in formulating treason-ous ideas brought on the confrontation between them. This was evident in their contrasting toasts to the Union during Jefferson's birthday anni-versary in February 1830. The break between them became clear after Jackson discovered that as secretary of war in James Monroe's cabinet, Calhoun had opposed Jackson's military actions in Florida. A long and convoluted correspondence between Jackson and Calhoun followed, which the latter had published to prove his innocence. Calhoun blamed Van Buren, who had nothing to do with the imbroglio, for engineering the controversy. The president kept Calhoun at arm's length, but the so-called Eaton malaria led to a complete severance of relations between the two. The Washington boycott of the hapless Peggy Eaton, wife of John Eaton, resulted in a cabinet reshuffle in which members who had partici-pated in the ban and had evoked Jackson's ire were consigned to political oblivion. Calhoun lauded "that censorship, which the [female] sex ex-ercises over itself." This censorship was "too high" to be tampered with by "political considerations." However, the cabinet members who were forced out not only valued female purity with a fearful ardency but were also Calhoun's sympathizers. With his own resignation, Calhoun's influ-ence in the administration reached a complete nadir. He and his fol-lowers now claimed that the omnipotent Van Buren had manipulated the entire affair and even used his single status to gain an upper hand in this social drama. Van Buren thought it wise to extricate himself from the entire controversy and accepted an appointment as minister to England against which Calhoun cast the deciding vote in the Senate. Calhoun thus had the satisfaction of denying his rival the diplomatic post. General Jackson, he now concluded, was too "odious," "weak," "suspicious," and "ignorant" to be supported.[40] Rather than personal differences, however, political and constitutional issues instigated the confrontation between nullifiers and Jacksonians.

The tariff issue lay buried as the nation's leaders discussed nullifica-tion, states' rights, the federal nature of the United States government, the Union, and the Constitution. The first public airing of nullification, during the 1830 Hayne-Webster debate, revealed the rise of two opposing political theories based on a reformulation of the young republic's political traditions. On the one hand, Hayne put forth the case for nullification that recast states' rights theory as a critique of democracy. On the other, Senator Daniel Webster unveiled a concept of the Union as the irreplaceable and permanent repository of its citizens' freedoms, in contrast to the old federalist nationalism, which viewed the federal government as a check on local democracy. Webster's construction of a democratic nationalism would inspire both Jackson and Lincoln. The Hayne-Webster debate, as most contemporaries recognized, represented a struggle between important new political notions.

Webster changed the terms of a debate on the disposition of western public lands by praising the Northwest Ordinance for restricting slavery. Hayne protested the Massachusetts senator's "premeditated and unprovoked attack on the South" and reacted strongly to Webster's rather mild economic argument against slavery. He accused, "Shedding weak tears over sufferings which have existence only in their own very sickly imaginations, these 'friends of humanity' set themselves systematically to seduce the slaves of the South from their masters." Liberty did not suit black people, he said, and, repeating the famous Burkean argument that seems to have found much favor among present-day historians, he contended that the "haughtiness of domination fortifies the spirit of liberty." Rather than a curse, slavery, he claimed, was a blessing to southern society. Webster answered that while he like most northerners thought that slavery was "one of the greatest evils, both moral and political," the North had no intention of interfering with it.[41]

However, constitutional theory, and not slavery, was the focal point of the debate. Some have speculated whether Calhoun helped Hayne prepare his rebuttal. Whatever the case may be, it is evident that the latter was defending an idea that had been created and perfected by the former. Hayne insisted that a state veto was based on the Constitution and the 1798 resolutions. Trying to reverse the charge of disunion, he argued that South Carolina had been devoted to the Union while New England had contemplated disunion in the Hartford convention. Webster argued that not only was the Constitution formed by the people of the United States as a whole but that the federal government, just as much as the state governments, was an "independent offspring of the popular will." A state veto would flout the people of the nation and convert their beloved Union into "a rope of sand." In a stirring, patriotic tone, he lauded the Union created by the "discipline of our virtues" and "the severe school of adversity." He concluded with the sentiment, which was soon immortalized, "Liberty *and* Union, now and forever, one and inseparable!"[42]

THE POLITICAL IDEOLOGY OF SLAVERY

The *Charleston Mercury* claimed that Webster had heaped "a torrent of sarcasm, ridicule, and abuse upon the South." Why, it asked plaintively, did he "go out of his way to taunt the South upon slavery and disunion?" As opposed to his, the conduct of Hayne in defense of the maligned region was "patriotic and chivalrous." But the unionist *Greenville Mountaineer* felt that Webster had outshone Hayne. It epitomized the reaction of states' rights Democrats, who rejected Webster's nationalistic interpretation of the Constitution but embraced the concept of primary allegiance to a democratic Union. Earlier, the upcountry paper had declared its Jacksonian constitutional faith: "The consolidation of all power in the general government on the one hand, and the disunion of the several states on the other, are equally fatal to the liberty of America."[43]

The Jacksonian states' rights view was clarified by Senator Edward Livingston of Louisiana, whose career spanned the life of the young republic. He noted that both Webster and Hayne were mistaken in their theories of the United States government, which contained an optimum mixture of both popular and federal characteristics. Nullification went against states' rights and had no authority in the Constitution or the Virginia and Kentucky resolutions. At the same time, Livingston, unfairly accused of being a nationalist, took Webster to task for referring to the American people as one consolidated national entity instead of in separate communities in the states. In cases of extreme oppression, he argued that the people of a state had the revolutionary right to resistance after exhausting all constitutional remedies. But he warned that the Union was a "Gordian knot" that could not be torn asunder without violence. His argument, which represented states rights and a democratic faith in representative government, had been approved by Madison and was the basis of Jacksonian Democrats' response to nullification.[44]

In 1831, unionists in South Carolina cemented their position in the Jacksonian coalition even as Calhoun and his followers deserted the Democratic standard. Being well aware of Jackson's suspicions of the Carolina doctrine, they invited him to join their Independence Day celebrations to quell the spirit of separatism. Though the president declined the invitation, in a letter he called upon Carolinians to safeguard the "palladium of your safety and prosperity" and to discountenance any attempt at disunion. He also promised that the tariff would be lowered with the payment of the public debt. Delighted at Jackson's response, unionists adopted "Union, States Rights and Jackson" as their party title and endorsed him for a second presidential term.[45]

As late as the legislative elections of 1830, both sides had used Jackson's name for electioneering purposes. But the nullifiers had also started complaining of his unfair treatment of Calhoun. Now they publicly launched a full-scale attack on the president. A nullifier pamphlet even presented an imaginary conversation between Jackson and the ghost of Jefferson in which the latter upbraided the former. The most bitter response came from the nullifier-dominated state senate, which condemned the Independence Day letter as "a manifest and most unauthorized interference of the Executive of the Union with the domestic parties of a separate State." Despite the protest of sixteen unionist state senators, led by Smith, the senate passed resolutions condemning the letter. The house passed a more moderate and ambiguous resolution stating that while it was ready to criticize the president when he was wrong, they would approve of him when, in their opinion, he was right. Calhoun wrote Pickens that he was glad a "movement" against Jackson's letter had been made as it revealed "how little worthy he is of his station."[46]

As Calhoun's faith in the president receded, his determination to put nullification into practice grew. Throughout the summer of 1830 he disavowed any control over the Carolinian nullifiers who had stepped up their demand for a state convention to nullify the tariff. But he confessed that he would be loath to curb them when he felt that "she [South Carolina] is struggling to preserve her reserved powers." If the tariff was submitted to any longer, he wrote, the South would one day have to acquiesce in the destruction of its "domestick institutions." Clearly, the picture that some historians have painted of Calhoun being dragged against his will into nullification by his followers is slightly overdrawn. Calhoun actually wrote an address during this year calling for a state convention and asserted that there was no reason to entertain any hope of relief from President Jackson or Congress. And by a singular coincidence, he issued his Fort Hill Address recommending nullification when his break with Jackson became final in 1831.[47]

Unlike Jacksonians, who were against all aspects of economic nationalism, nullifiers concentrated their fire on the tariff. Jackson had made clear his wish to reduce the tariff once the public debt was paid off. However, Calhoun and his followers criticized the president's support for the revolutionary soldiers' pension list and the distribution of surplus revenue, which they claimed would not lead to the lowering of the tariff even after the public debt was retired. Pickens referred to Jackson's recommendations as "the most stupendous schemes of bribery devised by the wits of man." Calhoun even looked askance at Jackson's Maysville veto, which was authored by Van Buren and hailed as a blow to internal improvements, as having been made "with too much art, and looked too much like courting all sides." Calhoun thought that nullification and his dispute with Jackson would not reduce his chances for the presidency, which he still hoped to acquire by throwing "himself entirely upon the South and to be more Southern if possible."[48]

Carolinian nullifiers' espousal of a state veto as well as their reliance on proslavery and separatist ideas also distinguished them from other free traders in the country. At the 1831 Free Trade Convention in Philadelphia, they found themselves isolated. Even southerners balked at the extent to which some Carolinian politicos were willing to go in their opposition to the tariff. The South Carolina delegation, composed of prominent unionists and nullifiers, was itself divided. Unionist meetings at Sumter and Abbeville looked to the free trade convention to save the state from nullification. The memorial of the convention to Congress challenged the tariff as being harmful to all consumers, particularly the "poor and industrious classes." As a concession to the southern delegates, it seconded the charge that duties operated unequally on the sections. However, this was not sufficient for the nullifiers, who supported an additional report written by Harper and Dew that claimed the tariff operated particularly at the expense of the planter class and was unconstitutional. The nullifier press summarily dismissed the effectiveness of the convention.[49]

Protectionists and free traders criticized Carolinian planter politicians for their adherence to nullification. Protectionists in the country quickly met to counter the effects of the free trade memorials. Matthew Carey, the untiring propagandist of a home industry, warned the citizens of South Carolina of the danger of being led to disunion and civil war and asserted that overproduction of cotton and not the tariff was the cause of their economic distress. In a public letter to Drayton, New York Democrat Gullian Verplanck pointed out the harmful effects of high duties on laborers, farmers, and mechanics but argued that the tariff laws were constitutional. What both the protectionist Carey and the free trader Verplanck failed to realize was that the Carolinian doctrine of nullification encompassed far more than the issue of the tariff.[50]

When the movement for tariff revision strengthened in Washington, nullifiers were not impressed. Introducing resolutions for the reduction of duties on foreign goods that did not come into competition with domestically produced articles, Clay defended the American system. His view of slavery as a necessary evil, his Hamiltonian economic policies, and his devotion to the Union made him seem remarkably unsouthern to nullifiers. Senators Ewing of Ohio and Sprague of Maine stated that the real cause for the depression in the South was the "withering curse" of slavery. Miller responded that abolitionists and protectionists were trying to divest slaveholders of their property. A tariff reform bill introduced by

Adams, now chairman of the Committee of Manufactures, became law in 1832. Most southerners voted for it and, with the exception of W. T. Nuckolls, Carolinian unionists also voted for the reductions.[51]

Nullifiers led by Hayne and McDuffie denounced the reform for further strengthening the principle of protection. Congressman John M. Felder felt that "State rights and Nullification doctrines are gaining ground here" and warned that "the majority have no idea of giving up the protective principle." The South Carolina congressional delegation claimed that the Adams bill was not a compromise since it increased the burdens of the slave South. The rest of the party were quick to pick up this refrain. The Carolinian State Rights and Free Trade Party declared the 1832 tariff unconstitutional. Nullifiers proclaimed, "All argument is now at an end." Calhoun had argued that "the General Government will not relax its hold, unless compelled, and that she cannot be compelled unless the South should unite . . . or some one of the States nullify the unconstitutional Tariff acts." Acknowledging that "an united appeal of the South is hopeless at this time," he recommended nullification. Nullifiers claimed that there was no difference between the policies of Jackson or the party of Clay and Webster and "if redress must be sought for, it will be found, not in the theory but in the practice of the South Carolina doctrines alone."[52]

By 1832, a majority of Carolinian planter politicians, led by Calhoun, were determined to act on nullification. The discourse of slavery and separatism perfected by the state's political elite had imparted an urgency and a broader dimension to the controversy, which the tariff by itself could never have generated. And Calhoun's break with Jackson pushed him to vindicate his pet theory. He best understood the political and constitutional implications of nullification. State interposition would not only nullify the tariff but it would also act as a permanent constitutional mechanism to protect the southern slaveholding minority in a democratic republic.

2

Nullification

[I] prefer a monarchy to a consolidated republic.
— JAMES HENRY HAMMOND, 1833

In the three decades before the Civil War, the proslavery, antidemocratic discourse pioneered by Carolinian planter politicians during nullification would form the theoretical foundation of southern nationalism. But it was only with secession that the Carolina doctrine would be fully vindicated in the South. By then most slaveholders had been converted to the notion of absolute state sovereignty that undergirded nullification, if not to nullification itself. In this sense, nullification was indeed a dress rehearsal for secession. Nullifiers' Jacksonian and proto-Whig opponents, though, despite their diverse political outlooks, would appeal for loyalty to the Union and the American experiment in republican government.

The appeal to these ideals was also pervasive among Carolinian unionists and was the dominant ideological framework that held together a heterogeneous antinullifier coalition. While a few planter politicians chose to reject nullification, the yeomanry of the nonplantation districts formed the base of the Union Party. The nullifiers derived their greatest political strength from the black belt, especially the planter-dominated lowcountry parishes and cotton districts of the middle- and upcountry. The final losers during nullification were the unionist mountain yeomanry, who were further marginalized politically, and the slaves, whose enslavement and rigid subordination was the sine qua non of the Carolina doctrine.

The nullification crisis did not lead to the democratization of state politics. For all the political mobilization that took place, the basically undemocratic structure of the state government remained unchanged though not unquestioned. The eventual victory of the nullifiers, which created the Calhoun-led political machine, ensured that no other issue would be debated quite so vigorously. Nullification helped the Carolinian planter class solidify its rule at home and present a virtually monolithic stance on all slavery-related issues in national politics.

The politicization of everyday life that began in 1828 and did not subside until 1834 was unsurpassed in the state's antebellum history. Newspaper wars, duels, political harangues, and barbecues changed the state, in the oft-quoted words of nullifier William Grayson, into "a great eating and talking machine." Whether this was a flowering of democratic politics, as is contended by some historians, can be disputed. Certainly various right-wing movements reveal that populism cannot be equated with democracy. And the antitariff agitation remained largely a top-down affair, led by planter politicians who never failed to make appeals to state and sectional patriotism.[1]

Calhoun's lieutenants, George McDuffie, Robert Y. Hayne, and James Hamilton, were instrumental in developing the Carolina brand of separatist and proslavery politics in which any dissent was delegitimized as submission to the North, as protariff and antislavery. Young and ambitious Calhounite planter politicians such as William Campbell Preston in Columbia, Francis W. Pickens and Andrew P. Butler in Edgefield, Warren Davis in Pendleton, Armistead Burt in Abbeville, Waddy Thompson in Greenville, Robert Barnwell Smith (later Rhett) in Colleton, James Henry Hammond, editor of the *Southern Times*, and Henry L. Pinckney, editor of the *Mercury*, vigorously took up the antitariff cause. Benjamin F. Perry charged that many nationalists and former defenders of the tariff had metamorphosed into ardent nullifiers. Older proslavery radicals such as Dr. Cooper, Robert Turnbull, and Whitemarsh Seabrook and future proslavery theorists such as William Harper, Grayson, and Hammond also emerged as leaders of the new nullifier party.[2]

The nullifier discourse, based on opposition to majority rule, bucked the national trend toward mass democracy and democratic rhetoric. Hayne made a fiery speech in the Senate against the "many headed potentate," or the tyrannical majority. And Hammond wrote that he would "prefer a monarchy to a consolidated Republic." Harper, in his explication of nullification, argued for the vindication of the "*great principle*" of minority veto. It would "obtain all the good which has resulted from monarchies and aristocracies without any mixture of the evil." McDuffie, who had initially attacked the tariff in typical Jacksonian fashion as oppressive to most people and favorable only to a "monied aristocracy," switched to Calhoun's position. He argued that the majority had no "natural right" to rule over a minority. A "single despot" was better than "King numbers," whose appetite for oppression exceeded that of the former. Moreover, nullifiers were "federalists" in state politics, opposing democratic reform within South Carolina.[3]

Nullifiers also tended to concentrate on planter woes and the sectional implications of the tariff laws. They were "all aristocrats by choice if not by origin." James Petigru, the distinguished unionist, regretted the susceptibility of the planter class to nullification. McDuffie's "forty bale" theory, or the notion that each cotton planter lost forty out of every hundred bales he produced to the tariff, became a powerful slogan for nullifiers. Calhoun had anticipated him, as he had argued earlier that cotton planters lost 40 percent of their income to the tariff. And like Cooper, McDuffie conflated class and section to portray the tariff dispute as one between manufacturers and planters, and hence, between the North and South. He attacked all forms of democracy that sought to exercise despotic sway over the southern planter. He defended the principle of racial and class inequality embodied in slave society and peppered his opposition to the tariff with strong proslavery statements. In an antitariff speech in Congress, he claimed that "by conferring the right to suffrage" on workers, "whatever may be their color, you do not elevate them to the character of freemen, but degrade liberty to their level." McDuffie's precocious conservatism celebrated the strict subordination and disfranchisement of labor. The style of his speech was vintage nullifier, beginning with an attack on the tariff and ending with a defense of slavery.[4]

Nullifiers issued an urgent plea for the protection of slavery. According to Pickens, the tariff controversy was really "an exterminating *war*" upon the property of slaveholders by nonslaveholders. The Colleton antitariff address argued, "All the property we possess, we hold by their boon; and a majority in Congress, may, at any moment, deprive us of it and transfer it northward, or offer it up on the bloody altar of a bigot's philanthropy." The Columbia antitariff address claimed that "It is known to be one object of the most conspicuous and efficient advantages of the Tariff, to effect by its means, the abolition of slavery throughout the southern states." The tariff would reduce the value of slave property and force slaveholders along the path of emancipation. As Preston confided to Thompson, slavery rather than the tariff was the real issue between the North and the South. John Hemphill of Sumterville felt, "We must retain unmutilated all our privileges; or we must be the slaves of our own slaves." At the Charleston antitariff meeting, Hayne cautioned, "Look at the condition of the Southern States, having the system of *slavery* so interwoven with their institutions that even to touch the subject is to involve them in ruin." Turnbull exulted that the "principles of Brutus" had finally been publicly affirmed.[5]

The incipient language of southern nationalism was also a powerful tool in the hands of pronullification planter politicians, who were able to use it to unite different classes in defense of their particular interests. William Henry Drayton, a unionist, referred to "a very small number of individuals, who are zealous of a severance of the State from the Union, and erecting ourselves into an independent sovereignty." Meetings in Cooswatchie, Laurens's courthouse, Edgefield, St. Helena's Parish, All Saint's Parish, and at the Pee Dee muster ground passed resolutions for non-consumption of northern manufactured goods and western hemp and livestock and looked to state action against the "tyranny of the north." Congressman W. D. Martin declared to his constituents in Barnwell that the state had the same relation to the federal government as Ireland did to England. The *Columbia Telescope* decried those who bore "southern degradation" and the "cunning bawlings" of the North. Nullifiers' use of separatist language pinned the label of disunion on them. The Colleton gathering, organized by Smith, advised "an attitude of open resistance to the laws of the Union." Later, he would announce, "The Union must be dissolved under its present course of administration" and "I am a disunionist and a traitor." And when Hayne proclaimed "I GO FOR MY COUNTRY," everyone knew which country he meant. McDuffie argued that the Union was being used as an "eastern idol" to prevent Carolinians from opposing the tariff. He would assert dramatically, "When I hear a Southern man cry 'Union'" methinks I smell treason on the tainted gale; but when I hear a Northern man shout 'Union,' I think I hear the trumpet blast of a robber band." At a Sumter meeting, Henry G. Nixon even predicted a war between the states over slavery. Unionist Christopher G. Memminger reported that nullifiers were being "classed in the same ranks as the Hartford convention" in the rest of the nation.[6]

Nullifiers stole a march over their opponents not only in agitation but also in organization. In 1831, the South Carolina State Rights and Free Trade Party was born under the auspices of Calhoun, the philosopher of nullification, Hamilton, the manager of the party, and McDuffie, the orator of nullification. Richard Yeadon, editor of the unionist *Charleston Courier*, complained that the nullifiers moved like a "Macedonian phalanx," as they "submit implicitly to their leaders." Hamilton's talent for "intrigue and management" and the "inflammatory nature of their cause" was sure to set the whole state on fire. As governor, on the pretext of reviewing the militia, Hamilton formed State Rights and Free Trade Associations in every district and parish. Some complained that he demeaned his office by his partisanship. He revealed the purpose of these associations as follows: "there is yet in the mass of the people an ignorance which leads to an apathy in regard to the proper means of preserving their rights. . . . The people *expect* that their Leaders in whose honesty and public spirit they have confidence will *think* for them — and that they will be prepared to *act* as their Leaders *think*." Calhoun also gave expression to the top-down philosophy of the nullifiers. He wrote that "most of our leading men out of Charleston have correct conceptions on the subject. . . . From them, truth will diffuse itself down among the people." Pickens argued with Hammond's assessment that "the 'people' are below many of 'our leaders' & particularly as regards 'disunion.' " But most nullifiers realized that they would have "to convert the people," or at least "a goodly portion of them."[7]

Nullification split the new states' rights, antitariff consensus in South Carolina. At the Charleston meeting in 1830, Drayton disavowed state interposition. And Cheves argued that they should act in concert with the rest of the South. Disagreement over nullification between the state's foremost legal minds, Harper and Judge John S. Richardson, marred the Columbia meeting. Drayton and Richardson, a states' rights theorist of some repute, condemned nullification as disunionist, unrepublican, and unconstitutional. As the former argued, "Is it republican, is it rational, that a single state should be able to controul [*sic*] 23 states?" William Smith and his followers rejected the concept of state veto and would give the Union party its distinctive claim to states' rights orthodoxy. Perry noted, "Mr. Calhoun had jumped over Judge Smith in the States' Rights school, and went far beyond what the judge had dreamed of in his opposition to national powers." In an address to the people of the state, Smith asked them to have faith in Jackson. Ex-governor David Rogerson Williams noted that the "new converts to state rights" were only concerned with the tariff and not with the bank and internal improvements.[8]

The course of Stephen D. Miller, a former Smith states' rights man, was more peculiar. At a public dinner in 1828, Miller had contended that the "road makers," "manufacturers," and the "Religious and Political fanatics" of the North really owned the land, cotton, and slaves of South Carolina. The Calhoun group had gained enough confidence in Miller's position to endorse him for the governorship. Miller's friends warned him, "Surely, the State will not be dictated by those men at the very time they should be interceding for forgiveness of their manifold sins. . . . They intend to out Dr. Cooper, and thereby take the lead." Miller proved his worth to nullifiers when as governor in 1828 he did much to arouse the state on the dangers of federal power to slavery. Pickens wrote Hammond, "Miller can be so flattered as to be induced to oppose Smith. . . . Their party will then be divided, & we will have the power of the State in our own hands." In 1830, as the nullifiers' candidate for the U.S. Senate, Miller defeated his former mentor, Smith. According to Perry, his conduct toward his old friend was less than "fair" and "open."[9]

Old states' righters, however, formed a vital segment of the unionist coalition, which was gradually taking shape on the basis of opposition to nullification and a broad allegiance to the republic. Its leadership consisted of states' rights men such as Smith, Richardson, John Taylor, James Blair, and Williams; nationalists such as Daniel E. Huger and Petigru; and staunch Jacksonian Democrats such as Perry, Joel R. Poinsett, and Memminger. Some of the Union Party leaders were the most moderate and reform-minded men when it came to the issue of slavery. Thomas S. Grimké, brother of the famous Grimké sisters, who was known for his patriotic 1809 Fourth of July oration, supported colonization and entertained grave doubts about slavery. Petigru and John Belton O'Neall were known to take up the cause of slaves and free black people in the courtroom. O'Neall was critical of South Carolina's antimanumission laws. Grimké and O'Neall were also involved in the temperance movement and the latter tried to launch a crusade against dueling. William Hemphill was accused of entertaining "cant and sickly sentiment" about slavery. Petigru and Poinsett never subscribed to the dominant positive good view of slavery.[10]

Unionist reformism never got translated into antislavery, and a few party leaders, especially lowcountry aristocrats such as Drayton, Langdon Cheves, and Hugh Swinton Legaré, would become as rabidly proslavery and separatist in their politics as their erstwhile opponents. Cheves, an early advocate of southern nationalism, flirted with the nullifiers. A contemporary observed about Legaré, "In feeling he was with the dominant party, yet in principle and on reason, he was with the opposition." Even though Legaré came out against nullification, he stayed aloof from the bitter political conflict over it that engulfed South Carolina. William Gilmore Simms identified himself as a unionist and states' rights man. Later, when he became known for his proslavery and southern nationalist views, his opinion of nullification would also change.[11]

Unionists were nostalgic for a bygone era when the toleration of slavery as a national evil had hardly interfered with its practical functioning. They were lost in the virulent politics of slavery. In a belated review of the *Crisis*, Hamilton felt that since the "civilized world" was opposed to slavery, the South should not agitate this question. As late as 1829, the *Greenville Mountaineer* was still characterizing slavery as "an evil and a curse, which has been entailed upon us by our ancestors." Some moderate papers such as the *Winyaw Intelligencer* and the mountain papers *Greenville Republican* and *Yorkville Pioneer* especially deprecated the use of slavery to alienate the people from the Union. The *Charleston City Gazette* chose to remind Carolinians that they had a higher stake in the republic than in slavery. [12]

The Union party effectively appealed for loyalty to the American experiment in republican government to stem the tide of nullification. The terms of unionist discourse had been set as early as 1827. Old '76 argued that he who opposes the principle of majority rule "denies the *virtue of the people*, on which all hopes of Republicanism rest. He is a monarchist, and only fit to hymn the praises of despotism." The *Charleston Courier* pointed out, "Many of our declaimers have abandoned without ceremony, this fundamental principle [majority rule] of all republican governments." And Washington lamented, "Shall it be said in after times, that for *this*, the beautiful system of Government, the ornament of an age; the example for a world; the boon purchased with the best blood of our fathers, was rudely torn to pieces and trampled under foot as inefficient and worthless; as poor, weak, and unfit to prove that man is capable of self-government?" Another unionist asked, "Shall South Carolina be the first to abandon that experiment, the last hope of freedom, and for what?" Nullification was the theory of Sir Robert Filmer and "precisely that principle which puts kings on thrones!" There were, according to one writer in the *Camden Journal*, "only 3 ways to be governed — either by the will of the individual — by the will of a small number of individuals in the body politic, or by the largest number of that body. The Nullifier of South Carolina, seems inclined to the *oligarchical* form. He is constantly thundering forth his anathemas upon the 'unprincipled majority,' and hence of course is presumed to entertain the opinion that the minority ought always to govern."[13]

Nullifiers and unionists would lay claim to the heritage of 1776. Nullifiers particularly played up the alleged support of Thomas Sumter for their cause. But the nature of the then ninety-six-year-old Sumter's letter on nullification led at least Perry to suspect that "one of his grandsons had something to do in its composition." Sumter died in 1832 and unfortunately could not clarify the issue. However, Colonel Taylor, a revolutionary hero and the father of Governor John Taylor, presided over the 1832 Union Convention in Columbia. Some unionists accused nullifiers of being Jacobins espousing anarchical doctrines. Nullifiers such as Harper reacted strongly to the Jacobin epithet, arguing that their remedy was safe and conservative. Harper in turn accused unionists of jacobinism for believing in "the government of lawless numbers."[14]

In order to combat nullification, Charleston unionists developed an explicit antiplanter rhetoric. They made appeals to city mechanics, who were told that the "Disunion party" desire "only masters and slaves, they despise a mechanic." They argued, "The lordly planter only swears more, about 'plunder, robbery and protection,' and d——ns the Government, and the Country, votes for Nullification, Disunion, British Protection and times as they *were before the Revolution*, when the King built the Exchange, Dungeons and all." The nullifiers "live like Patricians, rolling in their carriages, and luxuriating in the refined enjoyments of wealth and ease; only coming among the people *periodically* as elections are approaching." They were mainly planters who "live upon the fat of the land, and *discuss Nullification* over Champagne and Burgundy," have houses filled with "fine furniture" and could "spread a board fit for a Persian King." Planters were asked to raise their sons as men of labor rather than "as gentlemen of elegant leisure." Nullifiers replied that planters did not merely live off the labor of their slaves but supervised them in the fields. The more effective response was an appeal to state loyalty and southern nationalism to undermine challenges to planter rule. As the *Mercury* stated, "As Carolinians we enter our protest against this *anti-Carolina spirit* which is growing up against us. Southern opinions and Southern feelings, are falling into disrepute, and Northern notions, and Northern policy, are springing up amongst us."[15]

Charleston was a hotly contested area for both sides rather than an unionist stronghold. Contrary to accepted wisdom, the merchants of the city were also divided in their loyalties. In 1829, Pinckney defeated Grimké in the elections for the intendant of Charleston by a vote of 560 to 457. This was the start of the rivalry between the Mercury and disunion party and the Courier and Union party. In 1828 Grimké had represented the Charleston parishes of St. Philip's and St. Michael's in the state senate, where he had made a powerful speech against nullification. His defeat in the city elections, in which voter apathy dominated, was a major victory for nullifiers. In 1830, incumbent Pinckney was defeated by unionist James Pringle. Pringle defeated Pinckney by only eighty votes, but the nullifiers had their revenge when Pinckney was elected to the state house, where he was made Speaker. The unionist slate for the legislature did well, but Richard Cunningham, descendant of a prominent Tory family, defeated Petigru for the state senate by merely twenty-five votes. Later, Petigru would defeat the nullifier candidate for Legaré's vacated seat. In 1831, Pinckney avenged his defeat at Pringle's hands by winning the intendant elections by a margin of 108 votes. When he won the city elections again in 1832, the *Mercury* announced, "The spirit of Nullification is fixed and settled."[16]

The staunchly unionist and yeoman-dominated northwestern section of the upcountry also generated challenges against the undemocratic rule of the lowcountry planter elite. Perry emerged as the leading politi-

cal figure in this area and took over the editorship of the *Greenville Mountaineer* in 1830. In his youth he had entertained some antislavery notions,
but as an ambitious man seeking to gain acceptance in the charmed
circle of state leaders he soon shed these ideas. Hamilton referred to
Greenville district, the center of nonslaveholding-yeoman opposition to
nullification, as "the enemy's territory." Waddy Thompson failed sin-
gularly in his attempt to engineer nullifier success in this heartland of the
mountain yeomanry. Greenville proudly asserted that his district had
dismayed "the nullification gentry" by its opposition to their plans. In
Spartanburg, the aristocratic slaveholding Smiths, who had dominated
local politics and were for nullification, lost political power for the first
time in a unionist revolution. Nullifier Benjamin Whitner reported that
among the "plain but intelligent farmers. . . . I find the apprehension
universal that the friends of the Convention do not propose it as a peaceful remedy."[17]

Upcountry opposition to nullification revolved around the question of
unequal representation in the legislature. The *Mountaineer* complained
that the state's constitution was "more aristocratic in its fundamental
principles, than that of any other State in the Union," and that it was
"anti-republican" and "unwise." It objected to the idea that property
should be given greater weight than population in representation as a
"doctrine" that "may suit the genius of a European aristocracy, but we
doubt whether it will be palatable to the republican taste of Americans."
Nullifiers tried to respond by appealing to state and sectional loyalty. The
Mercury asked, "Would the upper country . . . virtually give up the contest
with the Federal Government, for the pitiful purpose of conquering the
Parishes? Would it give up the great cause of the South?"[18]

Both parties produced another flood of pamphlets and numbers in
newspapers for and against a state convention during the 1830 election
campaign for the legislature. The division on the convention bills revealed clearly the emergence of the two parties, and Hamilton recommended that the voting in the assembly be used to know "who is who."
Inaugurating the debate in the senate, Seabrook announced the "unyielding determination in the majority, to rivet their chains on the pa-
tient and unresisting slave-holder." The answer was a convention. While
Seabrook was supported by John L. Hunter and Grayson, no senator
presented the case for the opposing side. His bill passed by a vote of
twenty-three to eighteen but was still short of the required two-thirds
majority. The senate also passed William Pope's resolution affirming the
right of state veto by a vote of twenty-six to twelve. Each house formed a
Committee on Federal Relations. The house committee, headed by Preston, introduced seven resolutions, one calling for a convention. While

the first three states' rights resolutions were unanimously agreed to (115 votes to none), three resolutions calling for a convention and recognition of the right of a state to nullify a federal law were agreed to by only sixty to fifty-six votes. Huger led the house unionists against the convention. Opposing the notion of minority rule, he argued that a majority was less likely to be wrong than a minority, and if this was not so "then republicanism must be a dangerous fallacy, and the sooner we return to the 'divine rights' of the kings the better." He was seconded by John P. Richardson, while Thomas R. English, William R. Hill, and Butler put forth the case for nullification. Speaker Pinckney asked whether slaveholders should wait for emancipation with money "extorted from us by iniquitous taxation?"[19] By now, nullifiers were determined to establish the precedent of state interposition.

During the summers of 1831 and 1832, nullifiers waged an intense campaign to secure a two-thirds majority in the legislature in order to call a convention to veto the tariff laws. Appeals to state and sectional loyalty won more converts to the cause of nullification than cries of the oppression of planters. They asked Carolinians, "Are you willing to be the hewers of wood and drawers of water for the people of the Tariff States?" Just when the nullifiers stepped up their activities to a fever pitch, the Union Party's campaign lagged. This can be partly explained by the fact that most unionists accepted the 1832 tariff reform. The organization of the party also remained amateurish compared to the nullifier network. The disparate groups of unionists, the mountain yeomanry, Charleston merchants and mechanics, and planter leadership made concerted action difficult. Even more significant than all these factors was the decisive element in South Carolina politics: the support of the majority of the planter class, which lay with the unionists' opponents. Nullifier I. W. Hayne wrote confidently, "Why sir the gentry, with all of them their hearts [are] just where they should be . . . and the rabble, to a man of fortune, the most manageable I ever saw."[20]

The failure of the Union Party also lay at a more fundamental level. Nullifiers' strategy of portraying unionists as protariff and antislavery put them on the defensive. They spent their time proving their southern bonafides instead of continuing to emphasize the disunionist and unrepublican nature of nullification. Unionist leaders seized upon the idea of a southern convention as a substitute for the single-state action advocated by nullifiers. Cheves argued that the power of one state was not sufficient to meet the northern threat. Robert Witherspoon confessed that he preferred "the struggle of seven states to that of one state."

Unionist pamphlets espousing the "distinct and highly important interests" of the South versus the "aggressions of an uncontrolled majority" could well be mistaken for nullifier documents. The party met in Columbia in September 1832 and sent representatives to the southern states to implement the plan.[21]

Nullifiers now claimed that the southern convention plan was a plot for disunion while nullification was an unionist measure. Miller rejoiced that unionists had "jumped from Union! Union! *beloved* Union!" and Robert E. Yates noted that Richardson's advocacy of a southern convention had "neutralized" many of his followers. James Hemphill reported that "one half of their toasts are Convention, Revolution, Southern Confederacy &c. The other is Submission, peace &c." As James Clark informed Hammond, "There is much division among themselves as regards a Southern Convention — that all the discussions (on this [to] them [a] painful subject) will be kept from our ears; it is the wish of their leaders." The bankruptcy of the southern convention strategy was highlighted when Richard I. Manning, former governor of South Carolina and a rich upcountry planter, wrote to Calhoun asking whether the two opposing parties could now unite on a common platform. Calhoun wrote back refusing to entertain the idea of giving up his cherished scheme of state interposition.[22] The retreat of the Union party, just before the crucial legislative elections of 1832, was a triumph of one of the central ideas behind the Carolina doctrine, southern separatism. It was not their alleged conservatism that led to the defeat of the unionists, but their inability to formulate an alternative to the nullifier mix of southernism and proslavery.

Some unionists tried to respond to the nullifier onslaught by repeating the charges of elitism and disunionism. The nullification party was a "gentlemen's party" they argued. "The oppression so loudly complained of, is only felt in imagination — its effects are confined principally to the planting interest, the aristocrats of our country — those who unmindful of the superior blessings they enjoy, would for the sake of a few additional pence to their income, involve the country in war. And will the people of the state, the democratic people — the bone and sinew of the country — the stamina — will *they* sacrifice *their* peace and *their* lives — will they render desolate *their* firesides, and expose to ruthless invasion their families, merely to gratify a *proud* and *pampered* aristocracy?" In the yeoman-dominated mountain section of the upcountry, the movement for a southern convention had made little headway. Greenville had not even sent a delegation to the southern convention gathering, though local unionists endorsed the meeting. Picking up on the traditional upcountry complaint, they criticized the legislative apportionment. The "rotten boroughs" of the lowcountry parishes were more "clamorous for nullification," thus the system of representation ensured that the voice of a minority would dominate over that of the majority. Carolinians were called upon to "nullify" the parish elite who were against republican government. A meeting at Pickens's courthouse criticized "wealthy and influential men" for plotting to subvert "the liberties of the people" and "to deprive the voters of the District of the *free* choice of Representatives, the dearest and greatest privilege of freemen." John Barrillon wrote that the contest was between "*people's rights*" and the "aggressions" of the aristocracy.[23]

The election campaign of 1832 was the bloodiest in the state's history. Duels, which were usually personal affairs of honor, became the stuff of politics. Two years before, a duel between James Blair and Hammond had barely been averted. Perry shot Turner Bynum, a rival editor, in a duel. Bribery, murder, and mayhem stalked the streets of Charleston, where unionists and nullifiers came to blows and unionist leaders barely escaped being roughed up. One nullifier refused to attack a unionist "common laborer" because he did not want to spill his "base plebeian blood." Clark boasted, "And as for fighting, by God we always whip them."[24]

The outcome of the elections revealed that, with a few exceptions, nullifiers gathered a majority of their votes from districts and parishes where plantation agriculture and slavery flourished. They swept the statewide plantation belt, the lowcountry, the middlecountry, and the piedmont districts dominated by cotton cultivation, such as Richland, Edgefield, and Fairfield. In Prince William's, St. Bartholomew's, St. Paul's, St. John's Colleton, St. Andrew's, and St. Stephen's Parishes and the districts of Lexington and Marlboro unionists did not receive a single vote. The voting population in the parishes was exceedingly small, sometimes a couple hundred, giving substance to unionist complaints of minority domination. The city of Charleston gave a bare majority of its votes to nullifiers, 1448 to the unionists' 1316. Northern upcountry districts that lay outside the plantation belt, such as Greenville, Spartanburg, Chesterfield, Lancaster, and the nonplantation lowcountry district of Horry, remained strongly unionist. In Horry, unionists received 363 votes to the nullifiers' 58; in Greenville, 1,311 to 500, and in Union, 1,352 to 549. A prominent exception was Pendleton, where slaves comprised less than 30 percent of the population but which went for nullification, apparently because of the influence of Calhoun, who had established his Fort Hill plantation there. In two other notable exceptions, the nullifier slate in upcountry York won by merely forty-six votes, and in black belt Darlington, unionists received 698 votes to the nullifiers' 497. While most of the parishes went for nullification, in Prince George Winyaw, unionists outpolled nullifiers by one vote and in Williamsburg the vote was evenly

TABLE 2. Election for the State Legislature, 1832

Districts	Nullifiers	Unionists	Total
Abbeville	1,666	946	2,612
Barnwell	1,101	595	1,696
Beaufort	622	105	782
Charleston	2,028	1,675	3,703
Chester	1,096	757	1,853
Chesterfield	343	559	902
Colleton	433	88	521
Darlington	497	698	1,195
Edgefield	1,629	640	2,269
Fairfield	1,747	103	1,850
Georgetown	348	221	569
Greenville	500	1,311	1,811
Horry	58	363	421
Kershaw	358	556	914
Lancaster	427	626	1,053
Laurens	1,484	985	2,469
Lexington	761	0	761
Marion	772	500	1,272
Marlboro	271	0	271
Newberry	1,157	137	1,294
Orangeburg	1,440	145	1,585
Pendleton	2,494	1,255	3,749
Richland	784	259	1,043
Spartanburg	833	1,839	2,672
Sumter	983	776	1,759
Union	1,352	549	1,901
Williamsburg	283	283	566
York	1,116	1,062	2,178

Sources: Chauncey Samuel Boucher, *The Nullification Controversy in South Carolina* (New York, 1916), 203; *Charleston Mercury*, Oct. 11, 12, 13, 15, 16, 17, 1832.

divided between the two parties. Unionists also won in a handful of parishes — Clarendon, St. George's Dorchester, St. James's Goose Creek, and Christ Church. In the state as a whole, nullifiers had a majority of approximately 26,583 votes to the unionists' 17,033. Voter turnout tended to be low in areas where nullifiers won handily, a fact that casts doubt on the democratic upsurge for nullification theory.[25]

The election revealed that far deeper causes than momentary political excitement underlay the success of nullification. Despite the exceptions, a broad pattern linking nullifier strength to areas with the greatest in-

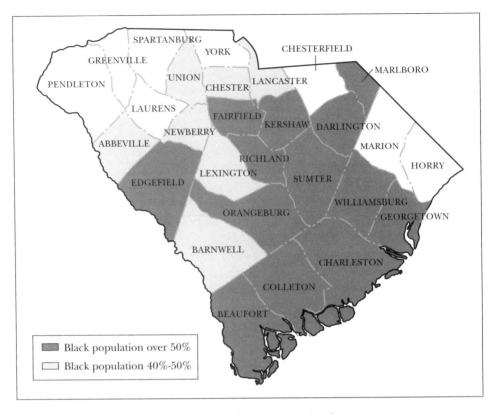

MAP 2. South Carolina Black Belt, 1830

Source: William W. Freehling, *Prelude to Civil War: The Nullification Controversy in South Carolina, 1816–1836* (New York, 1965) 365–67.

volvement in the plantation economy and unionist support with relatively slaveless areas is clearly discernible. Of South Carolina's twenty-eight districts in 1830, thirteen had a slave population of over 50 percent and seven had a slave population between 40 to 50 percent. Nullifiers had garnered their greatest support from the black belt. The average nullifier thus was either a slaveholder or lived in a predominantly slaveholding area and, more than likely, participated in the staple economy. A high incidence of slaveholding, a widespread slave economy, and planter-dominated politics gave nullifiers the popular edge they were looking for, and the unequal system of representation converted this edge into an overwhelming domination of the legislature, which made nullification possible. Nullifiers won a two-thirds majority in each house of the assembly even though they did not win two-thirds of the popular vote. The state government structure propped up the political dominance of the planter class, a majority of which were for nullification.

Governor Hamilton was so sure of a nullifier victory that he had written his proclamation convening an extra session of the legislature, even before the results were announced. He warned his friends, however, that this fact should not be revealed as it may influence "some timid and weak minded voters." The senate passed the convention bill by a vote of thirty-one to thirteen; and the house of representatives, by a vote of ninety-six to twenty-five. The campaign for the convention was desultory. Unionist legislators complained of the nullifiers' "precipitancy," noting, "In twelve days from the declaration of the Elections the Legislature has been convened — in four days a law was passed calling a Convention — the election of Delegates is ordered on the 12th and 13th of next month, and the Convention will assemble on the Monday following. All this is done in the short space of forty days from the conclusions of the Elections in October."[26]

The Union Party was divided on what strategy to follow for the convention elections. While lowcountry leaders advised against participating, upcountry leaders wanted to contest the elections. The result of this division was that nullifier candidates ran unopposed in many parts of the state. In Charleston, unionists' last-minute decision to contest the elections resulted in a narrow nullifier majority. The State Rights and Free Trade Party asked the voters of Greenville not to vote in the elections, as the presence of unionists would merely embarrass the proceedings of the convention. Despite all the confusion, unionists managed to elect their nominees in Greenville, Spartanburg, Lancaster, Chesterfield, Kershaw, Horry, Clarendon, Darlington, and from the parishes of St. James Goose Creek, St. George Dorchester, and Christ Church. Lowcountry leaders were elected from unionist strongholds — Alfred Huger from Spartanburg, Henry Middleton from Greenville, and Daniel Huger from Horry. Since the convention was formed on the basis of the legislative apportionment, the number of unionists in it was minuscule. In the 162-strong convention only 26 delegates were from the Union party.[27]

As one historian has noted, the planter aristocracy, which controlled the political "machine" of the state through unequal representation, inevitably controlled the convention. Huger felt that the unionists should not take their seats. Others proposed that the convention remedy inequitable representation and institute reforms such as the popular election of the governor. Middleton introduced resolutions stating that the supreme will of the freemen of South Carolina could only be represented by their own votes or by a convention elected solely on the basis of the white population. The present convention represented a "manifest and palpable usurpation of power" and should deem itself incompetent. Samuel R. Gibson of Lancaster presented a memorial from his district asking for a constitutional amendment on representation.[28] But democratic reform was certainly not a part of the nullifying gentry's agenda.

Given the composition of the convention, its actions were a foregone conclusion. It met in Columbia on November 19 and Governor Hamilton was elected president. Some developed cold feet at the last minute and advised delay, but P. M. Butler exemplified most nullifiers' impatience: "I wonder that it is a question—which is as to the time of the application of this act of Nullification. I *say without further delay*. . . . if we mean to *act* let us *act* at once *come what will*." Calhoun had already given his blessings for immediate action. A Select Committee of Twenty One, including such prominent nullifiers as Harper, Hayne, Miller, McDuffie, and Turnbull, presented an ordinance for the nullification of the tariff laws. A report, written by Hayne, claimed that the tariff had rendered "one portion of the Confederacy tributary to the rest." Given this state of things, the Union, "instead of being a blessing, must soon become a curse." The ordinance, also drafted by Harper, declared the 1828 and 1832 revenue laws null and void within South Carolina. It asked the legislature to implement the ordinance, which would take effect on February 1, 1833. Appeals to federal courts on the subject were forbidden and all state officials would be required to take a loyalty oath to enforce nullification. An amendment by C. J. Colcock exempted members of the legislature from taking this oath of allegiance, which would become the focus of controversy. Finally, the ordinance declared that any attempt to enforce the nullified laws would be deemed "inconsistent with the longer continuance of South Carolina in the Union." An elaborate signing ceremony was followed by the reading of an address to the people of South Carolina, written by Turnbull, and an address to the people of the United States, drafted by Calhoun and McDuffie. The address to the people of the state commanded the obedience of all citizens. The address to the people of the United States ended with the threat of secession. Governor Hamilton announced that the voice of the convention should be next to the voice of God for Carolinians.[29]

Forwarding convention documents to the legislature, he said that "the die has been at last cast" and asked the federal government to remove all troops from Charleston. The legislature passed two laws that gave effect to nullification. The first act ensured that importers could recover goods seized for nonpayment of duties with a writ of replevin. If this procedure failed then the sheriff could seize the personal property of the collecting agent through a writ of capias in withernam until the imported goods were returned. The legislature prescribed hefty fines and terms of imprisonment for any officer or person who obstructed nullification. The second act prescribed an oath of primary allegiance to the state for all civil and judicial officials and militia officers. To ensure that federal courts would not be able to challenge the legality of these actions, the rulings of federal courts could be overturned by that of the state courts. This provision was a direct violation of the appellate section of the Judiciary Act, but the unconstitutionality of nullification itself overshadowed the illegalities of executing it. The legislature also redistributed the top state offices among leading nullifiers. It selected Hayne for the governorship and Calhoun for Hayne's Senate seat. It also passed resolutions calling for a convention of all states. As if to illustrate the futility of this gesture, both houses passed bills to amend the militia laws and to provide for the security of the state. The governor was authorized to raise volunteer companies and to purchase arms and ammunition.[30]

As the actions of the convention and legislature made clear, armed confrontation between the state and the federal government was an eventuality that many were prepared to face. Nullifiers may not all have been disunionists but they were not unqualified unionists. The political discourse of slavery and separatism that they had popularized made secession a viable, and to some an attractive, option to majority oppression. Disunion might well have been a dreaded alternative for most nullifiers. But it was an alternative that flowed directly from Calhoun's theory of state sovereignty, which justified nullification and the constitutional right to secession.[31]

The national response to nullification centered around the issues of the Union and the Constitution rather than the tariff. The breathtaking speed with which nullifiers had acted stunned the country, and many feared for the future of the American republic. One writer noted, "*Nullification* is not the invention of the statesmen of South Carolina, for it is the seed of death which every republic has carried with it in its career of glory, prosperity, and freedom, and which has finally induced disgrace and ruin." Nullifiers planned to subvert the "distinctive republican character" of American government. Only civil war, anarchy, and tyranny could follow their scheme of minority rule. The opposition of the leading statesmen of the day, Madison, Webster, Clay, and Jackson, discredited the Carolina doctrine among groups with varying political opinions. Like Carolinian unionists, a majority of antebellum Americans saw nullification as unconstitutional, unrepublican, and disunionist.[32]

However, few were prepared for Jackson's strong reaction to nullification. After all, he had tolerated Georgia's defiance of the Supreme Court in its Indian removal policy. In his message to Congress, Jackson, congratulating the country on the approaching payment of the public debt, asked for the immediate lowering of duties to the revenue standard. But a few days later came the president's proclamation denouncing nullification as disunion. Historians have remarked on the completely different tone of these two presidential documents, which were issued virtually simultaneously. The reason for this apparent anomaly lay in the fact that in Jackson's mind the reduction of the tariff and nullification had always been two separate issues. Given the approaching extinguishment of the debt, the precipitous action of the nullifiers was, according to him, nothing more than a plot to destroy the Union and subvert republican government.[33]

Jackson, even more than Webster, espoused a new notion of the Union as the permanent embodiment of popular will. By this standard, rebellion against the Union was nothing short of defiance of the people's wishes, the sacred dictum of Jacksonian rhetoric. This was hardly "high federalism." Jackson defended majority rule and democracy and denounced the notion of a minority veto. For him it was a mockery that "a small majority of voters in a single State" claimed to have the power to decide the constitutionality of federal laws. Dismissing nullification as disunionist, he admonished nullifiers for raising the specter of civil war. For him, nullification represented "the approach of a crisis in our affairs, on which the continuance of our unexampled prosperity, our political existence, and perhaps that of all free governments, may depend." By endorsing the vision of a perpetual and democratic Union and challenging the constitutionality of secession, he created an important precedent for Lincoln, just as Calhoun and the nullifiers had laid the political and ideological groundwork for southern secessionists.[34]

Jackson became convinced that nullifiers were using the slavery issue to foment disunion. This does not mean that the president, a slaveholder who vigorously opposed abolition, was antislavery. The Democratic Party was, in the words of Van Buren, based on an alliance between southerners and the "plain republicans" of the North. And the Jacksonian-led democratic reforms for white men in New York, New Jersey, Connecticut, and Pennsylvania were accompanied by a curbing of African-American rights. But the political principles of Jacksonianism were not based on the defense of slavery but on the much broader intersectional ideals of democratic republicanism. Jacksonians accommodated and even protected slavery but did not make the vindication of slavery the centerpiece of their political philosophy.[35] Jacksonian democracy was clearly a white man's democracy, but Carolinian leaders were averse to any kind of democracy. What set the nullifiers apart from the Jacksonians was their ideological commitment to a proslavery, antimajoritarian theory.

Nullifiers' ferocious reaction to the proclamation revealed their acute suspicions of the democratic nationalism it represented. Hammond was apprehensive of its effect on "the timid & ignorant of our party" and felt that "it will have great influence, which . . . will require much caution to counteract." The legislature claimed that the president had no constitutional power to challenge the action of a state that possessed the right to secede from the Union. Governor Hayne in his counterproclamation warned Carolinians against Jackson's attempt to "seduce" them from their "primary allegiance to the state." Hayne planned to have a hundred men in every district and parish ready to take up arms, and he called for volunteers "to SUPPRESS INSURRECTION, REPEL INVASION, or SUPPORT THE CIVIL AUTHORITIES in the execution of the laws." He instructed his aides-de-camp to acquire powder, rifles, cannon balls, and muskets, and he ordered that the arms in the state armory be cleaned. He wanted an army of 10,000 ready to fight.[36]

Not only the frenetic military preparations but the renewed vigor with which nullifiers started justifying secession as a reserved right of the states gave an ominous cast to the crisis. Preston wrote that Representative Robert Barnwell had come "to the conclusion that no remedy is left but a dissolution of the Union," and that even though he had a "deep devotion" to the Union, "I consider it like every other political question as open for consideration." The United States, nullifiers argued, was merely a league of independent states that any one of them could leave when they wished. The *State Rights and Free Trade Evening Post* proclaimed, "At all events, let the RIGHT OF SECESSION never be abandoned. Let the Southern States cling to it as their political salvation." Nullifiers' threats led Perry to believe that they would secede from the Union at once.[37]

Carolinian unionists were also pushed to assume a more aggressive posture as prospects of an armed conflict increased. They complained that the nullification laws, especially the test oath, violated every principle of republican government by disenfranchising citizens, interfering with freedom of conscience and opinion, undermining the independence of the judiciary, and by legislating a "standing army." Local union meetings in Greenville and Spartanburg vowed that they would resist the "tyrannical" oath and that they would "never . . . consent to be disfranchised in the land of our nativity, nor proscribed from office for opinion's sake, while we have the powers and means of resistance." Apprehensive of the warlike preparations of the nullifier-dominated state government and encouraged by Jackson's proclamation, the convention of the Union and State Rights Party at Columbia in December 1832 issued a strongly worded report written by Poinsett and Memminger and a protest written by Petigru against nullification.[38]

The aroused mood of the unionists also produced some practical results in terms of party organization. Memminger and Poinsett, the manager of the party, set up Washington and Union societies all over the state. While the citizens in the predominantly nonslaveholding districts of Greenville, Spartanburg, Lancaster, and Horry were mostly unionist, unionist societies also had over 900 members in Pendleton, Abbeville, and Laurens. These societies managed to get a foothold even in some nullifier districts. In the lowcountry parishes, except for Charleston, they were not so successful. Poinsett firmly believed that "the heresies of nullification and right to secession must be combated manfully and be put down or ours is not a government for freemen to live under." He had urgently asked for Jackson's help and reported that he had nearly 7,000 Union men ready to bear arms. In some of the mountain districts, the local militia was completely dominated by unionists. The willingness of both nullifiers and unionists to fight for their beliefs turned the state into an armed camp. According to Rebecca Rutledge, "collecting of arms, drilling the militia, and raising and equipping new companies, these are the most engrossing occupations of most of the southern gentlemen."[39]

An atmosphere of impending civil war pervaded the state. Jackson assured Poinsett of support and denounced Hayne's military preparations as treasonous. He ordered troops to Castle Pinckney and Sullivan's Island and sent the sloop Natchez and General Winfield Scott to Charleston in case nullifiers stormed customhouses. In an elaborate set of instructions to the collectors of Charleston, Beaufort, and Georgetown, Secretary of Treasury Louis McLane asked them to enforce the revenue laws without provoking a confrontation with nullifiers. He recommended that they employ revenue cutters to collect duties onboard ships rather than in the ports and to shift the customhouse at Charleston to Castle Pinckney, where nullifiers would be powerless to prevent the collection of duties. Jackson also asked Congress for additional powers to enforce the revenue laws in South Carolina. In his State of the Union message of January 16, 1833, he noted that nullifiers had embarked on military preparations. He asked for military powers to be used in "self defense."[40]

Jackson's followers also made sure that nullifiers lost the battle for public opinion. Nearly every state issued its own report and resolutions on nullification and the proclamation. Northern states such as New Hampshire, New Jersey, Connecticut, Ohio, Illinois, and Indiana, including the border state of Delaware, gave their unqualified approbation to the proclamation and offered the services of their citizens to quell nullification. Nullification was condemned as a "heretical," "dangerous," and "anti-republican" doctrine that threatened to destroy the only "temple of liberty" known to mankind. The response of legislatures dominated by states' righters was more reserved. While rejecting the idea that nullification was an offspring of states' rights theory, Pennsylvania and Maryland were reluctant to endorse the new nationalism of the proclamation. Maine approved of it but also declared its devotion to states' rights. The New York report, drafted by Van Buren, gave a lengthy account of the development of Jeffersonian states' rights and illustrated the deviation of the Carolina doctrine from the original theory. At the same time, it did not endorse the proclamation. Old states' righters such as Nathaniel Macon condemned the proclamation and nullification as containing new heresies "unfit for use in the United States."[41]

Southern states' reaction to nullification gave little indication of their future conversion to Calhoun's ideas of absolute state sovereignty and the constitutional right to secession. Jackson claimed that the nullifiers had "been encouraged by a few from Georgia and Virginia but the united voice of the yeomanry" was against them. Mississippi, Louisiana, and Tennessee, Jackson's home state, were most supportive of the president. North Carolina and Alabama condemned the high tariffs and the latter called for a federal convention. The southwestern states, especially Louisiana, which was a high tariff state, were less likely to bemoan the tariff than the depressed south-Atlantic states. But antitariff feeling in the South, free from the discourse of slavery and separatism, did not translate into an endorsement of nullification. Georgia and Virginia were most sympathetic to the nullifiers. In the Milledgeville convention, a strong minority in Georgia came out in support of the nullifiers, though the legislature rejected nullification and issued a call for a southern convention. In Virginia, Governor John Floyd condemned Jackson's "warlike recommendations" and the proclamation. The slaveholding, planter-dominated tidewater section of the state was particularly supportive of nullification. The Jacksonians, who controlled the assembly, following the lead of Thomas Ritchie's *Richmond Enquirer*, refused to accept it. Like New York, Virginia condemned nullification but could not endorse the proclamation. It appointed Benjamin Watkins Leigh as commissioner to South Carolina. The aristocratic Leigh, a proslavery spokesman in the Virginia slavery debates, was a good choice to send to the Palmetto state.[42]

Despite the official reactions of states below the Mason-Dixon line, some prominent southerners such as George M. Troup and John M. Berrien of Georgia, Dixon Lewis of Alabama, John Branch of North Carolina, George Poindexter of Mississippi, and Littleton Tazewell, Abel P.

Upshur, and John Tyler of Virginia flirted with the notion of state interposition or were wary of Jackson's unequivocal assertion of federal jurisdiction. Unionists such as Petigru worried that the South would be converted to "the new superstition" of Carolina. As for Jackson's proclamation, Preston noted significantly, "Virginia denounces it. Boston approves it." For Calhoun, nothing could reveal the "depth of the conflict than the different sperit [*sic*] in which the Proclamation has been received in the two sections." Rebecca Rutledge wrote to her husband, "the two sections of the country will never return to their former harmony . . . that we shall be no longer brothers, but rivals." The southern states' response indicated that it would take more than the tariff to convert them to the Carolina doctrine. Cooper in his second consolidation essay argued that the South would have to choose between the true "southern doctrines" of the nullifiers and the "northern doctrines" that would reduce them to penury and destruction. Hammond remained convinced that "Our cause *is* the cause of the South & it must be sustained." Like Calhoun, he felt that adherence to the Jacksonian party line had caused southern states such as Virginia and Georgia to disavow nullification. Carolinian planter politicians' legendary aversion to the party system was not induced solely by a republican suspicion of factions but by a realization that mass-based intersectional parties and democratic politics worked at counterpurposes with sectional consciousness.[43]

The state's political isolation eventually served to dissipate the crisis. Without any assurance of southern support, starting a conflict was foolish at best and suicidal at worst. Nullification was suspended by an informal gathering of nullifiers at Charleston on the "fatal first" of February, giving Congress more time to work out a compromise over the tariff. The retreat was effected with much bravado. Hamilton defiantly declared that nothing would stop him from getting his sugar, which he had imported to put nullification into practice. Fortunately for "Sugar Jimmy," Jackson's removal of the customhouse to Castle Pinckney prevented him from going "to death" for his sugar. Preston claimed that the women of Carolina laughed at the proclamation.[44] Despite this display of invincibility, nullifiers realized that the game was out of their hands.

They were now prepared to entrust tariff reform to Congress, but they would rather cooperate with the anti-Jackson tariff men than with free traders in the administration. Verplanck had introduced a bill in Congress in December 1832 to drastically reduce the tariff. The bill was voted down in the Committee of the Whole House due to the opposition of protariff congressmen. Calhoun and his followers were also loath to let the Jacksonians take credit for tariff reduction. Nullifiers supported Clay's proposals, which were less favorable to free trade. His bill provided for the gradual reduction of the tariff to the revenue standard by 1842. He ensured that the tariff would last for another nine years and won plaudits as the savior of the Union. Overcoming reservations about a home-evaluation clause, Calhoun actively cooperated with the architect of the American system to push through the compromise tariff of 1833.

The furor surrounding the Wilkins bill overshadowed the debate over the compromise tariff. Congress responded to Jackson's request for additional powers when Senator William Wilkins of the Judiciary Committee reported the revenue collection bill or, as the nullifiers called it, the "Force bill." The Verplanck and Wilkins bills represented the carrot-and-stick or olive-branch-and-sword strategy of the administration, but they also represented Jackson's longstanding views on the tariff and nullification. The Wilkins bill had nullifiers up in arms but "the shock that was felt upon the first intimations of settling our controversy with the sword is wearing off." Calhoun desperately tried to get resolutions vindicating the Carolina doctrine passed in the Senate. The crucial issue for nullifiers now clearly transcended the tariff. However, the bill passed by a vote of thirty-two to one in the Senate, the lone dissenting vote coming from Tyler. Senators from North Carolina, Alabama, and Mississippi, including Troup of Georgia joined the Carolinians in abstaining from voting on it. In the House, McDuffie led the opposition to the bill. Future southern rights' men such as John Y. Mason of Virginia, Clement C. Clay of Alabama, and Henry W. Conner of North Carolina opposed it. Southerners' reservations on the Wilkins bill were an indication of their future susceptibility to the Carolina doctrine. It became law the same day as the compromise tariff, March 2, 1833, when the president signed both acts.[45]

The Wilkins bill sparked another memorable debate on the political and constitutional issues raised by nullification. In his speech against the bill, which lasted two days, Calhoun embarked on a long justification of his own and his state's course. Jackson, who had been identified with "the staple states," had proven false to the hopes vested in him by allowing "an individual" (Van Buren) to turn his attention to "mere party arrangements." Laying the blame for the tariff impasse squarely on the president, Calhoun contended that South Carolina had not acted hastily, but rather its sister states in the South had acted "tardily." He called upon the South as the "natural guardian" of the reserved powers of the state to come to the defense of nullification. In his refutation of Calhoun's speech, Webster argued, "those who espouse the doctrines of nullification, reject, as it seems to me, the first great principle of all republican liberty; that is, that the majority must govern." According to Webster, a northern conservative who was not a champion of unfettered democracy, the traditional checks and balances provided by the Constitution were sufficient to protect minorities. In the most salient part of his rebuttal, Calhoun outlined the need for state interposition. He stated, "There exists in every Southern State a domestic institution, which would require a far less bold construction to consider the government of every State in that quarter, not to be republican." Calhoun predicted that a day might arrive when a sectional majority would endanger slavery. If Webster's and Jackson's constitutional ideas were to prevail, he dramatically concluded, they would "drive the white population from the South Atlantic States."[46] For him states' rights theory was not a vindication of local democracy but a safeguard for the distinct interests of the southern slaveholding minority.

Calhoun was more interested in establishing state interposition as a legitimate constitutional doctrine than in provoking an armed conflict. He had advised nullifiers to give Congress time to act. The Clay compromise allowed him and his followers to claim a dubious victory for free trade. At the end of the congressional session, he rushed home to attend the state convention, which reconvened on March 11, 1833. According to Perry, Calhoun looked "thinner and had lost much of the greatness of his appearance."[47] Nullification had taken its toll on him.

The convention hastened to undo the work of nullification. Noting that "great truths should be independent of the human agents that promulgate them," the convention's report on the Leigh mission claimed presumptuously that South Carolina rather than Virginia and Madison had given the correct interpretation of the 1798 resolutions. The convention revoked nullification by an overwhelming vote of 153 to 4. A small minority led by Robert Barnwell Smith felt that none of the state's demands had been satisfied. The tariff was still in place and the Wilkins bill had been enacted. He argued that "South Carolina must be an armed camp" and concluded, "I fear that there is no longer hope or liberty for the South, under a Union, by which all self government is taken away. A people owning slaves, are mad, or worse than mad, who do not hold their destinies in their own hands." It must be noted, though, that historians have made too much of the differences between radical and moderate nullifiers. Smith's resolutions calling for the state to keep up its military preparations were passed by the convention, and 20,000 volunteers who composed the new military companies were asked to "retain their existing organization." His reasoning found wide favor in the party and he emerged as Calhoun's protégé and one of the leading figures in the state after the nullification crisis. Harper argued that it was the convention's duty to challenge the "consolidation" of powers in the federal government, as the government may use them "to relieve another 'disfranchised class,' whom your laws are alleged to oppress, your free negroes first; and afterwards, your slaves." The unrepentant convention nullified the Wilkins Act, which would "bring the utter ruin and debasement of the Southern States of this Confederacy."[48]

The more significant opposition to the actions of the convention came from unionists. Some such as Judge Richardson had already scoffed at the nullifiers' attempt to portray the Clay compromise as a victory over the policy of protection. Others felt that Calhoun had entered into his own corrupt bargain with Clay to secure the presidency. But it was the new nullification ordinance with its provision for another oath of exclusive allegiance to the state that irked them the most. This second test oath was even more objectionable than the first as it allowed the legislature to incorporate the oath into the state constitution by a simple majority. Normally, amendments to the constitution had to be passed twice by a two-thirds majority. Some nullifiers such as Miller also felt that an oath was not necessary. His resolution to strike out that section from the ordinance lost by a close vote of seventy-three to seventy-nine. The new ordinance of nullification with the test oath provision passed by a vote of 132 to 19. Satisfied, Hammond declared, "The Force Bill was nullified & the *allegiance* of every Carolinian declared to be due to the State & *obedience* only to the constitutional acts of the General Government."[49]

The crisis did not come to an end, as the oath of allegiance, which was clearly geared to cripple political opposition, gave new life to the controversy. Nullifiers felt that the oath was necessary because of the "secret military organization" of unionists and their willingness to cooperate with Jackson. They claimed that South Carolina had just as much right to demand an oath of allegiance as did England, France, or any other independent country. For unionists, this was merely proof of the unrepublican and disunionist nature of nullification. Nullifiers had shown that they "DARE NOT TRUST THE PEOPLE." In his farewell address, Drayton argued that the oath was designed to proscribe unionists from state offices. The 1833 Militia Act incorporated the test oath for all officers. Union party senators led by Daniel Huger entered a protest against the bill. It argued that the oath was unconstitutional and that the state had no right to demand the exclusive allegiance of its citizens to "any Prince, Potentate, State or Authority whatsoever."[50]

The passage of the test oath by the assembly galvanized unionist opposition. The *Greenville Mountaineer* reported that hundreds of farmers had migrated out of the state rather than take the "tyrannical Test Oath." Meetings in the unionist heartland, areas dominated by the nonslaveholding mountain yeomanry such as Greenville, Spartanburg, Pickens, Lancaster, Chesterfield, Anderson, Union, Chester, and lowcountry Horry, denounced the oath as a feudal concept since allegiance was owed only to kings by their subjects. The oath would end freedom of conscience and opinion, essential features of a republican polity. It disqualified duly elected officers from serving in the militia, which was "degrading and humiliating to freemen." Subversion of locally elected militias went hand in hand with the effort to create "a standing army." Greenville citizens elected an entire slate of unionist officers for the militia. Many were alarmed at the militancy of the nonslaveholding mountain farmers who promised opposition "*to death.*" The Union party convention, which met in Greenville on March 24, 1834, passed resolutions asking for resistance to the oath through peaceful and judicial means.[51]

Two cases challenging the constitutionality of the test oath came up before the state courts. Edward McCready and James McDaniel had been denied their commissions because of their refusal to take the oath. While the oath was upheld by nullifier Judge Bay in the McCready case, unionist Judge Richardson declared it unconstitutional and ordered McDaniel's superior to give him his commission. Both cases, *McCready v. Hunt* and *McDaniel v. McMeekin*, were brought before the Court of Appeals in the summer of 1834. They were argued by Grimké and Petigru versus Smith, whose extremism had been rewarded with the post of attorney general. Grimké hammered home the point that the oaths of allegiance were unrepublican and to be found only among the politically intolerant European monarchies. Representing the state, Smith argued for Calhoun's conception of absolute state sovereignty, which would allow for sole allegiance to the state and the constitutional right to secede from the Union. Finally, Judges O'Neall and Johnson pronounced the oath unconstitutional with Harper dissenting. The presence of two unionists on the bench had won the day for the Union party. Nullifiers responded with wild ideas to impeach the two judges, abolish the court, and enact state treason laws. The Court of Appeals would be abolished in 1835. For now, Governor Hayne advised restraint.[52]

Nullifiers, who remained adamant to enforce the oath, stepped up their campaign for the elections of 1834. The *Greenville Mountaineer* estimated that the nullifiers had received 20,000 votes to the unionists' 15,000. Again, this relatively close popular plurality translated into overwhelming nullifier domination of the malapportioned legislature. In an added blow to the unionists, Davis defeated Perry in a congressional election that "passed off very quietly," by only seventy votes in a district that included the nullifier-dominated Pendleton and the unionist stronghold Greenville. In the other mountain congressional district, which included York, Chester, Spartanburg, and Union, unionist James Rogers defeated nullifier William Clowney.[53]

Unionists now deluged the legislature with petitions against the oath, signed by thousands from Greenville, Union, Pendleton, Abbeville, Lancaster, and Kershaw. But nullifiers including Calhoun were determined to act. As Petigru noted, "Calhoun . . . wished to have his last revelations incorporated in the [state] constitution." Calhoun argued that if the oath was not enacted, it would be perceived as a sign of weakness rather than moderation. At the last minute, a compromise was worked out. The compromise report merely stated that the oath of allegiance to the state was consistent with allegiance to the U.S. Constitution. It passed by a vote of thirty-two to four in the senate and ninety to twenty-eight in the house. W. R. Hill, a nullifier from York, was disappointed that the state did not pass a treason bill. Union leaders issued an address to explain why they had accepted the compromise. I. W. Hayne wrote triumphantly, "The day is won. . . . The Union party have capitulated," and that the compromise was "*really conceding nothing*, on the subject of the Union." Perry predicted that the establishment of the principle of primary allegiance to the state was the first step toward the dissolution of the Union and the formation of a southern confederacy.[54]

The aftermath of nullification proved to be fatal for the Union Party. In the 1830s, the rise of the antislavery movement and emancipation in the British West Indies converted some unionist planter politicians into rabidly proslavery southern nationalists. Others such as Smith and Drayton simply left the state. Smith continued to accuse Calhoun of committing "a series of outrages upon the peace, tranquility, and social harmony of the people of these United States, and upon the stability of the Union itself." But Drayton wrote a passionate defense of slavery in his new home in Pennsylvania. Simms, whose literary skills were once employed in the service of the Union, became an ardent secessionist and the author of a well-known proslavery response to Harriet Martineau's critique of slavery. William Lowndes Yancey, the famous Alabama secessionist, had been a Greenville unionist and editor of the *Mountaineer* in 1834. Legaré and Daniel Huger were elected to Congress, where they spoke out on the necessity and advantages of racial slavery. Unionist editor Yeadon would demand that abolitionists be extradited to the South to stand trial for libel. A grand reconciliation between the two parties took place in 1840 when unionist John P. Richardson was elected governor over Hammond and became one of the leaders of the secession movement in 1850.[55]

Planters would reveal the limits and ambivalence of their unionism throughout the antebellum period with the rise of the sectional controversy over slavery. The unionism of Alfred Huger, postmaster of Charleston, was severely tested over the mailing of abolitionist literature in 1835. He warned, "the most Ultra Nullifier and the most confirmed Unionist, will go together Shoulder to Shoulder — and for once the Nation will see the Extraordinary Spectacle of a whole state; unanimous." Even though Huger continued to bemoan disunion, he made it clear that he was first a "Southern" man and a "Slave holder." Grayson became a unionist in 1850 but would go on to produce a proslavery poem and an influential vindication of secession in 1860.[56]

Petigru, Poinsett, O'Neall, and Perry were perhaps the only leading unionists whose beliefs survived in the postnullification era. More important, the nonslaveholding mountain yeomanry remained staunchly unionist throughout the antebellum period. This small group of mountain unionists remained an anomaly, unable to affect the course of the state. The continual spread of slavery and cotton in antebellum South Carolina and the politics of slavery and separatism inaugurated by the nullifiers resulted in their political impotence, even as it enhanced the political domination of planters and slaveholders.[57]

History and geography had indeed conspired to place the state's planter gentry at the forefront of the secession movement. Petigru wrote, "It is clear that our nullifiers mean to pick a quarrel with the north about negroes. . . . Nullification has done its work. It has prepared the minds of men for a separation of the States — and when the question is moved again it will be distinctly union or disunion." The nullifiers "are determined not to rest, until a Southern confederacy is formed," accused the *Camden Journal.* Efforts were clearly being made to rally a "southern party" over the "slave question." The words of the nullifiers themselves confirmed the worst fears of unionists. Pinckney argued, "Already the omens are alarming. The enemy defeated on one point, are preparing for another and a more dangerous assault. Already political mischief whets its knife, and the demon of fanaticism lights the torch. . . . Our rights and liberties may soon be subjected to a more fiery trial than they have sustained." Hammond also argued that the federal government "might well produce a monster that will devour our Institutions." Articles proclaiming the advantages of slave over free society began appearing regularly in the nullifier press. Pamphlets defending slavery as a Christian institution and a political and moral good also became commonplace. And Governor McDuffie proclaimed that slavery is "the cornerstone of our republican edifice."[58]

Nullification crystallized Carolinian planter politicians' early ideological commitment to slavery and southern nationalism. The failure of unionists prevented the growth of a viable political opposition and an alternative politics to the proslavery, separatist discourse pioneered by nullifiers. The politics of slavery and separatism checked democratic reform and stymied political dissent. After the crisis, the lack of a two-party system, the retention of an undemocratic state government structure, and Calhoun's personal sway made the state exceptional even in the context of southern politics. By the time the slavery expansion issue resulted in the sectional polarization of the nation, Carolinian planter politicians presented a virtual monolith on the questions of slavery and secession. They were well positioned to lead the movement for an independent southern nation.

3

The Discourse of
Southern Nationalism

. . . Southern views on the subject of slavery.
— SOUTHERN RIGHTS CIRCULAR, Charleston, 1847

The explosive sectional controversy over the expansion of slavery into newly conquered territories, which tore at the heart of mid-nineteenth century America and paved the way for the Civil War, presented a golden opportunity for Carolinian planter politicians to impart to their section the political ideology of slavery, with its ideal of an independent southern nation. The territorial crisis of 1846–50 embodied not only the "ominous fulfillment" of American nationalism but also the coming of age of southern nationalism based on the defense of racial slavery. The slavery expansion issue brought into sharp relief the dichotomy between free and slave societies that had subsisted within the framework of the American republic for over half a century. Just as the northern vision of free soil and free labor reflected the deeply held beliefs of its society, the southern argument for slave soil was based on a vindication of slavery and the values of a slave society. This ideological polarization, spurred by the territorial controversy, would make the problem of slavery obtrude decisively into the national political arena.[1]

It is in this context that South Carolina's exceptionalism became pertinent and influential. Not bound by party allegiances or democratic practice, Carolinian planter politicians championed the cause of their class and section. Calhoun's notion of state sovereignty became the basis of the southern position on slavery in the territories and on the right to secession. Not just formal constitutional and political arguments, but the vindication of slavery as a superior way of ordering society and of a separate southern identity based on slavery would constitute the discourse of southern nationalism. During nullification, Carolinian politicos had developed a systematic defense of slavery and the slaveholding minority in a democratic republic. The slavery expansion conflict fostered southern nationalism, which pointed to the inescapable conclusion that slavery was a higher good than the American republic.

The proslavery argument, which grew in scope and sophistication during these years, provided ideological coherence and unity to southern nationalism. A very basic and unequivocal commitment to slavery undergirded southernism. Talk of southern rights and honor was inextricably bound to the issue of slavery. It is false to create an artificial separation between this rhetoric and the defense of slavery, a distinction emphasized by some recent historians but that certainly eluded contemporary Carolinian and southern slaveholding politicians.[2] Southern leaders started contending with increasing frequency that the enslavement of African Americans had divine sanction and that slavery was the basis of all good society. And Carolinian planter politicians were on the cutting edge of this movement.

During the years between nullification and the first secession crisis, Carolinian planter politicians, under the leadership of Calhoun, emerged as the ideological watchdogs of the slave South. Influential outsiders, they were particularly important in developing the southern territorial position with the inauguration of the controversy over the expansion of slavery. If the nation witnessed the concerted rise of political antislavery with the introduction of the Wilmot Proviso in 1846 and the formation of the Free Soil Party, it also saw the growth of political proslavery with the birth of the Carolina-led southern movement.

A combination of the most advanced proslavery orthodoxy and the ability to shake the foundations of the Union on the slavery issue made even allegedly moderate Carolinian planter politicians stand out in national politics. In the aftermath of nullification, they had led the southern crusade against abolition, demanding an end to the movement and the persecution of its leaders. During the Gag Rule controversy, when southerners and their allies in Congress called for the tabling and nonreception of abolitionist petitions, Calhounite demands generally stood at the extreme of the proslavery spectrum. Calhoun's stance on slavery represented a standard by which southern political leaders could measure their own commitment to the peculiar institution. As early as 1837, he warned that "Abolition and Union cannot co-exist" and laid out the terms for slaveholders' adherence to the Union.[3]

The repeal of the Gag Rule in 1844, the enactment of a new tariff in

1842, and northern opposition to the annexation of Texas further provoked the separatist aristocracy of South Carolina. "Texas or Disunion" became a popular slogan during the so-called Bluffton movement. While Calhoun helped put down this abortive call for state action, he shared Blufftonites' suspicions of Van Buren Democrats and their enthusiasm for Texas. The Blufftonites, unlike many before them, emerged unscathed from their temporary falling-out with him. Robert Barnwell Rhett, the leader of the movement, was enlisted to check criticism of Calhoun's advocacy of internal improvements and to support his bid for the presidency. He and Franklin Harper Elmore, president of the Bank of the State of South Carolina, controlled the Calhoun political machine in the state. Some of Calhoun's closest followers, George McDuffie and Armistead Burt, flirted with Blufftonism. Governor James Henry Hammond blamed Calhoun's presidential ambitions for the failure of the movement,[4] but the Carolina leader differed with the Bluffton boys in policy and not principles.

Calhoun played a significant role in fulfilling one of their major demands, the annexation of Texas. He had long argued for annexation as especially beneficial to "the southern portion of our Union" and as a counterweight against the admission of future nonslaveholding states. Two states' rights Whigs — President John Tyler, who had cast a lone vote against the Wilkins bill, and Secretary of State Abel P. Upshur, a proslavery writer and admirer of Calhoun — helped to make it a reality. They acted on the thesis of a worldwide British abolitionist plot against slavery in Texas, Cuba, and the South that could be aborted only through the admission of Texas as a slave state into the Union. Calhoun not only advised Upshur, but Duff Green, his longtime ally, first called the administration's attention to this theory. Calhoun succeeded Upshur on his death in 1844 and had the personal satisfaction of carrying through the policy of annexation. The Texas issue also led to the political death of Calhoun's old rival, Van Buren, and tilted the Democratic Party toward the South. Even though most Democrats favored annexation, northern and southern states passed opposing resolutions with slave states for and free states against it.[5]

Calhoun did not hesitate to battle for Texas along sectional and proslavery lines. He warned, "If the annexation of Texas is to be defeated by the same sperit [sic], which has induced the reception of abolition petitions, it is difficult to say, what may be the consequence." In his exchange with Richard Pakenham, the British minister to the United States, he made the defense and perpetuity of racial slavery the primary justification for annexation. He used spurious census data to illustrate the supposedly higher degree of pauperism and criminality among free blacks as compared to southern slaves. He concluded predictably, "Experience has proved that the existing relation, in which the one [race] is subjected to the other, in the slaveholding States, is consistent with the peace and safety of both, with great improvement to the inferior." Calhoun explicitly made slavery rather than freedom the manifest destiny of the American republic. His arguments, which linked Texas annexation with the perpetuation of slavery, contributed to the defeat of the annexation treaty in the Senate in June 1844, but the electoral victory of James K. Polk on an expansionist platform rescued the project of annexation by the end of the year. Calhoun and Tyler, despite their reputations for constitutional purity, devised a joint resolution for annexation. The House of Representatives passed it in 1845 along sectional and partisan lines: southerners and Democrats tended to vote for it. However, twenty-seven northern Democrats voted against it and eight southern Whigs bucked their party to support it. Senate Democrats and three southern Whigs voted for a revised resolution and the House approved of the revised resolution. Hammond applauded, "It strengthens the South and the Slave Interest."[6]

Texas raised the specter of sectional differences that would become more evident during Polk's presidency, which was committed in policy to continental expansion. The Oregon question and the Mexican War, the two major territorial issues of 1845–46, had inevitable sectional repercussions. Calhoun led southern opposition to American occupation of the whole of Oregon. He had long favored a policy of "masterly inactivity" in Oregon as opposed to "masterly activity" in Texas and had established himself as a sectional rather than a national advocate of expansion. In South Carolina, northern support for all of Oregon was decried "as only a new phase of Abolition or rather it is Abolition developing its ultimate design and real character." Rhett claimed that it would destroy the South "by invasion from abroad, and insurrection within." When Polk accepted the division of Oregon at the 49th parallel, it was a particularly bitter pill for northern Democrats to swallow after the annexation of Texas and the outbreak of the Mexican War.[7]

Calhoun's position on the Mexican War was more anomalous. Hammond was convinced that his reservations on the acquisition of Mexico were a result of his desire "to revenge himself on those who will not run him for the Presidency." Neither Calhoun's presidential hopes nor Polk's rebuff in not letting him remain in the cabinet can entirely explain his position. And his alleged prescience, which made him see the disunionist consequences of territorial acquisition, had little to do with his stance on the war. Calhoun's moderate unionism had never prevented him from espousing immoderate measures on behalf of slavery. Rather, he was convinced that Polk's wish to incorporate all of Mexico would not extend but spell the death of slavery. While abolitionists and anti-expansionists opposed Polk's policies for extending slavery, Calhoun's criticisms were founded on the opposite premise. He argued that the American government was that "of the white man" and to incorporate the "mixed races of Mexico" would be "degrading to ourselves, and fatal to our institutions." No "civilized colored race" had proven themselves to be worthy of self-government. If Mexicans were made American citizens, they would undermine the racialist logic behind slavery. Carolinian Henry D. Gray also argued that the South did not need the "racial acres" of Mexico. Waddy Thompson, nullifier and former minister to Mexico, opposed the incorporation of "degenerate" Mexicans. Mexican law had also abolished slavery, and many believed that the southwestern deserts would prove to be inhospitable to a plantation economy. Unlike other critics of the war, however, Calhoun favored a defensive war and acquisition of some territory. The *Charleston Mercury* argued that only "rank abolitionists" were completely opposed to the war. Others such as Francis W. Pickens, Hammond, and William Gilmore Simms voiced their support for the war.[8]

Calhoun's differences with southern expansionists were eclipsed by his leadership role in claiming Mexican territory for slavery against northern demands that this area remain free. He argued, "It seems to be resolved on by both parties at the North, that no part of the territory to be acquired by the war shall be for the benefit of the South. . . . We are to be made to dig our own grave." W. F. DeSaussure wrote, "It is plain if territory is acquired from Mexico, the North will insist upon the exclusion of Slavery, & she has the majority. . . . Then the acquisition of territory becomes a curse to us." Some southern Whigs revealed the same fears. Calhoun's correspondents warned that the conquest of Mexico would result not in the expansion of slavery but in the creation of new free states. As the *Mercury* described it, "A belt of new States is to be drawn all around them as a wall of fire, within whose Anaconda embrace they may writhe and struggle . . . but they will be inevitably crushed and swallowed up at last" — a nightmare scenario for slaveholders.[9]

Calhoun had also developed a substantial following among some southern politicians over the years. Virginians Tyler and Governor Littleton Waller Tazewell, Georgian John M. Berrien, Henry Conner of North Carolina, and Senator Dixon Lewis of Alabama respected his opinions. Younger southern firebrands such as James Mason and James Seddon of Virginia, Abraham Watkins Venable of North Carolina, William L. Yancey of Alabama, Jefferson Davis and John Quitman of Mississippi, Charles McDonald and Walter Colquitt of Georgia, David Atchison of Missouri, David Yulee of Florida, and Pierre Soule of Louisiana would look to him for leadership. The slaveholding chivalry from the tobacco, rice, and cotton belts tended to be Calhounite. This group of rabidly proslavery men would have a lightning-rod effect on southern politics during the territorial controversy.[10]

The face-off between northerners and southerners began on August 8, 1846, when Representative David Wilmot of Pennsylvania attached his famous proviso, modeled after the 1787 Northwest Ordinance, prohibiting the introduction of slavery into Mexican territories to a war appropriations bill. The antislavery proviso passed the House by a clearly sectional vote of eighty-three to sixty-four. Presenting a nearly solid front, southern representatives voted against it. In a long filibuster, John Davis of Massachusetts prevented the voting down of the antislavery amendment in the Senate. The Carolina press ridiculed "the absurd proviso." Governor David Johnson of South Carolina in his inaugural message applauded the fact that conflicts and threats to the Union "are in a great measure happily quieted." According to DeSaussure, "the Wilmot proviso has brought up that horrid question, the specter of which is always haunting the South." Calhoun predicted that "Wilmot's proposition will prove [to be] an apple of discord." President Polk was dismayed at the defeat of the war appropriations bill, to which the proviso was attached, and vowed to veto the proviso. In 1847, Representative Preston King reintroduced the proviso, which was added to the "Three Million Dollar" war appropriations bill. Virtually to a man, regardless of party, southern representatives stood united in the debate and the voting over the proviso. Many threatened secession at the passage of any slavery-restriction law. Calls for disunion were no longer the exclusive preserve of Carolinians, who commended this "harmony of sentiment and determination that augurs well for the cause."[11]

Carolinian planter politicians counterattacked by challenging slavery restriction in the organization of Oregon territory. Representative Burt moved to amend the Oregon bill and replace the antislavery clause with a recognition of the Missouri line. He recommended it only as a suitable compromise and denied the right of Congress to exclude slavery from any territory. He pleaded for southern unity on this issue dramatically: "Should they wait till their hearthstones should be drenched with the blood of their wives and children?" Burt's amendment was defeated, with most northerners voting against it. Polk and other administration Democrats also advocated applying the Missouri line to the territories as a compromise. The only problem with this solution was that since the bulk of the Mexican territory was to the south of the line, slavery would be the clear victor. Southern leaders therefore quite willingly accepted and most northerners rejected this compromise. Calhoun and his followers viewed the passage of the Oregon territorial bill with its slavery restriction clause in 1848 as the passage of the proviso. The desertion of three southern "traitors" in the Senate—Sam Houston of Texas, Thomas Benton of Missouri, and Peleg Spruance of Delaware—had resulted in its enactment. Despite pleas from Calhoun for a veto, the more pragmatic Polk signed the bill, as Oregon lay well above the Missouri line.[12]

Carolinian politicos tried to establish an important principle to rally southern slaveholders, that slavery could not be excluded from any new territory acquired by the United States. In 1848, the Treaty of Guadalupe Hidalgo ended the Mexican War and resulted in the acquisition of California and the Southwest. Calhoun predicted, "the slave question will now come up" and "the south will be in the crisis of its fate." Simms, who now visualized a separate slaveholding nation that would include Mexican territory, advised Calhoun to seek specific guarantees for slavery in the territories. Calhoun had also informed Polk that he would not acquiesce to any restrictions on territorial slavery. Another attempt at compromise, backed by him, decreed that the federal courts should decide on the legality of slavery in the territories. But Calhoun also contended that the Constitution protected slavery and that it would overturn Mexican antislavery laws. This compromise, which was backed by John Clayton of Delaware, like the Missouri line was also stacked against free soil, as the federal judiciary was dominated by southern appointees. The fear of southern judicial intervention on behalf of slavery would be realized by the famous Dred Scott decision of 1857, which denied Congress the power to legislate on slavery in the territories. The Clayton bill was opposed by most northern congressmen and a few southern Whigs, who thought that the courts would uphold Mexican laws abolishing slavery. It was therefore tabled in the House.[13]

More important than these congressional maneuvers was the emergence of two clear-cut and opposing sectional positions on the expansion of slavery. The nonextension principle had already been well articulated by Barnburner Democrats like Wilmot and King. It proved to be far more popular among the northern electorate than the demand for the abolition of slavery and eventually succeeded in creating an antislavery majority in the North. Unlike a direct attack on slavery, nonextension came clothed in constitutional legitimacy and reaffirmed freedom rather than slavery as the cardinal doctrine of the republic—or, in the slogan of its exponents, "freedom national, slavery local." The withering away of slavery as a result of its restriction and the expansion of freedom lay far enough in the future not to disturb the racist complacency with which the nation had lived amidst the anomaly of slavery in a republic committed to universal freedom and equality. And unlike abolition, nonextension could attract those who were more concerned with white man's democracy than the rights of African Americans.[14]

Carolinian planter politicians were quick to detect the "politico-fanatical spirit" in free soilism, and it was not long before they developed the southern platform, a demand for the recognition of slavery in the territories. Rhett first articulated the slave South's position in an important speech on the Oregon bill. His arguments were based on Calhoun's conception of absolute state sovereignty. According to Rhett, the states as cosovereigns owned all territories belonging to the United States and Congress could not interfere with their rights. This theory achieved further refinement when Calhoun presented his 1847 resolutions declaring that the territories were the "joint and common property" of the states, that Congress, as merely the "agent" of the states, could make no laws infringing on their "equal right," and that the enactment of a slavery restriction law "would tend directly to subvert the Union itself." These resolutions formed the platform of the South. Declaring that he was proud to be a slaveholder, Calhoun warned that he would go to "any extremity" rather than give up the slave states' "equality."[15]

Calhoun's dictum of equal rights for the slave South, repeated uncritically and ad nauseam by many political historians, was particularly deceptive. Equality for the slave states actually translated into the establishment of slavery in the territories, and all slave territories in the history of the republic had become slave states. Only those areas where slavery had been specifically prohibited by the 1787 ordinance (and even there it was a long struggle to completely eliminate it) had entered the Union as free states. Calhoun's idea of common property decreed that slavery should spread nationally in the territories until it was prohibited by a state entering the Union. His theory of cosovereignty in the territories bore little resemblance to the fundamental principle of states' rights, the equality of the states. It actually decreed the sectional dominance of the slave states in the territories.[16]

Carolinian leaders further developed the southern platform as the sectional conflict grew. Representative J. A. Woodward claimed that the Constitution "carried" slavery with it to the territories. Congress, he said, must actively protect territorial slavery as its constitutional duty. Giving substance to northern fears of slavery expansion, Woodward claimed that slavery was indeed "national" and legally possible in every place under the Constitution. This principle of slavery expansion by constitutional fiat, reminiscent of Calhoun's claim that the Constitution invalidated Mexican antislavery laws, was a precursor to the demand for congressional protection of territorial slavery in the late 1850s. The state sovereignty theory was sounding more and more like an argument for the national sovereignty of slavery. Woodward also alluded to the individual property rights of slaveholders to carry their human property with them to the territories. Under the banner of equality of the states, the constitutional protection of slavery, and slaveholders' property rights, the southern platform contained an unambiguous demand for the expansion of slavery into the territories.[17]

One of the most interesting critiques of the southern platform came not from northern free soilers but from Hammond, who voiced serious states' rights objections to Calhoun's ideas. He predicted that it would lead directly to the demand that Congress ensure the spread and safety of slavery. He argued, "It would do very well not to allow the territories to decide the question of Slavery before they become States. . . . But who is to restrain them? Congress. Then it has power over Slavery in the Territories. A doctrine as false as dangerous." Hammond, very much out of character, also voiced some democratic objections to the southern platform. He wrote, "It is a fundamental principle not only of republican but of all sound political centers — that the majority of the people may establish their own government & make their own laws. We are not to overturn this principle because of Slavery." Calhoun's purpose, he accused, was "to say but nigger to the South to set it on fire" and "to be made an independent Slavery Candidate" for the presidency. He thought that the southern position was "weak . . . & had better not be raised." Unlike a majority of Carolinian politicians, he never fully grasped the significance of the slavery expansion issue.[18]

Initial reaction to Calhoun's southern platform revealed that many were willing to follow his reasoning. On March 8, 1847, the Virginia assembly passed resolutions supporting the common property of the states' theory and advocating resistance to the Wilmot Proviso. The delegates also urged a project dear to Calhoun — "firm, united and concerted action in this emergency" by the southern states. The resolves, a coup for Calhounite Virginians, became the prototype for southern resolutions on the Wilmot Proviso. During 1847–48, the Democratic Party conventions in Alabama, Georgia, and Florida as well as the legislatures of Alabama, South Carolina, and Texas passed similar resolutions. Governor Brown of Mississippi wrote that both parties in his state would endorse the Virginia resolutions. Even Whigs such as Georgia Senator Robert Toombs told Calhoun that they looked to him for direction. Southern endorsement of Calhoun's ideas was well represented in James D. B. De Bow's influential magazine, the *Commercial Review of the South and West* (later *De Bow's Review*): "we the people of a State, we the people of half the States of the Union, in our sovereign capacity, in our sovereign right, in our sovereign independence of all other people or peoples upon earth, of all mortal men, have decreed our institutions as they are, *and so will dare maintain them!*"[19]

Southern ultimatums on the Wilmot Proviso represented a triumph that had eluded Carolinian planter politicians during nullification. They applauded this show of unity but called for a still greater level of southern political consciousness on slavery that would lead to an abandonment of national parties and create a united sectional front. The *Mercury* issued many calls to slaveholders to protect their "rights of property" and to abandon the politics of "president making." As Calhoun admonished, "The great point is to rouse the South, to unite it." Carolinian politicos also had to walk a fine line, giving a spurt to the southern movement while not appearing to take the lead, given their well-known penchant for extremism. I. W. Hayne explained, "It is with great reluctance that South Carolina has led off, in this matter, and she will gladly yield her place to any Southern State." In his letter to Governor Johnson, Calhoun warned against any precipitancy that might jeopardize southern unity. His strategy of providing ideological leadership to the South had worked and the Virginia resolves let the state off the hook. Despite Johnson's recommendations, the legislature failed to pass resolutions against the Wilmot Proviso in 1847 because the senate hinted at secession by asking the governor to convene the legislature immediately on the passage of any slavery-restriction law. The lower house refused to agree to this resolution, which went further than the Virginia resolves and raised the specter of Carolina precipitancy. In 1848, after a number of fire-eating resolutions had been presented in both houses, the assembly recommended cooperation with "sister States in resisting the application of the principles of the Wilmot proviso" to Mexican territory "at any and every hazard."[20]

South Carolina's planter aristocracy formed the nucleus of the Calhoun-led southern movement. Their first effort was to raise funds and establish a nonpartisan, independent newspaper in Washington that would represent "Southern views on the subject of SLAVERY — Southern views of Southern Rights and Interests, growing out of, and in connection with, this institution." Calhoun's lieutenants such as Henry W. Conner, Elmore, Hayne, and Green were enlisted for this project. Some of the richest planters and merchants in the state, including R. F. W. Allston, Wade Hampton, DeSaussure, Charles T. Lowndes, John Rutledge, N. R. Middleton, Gabriel Manigault, Nathaniel Heyward, William Aiken, J. Harleston Read, Henry Gourdin, Whitemarsh Seabrook, and John L. Manning, donated two hundred to a thousand dollars each for the newspaper, and letters seeking support and subscriptions were sent all over the South. Hayne reported that the response in Charleston and in the neighboring parishes had been overwhelming. In one month, $20,000 was raised in

Charleston. The aim was to raise $100,000, and Hayne was confident that if the southern states "contributed proportionately to South Carolina, there can be no difficulty in raising the amount." Most of the signers, he wrote, were "gentlemen" who had distinguished themselves in public service; they were "men of fortune, large slave holders, or factors for the sale of rice and cotton in the city of Charleston." The project was finally realized in 1850 when the short-lived disunionist *Southern Press* was established.[21]

Under Calhoun's lead, planter politicians such as Rhett, Elmore, A. P. Butler, Hayne, Peter Della Torre, Laurence M. Keitt, I. E. Holmes, and R. W. Barnwell launched a circumspect yet widespread movement for southern resistance. Printed circulars warning of the dangers of antislavery and free soilism and asking southerners to unite on the principle of devotion to slavery were distributed among noted southerners. Members of the chivalry kept Calhoun regularly apprised on the state of southern feeling. Conner reported that he had sent five thousand copies of a *Mercury* edition on the Wilmot proviso to friends. At a Charleston meeting, Calhoun had held up the abolitionists as a model for slaveholders. The abolitionists had become influential as the "balance of power" party in the North by their commitment to principle. Similarly, slaveholders by uniting and maintaining their commitment to slavery in principle could vanquish their foes despite their minority position. He argued, "let all party distinction among us cease" and "let us make its [slavery's] safety the paramount question." The Charleston report stated that the nonextension principle not only condemned slavery as a political evil but was designed to destroy slavery in the states. D. F. Jamison, a secessionist planter from Orangeburg, commended "the first measure which has yet been adopted towards the Union of the slave-holding States on that vital question."[22]

Anti–Wilmot Proviso agitation soon engulfed the state in a manner clearly reminiscent of nullification. Numerous articles in Carolinian newspapers and district-level meetings presided over by state leaders in Anderson, Barnwell, Edgefield, Laurens, Fairfield, Orangeburg, Chesterfield, and Darlington tried to arouse the people on the perils to slavery, South Carolina, and the South. Senator Andrew P. Butler made a number of speeches and Calhoun was suspected of having written the Barnwell report. The rash of articles, speeches, reports, and resolutions recounted new signs of northern perfidy such as defiance of the fugitive slave law and petitions for the abolition of the slave trade in the District of Columbia and revealed the rationale behind the demand for the extension of slavery. They condemned the Wilmot Proviso as "Abolition in its Revolutionary and Most Dangerous form." Carolinian planter politicians also alluded to the economic conditions of the old slave states and Malthusian laws. Not just southern rights or honor but the very survival of the slave South was at stake. As Hayne argued, "The impending danger threatens an institution inextricably interwoven with our social as well as political system. The subject suggested involves not only the prosperity but the safety and very existence of the whole slave holding population."[23]

The state achieved a remarkable degree of political unity on the platform of proslavery and southern nationalism. Even unionists such as Christopher H. Memminger and Benjamin F. Perry looked to Calhoun for political direction. Perry took the lead in organizing anti–Wilmot Proviso meetings in Greenville, the one unionist stronghold in the state. The Fairfield meeting, chaired by John H. Means, soon to become governor, threatened state action and appointed a committee to correspond with other southerners. The Fairfield resolutions would form the program of the Carolinian secession movement. A writer using the appropriate pseudonym Turnbull warned the citizenry of a new "crisis" in their affairs when southerners unthinkingly paid homage to the "holy shrine of the Union." Simms felt that the only solution lay in the immediate secession of the southern states "en masse." Carolinian leaders remained sensitive to southern accusations of disunion and dictation. "The South Carolina Platform," they responded, was not so much against the present "political union" as it was for the "national union" of the South.[24]

Carolinian slaveholders' devotion to an ideologically pure brand of the politics of slavery was marred by the rise of the presidential question in 1848. Intersectional party politics hindered rather than fostered the growth of the southern movement. Much to Calhoun's dismay, neither his dream of a southern party united on a proslavery platform nor his candidacy matured. The *Mercury* had declared its favorite son, Calhoun, as "our entire choice" for the presidential elections. Many like Polk thought that the southern movement was a last bid by him to create a sectional party around the question of slavery in order to secure the presidency. James Clark, a former nullifier, asked Hammond not to repeat this "Political Sacralige [*sic*]" for fear of being "sacrificed." Hammond also felt that Calhoun was "utterly abominable" and that his "desperate ambition for the Presidency has not only prostituted his judgement, but sapped his patriotism."[25]

Calhoun, however, was guided by his basic concern for the safety and perpetuity of slavery as much as his desire for the presidency. He repudiated the idea of popular sovereignty, developed by conservative Hunker Democrats such as Daniel S. Dickinson, Vice President George M. Dallas, and Democratic presidential nominee Lewis Cass, which left the decision on slavery to the people of a territory. It gave no details as to the timing of this determination and could be interpreted differently North and South of the Mason-Dixon line and could therefore unite the Democratic party for the 1848 presidential elections. Squatter sovereignty, as Calhoun dismissively referred to this formula, affirmed to him that "It is impossible for the South to unite with the North on any of their prominent men as a candidate, without making dangerous concessions on the slave question." Democrats clung to the safety of popular sovereignty despite Yancey's efforts to pledge the party to the Calhoun-inspired Alabama platform. The platform had been endorsed by Alabama and Georgia and the Virginia and Florida Democratic conventions. When it failed to pass, most southern Democrats did not follow Yancey, who walked out of the Democratic convention. Calhoun had refused to let South Carolina participate in the convention, tainted as it was by the presence of a northern majority. A rump meeting at Georgetown nominated J. M. Commander as delegate to the convention, authorizing him to cast the nine votes of the state. This attempt at party politics was condemned "as a curiosity in South Carolina," where sectional loyalty to slavery superseded partisan affiliation. The reviled Commander joined forces with Yancey to try to push through the Alabama platform.[26]

Worse still in the eyes of Carolinian planter politicians, Barnburner Democrats, Conscience Whigs, and the abolitionist Liberty Party united to form the Free Soil Party, which nominated ex-president Martin Van Buren and Charles F. Adams on the platform of nonextension of slavery. Benjamin F. Whitner warned, "a separation of the Union, with all its consequences, will be inevitable" if the Free Soilers came to power. James Gadsden thought that Van Buren's candidacy illustrated the bankruptcy of all northern Democrats. He argued, "The tendency of Northern Democracy is to the extremes of disorder — anything but conservative — Fourierism, Socialism, Agrarianism, & all the isms which must and do end in abolitionism." The Free Soilers embodied, according to the *Mercury*, "death to Southern Slavery! desolation to the South!" This, if nothing else, should be a call to arms for southerners, who were "distracted" by the presidential elections. Why couldn't the South, it asked plaintively, band together like its foes?[27]

The southern slaveholder who seemed to reap the benefits of this call for unity was not Calhoun but Zachary Taylor, the Mexican War hero and the Whig presidential nominee. His selection over Henry Clay in 1848 was the result of a "southern insurgent movement" within the Whig Party. Even so staunch a southern nationalist as Virginian Beverly Tucker greeted Taylor as a "God send" and began many of his epistles to Hammond with an enthusiastic "Hurrah! for Old Zack!" Hammond argued that no slaveholder should "hesitate" in choosing the Louisiana planter over Democratic Presidential nominee Lewis Cass. Besides the handful of Carolina Whigs who supported Taylor, a group of Charlestonians launched the Taylor Democrat movement. They nominated Taylor with William Butler, the Democratic vice presidential nominee, as his Whig running mate, Millard Fillmore, was reputed to be an antislavery man. Calhoun's public stance of neutrality encouraged this movement, and Holmes, James L. Orr, A. G. Magrath, and Simms came out for Taylor. According to Thomas W. Bacot, "the Democrats have not taken him up because he is a *Whig*, but because he is . . . a slaveholder, who will not countenance your Wilmot Provisos, or pursue any other course detrimental to Southern Interests." Gadsden contended that rallying around Taylor would achieve the much-sought-for southern unity on slavery. But Calhoun refused to support Taylor. According to Hammond, he was merely sulking at not being a candidate himself. Calhoun probably had doubts about Taylor, who, unlike Cass, had not given any assurance about vetoing the Wilmot Proviso. Barnwell planter Lewis M. Ayer feared that Taylor may be contaminated by the antislavery wing of the Whig Party and like Clay and Benton, both slaveholders, prove to be untrue to the slave South. Like Jackson, Taylor was also suspected of being a nationalist. Calhounites led by Hayne, Rhett, Huger, Burt, and Butler repudiated Taylor despite their aversion to popular sovereignty. Though the Taylor movement was fairly successful in Charleston, the legislature went for Cass by a vote of 129 to 27.[28] Taylor's subsequent victory at the polls scarcely dented Carolinian planter politicians' determination to jump-start the southern movement.

The reemergence of sectional polarization over territorial slavery during Zachary Taylor's presidency breathed new life into the southern movement, and it would constitute Calhoun's dying legacy to the South. Calhoun was becoming convinced that it was time for slaveholders to either "give up our slaves" or their political connections with the North. He wrote, "The only real practical question is; What should be done to bring the South to the same conclusion, and to [make her] rally in support of her domestick institution?" His solution lay in Rhett's long-held notion of a convention of the slaveholding states that could either save the Union or "save ourselves at any event." Just as profound personal disappointment had preceded his previous incarnation as nullifier, the forever lost hope of winning the presidency drove Calhoun into an openly separatist stance. He had a circular calling for a meeting of southern congressmen distributed immediately after the passage of a resolution for the abolition of the slave trade in the District of Columbia in the House. Nearly 80 of the 121 Congressmen representing the slave states except Delaware met on December 23, 1848, in the Senate chamber. Thomas Bayly of Virginia presented a series of fire-eating resolutions that threatened dissolution of the Union over any attempt to interfere with slavery in the District of Columbia and the territories. A special committee, chaired by a Georgia Whig, Alexander Stephens, and containing one member from each of the slaveholding states, was created and a subcommittee, headed by Calhoun, formulated an address to the southern people, which was reported at the second meeting of southern congressmen in January 1849. It was adopted by a vote of forty-two to seventeen over John M. Berrien's alternate address to the people of the United States.[29]

Southern Whigs supported Berrien's address. With Taylor in the White House, southern Whigs, led by Toombs and Stephens, who resigned as chairman of the special committee, had good reason to shun Calhoun's call for sectional unity. They hardly felt the need for an insurgent southern movement. Hammond immediately branded them as "infernal traitors." Calhoun blamed partisan politics for putting obstacles in the way of southern unity. He wrote, "We ought rather than yield to one inch take any alternative, even if it should be Disunion, & I trust that such will be the determination of the South." He regarded the whole event as a success and pronounced, "The South is more aroused than I ever saw it on the subject." Given the fact that only forty-eight southern congressmen signed the southern address, of whom merely two were Whigs, Calhoun seems to have overstated his triumph. But southern Whigs' alienation from Taylor and the continuing sectional fight over slavery in the course of the year would soon give his statements the character of a self-fulfilling prophecy.[30]

Calhoun's southern address provided the rationale for a proslavery movement. He drew attention to "the conflict between the two great sections of the Union, growing out of a difference of feeling and opinion in reference to the relations existing between the two races . . . and the acts of aggression and encroachment to which it has led." Placing slavery at the center of a lengthy statement of southern grievances, Calhoun alluded to a host of concerns regarding the security of slavery, including free states' unwillingness to render fugitive slaves and efforts to end slavery in the District of Columbia. And he chastised the North for failing to suppress abolitionists, whose "avowed intention is to bring about a state of things that will force emancipation on the South" by uniting free society in hostility to slavery and creating "discontent" among the slaves. Calhoun contended that he was merely asking for the "right" of slaveholders to travel with their "property" to the territories, which were open to "citizens and foreigners, without discrimination as to character, profession, or color . . . savage, barbarian, or civilized." Northern demands for the nonextension of slavery were part of an insidious plan to create a sufficient number of free states to abolish slavery by a constitutional amendment. Anticipating Bourbon reaction to Reconstruction, he argued that on emancipation, "blacks, and the profligate whites that might unite with them" would, with northerners, oppress the "white race" in the South. He advised that only an united South willing "to resort to all means necessary" could prevent this outcome.[31]

The separatist implications of Calhoun's address led Berrien to write an alternate address to the people of the nation. Berrien's catalog of southern grievances was quite similar to Calhoun's. Basing his arguments on the claim that slavery was "an elementary principle of the Constitution," he called on the citizens of all the states to recognize southern rights, avoid agitation, and preserve the Union. Berrien represented the proslavery southern unionist position far more accurately than Calhoun, who had given up hope of securing slavery within the Union without some fundamental changes in the Constitution. As in the case of many states' rights Whigs, Berrien's stridently proslavery views made an odd combination with his unionism, and it was only a matter of time before the disjuncture between the two would become apparent. Of the two men, the supposedly metaphysical Carolinian was clearly the realist.[32]

The Calhoun-led southern movement made remarkable progress in 1849, given the extent of opposition to it. Encouraged by these events, Tucker wrote that the "end" of the agitation should be a "Southern Confederacy" and the "means," concert of action, the press, and "boldness." The Virginia assembly asked the governor to convene the legislature on the passage of the Wilmot Proviso or any law interfering with slavery and the slave trade in the District of Columbia. These resolutions were presented by John B. Floyd, son of the elder John Floyd, the Virginia governor with sympathies toward South Carolina during nullification. Despite Whig opposition, the resolutions passed the legislature. The assembly demanded an effective fugitive slave law and excoriated northern personal liberty laws. The Democratic conventions of Georgia and Alabama endorsed the Virginia resolutions and the Whig-dominated legislature of Florida recommended a southern convention. The Missouri legislature also came out for joint resistance by the southern states, and, besides recommending a southern convention, the Tennessee Democratic convention called for commercial nonintercourse with the North. The North Carolina assembly passed more moderate resolutions, but which also promised resistance to northern interference with slavery. Proposals for the gradual abolition of slavery inspired by Henry Clay and Cassius Clay, his antislavery cousin, proved to be stillborn in the Kentucky state convention. Besides formal action by the states, local meetings led by proslavery separatists sounded the cry for southern unity and resistance.[33]

Most Whigs and unionist Democrats such as Sam Houston of Texas, Howell Cobb of Georgia, and Thomas Benton of Missouri, however, steered clear of Calhoun's southern movement. Polk condemned it as disunionist in tendency. Cobb issued a "minority address" in which he looked to the Democratic Party for southern redemption. Most remarkable was the opposition of Benton, who cordially disliked Calhoun and was known for his fierce Jacksonian devotion to the Union. Benton attacked Calhoun as the inspiration behind the David Atchison–led proslavery movement in Missouri. He charged Calhoun with disunionism and unprincipled ambition. This evoked a long response from Calhoun, who recalled Benton's "treachery" in the Oregon bill vote and charged him with free soilism. The personal feud between the two men represented a clash between the politics of slavery and separatism and the old-style Jacksonian aversion to nullification and secession. This time, in much of the slave south, including Missouri, the Carolina doctrine was clearly ascendant.[34]

The agitation reached its peak among Carolinian planter politicians, the instigators of the southern movement. The state press had long argued for a bipartisan southern convention. Governor Johnson recommended a southern convention in his outgoing address in 1848, as did his more fiery successor, Whitemarsh Seabrook, a former nullifier and proslavery pamphleteer. Calhoun asked prominent Carolinians to start a movement for a southern convention though Hammond remained averse to his suggestions "to *agitate* in SoCa." Carolinian leaders held large public meetings in Fairfield, Edgefield, Richland, Barnwell, Kershaw, Sumter, York, Spartanburg, Laurens, and Orangeburg endorsing the southern address. At the Greenville meeting, Perry supported the idea of a southern convention. As during nullification, these meetings were top-down affairs orchestrated by local potentates. The lowcountry, except for Charleston and St. Stephen's Parish, was remarkably quiescent at this time, probably because its well known ultra temper needed no goading. Most of these district meetings created committees of safety and vigilance, as did the parishes, putting into place a network of organizations to coordinate the movement and suppress dissent.[35]

The vigilance and safety committees, composed of large and prominent slaveholders, ensured political conformity by conducting random acts of vigilantism against persons suspected of having unorthodox views on slavery. One John L. Brown and his son, James Brown, were arrested as suspected abolitionists. A Dr. Major was expelled from Barnwell merely for professing that slavery was wrong "in abstract." In Abbeville, a Reverend R. C. Grier was accused of holding antislavery views. In 1850 alone, three cases of tarring and feathering were reported in South Carolina. A slave patrol beat Junius Smith, a Greenville farmer, at his home in December 1851 for being a member of the American Colonization Society and a suspected abolitionist. Between 1847 and 1853, eight Carolinians were convicted of abolitionism. Neither white democracy nor mastery of their households protected these men from being assaulted for their views.

Perceptions of slave behavior also generated political anxiety. The South Carolina Association was once again enlisted to monitor slaves and the free black population and stringent measures were enacted to guard against a slave uprising. Elmore was concerned about the two thousand "able bodied" free black men within reach of Charleston's arsenal. Apparently, "the slightest disturbance" could render the slave population "moody" and "seditious." The North could thus conduct a covert war against slavery by merely offering to the slaves the "sympathy and aid of a greater authority than the master" and by giving them "political hope." Only a few years before, Hammond had written to Calhoun that he was "astonished & shocked to find that some of them [slaves] are aware of the opinions of the Presidential candidates on the subject of Slavery & doubtless of much of what the abolitionists are doing. . . . I fancy—it may be fancy—there is a growing spirit of insubordination among the Slaves in this section. . . . A *quick & potent* remedy must be applied. *Disunion* if *needs* be." In the Senate, Butler alluded to the case of a "Mr. Babbit" who was indicted for spreading "incendiary publications" and encouraging slaves to rebel in Spartanburg. He was referring to the case of J. M. Barrett, who was arrested for possessing antislavery literature and letters written in code. As he scolded, "Is it not notorious, I ask Senators, that the slaves in the slaveholding States have become dissatisfied in consequence of your inflammatory publications and harangues, made even here within the walls of Congress?"[36]

South Carolina's peculiarly slavery-dominated society and planter-dominated polity also served to stifle divisions that plagued the rest of the South. As Tucker noted, "There are circumstances peculiar to South Carolina which qualify her to lead in an enterprise of this sort. Chief among these is her number of educated and aspiring gentlemen of large property." Many younger planter politicians, such as Keitt, Milledge Luke Bonham, William P. Miles, John H. Means, W. A. Owens, and John McQueen, would lead the secession movement. The beau ideal of these young Hotspurs was not Rhett, but Calhoun, who advised, "I deem it due to candour and the occasion to state that I am of the impression, that the time is near at hand, when the South will have to choose between dis-union, and submission. I think so, because I see little prospect of ar-resting the aggression of the North." On Calhoun's suggestion, 109 delegates representing the committees of safety from the districts and parishes assembled in Columbia on May 14, 1849. Resolutions called for concerted action by the southern states and created a Central State Com-mittee of Safety and Vigilance. An Executive Committee of Five chaired by Elmore was also formed, and the various local committees were in-structed to "spread useful information" among the people and bring to justice all "offenders against our peace and institutions." While the local committees served as a propaganda cum vigilante machine, the central committee acted as a "quasi official advisory body" to Governor Sea-brook. It is worth noting that the governor spent much of his time review-ing the militia and spent $30,000 acquiring arms and buttressing state defenses.[37]

The southern movement in South Carolina was directed against per-ceived external and internal threats to slave society; it was the possibility of a link between the two that alarmed many a slaveholder. It was not just the legendary southern attribute of honor that made Carolinian planter politicians so sensitive to antislavery. The very real perception that slave society would not be able to survive the political contradictions engen-dered by free soilism lay at the heart of Carolinian slaveholders' reaction to the territorial conflict. An antislavery movement was threatening be-cause it challenged the survival of slavery and because it could possibly appeal to nonslaveholders, slaves, and the free black population. It was a direct attack on slaveholders' and planters' regional hegemony.

Carolinian planter politicians again had to walk the line between lead-ing and appearing to lead the southern movement. Calhoun, well aware of the popular prejudice against his state, felt that the first call for a southern convention should emanate from some other state. Virginia, which had led in formulating proslavery resolutions, could not be relied on to take any concrete action, R. K. Cralle advised. It would "submit" after a few "patriotic groans," and he told Calhoun to look "further south" for the task of engendering sectional unity. Mississippi, an emerg-ing stronghold of lower south separatism with many Carolinian émigrés, seemed ideal to issue the call for a southern convention. By the 1850s, Mississippi and Louisiana, along with South Carolina, had the highest levels of slaveholding and the most widespread plantation belts. The entire state delegation had signed the southern address. Of all the states of the Deep South, its planter politicians, after the South Carolinians, were leading proponents of southern interests.[38]

The behind-the-scenes Carolinian maneuvering in Mississippi illustrated that Carolina's planter aristocracy still stood at the head of the southern movement. In his letter to Col. Collin S. Tarpley, Calhoun expressed his desire that Mississippi should issue the call for a southern convention. He also hoped that the southern states would follow the example of South Carolina in organizing committees of safety. Calhoun's letters were circulated among prominent men of the right sympathies in Mississippi. In May 1849, a public meeting at Jackson recommended a state convention to consider North-South relations. When the bipartisan convention met in October under the presidency of the Whig judge William Sharkey, it issued the call for a southern convention to be held in Nashville on the first Monday of June 1850. The Mississippi platform repeated Calhoun's theory of joint ownership of the territories and threatened disunion. Governor Seabrook, on Calhoun's prompting, sent Representative Daniel Wallace to attend the convention and to get a pledge of action from the governor. Wallace, unaware of Calhoun's role in instigating his mission, reported that he "saw clearly *that our Old Statesman*, was perhaps at the bottom of this movement." However, because of the strong anti-Carolina prejudice in Mississippi, he had to be extremely circumspect in his conversations with state leaders. The authorship of the convention resolutions was also kept a secret as they were drawn up by Col. William Hill, a native Carolinian who had been a prominent nullifier in York.[39]

Throughout this time Carolinian leaders and the press remained relatively calm so as to not jeopardize the Mississippi situation. As soon as the call came through, they broke their silence. Calhoun wrote, "I would regard the failure of the Convention called by Mississippi, to meet from the want of endorsement by the other Southern States to be a great, if not fatal misfortune. . . . I do not think that our State should hold back. . . . If we do not move, other states will be backward to move. As jealous as they may be of us, they still look to us to give the signal." As per his wishes, Governor Seabrook in his annual message and the legislature endorsed the southern convention. The assembly provided for the selection of four delegates at large and two delegates from each congressional district to represent South Carolina and declared, "if Slavery be abolished in the District of Columbia by Congress; or the Wilmot Proviso adopted, the Union would be dissolved."[40]

The convention movement received a further boost from the events of the Thirty-First Congress. The moderation of southern Whigs had been dispelled by the course of the Taylor administration. Taylor's closeness to William Seward and antislavery Whigs and his aversion to slavery extension came as a rude shock to most southern Whigs. His plans for the immediate admission of California and New Mexico, which assured their entrance as free states, his refusal to give an explicit guarantee to veto the Wilmot Proviso, and his determination to secure New Mexican lands from Texan claims angered most southern congressmen. The Georgia duo, Toombs and Stephens, Alabama's Henry W. Hilliard, and North Carolina's Thomas L. Clingman and Willie P. Mangum led a southern revolt in the Whig caucus and made the election of nearly every House officer starting with the Speaker a sectional issue. Carolinians applauded this chaotic state of affairs, and the Carolina press, after raining abuse on southern Whiggery, did a complete about-face to praise its "lofty tone." Southerners seemed more united than ever against Taylor's plans for the organization of the territories, which they dubbed the "Executive Proviso."[41]

Sectional division over slavery expansion had also reached down to the state and local levels and seemed to be complete. By 1850, fifteen northern states and Delaware would endorse nonextension of slavery and ten southern states would come out against it. The Free Soil Party sent nine representatives and one senator to Congress. Free Soilers continued to bring forward proposals for the abolition of slavery and the slave trade in the District of Columbia and for the admission of California and New Mexico. Joshua Giddings's resolution allowing free black men to vote in a referendum on slavery in the District of Columbia especially outraged southerners. Calhoun noted, "The South is more united, than I ever knew it to be, and more bold and decided. The North must give away, or there will be a rupture," and many southern congressmen "avow themselves to be disunionists, and a still greater number admit, that there is little hope of any remedy short of it."[42]

The politics of compromise, however, posed a new obstacle to the Calhoun-led southern movement. On January 29, 1850, Henry Clay presented resolutions that pulled together various issues: the territorial conundrum, Texan claims to New Mexican land, a new fugitive slave law, and abolition of the slave trade in the District of Columbia. He upheld the Mexican antislavery laws in the territories and stated that he would never vote for the introduction of slavery in areas where it did not exist. By wrapping his compromise proposals in a mildly free soil garb, he probably did not win any overnight converts among southerners, aroused by a year-long proslavery, separatist agitation. In the long run, the politics of compromise, shorn of any free soil implications, effectively appealed to southern unionists and won the backing of politicians such as Mississippi's Henry Foote, Alabama's Jeremiah Clemens, and Georgia's Toombs, Stephens, and Cobb. But Carolinians denounced Clay's "mongrel propositions" and his "mania" for compromise.[43]

Calhoun's dying hopes were vested with the movement that he had inaugurated and he led southern opposition to the compromise. He wrote that "the South . . . cannot with safety remain in the Union as things now stand & that there is little or no prospect of any change for the better . . . disunion is the only alternative left to us." In the near-mythic accounts of his speech read by Senator Mason, the grim Carolinian, haggard, ill, and at death's door, made a last, superhuman effort to save the Union. Actually, an examination of the speech reveals his prior conviction of the impossibility of reconciling the two sections on the question of slavery. He claimed that he had always worked to save the Union, "if it could be done; and, if it cannot, to save the section where it has pleased Providence to cast my lot." He argued that the admission of California would be the "test question" for the slave South to choose between "submission or resistance." He had always stated that admitting California into the Union would be "worse than the Wilmot Proviso." In resolutions dictated from his death bed, Calhoun contended that the admission of California would be based on the principle of territorial sovereignty, a "revolutionary and anarchical" doctrine that would subvert "state sovereignty." But if California entered the Union with a state constitution abolishing slavery, then it should presumably have been entitled to the claim of state sovereignty as developed in proslavery territorial theory. In this case constitutional niceties escaped him and other southern leaders who opposed statehood for California, arguing that it had been achieved fraudulently. Calhoun further claimed that the founding principle of the American republic was no lofty ideal but the rather mechanistic notion of political "equilibrium" between the two sections. This equilibrium had been disrupted by the conscious acts of the federal government, which had excluded the slave south from the territories and pursued economic policies to the detriment of its interests. It would be destroyed by the admission of a free state and "require the South to secede, to dissolve the Union." Tracing the history of the slavery controversy, Calhoun blamed the rise of abolition and a "national consolidated democracy" for forcing southern slaveholders to question the value of the Union.[44]

Calhoun's dying pronouncements could not stem the tide of compromise in Washington. One of the most decisive voices lifted in favor of adjustment was that of his old adversary, Daniel Webster. He argued that no laws against the introduction of slavery were needed as the "ordinance of nature" would bar it from the Mexican territories. He even suggested the formation of four new slave states in Texas as laid out in its annexation resolution and argued strongly for the rendition of fugitive slaves. In his reply to Webster, Calhoun criticized his statement "that this Union cannot be dissolved." But on the whole, even Calhoun and Carolinian newspapers had warm words of praise for Webster's "great" and "noble" speech. His concessions on slavery paved the way for the acceptance of the Compromise of 1850 among many southern politicians.[45]

Seward, not Webster, formulated a more complete rebuttal of Calhoun's speech. He argued that Calhoun's demand of "equality" for a slaveholding minority was "entirely subversive of democratic institutions." He agreed with the old Carolinian that emancipation would be a "democratic revolution" against "capital," and, like Calhoun, he equated this struggle with the fight between reaction and democracy in the 1848 European revolutions, though obviously he was cheering for the opposite side. Freedom, he asserted, was the "universal principle" that underlay the American republic and its progress would eventually do away with slavery. And to drive home the point, he observed, "You may separate slavery from South Carolina and the State will remain; but if you subvert freedom there, the State will cease to exist." Hammond observed that Seward rather than Webster was the "true representative" of the North.[46]

The death of Calhoun on March 30, 1850, furthered the cause of a sectional truce. In a letter that was returned to him after Calhoun's death, even Hammond had written, "I would regard your retirement at this moment as a peculiar calamity to the South." Reverend James Henley Thornwell, proslavery theologian, thundered in the imagery of the Old Testament that South Carolina's love for its leader had provoked the retribution of a jealous God who cannot share His glory with another. However, the majority of Carolinians, the slaves, perhaps felt differently. One black man is reported to have said, "Calhoun was indeed a wicked man, for he wished that we might remain slaves." Perry noted that his death had "relieved South Carolina of political despotism," and Poinsett, an old adversary, believed that he had been "bent on the destruction" of the republic. Calhoun's old opponents such as Clay and Webster delivered suitable eulogies on him, but Benton is reported to have remarked that the "country is *now* safe."[47]

Calhoun's death became another occasion in South Carolina to reiterate southern nationalist ideals and recall his legacy of political loyalty to slavery, even as it plunged the state into official mourning. The funeral procession in Charleston led by Governor Seabrook and the signs of mourning that hung from private homes, as required by the committee of arrangements, were testimony to his hold over the state. The legislature appropriated ten thousand dollars to publish his two manuscripts posthumously. Seabrook desperately searched for a candidate to fill his senatorial seat, which was offered at various points to Langdon Cheves and James Hamilton. Hamilton was offered the job first but the offer was rescinded when his closeness to the Texas bond lobby and support for the compromise was revealed, the pretext being that Hamilton did not meet the state's residency requirements. On Cheves's refusal, Elmore was selected, but his death led to another search. Finally, Robert Barnwell, former nullifier, agreed to fill the senatorship for the rest of the term. Heirs apparent Rhett and Hammond delivered rousing eulogies on the departed leader. In his official address to the assembly, Rhett pointed out that Calhoun was the discoverer of two great principles, nullification and the constitutional right to secession. He defended slavery as the natural outcome of inequality among men and "races" and praised Calhoun for being the first "great Statesman in the country, who denounced the cant — that slavery is an evil — a curse." While both Rhett and Hammond took pains to illustrate Calhoun's love for the Union, they recommended disunion based on his pronouncements. They alluded to his vindication of slavery and his political theories as his greatest contributions to the South.[48] The spread of a slavery-based southern nationalism owed much in political and ideological inspiration to Calhoun.

The discourse of southern nationalism was constructed around Calhoun's constitutional theories and the fully developed proslavery argument. Since nullification, Calhoun had devoted much of his intellectual energy to devising political mechanisms that would guarantee the permanence of slavery and the interests of the southern slaveholding minority in a democratic republic. In attempting to solve these issues, Calhoun wrote his two works on political theory, *A Disquisition on Government* and the much longer *A Discourse on the Constitution and Government of the United States*.

Despite his reluctance to allude to slavery, Calhoun's books were geared to address the specific political dilemma of the slave South. He developed the concurrent majority theory, which he had first conceived of during nullification, in the *Disquisition*. A concurrent or "constitutional" majority would take into account the "dominant" interests of a community and allow each a "negative" over the other. According to him, only the wealthy and the powerful would qualify as the dual components of concurrent majority. He argued, "the wealthy and intelligent being identified in interest with the poor and ignorant of their respective portions or interests of the community, become the leaders and protectors." Not only was this idea a central tenet of proslavery ideology, it also shows he was hardly advocating a political alliance between southern slaveholders and northern labor. Concurrent majority clearly postulated a political system dependent on northern capitalists and southern slaveholders taking care of the interests of their respective societies. Calhoun's lengthy attempt in the *Discourse* to prove that the Constitution was based on his idea of concurrent majority and absolute state sovereignty and that it granted the states the right to secession shows the practical bearing of his political theory. His suggestion of a dual executive had relevance only for the sectional conflict. It failed to establish any general principle for the protection of minorities in democratic polities.

Calhoun's ideas represented a conservative reaction to the democratization of national politics. According to him, the "right to suffrage" only aggravated the problem of majority domination. Criticizing the development of democracy and mass-based political parties in the Jacksonian era, he contended that numerical majorities produced absolute governments and selfish partisan warfare. A government based on concurrent majority would have acted as an effective check on popular democracy and majority rule. It would have given southern slaveholders veto power over any act of the federal government. Archconservative Alfred Huger, a conditional unionist whose disdain for democracy was legendary, praised both treatises as "the ablest American production." George Fitzhugh, slavery ideologue par excellence, wrote that Aristotle's and Calhoun's works were the only sound "text books" on political theory for the slave South.[49]

Calhoun's definition of liberty as a "reward" for the few rather than a universal right also had great affinities with proslavery ideology. "Liberty" he felt, "when forced on a people unfit for it, would, instead of a blessing, be a curse . . . the greatest of all curses." He criticized natural rights theory, arguing, "These great and dangerous errors have their origin in the prevalent opinion that all men are free and equal. . . . [N]othing can be more unfounded and false." Instead, "inequality of condition" was necessary for "progress." Slavery and its exigencies shaped Calhoun's political thought. Merely the fact that he chose to address the workings of the United States government or used concepts common in the political vocabulary of the time does not incorporate him within either a preexisting republican or liberal discourse, as some scholars have contended. Nor is it adequate to portray Calhoun's work as being within the tradition of Madisonian constitutionalism with its concern for minority rights. Calhoun used and deviated from American political traditions. That is what made him an original thinker on the problem of slavery and democracy. If his thought must be categorized, it would not be under classical republicanism or a compromised liberalism, but under the political philosophy of the slave South. As such, his stature as a political theorist is intrinsically connected with the institution he so well defended.[50]

Calhoun's contributions to the ideological defense of slavery also formed an important part of his legacy for southern slaveholders. As a prominent political leader, his views on slavery had a far greater impact than similar arguments voiced by other proslavery ideologues. In his speech on the reception of abolition petitions, Calhoun had announced that southern race relations were "a good — a positive good." His argument for slavery was explicitly racial, but Calhoun also praised slavery or the "patriarchal mode" of extracting "the labor of the African race" as superior to other forms of labor relations. He argued that the enslavement of labor was the only solution to the inevitable conflict between labor and capital. For him belief in racial and class inequality went hand in hand. He justified the principle of inequality embodied in the institution of racial slavery. His defense of racial slavery was also an integral part of his broader critique of revolutionary egalitarianism and the spread of democracy. In a speech on the Oregon bill, he began with an attack on Free Soilers' use of Jefferson to justify slavery nonextension, only to end with a full-blown Aristotelian critique of the Declaration of Independence and of Jefferson's opinions on slavery. He opposed all democratic movements of the day — Dorrism in Rhode Island, Chartism in Britain, and the 1848 European revolutions. Abolition, he pointed out, sprang from the same principles. The "South Carolina doctrine," his critics argued, was against "the very idea of liberty itself. . . . [H]e [Calhoun] strikes at the very heart of democracy." The *Charleston Mercury* approvingly quoted the abolitionist *National Era*'s description of Calhoun as "denying the doctrines of the Declaration of Independence" and maintaining that slavery "is the rightful condition of the laboring man, irrespective of color." Calhoun did not advocate the enslavement of white workers and even labored to argue that slavery created perfect equality among whites. But he defended slavery as a system of labor and praised the slave South's role as a conservative bulwark against the spread of democracy.[51]

Proslavery thought provided Carolinian planter politicians with a viable ideological foundation for a southern nation based firmly on racial slavery and the distinct values of a slave society. By 1850, it had crystallized into a pat set of arguments that lauded the superior and conservative nature of slave society, as opposed to societies based on free labor, and that sought to put slavery above mortal criticism by pronouncing it a biblical institution sanctioned by God.[52]

Proslavery ideology in South Carolina reflected the deeply reactionary values of a slave society and departed fundamentally from both the revolutionary heritage and contemporary notions of democracy. Like Calhoun, the state's proslavery thinkers developed a systematic critique of the Declaration of Independence and natural rights theory. Thomas Cooper, who argued that Jefferson was a slaveholder and that the Declaration was clearly not meant for the "black race," went on to conclude, "We talk a great deal of nonsense about the rights of man. We say that every man is born free, and equal to every other man. Nothing can be more untrue no human being ever was, now is, or ever will be born free." According to William Harper, man in fact was "born to subjection," and inequality was necessary for "civilization." And Hammond declared, "I repudiate, as ridiculously absurd, that much lauded but nowhere accredited dogma of Mr. Jefferson, that "all men are born equal." For Simms, the "doctrine of majorities" and "levelling" democracy as well as the notion of natural rights were false. Carolinian planter politicians such as Hammond and Woodward regularly denounced the "metaphysical inductions" of the Declaration in Congress. Carolinian secessionist William Porcher Miles, following Calhoun, developed an eviscerated version of liberty as a privilege for the few rather than a right of all.[53]

While Carolinian proslavery theorists challenged the notion of universal individual rights of liberty and equality, they defended the right to property with an ardor that would have put to shame its bourgeois adherents. In 1848, when a minority in the House Committee of Military Affairs challenged the notion of human beings as property contained in Burt's report, which granted one Antonio Pacheo compensation for his slave property, the Carolina press launched into a long defense of the right to property. The proslavery position consistently valued slaveholders' right to property at a much higher level than the slaves' right to liberty. Justification of human property, even more than any capitalist logic, demanded such priorities. For instance, Hammond pointed out that man's right to "property in man" had been "consecrated" by the Bible. Woodward argued that restriction of slavery would violate southern slaveholders' individual property rights. And Cheves likened abolition to communism and the antiproperty theories of the great anarchist thinker Proudhon. As Calhoun had also noted, "A very slight modification of the arguments used against the institutions, which sustain the property and security of the South, would make them equally effectual against the institutions of the North, including Banking, in which so vast an amount of its property and capital are invested." Hammond predicted that antislavery would ultimately challenge northern capital after vanquishing slaveholders and he emphasized the threat to all property relations embodied in it. Louisa McCord, a proslavery essayist of some repute, enlisted the principles of liberal political economy to fight against abolition, which she argued was akin to socialism.[54]

Carolinian slaveholders did not always take the supposedly high road in their vindication of African slavery. Brutal racialist notions buttressed their arguments. Most like Keitt defended slavery as a system of race relations as well as the basis of all good society. Racism did not make them white egalitarians nor did its alleged absence lead to a purely class-based analysis. Instead, belief in racial inequality bolstered a commitment to the general principle of inequality. McCord, a virulent racist, felt that "the assumed position of equality even in the limited sense which we adopt [for white men] is plainly a false one." Hammond argued that slavery gave rise to the best kind of aristocracy and condemned "agrarianism" and "sans culottes." He included all whites in this aristocracy, but the logic behind his position reflected the hierarchical world of the planter class. He and other southern nationalists such as De Bow and Tucker remained highly skeptical of the benefits of mass democracy and universal suffrage. William Henry Trescot, secessionist planter and historian, prayed for the emergence of a statesman who would "take slavery with all its feudal necessities as the basis of his domestic policy. . . . [S]lavery has either to be abolished or made the acknowledged basis of a consistent government."[55]

Just as belief in race and class inequality complemented each other in Carolinian proslavery discourse, the justification of racial slavery led slavery ideologues to champion gender inequality. For most Carolinian slaveholders, the supposedly natural and divinely ordained differences of race and sex further proved that the principle of inequality was the basis of all civilization. And defenders of slavery needed to look no further than to Aristotle to expound on the natural position of women and slaves in the household. Simms was as harsh in his condemnation of Harriet Martineau's advocacy of women's rights as her antislavery pronouncements. But it was McCord who penned the most powerful critiques of the antebellum women's movement and embraced the role of an anti–women's rights crusader. She also evoked bourgeois Victorian notions of separate spheres and women's distinct nature and criticized the advocates of "equal rights without distinctions of sex or color."[56]

Carolinian proslavery thinkers' critique of bourgeois ideas and capitalism was highly uneven and attenuated. Their alleged sympathy for the plight of free labor was outweighed by their fears of its potential for mischief. They argued that the lot of the black slave was better than that of the free laborer, especially in Britain, because unlike a capitalist employer a master was guided by the dictates of self-interest, humanity, and custom to provide for his slave's well-being. And like Calhoun, they concluded that the enslavement of labor was the only solution to the conflict between capital and labor. Harper worried that if labor was not kept in a state of strict "subordination," it would pose a grave danger to society.

"Imagine," he wrote, "an extensive rice or cotton plantation cultivated by free laborers, who might perhaps *strike* for an increase in wages, at a season when neglect of a few days would insure the destruction of the whole crop." William J. Grayson, the lowcountry planter who compared the condition of the free laborer unfavorably with that of the slave in his famous poem *The Hireling and the Slave*, noted,

> No mobs of factious workmen gather here,
> No strikes dread, no lawless riots fear;

Free labor's "anarchic" and "communist" response to its conditions, he warned, threatened to destroy all property relations. In his secessionist pamphlet, Trescot went so far as to argue that "The political majority of the North represents labor — the political majority of the South represents capital — can the latter suffer the power of legislation in the hands of the former?"[57]

The Christian defense of slavery reinforced the conservative and antidemocratic nature of proslavery discourse in the state. Proslavery theologians contended for the superiority of slave society in comparison to an abolitionized northern society in which, they argued, property, marriage, female subordination, the sabbath, and other such pillars of social order were constantly challenged and overthrown. Communion and certainly subjection to such a society was anathema. As Thornwell wrote, "The parties in this conflict are not merely Abolitionists and Slaveholders; they are Atheists, Socialists, Communists, Red Republicans, Jacobins on the one side, and the friends of order and regulated freedom on the other." Proslavery Christianity also facilitated the repudiation of revolutionary egalitarianism. Reverend Richard Fuller in his letters to Francis Wayland, the antislavery clergymen, argued that "despotic power is not a sin" and drew a connection between the "benevolent" despotism of slavery and that of God. Reverend Iveson Brookes pointed out that northern clergymen drew their conclusions against slavery from Jefferson's "infidel" and "nonsensical" dogmas on human equality rather than from the Bible. Reverends Whitefoord Smith and Ferdinand Jacobs preached that inequality was a condition ordained by God. Smith defended slavery against "a spirit of insubordination and lawlessness, of infidelity and atheism," and Jacobs argued, "*Liberty is not an inalienable right.*" And Thornwell asserted that the sectional controversy over slavery represented a fight between the revealed truth of the Bible and the "modern speculation in the rights of man."[58]

The cardinal dogma of Carolinian proslavery clergymen was scriptural fundamentalism. This was not only orthodox theology, but it also best vindicated human bondage. Thornwell argued, "Beyond the Bible she [the Church] can never go, and apart from the Bible she can never speak." Hammond claimed that abolitionists "*deny the Bible, and set up in its place a law of their own making.*" If we accept that biblical literalism is the highest form of theological inquiry, then indeed, these men won the Christian debate on slavery in antebellum America. But in one case, proslavery theologians seriously undermined fundamentalist doctrine in their ardor to defend African slavery. In their interpretation of Noah's curse on Ham's son Canaan, they not only extended the curse to all of Canaan's posterity but also equated them with "the black race." While they were not the first to make this claim, this whole theory certainly went beyond the given word of the Bible. According to Brookes, God had personally cursed Ham with African features and ordained that "the negro" would never rise to intellectual greatness. The Ham story underwent wilder and more far-fetched transformations in the eager hands of lesser minds in the Old South. It also illustrated that proslavery Christian discourse was hardly free from racialist thinking, though some clergymen such as John Bachman, Thornwell, and John Adger fought against the heretical and pseudoscientific theory of the polygenetic origins of man supported by racist slavery apologists such as Josiah Nott and De Bow, native Carolinians, and McCord. Even when positing the unity of mankind, proslavery clergymen were hardly free of racism. Adger argued that while black people were of "Adam's race," they were of an "inferior variety."[59]

The most sophisticated versions of proslavery Christianity tried to make the whole notion of human bondage far more palatable than it actually was. Thornwell claimed that slavery sanctioned the slaveholder's right to the labor of his slave and not to his or her person. He argued that slavery and many other earthly imperfections were a part of the fallen state of man, a condition ordained by God. The religious duty of slaveholders was not to abolish slavery but to work for reforms. His reformism went far enough to contemplate eventual emancipation. These arguments revealed to what extent the southern slave system would have to be changed before any effective defense of it could be mounted. We would do well to remember that the proslavery literature on the duties of Christian masters was prescriptive rather than descriptive of slavery and was geared to answer the abolitionist view of slavery as a violation of Christian brotherhood.[60]

Just as Carolinian slaveholders' early vindication of slavery had spurred nullification, proslavery ideology, including the Christian defense of slavery, would inspire their fight for an independent slave nation. Regardless of the individual political beliefs of proslavery writers, their works were indispensable in the construction of a separate southern identity based on slavery.

The Calhoun-inspired southern movement rested on a clear vindication of slave society. The extension and perpetuity of slavery lay at the heart of the southern nationalist agenda. A firm belief in the essential rightfulness of slavery and the superiority of slave society undergirded this practical or policy aspect of southern nationalism. This was evident in the coming of age of proslavery ideology during these years and in the argument for southern independence that revolved around the safety and protection of slavery. The proslavery argument and Calhoun's political theories constituted the twin pillars of southern nationalist discourse in South Carolina.

Relatively free of partisan and intersectional divisions, the state was poised to lead the secession movement of 1850. Southern nationalism had made much headway in most of the slave South in the context of the sectional struggle over the territories. Southern disunionist ultimatums on the Wilmot Proviso and any restriction of slavery in the territories revealed this. The sectional controversy popularized the discourse of southern nationalism for the first time in the slave states. It also gave Carolinian planter politicians new authority as the most vigorous and consistent exponents of slavery and southern separatism. Calhoun's willingness to contemplate disunion rather than to compromise on the extension of slavery would inspire the South's first secession movement. A Carolina-initiated movement for southern independence would soon bring some lower south states to the brink of disunion.

4

South Carolina and the First Secession Crisis

We shall be a fire ship in the Union if they will not let us go out of it.
I do not believe that this Union as administered now will tolerate slavery
& slavery therefore must not tolerate this Union.
— ROBERT BARNWELL, 1850

Carolinian planter politicians, with their ideological purity on slavery and extreme separatism, were perfectly poised to lead the movement for a southern nation. The failure of partisan politics to settle the question of territorial slavery bode well for them. Their ideas, political fidelity to slavery, and disunionist threats became increasingly influential in the rest of the South and put the Union, in the eyes of most contemporaries, in serious jeopardy. Carolinian separatists' opposition to the Compromise of 1850 would also form the program of the first secession movement.

The social geography of the slave South shaped the contours of southern nationalism. The equation of slavery with regional identity distributed the cause of a new southern nation unevenly along class, state, and sectional lines. The secession movement would gain many more converts in the Deep South, where slavery and slaveholding were more widespread and nonplantation belts were smaller, than in the upper south and border states. Sectional consciousness also worked at cross-purposes with partisan loyalties. In the lower south states where secession was hotly contested, party lines broke down. Political differences along geographical cum class lines were evident, as in most slave states predominantly nonslaveholding hill areas proved to be far more immune to the lures of southern nationalism than the plantation belt.[1]

The case of South Carolina reveals that planter leadership, a statewide plantation belt, widespread slave ownership, and participation in the staple economy among the yeomanry were decisive factors in making the state a stronghold of southern nationalism. The exceptional and advanced nature of the political culture of slavery in South Carolina is illustrated by the fact that while the slavery expansion controversy in other southern states raged between unionists and secessionists, in this state a difference arose between those who advocated the secession of the state by itself and those who championed the combined secession of the southern states. The latter party contained a small group of outnumbered and outgunned unionists, who were forced to act under the auspices of cooperative secession.[2] The terms of political debate were therefore quite different from those during nullification. Loyalty to the ideal of a southern nation, rather than to the Union, checked the immediate secession of the state.

In South Carolina, overt appeals for the protection and extension of slavery rather than notions of southern liberty and honor inspired the secession movement. Under Calhoun's leadership, state leaders had established the ideological and constitutional principles behind the demand for the extension of slavery to the territories. Even those southern politicians who accepted popular sovereignty and the compromise interpreted this formula according to Calhoun's theory of state sovereignty and made the security of slavery the condition of their unionism. Carolinian planter politicians, political losers in the struggle for southern nationhood in 1850, would emerge as the long-term ideological victors in much of the slave South.

During the early months of 1850, the Carolinian-led movement for southern unity made remarkable progress. Nine southern states were represented in the Nashville convention in June 1850. Tennessee, being the host state, had the largest delegation and Texas with one delegate had the smallest. Of the states that were to form the Confederacy, only Louisiana and North Carolina were unrepresented. Louisiana was the one state in the Deep South where the secession movement failed to make much headway in 1850, except among a small faction of Carolinian émigrés led by Pierre Soule. The border states of Delaware, Maryland, Missouri, and Kentucky also stayed away from the convention. In Missouri and Kentucky, the unionist leadership of Thomas Benton, Henry Clay, and John J. Crittenden prevailed, and Delaware had long been regarded as almost a free state. In Maryland and North Carolina, Whigs and unionists blocked participation, but a Whig-dominated Florida legislature sent six delegates to Nashville, of whom four attended the convention. The introduction of the compromise had already created some dissensions within southern ranks. The divisions in the 1850 southern movement would reemerge in 1861. Procompromise feeling was strong among unionists and Whigs and the Lower South tended to be far more separatist than the Upper South. Intersectional divisions between the nonslaveholding yeomanry of the upcountry and the planter-dominated black belts were also apparent, as most delegations represented the plantation belts. The arbitrary selection of delegates to the convention revealed the undemocratic, top-heavy nature of the southern movement. The average citizen had yet to be converted to the cause of southern nationhood and the democratic credentials of the 1850 movement were suspect.

Only South Carolina seemed impervious to partisan and sectional divisions. It sent a delegation of sixteen members led by three delegates at large, Langdon Cheves, Robert Barnwell, and James Henry Hammond. I. W. Hayne, appointed by the governor as a substitute for Franklin Harper Elmore, did not attend. The delegation contained seven former nullifiers and many unconditional secessionists such as Robert Barnwell Rhett, Maxcy Gregg, James H. Adams, and D. F. Jamison. The Carolinian group also stood out for the large number of wealthy planters in it. Local meetings, presided over by the state's planter politicians, had nominated most of South Carolina's delegates to the convention. Speeches by prominent men in these meetings proclaimed secession as the only remedy.[3]

The secessionist leadership of the South, with some exceptions such as Alabama's William Lowndes Yancey, was well represented at Nashville. Despite his doubts about the convention, Hammond noted, "To me it seems to be the one thing needful [is] to *unite the South* on some measure of resistance looking to action." William Gilmore Simms, who was even more optimistic, wrote, "I regard the Southern Convention as, in fact, a Southern Confederacy. To secure the one it seems to me very certain is to secure the other." The convention was presided over by William Sharkey, who like many southern Whigs had moved to a procompromise position. The choice of Nashville as a meeting place had been strategic because Tennessee and much of the Upper South were far more unionist in sentiment. The convention met at McKendree church with the South Carolina and Mississippi delegations appropriately occupying the front pews. The Carolinians "were studious in yielding precedence to all others" and won high praise for their restraint. Francis W. Pickens and Rhett disagreed with this strategy—the former made two fire-eating speeches and the latter wrote the address of the convention. But the strongest disunion pronouncements came from Beverly Tucker, of whose speech Hammond wrote, "such a phillipic has not been seen lately."[4]

The Nashville resolutions and address laid down very clearly the preeminence of slavery in southern nationalist discourse. Alabama's John Archibald Campbell, one of the leaders of the southern movement, presented the resolutions. They reiterated Calhoun's theory of the territories as the joint property of the states and contended that Congress was obliged to make laws for the protection of territorial slavery. They further stated that the federal government had no right to "denationalize property" recognized by the Constitution and that the slaveholding states would not submit to any act of Congress infringing on the "rights of masters." While the resolutions were based on proslavery constitutional theory, they also noted that "slavery exists in the United States independent of the Constitution." The address, composed by Rhett, embodied the secessionist argument against the compromise. Addressed to the people of all the slaveholding states except Delaware, it was even more separatist in tone than the resolutions and led to a minority protest. Rhett argued that the dilemma of the South was "progressive," as the northern goal was to abolish slavery by the creation of new free states. Like Calhoun, he described the irreconcilable differences between the sections based on slavery and decried majority domination. He criticized attempts to provide fugitive slaves with a jury trial as an interference with a slaveholder's personal dominion over his slave. The address and the resolutions recommended the adoption of the Missouri line as an ultimatum and pointed the way to secessionists' rejection of the compromise. Whether the convention led to the eventual passage of the compromise measures is debatable. Most unionists and Whigs who supported the compromise opposed the convention and stayed away from it.[5]

In South Carolina, the outcome of the convention was hailed enthusiastically. The *Charleston Mercury* called it "one of the great events of our times" and argued that it was composed of southern patriots devoted to the safety of their region. Skeptical as he was, Hammond wrote, "The great point, is that the South *has met*, has acted with great harmony in a nine day Convention & above all *has agreed to meet again*." Flushed by his success, Rhett predicted disunion and the formation of a southern nation in a speech at Charleston's Hibernian Hall.[6]

The politics of compromise, however, marred Carolinian secessionists' triumph. The final shape of the compromise proved to be more favorable to the South than Clay's proposals, as it left the territory of New Mexico and the Mormon enclave at Deseret (Utah) open to slavery. The new fugitive slave law was stringent to the point of making a mockery of the due process of law. In return the North received the admission of free California and the abolition of the slave trade in the District of Columbia. Texas agreed to give up claims to New Mexican land for five million dollars and assumption of its public debt by the federal government.

Sectional differences had doomed Clay's omnibus bill. Aggressive political management by Stephen Douglas, Democratic senator from Illinois, culminated in the passage of the compromise in September 1850, now broken up into distinct parts. Taylor's death and the accession of his conservative vice president from New York, Millard Fillmore, expedited the process. A look at the roll call voting in Congress reveals that each measure passed by a sectional vote and as such the compromise was indeed an armistice. Even moderate groups showed signs of sectionalism. Border-state Whigs voted against the abolition of the slave trade in the District of Columbia and some procompromise northern Democrats abstained from voting on the Fugitive Slave Act.[7]

The long debates over the compromise measures gave Carolinian congressmen ample opportunity to air their objections to the sectional adjustment. Following Calhoun, they argued that the nonextension of slavery meant death to the institution and that the admission of California would be resisted to the "last extremity." On the passage of the California bill, ten southern senators, including Senators A. P. Butler and Barnwell, presented a formal protest. Butler reported, "The prospect of the South is indeed gloomy indeed." The compromise, Carolinian planter politicians contended, was an "unconditional surrender" on the part of the slave South. Not only did it decree the "dismemberment" of Texas, a sister slave state, but the prohibition of the slave trade in the District of Columbia would lead to abolition. The territorial bills allowed "squatters" and "foreigners" to outlaw slavery. Proslavery nativism, an issue neglected by most historians, was an important ingredient in Calhoun's and Carolinians' rejection of popular sovereignty. Carolinian secessionists argued that the "channels of separation" had been made deeper and that the "die was cast." They felt, "Compromise is not peace, it is war under the semblance and garb of the law." Simms had "no hope, and no faith on compromises of any kind" and argued that disunion was an "inevitable necessity." Unionists such as Henry Foote and Sam Houston enjoyed baiting Carolinians for their extremism. "No southern man can open his mouth in defense of his section," Barnwell complained, "that this brawling blackguard [Foote] is not immediately up howling some thing against disunion and traitors."[8]

Carolinian congressmen had voted for only the Fugitive Slave Act but they predicted that it would be repealed or not enforced. Reports of so-called mob action in the North against the capture of fugitive slaves was given prominent coverage in the state press, which dismissed President Fillmore's proclamation to enforce the law as another example of pulling wool over southern eyes. In Congress, Rhett caused some consternation among fellow southerners when he declared that the fugitive act was unconstitutional as it transferred state power to the federal government. Rhett's argument, Hammond contended, was "fatal" for a disunionist because it delegitimized the very law whose nonenforcement could lead to southern secession. Senator Butler, in a more measured speech, pointed out the futility of breathing "life into an extinct article of the Constitution of the United States." He argued that northern defiance of the fugitive law particularly incited slaves to revolt. "A descendant of a secessionist" warned, "*If South Carolina does not secede from the Union, the effect upon her peculiar population will be disastrous in the extreme.*" Rhett claimed that Congress was nothing more than a "grand abolition convention" teaching and "inspiring" insurrection among the slaves.[9]

Only a handful of Carolinian unionists such as Joel R. Poinsett, James L. Petigru, John Belton O'Neall, and Benjamin F. Perry demurred. Richard Yeadon, who had flirted with secession earlier, thought that the compromise was "in great measure a Southern triumph," and his paper, the *Charleston Courier*, was perhaps the only one in the state to advocate its acceptance. Poinsett, whose name came up and was quickly dropped as a possible choice for the state delegation to the southern convention, affirmed that he would never sanction disunion. Perry felt that the compromise ceded much to the slave South by opening all territories to slavery, and he supported the convention movement in the hope that the rest of the South would check Carolinian extremism. But he also realized, "the whole of South Carolina is opposed to it — and a large portion of the State [is] for Disunion *per se*."[10]

Carolinian secessionists organized Southern Rights Associations to lead their movement. The "most respectable and influential citizens" made up these associations. As Governor Whitemarsh Seabrook proclaimed, "Let agitation concerning the remedy forthwith commence in every Parish and District of the State." The state press stepped up its campaign for disunion. A newspaper essayist, "Cincinnatus," concluded, "the Union is no longer our shield but a sword in our vitals." Only secession, according to another writer, would provide security to slavery and increase the value of southern slaves and lands. Hammond also argued, "I trust that a cordial union will soon be established among the Slaveholding States for the defence of their common & *vital* interests now in such imminent danger." Prominent Carolinians made speeches urging a separation of the states.[11]

The South Carolina–led secession movement drew its ideological inspiration from proslavery ideology. The proslavery argument was thus neither aberrant nor without any political significance. This was most evident in the barrage of propaganda produced by the state's Southern Rights Association encouraging the South to secede from the Union.

Virginia planter Muscoe R. H. Garnett's pamphlet painted on the one hand an idyllic picture of economic prosperity, political clout, and geographical expansion for an independent slave confederacy. On the other hand, the North would wither and decay without the conservatism of the slave South to protect it from labor radicalism, agrarianism, and anti-rentism. The lot of the African slaves, he felt, was far better than not only the paupers and laborers of the North but also its farmers. Garnett's homilies prompted a "citizen of Boston" to refute his picture of free society on the verge of collapse. The Bostonian probably added fuel to the fire when he sought to assure slaveholders that while most northerners did not want to interfere in slavery, they regarded it as an evil that they hoped would gradually disappear. This would hardly pacify southern nationalists who were by now waxing lyrical on the blessed advantages of slavery and seeing it as the most vital and cherished part of a separate identity.[12]

The secessionist pamphlets of the 1850s represented a fine mixture of southern separatism and proslavery ideology. By the end of the year, the association published four pamphlets by Carolinian planters William Henry Trescot, John Townsend, Peter Della Torre, and Edward Bryan, staunch believers in the cause of a slavery-based southern nation. Townsend and Della Torre were also members of the legislature. In his review of Garnett's work, Della Torre argued that the federal government was "an antislavery, abolition government" that was determined to prevent the expansion of slavery and to eventually destroy it. Townsend asserted that the North was marching steadily toward the goal of emancipation and that the South should make no compromises in this question of its "political life and death." He went on to spell out the implications of the nonextension of slavery: "This scheme of self-destruction, — this species of political suicide, is the mildest form, the slowest process, by which our enemies propose to abolish slavery among us." Similarly, John A. Campbell contended that the compromise measures were merely a disguise for free soil sentiment and that slavery under these conditions would never last within the Union. Like Garnett, Townsend sanguinely predicted that the peaceful secession of the slave South would bring it untold prosperity, once freed from its colonial position in the Union. Evoking Clio for the cause of southern nationhood, Trescot concluded that the American republic had achieved its destiny and that it was now a "historical necessity" for the slave south to seek its own. Another Carolinian separatist warned, "Secession has now become inevitable. We are no more the same nation. Interest, opinion, laws, divide us, and the breach can only be widened — for fanaticism, that lever of hell, is at work." Bryan argued that the American nation was no different than the human body, subject to inevitable processes of decline. Slaveholders, he wrote, hated "the op-pressive Union."[13]

Unlike some recent historians who have claimed that slavery itself had little to do with slaveholders' fight for nationhood, these propagandists made no bones about connecting their movement with the preservation and celebration of human bondage. Trescot argued that slavery lay at the basis of the best system of labor, society, and polity. He and Bryan felt that the South's superiority lay in the fact that labor was dependent and infe-rior to capital while in the North political equality between labor and capital produced ceaseless strife. Bryan contended that inequality and slavery were the universal conditions of labor, which formed the "de-graded" and "dangerous" element of society. Carolinian secessionists were confident that the slaves would be faithful to their benevolent mas-ters in a civil war. The more practical Townsend suggested the time-honored measures of striking down "deluded" slaves and hanging "dia-bolical" agents. Bryan claimed that slavery was sanctioned by both the Bible and the Koran. Alabama secessionist John A. Campbell also under-took a long historical analysis to illustrate that slavery had been an essen-tial feature of most "civilized" nations in the world. According to Della Torre, slave society "obeys and displays the great law of nature — series, gradation, order." Bryan paraphrased and simultaneously subverted the famous revolutionary cry "Give us SLAVERY or give us death." Such a slogan could hardly have emanated from a movement guided merely by fears for southern liberty and political slavery to the North. As Della Torre asserted, "hostility to slavery is hostility to the South. You can-not speak, you cannot think of the South, without slavery. It is included in her idea."[14]

Proslavery ideology provided secessionists with an alternative political identity and successfully challenged their fealty to the American repub-lic and the principles on which it was founded. There was a direct con-nection between the growth of the proslavery argument and southern separatism. Many contemporaries connected southern acquiescence to northern "aggression" with the fact that too many of the section's leaders had been "morbidly diseased in opinion" with regard to slavery. Della Torre argued that the Jeffersonian view of slavery as an evil necessity was "fatal" to the southern demand for independence. De Bow firmly based "The Cause of the South" on the protection of "social forms and institu-tions, which separate the European and the African races, into distinct classes, and assign each a different sphere in society."[15]

Carolinian clergymen composed many of the proslavery tracts in the sectional war of words and ideas and some sanctified the cause of south-ern nationalism. As Reverend Iveson Brooks wrote, "we would be reckless to the divine trust committed to us to submit to the encroachments of any fanatical movement against Slavery as God's institution." The division of the Baptist and Methodist churches into northern and southern wings in 1845–46 was a precursor to disunion in more ways than one. Southern clergymen used Calhoun's constitutional theories to justify the schism. In *A Defence of the South*, Brooks called for the peaceful separation of the two sections should the Union continue to oppress slaveholders. The pamphlet assured slaveholders that even though the world was against slavery, God supported his "favorite" institution. Whitefoord Smith, in his sermon to the assembly, called for resistance, arguing that South Carolina had been "traduced" and "mocked." Few revealed, as John Adger did, any uneasiness about the politicization of southern Christianity when he admitted that he now prayed to God as a "partisan." Many Carolina ministers were as rabidly secessionist as the state's politicos. James Henley Thornwell confessed, "But I am sorry to say that many of our clergy are as rash and violent as the rashest of their hearers."[16]

Even conditional unionists such as Thornwell contributed to the sectional discourse by condemning free soilism and warning that the South would not tolerate any interference with slavery, which "is implicated in every fibre of Southern society; it is with us a vital question, and it is because we *know* that interference with it cannot and will not be much longer endured we raise our warning voices." While Thornwell opposed secession in 1850, he made it clear that the "responsibility" for alienating slaveholders from the Union lay with the "non-slaveholding States." Echoing Calhoun, he claimed that the southern position on territorial slavery was constitutional. He wrote, "But the Union is the creature of the Constitution. The destruction of one is, and must be, sooner or later, the destruction of the other. The guilt of dissolving it must rest on those who trample the Constitution in the dust."[17]

The southern movement derived its ideological unity from the proslavery argument, a body of thought whose hold on the state's leadership was apparent. Thornwell became the president of South Carolina College and exercised the same intellectual influence on the state's aspiring leaders that the atheist Dr. Cooper had during nullification. In his speech on the Compromise of 1850, Representative I. E. Holmes argued that the Bible clearly recognized the master-slave relationship. And in his pamphlet, Bryan contended that God had ordained slavery on earth and that the curse on Ham justified the enslavement of Africans.[18]

Politically, the southern nationalists of 1850 pinned their hopes on the joint secession of the slave states. Bryan advised all southern states to send delegates to the second session of the Nashville convention to commence the work of disunion. The *Southern Press* proclaimed that it was no treason for the South to meet in convention and consider changing or abolishing its government. Senator Barnwell wanted the convention to formulate an address "making slavery the issue and defending it as a social institution claiming the right of secession and recommending a Congress of the Slaveholding States and perhaps as an irritant and a popular mode of bringing about disunion recommending non-intercourse with the North until the meeting of the Congress." As a strategy, however, joint secession was doomed to failure. Partisan, sectional, and class differences in the slave South were bound to check any concerted action. And with the exception of the four cotton states, southern nationalism had failed to make much headway in the rest of the South after the passage of the compromise.[19]

The second meeting of the Nashville convention in November 1850 proved to be the last hurrah of secessionists. In the absence of Sharkey, it was presided over by Charles McDonald, a secessionist from Georgia. The delegates, with the exception of those from Tennessee, were far more separatist in temper than their predecessors and this gathering was smaller. Arkansas and Texas had dropped out and Virginia sent one delegate. Most state delegations were trimmed in size and only South Carolina still retained a respectable representation, though R. F. W. Allston did not attend. Hammond felt that the convention would do nothing but "harm" the cause and hoped that a new southern congress would lead the slave states out of the Union. He concluded that the convention was "an abortion, which had neither awed the North nor harmonized the South and which should be allowed to sink into oblivion as soon as possible." He feared that the "Union men would crowd in and pervert the convention" but later conceded that it had been dominated by "Resistance" and "ultra" men and openly led by the Carolinians.[20]

The convention articulated the secessionist agenda of 1850. The seventy-four-year-old Cheves gave the most memorable speech, a classic statement of the antidemocratic, proslavery discourse of southern nationalism. He condemned the free states as the "most unjust oppressors" and the "bitter and unappeasable enemies" of the slave South, bent on the "destruction" of its "most valuable property." The "manyheaded" and "popular tyranny" of the North was waging a war against slavery, which was recognized in the Constitution and supported by the Scriptures. He argued that antislavery was actually the "doctrine" of communism and anarchism as it advocated that all "property is a crime." The slave South would have to resist these "wild" theories "as a nation" or it would be "subdued as a nation." Cheves concluded, "Secession — united secession of the slaveholding States, or a large number of them. Nothing else will be wise — nothing else will be practicable. The Rubicon is passed — the Union is already dissolved!" The preamble and resolutions adopted by the convention justified the right to secession. They recommended a southern congress to "provide for their future safety and independence." Of the seven states, only Tennessee rejected the report and resolves.[21] The first few months of the southern movement seemed to be proceeding according to a well-orchestrated Carolinian plan.

Southern nationalism found its first home in those states that had the greatest stakes in slavery. Lower south separatism was fed not only by a rejection of the compromise measures but by the conviction that southern independence was crucial for the growth of slavery. While the Upper South, Florida, and Texas, with the exception of some southern rights leaders, accepted the Compromise of 1850 as a rejection of the slavery nonextension principle, a significant secession movement arose in Georgia, Mississippi, South Carolina, and, to a lesser extent, Alabama. Of the deep south states, only Louisiana failed to produce comparable agitation. Georgia's legislature had called for a state convention on the admission of California. Simms wrote that if Georgia raised a "finger" in resistance, his state would "lift her whole hand and the fist shall be doubled." Butler recommended sending a committee representing South Carolina to the Georgia convention and Barnwell asked Hammond to use his influence in that state for the southern cause and to disregard "the cry of So Carolina, they will raise it any how, give them cause to do so." He wrote, "If it were not for the cheering indications from Georgia Alabama & Miss I should at once make up my mind that if South Carolina acts at all she must act alone, but I will hope for better things." For Barnwell, the state's role was clear. He argued, "we shall be a fire ship in the Union if they will not let us go out of it. I do not believe that this Union as administered now will tolerate slavery & slavery therefore must not tolerate this Union."[22]

Carolinian planter politicians studiously followed the strategy laid out by Calhoun for southern unity: they sought to avoid isolation by encouraging other slave states to take the lead. Governor Seabrook commenced a correspondence with the governors of Virginia, Mississippi, and Alabama asking what steps their states would take on the convening of the Georgia convention. He also assured them that South Carolina would not take any action unless at least two states moved ahead first. The secessionist-minded Governor Towns of Georgia advised Seabrook to delay formal action until after the convention elections, as he felt that any precipitousness on the part of the Carolinians would hurt the "true Southern party" in his state. Seabrook had already decided to postpone all state action until the Nashville convention reconvened in November. He warned his friends that "a false step" might destroy the whole southern cause. Governor John Quitman of Mississippi wrote to Seabrook about his intentions to call a state convention "with full powers to annul the Federal compact." Quitman also wrote to Rhett asking for his suggestions on "the proper course to be pursued by the south in this emergency." Rhett and Yancey addressed meetings in Alabama and Georgia, commencing their decade-long cooperation for disunion.[23]

South Carolina's romance with southern nationalism soon received some major jolts. The rise of a Union Party under the leadership of such ardent defenders of slavery as Robert Toombs, Alexander Stephens, and Howell Cobb of Georgia, Henry Foote and William Sharkey of Mississippi, and Henry Hilliard, Jeremiah Clemens, and William R. King of Alabama seriously challenged southern nationalists like Yancey, Jefferson Davis, Quitman, Walter Colquitt, and Charles McDonald. The secession crisis dissipated party lines and eventually spelled the demise of the Whig Party in the cotton states. New parties — the Constitutional Union Party, consisting of Whigs and unionist Democrats, and the Southern Rights Party, composed of secessionist Democrats and some states' rights Whigs, engaged in a fierce political battle over the compromise and secession. The Mississippi legislature called for a state convention and rebuked Foote's championship of the compromise. The convention was to convene only in October 1851, giving unionists ample time to marshal their forces. Accusations that the southern movement was merely an old Carolinian ruse for disunion undercut the strength of secessionists. Southern nationalists were soon reduced to defending the constitutionality of secession rather than advocating disunion.[24]

Unionists first rode to victory in the Georgia convention elections. The 1850 platform of the Georgia convention epitomized the conditional unionism of lower south politicians. While it said that the state regarded the compromise as a "permanent settlement of this sectional controversy," it threatened secession if slavery was abolished in the District of Columbia or any area under the control of the federal government. It further specified that if the interstate slave trade, the entry of any slave state into the Union, or slavery in Utah and New Mexico were prohibited or if the Fugitive Slave Act was not enforced, secession would be justified. While secessionists suffered a serious setback, the ideological triumph of the discourse of southern nationalism was evident. Many lower south unionists also admitted the "constitutionality" of the "right to secession" while others such as Cobb hedged the question.[25] Lower South leaders, while rejecting the remedy of secession, adopted the proslavery discourse of southern nationalism.

The elections of 1850–51 revealed that the real laggards in the fight for the slave South were not its political leaders but its ordinary citizens. Procompromise forces and an upsurge in unionist sentiment among voters defeated secessionists. The Georgia platform acted as a check to immediate secession and was a prelude to the electoral triumph of the constitutional unionists in Mississippi and Alabama. Most southern states endorsed the Georgia platform rather than the Carolinian plan for secession. In 1851, the Virginia assembly, spurning the call for a southern congress, asked "South Carolina to desist from any meditated secession upon her part, which cannot but tend to the destruction of the Union and the loss to all of the States of the benefits that spring from it." Yancey's attempts to promote secession in Alabama also ended in dismal failure. A unionist majority in the Mississippi convention elections ended all hopes of South Carolina leading even a single southern state out of the Union. Over the protest of a vocal minority, they added insult to injury by denying the constitutionality of secession. Subsequent unionist victories in state elections in Alabama, Georgia, and Mississippi confirmed the isolation of Carolinian secessionists.[26]

The rise of lower south unionism did embolden the handful of Carolinian unionists to come out against secession. Poinsett in a public letter defended the compromise and challenged the constitutionality of secession. Petigru, who had been advised to restrain his unionism for the sake of prudence, could barely contain himself when a toast was drunk "to the health of South Carolina." He responded, "With all my heart, and her return to her senses." Francis Lieber, a German political scientist at South Carolina College, lamented that the "simple grandeur and deep wisdom" of American representative government should be threatened by disunionism. In contrast to the unconditional unionism of Poinsett, Petigru, and Lieber, Yeadon suggested that the South should issue a disunion ultimatum to the North if it did not abide by the compromise, especially the Fugitive Slave Act. According to Perry, only four or five members of the state house, representing the northern nonplantation districts, were unionist. The only lowcountry unionist was Henry Lesesne of Charleston, a former law partner of Petigru's. The entire legislature, Petigru felt, "are declared disunionists." He observed, "There seems to be a current in favor of Union everywhere but here." Perry's ambitious wife lamented the "stigma" attached to her husband. Unionists complained about the state's "proscriptive" and "intolerant" political climate. One southerner noted, "In S.C. the great difficulty is that the people never have but [one] side of the question."[27]

As W. J. Grayson discovered, in South Carolina in 1850, being a unionist carried the same opprobrium that being a disunionist did in other parts of the country. Rumors that the state would secede immediately prompted him to address the governor in a public letter, reminding him that South Carolina might be as isolated as it was during nullification. He also wrote the only unionist pamphlet and had it printed at his own expense. Grayson, a proslavery writer, espoused an extremely conservative view of the Union, designed to appeal to slaveholders apprehensive of the effects on slavery of any political upheaval. Like Berrien, he recommended a program of economic nonintercourse with antislavery states. Disunion would not only lead to war but it also could not guarantee a uniformity of opinion on slavery among southerners themselves. The nonslaveholders of the Upper South might prove to be the new North within a southern confederacy. The barrage of criticism that greeted his statements was enough to deter any strong-hearted unionist. Secessionists accused him of inconsistency because of his participation in nullification, of treachery for being a federal office holder, and finally of temerity, for daring to address the governor.[28]

Only in the Palmetto state did an overwhelming majority of planter politicians come out for secession. But with the defeat of the southern movement elsewhere, Carolinian secessionists were soon divided on tactics, whether the state should secede by itself or with the rest of the South. They had tried hard to goad the South and their failure convinced some of the desirability of separate secession. Fillmore's message asserting the finality of the sectional settlement was dismissed as "the essence of respectable platitude and constitutional ding-dong." The assembly through Governor Seabrook provoked a hostile correspondence with the administration demanding an explanation for the movement of federal troops into Charleston. However, Rhett's recommendation that the state provoke a military conflict was one at which even his friends balked. Edmund Rhett despaired of the rest of the South and D. F. Jamison feared that they would end up doing "nothing." Petigru shrewdly predicted a "reaction" against the idea of single secession.[29]

Some Carolinian planter politicians thought that they must avoid rash action. Simms wrote, "Were I to trust my feelings, I should say to South Carolina secede at once. Let our State move *per se*. But here's the danger. None of the Southern States stood to the rack in 1833 when South Carolina threw herself into the breach." James Hamilton also wrote a series of public letters in which he warned about the dangers of lone action by the state. The high price of cotton, he wrote, had "neutralized" all feelings of resistance in the Lower South. Secession should be the result of united southern action, and "for a single state like South Carolina, so suspect in her loyalty to the Union, to make the issue at once, would be a calamity I cannot but think to be greatly deplored." He made the southern nationalist case against separate secession: "I believe that SoCa will ultimately have to take the lead in seceding — perhaps to secede alone. . . . In a few years, who can say when or how soon, the voice of the South will call us to take the lead." Hammond denounced immediate secession as "an act of madness." For Hammond, the issue took on a personal coloring when Rhett defeated him for Calhoun's senatorial seat in the assembly. The separatists were powerful enough also to select John H. Means for the governorship.[30]

Carolinian secessionists soon divided over their course of action. In his inaugural address, Governor Means asserted that if the state failed to unite the South on secession, it must make a lone stand. He blamed southern prejudice against South Carolina and attempts to isolate it for the failure of joint secession. While the lowcountry-dominated senate was for single-state action, southern cooperationists formed a substantial contingent in the house. The cooperationists, led by Christopher Memminger and Perry, wanted to elect delegates for the southern congress as recommended by the Nashville convention. In his speech, Perry assured his colleagues that his fealty to the South and its "institutions" exceeded his love for the Union. Secessionists Laurence M. Keitt and John P. Richardson supported the call for a state convention. Intermediate measures such as nonintercourse with the free states and recall of the congressional delegation as a step "preparatory" for disunion were also advocated. The deadlock was finally resolved when an "omnibus bill" calling for both a state convention and a southern congress passed the house by a vote of 109 to 12. It passed the senate with only three dissenting votes. Elections for the state convention and the congress were scheduled for February and October 1851, respectively. Barnwell, Richardson, Cheves, and Wade Hampton were selected as statewide delegates to the Southern congress, to be held in Montgomery. At the end of 1850, the veneer of unity over the Southern Nationalist Party still held and the legislature could unanimously declare that it regarded "a dissolution of what is still called the Union, as a certain event — an inevitable necessity. The only question is as to the *time*." It also passed an act for the defense of the state that provided for annual brigade encampments and established a Board of Ordnance to examine the state's stockpile of arms and ammunition and boost its coastal defense. Hammond wrote that "the Legislature have given *their approbation for abortive violence*."[31]

It was evident that South Carolina would once again follow its unique calling in national politics. In February 1851, separatists scored an overwhelming victory in the sparsely attended convention elections. As John Russell had predicted, "The election for delegates to the Convention from these Parishes, will pass off without exciting the slightest interest."

Over 50 percent of the voting population in many districts had not exercised their franchise, casting serious doubts on the popular basis of disunion even in South Carolina. In Horry, "that Damned Independent Republic" of mostly nonslaveholding unionist farmers, not a single person had voted because the polls had not been opened. Some polls in Spartanburg and Chesterfield were not opened, many people did not vote in Sumter and Fairfield, and not even a quarter of the vote was cast in Pendleton and Charleston. If secession was to be successful, disunionist leaders realized, they would have to combat the "listless inactivity pervading the masses." Voter apathy insured that the most hot-headed secessionists dominated the convention. While 127 of the 169 elected delegates were for single-state action, only ten of the minority could be properly called unionists. Not only was representation in the convention based on the skewed legislative apportionment, but only one-third of the citizenry had voted in the election of its delegates. Both unionists and joint secessionists charged that the separatists had deliberately held the elections in a surreptitious and hurried fashion to bypass public will. Barnwell feared that the separatist-dominated convention would go ahead and vote for immediate secession. One separatist argued that nonvoters were bound to abide by the decision of the convention according to the "theory of elections." But it was now tacitly understood that another gauge of popular sentiment was needed. Hamilton suggested holding a referendum on secession. Eventually, all sides agreed to make elections to the southern congress a "test election" for separate or joint secession.[32]

The Carolinian brand of the politics of slavery and separatism had long placed the Palmetto state in a "state of political expectancy," with disunion as a cherished goal. Benjamin F. Whitner probably echoed the sentiments of most Carolinian leaders when he remarked, "Nothing but secession, separation, dismemberment (call it what you will) of the South from the North — the 'Slave States' from the 'Hireling States' will save our independence — or slave institutions." Lieber wrote to Perry that secessionists were more united and determined than before. Thornwell observed, "South Carolina . . . seems bent upon secession. The excitement is prodigious. Men, from whom one would have expected better things, are fanning the flame, and urging the people to the most desperate measures." Southern nationalists also argued that Carolinians should lead in creating an alternative to the Georgia platform. Quitman urged South Carolina to take "prompt and bold action" for the sake of all the slaveholding states. Tucker wrote repeatedly to Hammond that the state must take the lead, if a southern nation was to become a reality. In an article for the *Southern Quarterly Review*, he exhorted it to throw off "the yoke of this fatal Union."[33]

To spur the state to secession, the Southern Rights Association of Charleston issued an invitation to all the local organizations to meet in convention in May 1851. Separatists appealed to the more cautious in the disunionist party to come over to their side. Unionists, they contended, were too "small" and "paltry" to merit any attention. They should be treated like a "worm," a writer suggested, which one should avoid rather than kill. The gathering of 431 delegates, representing all districts except Horry, was dominated by separatists. Its unrepresentative nature was evident from the fact that even the Greenville delegation was rabidly disunionist. John P. Richardson was chosen to preside over the meeting and other separatists such as Maxcy Gregg and Edmund Rhett controlled its proceedings. W. H. Gist's resolution stating that "South Carolina would present an undivided front to her enemies" passed unanimously. Gregg, as chairman of the Select Committee of Twenty One, presented a report and resolutions recommending secession with or without the other slave states. The address to the Southern Rights Associations of the South argued that the Compromise of 1850 would result in not only the "abolition of negro slavery" but would also reduce "the free white population of the South to the same level with the agrarian rabble" that before long would be "the controlling power of the Northern States." It noted that the state had followed the rest of the South to avoid charges of dictation but that it now had the "right" to secede. Secessionists also formed a Central Southern Rights Association of South Carolina with a Committee of Nine to coordinate the actions of the local organizations. This committee issued a confidential circular to all the presidents of the local associations suggesting that "the utmost respect should be shown, and the most conciliatory conduct adopted, on the part of the majority, towards the minority, of the great resistance party." Separatists wanted to maintain "an unbroken front." Gregg asked Hammond not to come out publicly against separate state action. And the state press desperately tried to gloss over differences among southern nationalists.[34]

Far from uniting secessionists, the convention precipitated an irrevocable split in their ranks. The opposition of some prominent secessionists to separate secession had become clear. Representative W. W. Boyce had refused to even participate in the convention. Cheves, whose defection was a serious setback for the separatists, declared that he was opposed to secession without the other southern states. Barnwell argued that separate action defeated the very ends it was supposed to serve, the safety of slavery and the formation of a southern nation. Senator Butler warned of taking any step that would isolate the state from the rest of the South. Even Della Torre came out against separate secession, though he pleaded for unity among Carolinian disunionists. Armistead Burt argued that even though slavery was of greater value to South Carolina than the Union and secession was the only remedy available, the state should not secede alone. These men argued that they were just as committed to secession as the separatists but they objected to jeopardizing the southern movement by lone action. As cooperationist James Orr stated, "There is no reasonable hope that the injustice of the past will be redressed, or that security for the future can be obtained, and our peace and prosperity both conspire to point to a Southern Confederacy as the only means left to us to perpetrate the institutions our fathers bequeathed to us."[35]

Some clergymen also came out against separate secession. Bishop William Capers wrote, in a widely publicized letter, that after traveling through the major southern states, he was convinced that the southern people did not desire secession and that if South Carolina seceded on its own then economic and political desolation awaited it. Reverend Robert Henry contended that the South was not prepared to follow the state and condemned southern weakness and division along with the notion of separate secession. In an article in the *Southern Presbyterian Review*, Thornwell questioned whether slavery would be safer in an independent South Carolina. Ardent defenders of slavery and the political dogmas of their state, these clergymen were convinced that single-state action would threaten slavery and the cause of southern nationalism. Separatists criticized them for interfering with the temporal affairs of government.[36]

In a bid to unite the secessionist party, Hammond proposed a "plan of action." It recommended severance of all ties between South Carolina and the federal government short of actual disunion. The state would not select presidential electors and congressional representatives, its citizens would not be allowed to hold federal office and would be taxed for visiting northern states, as would northern goods entering the state. Such a plan, Hammond felt, would illustrate their commitment to disunion and avoid the risks of a separate secession. He explained, "South Carolina will be morally out of the Union, and a blow stricken that will be fatal to the moral power of the Union itself."[37] Secessionists, however, refused to adopt Hammond's plan.

As the secession movement gathered steam, differences between the separate and joint secessionists became apparent. This division among the state's leadership was strategic rather than indicative of any major difference in ideology. It was over the mode of secession, and, while hopes for action by the cotton states lingered, it was not very significant. As cooperationist sentiment grew, it became increasingly apparent that the separatist-dominated state convention was extremely unrepresenta-tive. Elections to the southern congress, which was rejected by all other southern states and existed only in the political imagination of Carolin-ian planter politicians, would become the most crucial event during the state's first secession crisis.

During the summer and fall of 1851, the contest between cooperationists and separatists put South Carolina in the grip of an election fever. Not since nullification was any political campaign so keenly fought in the state, in which elections tended to be largely uncontested, nonpartisan affairs. However, the limits of political discourse and electoral choice were well drawn. The question at issue was not union or disunion but single or joint secession.

The secessionists were formally divided into two factions, separatist and cooperationist, and state leaders were forced to declare their alle-giance to one of the groups. Seabrook wrote to Butler expressing fears about the rise of a new opposition party led by him, Orr, and Barnwell. Butler, piqued at calls for his removal from the Senate by James H. Adams and Pickens, remained unmoved. Representatives Daniel Wallace, John McQueen, W. F. Colcock, and Chancellor George Dargan came out for the separatists, while ex-governor David Johnson, state legislators such as Alfred P. Aldrich, C. W. Dudley, and John S. Preston; Representative W. A. Owens; and Judge T. J. Withers supported joint secession. Hammond felt that cooperationists had the "large preponderance of talent." But the overwhelming majority of Carolinian newspapers continued to advocate single-state action. Many contemporaries felt that the separatists were a younger generation of politicians given to extremism and that the coop-erationists consisted of the established leadership of the state. Grayson balefully wrote that the separatists were a bunch of young hotheads who had no notion of the consequences of their rashness. Younger politicians such as Governor Means, Gregg, Edmund Bellinger, Gist, Adams, Col-cock, Keitt, Lewis Malone Ayer, Jamison, and Bryan did lead the sep-aratist movement, but it was also composed of prominent old nullifiers such as Rhett, Allston, Pickens, and Seabrook. And some younger politi-cians such as Orr, James Chesnut, Owens, and W. W. Boyce joined the cooperationists.[38]

Both sides hotly debated the advantages and disadvantages of separate secession through the medium of the press and pamphlets. In one of the more memorable confrontations, in Blacksville, Aldrich and Bellinger argued whether it would lead to the ruin of the state. Colcock felt that the South would secede only to defend slavery and that South Carolina as the leading "pro-slavery state" in the Union should head the secession movement. Adams claimed that once South Carolinians moved the rest of the South would be found behind them. Seabrook and Rhett argued that it was their responsibility to precipitate secession, now that "southern cooperation is at an end." But Simms noted that "South Carolina is again destined to be abandoned in the breach by her chivalrous sisters!" Louisa McCord wrote that secession would separate the state not only from "our oppressors" but also from "our sisters in endurance."[39]

Though heavily outnumbered, unionists were an active component of the cooperationist party. The old unionist network between Charleston and the nonplantation belt of the upcountry underwent a bit of a revival. While distinguished lowcountry unionists Petigru and Poinsett had consistently opposed South Carolina's drift toward disunion, Perry's flirtation with southern nationalism had long ended. Three Charleston papers, the *Southern Standard*, the *Charleston Evening News*, and the *Charleston Courier*, came out against immediate secession. James Harvey reported to Thomas Corwin, Fillmore's secretary of treasury, that while the inland planters had "little to do, but to excite morbid imaginations with imaginary wrongs," the merchants and mechanics of Charleston had no sympathy for disunion. The separatists in Charleston were forced to form an Auxilliary Southern Rights Association after failing to take over the main association. Antisecession sentiment was also strong among the nonplantation belt yeomanry of the northern most districts such as Greenville, Spartanburg, York, Lancaster, Pendleton, and the lowcountry district of Horry. Greenville had been the only district to elect a completely unionist slate to the state convention. Most of the upcountry newspapers, such as the *Greenville Mountaineer*, the *Spartan*, and the *Pendleton Messenger*, however, were rabidly secessionist. In February 1851, Perry started printing the *Southern Patriot*, the sole unionist paper in the state. Perry's unionism, tempered by his overtly proslavery stance, was reflected in the motto of his paper: "The Rights of the South and the Union of the States."[40]

A reaction against separate secession soon engulfed the state. While the first cooperationist meeting was held in Hamburg, the party received a major organizational boost from the huge rally at the Greenville court house and the "Great Cooperation and Anti-Secession" meeting held in Charleston on July 29, 1851. Separatists claimed that the Hamburg meeting was a gathering of Georgians rather than Carolinians. However, the cooperationist movement could not be dismissed so easily. Over four thousand attended the Greenville meeting and at Charleston around twelve hundred people signed a document opposing separate secession. Cooperationist meetings in York, Spartanburg, Lancaster, Sumter, Barnwell, and Newberry followed and the party grew rapidly in the upcountry.

Aldrich reported that besides the parishes, most of the state was against the idea of single-state action. The lowcountry, with the exception of Charleston and the relatively slaveless district of Horry, remained a separatist stronghold.[41]

Separatist meetings were held in the parishes of St. Stephen's, St. Bartholomew's, St John's Colleton and Berkeley, St. Mathews's, and St. James Goosecreek. Separate secessionists argued that they were the true southern nationalists, as a confrontation between the state and the federal government would evoke southern sympathy and ultimately lead to the formation of a southern confederacy. They completely romanticized the notion of their "little" state "facing the music" and carrying the banner of the southern nation all by itself. As Keitt claimed rapturously, "Our State is small in number and resources — yet around its head is the agricola of undying fame — Small as it is, it is classic ground — and has more weight in the federal councils than any State in the union." The Southern Rights Association of South Carolina College asked the state to fulfill its role "in the van" of the southern movement. J. K. Paulding, a northern proslavery ideologue, contended that South Carolina must secede alone as the Compromise of 1850 was a "pretended concession." D. H. Hamilton argued that the South would join the state as it had the same interests in slavery. The *Charleston Mercury* capped the agitation by publishing an ordinance of secession. Separatists published various tracts for secession and used the words of cooperationist leaders to justify immediate secession while dismissing the party as a small federal clique in Charleston. Aldrich voiced the dilemma of joint secessionists: "if we do nothing . . . we will be disgraced, and if we do act by separate secession we will be ruined."[42]

Separatists, however, soon relinquished southern nationalist ground, which would be the death knell of their party. They began defending the idea of a separate nationality for the state. Some thought that they would be an independent nation for at least a couple of years before the rest of the South joined them. The issue, as Lewis Malone Ayer told his Barnwell constituents, was secession by South Carolina or no secession at all. In a remarkably frank admission of the undemocratic nature of the movement, he stated that the reason the South was not as united on this question as South Carolina was "because they, by direct vote, elect all the high offices of the State and General Government." Democratic practice in the other states made them susceptible to partisan divisions and federal patronage, while the Carolinian planter elite apparently protected the masses from such scourges. He claimed that many small nations in Europe led an independent and prosperous existence. Ayer even went so far as to assert, "The fact is, I should have as great objection to South

Carolina becoming a part of a Southern consolidation of States, as of the consolidation she is presently threatened with." "Rutledge" noted that slavery would be as safe in an independent South Carolina as in a southern confederacy. Others argued that despite the dangers of separate secession, they would have to take the plunge.[43]

In their most damning argument against single-state action, cooperationists claimed that it would do irreparable harm to the cause of a slavery-based southern nation. They strongly criticized the idea of setting up South Carolina as an "independent nationality" as "braggadocio" and "suicidal." They argued that a federal blockade and prohibitive duties would destroy the economy of the state without a military confrontation and condemned Rhett's idea that the state would be able to sustain its economy through smuggling as politically bankrupt. Barnwell complained, "When they said that they would secede to force cooperation, I hoped that the elections in the other States would make it certain that in this mode cooperation could not be got that secession would be abandoned, but they instantly changed to this scheme of making a separate nation of South Carolina." Owens asserted that South Carolina would be ruined by the heavy taxes needed to support an independent government. William Elliot argued that Charleston would be particularly hurt, mechanics would be forced to migrate, banks and railroad stocks would fall, and capital would leave the state. To clinch their argument, cooperationists claimed that separate secession would lead to the destruction of slavery. The state would become an "object of ridicule" and be forced to "crawl back" into the Union. Moreover, secession would do more to exclude them from the territories than any number of provisos. Simms wrote that the "premature action of South Carolina" would actually discourage the formation of a southern confederacy. Separate secession, claimed "Fabius," was the "disunion of the south." Cooperationists ended their campaign in Charleston with another "monster" meeting in September 1851. Hayne, James Simons, and Memminger addressed the meeting and evoked Calhoun's legacy for their party.[44]

Both cooperationists and separatists laid claim to Calhoun's mantle. While cooperationists could cite Calhoun's efforts to procure southern unity, separatists argued that his advocacy of nullification and state sovereignty placed him in their camp. Matters became more complicated when Hamilton claimed that Calhoun had been for joint secession, while Calhoun's son revealed that on his deathbed, his father had told him that if California was admitted into the Union, South Carolina should secede, even without the South. Whatever may have been the case, it was certain that having given up on the Union in the last years of his life, Calhoun visualized a southern confederacy rather than an independent South Carolina in its place. For most separatists, however, an independent South Carolina was a prelude to the formation of a southern nation. As the wealthy secessionist planter John S. Palmer explained, "We all seemed bent on devising the speediest and most effective measures for insuring our exodus from the accursed union."[45]

While separate and joint secessionists bickered over who was more loyal to Calhoun, slavery, and the southern nation, unionists found a distinctive voice of their own. Poinsett, reviving the unionist discourse of nullification, asked Carolinians to weigh the cost of "the overthrow of this great republic, the seat of freedom, the hope of the world, the foundation of our strength and safety." Some complained that unionist leaders did not go far enough in their commitment to the republic and that they spoke "of the rights of the south too strongly." More interesting were expressions of a more radical sentiment. In Cheraw, a parade of thirty to forty men marched to the polls shouting "Damn the negroes and their masters," exhibiting an incipient antislavery sentiment that combined resentment of the slaveholder and the slave. Memminger also alluded to the free white laborers in Charleston who objected to "slave competition" and the "tyranny of Capital" as dangerous to the existence of slave society. They could become "hot abolitionists."[46]

The appearance of an antislavery pamphlet in Spartanburg may not have been representative of nonslaveholding yeoman sentiment, but it put Carolinian planter politicians on guard against the spread of free soilism. The writer, "Brutus," argued that wealthy Carolinian planters, "having the monopoly of the government of the State," were trying to break up the Union. While talking about state sovereignty, they trampled on the "sovereignty of the state," the people. He argued that the "bloated" aristocracy, by asking for "the dominion of this man-crushing power [slavery]" in the free territories and threatening disunion, cut off all hope for the "poor man of Carolina." He called for a convention to amend the state constitution and fulfill the guarantee of a republican form of government contained in the U.S. Constitution. Brutus concluded, "We must teach these masters of overgrown plantations that we cannot always endure this state of things."[47]

Brutus turned out to be William H. Brisbane, an ex-slaveholder and abolitionist who had left South Carolina, but at least some of his demands were part of the more mainstream unionism of the nonplantation belt. Perry, for instance, asked why one man from the swamps of St. Denis should command as much power as 120 men from the Pendleton mountains and condemned the state government as that of a minority and as antirepublican. Lieber also argued that a reform of the state constitution was long overdue. The *Patriot* charged, "The parishes declare war, vote us

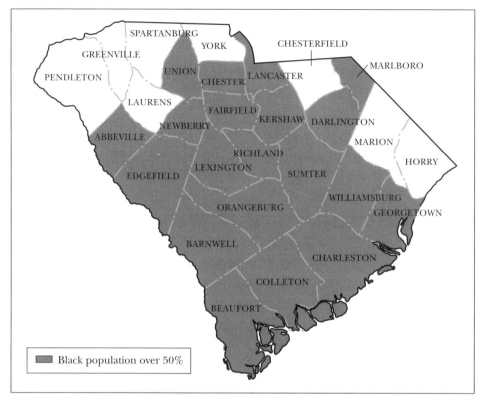

MAP 3. South Carolina Black Belt, 1850
Source: William W. Freehling, *The Road to Disunion: Secessionists at Bay,*
1776–1834 (New York, 1990) 212. Used by permission.

out of the Union, and then make the people of the upper country do the fighting and defray the expenses." The government of South Carolina was an "oligarchy" modeled after the "rotten borough system" of England, argued one writer. Soon unionists started alluding to a host of reforms. The state should spend money on a free school system rather than on the South Carolina College where the sons of the planter elite were educated and have popular elections for the governor and presidential electors. Unionists even challenged the sacrosanct image of Calhoun, which had reached spiritual proportions in South Carolina after his death. They repudiated his theory of concurrent majorities as unworkable and undemocratic.[48]

Unionists were forced to act under the auspices of the cooperation party, revealing their minority status and the tremendous odds against any form of oppositional politics in South Carolina, where a widespread plantation belt had led to the creation of a hegemonic and virulently

TABLE 3. Election for the Southern Congress, 1851

Congressional Districts	Cooperation	Secession	Total
First District	8,164	6,564	14,728
Second District	10,034	3,593	13,627
Third District	6,898	5,033	11,931
Fourth District	8,748	5,375	14,123
Fifth District	6,675	4,937	11,612
Sixth District	5,654	2,906	8,560
Seventh District	3,809	6,699	10,508
Total	49,982	35,107	85,089

Sources: John Barnwell, *Love of Order: South Carolina's First Secession Crisis* (Chapel Hill, 1982), 198–99; *Charleston Mercury*, Oct. 20, 28, 29, 1851.

Note: Numbers of votes listed above represent total numbers of votes cast for two cooperation and two secession candidates for each congressional district added together and not the number of voters who cast their votes in the election.

proslavery discourse of southern nationalism. Over 50 percent of white households in the state were slaveowning in 1850. Unionist sentiment dominated only the northern non–black-belt fringe; the rest of the up-country and Charleston were far more cooperationist in sentiment.[49]

The elections to the southern congress revealed how the spread of slavery had shaped the contours of southern nationalism in South Carolina. Both parties put up two candidates each in the seven congressional districts. The election results of 25,062 for the cooperationists and 17,617 for the separatists revealed that the latter had overplayed their hand in a state committed to disunion. The number of votes was the largest ever polled and cooperationists carried all the congressional districts except the seventh, which was Rhett's constituency. They won in the first, third, fourth, fifth, and sixth districts by over a thousand votes. The second district, which included unionist Greenville, went cooperationst by over three thousand votes.

A closer analysis of the vote reveals that a direct correlation existed between the greatest cooperationist strength and the nonplantation-belt. Cooperationists mustered their largest majorities in the nonplantation belt districts, Pendleton, Greenville, Spartanburg, York, Lancaster, Chesterfield, and Horry. In Horry only 12 votes were cast for the separatists as opposed to 734 for the cooperationists. Only the lowcountry district of Marion, which did not have a black majority, gave the cooperationists merely a slight edge of thirty-nine votes. As expected, Charleston went for cooperation. Separatists scored their largest victories in the oldest plantation areas, the lowcountry and the middle district of Orangeburg. Only St. James Goose Creek voted cooperationist; the rest of the parishes were overwhelmingly secessionist. Separatists also tended to lose by much smaller margins in the black-belt districts of the state. In Edgefield they lost by one vote and in many districts, such as Barnwell, cooperationists won by less than a hundred votes. In Laurens, Union, and Fairfield, all three part of the plantation belt in the upcountry, the separatist vote exceeded that of the cooperationists. In Spartanburg, the slavery-and-cotton-dominated southern half voted strongly secessionist, while the nonslaveholding northern half and the town of Spartanburg went for cooperation. The extremism of the lowcountry planter aristocracy had been the single most potent force behind the secession movement. In South Carolina, the conservatism of planters and large slaveholders on secession is a myth. The leadership of the cooperationist party like that of the separatists was composed of the planter elite and suggested a "badly divided gentry," but the plantation areas generally voted for cooperation in smaller numbers than the state's tiny nonplantation belt.[50]

In the aftermath of the cooperationist victory, Carolinian planter politicians moved to mend the breach among secessionists and isolate the unionist minority. Many, like Hammond, feared that unionists, who opposed reconciliation with separatists, planned to "organize a permanent party." Barnwell wanted to "make up as soon" as possible with "the secessionists to get rid of the unionists." Governor Means in his message stated, "I cannot believe that this result has been founded in a willingness to tamely submit to our wrongs, but in a difference of opinion as to the best mode of redressing them." O. M. Dantzler recommended passing a secession ordinance that would immediately go into effect at the next instance of northern "aggression." Gregg touted Hammond's short-of-disunion plan to prevent "the increase of a Union Submission party." As James Jones wrote, "*Secession is dead* and I fear *buried forever*. I am therefore anxious to see any plan which makes a single step towards disunion." Edmund Ruffin, the Virginian secessionist, also evinced a keen interest in Hammond's plan as a measure to keep the secession movement alive. Most cooperationists were averse to any action but supported unity among southern nationalists. Hayne echoed the sentiments of many: "in our *present* circumstances the plan proposed is I think beyond the mark. It cannot produce unanimity among ourselves, but on the contrary would if urged produce new distractions; and even if acceptable at home, comes too late to be effective in our sister States. In my opinion *no* very decisive step can be taken at this time. *The occasion has been lost*, and cannot be recovered." Aldrich recommended a resolution that simply declared that the state was ready for disunion but would wait for "a sufficient number of Southern States."[51]

The ideological similarities between the two wings of southern nationalists were illustrated strikingly during the next legislative session. Leaders of both factions opposed Perry's proposal for the popular election of presidential electors. Besides a shared commitment to a slavery-based southern nation and to the state's undemocratic political structure, the very realities of Carolinian politics dictated a coming-together. Despite the recent electoral triumph of the cooperationists, separatists still commanded a majority in both the legislature and convention. When the two factions met in legislative caucuses, they had been unable to agree on any definite plan. However, they united to pass a bill calling for the convention to meet in April 1852 by a vote of sixty-eight to forty-four in the house. The bill had passed the senate by a more unanimous vote of twenty-eight to nine. Unionists, having failed to stop the convention from meeting, argued that it should be used to end parish representation. Perry put out a list of reforms that the convention could undertake. The demand for political reform was loud enough to alarm secessionists, who insisted that the convention could act only on the subject it was called for. Unionists recognized that cooperationists would hardly be more amenable to their agenda than separatists were.[52]

In the end, southern nationalists united on a common platform of secession and made it clear that it was only the refusal of the rest of the South to abandon the Union that kept their state from disunion. Means was elected to preside over the convention as per political custom despite separatist suspicions that the cooperationists might bypass the governor. He called for an end to all "internal feuds" and "party strifes" so that the state could once again direct its attention against the "common enemy." A Committee of Twenty One, which contained cooperationists such as Cheves, Butler, Barnwell, and Perry and separatists such as Seabrook, Gregg, Pickens, and Richardson, presented a majority report declaring that the state was perfectly justified in wanting to dissolve the Union and that it refrained from doing so only on the grounds of expediency. An accompanying ordinance, asserting the right of the state to secede from the Union, was adopted by a vote of 136 to 19. Most of the negative votes were cast by unionists. Edward McCrady protested the ordinance's "unrestricted" right of secession, which did not specify any cause or the violation of the Constitution as a justification for disunion. A minority report written by Gregg, who voted for the ordinance, objected to the absence of "practical resistance." Another report by Perry declared a deep regard for the Union but threatened secession at any interference with slavery, the domestic slave trade, and the rendition of fugitive slaves. Its rejection revealed the extent to which South Carolina was ahead of even other lower south states in its commitment to southern nationalism.[53]

Most hailed the work of the convention as a reconciliation in the ranks of the secessionist party. And though Rhett resigned from the Senate because of the failure of separate secession, the separatist press rejoiced at the fact that secessionist doctrine was from now on the official creed of the state. Unionists, of course, were less than happy at the outcome. Not only was their program for political reform summarily shelved, but South Carolina had virtually repudiated the Union in theory if not practice. A few unreconciled separatists thought that the convention had been futile. According to William Huston, the state had looked the enemy in the eye and then retreated. Hammond, irritated by the rejection of his plan, felt that the work of the convention was "too pitiful for comment." But as the *Spartan* argued, "Is it no step forward to know, that hereafter if a citizen of South Carolina opposes secession, he opposes the Constitution and the laws of his State? Is it no step forward to have united all true resistance men of both parties and insolated [*sic*] and crushed the few noisy, arrogant unionists and Government hirelings, which are to be found in certain locations within our borders?"[54] Thanks to the clear espousal of secession in 1852, South Carolina would be well prepared to lead the South in 1860.

The aftermath of South Carolina's first secession crisis was an anticlimax. As Huston stated, "South Carolina now occupies neither the position of graceful acquiescence or indignant resistance, but of sullen, reluctant, discontented submission." By the end of the year, a group of cooperationists led by Orr, Memminger, and Perry came out for the election of Franklin Pierce, the Democratic nominee for the presidency, and seemed to be pushing for a closer, working relationship with the Democratic Party. This movement evoked the criticism of separatists and the more prosecession wing of the Cooperation Party under Senator Butler. Far from keeping one foot out of the Union, these men wanted to "rule the Union" through the Democratic Party. The selection of Josiah J. Evans for Rhett's Senate seat alarmed secessionists. They would have to deal with the National Democrats and the resurgence of the Democratic Party throughout the South.[55]

While Carolinian planter politicians had to face the realities of political defeat, they resumed their role as the ideological watchdogs of the slave South. Whether it was the "red republicanism" of the unsuspecting Hungarian patriot Louis Kossuth or the leveling and anarchic doctrines of democracy and female Bloomers, they trained their fire on all enemies of slavery and slave society. The conservative Thornwell and extremist Bryan could agree that government was a divine instrument not to be tainted with such blasphemous concepts as the sovereignty of the people. According to Hammond, "A Republican government develops more fully than any other the energy of its people & calls into exercise the character & talents of the underclasses beyond any other political organization. . . . I am inclined to think it the worst of all forms of Government. I speak of Democratic republics in which universal suffrage is adopted & offices are open to all." The British government with its monarch and a "rich, hereditary, permanent aristocracy" was the most "perfect" system of governance. His views were reminiscent of an archaic republican faith in mixed government but they were also a product of the antidemocratic world of Carolina planters. Slavery, as Keitt and Miles contended, rather than liberty for the many was the defining feature of good society and polity. Thornwell's "Report on Slavery for the Presbyterian Church" reinforced proslavery theological dogma. The publication of *The Proslavery Argument* in 1852 incorporated the works of Hammond, Harper, and Simms. During the same year, reaction to Harriet Beecher Stowe's *Uncle Tom's Cabin* single-handedly contributed to the renaissance of proslavery works in the state.[56]

The triumph of proslavery thought was no mean achievement and proved to be a far more permanent feature of southern politics than the defeat of the first secession movement. The demise of the Whigs in the Lower South and the desire to reshape the Democratic Party into a proslavery party revealed the success of the politics of slavery. Though the South repudiated secession in 1850, some of the cardinal tenets of Carolina politics — the constitutional right to secession; state sovereignty and the co-property theory, which justified slavery expansion; and the proslavery belief in the alleged superiority of slave society — were fast becoming southern political orthodoxy. A politically and ideologically resurgent slave South would have important ramifications throughout the 1850s when successive sectional clashes over slavery expansion reinforced the politics of slavery, pushing its goal of a slavery-based southern nation ever closer.

5

The Carolinian Movement to
Reopen the African Slave Trade

Slavery must spread in power and area.
— *Charleston Mercury*, 1854

During the last decade preceding the Civil War, Carolinian planter politicians fortified their reputation for proslavery extremism by spearheading the movement to reopen the African slave trade. The growth of this movement was not only the logical outcome of the premises of proslavery thought but also an integral phase of the sectional conflict over slavery expansion. Like other contemporary manifestations of southern nationalism and slavery expansionism, which included the dream of a southern slaveholding empire in Central America, the movement found a congenial home in the Deep South. With the exceptions of W. E. B. Du Bois's pioneering work and a 1971 monograph by Ronald Takaki, this chapter of Carolinian and southern history has been relatively unexplored. Southern historians generally have viewed the movement as an aberrant phenomenon. Scholars of the Atlantic slave trade, who have emphasized the minor role of North America in the trade, have also ignored it.[1] Even those historians who have studied this movement have not fully grasped its significance for the politics of slavery and separatism in the 1850s.[2]

In no other southern state did the African slave trade agitation assume the proportions that it did in South Carolina, the "storm-center" of the movement. The Carolinian movement to revive the African slave trade gained its largest following among the most rabid secessionists and slavery expansionists, men who may not have been representative of their region but who led the fight for an independent southern nation. Opposition to the movement centered among the national Democrats, who viewed it as a plot geared to destroy their strategy of dominating the federal government through the increasingly prosouthern Democratic Party.[3]

The movement to reopen the African slave trade was intrinsically connected to the politics of slavery expansion and secession in the 1850s. It paralleled closely the fight over Kansas. By not paying sufficient attention to the expansionist logic of slave traders' arguments, historians have missed the crucial connection between the slave trade movement and the sectional conflict over slavery expansion. Some of the foremost southern nationalists and slavery ideologues, such as George Fitzhugh, James De Bow, Edmund Ruffin, Henry Hughes, Edward Pollard, Louis T. Wigfall, William Lowndes Yancey, Robert Barnwell Rhett, and John A. Quitman also endorsed it. The agitation provided a congenial political home to secessionists, who remained unreconciled to their failure. By the end of the decade, the African slave trade movement had not only initiated a major rethinking on this issue in the Lower South but had also become an important part of southern nationalists' platform of disunion and slavery expansion.

The attempt to revive the African slave trade marked the coming of age of the politics of slavery and separatism. While isolated suggestions for reopening the African trade had been made earlier, most notably by the *New Orleans Courier* in 1839, Carolinian Leonidas William Spratt's single-minded advocacy inaugurated a full-fledged movement to legalize the African slave trade. In 1853, Spratt purchased the *Southern Standard*, a cooperationist Charleston newspaper, with the intention to make it a vehicle for the reopening of the African slave trade. Not much is known about Spratt before he plunged himself into the political limelight. He was an alumnus of South Carolina College and it is not known whether he owned slaves, even though many historians assume he was a nonslaveholder. With the exception of his paper, initial signs of support for the slave trade were indirect. The *Charleston Mercury* approved of John Slidell's resolution in the U.S. Senate recommending the rescinding of the eighth article of the 1842 Webster-Ashburton Treaty, which provided for the joint patrolling of the African coast by the British and Americans. It argued that the African squadron was a waste of men and money, given the demand for slaves in the Americas. John Clayton's bill to end American participation in the prolific Cuban slave trade, according to the *Mercury*, represented a backward slide from Slidell's resolution, which promised "the dawn of a better policy and truer philanthropy, than that which originated with the act of 1808, and committed the Government against a trade which had produced the most beneficent results to both the white and black race."[4]

The African slave trade movement got off to a slow start until the Kansas-Nebraska Act propelled the issue of slavery expansion back into national politics in 1854. Most Carolinian leaders saw the act's abrogation of the Missouri compromise as a triumph of Calhoun's co-property doctrine, which deemed any congressional restriction of slavery in the territories unconstitutional. They were also hopeful that Kansas might be admitted into the Union as a slave state, thus correcting the imbalance between slave and free states. Under A. P. Butler's leadership, the Carolinian delegation in Congress denounced the Missouri compromise as the source of "unnumbered woes" and "a thorn in the side of the southern portion of the Confederacy." They criticized northern opposition to the Kansas-Nebraska Act as new evidence of free soilism and abolitionism. Some started listing the obstacles that lay in the way of converting Kansas into slave soil. Spratt would argue that the expansion of slavery without an additional supply of slaves would weaken rather than strengthen slavery. That summer the slave trade movement gained its largest number of converts among prominent secessionists such as R. B. Rhett, Maxcy Gregg, Edward Bryan, John Townsend, O. M. Dantzler, Laurence Keitt, W. P. Miles, James H. Adams, Edmund Bellinger, Alexander Mazyck, John A. Calhoun, Andrew P. Calhoun, Gabriel Manigault, John I. Middleton, F. D. Richardson, C. W. Miller, Milledge Luke Bonham, and M. C. M. Hammond. Most of them were also substantial low-country planters, some owning more than a hundred slaves. This important accession to the movement would be reflected in the *Charleston Mercury* and in secessionist papers such as the *Abbeville Banner* and the *Camden Journal*.[5]

Slave traders, as advocates of this movement came to be known (not to be confused with men who actually conducted the slave trade), employed an explicitly expansionist logic in their call for the reopening of the African slave trade. The laws against the slave trade, they argued, were designed from the start as a way to restrict and end slavery. The southern states were engaged in a "war for life" with northerners, who were threatening to destroy slavery by excluding it from the territories and "cutting off" its labor supply. The South "cannot go backward nor stand still, while her foes are closing around her. She must press forward with her institutions and civilization. Slavery must spread in power and area. The preponderating power of the Free States, ever on the increase, must be counterbalanced by the addition of Slave States." Without reopening the slave trade the recent victory for the slave south in the shape of the Kansas-Nebraska Act would bring no "practical good." They would never be able to compete effectively with northerners, who were backed by foreign immigration. And if southerners tried to emigrate with their slaves they might weaken slavery in their native states, especially in old slave states such as South Carolina. If the rising demand for slaves were not met, the slave South would cease to flourish. The growing number of nonslaveholders also threatened to undermine slave society. Thus, not just the South's prosperity but its very survival depended on the legalization of the African slave trade.[6]

The growth of an expansionist mentalité among Carolinian planter politicians after the territorial crisis bolstered the slave traders' arguments. The cotton boom of the 1850s, which revived a stagnant slave economy, no doubt contributed to this mindset. Secessionists such as Keitt and national Democratic leader James L. Orr also advocated the annexation of Cuba and evoked the dream of a Caribbean slaveholding empire. Most Carolinian politicos were lukewarm about this project. While praising the Ostend manifesto, they argued against incorporating "racially mixed" Latin societies. Instead, many wanted the countries in the Gulf of Mexico and the Caribbean to form "one great slaveholding Mediterranean" alongside an independent southern nation. The plan to acquire Cuba, Carolinian secessionists felt, was a diversionary tactic supported by the Democratic Party. They argued that as the North would not tolerate the entrance of another slave state, Cuba would be "abolitionized" if it was annexed into the present Union. Slave traders argued that while the annexation of Cuba would solve the problem of the slave South temporarily, only the reopening of the African traffic would contribute to the long-term expansion of slavery.[7]

Many Carolinian secessionists committed themselves to a cause that reflected the most extreme side of proslavery sentiment. The argument for the African traffic was, as Takaki has described it, a quintessential "pro-slavery crusade," but it was not a result of an attempt to overcome any guilt or moral ambiguity over slavery. Slave traders argued that "African slavery, in the minds of the people of the South, is a very different thing now from what it was at the formation of the Constitution, when they consented to the measures against the slave trade." By logical extension, the African slave trade, they claimed, was as much a positive good as slavery since it had "civilized" and "christianized" the "savages" of Africa. Borrowing from proslavery arguments that compared the condition of slaves favorably with wage workers, they contended that the atrocities of the trade were a result of efforts to suppress it and that they paled next to the hardships suffered by European emigrants. "Let the minions of Abolition lead the war upon Slavery, by attacking the Slave Trade. It is their cause, not ours," they concluded. Opposition to the slave trade was a result of abolitionist "fanaticism" and was a preliminary to the "grand consummation" of emancipation. The trade was a "blessing" for the African and its inhumanities were merely the necessary costs of "progress" and "civilization."[8]

The Grand Juries of piedmont Richmond and lowland Williamsburg made full use of expansionist and proslavery discourse in recommending the reopening of the Atlantic traffic in their fall terms of 1854. The Richmond jury argued in a long presentment that all restrictions on the African slave trade must be removed, as the "political existence of the Southern States depend[s] on this important change in the present policy of the government on this subject." The much shorter Williamsburg presentment condemned the federal prohibition of the foreign slave trade as a "public grievance" and urged the legislature to work for the removal of the "evil," while emphasizing the morality of the slave trade. The secessionist press praised the juries' suggestions as "admirably proper at this particular political juncture."

In the House of Representatives, the Committee on the Colored Population, chaired by J. Harleston Read of Prince George Winyaw, a national Democrat, formulated an unfavorable report on the Williamsburg presentment but made some crucial concessions to it. The report argued that South Carolinians and southerners had agreed to the federal prohibition of the African slave trade and that its reopening would lessen the value of slave property, which may result in abolition in the border states, bringing South Carolina closer to the free states. But it admitted that the reopening of the trade would increase the political strength of the slave South by establishing slave territories and states and that the slave trade was indeed a "blessing" for the Africans as it resulted in their "moral social and physical elevation." As the *Mercury* pointed out, "the concession of this is, in fact, yielding the whole moral argument on the Slave Trade."[9]

The only public opposition to this new program of secessionists came from Benjamin F. Perry's *Southern Patriot*, the sole unionist newspaper in the state, which argued that the slave trade movement was a disunionist plot. It added, "If we have to turn pirates and kidnappers, and fight the whole civilized world under a red and black flag, in order to defend slavery in the Southern States, we are, indeed, in a most deplorable state of degradation as a people." Ignoring the *Patriot*'s opposition, slave traders claimed that much of the southern press had treated their views "with consideration, if not with assent."[10]

The outbreak of the Kansas wars between free and slave state settlers in 1856 again raised the issue of slavery expansion and the African slave trade. Carolinian planter politicians acted with great energy in the controversy, claiming that the right of the slaveholder to take his slaves to the territory was equal "to the right of a northern man to his horse." Kansas meetings, advocating plans to raise men and money to ensure the formation of a slave state, were held at Georgetown, Charleston, St. John's Colleton, Orangeburg, St. John's Berkeley, Abbeville, and Sumter. The Kansas association of Charleston asserted that not only did slavery need to expand into "unworn and virginal" soil to increase "slave money value," but that it also exercised a conservative influence on society as a whole by checking "the radical notions which beget, as is seen in our *Freesoil* sections, those *isms* which are disturbing and disgracing civilization." Carolinian congressman Preston S. Brooks, a national Democrat, brought notoriety to himself and his state for assaulting Senator Charles Sumner during the Kansas debates. In the wake of his newfound celebrity, Brooks called for disunion and also argued that the prohibition of the African slave trade was a mistake that had allowed the North to increase its political power at the expense of the slave South. Alfred Huger moaned, "Truly our pugilistic exhibitions in the Senate chamber of the United States and our love for freshly imported barbarians, must establish for us a reputation of being 'a peculiar people.'"[11]

The slave trade issue loomed large in state politics. Some secessionists and slave traders such as John Cunningham and F. D. Richardson flirted with the nativist Know Nothing movement but most Carolinian planter politicians remained committed to the state's antiparty creed. Unlike antislavery northern and unionist southern Know Nothings, Carolinian nativists were staunchly proslavery and secessionist. Nativism in South Carolina became somewhat of a political joke when one Carolinian reportedly informed Governor James H. Adams that the slaves had set up a Know Nothing society against competition from foreign African labor. Threats of disunion if Republican presidential candidate John C. Fremont were to be elected also ran rampant. In a public letter to the governor, Rhett called for immediate secession and boldly set out the secessionist agenda:

> we shall announce it, and here declare that we not only desire to make Territories, now free, slave Territories, and to acquire new territory into which to extend slavery — such as Cuba, North Eastern Mexico, &c — but we would re-open the African slave trade that every white man might have a chance to make himself owner of one or more negroes, and go with them and his household go[o]ds wherever opportunity beckoned enterprise. . . . At all events, if the attempt to re-open this trade should fail, it would give one more proof of how injurious our connection with the North was become to us, and would indicate one more signal advantage which a Southern

Confederacy would have over the present heterogeneous association called the Union.[12]

It was in this atmosphere of political extremism that the slave trade movement took off. Governor Adams officially endorsed the revival of the African slave trade in his notorious message to the legislature in November 1856. Adams, who had been a nullifier in 1832 and a separate secessionist in 1850, was a substantial planter with nearly 200 slaves and an early convert to the slave trade cause. His election to the governorship had been vigorously championed by the *Standard*, slave traders, and secessionists. National Democrats had opposed Adams's selection because of his opposition to electoral reform. In his inaugural address, Adams commended the fact that South Carolina had been "exempt from the baleful influence of the wild spirit of democracy which has run riot over the North" and asked Carolinians to "shut it out" as they would " 'the pestilence that walketh in darkness' and 'the destruction that wasteth at noonday.' "

Adams's more famous message of 1856 made two broad arguments to justify the revival of the African slave trade. First was the "outward pressure" on slavery, which demanded that all efforts be made to strengthen it. The only way to do this, he contended, was to "diffuse" slavery and widen the basis of slaveholding. Second, in a more novel argument, he claimed that high staple prices threatened the monopoly in cotton supply held by the slave South. Cheaper slaves and cheaper cotton were needed to ensure that the British would not abandon the southern states for other sources of raw cotton. The governor felt that the 1808 slave trade prohibition had allowed northern free society to grow at the expense of the South. Also, declaring the slave trade piracy was a "brand" upon the slave South because "if the trade be piracy, the slave must be plunder." Adams argued that slavery, "the most sacred obligation" of slaveholders, must be given "the means of expansion" so that it could have "a perpetuity of progress."[13] Like other secessionists, Adams espoused the African slave trade on expansionist and proslavery grounds.

The *Mercury* predicted that Adams's message would provoke "violent bursts of philanthropy and scolding from the Northern press, particularly as it is the first time that a high public functionary, in the discharge of his official duties, has made such a recommendation." Even some in the southern press thought that the document reflected the "political distemper" that habitually afflicted the state. But the reaction in South Carolina was rather tame. According to William C. Preston, the Whig nullifier whose career had self-destructed after he had opposed Calhoun, "no one dares denounce it in a high tone of indignation for fear of being suspected of abolitionism. In truth we are under a reign of terror and the public mind exists in a panic."[14]

Carolinian slave traders scored another coup when the house committed the slave trade part of the governor's message to a special committee chaired by M. C. M. Hammond, an advocate of the African traffic. Attempts to commit the message to the Committee on the Colored Population, which had presented an adverse report on the revival of the slave trade only two years ago, or to the Committee on Federal Relations, failed. Bryan, Dantzler, Hammond, Middleton, and Richardson led the offensive in the house. They were opposed by unionists and national Democrats such as Perry, Edward McCrady, and Richard Yeadon. McCrady dreaded getting into a "personal contest" with the governor and wrote that he was convinced that "the secessionists are about to make another move and perhaps again isolate the state." Yeadon's attempt to indefinitely postpone the slave trade question was defeated by a vote of forty-five to seventy. In the senate, matters proceeded even more smoothly for the slave traders and the governor's message was referred to a special committee chaired by Alexander Mazyck, another known advocate of the African slave trade. Both the house and senate committees received permission to present their reports during the next session. The slave trade issue, like the disputes over popular elections and South Carolina's role in the Democratic Party, reinforced sectional and factional divisions. National Democrats and legislators from predominantly non-slaveholding districts were most opposed to and secessionists and black-belt representatives most in favor of considering it.[15]

The 1857 house and senate committee reports on the governor's message, authored by Bryan and Mazyck, seconded his call for the reopening of the African traffic. Mazyck chose to remind his readers that "those who denounce the slave trade as a wicked and abominable traffic, are no less severe in their condemnation of slavery itself." In his report, Bryan traced the efforts against the African slave trade to the founding fathers' "love of liberty," which had carried them "beyond the limits of sound discretion." Both asserted that the branding of the slave trade as piracy and inhuman was inconsistent with contemporary southern feeling on slavery. Urging the expansion of slavery, Bryan and Mazyck pointed to uncultivated lands and the drain of slaves westward as evidence of shortage of slaves within South Carolina. The South, Bryan argued, was in competition with northern free society, which received thousands of immigrants, while southern slave society remained bound by the slave trade restriction. Similarly, Mazyck contended that the slave trade prohibition retarded the expansion and progress of the slave South. Unlike Bryan, Mazyck devoted a good part of his report to the effects of the slave trade on Africa. Not only had the slave trade resulted in the Christianization of Africans but, reminiscent of arguments made by some historians of the Atlantic slave trade, it had also relieved pressure on the "means of subsistence" in Africa by drawing away an excess of the population. The commerce was justified as apparently "three-fourths" of the African population was enslaved. Resolutions accompanying the house report asked Carolinian congressmen to secure the repeal of the eighth article of the Webster-Ashburton treaty and the 1820 law, which declared the slave trade piracy. In good nullifier fashion, Mazyck simply declared the 1820 law "unconstitutional, null, and void."[16]

Both reports were tabled but printed by the legislature. Bryan's motion to table the majority reports and print 2,000 copies of them passed the house easily. In the senate, the first effort to table Mazyck's report, of which a thousand copies were printed, was defeated by a vote of twenty-four to fourteen. But the second attempt to "indefinitely postpone" it carried by a nearly similar vote, twenty-two to fourteen. The senate vote reflected the sectional division on the slave trade issue, with the secessionist lowcountry voting overwhelmingly against postponement.[17]

The limits of a proslavery critique of the slave trade were illustrated by the dissenting house minority report written by J. Johnston Pettigrew, a National Democrat. Orr had him appointed to the special committee specifically to write a report against the revival of the foreign slave trade. Pettigrew was a good friend of Spratt's and had contributed articles to the *Standard*. He was in complete agreement with slave traders on the commerce's supposedly beneficial effects on Africans. He wrote, "the undersigned, as a friend of Africa, might well advocate the revival of the Slave Trade, and receive its agents as angels of mercy." Like his opponents, Pettigrew claimed that "even in its most barbarous days, the Slave Trade had some redeeming features; there was room for hope, if not an expectation of eventual good." He contended that since most Africans were slaves, the slave trade could not be seen as wrong, and even if that was not the case, nothing could impair the southern "right of property" to the "unwilling physical labor of another." The African slave trade was to be opposed not because of its inhumanity but because it was against the "best interests of South Carolina." Not only would it lessen the value of slaves and cotton but it would introduce "one hundred thousand idle, slovenly, insubordinate barbarians" who would increase the costs of running a plantation. The introduction of "untamed" Africans would force slaveholders to resort to the brutal physical punishments of colonial slave codes and provoke slave rebellions. Furthermore, the African slave trade tended to divide southerners and was therefore inadvisable. The piracy law had come into effect long after the South had ceased importing slaves and thus it could not apply to southern slaves. In a postscript to the report he stated, "I am in favor of abrogating the 8th Article of the Treaty of Washington, for a variety of reasons. I do not consider the Slave Trade piracy, indeed, the contrary is almost expressly admitted in the Report: but the propriety of making a sectional issue on these two points, is a different matter." Pettigrew would reiterate this in a public reply to his critics.[18]

The *Charleston Mercury* commended the legislature's action in raising the African slave trade issue and could barely hide its partiality in discussing the reports. It praised Bryan in fulsome terms as a true Carolina statesman and Mazyck's report as a "clear, logical and striking document." Pettigrew's report, discussed nearly a month later, was criticized for its narrow perspective and pronounced "untenable, technical and lawyer-like." However, the rival *Charleston Courier* refrained from taking an open position against the African slave trade at this time and argued that both sides of the question must be heard as it had been raised in the assembly and the southern commercial conventions. A few months earlier the *Courier* had even criticized those southern journals that, it noted, copied northern abolitionists in attacking southerners for discussing the revival of the African slave trade. The national Democratic press praised Pettigrew's report and fervently wished for "the removal from the Council of the State of a proposition frought with so much danger to Southern Union and harmony."[19]

The rivalry between the National Democrats and slave traders played an important role in the 1858 state elections. Even though the African slave trade was apparently not an issue in the assembly elections, Pettigrew lost his house seat from St. Philip's and St. Michael's after serving only one term, while Spratt was elected as a representative from the same parishes, which comprised the city of Charleston. But Adams's defeat in the legislature for Josiah J. Evans's seat in the Senate on the latter's death marred this victory for the slave traders. Even after leading decisively in the first three ballots and with Rhett withdrawing in his favor, Adams finally lost the election to James Chesnut. Chesnut, a compromise candidate, was supported by the National Democrats and moderate secessionists. Adams squarely blamed his defeat on Orr, who had made a couple of speeches against him and the slave trade earlier that year, and on the opposition of men such as Senator James Henry Hammond and Congressman W. W. Boyce. Hammond had threatened to resign if Adams was selected as his colleague. Cunningham criticized slave traders for dividing the states' rights party and contributing to the triumph of the National Democrats.[20]

The factional division between secessionists and National Democrats also reflected a sectional divide over the African slave trade, with the lowcountry parishes and areas with the highest proportion of slaves favoring it. Differences over the slave trade in South Carolina reveal that the notion that large slaveholders as a class opposed its reopening in order to safeguard the value of their human property is false. In fact, the secessionist-minded lowcountry aristocracy led the movement to reopen the African traffic. With the exception of Spratt, most slave traders were typically large slaveholders. Perhaps the appalling slave mortality rates in their rice plantations led some, such as Gabriel Manigault, to support the revival of the African slave trade. Voting patterns in the legislature reveal that support for the slave trade was less strong in the piedmont, with the nonplantation belt being most opposed to the Atlantic traffic. The northern fringe of nonslaveholding mountain yeomanry had historically opposed nullification and secession. They now emerged as the strongest opponents of the slave trade movement. Historians who view the African slave trade movement as geared primarily to serve the interests of nonslaveholders by increasing slave ownership have failed to fully grasp the social basis of the movement. With their well-known opposition to democratic reform and acute suspicions of nonslaveholders' loyalty, Carolinian slave traders, most of whom were large planters, were no champions of the common white man. If we accept the idea that slave traders intended to make slaveholders of all white men, they were most unpopular among the class they were supposed to benefit.[21]

Slave traders' call for the diffusion of slaveholding was based primarily on suspicions of nonslaveholding whites' loyalty to slavery. The increase in the number of nonslaveholders during the 1850s threatened to create an internal free-labor challenge to slavery. Even as plantation slavery tightened its grip on the state's economy and continued to spread, slaveholding, as elsewhere in the South, became more concentrated as the decade wore on. In 1850 slaveholders headed just over half of all Carolinian households, but by 1860 the percentage of slaveholding families had fallen well below 50 percent. The growth in the number of nonslaveholding whites, especially of free white labor in Charleston, and in the number of slaves exported to the Southwest posed a dilemma for Carolinian slave society. The decade between 1850 and 1860 was the only time in the history of antebellum South Carolina when the white population grew proportionally more than the black (see Table 1). Growing demands for popular elections and mechanics' petitions against "slave competition" made the planter elite skittish.[22]

Slave traders' call for the spread of slave ownership was also a part of a broader argument for the expansion of slavery and cannot be viewed in isolation. Adams, who most emphasized the idea of making slaveholders out of nonslaveholders, warned that the northern cry against "slavocracy" might appear in the South if slaveholding continued to shrink. While Mazyck had ignored this particular argument, Bryan and Spratt devoted only a few lines to it. Bryan noted that the reopening of the African slave trade would actually benefit big slaveholders as they alone had the means to buy additional slaves. He also pointed to the dangers of "hireling labor," which had already become a source of antislavery feeling in the border states. "A deadly war is waging against us; and while we are fortifying our position against external enemies, we should be careful to preserve our internal strength," he argued.[23] Like the movement for a southern nation, the African slave trade agitation was planter led and reflected the fears and concerns of this class. The movement was not just an extremist fantasy but derived its relevance from forces that had increasingly started to dominate South Carolina.

The African slave trade gained its largest following among secessionists, slavery expansionists, and proslavery ideologues. Slave traders represented the most disunionist and proslavery faction of secessionists. By ignoring the continued partiality of Carolinian secessionists for the African slave trade, most historians have failed to fully appreciate the nature and extent of the movement. In Congress, secessionists such as Keitt, Miles, and Bonham continually equivocated over the African traffic, arguing that they were against the violation of federal laws while they criticized them as unfair to the slave South. Bonham called the 1820 law "a blot on our statute book" and emphatically stated that he had "no scruples on the subject of the African slave trade." Both he and Miles felt that the foreign slave trade should be reopened once a southern nation was formed. For his part, Keitt pointed out that when Charles Cotesworth Pinckney had fought to extend the Atlantic slave trade until 1808, he had argued for sectional "equality."[24]

Even when they tried to distance themselves from the African slave trade, Carolinian secessionists' sympathies were clear. In an apparent about-face, the *Charleston Mercury*, organ of the Rhett-led secessionists, argued that while the South remained in the Union, it was futile to advocate the legalization of the African slave trade, as northerners would not assent to it under any circumstances. Moreover, since this issue was "impracticable" and tended to divide the South, "silence" would be its "better policy." At the same time, it claimed that the African slave trade should be discussed to allay "prejudices engendered by false teachings" and that it should not be branded as piracy nor be punishable by death. Clearly bringing out the contradiction between the federal laws and the southern view of slavery, it asserted, "We first brand it as a 'crime,' a 'piracy,' and worthy of 'death,' then advocate it as a divine blessing and God-send!" The *Mercury*'s new position was hardly an abandonment of the African slave trade. The editorial argued that its reopening should be advocated when it became a "practical measure" or with the establishment of an independent southern nation. In a letter to Hammond, R. B. Rhett Jr., the editor and Rhett's son, claimed that while he was personally against the African slave trade, he had to open his columns to all views. However, even a brief perusal of the paper after this editorial reveals its continued propagation of the African slave trade. Despite its proclamation of silence, the *Mercury*'s sympathy for the slave traders was hard to disguise. So much so, that it had to defend its "consistency" on this issue by making a fine distinction between the actual reopening of the Atlantic slave trade and its rather vocal opposition to the "suppression policies" of the federal government. But this facade would melt away as the agitation continued. In 1858, it praised Spratt's African slave trade pamphlet "as a repository of facts, important to the intelligent discussion of this important question" and as "timely and useful."[25]

Concerns for slavery expansion, fueled by a new round of sectional hostilities in Kansas, remained the central inspiration behind the African slave trade movement. Slave traders argued that the fight for Kansas and the *Dred Scott* decision would be useless if the South did not have the slaves to realize its territorial program. The British consul at Charleston, Robert Bunch, and John L. Manning, a National Democrat who opposed the revival of the African traffic, noted the growing success of the slave traders. In July 1858, replicating its 1854 offensive, the *Mercury* started publishing articles in favor of the foreign slave trade. "South" argued that the demand for slave labor in the slave states had become "*a political need of the first magnitude!*" Without more slaves it could not compete for new territories and the border states would become "Thayerised." The *Camden Journal* also argued for the need to reopen the African slave trade and for disunion. Even the *Charleston Courier* reprinted articles from the New York *Journal of Commerce* that justified African apprenticeship schemes. In a widely reproduced speech, state legislator C. W. Miller asked his constituents to consider the revival of the African slave trade on mainly expansionist grounds. He noted that "the South will be slow in attaining her full and due growth, in natural greatness without the necessary additional labor which is alone to be supplied by the re-opening of the African slave trade." Edward Bryan wrote that he would like to see slavery cover the entire area from Norfolk to Rio de Janeiro. Grandiose notions of southern progress exemplified the expansionist dimension of slave traders' arguments.[26]

Carolinian planter politicians' adherence to the African slave trade cause varied in direct proportion to their commitment to slavery expansion and southern nationalism. This was especially true of some states' rights men, who formed a middle group between extreme secessionists such as Rhett, Keitt, and Miles and national Democrats such as Orr, Pettigrew, and James Farrow. Boyce and Chesnut, former cooperationists, opposed the reopening of the African slave trade. Boyce argued against all aggressive schemes for slavery expansion, the congressional protection of territorial slavery, and the effort to reopen the African slave trade, saying the slave South must eschew all forms of "ultraism" and pursue a policy of "moderation." He pointed to South Carolina's isolation and the need to "ripen public opinion" for disunion. By advocating extreme measures, Carolinians would only alienate and divide the South. Similarly, Chesnut argued for southern unity and repudiated the call for a slave code in the territories and the reopening of the African slave trade.[27]

Like Boyce and Chesnut, Hammond surprised many when in his Beech Island and Barnwell court house speeches, he came out against not only the reopening of the African slave trade but also slavery expansion and secession. His political career spanned the state's tumultuous antebellum history and he had established his reputation as a leading proslavery theorist and southern nationalist. Long before the African slave trade agitation, he had advocated the reopening of the Atlantic traffic. On his selection to the United States Senate in 1857, Hammond was identified with the states' rights party, which included moderate and rabid southern nationalists. A year later he stunned his supporters by arguing that for now it was better for the slave South to remain in the Union than "incur the unknown hazards of setting up a separate government." He lauded the South's powerful position within the Union and expressed reservations on slavery expansion. The slave South had neither the population nor "suitable territory" within its reach for the creation of more slave states. He asserted that since much of the western territory was unsuitable for slavery, the South would have no place for the extra slaves imported from Africa. His views were bombshells for Carolinian secessionists and slave traders, who had counted him as one of their sympathizers. As Adams wrote to him, "I will not of course argue the [slave] trade question with you. You and I once thought alike on it. . . . Before however, you do take strong ground I beg in the name of old ties that you will remember your own antecedents on the subject." Criticisms of Hammond's apostasy began to appear in the state press. Hammond characterized his critics as "slave traders" and secessionists of the most "spasmodic school." His friend W. H. Trescot observed that either the slave South would have to submit to being surrounded by a cordon of free states or reopen the African traffic in order to expand. But he praised Hammond's unionism as a "logical correction" of Calhoun's views. Rhett's secessionism, he wrote, was a "logical consequence" of Calhoun. The *Courier* argued that Hammond was "fully up with the spirit of the state" and merely advised against "rash" action. However, Hammond would soon be isolated from the secession movement.[28]

The African slave trade proved to be especially seductive to southern secessionists, men who were at the cutting edge of the movement to form an independent slave nation. *De Bow's Review*, a journal devoted to slavery expansion and southern nationalism, inaugurated the southern debate over the African slave trade. Articles illustrating the alleged barbarity of Africans and "scientific" proof of their racial inferiority had already appeared in it with monotonous regularity. The African slave trade, it now argued, was "the greatest missionary enterprise in the cause of religion and civilization." James D. B. De Bow, its editor, had fashioned the magazine as an outlet for proslavery pieces in the 1850s, and it seemed only natural that he would take up the African slave trade cause. Besides, the economic regeneration and expansion of the slave South was a lifelong obsession of his. As early as August 1856, De Bow started arguing for the reopening of the foreign slave trade. According to him, the 1808 prohibition of the African traffic illustrated the injustice of a common policy for the two sections, as it had slowed southern economic growth while the North grew in population, wealth, and power. Like Carolinian slave traders, he pointed out that the Kansas-Nebraska Act had actually inaugurated an unfair competition between the two sections, as without an additional supply of African slaves, southerners could not compete with northern immigration. An article on "African Slavery Adapted to the North and North West" in the *Review* sought to prove that the reopening of the African slave trade would also supply slaves for northern territories.[29]

The slave traders also added other prominent secessionists and slavery ideologues to their ranks. Edmund Ruffin contended that he was against the African slave trade for "practical" reasons. But he opposed its categorization as piracy and saw the movement as a way to promote disunion. He strongly criticized a *Richmond Enquirer* editorial opposing the African slave trade and questioned the legitimacy of the federal laws against it. In a speech to rally secessionists behind the demand for a territorial slave code, William Lowndes Yancey complained that from 1808 the "power to increase its labor has been denied to the South by the act of our government." Louis T. Wigfall, the Texas fire-eater and a native Carolinian, would also come out in favor of reviving the Atlantic traffic in human beings. Some secessionists argued that the slave trade was "impolitic" but objected to it being called "infamous" or morally despicable.[30]

The advocacy of the African slave trade by the most theoretically sophisticated proslavery ideologues revealed the inhuman underside of even the most advanced arguments for slavery. George Fitzhugh, who had opposed the revival of the foreign slave trade in his 1854 proslavery polemic, *Sociology for the South; or, The Failure of Free Society*, now advocated it as an essential part of the propagation of the "conservative principle" of southern slavery and demanded "a re-hearing" on the Atlantic slave trade in the name of the slave South. He declared, "The successful assertion of her [the South's] equal right of expansion and protection in the territories with her peculiar institutions, will be a great point gained. It prepares the way for the African slave-trade . . . there is no liberty, no independence, no State equality, until our equal right to *increase, expansion*, and *protection*, is fully admitted and acted on." He contended that the African traffic could never be suppressed, as it was apparently "a natural operation, as old and constant as the tides." Edward Pollard, another proslavery theorist from Virginia, also recommended the reopening of the Atlantic trade as a way to keep the "*slave gentry* of the South" in their place. Henry Hughes's endorsement of the African slave trade was slightly more complicated. Just as he chose to describe slavery with the euphemism of warranteeism, he argued for the immigration of African contract labor rather than for the slave trade. In 1859, he would form the "African Labor Supply Association" to import "apprentices" from Africa. Unlike Hughes, Pollard and Fitzhugh quixotically felt that the revival of the African slave trade was a unionist measure as it would restore the balance of power between the sections and strengthen the Union.[31]

Even more than these well-known proslavery ideologues, Spratt, appropriately dubbed the "philosopher of the African slave trade" by Horace Greeley, best articulated the proslavery rationale behind the movement. His ideas reveal that he has been strangely neglected by historians of proslavery thought. According to Spratt, "The American Revolution vindicated the great truth that all men are were born free and equal, but society in its secret movements vindicated a still greater truth that inequality was necessary to man's progress." He characterized the reopening of the African slave trade as a correction of the revolutionary dictum that "*equality is the right of man*." Inequality, he stated, was "objectionable in theory," but "necessary in practice." Bryan, who was second only to Spratt in his devotion to the movement, argued that "in venerating the memory of a past generation, let us avoid a blind subserviency to its prejudices and fallacies." The very "first line" of American history, which stated that all men are created equal, was false.[32]

Spratt characterized the reopening of the African slave trade as the final justification of the values of slave society, and, like Fitzhugh, he wanted to defend not just slavery but "the slavery principle." He contended that the North and South represented "two distinct and antagonistic forms of society." But his argument went beyond a southern version of the irrepressible conflict. He felt, "wherever there has been social power and progress there has been articulation [of] a ruling and a subject class, if not a ruling and a subject race — an artificial if not a natural dualism." He went on to point out that no society in history had ever progressed through "an unarticulated mass of pure democracy." The slave South, by basing its aristocracy on the so-called "natural" distinction of race, provided the best hopes for the future of mankind. It must be noted that Spratt's vindication of racial slavery provided the basis for his celebration of inequality and aristocracy. He was no Herrenvolk theorist. Far from acting as opposing values, belief in racial inequality bolstered his belief in inequality in general. To be in favor of slavery and against the African slave trade, he wrote pungently, was to be in favor of the state of matrimony and against marriage. Nor could anyone make a principled distinction between the legal domestic and illegal foreign slave trades. The revival of the African slave trade would solve all the problems of "progress" and northern domination confronting southern slaveholders. Not only did the Union facilitate the North's parasitic hold on the South, free society represented principles directly antagonistic to the "aristocratic" South.

Spratt also revealed the expansionist mentality of slave traders, arguing that the foreign slave trade would give the slave South the population and power to "take another State in Texas; so, also, we might take, perhaps, Nebraska, Utah, and Oregon; and it is even possible that, with slaves at importers' prices, we may stop the hungry mouth of free society in older States, and lull it to repose as far back as the sterile regions of New England." Ten thousand of the "rudest Africans" would have won Kansas for the slave South, he claimed. He also attributed the decline of Charleston, the colonial entrepôt of the African slave trade, to its suppression. The foreign slave trade was necessary for the economic, political, and geographic expansion of the slave south. Alluding to the fact that slavery was on the retreat in the border states as well as to the growth in the number of nonslaveholding whites, he argued that it might even be necessary for the survival of slavery. Spratt was hardly advocating the democratization of the slaveholding order. An increase in the supply of slaves was to prop up and expand this order rather than to change it.[33]

Slave traders' arguments illustrate that the revival of the African slave trade embodied the ultimate rejection of the revolutionary generation's compromises on slavery and represented the most audacious proposal for the expansion and perpetuity of slavery. The dynamic of the political discourse of slavery and separatism, infused as it was with vindications of slavery and ideals of an independent slave nation, encouraged the African slave trade agitation. And the continuing fight over slavery expansion embodied in the battle for Kansas gave the movement a compelling practical resonance.

By the end of the decade, the African slave trade movement spread beyond the borders of South Carolina to other lower south states. The issue, having been aired in *De Bow's Review*, was taken up by certain secessionist newspapers. A handful of newspapers in Texas and Louisiana and twenty Democratic papers in Mississippi came out for the reopening of the African traffic. Somewhat unusual was the *Southern Citizen* of Knoxville, which propagated the African slave trade despite widespread opposition to the movement in Tennessee and the Upper South. In the Deep South, the African slave trade cause was increasingly put forward as part and parcel of the southern nationalist agenda. As the *New Orleans Delta*, the secessionist newspaper that launched the movement in Louisiana, summed it up, "the South should assert all her rights and defend all her interests political or commercial. She should ignore no question—neither slave-extension nor the slave trade—which concerns her present or future welfare."[34]

The African slave trade was also deliberated for the first time in southern legislatures. In the Mississippi senate in November 1857, Hughes introduced a bill calling for the formation of an African Labor Immigration Company. In early 1858, state senator Henry St. Paul of Louisiana presented a resolution authorizing the governor to issue a contract for the labor of 2,500 "free" Africans. A few days later, representative J. W. Taylor introduced a bill to authorize the company of Brigham and Associates to transport indentured African laborers. Both the Mississippi and Louisiana bills were rather obvious attempts to circumvent the federal laws against the Atlantic slave trade. For some Carolina purists the apprenticeship schemes were merely a "subterfuge" for the African slave trade. They felt that the southern states should instead simply nullify the federal laws "and carry on a direct importation under the original and proper form." The Mississippi apprentice bill was narrowly defeated in 1858. The Louisiana bill was indefinitely postponed by a close vote of fifteen to thirteen in the senate. At the end of the session, 10,000 copies of the bill and a favorable committee report were printed. Later in the year, an effort in the Georgia legislature to rescind a clause prohibiting the external slave trade in the state constitution failed. Similarly, resolutions for the reopening of the African slave trade in Alabama seemed to have fallen on deaf ears. In Texas, the legislature did not act on a 1857 resolution calling for an end to the federal ban on the African slave trade, but the majority report on the resolution conceded that the trade was a blessing to Africans and upheld slavery as a just institution. Some Texas county conventions of the Democratic Party passed resolutions in favor of the slave trade, and Hardin R. Runnels, a secessionist and advocate of the African slave trade, defeated unionist Sam Houston in the gubernatorial elections.[35]

Lower south slave traders were more successful in the realm of propaganda than in the passage of measures to reopen the Atlantic slave trade. Edward Delony, a state senator from Louisiana, published an article in *De Bow's Review* characterizing the federal prohibition of the slave trade as unconstitutional and designed to retard the growth of the slave states. Delony's expansionist logic was evident in his plans to "expand the area of slavery" and for the "regeneration" of Haiti, Cuba, and Central America. However, in 1859 another apprentice bill and resolutions demanding the repeal of the federal laws were tabled in the Louisiana house of representatives, and Delony moved to table his own bill, providing for the outright importation of Africans, in the senate. The *Natchez Free Trader* argued that there was no use in trying to stop the traffic as the "people of the Southern States will have" more slaves. But a bill for the repeal of the prohibition of the external slave trade was defeated in the Mississippi legislature in 1860.[36]

Southern unionists, veterans of the battle against secession in 1850, opposed the slave traders. In Texas, Governor Runnels was defeated by Houston, who was a firm opponent of the African slave trade, in 1859. The state Democratic convention also voted down a proposal for the revival of the African traffic and Peter W. Gray, a distinguished Texan jurist, gave an influential address against it. Later H. W. Hilliard of Alabama and Henry S. Foote of Mississippi would lead unionist opposition to the African slave trade movement. Georgian Robert G. Harper, in his pamphlet, warned that many men of the "Southern Rights School" were enamored of the African slave trade. Harper argued that the slave trade laws were constitutional, and that even though the states were theoretically sovereign, practical sovereignty in these matters lay with the federal government. The reopening of the Atlantic trade would reduce the value of slaves and result in the contraction rather than the expansion of slavery.[37]

Some southern leaders who claimed to be against the African slave trade conceded many of the arguments made by its proponents. The anomalous position of lower south planter politicians on the African slave trade was a result of the widespread rethinking on this issue initiated by the slave traders. In a public speech, Alexander Stephens stated that the South could not create any more slave states unless it received a fresh supply of slaves from Africa. Whether Stephens meant to endorse the reopening of the African slave trade is not clear, but he had given wide publicity to one of the major arguments of the slave traders. Another prominent Georgian, Robert Toombs, condemned both the 1842 treaty and the piracy law. Alabama governor A. B. Moore declared that he was for the repeal of the piracy law but was unwilling to make the African slave trade an issue of contention in the South. Jefferson Davis, future president of the Confederacy, felt that the African traffic should be reopened in the territories.[38]

The slave trade question was more fully debated in the southern commercial conventions, which gradually became a meeting ground for southern nationalists and a forum for their agenda. Southern commercial, manufacturing, railroad, and planters' conventions had proliferated since the 1830s to devise programs for the economic regeneration of the slave South. By the 1850s, the commercial conventions had emerged as the dominant organization for voicing not only economic but also the political concerns of the slave South. The Charleston convention in 1854 was attended by nearly 900 delegates from all the southern states except Delaware. Realizing that the conventions provided the best sectional forum for their cause, slave traders tried unsuccessfully to introduce the question of reopening the African traffic at the Charleston gathering. In the New Orleans convention of 1855, J. W. P. McGimsey, a Louisiana planter and a friend of Spratt's, declared that slavery was a divine institution and asked for the repeal of the African slave trade prohibition. Carolinian slave traders rejoiced that the slave trade issue had been raised in "the highest tribunal of southern sentiment," but McGimsey's resolution appears to have been stillborn, as it was a subject neither for debate nor action.[39]

As the conventions became more secessionist in sentiment, slave traders were more successful. At the 1856 Savannah convention the revival of the African slave trade was a major topic of discussion. Charles Colcock Jones wrote from the convention that "[the African slave trade] is thought to owe its paternity to South Carolina — and to be a measure looking towards disunion." Indeed, the convention was seen "as thoroughly treasonable as the vilest conclave that ever polluted the soil of South Carolina." W. B. Goulden, the largest slaveholder in Georgia and another Spratt confidante, introduced a resolution to repeal tariff and African slave trade laws and to form a treaty with Canada for the return of fugitive slaves. The resolution was apparently tabled by a "decided vote," but the next day Jones recalled the slave trade part of Goulden's resolution. It was then voted on and tabled by sixty-seven to eighteen votes. Only the delegates from South Carolina, Texas, and Tennessee voted against the motion. Another attempt to revive the slave trade issue was made by A. L. Scott of Virginia, who introduced a resolution calling for the appointment of a committee to consider reopening the African traffic and to report its findings to the next convention. Scott claimed that he was not trying to revive the external slave trade but wanted to remove the "stamp of disapprobation" that had been placed on it. However, he argued that "[t]he leaders of the freesoil movement no doubt smiled in secret to think, that in order to overspread Texas, New Mexico, and Kansas, we were preparing to make them a present of Maryland, Virginia, Kentucky, and to illustrate our generosity, to throw Missouri into the bargain." Goulden, Jones, McLeod of Texas, and Spratt pressed for a consideration of the African slave trade. Only the convention, Spratt contended, could be seen as representative of southern opinion, as Congress merely acted according to the wishes of its free soiler majority.

A group of lower south unionists, as well as most upper south representatives, resisted slave traders' efforts. Albert J. Pike of Louisiana referred to the inhumanity of the trade. To make sure that he would not be assailed as a traitor, he assured his audience that even though he was northern by birth, he was southern in sentiment and had written widely in defense of the slave South. Whether those present were impressed by Pike's southern bonafides or not, they spent much time distancing themselves from his moral condemnation of the African slave trade and his rather outdated Jeffersonian conviction that the diffusion of slavery would eventually lead to its demise. Alabama delegates Cochran, Baker, and Mason, for instance, were against the African traffic, but they repudiated Pike's position. Opposition to the slave traders' agenda was voiced mainly by the upper south representatives, a portent of the intrasectional split on this issue. Except for a few, most upper south representatives felt that such proposals would result in a new and unwanted controversy over slavery. Funsten of Virginia argued that the people of his state saw slavery as a "positive good" but thought that reopening the African slave trade would be counterproductive. Scott's resolution was defeated by a vote of sixty-one to twenty-four, with South Carolina, Alabama, Louisiana, and Texas voting for it. As if to assure the world that this was not the result of any wavering over slavery, the convention passed a resolution stating that the African slave trade decision "was not prompted by any shrinking doubt of the justice of our cause, or any unmanly fear of looking those facts in the face."[40]

Carolinian slave traders decided to make their goal the abrogation of the African squadron clause of the Webster-Asburton treaty, an issue on which they enjoyed more widespread support, rather than the immediate revival of the African slave trade. They hailed reports of British and French plans to introduce indentured laborers and African apprentices in their colonies as evidence of the failure of both emancipation and the effort to end the Atlantic slave trade. They claimed that the "coolie trade" was actually a revival of the slave trade and berated Europeans for their hypocrisy. The *Courier* and *Mercury*, in a rare show of unity, now argued for the recall of the African squadron. Bryan in a popular pamphlet called for the repeal of the piracy law and the annulment of the slave trade treaties with Britain. In an accompanying letter to Secretary of State Lewis Cass, he praised Cass's opposition to the British demand to search and visit American ships suspected of participating in the illicit trade but argued that the British would be forced to give up their visitation rights if the piracy law was repealed. Prominent Carolinians not associated with the African slave trade movement, such as W. H. Trescot and W. G. Simms, endorsed Bryan's call for the withdrawal of the African squadron. Trescot pointed out that the government "wants to please the North by keeping the Treaty and the Squadron and the South by making them practically inefficient." However, he criticized Carolinian politicians' opposition to the piracy law as ahistorical. But Simms attacked the piracy law, arguing that "if the *trade* in slaves be piracy, the *retention* of the *same people in slavery* is crime!" The *Mercury* repeated almost verbatim Bryan's argument that the designation of the African traffic as piracy had given the British grounds to search and visit American vessels.[41]

The Knoxville convention of 1857 repudiated the eighth article of the Webster-Asburton treaty and gave slave traders their first symbolic victory. It was presided over by De Bow, who put forth the new idols of southern orthodoxy: disunion, the acquisition of Central America and Cuba, and the legalization of the African slave trade. Bryan introduced a resolution calling for the annulment of the African squadron article of the Webster-Ashburton treaty. Those against the slave trade failed to table his proposition, their motion being voted down by sixty-two to forty-two votes. All the votes to table Bryan's resolution came from the upper south states. Virginia was the only one to vote with the Lower South. Bryan stated that the slave South was engaged in a battle for public opinion and that most of the efforts against the African slave trade were motivated by antislavery feeling. He claimed that the African squadron had failed to check the trade and to stop the British from searching

American vessels. Recalling Calhoun's opposition to this article, he argued that the 1842 treaty would not have received a single southern vote if it had consisted of only the eighth article. Southern money would be better spent in apprehending "negro stealers" and hanging abolitionists and "incendiaries." Bryan's resolution passed by a vote of fifty-two to forty, this time with Georgia joining the Upper South in opposition. The convention's action elicited a response from former president John Tyler, who defended the treaty as an act of his administration. Tyler argued that joint policing was a substitute for the right to search claimed by the British. He went on to suggest that the convention would be better served by first considering the repeal of the piracy law. Bryan seized on Tyler's suggestion as appropriate and timely.

Those opposed to the African slave trade were anxious to separate the treaty annulment issue from the reopening of the slave trade. William Sneed, a Tennessee delegate, introduced a resolution stating that while the eighth article of the 1842 treaty should be abrogated, it would be "inexpedient and contrary to the settled policy of the country" to end the African slave trade prohibition. This resolution was voted down. And Spratt's resolution calling for the formation of a committee to report on the African slave trade at the next session passed handily.[42]

After their success at the southern convention, Carolinian slave traders decided to raise the issue of antislave-trade federal laws and treaties in the legislature. As state senator W. D. Porter wrote, the slave traders were determined to push their agenda even at the risk of dividing the state. In the house, Spratt introduced resolutions asserting the South's supremacy over all questions affecting slavery and called for the repeal of the African slave trade laws. His resolutions were indefinitely postponed by a vote of sixty-three to forty-seven, with a majority of lowcountry representatives voting against postponement. The relatively close vote illustrated the growing popularity of the African slave trade cause among Carolinian planter politicians. This was even more evident in the parish-dominated senate, where Mazyck and Bryan introduced resolutions declaring all laws interfering with the African slave trade between two foreign countries and the 1820 piracy law unconstitutional and demanding the repeal of the eighth article of the 1842 treaty. The Committee on Federal Relations tried to separate Mazyck's resolutions on the foreign slave trade and the piracy law and recommended the passage of the latter. Mazyck resisted this effort and in the end both his resolutions were tabled by a vote of nineteen to fourteen and twenty to fifteen, respectively. However, Bryan's resolution for the repeal of the eighth article of the 1842 treaty passed by a nearly unanimous vote of thirty-eight to one. An additional resolution stating that the legislature did not wish to express any opinion on the reopening of the African slave trade also passed by thirty-four to five votes, even though Mazyck tried to have it stricken. The house concurred in these resolutions. Despite the qualification, the passage of Bryan's resolution was a legislative triumph for the slave traders. South Carolina was the only state to endorse the convention's repudiation of the African squadron clause of the Webster-Ashburton treaty.[43]

The African slave trade dominated the proceedings of the 1858 Montgomery convention, as Carolinian planter David Aiken noted. Andrew P. Calhoun, son of the late Carolina leader and an advocate of the slave trade, presided over it. Spratt presented his report, which argued for the reopening of the Atlantic slave trade. Roger A. Pryor of Virginia dissented, admitting that he had been initially "captivated" by the idea. He argued that the South could ill-afford to alienate its northern allies in the Democratic Party and accused slave traders of trying to bring about disunion. H. W. Hilliard also spoke at length against discussing the African slave trade because of its disunionist implications. Other moderates warned against the divisions that the issue had created and referred to southern acquiescence to the slave trade laws and to the fact that the piracy law had been enacted under Virginian James Monroe. Yancey, who criticized Jefferson's and Virginians' views on slavery, pointed out that the Missouri compromise, now regarded as unconstitutional by all southerners, was also passed during Monroe's term. He accused Pryor of pandering to northern Democrats against the slave South's true interests. The debate quickly degenerated into a question of whether or not Virginia had been true to slavery and the South. Rhett tried to diffuse the situation by recommending that Spratt's report be published to spread information on the subject and tabled. While the convention unanimously agreed to this expedient, a resolution offered by Breckinridge of Louisiana praising the African slave trade as a blessing to both the black and white "races" but stating that the South was "honor bound" to abide by the Constitution until the Union was dissolved was also tabled. The alienation of the Upper South on the African slave trade issue was illustrated by an editorial in the influential *Richmond Enquirer*. It asked, "If a dissolution of the Union is to be followed by the revival of the slave trade, Virginia had better consider whether the South of the Northern Confederacy would not be more preferable for her than the North of a Southern Confederacy."[44]

Yancey, rather than Spratt, was the leading spokesman of the African slave trade in the convention and he made an original contribution to the debate by developing a constitutional argument for the Atlantic commerce. He pronounced the federal laws against the African slave trade unconstitutional on the grounds that the Constitution had not granted

Congress the power to end the trade. The exact wording of the constitutional clause on the African slave trade allowed for its continuance until 1808 and did not specify its abolition. According to Yancey, only through liberal construction could Congress be said to have the power to end the Atlantic traffic. Yancey's rather ingenious rationale revealed how an overly literal reading of the Constitution could be used to subvert its meaning. He also utilized states' rights theory against federal prohibition of the Atlantic slave trade by proposing that the congressional slave trade laws be repealed so that individual southern states could decide on whether to reopen the commerce.[45]

Most slave traders repeated his constitutional and states' rights argument for the African slave trade and hardly ever resorted to the higher law ideas that their critics accused them of espousing. They engaged in the kind of detailed quibbling that was a hallmark of southern constitutionalism. The *Charleston Mercury* argued that the constitutional clause on the African slave trade was merely a "negative pregnant" to prevent the government from passing a law against the African slave trade before 1808, and not a positive grant of power to the federal government to abolish the trade. Mazyck had stressed states' rights objections to the federal laws, arguing, like the nullifiers, that the Constitution provided for congressional regulation and not prohibition of commerce. D. S. Troy of Alabama pointed out that the African slave trade was not considered illegal when the Constitution was written. Congress had no power to define it as piracy under the Constitution or the international laws of nations. Fitzhugh also challenged the constitutionality of the African slave trade laws. Thomas Walton of Mississippi undertook a long examination of the African slave trade prohibition and predictably concluded that it was unconstitutional. Furthermore, he claimed that the prohibition had become unjust because it prevented the South's "onward march to the establishment of more slave States, and to the restoration of their political equality" with the North. Walton argued that formal nullification of the federal slave trade laws by the southern states was the only course left to them.[46]

The 1859 Vicksburg convention, which was dominated by lower south secessionists, handed slave traders their biggest victory by endorsing the overthrow of the African slave trade laws. The absence of upper south states such as Virginia, North Carolina, Maryland, Kentucky, Missouri, and Delaware made it an especially auspicious gathering for the slave traders. While proposals for immediate secession on the election of a Republican president and for a congressional slave code were also discussed, the African slave trade again dominated the proceedings of the convention. On the second day of the meeting, Spratt recalled his report and resolutions on the Atlantic slave trade. His advocacy of the African traffic included a dramatic appeal for disunion. He argued that while northern society was based on the principle of the "perfect equality of man," the cause of the South was that of slavery. The contest between them was inevitable and he hoped that the election of a "Black Republican" would goad the South into resistance. The slave South must declare, "We must be free — free to expand according to our own nature — free of the touch of any hostile hand upon us. We are right in that existence which it has pleased Almighty God to give us, and we can admit of no declaration of a wrong in the means to our advancement!" De Bow also pointed out that if the Union "cramped . . . Southern energy, destroy[ed] Southern industry, and diminish[ed] Southern wealth," then it was "legitimate" to ask "whether there was not some other government better adapted to their condition."

This time a division developed between those who argued for the repeal or nullification of the African slave trade laws and those who wanted to establish an African apprenticeship system. Hughes was the leading advocate of the latter group. In his article "State Liberties, or the Right to African Contract Labor," he had argued that the Constitution prohibited only the importation and not the migration of Africans. He recommended the establishment of a contract system as a perfectly legal way to supply African labor to the South. John Humphreys of Mississippi also claimed that this would be the "state rights" way for the South to secure a "prompt and practical supply of African labor." Humphreys pointed out that all the northern states, the Upper South, and the Democratic Party would oppose the repeal of federal slave trade laws. While De Bow decried the division between slave traders and the apprenticeship advocates, he along with Hughes formed the "African Labor Supply Association" to implement this plan. Several resolutions on the African slave trade were offered at the convention. The slave traders' resolution — "That in the opinion of the Convention, all laws, State or Federal [the word 'judicial' here instead of the original 'federal' appears to be a misprint], prohibiting the African slave trade, ought to be repealed" — was adopted by a vote of forty to nineteen. Of the nine southern states present, only Tennessee and Florida voted in the negative. The South Carolina delegation, reflecting the opposing views of secessionists and national Democrats on the African slave trade, was divided evenly with four votes for and four against the resolution. Clearly, the absence of most of the upper south states had contributed to the slave traders' triumph.

Foote, unionist leader from Mississippi, led the comparatively small opposition to the slave traders at the convention. He especially objected to Spratt's philosophy. Just as he had criticized Calhoun and Carolinian secessionists during the congressional debates over the Compromise of 1850, Foote now proceeded to attack the new heresy from the Palmetto state. He asserted that he could agree to no resolution that claimed that slavery in the abstract is right, as he had always believed freedom and liberty are right. Referring to Spratt's criticism of the principle of equality, he mocked, "Democracy, how your glory is passed away!" African slavery, Foote qualified, was a "noble system" and left alone, it would expand on its own. He criticized slave traders' disunionism and their "aggressive" views on slavery. Farrow, a national Democrat from the upcountry district of Spartanburg, defended his state from charges of endorsing the African slave trade. The formal protest against the action of the convention, however, was signed by only ten unionist delegates from Mississippi led by Foote. The protest stated that the convention was unrepresentative and had no right to take such action in the absence of "great slave States" such as Virginia, Kentucky, Missouri, and North Carolina. It also argued that the convention would contribute to the election of a Black Republican president, hastening the dissolution of the Union. One signer, J. S. Holt of Natchez, stated that he was against the African slave trade for reasons of political economy and did not endorse the opinions expressed in the protest. Most of Foote's associates were just as perturbed by the convention's rampant disunionism as by its championship of the African traffic. Foote complained that they were seen as "*traitors* to the best interests of the South, and only worthy of expulsion from that body."[47] Vicksburg was the high point in the South Carolina–led southern movement to reopen the African slave trade.

The debates over the African traffic in the conventions and in lower south states and the partiality of southern nationalists and slavery ideologues for the African slave trade illustrated the importance of this issue in the fight for an independent southern nation. As Du Bois noted long ago, the slave traders did not "carry a substantial majority of the South with them in an attempt to reopen the trade at all hazards, yet the agitation did succeed in sweeping away nearly all theoretical opposition to the trade, and left the majority of Southern people in an attitude which regarded the reopening of the African slave-trade as merely a question of expediency." According to Du Bois, a substantial minority in the slave South and a majority in the Gulf states were for the revival of the foreign slave trade.[48] It would be fair to assert that a majority of secessionists in the Lower South actively promoted or sympathized with the slave trade cause on the eve of disunion. Opposition to the African slave trade treaties and laws, if not the demand for the outright reopening of the traffic, had become a part of the southern nationalist platform. For no matter how hard some slaveholders would try, they could not completely disown this unwelcome offspring of proslavery thought, secessionism, and southern expansionism.

6

Judicial Nullification

The African slave trade is not piracy.
— JUDGE ANDREW G. MAGRATH, 1860

On the eve of disunion, efforts to overturn the African slave trade laws with the demand for federal protection of territorial slavery lay at the forefront of slavery expansionism and southern nationalism.[1] Though the slave traders failed to gain their objective both in and out of the Union, they precipitated an unprecedented rethinking on the African slave trade in the cotton states and effectively undermined the national consensus on its heinousness. Even those Carolinian and southern planter politicians who were against the revival of this traffic made clear their opposition to federal suppression policies and the slave trade laws and treaties. By arguing mainly on the grounds of policy and conceding the principle to slave traders, southern opponents of the African slave trade movement unwittingly recognized that the rationale behind the argument for the slave trade was based on the discourse of slavery and separatism to which they also subscribed. The limits of a proslavery critique of the African slave trade movement would become apparent when most southern critics of the movement refused to endorse a moral condemnation of it.

The slave traders' triumph thus lay more in the realm of ideology and propaganda than in the passage of measures reopening the external slave trade. It did, however, prepare the grounds for the flouting and the judicial nullification of the African slave trade laws in South Carolina and the Lower South. The first public instance of illegal importation of Africans, in violation of the 1808 African slave trade prohibition, took place under the auspices of the slave traders. Not only did Carolinian and southern juries fail to punish those involved, but Judge Andrew G. Magrath declared the 1820 piracy act null and void as far as the African slave trade was concerned.

South Carolina's 1860 judicial nullification went unnoticed due to the onrush of events leading to secession, and historians have yet to examine its import. When the Confederacy adopted a constitution prohibiting the foreign slave trade, South Carolina was the only state to protest. It is an irony of history that the ideological purity of Carolinian fire-eaters proved to be a liability in governing the slave nation they had done so much to create.[2] But the African slave trade agitation was by then already an important part of the stream of events that fed into the vortex of sectional conflagration.

In the years preceding the Civil War, the decisive arena for the African slave trade agitation would be not the state houses but the courts of the Lower South, where instances of illegal importation of Africans were tried. In 1858, the U.S.S. *Dolphin* commanded by Lt. Maffite captured a slaver by the name of *Echo*, originally the *Putnam* of New Orleans, off the Cuban coast and brought it to Charleston. While the captain of the ship was taken to Boston by Mafitte and detained there, the rest of the crew, consisting of Spaniards and Americans, were imprisoned in Charleston. Two sick "passengers," probably also crew members, were left at Key West, Florida. The *Echo*'s human cargo, around 318 Africans, most of them young boys and girls, were packed nude in the notorious "spoon fashion." Nearly 170 Africans had died during the Middle Passage. Carolinian papers contained reports of the appalling state to which the survivors were reduced, referring to their skeletonlike and diseased appearance oddly mixed with fanciful accounts of their joyous singing and dancing and their alleged desire to remain in America.

The sensational arrival of the *Echo* in Charleston seemed to be almost providential, as it brought the slave traders' arguments down to a human and palpable level. At least one of the slave traders, D. H. Hamilton, the marshal to whose protection the Africans were entrusted, had a change of heart: "No one who has witnessed the amount of misery and suffering entailed upon these creatures by the horrors of the African Slave Trade, as I have been compelled, could for one moment advocate a traffic which ensures such inhumanity, to any family of the human race — I acknowledge most frankly to have been an advocate for the re-opening of the Slave Trade — but a practical, fair evidence of its effects has cured me forever." Francis Lieber, the unionist German professor, wrote, "Do angels weep? If they do, if pain is known in their regions, they weep over such a cargo of unutterable suffering as the Echo carried to our hemisphere." But there were others, such as a "Charlestonian" who described the death of a young African boy, and argued that the prohibitory laws should be repealed and the African slave trade regulated to avoid such abuses. He stated that even though "the slave trade, as conducted, is a great crime," it was sanctioned by the Bible and "coeval" with the African "race." "Charlestonian," however, opposed the immediate importation of Africans on the grounds of "expediency." Even more forthright and hardened was "So. Ca.," who repeated the canard that the African slave trade actually saved lives, as it rescued doomed prisoners of war from Africa. Some even suggested that the captured Africans should be studied to improve "ethnological information."[3]

The *Echo*'s arrival provided a fresh impetus to the African slave trade movement in South Carolina. Almost immediately, slave traders started demanding that the Africans not be sent back to Africa as required by federal law. For instance, "Festina Linte" claimed that the president had no right to send the Africans back to their homeland, as the *Echo* might very well have been involved in the domestic slave trade of Cuba. "Curtius" argued in the *Charleston Courier* that to return the Africans was a "wanton insult" to slavery. He pointed out that there were men ready to offer $50,000 for the Africans to let them partake of the blessed condition of slavery in the southern states. C. A. L. Lamar, the Georgian planter and slave trader, offered to do precisely that. One Charleston widow was willing to exchange her fifteen slaves, whose alleged pretensions she complained of, for the "barbarians." "Conservative" felt that southerners should not be called upon to do the "dirty work" of punishing slave traders for an offence that was carried on daily in their streets. He also warned of the effect such a proceeding would have on their slaves. He asserted that Charleston slaves were already discussing the immunity of the *Echo* Africans from enslavement and the marching of fifteen manacled "white men" down the streets of the city. Such demonstrations he felt were bound to make them look with hope to the "powerful friends of 'freedom' " for their own "deliverance." A certain "A. W. D." from Williamsburg offered to contribute $50 and raise $1,000 to $2,000 to defend the *Echo* crew because he felt that the issues involved were of great significance to the slave South. According to a sample of the state press, only one newspaper, the national Democratic *South Carolinian*, was in favor of returning the Africans. Most, including the *Southern Guardian*, *Camden Journal*, *Yorkville Enquirer*, *Southron*, *Pee Dee Times*, and *Cheraw Gazette*, were in favor of "keeping" the Africans.[4]

Carolinian slave traders were quick to take advantage of this sentiment. Leading figures in the movement such as Leonidas Spratt and F. D. Richardson offered their legal services gratis to the imprisoned crew of the *Echo*. Even before the prisoners could be arraigned, slave traders put in writs of habeas corpus and certiorari to have them released, as they had not appeared before a commissioner of the court to be charged for their crimes. The *Echo* case was prosecuted by James Conner, the district attorney, and presided over by Justice Andrew G. Magrath, who had written a secessionist pamphlet in 1850 and later joined the cooperationists. Conner showed that the crew had been imprisoned on the basis of an affidavit of the naval officer who had captured them. He alluded to the seriousness of the charge under the 1820 piracy law, which prescribed the death penalty as punishment. The counsel for defense declaimed at length on the arcane details of habeas corpus laws and demanded that the arresting officers appear in court, knowing full well that the *Dolphin* had sailed away. Magrath denied the petition of habeas corpus. He also claimed that the discovery of Africans in a slaver was not conclusive evidence of its involvement in the Atlantic slave trade, but that this fact was not important at this stage of the case.[5]

The slave traders did not have a legal leg to stand on, but they made full use of the *Echo* proceedings for their cause. Clearly encouraged by Magrath's judgment, Spratt and Richardson presented another writ of habeas corpus, this time for the *Echo* Africans who were in the custody of Marshal Hamilton. They had been virtually challenged to do so by "Non Ego" of the *Courier*, who suggested that since the slave traders had tried to make a case for importing "free African emigrants," they could apply the law of habeas corpus to the *Echo* Africans. In the writ, Spratt stated that Hamilton had denied Richardson the right to visit his clients. The slave traders' new role as self-appointed counsel for the Africans was a bit like having a wolf defend sheep. Conner asked why the Africans themselves had not put in the writ. While slave traders argued for the "personal liberty" of the Africans, Magrath refused their petition on the basis of the *Dred Scott* decision. He stated that the Supreme Court had declared "a perpetual and impassable barrier" between the "white race and the negro" and that the latter were not entitled to any of the rights and guarantees of U.S. citizenship, including habeas corpus. Cleverly, Spratt then concluded that since the court had denied liberty to the Africans, it could not convict their enslavers.[6]

Rumors were rife in Charleston that slave traders intended to get control of the Africans by hook or by crook. Hamilton wrote that "but for the disagreeable necessity of firing upon our own citizens, I would like no better fun, than to accommodate those pugnacious and valorous gentlemen, who are planning attempts to rescue the Africans from my hands." George A. Gordon noted, "But the great topic of conversation, the great theme of interest are the raw niggers, the freshest foreigners in our port. All sorts of plans, schemes and projects, legal and illegal are broached and discussed, as to the best means of getting them on shore, for once on shore they are free from U.S. laws and must come under the jurisdiction of the State. They would find their way to the plantations rapidly then." Probably this talk, as much as the yellow fever raging in Charleston, prompted the removal of the *Echo* Africans to Fort Sumter by the federal government, which made hasty arrangements for their departure. Thirty-five Africans would perish before they boarded the U.S.S. *Niagara* to Africa and fifty-seven more would die on the journey back. Dr. Rainey, the agent in charge of the Africans' return, predictably concluded that they would have been better off as slaves in the South.[7]

The case against the *Echo* crew, which was heard in December 1858 in the United States District Court at Columbia, provided slave traders with a judicial forum for their arguments. Judge Magrath and Judge James M. Wayne, a Georgia unionist who had coauthored the *Dred Scott* decision, presided. The Richland Grand Jury had refused to indict the prisoners, and Spratt again made a motion for their release on a writ of habeas corpus. He tried to illustrate the unconstitutionality of interfering in the slave trade between two foreign countries and of the 1820 piracy law. Spratt's arguments were answered by Isaac W. Hayne, the state's attorney general, and Conner, who pointed out the perfect legitimacy of taking action against slavers owned and operated by United States citizens. Conner emphasized that the Constitution explicitly granted the power to regulate commerce to Congress. The African slave trade exception to this power, he argued, had expired in 1808. Hayne, forgetting his nullifier days, argued that if opponents of the African slave trade laws objected to its antislavery implications then they should work for its repeal rather than declare it unconstitutional. Not wanting the slave traders to paint themselves as defenders of the slave South, Hayne claimed that the owner and American crew members of the *Echo* were "foreigners" and northern men and therefore of no interest to Carolinians. In their decision, Magrath and Wayne agreed with the prosecutors that the prisoners should be recommitted and retried at the next session of the court. The Grand Jury's refusal to indict the crew revealed that slave traders had made headway with their argument that the African slave trade prohibition, especially the piracy law, was an insult to the South. Oscar Lieber, estranged son of Francis Lieber, noted the growing sentiment in the state in favor of the foreign slave trade.[8]

The *Echo* case rekindled the African slave trade agitation. The *Charleston Mercury* inaugurated an extensive press campaign questioning the constitutionality of the federal slave trade laws. It argued that the Atlantic slave trade was a "legitimate trade" under the "laws of nations" and that for Congress to interfere in the trade between Africa and Cuba was "rank usurpation." Spratt added that the Constitution had not even granted the federal government the power to end the African slave trade to the United States. The constitutional clause, he reiterated, merely allowed for the continuation of the foreign slave trade until 1808; it gave no "express authority" to Congress to end this traffic. The federal prohibition was an infringement of the sovereignty of states, who alone had the power to legislate on it. The almost incessant din that the *Mercury* kept up on the African slave trade question reached a crescendo by the end of the year. The paper contended that under no circumstances could the imprisoned crew be condemned to death under the piracy law. No slaveholder would convict men of buying and selling slaves. "F.A.P." (Professor Frederick A. Porcher of the College of Charleston) claimed that the real pirates were the United States Navy, which had apprehended the *Echo* under false pretexts, by flying a different flag to fool its crew, and which had no authority to capture a ship in Spanish waters. He felt that the slave South should not condemn its institutions by punishing those whose only offense was that they were "negro traders." Southerners should not bear the cost of the *Niagara* and pay the Colonization Society for the return of the Africans. He strongly criticized the "indecent haste" with which the president had the Africans transported back to Africa, as their captors had not yet been convicted. Similarly, "Africanus" argued that the Africans should have been left in South Carolina to be "assimilated" with the slave population. "P.A.F.," probably another pseudonym used by Porcher, declared that the government should pay reparations to the *Echo* crew for their "sufferings." Harking back to the spirit of Carolina statesmen John Rutledge and Rawlins Lowndes, who had objected to the African slave trade prohibition, slave traders asked fellow Carolinians to resist the laws, and they called on southern juries to "assert the integrity of the constitution." A letter from "Edgefield," who advocated a policy of "let well alone" for the African slave trade, reminded the *Mercury* of its earlier decision to cease agitation on the slave trade and halted the paper's flaunting of the slave traders' cause. In December, a chastened editorial on Maxcy Gregg's "Appeal to the State Rights Party" admitted that the revival of the African slave trade was impractical within the Union.[9]

The slave traders' campaign against federal suppression policies and laws, however, was extremely successful. Referring to the 1819 and 1820 slave trade acts, the *Mercury* continued to declare that "the acts of Congress prohibiting the slave trade *between foreign countries*, and declaring that trade to be *piracy*, are unconstitutional." The 1819 act actually only banned American citizens from participating in the slave trade between foreign countries, but such details escaped slave traders. "Van Tromp" reiterated that Congress had no power to enact laws on the slave trade. Alluding to the *Echo* case, Alexander Mazyck argued that if southerners ceded the power to regulate the slave trade between two foreign countries to the federal government then the government could also define the coastal slave trade between Virginia and Louisiana as piracy. In his message to the legislature, Governor R. F. W. Allston deprecated American "interference" in the Cuban slave trade.[10]

The *Echo* case also aroused opposition to the slave traders in the national Democratic press such as the Columbia *South Carolinian* and the *Edgefield Advertiser*, the once staunchly secessionist paper. The *Advertiser* had been criticized for its recent wavering in the cause of southern nationalism, and its disavowal of the slave traders reflected its newfound moderation. The *South Carolinian*, appealing to old sectional rivalries, argued that the reopening of the African slave trade would benefit the lowcountry at the cost of the upcountry. Its opposition prompted the slave traders to publish the Columbia *Carolina Times*, a "thorough going state rights, slave trade, and anti-Northern paper," as an alternative. Some other newspapers, including the *Charleston Courier* and the *Charleston Evening News*, also came out against the African slave trade. But John Cunningham, the maverick secessionist editor of the latter paper, also admitted that no southerner would ever convict a slave trader. The *Courier* had established a reputation for moderation since nullification. Richard Yeadon, its former editor, had led the opposition to slave trade proposals in the state house of representatives. In September 1858, it announced its opposition to the reopening of the African slave trade. While the *Courier* editorial admitted to having published several articles in favor of the foreign slave trade, it now denounced the Atlantic traffic. The editors argued that it would reduce the value of southern slaves and the price of cotton and thus "abolitionize" the border states and destroy cotton culture in the older slave states of the Atlantic seaboard. The African slave trade would "distract and divide the South." Harking back to its opposition to nullification as an ultra and unconstitutional measure, the *Courier* now condemned the African slave trade agitation as against the spirit of "the conservative and the Constitution-loving South." One of its writers, "Publius," observed that Calhoun had never asked for the repeal of the slave trade laws. Publius was only half right; Calhoun had expressed reservations about the piracy law.

The *Courier*'s disavowal of the African slave trade stoked its ancient hostility with the *Charleston Mercury*. For example, "Free Trade" accused the *Courier* of using abolitionist reasoning in pointing to the horrors of the trade and its brutalizing effect on traders and slaveholders. Similarly, "Conservatist" chose to remind the *Courier*'s editors of the fact that there were thirty respectable "gentlemen" in Charleston engaged in buying and selling slaves daily and that most Carolinian slaveholders had traded in slaves at one point or another. These correspondents of the *Charleston Mercury*, like the proslavery ideologues who claimed that self-interest, sentiment, and law checked abuses in the master-slave relationship, argued that the legalization and regulation of the Atlantic slave trade would eliminate its brutalities. Another *Mercury* writer, with the appropriate pseudonym "Las Casas" (the Spanish priest who had advocated enslavement of Africans instead of Native Americans), launched a sustained attack on the *Courier*'s mild editorial comments. The reopening of the African slave trade, he contended, was opposed only by those papers and politicians associated with the national Democrats. "Las Casas" concluded, "It [the African slave trade] has on its side every consideration of Christian benevolence, of sound political economy, of agricultural and commercial progress, and of sectional power and security; and nothing but time is required to bring to its support a large majority of the people of this State and of the States south and west of it."[11]

"Las Casas'" confidence was borne out when the *Echo* case was retried in the Charleston Circuit Court in April 1859. The jury issued bills against the crew after the *Mercury* pointedly suggested that the prisoners should be indicted in order to test the constitutionality of the federal slave trade laws. The crew was represented by Spratt and such leading secessionists as Maxcy Gregg, Richard De Treville, and Edmund Bellinger. The sixteen crew members of the *Echo* were tried in two separate trials presided over by Magrath and Wayne. This time the naval officers from the *Dolphin* were present to give detailed testimony on the capture of the *Echo* and the deplorable state of the Africans found on board. District Attorney Conner also presented evidence of American ownership of the vessel. The owner was apparently the captain, Edward C. Townsend of Rhode Island, and the slaver was originally the *Putnam* of New Orleans. In his summation, Conner not only argued for the constitutionality of the slave trade laws and southern acquiescence in the prohibition, but also stressed the brutality of the trade brought out in the testimony of witnesses.

The counsel for defense, after attempting to block testimony on the condition of the *Echo*'s human cargo, rarely referred to the facts of the case. Instead, they rehashed time-tested arguments that slave traders had used since 1854. Gregg, whose attempt to illustrate that the Mr. Townsend of Rhode Island was not the Mr. Townsend of New Orleans was rather thin, based the major part of his argument on the contention that slavery was the "general condition" of Africans and that the 1820 piracy law was unconstitutional. De Treville claimed that this law was a "mark of vassalage" for the slave South. Both appealed to the jury to protect Carolinians from federal usurpation. As De Treville stated, "*You are the inter-*

vening power which stands between the *State of South Carolina*, her institutions and her policy on the one hand, *and the Government of the United States on the other*—a government as foreign to you as is the Government of France on all matters of internal polity, but more especially on the subject of slavery." Bellinger invoked the Constitution, international law, and the Mosaic code to argue that no southern state was obliged to restrict the entry of slaves from foreign countries. Drawing attention to Republican efforts against the African slave trade, he warned dramatically that the "Black Republican blood-hound" was getting ready to attack slavery. Bellinger and Spratt argued that the African slave trade issue was a part of the war of principles between the free North and the slave South. The North, according to the latter, had "circumscribed" and "restricted" slavery by excluding it from "vacant territory" and "a supply of foreign slaves." Moreover, it was "repulsive to the feelings of the South, that men shall be hanged for trading in slaves." Substituting illusion for reality, in answering the vivid testimony on the plight of the Africans, they pointed to the supposed benefits that would accrue to them on their redemption by southern slavery.

In his charge to the jury, Judge Wayne stressed the distinctly un-Carolinian notion that only the Supreme Court could rule on the constitutionality of federal laws. The jury's duty was to make a decision based on evidence rather than on questions of constitutionality. However the jury returned after barely an hour of deliberation with the verdict "Not Guilty." In the second case, a similar verdict was given after half an hour. In the latter case, the prosecution had challenged in vain the presence of certain jury members, including the foreman, from the first case as prejudicial. In a footnote to the *Echo* trials, the notorious Captain Townsend was repatriated to Key West, Florida. The Florida judge and jury, in emulation of their Carolinian brethren, set Townsend free. The only just result had been the confiscation and sale of the *Echo* and the return of the Africans according to the 1819 law, despite southern opposition.[12]

In its triumphant vindication of the verdicts for the "simple seamen" of the slaver, an editorial in the *Charleston Mercury* explained that it would be "cruel and hypocritical" for "members of a community where slaves are bought and sold every day, and are as much and as frequently articles of commerce as the sugar and molasses which they produce, to pass condemnation, and a verdict of guilty of death upon men whose only crime was that they were going to a far country, to bring in more supplies of *these articles of trade, these commodities*" [my emphasis]. The *Mercury* also defended the jury's action as an act of legitimate "resistance" rather than one of higher lawism. Furthermore, it ventured to predict that prosecution was useless as the verdict in all slave trade cases would be an "*Echo* to this." In another slave trade case, a Charleston ketch, *Brothers*, had been apprehended in 1858 on suspicion of being a slaver. Not only was the *Brothers* crew not indicted by their Charleston jury, but in the admiralty case, Judge Magrath ruled that there was not sufficient evidence to libel the ketch and returned it to its owners. Punning being a favored form of expression in the secessionist press, one newspaper declared, "From present prospects it is quite likely that the Federal Government will soon have as many sable boarders as it will be able to cater for, since Africa's sooty sons seem to be still *Wander*-ing over. It is quite possible, however, that they may fail to *Ketch* every *Wanderer*, notwithstanding they have located the *Echo*."[13] With the arrival of the slaver *Wanderer*, slave traders stepped up their activities from defending those participating in the African slave trade to participating in the nasty business themselves.

By sponsoring the open violation of federal laws and by conducting the African slave trade, slave traders lived up to their designation. The seriousness of their intent is evident from a printed questionnaire that Bryan circulated among prominent Carolinian planters seeking information about "the efficiency and docility of native Africans and their descendants," accompanied by detailed questions on the management, health, and skills of Africans. The central figure in this story, however, was Charles Lamar, a capricious Georgia rice planter who had displayed his penchant for slavery expansionism by supporting southern filibustering or illegal invasions of neighboring countries (not to be confused with stalling tactics in Senate debates) in Central America and by his advocacy of the African slave trade. His correspondence reveals that by 1857 he was involved in the fairly extensive illicit slave trade business in New Orleans and New York. A friend of Spratt's, Lamar kept track of the Carolinian slave trade movement and decided to test federal prohibition of the traffic in the state. In the summer of 1858, the Charleston firm of E. Lafitte and Co. applied for a clearance for Lamar's ship, the *Richard Cobden*, to bring African "emigrants" to the United States. W. F. Colcock, the Charleston collector who had been a prominent secessionist in the 1850 crisis, admitted Lamar's "right" to transport African emigrants but as he was a "government official" referred the application to Washington. Secretary of Treasury Howell Cobb, the Georgia unionist, replied that the ship should be refused clearance as it intended to violate the law prohibiting the Atlantic slave trade. Cobb ridiculed the notion that Lamar intended to transport African emigrants to South Carolina, whose laws banned the entrance of free black people. Undaunted, Lamar applied for another clearance for his ship to take African "emigrants" to Cuba. Cobb's letter also provoked rebuttals from Lafitte and Co. and Lamar.[14]

Slave traders succeeded in creating a controversy over the clearance of the *Richard Cobden*. As Lamar complained, "The ship was . . . entitled to a clearance, unless indeed Northern public opinion is entitled to prevail over the legal rights of Southern citizens. . . . You have undertaken to condemn the proposed voyage as illegal, and have closed the courts of the country against me, by depriving me of the only possible means of obtaining a hearing on the question." The prohibition of the Atlantic slave trade was "a badge of servitude" for the South and most "gentlemen of prominence and influence" in the southern states sympathized with him. He threatened, "I will re-open the trade in slaves to foreign countries, let your cruisers catch me if they can." The *Charleston Mercury*, while repeating its official policy of not agitating the revival of the African slave trade, criticized Cobb's decision as an usurpation of executive power. When the *Charleston Evening News* accused it of sympathizing with slave traders, the *Mercury* protested that while it was against the piracy law as "an ebullition of fanaticism" and "a brand of moral reprobation on the institution of slavery in the South," it had no definite position on the reopening of the Atlantic slave trade. It concluded, "*the African slave trade can never be wisely and safely re-opened except by those who are immediately interested in slavery. They, alone, have the power to control and regulate it, as their welfare shall require, free from the influence and interference of those who are not interested or are positively hostile to the institution.*"[15]

Lamar's exploits gave slave traders a new cause célèbre. According to rumors, his ship, the *E. A. Rawlins*, apprehended many times on suspicion of being a slaver, had landed hundreds of Africans in Georgia. But the documented arrival of the *Wanderer* in November 1858 with over 400 African boys on board created a sensation throughout the country. The *Wanderer* had been sold to Lamar and his associates — N. C. Trowbridge of New Orleans, Capt. McGhee of Columbus, Georgia, Richard Dickson of Richmond, and Benjamin Davis of Charleston — by John Johnson, a Louisiana planter and a member of the New York Yacht Club. Its captain was William Corrie of Charleston, who also had a share in its ownership. The *Wanderer* had been seized on suspicion of being a slaver in New York but it managed to elude prosecution. Apparently, it was feted in Charleston harbor with a gun salute before setting out on its slaving mission, and the Carolina press only had praise for the manly bearing of its captain. After fooling and out-sailing naval patrols in Africa, the *Wanderer* completed its voyage, landing its human cargo on Jekyll Island off the Georgia coast, which was owned by the Dubignons, a planter family. Reports of the landings led to the imprisonment of three crew members and their subsequent trial in the Savannah district court. The next year Lamar and his associates were indicted in Savannah. Corrie managed to escape to Charleston, where he was tried for violating the African slave trade laws.[16]

Numerous reports of Africans smuggled into the Gulf states continued throughout 1859. Senator Stephen A. Douglas claimed that at least 15,000 Africans had been illegally transported to the slave South at this time. But except for the *Wanderer*, the Buchanan administration failed to confirm any other landing. There were, however, at least two more instances when it seems likely that the federal prohibition had been violated. In 1859 the *E. A. Rawlins*, Lamar's ship, was finally libeled for being a slaver. No Africans were found on board, but rumors were rife that it had landed hundreds of Africans in Florida just before it was apprehended. In the second case, Captain Timothy Meagher, a rich planter from Alabama, was said to have tried to land the *Clotilde*, with nearly 200 Africans on board, near Mobile. These reports of the flagrant violations of the law and the failure of southern juries to convict men implicated in the illicit slave trade was, as Edmund Ruffin admitted, a virtual repudiation of the African slave trade prohibition. Spratt boasted that "foreign slaves have been introduced" into the country and that his "friend Lamar already hoists the slave-trade flag and floats it from his masthead." He observed that "southern juries" had acted as "the only bulwark against physical aggression" and that the federal government dare not "send its agents to enforce the law" and "search our homes and seize our citizens for acts we recognize as right."[17]

The actual importation of Africans under horrific circumstances provoked some religious opposition to the slave traders. A meeting of the Rocky Creek Baptist Church in Edgefield district, where many *Wanderer* Africans were held, resolved that while they would defend slavery "with all the means God has given us," they would oppose the reopening of the African slave trade with "all the legal means within our power." They further invited their "Sister Churches to co-operate" with them "in this laudable venture." The Rocky Creek resolutions were stillborn. Not a single congregation in the state responded to the church's request for cooperation and the members had to recant their resolutions due to local pressure. A month later, the only recorded antislave-trade meeting took place in Edgefield. This meeting also produced resolutions avowing complete fidelity to slavery but condemning the African slave trade agitation for creating "discord at home and increased opposition abroad." The presence of the Africans in Edgefield created some turmoil when a "northern woman" was ordered out of town on suspicion of holding antislavery views. James Hemphill, alluding to efforts to reopen the African trade wrote, "one hardly knows now what constitutes heterodoxy on the subject of the peculiar institution."[18]

The proslavery Christian criticism of the African slave trade was constrained by its premises. In his influential review of the Carolinian legislative reports on the African slave trade, John B. Adger had claimed that while the Europeans had hypocritically started a new slave trade under the guise of "coolie" labor, the southern demand for the reopening of the African traffic was a mark of "the upright and honest spirit of the slaveholder." Reaffirming proslavery dogma, he claimed that slavery is "a necessary, a just and a good relation" and the best form of extracting "the involuntary labor of certain classes of people." Slaveholders, he continued, were "God's agents in partly reclaiming" Africans from their alleged savagery. Seconding Pettigrew, Adger called the plan to revive the foreign slave trade "a signal failure, viewed simply as the discussion of a great question of state policy." The slave traders, he felt, created divisions in the South just when southerners needed to stand "shoulder to shoulder."[19]

Proslavery divines like Adger and James Henley Thornwell took their biblical literalism seriously enough to repudiate the African slave trade as "man stealing." Pope Gregory XVI had condemned the trade on these grounds earlier, as Bishop John England had demonstrated in letters published in a pamphlet in 1844. England, trying to justify the Catholic Church's position, had attempted to distinguish slavery from the slave trade. Similarly, the *Southern Episcopalian*, edited by Reverends C. P. Gadsden and J. H. Elliot of Charleston, claimed that the "right" to hold slaves was different than the "right" to enslave them. The Bible condemned man-stealing and slaveholders must revere the Bible even when it went against them. However, they claimed that the domestic slave trade was justified on the distinctly unbiblical notion of the right to property, which carried with it the "right to transfer." Calling the slave trade the least "defensible" part of slavery, they argued that there could be no comparison between the foreign and domestic trades if the latter was conducted on a "Christian" basis. The *Episcopalian* had been earlier reproached by "a northern religious journal" for "speaking with too much calmness" about the inhuman commerce. Its editors took the opportunity to clarify their position on the African slave trade after the landing of the *Wanderer*. They argued that the revival of the African slave trade must be opposed all the more strongly since it was perceived to be a "southern measure." They astutely attributed the agitation to a change in the southern view of slavery: "The sentiment of the South, and especially of South Carolina, seems verging toward the opposite extreme of a national oscillation, passing from morbid sensitiveness into aggressive assertion."[20]

In a stronger vein, Reverend J. Leighton Wilson wrote a passionate article against the African slave trade. Unlike most Carolinian clergymen, Wilson was a supporter of the Colonization Society and had been a missionary in Africa. He was also identified with antislave trade efforts long before its reopening was contemplated. In 1850, he had written a pamphlet strongly defending the British naval squadron in Africa and the colony of Liberia and had recommended strong measures against the Atlantic slave trade. In his article against the reopening of the African traffic, Wilson, unlike other proslavery ministers, emphasized the harm done to African nations from the trade. He argued that the African slave trade had led to wars and destroyed life and property in western Africa and that it would be far better for Africans to be "christianized" in their homeland than to be subjected to the horrors of the Atlantic slave trade.[21]

However, it would be wrong to conclude that the entire religious community was against the African slave trade. A critic of Adger's, in good proslavery fashion, quoted the Bible to show that the Israelites had participated in the African slave trade and that neither Moses nor Christ had explicitly condemned it. He also claimed that not all Carolinian clergymen, including Presbyterians, would agree with Adger. In reply to the *Episcopalian*, one writer in the *Charleston Mercury* claimed that the editor had "failed to give any direct Scripture authority for his denunciation of the trade." The Southern Methodist Episcopalian Church rescinded its rule against the enslaving and selling of free persons in 1858, but it declared coyly that it did not wish to express an opinion on the reopening of the African slave trade. Some southern clergymen showed no such compunction. Iveson Brookes, the vocal proslavery Baptist minister, argued that the "sin" of the slave South lay not in its participation in the inhuman traffic but in the part it had played in its suppression. He wrote, "Had not the foreign slave trade been broken up in this country and the slave forbidden to enter, the millions of acres of western territory of which we have suffered ourselves to be robbed of all participation, the greater part of this whole continent would be now filled with slaveholders and their civilized and Christianized African slaves."[22]

Like some clergymen, Carolinian unionists were also horrified at the actual landing of Africans in the United States. James L. Petigru wrote, "[History's] pages will be defiled by recording the depravity of the present day, when the laws against the kidnaping of Africans, and robbery of our neighbors by Filibusters, cannot be enforced." Lieber, who had escaped to New York by now, wrote that the "African slave trade is a godless, unchristian crime and infamy—the blot of our race, and renewing it would be high handed rebellion against civilization, religion—against our God." Alfred Huger, astounded at the slave traders' constitutional arguments, wrote caustically that they would soon be waging "war against the simplest arithmetical proposition." W. C. Preston bemoaned that the plan to reopen the African traffic was a result of "that prurient temper of the times which manifests itself in disunion schemes. . . . My state is strangely and terribly infected with all this sort of thing."[23]

None was more dismayed than Hammond, who had by now staked his career on a newfound conservative unionism and opposition to slavery expansion. "The South has done nothing but stab herself. . . . The Echo, the Wanderer cases and all their incidents; and the demand made here for Congress to pass laws protecting Slavery in the Territories—ideal, impracticable, and injurious all, they strip us of every supporter in the free states, for no man there can stand on them." He blamed the "infatuated and besotted 'fire eaters' " of his state for tolerating and even encouraging the "vile proceedings" of slave traders. He condemned filibustering, the revival of the African slave trade, and the demand for a territorial slave code. Not only did they damage the "prestige" of the South but they also encouraged the spread of abolitionism. The "Rhetts and Spratts" along with "Brown, Davis, Slidell &c" are "recruiting sergeants for Seward and his gang," he wrote.[24]

Despite such criticisms, the *Wanderer* incident showcased slave traders' audacity and support for their illegal activities. The most amazing aspect of the case was the relative ease with which Lamar and his associates managed to distribute the *Wanderer* Africans in the plantations of the Lower South. Accounts of the unfortunate "wandering Africans" came in from all parts of the South, though a majority were said to be distributed in Georgia and South Carolina. It became common knowledge that the Brooks and the Tillman plantations in the Edgefield district housed some of the Africans. Oscar Lieber left behind a detailed description of one of these Africans. In a letter to Senator Chesnut, James H. Adams wrote that "many of the first men and families in our state and men of equal standing in Georgia, Alabama, and Mississippi" held the *Wanderer* Africans. He warned that if the federal government tried to recover them, it would precipitate "an issue of blood" with the state. Such a conflict, he predicted, may create trouble among the slaves, many of whom "in our cities and towns are now looking forward to the coming of their Messiah of deliverance with as much confidence as the Jews of old." For now at least, Adams's fears came to naught. Slave traders even managed to whisk away an African boy recovered by authorities from the Savannah jail. Bribes, vigilante action, and intimidation seem to have been the stock practices of Lamar and his allies in foiling the prosecution of the case. As the local grandee, Lamar illustrated that he could get away with murder. In February 1859, the government libeled and confiscated the *Wanderer* for being a slaver. At the government auction, Lamar easily rebought his schooner and knocked down the one hapless Georgian who had dared to bid against him.

The incompetent prosecution of the case by the Buchanan administration also contributed to the slave traders' triumph. District Attorney George Ganahl accumulated and presented enough evidence in court to have the three crew members and Lamar and his associates indicted in the Georgia district court. The latter were indicted for illegally holding Africans as their ownership of the *Wanderer* could not be proved. The Savannah jury protested that it had been forced by the court to indict Lamar and declared that the South was no longer willing to acquiesce in the federal slave trade laws "because they directly or indirectly, condemn this institution [slavery], and those who have inherited or maintain it." Besides these ad hominem declarations, Ganahl also had to contend with the peculiar Henry R. Jackson, a relative of Cobb's, who was appointed as a special prosecutor for the *Wanderer* case by Attorney General Jeremiah Black. Jackson, who became obsessed with the fantastic idea that the plan to reopen the African slave trade was a New England plot, spent most of his time hunting down one of the members of the *Wanderer* crew, a northerner by the name of Farnum, in order to prove his theory. He also worked at cross-purposes with Ganahl, seriously weakening the prosecution's case. Moreover, not only did the federal government fail to recover the *Wanderer* Africans but it ignored pleas for assistance by local authorities. Hamilton refused to search for the *Wanderer* Africans in Edgefield despite numerous reports, since he had not received compensation for his services in the *Echo* case. Conner threatened to resign for similar reasons and Ganahl resigned after the first *Wanderer* case.[25]

The *Wanderer* trials illustrated slave traders' success in the Lower South at emasculating the federal laws against the African slave trade. When the case against the crew came up for trial in November 1859, Judge Wayne, a staunch unionist, gave a clear charge to the jury that dwelt on the constitutionality of the African slave trade laws and the abhorrent nature of the traffic. Wayne went to great lengths to illustrate that the African slave trade laws could not be construed as an insult to the slave South. Despite his assertion that there was adequate proof connecting the accused to the slaver, the jury returned a verdict of not guilty. The case against Lamar, Trowbridge, Farnum, the Dubignons, et al. would drag on for another year. Hamilton Couper replaced Ganahl as the district attorney in the cases against Lamar and his seven associates. Jackson also managed to apprehend Farnum, who was brought to trial at the Savannah court. Lamar and his cohorts kept up their familiar antics of intimidation. Lamar fought a duel with one of the witnesses and challenged Couper to one. At one point, he and his supporters coolly spirited Farnum away from the county jail. It came as no surprise to anyone when the Savannah juries failed to convict any of the accused. In May 1860 the Georgia trials came to an abrupt end with mistrials and nolle prosequi entered for the remaining defendants.

Lamar and his associates were tried, however, for breaking into the county jail and kidnapping Farnum. They were sentenced to thirty days in prison and fined $250. But the "jail being considered unfit and unwholesome for the local gentry," the prisoners lived up their jail time in Lamar's Savannah quarters in style. Illustrating exactly what he thought of the whole affair, Lamar angrily replied to a letter addressed to him "in jail," "I am *not* in jail, and the damned Government has not the power to put and keep me there. I am in my own rooms, over my office, and go home every night, and live like a fighting-cock at the *expense of the Government.* . . . I can *whip* the Government any time they make the issue, unless they raise a few additional regiments." Ironically, that is exactly what the federal government would do, and Charlie Lamar, after some blockade running, would die a Confederate hero. The *Wanderer* saga continued when the ship was stolen by Lamar's captain for another slaving expedition. It was finally confiscated by federal authorities, and the Lamar family's attempt to recover it failed signally in the Boston courts.[26]

While the Georgia trials were considerably more entertaining, an interesting side show to them developed in Charleston in the case against the *Wanderer*'s Carolinian captain, William Corrie. When the New York Yacht Club expelled Corrie from its membership for his slaving activities, even the *Courier* expostulated that the action was "political" and "sectional" as he had yet to be found guilty in the courts. Corrie was also the one person against whom irrefutable proof of ownership existed. Georgia authorities therefore made repeated attempts to arrest him and make him appear before the Savannah court. In January 1859 Magrath had ruled that Corrie was not liable under Georgia's jurisdiction, and that if arrested in South Carolina, he would have to be tried there. Magrath even felt that there was not enough evidence to indict him. Finally, when Corrie was arrested for piracy on the basis of Ganahl's affidavit, the Georgia prosecutors renewed their petitions for repatriation, which Magrath repeatedly denied. The peculiar circumstances of the case against Corrie make one suspect that the Carolinian judge had other motives besides the trial of the defendant in refusing the Georgia court's request. It soon became apparent that Magrath, who claimed to be against the African slave trade, planned to challenge the piracy law, which by now was widely seen as an insult to the slave South, thanks to the slave traders' propaganda. In one of his decisions, Magrath had declared that it was not the time for him to render his interpretation of the 1820 law, implying that he would do so if a case came up in his court. Moreover, in May 1859, after finding no bill against Corrie, the dismissed Charleston jury oddly asked permission to reconsider its decision. This request was refused by Judge Wayne with Magrath dissenting. The jury probably changed its mind after being informed by Magrath that if Corrie was not indicted in South Carolina he could be extradited to Georgia to stand trial there. He further hinted to the jury that having been refused permission to change their bill they could introduce a presentment. In a highly unusual step, the jury then made a presentment initiating criminal proceedings against Corrie on the charge of piracy. Magrath then proceeded to free Corrie on bail even though he was charged with a capital offence.[27]

The trial of William Corrie became the most significant *Wanderer* case when Judge Magrath used the opportunity to proclaim the judicial nullification of the 1820 African slave trade piracy law. On instructions from Attorney General Black, Conner entered a nolle prosequi in the case so that Corrie could be tried in Georgia. In his decision, Magrath went over his past refusal to extradite Corrie to Georgia. The 1820 law, he claimed, made an exception for the time-honored rule that a criminal should be tried in the place where the crime was committed. But this was not the only peculiar construction that Magrath gave to it. In the more astounding part of his decision, Magrath claimed that the 1820 piracy act did not apply to the African slave trade at all. He contended that unlike previous acts relating to the African traffic, the title of the 1820 law contained no direct reference to it. He then went on to argue that "the slave trade itself, and such acts of violence and spoliation" covered by the piracy act were "distinct." Magrath stated that the Atlantic slave trade was prohibited and regulated as a "trade" or a "business" punishable by imprisonment or fines but not by the law of piracy, which referred to specific criminal acts including enslaving or decoying a free "negro or mulatto." To make sure that this argument could not be applied to the African slave trade, he claimed that to purchase a slave on a "foreign coast" was not equivalent to enslaving a free person. And while such an act was prohibited by the laws of the country, it was not piracy. It was clear that all any person involved in the African slave trade had to do was to produce a bill of sale to escape being hanged as a pirate. This he contended was the same law that was applicable to slaves and free black people.

Local southern laws on slavery, which had already been nationalized by Calhoun's common property and constitutional theories, were to span the high seas and even the continent of Africa. Magrath's remarkable decision was upheld by the tortuous and convoluted reasoning that had become a hallmark of southern constitutional thought, especially the Carolinian brand of it. Supposedly based on the twin idols of literalism and strict construction, he distorted both the Constitution and federal laws at will to suit secessionists' political prejudices. The rule of strict construction thus produced the most obvious distortion of intent and law. This kind of legal reasoning had been established as a respectable precedent in South Carolina since its first nullification. And it sustained and protected the flagrantly illegal acts of slave traders.

Magrath's decision also more than met the moral demands of slave traders — the slave trade was not piracy and slaves were certainly not plunder. His decision virtually repeated the arguments of the counsel for defense in the *Echo* trials. By nullifying the application of the 1820 law to the African slave trade, he had wiped out the insult to the slave South contained in the federal slave trade laws. To reconcile this construction of the piracy law with his and Wayne's joint decision in the *Echo* case upholding the constitutionality of the African slave trade laws, including the 1820 act, Magrath concluded that while he conceded to Congress the constitutional authority to declare the slave trade piracy, in his opinion, Congress had yet to exercise this authority! As if this bit of grandstanding was not enough, he also refused Conner's plea of nolle prosequi on the grounds that it was an unwarranted interference by the president in the prosecution of the case. "Federal usurpation" was after all a favorite theme among Carolinian planter politicians. Reacting to northern criticism, Magrath, presumably thinking that his decision was a model of objectivity and independence, wrote, "If a Judge in the Courts of the United States, is to be obedient to a handful of the representative of the Anti Slavery party of the Free States, heaven save the States, in which, under such prejudice Justice is administered." A couple of months later Magrath and Wayne agreed to Conner's request for the discharge of the Grand Jury, and Corrie, like the rest of the *Wanderer* defendants, got off scot-free. Magrath's decision was hailed in South Carolina. The *Charleston Mercury* pronounced that the 1820 law was from now on a "dead letter."[28]

Magrath's slave trade decision and the universal applause with which it was received in the state revealed the real nature of the slave traders' victory. Not a single criticism of the decision appeared in the state, not even by national Democrats or moderate states' rights men such as James Orr, J. H. Hammond, W. W. Boyce, James Chesnut, and J. H. Thornwell. In his speech at the Vicksburg convention, James Farrow pathetically claimed that Carolinian juries in the slave trade trials had based their decision on evidence rather than on the constitutionality of the slave trade laws. When Massachusetts senator Henry Wilson charged that Corrie "struts the streets [of Charleston] amidst the caresses of applauding thousands, shielded from a felon's doom by the monstrous perversions of the laws of the land by a faithless, if not by a perjured judge," Hammond defended Magrath's decision and weakly argued that Corrie was popular because of his "personal qualities" rather than for slaving. Only W. H. Trescot privately protested the decision to W. P. Miles: "Whatever our interests may be, there is such a thing as right and it will not do to 'blacken' the truth even for the sake of cheap labor." But most Carolinian politicos were no longer willing to condemn the Atlantic trade as a crime against humanity or to take part in its suppression.

While slave traders may have been in the minority, many Carolinian planter politicians accepted their rationale, if not their demand, for the immediate reopening of the African slave trade. Hamilton, who had been so moved by the plight of the *Echo* Africans, now argued that "the amendment of the Slave Trade Acts is of more importance practically, to the South, than any which has arisen since the formation of the Confederation, not even excepting 'the Missouri Compromise.' " W. D. Porter, president of the South Carolina senate, who opposed the legalization of the African traffic as being especially harmful to his state, acted as a lawyer for Corrie. Magrath himself is a case in point as he claimed to be opposed to the African slave trade. In a letter to Hammond in 1859, he wrote that the "Judicial department" was "in the van[guard]" as far as the African slave trade agitation was concerned and that he would "maintain the Laws with all the energy" he had. He did not specify, however, what the vanguard role of the judiciary was. But he did elucidate his judicial philosophy: "Why in South Carolina, the jurisdiction of the United States does not even prevail in the Court House itself! Except for such matters, as would be classed among contempts, there would be no exercise of jurisdiction. The most narrow kind of tenancy; from year to year; a tenancy which no one takes, but rarely upon compulsion; it is the only kind of tenancy, which in this State, the United States, will take." He ascertained that while most were opposed to the revival of the foreign slave trade, "it is yet to be seen whether that majority will go to the extent of enforcing the Laws." It should hardly be surprising that on Lincoln's election, Magrath set the ball rolling for the state's secession by melodramatically tearing off his robes and stamping on them while announcing his resignation from the federal judiciary.[29]

South Carolina, with its ideological purity on slavery and political separatism, had proven to be fertile ground for the movement to reopen the African slave trade. Public opinion in the state was adverse to implementing federal laws on the traffic. Carolinian planter politicians' equivocal position on this issue acted as a shield for slave traders' illegal activities. The state's less well-known second act of nullification by Magrath symbolized the extent to which slave traders had managed to popularize their cause and make it respectable to an assorted group of southern nationalists.

Congressional debates over the African slave trade revealed that on the one hand, many Carolinian and southern planter politicians, who were on record for opposing the revival of the foreign slave trade, questioned federal suppression policies and laws. On the other hand, the newly formed Republican Party emerged as a strong critic of the southern agitation to reopen the Atlantic slave trade and as an advocate of the strict enforcement of the African slave trade laws. The emergence of the African slave trade as an issue of sectional contention a couple of years before the Civil War illustrates clearly how slave traders had managed to overturn the revolutionary consensus on the prohibition of this traffic. By failing to take note of the congressional debates over the African slave trade, historians have also failed to fully grasp the dimensions of the movement to legalize the African slave trade in the 1850s.

The ambivalence of some southern politicians on this issue was evident from the start. As early as 1854, John Slidell had recommended the rescinding of the eighth article of the Webster Ashburton treaty in the Senate. Allusions to the African slave trade had also been made in Congress during the Kansas debates. A. P. Butler and L. M. Keitt pointed to northern complicity in the African slave traffic to South Carolina when it was revived in 1803. Keitt contended, with an interesting qualification, that "to the North belongs the sin (if sin there be) of the capture and transportation of the African, and to the south, the virtue of civilizing him." While northerners pointed out that it was the insistence of South Carolinians that allowed the Atlantic traffic to flourish until 1808, others such as Senator John P. Hale of New Hampshire, known for his antislavery beliefs, disarmed Carolinian planter politicians by acknowledging northern participation and arguing that it was all the more reason for northerners to take measures against the inhuman trade.

Many southern politicians who opposed the reopening of the African slave trade refused to countenance strong moral condemnations of it. In 1857 Emerson Etheridge of Tennessee, a unionist, introduced a resolution in Congress strongly condemning any proposal for the revival of the African slave trade as "shocking to the moral sentiment of the enlightened portion of mankind." His resolution was clearly directed at Governor Adams's message recommending the reopening of the African slave trade. Most southern representatives argued that while they did not advocate the reopening of the African traffic, they could not vote for a resolution that branded the slave trade as inhuman and immoral. Still others, such as two Pennsylvania representatives, felt that Etheridge was merely trying to create a division between the northern and southern wings of the Democratic Party. Etheridge's resolution passed by a vote of 140 to 57, with 54 out of the 71 southern representatives voting against it. Carolinian representatives of differing political beliefs—James Orr, David Aiken, Preston Brooks, John McQueen, and Keitt—united to vote against the resolution. Orr and W. W. Boyce tried to substitute milder resolutions. Orr's resolution, which simply declared that it was inexpedient to reopen the African slave trade, passed by a more overwhelming vote of 183 to 8, the dissenters including Brooks and Keitt and some other cotton states' representatives. The passage of Orr's resolution has been seen by some historians as evidence of the fact that most southerners were unalterably opposed to the Atlantic slave trade. Actually, it indicated just how many southerners, especially those from the Lower South, opposed an explicit condemnation of the African traffic.[30]

Etheridge's moral condemnation of the foreign slave trade clearly reflected a minority position in the slave South. A year later, he had to fight against being branded a free soiler and a Black Republican. He was convinced that southern disunionists had launched a concerted movement to reopen the African slave trade. Responding to charges that he was trying to divide the Democratic Party, Etheridge argued that the party itself had brought about all the sectional divisions plaguing the country with the Kansas-Nebraska Act and the Ostend manifesto. He also distanced himself from the view of slavery that had become dominant in the South. He stated that he "emphatically" objected to slavery being portrayed as a Christian and divine institution and as a necessary foundation of society and polity. Instead, like the founding fathers, he saw slavery as a given "fact" of political economy that should be left to those concerned with it. Carolinian slave traders immediately condemned Etheridge as a southern man with "British-abolition" principles.[31]

The landing of the *Wanderer* and the public flouting of the slave trade prohibition goaded Republican senators such as Henry Wilson and William Seward to call for federal action against violations of the law. Carolinian secessionists, referring to the Republican Party's championship of the Homestead bill and the slave trade laws, called it a party of "land for the landless" and "niggers for Niagara," an allusion to the U.S. vessel that had transported the *Echo* Africans back to Africa. In December 1858 Wilson's resolution demanding more information and release of the official correspondence relating to the *Wanderer* affair passed the Senate.

President Buchanan replied a month later, but only to state that the government was making full efforts to apprehend the criminals. Seward introduced a bill in early 1859 for the more effectual prohibition of the African slave trade. The Committee of Judiciary reported on the bill that since it was of "great moment" and would result in a debate, there was not enough time to act on it.[32]

During a Senate debate, Wilson referred to the rise of the African slave trade movement "in portions of the country" where "grand juries cannot be relied on to indict persons if caught in that trade." When Hammond challenged Wilson's assertion that southern juries could not be depended on to enforce the slave trade laws, he replied, "No doubt, a large portion of the people of the Southern States are opposed to the African slave trade; but there is a party, young, vigorous, and active, that wishes to open the slave trade; a party that wishes to extend the country into the tropics; a party that believes not only in compulsory labor in the tropics, but everywhere else; a party that wishes to govern this country under that policy, and failing to do that, to establish a Southern Confederacy and dissolve this Union, there is evidence." If Wilson's speech contained an acute sense of an encroaching slave power, it also listed accurately the assorted varieties of slavery expansion schemes championed by southern nationalists.

Sectional cleavages over the African slave trade became clear when an obscure clause in the consular and diplomatic bill appropriating $75,000 for the suppression of the African slave trade became the subject of an acrimonious debate in the Senate. Of this amount, $45,000 was for the African squadron and $30,000 for expenses incurred in the repatriation of the *Echo* Africans to Liberia. Senator Clement Clay of Alabama moved that the entire clause be struck out because Congress had no constitutional authority to make the appropriation. He was seconded by Senator Albert G. Brown of Mississippi, who opposed the revival of the African slave trade. Brown contended that the *Echo* Africans should not have been sent back to Africa as "Slavery here is better than the sort of freedom they enjoyed at home." Two senators from the Upper South, R. M. T. Hunter of Virginia and Thomas Clingman of North Carolina, argued in favor of the constitutionality of the African slave trade laws and the appropriation. Both also defended the efforts of the Colonization Society in their work of repatriating and "educating" the *Echo* Africans. In his Barnwell court house speech, Hammond had accused the Liberian government of participating in the African slave trade. The Colonization Society and Liberians vigorously denied this charge, and even antislavery men such as Wilson, who stated that he was no friend of the Colonization Society, acknowledged that the Liberians had played a major role in suppressing the slave trade near the colony. Southern attacks on appropriations for the Colonization Society were taken as indications of sympathy or at least tolerance for the slave trade agitation. Opposition to the bill was even more glaring because more than half of the appropriation was for the African squadron and the bill was an administration measure.

Slave traders had succeeded in making their cause a sectional issue among those southerners opposed to the revival of the Atlantic slave trade. Clay's resolution was defeated by a vote of forty to twelve. Significantly, the twelve votes against the African slave trade appropriation came from such prominent southern leaders as Robert Toombs, Jefferson Davis, James Mason, Clement Clay, Hammond, and the freshman senator from South Carolina, James Chesnut. In the house, Carolinian representatives opposed the measure, which passed by 101 to 98 votes. Republican representative David Kilgore's resolution condemning the African slave trade failed to pass the house by a two-thirds majority. Lamar declared, "Even the politicians, and those, too, who have been in that corrupting atmosphere of Washington City, are coming to us."[33]

During the next session of Congress, Wilson once again spearheaded the effort to suppress the Atlantic commerce in slaves. He proposed a comprehensive bill that would have increased the number of American ships policing the African coast, offered bounties to persons giving information on the landing of Africans in the United States, and checked the use of the American flag and vessels in the African slave trade. He argued for the necessity of his bill by pointing to the impunity with which juries "misconstrue, misinterpret and pervert" the laws and to the rising sentiment in favor of the African slave trade in the lower south states. After failing to secure the passage of this bill, Wilson proposed an amendment to a naval appropriations bill to secure three steamers for the African squadron, which was also defeated by a "party vote." The increase in illicit American participation in the Cuban slave trade stirred even the Buchanan administration to take some action by increasing the number of guns employed in the African squadron. But the administration also forced the British to formally give up the right to search and visit American ships in 1858. In his 1859 message to Congress, Buchanan argued unabashedly for Cuban annexation as a way to end the African slave trade to that country.[34]

However, sectional more than partisan divisions continued to mar the African slave trade debates in Congress. In May 1860, the United States Navy captured an American slaver and transported the more than 1,000 Africans it was carrying to Key West, Florida. This incident gave rise to another debate in Congress over the African slave trade and the suppression policies of the United States government. Sensitive to southern criticism over the Buchanan administration's handling of the *Echo* Africans, Judah P. Benjamin of Louisiana, chairman of the Judiciary Committee, introduced a bill on behalf of the administration to authorize the president to enter into a contract with the agents of the Colonization Society to transport the Africans back to Africa and make provisions for their care. The administration's request once again exposed sectional divisions over the handling of the African slave trade cases. Southern senators, even those who agreed that the government was responsible for repatriating the Africans, firmly opposed amendments increasing the amount appropriated and the period of care of the Africans. Some staunchly opposed the entire appropriation, which merely implemented the law of 1819. David Yulee of Florida, for instance, generously offered that the people of his state would "take care" of the Africans at no charge. His colleague, Stephen R. Mallory, offered an amendment stating that the Africans be returned only after the expiration of their "terms of servitude."

More remarkably, Senator James Mason of Virginia, who apparently was against the revival of the foreign slave trade but was known for his commitment to southern separatism, fully substantiated slave traders' constitutional arguments. He declared, "all the differences attending this subject grow out of the fact that the legislation upon this subject commenced on the wrong basis. I am one of those who could never see any warrant in the Constitution by which the United States undertook to suppress the slave trade — never. . . . I never did see in the Constitution any warrant for the United States to put a stop to the slave trade." Congress, Mason contended, had usurped southern states' jurisdiction over the African slave trade. Robert Toombs of Georgia took this opportunity to criticize the Webster-Ashburton treaty and claimed that while it was their duty to abide by the African slave trade prohibition, the government had no right to "interfere" in the slave trade to Brazil or Cuba. Like the slave traders, Toombs chose to ignore the fact that American participation in the African slave trade to any country had been declared illegal by the 1819 law. Jefferson Davis also opposed the appropriation. He offered an amendment that would simply provide for the Africans' return to their point of departure in Africa, even though Benjamin pointed out that that would leave them in the barracoons at the mercy of their captors. Brown argued that the Africans must be returned as required by law, but that he did not believe that the African slave trade was in any way inhumane. While Davis's amendment was defeated by a vote of thirty-eight to seventeen, the bill passed by forty-one to fourteen votes, with Davis, Brown, Mason, Toombs, Slidell, and Clay voting against it. Hammond was absent for both votes and Chesnut voted for Davis's amendment and the bill.

In the House of Representatives, the African slave trade appropriation was increased and the bill passed by a vote of 122 to 56. Carolinian representatives such as secessionists Bonham, Keitt, and even the antislave-trade Boyce voted against it. Pryor, who had so eloquently opposed Yancey at the Montgomery convention, now contended that "instead of returning these negroes to the unrelieved and sterile slavery of Africa, let us reduce them to a mild and profitable subjection in this country." Representative Millson, also of Virginia, accused Pryor of claiming to be against the African slave trade but voting against all laws to put it down. Millson accurately complained that "every attempt to arrest the slave trade" and "every attempt to punish" slave traders seemed "to excite the sensibilities of some gentlemen."[35]

The congressional debates showed not only the emergence of the African slave trade as a sectional issue but also the growing opposition of southern nationalists to the enforcement of federal laws against it. Irrespective of their position on the African slave trade, these southern leaders claimed that nearly all Africans were slaves and the Atlantic slave trade merely transferred them to a better condition of servitude. According to most of them, the transatlantic traffic in human beings was not a heinous crime but, rather, a mere transfer of property that only happened to be prohibited by law. Southern nationalists' opinions on the African slave trade were hedged with so many qualifications, contradictions, and concessions to slave traders' arguments as to make their position not only inconsistent but untenable. The congressional debates over the suppression policies of the federal government revealed the bankruptcy of their position. The real dilemma that the African slave trade movement presented to southern slaveholders was not so much how to "get right with slavery" but "how to get right" with the hitherto widely condemned Atlantic traffic.

Sectional divisions over the African slave trade marked the road to disunion, although in the end secessionists tried to bury the issue in order to engender southern unity. Secessionists' ambiguity reflected their attraction to the African slave trade and their fear that it would damage the much-sought-for southern unity that had hampered secession in 1850. The *Charleston Mercury* advised, "Speak of the suppression of the African slave trade as an evil, if you please — advocate its being reopened by Congress, if you have such imagination — denounce its condemnation as piracy — discuss it as a wrong or a grievance, if you please, but make *no distinctions, no divisions, no parties upon it,* in the South." The South may reopen the slave trade, it hinted, when it became "*practicable and within our control.*" An imminent Republican victory made it imperative that all questions take a backseat to secession. The *Camden Journal,* which had supported the African slave trade movement from the beginning, now stated, "The slave trade may very well be permitted to 'sleep' for the present." The *Yorkville Enquirer* argued that even though the reopening of the African slave trade would be viewed with "much favor" by southerners, it was improbable that Congress would ever pass legislation to that effect. The real remedy, it felt, was the immediate creation of a southern nation.[36]

A few secessionists felt that the African slave trade issue could be made the cause of disunion. The *Southron* of Orangeburg recommended that the state formally nullify the federal laws and put the African slave trade under the control of the "sovereign states." It concluded, "if the North will not come up to such a construction of the compact of the Union it is the true issue on which we should dissolve it." Why should the slave South, Joseph P. Lovejoy asked, "stand aghast with reverence — paralyzed by conscience" at the constitutional prohibition of the African slave trade when the North defied the fugitive slave law? The southern states must dissolve the Union and decide for themselves whether or not they should reopen the foreign slave trade. A slave trade meeting was held at Mt. Pleasant, Christ Church Parish on October 17, 1859. "Waccamaw" suggested that the meeting pass resolutions stating that they would aid anyone who landed Africans in the state, "in spite of the Constitution or laws of 'the glorious Union.' " Spratt and Bryan addressed the meeting, which issued a long report and resolutions for the African traffic. Another slave trade meeting at Charleston passed similar resolutions.

This time the *Mercury* issued a strong reprimand to slave traders for "playing into the hands of the Unionists of the South." For the first time, the Rhetts also opened their columns to both sides on the African slave trade issue. Earlier, they had published the *Southern Episcopalian* editorial on the African slave trade at the request of a correspondent. By the end of the year, the *Mercury* had a couple of letters arguing that the African slave trade agitation was damaging plans for a concert of southern action. After carrying Mazyck's long letter to the Mt. Pleasant meeting in favor of the Atlantic trade, it reproduced Cunningham's equally long reply. Carolinian secessionists were increasingly fearful that this agitation would isolate their state. While they did not completely forsake the movement, they insisted that it not be made a "party issue."[37]

Slave traders, who received their largest vote during the 1859 legislative session, also decided to postpone all action. Bryan recalled slave trade resolutions sent to the Committee on Federal Relations, and O. M. Dantzler of St. Matthew's Parish and Spratt reintroduced their 1858 resolutions in the state senate and house. In a speech that the *Mercury* characterized as "thoughtful and able," Dantzler argued that the African slave trade issue may divide a "national president making organization" or the Democratic Party but that it could not alienate true southerners. Dantzler was opposed by Wade Hampton, the rich cotton planter and senator from Richland district and future Confederate general and governor of the state. Hampton had opposed secession in 1850 and was associated with the national Democratic group. At the previous session, he had presented an antislave-trade resolution. He argued against the introduction of African "barbarians" who would "demoralize" southern slaves. He criticized the higher-law doctrines of slave traders and repeated that the African slave trade would divide the South. The Committee on Federal Relations recommended the passage of a resolution that simply stated that it was impractical to reopen the African slave trade and that all agitation on the subject was "unwise, inexpedient and impolitic." Edmund Rhett, making it clear that he sympathized with Dantzler, recommended the tabling of all the slave trade resolutions. His motion was seconded by Mazyck and carried by a vote of thirty to twelve. The legislature also returned without comment resolutions passed by the New York assembly condemning the "virtual reopening within the Federal Union of the Slave Trade" and vowing to protest this at the "ballot box."[38]

The New York resolutions were a reflection of the growing northern concern that the cotton states were determined to reopen the African slave trade. The Vicksburg convention and the results of the *Echo* and *Wanderer* trials furthered this conviction. In 1860, Reverend Rufus Clark, an antislavery minister, published an influential book against the movement to revive the African slave trade. Clark recounted the evils of the transatlantic slave trade and its devastating effects on African nations. He argued that the African slave trade was intrinsically connected to the question of slavery and the domestic slave trade. Americans, he wrote, had "retrograded" from the revolutionary generation's desire to end slavery by tolerating and encouraging the system of southern servitude. "The extension of slavery and the encouragement of the slave trade are the natural growth of the institution of slavery among us," he observed. The slave traders wanted to ensure the expansion and permanence of slavery and thus struck at the "vitals of the republic." The 1860 Republican Party platform contained a strong denunciation of the Atlantic commerce: "That we brand the recent re-opening of the African Slave Trade, under the cover of our national flag, aided by perversions of judicial power, as a crime against humanity and a burning shame to our country and age; and we call upon Congress to take prompt and efficient measures for the total and final suppression of the execrable traffic." The Lincoln administration would prosecute the only American citizen hanged for participating in the African slave trade.[39]

By 1860, however, Carolinian secessionists had decided to cease the slave trade agitation for the larger cause of secession. The movement gradually petered down into occasional grumbling about the federal government's suppression policies and the European "coolie trade." Trescot, in a letter to Miles, argued that slavery was "just beginning its career and to develop naturally will require freer scope than is allowed by the bandages of the Federal Constitution." Southerners should, therefore, avoid "skirmishes" over the African slave trade and concentrate on the real "battle." Governor W. H. Gist had assured Hammond that he would not tolerate any violation of the African slave trade laws that would distract "the State by party strife" at this crucial stage. In November 1860, Oscar Lieber wrote that he had not heard of the African slave trade for "at least a year" and that it had "long disappeared in the grand issue of the day." Carolinian planter politicians were now preparing to "unite the South" for secession and were "unwilling to allow themselves to be rendered inactive or impotent by issues, which the hottest would regard as not pertinent to the great question of the day." Despite the burial of the African slave trade agitation, on the eve of South Carolina's secession, "A Southern Planter" was nervous enough to write a public letter asking the state convention not to adopt any measure "by a divided vote on as exciting a subject" as the slave trade. Arguing that he was neither for nor against the Atlantic slave trade, he advised the convention not to take any step that would destroy the unanimity of the state on secession, "keep any of our Southern States from us," or jeopardize recognition from the "great nations of Europe." There would be time enough to deliberate on the reopening of the African slave trade once the slave states had acted and a southern confederacy was formed.[40]

The idea that the slave traders would ram through a slave trade proposal in the secession convention, after a year of self-imposed silence for the cause of the southern nation, was unlikely. But perhaps such fears originated from the fact that in spite of slave traders' quiescence, the African slave trade issue had continued to pop up in the events that led to secession. Before the fateful Democratic convention met in Charleston in 1860, Stephen A. Douglas wrote, regarding his opposition to the southern platform, "If . . . the convention shall interpolate into the creed of the party such new issues as the revival of the African slave trade, or a Congressional slave code for the territories or the doctrine that the Constitution of the United States, either establishes or prohibits slavery in the territories beyond the power of the people legally to control it as other property—it is due to candor, to say, that in such an event, I could not accept the [presidential] nomination tendered to me." The fact that Magrath announced his controversial decision on the *Wanderer* even as the Charleston convention became irrevocably divided between Douglasites and lower south secessionists did not help matters. And at the convention, W. B. Goulden was deluded enough to ask northern Democrats to join southerners in repealing the African slave trade laws, a demand that was greeted with much laughter in the galleries. He claimed that if the African slave trade was revived then southerners could afford to ignore the territorial question (Goulden was that odd and rare commodity, a unionist and a slave trader). Leroy Pope Walker of Alabama, a future member of the Confederate cabinet, offered a resolution, the basis of the majority report on the party platform, stating that the federal government must provide "protection and equal advantage to all descriptions of property recognized as such by the laws of any of the States as well within the Territories as *upon the High Seas*." Benjamin F. Butler of Massachusetts complained that this resolution could be viewed as a demand for the reopening of the Atlantic slave trade. These words were deleted from the second majority report, which only alluded to slavery in the territories.

Southern nationalists had abandoned the reopening of the African slave trade long before the meeting of the Charleston convention. Lower south fire-eaters who had argued for the African slave trade, such as Yancey and Eli Shorter of Alabama, Ethelbert Barksdale of Mississippi, and Wigfall of Texas, gave it up for fear of endangering southern unity. It was clear that the Upper South, already relatively unresponsive to southern nationalism, would never concede the reopening of the African traffic. In his speech to the Alabama state Democratic convention, Yancey had made it clear that while he was for the repeal of the African slave trade laws, he did not want to make it an "issue" for the South. Yet he argued that all matters relating to slavery should be taken out of the hands of the federal government and again challenged the constitutionality of the piracy law.[41]

When it became clear that South Carolina and the rest of the cotton states would secede from the Union after Lincoln's election, Henry J. Raymond, editor of the *New York Times*, wrote a series of public letters to Yancey charging lower south secessionists with secretly conspiring to reopen the African slave trade. He wrote, "What you and your associate conspirators seek is the restoration of the African Slave-trade. 'CHEAP NEGROES' is the grand consummation at which you aim, — the mighty motive which rouses you to the task of destroying a Government which was formed to 'secure the blessings of Liberty to ourselves and our Posterity.'" Northern journals and upper south unionists repeated Raymond's charges.[42]

Southern nationalists moved quickly to allay the fears to which such accusations gave birth. The seceding conventions of Alabama, Mississippi, and Georgia had passed resolutions endorsing the restriction of the African slave trade, though in Mississippi some slave traders entered a written protest. Similar resolutions, however, had been voted down in the Louisiana convention. In the Alabama convention debates, the reason for lower south secessionists' endorsement of the African slave trade prohibition became clear. The fear that the Upper South, especially Virginia, would not join the slave nation seems to have dominated their discussion of the African slave trade. Yancey, who sympathized with the African slave trade cause, now vigorously supported its prohibition.

The revival of the foreign slave trade by the Confederacy or even leaving it an open question would have seriously impaired the secession movement in the upper south states. Not only did the secession movement lose steam after the dramatic exit of the cotton states, but secessionists faced electoral defeat in the upper south states. Unionist opposition and the several proposals for compromise from the border states made for a period of excruciating uncertainty for secessionists. Without the Upper South, the chances of survival of a "Gulf coast confederacy" would be slim indeed. George W. Bagby, secessionist editor of the *Southern Literary Messenger*, assured his readers that he knew "upon the authority of leading men in every one of the Gulf States" that the Confederacy would enact a constitutional prohibition of the foreign slave trade. He queried, "Can Virginia ask more?" But along with the carrot, the Confederacy also offered a stick. Its constitution banned the African traffic and granted the Confederate Congress the power to prohibit the slave trade between the Confederacy and the slave states still in the Union.[43]

The second consideration that guided secessionists was the need for European and British recognition. When Robert Bunch, the British consul at Charleston, expressed his government's concern that a southern confederacy would reopen the slave trade, Rhett had answered that "no Southern State, or Confederacy, would ever be brought to negotiate on such a subject; that to prohibit the Slave trade was, virtually, to admit that the Institution of Slavery was an evil and a wrong, instead of, as the South believed it, a blessing to the African Race and a system of labor appointed of God." Rhett claimed that while he personally and leaders from the old slave states were against the African slave trade, others would demand it. He told Bunch that a southern nation would probably revive the African slave trade for a limited period. But the legalization of the African slave trade by the Confederacy would alienate European countries; it could even involve the slave nation in open hostilities with Britain's naval fleets charged with the suppression of the trade. The slave South could ill afford to alienate the largest buyer of its cotton, and for it to make new enemies when Civil War was imminent would have been politically un-wise, to say the least.[44]

However, it was also clear that the new slave nation would never de-nounce the Atlantic slave trade as piracy or enter into treaties with for-eign countries to suppress the traffic. This was small consolation for Carolinian purists. Repeated efforts by Rhett and Chesnut to remove the constitutional prohibition and give the Confederate Congress control over the African slave trade had failed, with only the South Carolina delegation voting for the change. The African slave trade prohibition passed with South Carolina and Florida voting against the clause. Caro-linian secessionists could barely reconcile themselves to these develop-ments. While commending the constitution as the best ever devised by man, they criticized some of its features, such as the absence of a clause prohibiting the entrance of free states to the Confederacy, the retention of the three-fifths clause instead of full representation of the slave popu-lation, the popular election of the president, and the external slave trade prohibition. The *Courier*, which supported the Confederacy's decision on the African slave trade, accurately predicted that the slave trade prohibi-tion would "excite at present more discussion" than any other part of the constitution. The *Mercury* loudly protested the prohibition, asking, "Were our Constitution makers looking Northward or to Europe rather than to the requirements of their own country and dignity?"

The African slave trade prohibition caused more consternation during the ratification of the Confederate constitution in the state convention. The most protracted debate over the new constitution took place in South Carolina. Gabriel Manigault and John Izard Middleton offered resolutions for amending the constitution so as to allow the African slave trade. Suggestions that South Carolina should be the first to ratify as it had been the first to secede fell on deaf ears. Finally, on April 3, the Confederate constitution was ratified by a vote of 138 to 21, with only some diehard slave traders such as Spratt, Adams, Mazyck, Middleton, and Manigault voting against it. The stand-off over the forts and a proba-ble military confrontation with the United States government no doubt expedited ratification. As Hammond said, "I see the Constitution has been adopted by an overwhelming majority against Rhett & Co., Slave traders, Free Traders, fire eaters, and extremists, and I suppose this is an end of them. It is certain that these men brought on this great movement. They were instruments in the hands of God (as Judas was) — though it was denied me to see it then." The convention passed a resolution stating that as soon as the Confederacy was established, South Carolina should call for a constitutional convention to repeal the African slave trade prohibition, amend the three-fifths clause, and prohibit free states from entering the Confederacy. In 1861, eight years after the start of the movement to revive the foreign slave trade, the state was officially on record for the reopening of the African traffic.[45]

The most trenchant critique of Confederate policy on the foreign slave trade came from Spratt. In a public letter to John Perkins, a Louisiana delegate to the Confederate convention, he argued vigorously for the reopening of the African slave trade. Spratt wrote that the South was in the process of founding a "Slave Republic" and that it could not afford to repudiate the principles for which it had gained independence merely to conciliate the border states and "foreign sentiment." The Union, he reminded the founders of the Confederacy, "*has been disrupted in the effort of slave society to emancipate itself.*" If the slave South did not reopen the African slave trade, it would not escape the cankers of democracy, equality, abolition, and the "rights of man" that plagued the American republic. He warned that perhaps "another revolution" might be needed to fully vindicate slavery if the Confederacy insisted on imposing a constitutional ban on the African slave trade. Blinded by his single-minded advocacy, Spratt ignored the threats to the survival of the very slave republic he lauded. As his critics countered, "we are already sufficiently a 'Slave Republic,' for all good and substantial purposes."[46]

It is difficult to predict what would have become of the "slave republic" and the African slave trade issue if the Confederacy could have maintained its independence. After all, amending the Confederate constitution was a fairly simple process and many southern leaders were convinced that the African slave trade was neither a crime against humanity nor immoral but merely a matter of policy. And if the reopening of the African slave trade was merely a matter of policy, who could say what policy or interest would dictate in the future? In 1863 northerners were still charging the Confederacy with harboring a secret plan to revive the African slave trade. A diplomatic despatch of Secretary of State Judah P. Benjamin containing the refusal of the Confederate government to enter into any treaty for the suppression of the Atlantic traffic was taken as further evidence of such nefarious aims. The Confederate Congress even passed a law that would have allowed the sale of Africans imported illegally, but it was vetoed by Confederate President Jefferson Davis.[47]

The Civil War insured that racial slavery and the African slave trade would be consigned to the dust heap of history. While the attempt to reopen the African slave trade was not successful in realizing its final goal, it had played an important role in the development of proslavery thought and southern nationalist politics in South Carolina and the

Lower South. Slave traders had successfully initiated an ideological re-evaluation of the African slave trade there. Many southern politicians who opposed its reopening refused to condemn the Atlantic traffic in slaves or to support federal suppression policies and laws. And while it represented the most controversial side of slaveholders' commitment to slavery, the movement to revive the African slave trade remains one of the best vantage points from which to view the politics of slavery and separatism in the 1850s.

7

The Coming of Secession

Slavery is our king — slavery is our truth
— slavery is our Divine Right.
— JOHN S. PRESTON, 1860

The rise of a slavery-based southern nationalism was a testament to the antebellum ideological and political leadership of Carolinian planter politicians. The rhetoric of democratic republicanism, perfected by mainstream politicians north and south of the Mason-Dixon line during the antebellum period, did not play a key role in propelling secession. Secession was an overthrow of politics as usual and a result of the demise of the Second Party System. Historians have failed to recognize the ideological and political departure that secession represented in southern politics and concomitantly the pivotal role of South Carolina in its onset.[1] After all, Carolinian planter politicians had pioneered in the formulation of proslavery ideology and constitutionalism that would lead to disunion. And the Carolinian brand of politics had long presented an alternative to Jacksonian democracy and the Second Party System in the South. The waning of the Jacksonian era and the ultimate triumph of Carolinian ideas propelled the secession movement in the Old South.

If South Carolina was the secessionist state par excellence, then resemblance to its politics is an adequate gauge of secessionist strength in other southern states. By 1860, the destruction of the two-party system, the growing commitment to slavery expansionism, the ubiquitous acceptance of the Carolinian doctrine of proslavery and state sovereignty, the geographical spread of slavery, and the domination of the plantation economy underlay the southern movement toward an independent nation in the Lower South. However, the upper south and border states, which retained more than a semblance of partisan rivalries and faced significant internal challenges to slave society, remained far more resistant to the lures of southern nationalism. The conditional nature of upper south unionism would be illustrated by the firing on Fort Sumter and throughout the Civil War.[2] As long as slaveholders and planters remained committed to slavery and were heavily overrepresented in the political leadership of their region, Carolina-style politics would not go out of fashion in the slave South.

Carolinian planter politicians perceived the triumph of the Republican Party with the election of Lincoln to be nothing short of a declaration of war against slavery and sought to unite the rest of the South behind this conviction. External challenges to slavery threatened to expose internal contradictions within slave society, seriously compromising a system whose integrity and security depended on the undisputed sway of its master class. After John Brown's raid on Harpers Ferry in 1859, Carolinian secessionists unleashed a campaign of terror to check dissent and mobilize their state for disunion. The identification of the Republican Party with efforts to undermine planters' and slaveholders' mastery over the subaltern classes of slave society made secession, according to these men, imperative for the very existence and survival of slavery.

South Carolina's unanimity on secession reflected the unified sentiments of its planter class and political leadership. Factional divisions over the mode of secession, the African slave trade, and allegiance to the Democratic Party only masked the underlying political unity of a great majority of Carolinian planter politicians. Throughout the 1850s, they were divided over the extent to which the state should participate in the Democratic Party. This difference between the so-called National Democrats and states' rights Democrats, a group which included moderate and extreme secessionists, marked state politics. After the passage of the Kansas-Nebraska Act and the rise of the Republican Party, many started viewing the Democratic Party as a vehicle for southern interests. But most Carolinian planter politicians still followed Calhoun's dream of creating a sectional organization that would lead the slave South in or out of the Union. In the long run, it would be the mixture of both these policies that would prove fatal to the national organization of the Democratic Party and result in secession.[3]

The rise of the party men in South Carolina was a testimony to the southern tilt and increasingly sectional nature of the Democratic Party rather than of a newfound moderation among Carolinian politicos. In 1856, for the first time a state Democratic convention met and undertook to send delegates to the national party convention. Nearly all the districts were represented at the convention, but, with the exception of

Charleston, most of the secessionist lowcountry parishes did not send a single delegate. Francis W. Pickens, who was chosen to preside, confidently argued that "with the *South united* and the North *divided, we can control this Union.*" Party leader James L. Orr stressed the necessity of South Carolina acting with sister southern states in the Democratic Party to check the election of a Republican president. He reminded Carolinians that the Kansas act had lifted "an odious restriction" on the slave South and told them that they only had to "persevere" to "build up there a slave holding community." He declared dramatically, overturning the age-old Carolinian conviction, "The Government has ceased to be the despoiler of our rights. It is now our protector."[4]

States' rights men such as A. P. Butler, R. B. Rhett, L. M. Keitt, and John McQueen lamented that the convention movement had subverted the ancient policy of South Carolina in one blow. W. W. Boyce noted that partisan affiliation would compromise the state's vanguard position in the movement for a southern nation. He pointed out, "The time is rapidly approaching when it may be of the most vital importance to have at least one State at the South ready with united counsels to urge a great policy on the South. The only State that could fulfill this requisite is South Carolina and it would be a matter deeply regretted if she should be in such distracted condition as not to be able to fulfil this mission." Governor R. F. W. Allston recommended that Carolinians should act with the Democracy as long as it respected the "principles" advocated by the state for the "last thirty years." But he cautioned against drifting "into the smooth current of nationalism," and he asserted that the state's "political position" was "well settled" since 1852.[5]

A secessionist consensus among the state's leaders in case the Republicans won the presidency existed as early as 1856. During the presidential campaign, Orr worked feverishly for Democratic candidate James Buchanan's election "to save the government from revolution and ruin." Pickens wrote to Armistead Burt, "If Buchanan is defeated we will be near the beginning of the end and we must solemnly prepare to meet great events." Samuel McGowan, a National Democratic legislator from Abbeville, felt that South Carolina should fight "that motley mob of Free Soilers, Fremonters, free niggers and free booters." Preston Brooks asserted that "the only mode of meeting it [free soilism] is, just to tear the Constitution of the United States, trample it underfoot, and form a Southern Confederacy, every State of which will be a slaveholding State." And Butler tried to develop Calhoun's notion of "concurrent majority" into one of "concurrent nationhood." He argued that after separation, the two sections should confederate under a "conjunctive congress" that would have little more than "advisory powers." Conservative planters such as Alfred Huger flirted with the prospect of disunion in the event of a Republican victory. He initially argued that "even if Fremont . . . gets elected it has nothing to do with the Union," but with the approach of the elections, he changed his mind and wrote that only the election of a Republican could "dissolve the confederacy if anything can dissolve it."[6]

A hollow debate about the nature of the right to secession also reflected the secessionist consensus among most prominent Carolinians. In 1857, Richard Yeadon started publishing lengthy articles in the *Charleston Courier* challenging the sacrosanct Calhounian doctrine of state sovereignty on which the constitutional right to secession rested. John Cunningham, secessionist editor of the *Charleston Evening News*, in response, repeated nullifiers' arguments for the constitutionality of the right to secession as one of the reserved rights of the states. Secessionists roundly attacked the *Courier* for giving up the cardinal doctrine of state sovereignty and for its alleged unionism. On the defensive, Yeadon replied that he believed "*original sovereignty*" to lie with the states and "derivative sovereignty" to lie with the Union, and though the right to secession was a "revolutionary" right, the federal system endowed it with "character, dignity and even sanction."[7] In the end, his understanding of secession as a revolutionary right did not seem less effective than Cunningham's espousal of the constitutional right to secession.

Buchanan's election and doubts about the willingness of the rest of the South to secede stymied disunionist plans. Leonidas Spratt claimed that the cause of the slave South in the Union was hopeless and that it was merely a matter of "prudence" for slaveholders to prepare themselves for a final separation. In a letter to Governor Adams, Rhett called on the southern states to dissolve the Union "in their sovereign capacity" and form a southern confederacy "united together by a common bond of institutions and pursuits." Released after the defeat of the Republicans, Rhett's letter was largely ignored. The legislature tabled secessionist resolutions offered by John I. Middleton and Alexander Mazyck. B. F. Perry rejoiced that the Republicans had been "crushed, and the broad, bright banner of Democracy waves victoriously over the North and the South, the East and the West." Simeon Corley, a unionist, wrote that "the demagogues of our State will have to set their wit to work, in order to hit upon some other *pretended* cause for a dissolution of the Union."[8]

Many Carolinian planter politicians felt that Buchanan's victory secured the sectional dominance of the slave South. The year 1857 "marked the high tide of the proslavery south's national political power" in the Democratic Party and the federal government. Orr was elected Speaker of the House of Representatives by a solid Democratic vote, despite his states' rights colleagues' refusal to vote for him. The *Dred Scott* decision, which endorsed the southern territorial program, strengthened Carolinian Democrats' conviction of the rightfulness of their policy. Adherence to the Democratic Party was therefore not a repudiation of the politics of slavery and separatism. In a letter to Perry, Pickens explained that "as long as the Government is on our side, I am sustaining it, and using its power for our benefit and placing the screws upon the thumbs of our opponents so as to make them feel." But, "If our opponents reverse the present state of things — seize the power of government — change the issues and overthrow the Constitution, then I am *for war*."[9]

Secessionists also started viewing party rivalries as a reflection of deeper sectional differences. They claimed that "the Democracy — for the first time in its annals, fighting under the banner of conservatism — overcame the hosts of Isms, headed and led on by" Republicans and abolitionists. They emphasized the deep divide between a conservative, God-fearing slave South and a North populated by "Socialists, Communists and Abolitionists, combined and urged on by abandoned political demagogues," and they argued that the growing strength of the Republican Party in the North revealed that northerners saw themselves as a "distinct people." Keitt predicted that the country was divided into sectional parties and that the "issue" would be made in the 1860 elections.[10]

Carolinian secessionists recommended that southerners reconstitute the Democracy as a proslavery organization. The *Charleston Mercury* argued that while the state's policy should be to "rally under the banner of the Democratic party, which has recognized and supported . . . the rights of the South," southerners should "sift and purify, the Democratic party, and strengthen it on the precise point of Southern Rights." W. H. Trescot wrote, "a few strong minds if they act in concert might give unity to the Southern feeling by embodying some policy which while it preserves the colour of a national system will be essentially based upon southern principles and look to sectional effect . . . to form a Southern party which would either succeed and thus govern the country or fail and thus form a compact Southern party ready for action." As William Gilmore Simms advised W. P. Miles, "Let all your game lie in the constant recognition and assertion of Southern nationality!"[11]

Carolinian planter politicians' honeymoon with the Democratic Party started to founder fairly early. The last stage of the fight for Kansas challenged the legitimacy of southern dictation within the Democratic Party. In South Carolina, the old fear of a free-soil cordon sanitaire strangling the slave South to death was a central concern. The state press also kept up its criticism of the territorial appointees of the administration when it detected any wavering on their part to make Kansas a slave state. When Kansas applied for admission under the proslavery Lecompton constitution, the work of men representing less than 10 percent of settlers in the territory, the *Mercury* trumpeted that a "mighty lesson" had been taught to southerners. They were apparently shown what unified determination could achieve. The Buchanan administration, hostage to the dominant southern wing of the party, backed Lecompton. While Carolinians showered praise on Buchanan, they lashed out at Stephen A. Douglas, who was unwilling to support such a perversion of popular sovereignty. D. F. Jamison pointed out the dangers of trusting northern Democrats and "squatter sovereignty" and Cunningham wrote that Douglas was "as dangerous as Seward."[12]

Carolinian politicians of all factions united to vindicate Lecompton and threaten secession. Most, including those who had reservations about Kansas such as Robert Barnwell and Cunningham, were determined that it be admitted under Lecompton. Perry claimed that the refusal of Congress to admit a slave state was "just cause" for disunion, as did Yeadon. A. G. Magrath argued that Kansas could be used to start a secession movement. The real issue between the North and South, Miles pointed out, was "slavery expansion" versus "slavery contraction." Slaveholders could not view the latter policy with "suicidal apathy" nor could they "worship" the Union "with blind devotion and superstitious attachment." Keitt and Trescot were confident that Lecompton would be accepted and the latter looked forward to the unchallenged reign of southern slaveholders in the Democracy, which would drive the Republican Party to extinction. James Henry Hammond also felt that the controversy would "blow over" and purge the Democratic Party of unsound northerners. At the same time, he wrote, "But if Kansas is *driven out of the Union for being a Slave State*, can any Slave State remain in it with honor?" As Simms advised him, "That Kansas, as an element of value to the South is of no moment; but that it rises into importance, of the most vital sort, when her recognition depends wholly upon the exclusion and denunciation of an Institution, which is inextricably wrapt [*sic*] up in the property, safety, prosperity and absolute existence of the South!" Growing indications that Lecompton could not be rammed through Congress pushed Hammond's newfound unionism to the background and he wrote that he was for "Lecompton or Separation." Only Boyce felt that slavery could never be established in Kansas and that in the end it would only divide the Democratic Party and ensure the ascendancy of the Republicans.[13]

The 1858 English compromise bill, which submitted the Lecompton constitution to Kansas voters for ratification, led to new calls for disunion in South Carolina. Milledge Luke Bonham, who along with McQueen voted against the bill, explained that he could not bring himself to compromise on the admission of a slave state and predicted disunion if Republicans won the next elections. At a public dinner in Cheraw, Mc-Queen argued that "abolitionists" and "red republicans" had teamed up with northern Democrats to prevent the admission of Kansas as a slave state. He asked his listeners to be prepared for secession. When a majority in Kansas rejected Lecompton, the *Mercury* intoned, "The South has been discomfited, beaten, cheated, and endangered."[14]

Carolinian secessionists, however, seized on the sectional division of the Democratic Party over Lecompton as the "hope of the south." Any "armistice with Douglas" and northern Democrats, they pointed out, would be giving up on the territorial position of the South. Secessionists predicted that the Democratic convention in 1860 would result in the "repudiation of Douglas and his insolent heresies, or the instant death of a party abandoning its cardinal principles." "Colleton" surmised, "The era of national parties is drawing to a close. The history of those parties is the record of southern wrongs; the overthrow of the survivor of them will be the re-establishment of Southern rights." These men felt that since the Democratic Party was stronger in the South, "why should it not turn its back on the North, and act only for the South?" They asserted, "the sectional organization will be completed by which the issue can be made." As another secessionist stated, "To herald forth the truth that Southern men would no longer be led and blinded by *Northern Democracy*, would to us be a proud day and one auspicious of future good, greatness and independence to the South." John A. Calhoun hoped that the "*National Democracy . . .* be blown to the winds" so that secessionists could confront Republicans.[15]

Maxcy Gregg issued the secessionists' manifesto in a pamphlet entitled "An Appeal to the State Rights Party of South Carolina" in 1858. The appeal based its argument on the fact that since the tariff controversy Carolinians had refused to be completely "incorporated" in the Democratic Party. Andrew P. Calhoun led off with his father's famous warning that the interests of the South should not be subordinated to that of the party. James Tradewell reminded the state of "the war of extermination" waged by the Democratic Party in 1832 against "state sovereignty" and "state rights." A. C. Garlington traced majoritarian despotism to the passage of Jackson's "Force Act" during the nullification crisis. W. E. Martin and Tradewell stressed that the Democracy could not be relied on "to uphold the rights of the slave-section" in case the Republicans won in 1860. Rhett indicated through the *Mercury* that the "Appeal" for the most part represented secessionist principles, though there is some evidence of personal rivalry between him and Gregg.[16]

Secessionists, however, failed in their attempts to form a separate sectional organization. As early as 1855, some had recommended the creation of a sectional party at a meeting in Fairfield. In 1858, William Lowndes Yancey's and Edmund Ruffin's efforts, supported by Rhett, to create a southern organization of fire-eaters, a "League of United Southerners," was largely stillborn. Responding to critics, Ruffin wrote, "The many & zealous recent defenders of the Union, & denouncers of its enemies, have been recently stimulated by the fear that . . . upholding the southern party will operate to overthrow the *national* democratic party, by driving off the smaller northern wing of that party. If the success of this party is to be best effected by injuring (& still more if by destroying) the supporters of southern rights, then I shall more anxiously wish for the speedy overthrow of the national democratic party, & its being beaten by the 'Black Republican' or abolition party, in the next presidential election."[17] But the fight for slavery would soon take place within the Democracy.

Southern advocacy of "federal protection of slavery in the territories" was not so much a conspiracy to break up the Democratic Party but a well-thought-out program to force it to adhere to the southern territorial position. As such, it was far more potent in putting nails in the coffin of the party. It struck at the heart of both Republicans' commitment to the nonextension of slavery and the northern Democratic belief that slavery was a matter of local self-government. For most southerners now demanded nothing short of ironclad federal guarantees for the extension and perpetuity of slavery as the price of their adherence to the party and the Union, a price that most northerners were unwilling to pay. Senator Albert Gallatin Brown argued for a congressional slave code as the only adequate protection for slavery in the territories. On February 2, 1860, Jefferson Davis presented his famous resolutions in the Senate asserting that if the federal judiciary and executive did not possess the "means" to protect territorial slavery then it would be "the duty of Congress to supply the deficiency." The Davis resolutions became the platform of the southern Democracy. On the other hand, Douglas insisted that territorial legislatures could prevent the growth of slavery by "unfriendly legislation" or by simply failing to pass laws for its protection. After the *Dred Scott* decision, the Lecompton controversy, and the demand for a federal slave code, the popular sovereignty theory could no longer obscure the fundamental difference between northern Democrats' advocacy of territorial sovereignty and southern espousal of territorial slavery and state sovereignty.[18]

While secessionists latched on to the slave code as a means to advance the cause of southern nationality, some deprecated the issue for dividing the Democratic Party. National Democrats repudiated both Douglas's popular sovereignty and the slave code. Pickens, who was now the American minister in Russia, argued that it was an "error" to think that Congress must protect slavery by law in the territories. At the same time he condemned "unfriendly legislation" as "mob law." The *Dred Scott* decision and the federal courts must "decide the issue." John Ashmore wrote that Douglas had been his favorite for the presidency, but since Lecompton had illustrated "his utter want of sincerity and fair-dealing," he was completely opposed to him. Earlier, Simms had charged that Orr was planning to get the vice presidential nomination on a Democratic ticket headed by Douglas. Orr's confidential letter to Hammond indicates that these speculations were without any basis. He wrote that "Douglass [*sic*] I think has settled his prospects for the Presidency and when the inquisition is held the verdict will be *felo de se*." While Orr condemned the congressional slave code as a "transparent and atrocious" ruse, he dismissed "squatter sovereignty" as an "absurdity" and Douglas's ideas as "ingenious but not profound."[19]

A few states' righters also voiced their opposition to the demand for a federal slave code. At a speech in the South Carolina upcountry district of York, Boyce argued that a "policy of moderation" was the best course for the slave South to follow in order to ensure the electoral defeat of the Republicans. He also expressed strong reservations about the practicality of slavery expansion, so much so, that the *Mercury* asked whether Boyce meant to take up the same position as the Republicans and the anti-Lecompton Democrats. Boyce, however, argued that moderation would also help "ripen public opinion" in the slave South for disunion in case a Republican was elected. James Chesnut dismissed the slave code as a "Trojan horse" and the African slave trade as "Pandora's box." He pointed out that the territories in the Southwest would become slave states as long as the federal government did not interfere. He concluded that federal courts should be left to enforce the *Dred Scott* decision. An admiring report concluded that his speech was a "triumphant answer to Judge Douglas' Squatter Sovereignty heresies."[20]

Hammond opposed the southern demand for a slave code as self-defeating and delusive but felt that Douglas should be "read out of the party." He confided to Simms, "we have been hunting elephants and caught a number—Slave Trade—Slave Code—Mexican protectorate." But when asked to speak out against them in the Senate, he replied, "Why not try to arrest a hurricane?" Trescot pointed out to Hammond that the slave code was a "logical consequence of Dred Scott." Nevertheless, Trescot argued that a slave code would be useless if the local population decided not to implement it. Also, Congress could use the precedent of federal legislation on slavery to "confer rights on blacks" and thus "[s]ubvert the power of the master and give the negro the power of perpetual destructive annoyance." But he rejected the "popular sovereignty of Douglas" for making "short shrift . . . of slavery by northern immigration." A majority of Carolinian and southern politicians, however, were not willing to retreat but wanted to push ahead in the struggle for the extension of slavery. A year later Chesnut reversed himself and argued that federal protection of territorial slavery was the "true constitutional doctrine." By the time the Democratic convention met at Charleston in 1860, most Carolinian planter politicians would be converted to the new shibboleth of a congressional slave code.[21]

Carolinian planter politicians' criticisms of popular sovereignty as mobocracy revealed an antidemocratic, proslavery perspective that put them at odds with northern Democrats. In his defense of Lecompton, Hammond argued with typical Carolinian logic that constitutions should be made by minorities as they are "administered by majorities." "Disunionist" argued, "her [the south's] claim is . . . that *no State shall be allowed to enter this Union with a Constitution prohibiting Slavery.* At any time previous it is only the people of a Territory who can speak, and they cannot derogate the rights of States. This may seem extreme, but it is extreme only inasmuch as it is the true and direct denial of the Republican doctrine, which proclaims that no State can enter with a Constitution recognizing slavery." Carolinians viewed the "hordes" of foreign immigrants as the main culprits in the move to restrict slavery. Proslavery nativism was the direct result of northern Democrats' espousal of popular sovereignty. As Rhett argued, the North ordained that "the South is to have no protection, whilst people, emigrants from Europe are to determine whether we have slaves or not, under the title of Squatter Sovereignty."

In a series of articles in the *Charleston Courier*, Douglasites upheld popular sovereignty as a defense of democracy. It is difficult to ascertain the author of these articles. One possibility was Arthur Simkins, editor of the National Democratic *Edgefield Advertiser*. "A Warning Voice" wrote that "squatter" or popular sovereignty was nothing but "the right of a people, great and small, to govern themselves." By resisting popular sovereignty or the right of the people of the territories to decide on slavery for themselves, southerners were denying the principle of democracy. "Outsiders" also chose to remind the state that "[u]niversal suffrage is an accomplished fact. The people are masters. They are sovereigns. . . . They rule in the Territories. The deluge is universal. It covers plain and hill top, valley and mountain. Who can resist it? What man—what party?" He added, "the attempt of our Southern leaders, in and out of Congress, by eloquent speeches, to stem the tide of popular supremacy is bold and spirited. It is worthy of all admiration. We know [of] nothing so plucky in history." James L. Petigru, South Carolina's only unconditionally unionist leader, argued that to "abuse" Douglas for defending the democratic right "of the people of the Territories . . . to be consulted as to the laws made for their government was the height of popular malignity and folly." He felt that Douglas should be criticized not for popular sovereignty but for his sponsorship of "the repeal of the Missouri compromise."[22]

Carolinian secessionists, however, hoped that the demand for a federal slave code would supersede partisan affiliation and loyalty to the Union. They were adamant in pursuing the territorial question as a testimony of the untrustworthiness of all northerners on the slavery question and an argument for an independent southern nation. In his 1859 Grahamville speech, Rhett assured his audience of the Third Congressional District, the only one in the state to vote for single secession in 1852, that they stood "vindicated by events." He argued that no northern party was ready to support the South and that the North, as a whole, had "become sectional." Expansion, he claimed, is the "law of all nations" and the slave South "must have expansion too." Disunion was the logical response to slavery restriction, as it was useless for the South to fight against the "despotism" of "an absolute democracy." In October 1859, the Rhetts, father and son, printed a proposed plan of action for southerners at the Charleston Democratic Party convention under the heading, "measures of southern resistance to northern rule." According to this plan, southern Democrats should support only those candidates who agree to the southern platform on territorial slavery.

Rhett's plans were part of the "fateful partnership" he had formed with Yancey to advocate a slave code. In a speech at Columbia, the state's capital, Yancey announced, "Slavery exists nowhere by law of Congress — its basis is a much higher law . . . but to exist in its perfection, to claim the full rights to which it is entitled, it demands that protection against felony to which every other species of property is entitled." He urged all "state rights men" in the South to participate in the Democratic convention to fight for the southern territorial program and to "secede from the convention" if their demands were not met. At the Alabama Democratic convention, Yancey argued that the main principle of southern Democrats was the "full protection" of slavery by the federal government. The convention recommended that its delegates withdraw from the national Democratic convention if it was not adopted by the party. The headlines from the *Charleston Mercury* literally screamed its approval: "Alabama in the Lead" and "Alabama All Right." In July 1859, the Mississippi Democratic convention announced that the party doctrine of congressional noninterference with slavery was not applicable to the protection of territorial slavery. Carolinian secessionists argued that their state would stand by Alabama and Mississippi and repudiate anyone who equivocated on the southern platform or who supported Douglas, as "[t]he Charleston convention may fill an important page in history. It may tell of the rebound of a great and free people in the maintenance of their rights, or tell of their final submission and downfall."

But secessionists felt that the state should stick to the old Calhounian policy of avoiding party conventions and support all such efforts from the outside. The Charleston convention, they reasoned, was tainted by northern participation, as northern Democrats were just as bad as Republicans when it came to the territorial position of the slave South; one was "Lucifer" and the other "Satan." Dismissing the National Democrats as representing only a handful from Edgefield and Anderson, they argued that South Carolina should not participate in any convention unless it was a southern convention. They feared that the convention would abandon southern "principles" and perhaps nominate a "supple, venal tool from the South" who would get southern support only because of his "nationality." The *Southron* of Orangeburg noted that the convention may nominate "Senator [Stephen Benedict] *Arnold* Douglas." Hammond also opposed the idea of the state being represented at the convention. However, heeding Orr's friendly yet emphatic warning, he kept his opposition to the convention private.[23]

A few secessionists, however, recognized the importance of the state's participation in the 1860 national Democratic convention. Paul Quattlebaum preferred to forge southern unity and to fight for the southern territorial program in the convention. As Trescot wrote to Miles, these men wanted "to either give the Democratic party a Southern character or else having demonstrated that impossibility to be in position to ask for concerted Southern action as the only alternative." And Cunningham wrote, "I am opposed to National or party conventions as a regular system of party machinery, but I am much inclined to think that it would be wise for the State Rights Democracy of South Carolina to supercede the nationals *for once*, and send an able and true delegation into the Charleston convention." Governor W. H. Gist felt each group should go ahead and follow their own course without criticizing the other. He was eager to avoid any conflict that would threaten Carolinian leaders' unity on disunion.[24]

The South Carolina legislature endorsed the policy of "backing Alabama" from the sidelines. Edmund Rhett presented resolutions in the senate stating that it was against the policy of the state to participate in "any caucus or convention with the people of the Northern States" for the nomination of presidential candidates. In the end, only 37 members of the 169-strong legislature endorsed the state's participation at the Charleston convention. B. H. Wilson of Prince George Winyaw, a National Democrat, declared that "the Union will *and ought to be dissolved*" and that "minor differences of opinion" on the "question of expediency should cease." W. D. Porter claimed that the only reason he did not join the convention movement was because he was president of the state senate, a body that disapproved of participation in party conventions.[25]

The conventionists, composed predominantly of the National Democrats, argued that the South should unite under the auspices of the Democracy to defeat the Republicans. In February 1860, James Simons, J. J. Pettigrew, and Michael O'Connor presided over a convention meeting in Charleston. National Democrats held other local meetings for the selection of delegates to the convention, which was to be held on April 16, 1860. At the convention in Columbia, seven of the state's twenty-nine districts, consisting mostly of the lowcountry parishes, were not represented and nine districts had sent only one representative each. The state's National Democratic leadership were present in full force. In his opening address, Orr stressed the importance of acting with the Democratic Party when "not only is the maintenance of our principles involved, but the fate of the Government itself for weal or for woe, for all time to come, is to be decided on the approaching Presidential contest." He broadly hinted at secession in the case of a Republican victory, arguing that such an eventuality would force the slaveholding states to "strike a blow." The convention nominated him for the presidency. In his acceptance speech, Orr argued that he was all for preserving the government as long as southern "interests" were respected. "If not . . . there can be no hesitation as to the course the people of the Southern States must pursue." Despite several attempts, the convention did not adopt the Alabama platform for the federal protection of territorial slavery. The resolutions adopted by the convention, based on those presented by J. D. Pope, Perry, and James Farrow, denied territories the power to act on slavery before statehood and endorsed the *Dred Scott* decision but did not demand a slave code or instruct its delegates to withdraw from the Charleston convention if the southern platform were not adopted. Perry wrote to his wife that the Columbia gathering had proceeded "harmoniously" for the most part. But the *Mercury* warned, "A trimming course cannot be acceptable to the people of this State, especially where great vital principles are at stake."[26]

Secessionists were nervous that the National Democrats would be willing to support Douglas. Trescot feared that if there was a choice between Douglas and a Republican, there might be a "strong party" for the former. Huger thought that Orr would "barter away" the state delegation to Douglas. But most conventionists felt like Quattlebaum that "if we have to triumph with Douglas as a leader, success will be little better than defeat." Even unionist John Belton O'Neall dismissed Douglas "as a drinking rowdy and bargaining politician." Hammond wrote that he had never heard of any South Carolinian support Douglas after Lecompton. Perhaps the only bonafide Douglas supporters in the state were Simkins and the ambitious Sue Keitt, who wanted her husband named as the vice presidential nominee on a Douglas ticket. Robert N. Gourdin, the secessionist Charleston merchant, was confident that no southerner would support Douglas or the Cincinnati popular sovereignty platform. Muscoe R. M. Garnett asked the question on everybody's mind: Would the Carolinians follow Alabama out of the convention?[27] The obduracy of secessionists had ensured that only the most moderate men represented the state at one of the pivotal events leading to secession.

The breakup of the Democratic Party took place appropriately on Carolinian planter politicians' turf. While Charleston, thanks to its disparate population of merchants and mechanics, had not been a stronghold of nullification and secession, it was also home to the planter aristocracy, the unrelenting *Mercury*, and the most advanced productions of proslavery thought. E. G. Mason reported that Charlestonians spent much time convincing outsiders that slavery was a "patriarchal institution" and the "best possible arrangement for the black man" and that "[e]very chance was seized upon to uphold the assumption of South Carolina's independence of the rest of the world. . . . [T]he disunion feeling was universal." Thomas Ravenel exemplified the attitude of separatist lowcountry planters when he noted in his diary, "Charleston was disgraced for a week by having her streets invaded at liberty by real genuine Abolitionists under the garb of National Democracy" and that it was "impertinence" on the part of others to force "the presence of the Convention" on the state. As one Douglasite said, "Charleston is the last place on Gods Earth where a national convention should have been held." "Many Citizens" wrote in the *Charleston Courier* that the "free State section" men had flooded the city to "control" the convention and counteract the "political atmosphere of South Carolina."[28]

Caleb Cushing, president of the convention, completed the irony of the Democratic Party meeting on Carolina soil when in his opening address he referred to Calhoun as a party leader par excellence. For Douglas's followers more was at stake than the presidency since Douglas epitomized the principle of popular sovereignty, the only territorial platform that northern Democrats were willing to adhere to. The lower south delegations, however, were prepared to stake the existence of the party on federal protection of territorial slavery. Administration or Buchanan men formed a small third group, whose bitter hatred of Douglas matched that of the southern fire-eaters. Douglas had already made clear that he would not accept the nomination of the convention if it adopted the slave code, and most southerners viewed Douglas's elevation to the presidency to be little better then the victory of a Republican president. There was, as Murat Halstead observed, "an irreconcilable difference in the doctrines respecting slavery in the Territories between the Northern and Southern wings of the Democratic party."[29]

The impossibility of constructing a bisectional consensus on the issue of territorial slavery became evident. The only unanimous decision made by all sides was to dispose of the troublesome question of slavery in the territories by working out the party platform before the selection of a presidential nominee. On April 27, the fifth day of the convention, the committee on resolutions presented three reports on the party platform. W. W. Avery of North Carolina presented the majority report, which embodied the southern position. It proclaimed that neither the federal government nor the territorial legislatures had the power to abolish slavery, and that it was the "duty" of the federal government to protect slavery in the "high seas" and the "territories." The Douglasite minority report, introduced by Henry B. Payne of Ohio, endorsed the 1856 Cincinnati popular sovereignty platform and promised to abide by the decisions of the Supreme Court. A third report, filed by Benjamin F. Butler of Massachusetts, simply readopted the Cincinnati platform. Payne pleaded with southerners not to insist on new guarantees for territorial slavery and "tie our hands" in the fight against Republicans. Yancey made the "speech of the convention," which set the stage for the secession of the Lower South. He recalled that the northwestern Democracy and their "leader" had not stood by the slave South during the fight for Kansas. But the biggest sin of northern Democrats was that they thought slavery was "wrong"; therefore, like free soilism, "squatter sovereignty" ordained the nonextension of slavery. Yancey received prolonged ovations from the galleries and the *Mercury* characterized his effort as "brilliant."[30]

The deep south secessionists were determined to make or break the party on the federal protection of territorial slavery. Some southern members of Congress, including Carolinians, were telegraphing their delegations to follow Alabama out of the convention if it did not adopt the southern platform. Predictably, on the adoption of the Douglas platform, the Gulf squadron, led by Alabama, chugged out of the convention. Leroy Pope Walker went over familiar grounds to explain the reasons for Alabama's withdrawal. Most revealing was his contention that the southern report represented the votes of those states in which the Democratic Party was in the ascendancy, but that the Douglas report represented a northern majority, a section where the party was sure to lose. As Burrows of Arkansas in his diatribe against the "half-and-half Free Soilism of the Northern Democrats" argued, the "Democratic party is the South, and the South is the Democratic party." Northern delegates replied that if this novel rule of party membership had been applied earlier, then much of the South would have been excluded from the 1852 Democratic convention on the basis of their vote for Taylor. The impasse broadened when Mississippi, Louisiana, South Carolina, Florida, Texas, and part of the Arkansas delegation left the convention. General James Simons presented the protest of the South Carolina delegation, basing their withdrawal on the fact that the platform adopted was contrary to the position on territorial slavery adopted by the state convention. The next day most of Georgia's and the rest of the Arkansas delegation walked out, making the cotton states' secession complete. Halstead wrote, "The Convention was under the frown of King Cotton, and his displeasure was upon it like a blight or deadly nightshade." With the exception of Arkansas, these states would also lead the secession movement.[31]

The ghost of Calhoun, whose grave lay in the city, had triumphed over Jackson's legacy. Charlestonians wildly applauded the seceders. Serenades, meetings, public orations, banners, and torchlight processions gave the city a festive air. At long last, Carolinian newspapers proclaimed, " 'Southern Rights' and 'Southern Interests' are not to be considered footballs for politicians and Janus-faced carpenters of ambiguous platforms." Ravenel proudly affirmed "the true Southern influence of Charleston and the State" that had "burst" open the Democratic convention and formed a "Convention of the Cotton States." While Carolinian secessionists had nothing but praise for the departing delegates, they vented their ire on the remaining southerners. They accused the Upper South of "squatterism" and sympathy for Douglas and declared that "the people of the cotton states must take care of themselves." Secessionists reserved their special disapprobation for the two Carolinian unionists who chose to remain in the convention, Perry and Lemuel Boozer of Lexington. Both were loudly booed and hissed by the Charlestonians in the galleries every time they spoke or cast a vote. Simkins, who was also against the withdrawal, had been called home on a family emergency.[32]

Carolinian secessionists' hopes were focused on the seceding delegations. Magrath wrote that "all of good or ill which is to follow depends upon the proceedings in the Southern convention." The seceders congregated at St. Andrew's hall and on Yancey's suggestion decorously named themselves "Constitutional Democrats" rather than "Seceding Democrats" or "Disunion Democrats." A new name was necessary, Yancey pointed out, because "this is not a Convention of the Democracy of the United States. It is palpable that it is not. This is a Convention of several Southern States—probably nine Southern States." John S. Preston of South Carolina was made chair of the convention, which adopted the southern platform.

Meanwhile, the upper south states played the same role that most of them would in the secession crisis: stalling and fighting the southern battle within the party before joining the Deep South. The Democratic convention deadlocked over the presidential nomination. On May 3 the national convention adjourned to meet again in Baltimore in June, as did the seceders' convention, to reconvene in Richmond. This was not before Bayard and his fellow Delaware delegate retired from the seceders' convention, carrying out the principle of seceding from conventions "reductio ad absurdum," according to one witty observer.[33]

Some Carolinian politicians expressed reservations at the breakup of the Democratic Party. Perry, Orr, and Ashmore, who were in the minority even among the National Democrats now, were confident that they could have defeated the Douglas forces and then gone on to defeat the Republicans. Perry blamed the "outside pressure" of "inflammatory speeches," southern caucuses, the galleries, and Charleston newspapers for putting added strain on the unity of the convention. He warned that Douglas's forces had been reactivated in the southern states in an effort to send delegations favorable to him. The Richmond convention, he felt, would be a "mischievous abortion," as the upper south states would not join it. Orr and Ashmore felt that if the seceders had stayed on in the convention they would have succeeded in nominating a suitable southerner.[34]

This analysis was shared by some southern Democrats in Congress who remained anti-Douglas and firmly committed to the southern position on the territories. They penned an address to the Democracy in the South recommending that they return to the Baltimore convention, but they also firmly endorsed the seceders' demand for the congressional protection of territorial slavery. The Southern Address was signed by senators from Georgia, Louisiana, Arkansas, and Virginia; Davis; and ten southern representatives. Carolinian secessionists such as Gourdin could hardly believe that southern leaders would refuse to fully "stand by" the Charleston walkout. The *Mercury*, while praising the fact that not a single Alabama or South Carolina congressman had signed the address, typically accused the signers of the Address unfairly of supporting "Douglas principles."[35]

Carolinian secessionists were determined to preserve the results of the lower south walkout at Charleston. Announcing a historic change in their policy, Rhett argued that the state must participate in the Richmond convention because it was a "sectional Convention, called by one section of the Union, to support rights and interests belonging to one section of the Union, and acknowledged but by one section of the Union." The "contest" was over the territories: the slave south would either have the territories or discard the Union. National Democrats agreed to a new state convention and delegation to Richmond. A public meeting at Charleston set the tone for local meetings by "heartily" approving of the Charleston walkout and demanding the federal protection of territorial slavery. The meeting chose nationals such as Pettigrew and Pope, secessionists such as Rhett Jr. and Martin, and a moderate states' righter, I. W. Hayne, to represent the district. Hayne applauded this political unanimity and Miles pointed to the insignificance of "political differences" in the state. Hammond emphasized the importance of maintaining the unity of "the eight seceding *Cotton* states." Similar meetings were held in Kershaw, Gilionsville, Christ Church, Sumter, Chesterfield, Kingstree, St. George's, St. Stephen's, and Beaufort. For the secessionist lowcountry aristocracy, the Richmond convention would be the first step in the formation of a southern nation. A St. Paul's gathering demanded that the state be freed "from the bonds of this unnatural alliance" to form a "*Southern Confederacy.*"[36]

The new state convention that convened at Columbia on May 30 was a very different body than its predecessor. Only 52 of the 161 delegates to the earlier convention were present. Representation to the convention was organized on the basis of the state's lopsided legislative apportionment, and as the parishes were present in full force, secessionists were clearly in the majority. John H. Means, South Carolina's governor during the first secession crisis, presided. On behalf of the fire-eaters, Edmund Rhett proposed that representatives from the state's election districts and parishes form the committee to select delegates. Rhett's proposal, based on the malapportioned representative system, would give the secessionists a decisive advantage. "The Parishes," he insisted, "wished to be heard." The National Democrats preferred a committee composed of representatives from the congressional districts. Reed, from the nonplantation-belt district of Anderson, strongly protested Rhett's scheme, evoking age-old sectional grievances: "Was it right that the 3600 of Spartanburg District, or the 3000 of another, should have no more voice in a popular election than fifty or a hundred gentlemen who live in a Parish below?" A resolution for choosing the state's delegation by a general vote in the convention was accepted as a substitute for Rhett's proposal. Since the convention itself was based on the malapportioned representative system, secessionists won their point.

The men who were at the cutting edge of southern nationalism in South Carolina would represent their state in Richmond. In the first show of strength, Rhett defeated Hayne by eighty-four to sixty-seven votes. It was clear that the secessionist offensive spearheaded by the Rhetts had been successful. Franklin Gaillard angrily charged that Hayne's smaller vote actually represented "three-fourths of the people of South Carolina." Adroit historians have calculated that according to the 1850 census Rhett's entire vote represented 11,000 fewer citizens than the vote for Hayne. If calculated according to the 1860 census the difference was even greater. One by one, the Charleston delegates withdrew their names from the ballot, taking Rhett's election "as a condemnation of the Convention party of South Carolina." In the end, along with Rhett, Middleton, Garlington, and Armistead Burt were elected as delegates at large with some of the upcountry districts refusing to vote. Burt, who had been inactive in state politics since the defeat of secession in 1852, proudly affirmed his nullifier and disunionist credentials. Rhett accepted his nomination in a conciliatory speech. Secessionists such as Martin, John Townsend, A. P. Aldrich, Jamison, Benjamin Waldo, and A. P. Calhoun made up the rest of the delegation.

National Democrats warned that sending such a flagrantly disunionist delegation to Richmond would damage southern unity, as most southern Democrats looked to the reconstruction of their party on the southern territorial platform. Huger resented "S.C. being put upon the Gallop, only to try the height and width, of 'bank and ditch' before others venture to 'take the leap!'" John Preston claimed that "the real state of Southern sentiment is misunderstood in South Carolina where a blind irritation exists." Secessionists made it clear that they were not going to Richmond for the "reintegration" of the Democratic Party but to uphold "southern principles" to the bitter end. Aldrich argued that they had participated in the convention not as members of the Democratic Party but as "southerners" and "slaveholders." In a meeting at St. John's Colleton, Townsend reiterated that the state needed "strong" representation at this stage. Alarmed at the difference of opinion, Ruffin reported that there was not much more support for secession in the northern part of South Carolina than there was in Virginia. But the nationals had been just as staunch defenders of the slave South as their more extreme counterparts. One of Hammond's correspondents explained, "The unpleasant jar which was recently developed in the convention in Columbia I cannot regard as important because all parties are agreed upon the majority platform of the Charleston convention — and the only strife seems to be — who shall keep the ball moving which was put in motion by the seceders from the Charleston convention."[37]

Carolinian secessionists understood their role perfectly. Ruffin noted that "not one of these [cotton] states will move in secession first & alone, unless S.C. will." Jamison asked, "what can an inflexible Southern man achieve in Richmond? Nothing I fear, but aid in preventing our State from the humiliating position of knocking for admission at the doors of the Baltimore Convention." Or as Simms asserted, "no more tampering with the enemy, no more compromise bolstering up a dwindling party to the ruin of the South." In Richmond, the South Carolina and Florida delegations alone were not instructed to seek admittance into the Baltimore convention. The "Constitutional Democratic convention" quickly adjourned after meeting for two days, even though Carolinians tried to contest the adjournment. Not only were most of the delegations following the plan of the Southern Address and the instructions of their state conventions, which had accredited them to Richmond and Baltimore, but the formation of contesting Douglas delegations from Georgia, Alabama, and Louisiana made it imperative for the southern cause that the Charleston delegations from these states fight for readmission in Baltimore. All the cotton states, except South Carolina, attended the Democratic convention. The Carolinian delegates instead met on June 21 and adjourned every day waiting for their southern brethren.[38]

The Baltimore convention proved that Carolinian secessionists had been right in smelling blood with the Charleston breakup. The upper south states, led by Virginia, insisted that all the seceding delegations be readmitted. The Douglasites proposed their own formula for readmission contained in the committee of credentials' majority report. It reseated the seceding Mississippi and Texas delegations, divided the votes of Georgia and Arkansas between the contesting delegations, and seated the Douglas delegations from Louisiana and Alabama. Northern Democrats were determined to punish Yancey and Slidell for the party split at Charleston but seemed to have presented the report in a spirit of compromise. At one point they even indicated their willingness to reseat the seceding Louisiana delegates as long as the odious Yancey delegation from Alabama was kept out. But southerners refused to back down, and on the adoption of the majority report, the upper south states seceded from the convention. According to Halstead, "The Democracy of the Northwest rose out of the status of serfdom. There was servile insurrection, with attendant horrors, and Baltimore became a political St. Domingo." The convention nominated Douglas for the presidency. In his acceptance speech, Douglas vowed to save the Union from "interventionists" — northern abolitionists and southern disunionists.[39]

Carolinian secessionists declared that the Democratic Party was dead and recommended the same remedy for the Union. The Charleston and Baltimore seceders met at the Institute Hall in Baltimore and speedily adopted the southern platform on the federal protection of territorial slavery and nominated John Breckinridge for the presidency and Joseph Lane of Oregon for the vice presidency. The main event of the meeting was an endless speech by Yancey pronounced to be a distinct "disenchanter." Apparently, his florid oratory and secessionist rhetoric made little headway outside Charleston, and he embarrassed those who were trying to rid themselves of the disunionist label. Some southern delegates then proceeded to Richmond and saved face for the waiting Carolinian delegation by attending the defunct cotton states' convention and rubber-stamping the Breckinridge ticket. A Douglasite at Baltimore fighting against the readmission of the seceding delegations had cleverly congratulated South Carolina for being "the only State that had preserved its dignity and stuck to its disunionist principles." Hammond wrote to Simms that he was glad that South Carolina was not part of the "pitiful political exhibition" by the southern states to "sneak back to Baltimore" and "humbly intreat [sic] to be re-admitted."[40]

The death of Jacksonian democracy resembled its birth. As in 1824, four candidates crowded the presidential elections. But it was the first time in the history of the Union that party politics represented values so much at war with each other. The two Democratic nominations completed the four-cornered presidential contest of 1860. While the Democratic Party was self-destructing under the pressure of the slavery issue, the newly formed Constitutional Union Party, composed of Opposition Party men mainly from the Upper South and conservative unionists from the North, met and nominated John Bell of Tennessee and Edward Everett of Massachusetts for the presidency and vice presidency. The Constitutional Union Party platform espoused a broad and nebulous commitment to "THE CONSTITUTION OF THE COUNTRY, THE UNION OF THE STATES, AND THE ENFORCEMENT OF THE LAWS" as the only principle that both North and South could agree on. In Chicago, Abraham Lincoln and Hannibal Hamlin were nominated for the Republican ticket. The Republican plank unequivocally declared "freedom" to be "the nominal condition of the territory of the United States."[41] In a very real sense, in 1860, the nation was presented with the choice to be all free or all slave.

On the eve of secession, several events revealed how vulnerable Carolinian planter politicians felt even in this stronghold of proslavery and separatist sentiment. Just as the Vesey conspiracy and Nat Turner's rebellion over three decades earlier had strengthened most Carolinian planter politicians' resolve for nullification, abolitionist John Brown's attempt to start a slave insurrection at Harpers Ferry bolstered the argument for secession. In October 1859, news of the raid and evidence of abolitionist involvement filled the state press. Harpers Ferry, the *Charleston Mercury* stated, was nothing more than a practical application of antislavery ideology. Secessionists dismissed Brown as a "treacherous and desperate hyena" and the raid as a "silly invasion of Virginia," but they claimed, "Our connection with the North, is a standing instigation of insurrection in the South." Trescot felt that Brown was merely a "symptom" of the country's "political disease." Secessionists used the raid to illustrate that they had been correct all along. The *Mercury* concluded, "The South must control her own destinies or perish."[42]

John Brown's raid also pushed moderates and conditional unionists to take an openly disunionist stand. Perry introduced a disunionist resolution in the legislature that stated that the "domestic institution of African slavery" is "in the best interests and happiness of the white and black races," which Carolinians would be willing "to protect and defend at any and every sacrifice of their political relations with the Federal Government and the Northern States, should it be invaded and assailed in any manner and form whatever." Another unionist, F. I. Moses of Claremont, declared that he never thought he would live to see the day when he thought of the Union as a "nuisance." In a speech on Senator James Mason's Harpers Ferry resolution in Congress, Chesnut warned, "We cannot permit the Union to be a mere badge of servitude . . . we will sunder the Union, pull it to pieces, column, base, and tower, before we will submit to be crushed by a Government, which is our own as well as yours." Huger declared, "We are on the verge of disruption! A Great Empire is to be overthrown! . . . [F]or once let the public mind be given to serious things — and let the little details of Revolution take care of themselves!" Hammond and Pickens felt that the time had come for the South to demand additional guarantees for slavery. C. G. Memminger claimed, "Every village bell [in the North] which tolled its solemn note at the execution of Brown proclaims to the South the approbation of that village of insurrection and servile war."[43]

A nagging conviction that antislavery forces would encourage internal challenges to slave society fueled Carolinian planter politicians' fears. Their perceptions of the Republican Party came to be guided by this fear and the very term "Black Republican" embodied it. When the Republican Party put up its first presidential candidate in 1856, parts of the slave South were aflame with reports of slave rebellion. John Brown, slave rebellion, abolitionists, and the Republican Party came to be indelibly connected in the minds of Carolinian slaveholders.[44]

During the speakership controversy in Congress in December 1859, Carolinians and southerners attacked Republicans for allegedly collaborating with Brown. Representative Clark of Missouri introduced a resolution that stated that no member of the House who had endorsed Hinton Rowan Helper's book *The Impending Crisis* should be considered "fit" to hold the office of Speaker. Helper, a native of North Carolina, had written an economic indictment of the system of slavery from the perspective of southern nonslaveholders. Clark's resolution was clearly aimed at John Sherman of Ohio, the leading Republican candidate, who had signed a written endorsement of Helper's *Compendium*, which contained pertinent selections from his book. While Helper was probably not an accurate representative of the opinions of most southern nonslaveholders, his proposal for a class revolt against the regime of slaveholders was particularly frightening to Carolinian secessionists, who condemned his book as the "black banner of treason." Not only did lower south representatives prove to be unbending in their opposition to the Republican majority, but the opposition of nine representatives from Alabama and South Carolina ensured the defeat of John A. McClernand, a Douglas Democrat, whose election as Speaker would have put an end to the impasse. Ashmore was the only Carolinian to cast his vote for McClernand, and he would be heartily abused by the secessionist press for his defection. Ashmore was, however, satisfied that he had "at least broken the back of JOHN SHERMAN, upon his Helper indorsement, if we have not broken his neck." The rest of the Carolina delegation held firm against all Republicans and Douglas Democrats. Repeatedly, southern representatives refused to adopt the plurality rule that had resolved similar deadlocks in 1849–50 and 1855–56. Ashmore wrote in despair, "We have no organization of the House yet, nor does there seem to be much prospect ahead."[45]

Carolinian secessionists hatched bizarre plans for disunion during the impasse. Governor Gist assured Miles that not only would he reconvene the legislature but he would "have a Regiment in or near Washington in the shortest possible time" if necessary. Apparently, Governor Henry Wise of Virginia was prepared to do the same. The atmosphere in the House was particularly volatile during this time, with most members carrying weapons to their seats. Ruffin described the scene in the House chamber: "The middle aisle is the separation of the two parties, of democratic & mostly southern members on the right (of the speaker,) and on the left, exclusively northern, & 'republican' or abolition, or Brown-Helper party men." A year earlier, Keitt had instigated a melee on the floor because Representative Galusha Grow, a "damned Black Republican puppy," had wandered over to his side of the chamber. Commenting on the incident and recalling Brooks's assault on Sumner, Trescot wrote, "I have a nervous apprehension of some new mortification whenever I hear that a South Carolinian has been distinguishing himself." Susanna

Keitt felt that "war" might break out at any minute. Keitt confessed that he had not ventured into the House for "fear of catching a stray bullet." He argued that southerners were not resisting an "individual" but rather the Republican Party and the antislavery crusade. Huger wrote that he "looked daily for the shedding of blood in the House of Representatives!" He felt that if Sherman were elected southerners could not remain in the House without "dishonoring themselves." Rhett recommended that they withdraw from Congress if any Republican were elected Speaker.[46]

The speakership contest was a good gauge of southern nationalist sentiment in the Lower South and South Carolina. In a speech before the house, Bonham declared that he received his "first political lesson" as a boy during nullification and that "disunion is not now the bugbear that it once was." He pronounced the elementary principle of southern nationalism: "*There is a treason, now known to the South greater than the treason of disunion, and that is treason to the South itself, and her constitutional rights.*" He went on to argue that if a Republican were elected president, his state would immediately secede and that slavery was a " 'moral, social and political' blessing and good" that would be preserved in or out of the Union. Northerners, he claimed, could not hope to arouse his slaves, who loyally tended to his family armed with guns, or the nonslaveholders, who knew that they had "the right" to possess slaves and would faithfully defend the slave South. Boyce argued that the Republican Party's identification with Brown and Helper confirmed that it was a "revolutionary party," a party committed to "perpetual war" against southern slaveholders. Keitt announced to the assembled House that he was willing to "shatter this Republic from turret to foundation stone." He proclaimed, "The South will resist, to the overthrow of the Government, the ascendancy of the Republican party, because its principles conduct to her destruction." Republicans, he claimed, intended to "build a wall of fire around the south till it succumbs to servile war, famine and pestilence." The Union, he noted, could be destroyed by the act of any one southern state and if the federal government waged war against that state then the rest of the South would come to its defense and organize a "slaveholding confederacy." Despite Carolinian threats of secession, southerners acquiesced to the election of William Pennington, a moderate Republican from New Jersey, as Speaker.[47]

The Helper controversy and John Brown's raid aggravated Carolinian slaveholders' suspicions about the loyalty of nonslaveholders and slaves to slave society. Brown and his allies, Carolinian newspapers warned, had other plans for instigating slave revolts all over the South that they could not publish because of their "incendiary nature." Descriptions of

Brown's maps of the southern states containing census figures led many to believe that he had planned several rebellions in areas containing a black majority. This logic indicated that virtually the whole of South Carolina was ripe for a slave revolt. The state was gripped by a paroxysm of fear of "northern agents" and servile insurrection. Random and planned acts of violence against anyone suspected of hostility to slavery punctuated the two years before disunion. A "lady" in Aiken was summarily ordered to leave the state because of a letter she wrote "filled with low abuse and palpable misrepresentation of slavery, southerners and southern life." British consul Robert Bunch, who sympathized with the secessionists, reported on the "reign of terror." He wrote, "Persons are torn away from their residences and pursuits; sometimes 'tarred and feathered'; 'ridden upon rails,' or cruelly whipped; letters are opened at the Post Offices; discussion upon slavery is entirely prohibited under penalty of expulsion, with or without violence, from the country." In the most dramatic incident, an Irish stonecutter was lynched and then tarred and feathered in Columbia. Reverend Iveson Brookes claimed that not a single slaveholder was involved in the incident, which he dismissed as the work of "city mechanics" and rowdy students. But he justified the action taken by "exasperated citizens" against "those suspected to be Brown's agents." In Charleston, Judge T. J. Withers condemned a black British sailor to death for hiding a slave beneath his ship berth, despite the sailor's protestations that he had nothing to do with the runaway slave. Petigru, who refused to get caught up in the hysteria engulfing the state, managed to persuade the governor to commute the sentence, much to Withers's ire.

The slaveholding gentry sanctioned, and at times coordinated, reprisals against suspected abolitionists even though they demurred at the disorderliness of vigilante activity. In Orangeburg, four men — a schoolteacher, two painters from New York and North Carolina, and a "book agent" — were ordered to leave the village by a committee of "gentlemen" in late November 1859. A few days later, "a portion of the most respectable gentlemen" in Kingstree, Williamsburg district, met and decided to expel two northern schoolteachers suspected of being abolitionists. While the teachers' employers vowed to resist the committee, about 250 armed men stood by to implement its decision. District notables presided over a public meeting at which it was decided that the teachers would be allowed to remain until the end of their school terms. A Committee of twenty was then constituted to carry out the decision. Reverend W. L. Wallace recommended the creation of "vigilant associations," as he felt "the conduct of some negro[e]s in this District very suspicious, and [they] should, therefore be watched." The fact that the people of Williamsburg nearly precipitated an armed clash in their eagerness to hunt down "incendiaries" alarmed some observers. Rhett presented a plan for "the safety of the south" and recommended that a Committee of Safety of "older" and "discreet" men and a Committee of Vigilance of "young men" should be formed in each district, county, or parish in the South. Soon committees started springing up all over the state supplementing the local militia cum slave patrols. The Orangeburg Vigilance Committee had to put a stop to the indiscriminate naming of suspected subversives, as some residents took advantage of the atmosphere to try to square old rivalries. David Gavin noted, "A good many persons who are suspected of abolition principles and abolition emissaries have been lynched and expelled from the country by Lynch Law." He felt that laws should be passed to legitimize such activities and for the better "regulation" of the free black population. Commenting on Brown's hanging, he wrote that if southerners had "the sense and judgement they had the reputation for," they would convict and hang many more who are abolitionists or who support abolitionists. The rice planters of St. John's Berkeley met at Black Oak to form a vigilance committee as the parish police system was "insufficient for the exigencies of the times." Abolitionists, they warned, could come in various guises — "the holy fire of the messenger of God," "the humble garb of poverty," "the school master warmly welcomed to the family hearth," or "the book or map agent hospitably entertained."[48]

The Helper controversy provoked fears of nonslaveholders' loyalty to the slave South. Harold Wyllys, a Greenville farmer, was arrested by the district vigilance committee for distributing copies of *The Impending Crisis*. A. B. Crook, president of the committee, reported to Perry that "a reading negro preacher" also had copies of the incriminating book. Helper's book and "other pamphlets of similar character" were found in Wyllys's home. Crook felt that he should be kept in jail and "tied and hung [*sic*]." Wyllys was sentenced to a year in prison, and we do not know what happened to the black preacher, who probably had a more dire fate awaiting him. Alluding to the fact that Helper's book was endorsed by the governor of New York and members of Congress, Crook concluded, "If we really live under a general Government incapable of protecting us from such attacks the sooner we get rid of it the better." In April 1860 a number of confiscated books and pamphlets were burned in front of the Greenville court house. A "non-slaveholder," who wrote long rebuttals of Helper's arguments, cleverly used the opportunity to ask for more appropriations for free schools, as it was "painful" for him to see a "white man" who could not "write his name." The obstinate unionism of Greenville's mountain yeomanry worried secessionists. As D. H. Hamilton argued, "I tell you, when the battle comes in earnest, when talking is at end, and we find ourselves fairly embarked in a contest which will shake the world, you will find an element of great weakness in our non-slaveholding population. Unfortunately this knowledge will not avail us now, we have chosen to bring the issue upon the question of Slavery, and we must take the consequences." He asked, "think you that 360,000 slaveholders, will dictate terms for 3,000,000 of non-slaveholders at the South. — I fear not, I mistrust our own people more that I fear all the efforts of the Abolitionists."[49]

These periodic outbursts belied Carolinian slaveholders' much-vaunted faith in slave society. The state's black majority, the relatively unsupervised slave population in isolated lowcountry plantations, and absentee masters fed anxieties in times of crisis. Customary privileges that slaves and the free black population had gradually won in defiance of the letter of the law became prime targets of proscription during such periods. Charleston's free black community was particularly vulnerable. A series of articles entitled "Where are we drifting to?" by "A Slaveholder" in the *Charleston Mercury* embodied such attacks. "A Slaveholder" evoked the draconian slave codes and laws passed in the aftermath of the 1739 Stono rebellion and the Vesey conspiracy. "Another Slaveholder" wanted to know what had happened to the South Carolina Association that had terrorized the streets of Charleston after the Vesey affair and demanded the immediate abolition of the practice of slave hiring.[50]

As if to make sure that the lesson of Harpers Ferry would not be forgotten, Ruffin sent a pike used by Brown and his men to Governor Gist and requested that it be displayed prominently in the state house. Gist complied and asked the legislature to thank Ruffin, much to the old Virginian's discomfiture, who thought that "[t]he Gov. of S.C. has taken more notice of the presentation of my pike to that state than the case required." The governor argued that since the state was "exposed . . . to secret emissaries inciting our slaves to insubordination and insurrection," a new law mandating the presence of the master or a "white man" throughout the year for "any quantity of negroes" was needed. The assembly passed a rash of legislation that reflected slaveholders' nightmares of subversion and slave insurrection. Bills creating a night police guard in Georgetown and a fire guard and a rifle regiment in Charleston were rapidly enacted. The Joint Committee on the Military reported a measure that strengthened the state's militia system to "meet any sudden emergency which may arise from the political condition of affairs." Three newly passed laws entitled "An Act to punish attempts to poison," "An Act to regulate the granting of licences to itinerant Salesmen and Travelling Agents," and "An Act to provide for the Peace and Security of this State" contained stringent provisions designed to check slave rebelliousness and "dangerous interference with slaves by foreigners and evil disposed persons." A bill for the reenslavement of free blacks died in committee but not before creating panic in the free black community. The Charleston Grand Jury wanted slaves and free blacks prohibited from using public transportation. Twenty bills aimed against the free black population remained on the docket.[51]

An atmosphere of terror and vigilantism limited the scope of political dissent and helped propel the secession movement. News of the Texas slave panic of 1860 and reports that most of the slaves were convinced that Lincoln's election meant emancipation made Carolinian slaveholders edgy. Keziah Brevard was convinced that the night of September 15, 1860, "if reports are true, had been set apart to cut us off," and she wished that "the Abolitionists & the negroes had a country to themselves." Brevard confessed that she did not know whether slaves "have any good feelings for their owners or not," and that they "were far more knowing than many will acknowledge — " A particularly wise little slave girl, playing on the fears of her mistress, assured her that she "did not know how my negroes hated white folks & how they talked about *me*." In Bennetsville, two "suspected John Brownites" were apprehended. One, Mr. Hitchings, had "northern arms" and a New York receipt on him and was asked to leave the state. An Abbeville woman wrote that in one village "[f]ive negroes are to be hung, twenty white men implicated all *southern born*, the poor white *trash* who have associated with negroes and are jealous of the higher classes and think insurection [*sic*] will place them on a footing and they get some plunder in the bargain." A Newberry paper reported that some runaway slaves were found with a Bible marked in a way that revealed that they were "misapplying the true meaning of certain passages of the scripture" and used the case to argue against teaching slaves to read. In Spartanburg, two slaves were subjected to "fifty lashes apiece" for conspiring to lead a rebellion and several more were apprehended on a variety of charges: petty crime, abolitionism, and arson. Keitt, whose brother had been killed by his slaves in Florida, wrote, "If Lincoln is elected — what then? I am in earnest — I'd cut loose, through fire and blood if necessary — See-poison in the wells of Texas and fire for the Houses in Alabama — Our Negroes are being enlisted in politics — With poison and fire, how can we stand it? I confess this new feature alarms me, more even, than anything in the past — If Northern men get access to our negroes to advise poison and the torch — we must prevent it at every hazard — the future will not 'down' because we are blind." Orr warned of "untiring fanatics" infiltrating the slave South.[52]

Carolinian planter politicians took extra precautions to guard against a slave uprising as a part of their mobilization for secession. A meeting in St. Peter's Parish again recommended the removal of the entire free black population from the state. Governor Gist asked for the "enactment of a law, punishing summarily and severely, if not with death, any person that circulates incendiary documents, avows himself an abolitionist, or in any way attempts to create insubordination or insurrection among the slaves." Prominent secessionists in the legislature such as Carew and Aldrich introduced bills for the "speedy trial" of all suspected subversives and for the increased policing of the free black population. Commenting on the hysteria gripping his state, Petigru wrote, "My own countrymen here in South Carolina are distempered to a degree that makes them to a calm and impartial observer real objects of pity. They believe anything that flatters their delusions or vanity: and at the same time they are credulous to every whisper of suspicion of insurgents or incendiaries." Henry Ravenel claimed that these apprehensions were "wrong and unnecessary" because slaves were attached to their masters. At the same time, he recommended increased "vigilance and police regulation."[53] Renewed fears of slave rebellion heightened the repressive quality of the secession movement. Moreover, in the minds of many Carolinian slaveholders, the Republican Party was the "Brown-Helper" party that would incite slaves and nonslaveholders and whose ascendancy would spell their doom.

In the year before the Civil War, Carolinian secessionists tried to unify the South on a strategy for disunion. They understood their own role as propagandists for secession, arguing, "Dissolution will never come by the voluntary act of the people. Some master-spirits must lead the way." Laertes pointed out that if any of the far south states would take the first step toward secession, the rest of the South was bound to follow. In his speech on the laying of the cornerstone of Calhoun's monument, Keitt invoked the "testament of the dying [sic] Statesman" to ask southerners to unite and meet "impending dangers." The *Camden Weekly Journal* noted, "A Constitutional Union is impossible; the South will have no other; dissolution must come, and a Southern Republic can then frame a constitution founded upon its organism, whose precepts will then naturally be obeyed." Martin Witherspoon Gary, the young legislator from Edgefield and future governor, was certain that southerners had "but to make a bold and united effort to become a great, independent and prosperous people." "Every consideration of duty and interest calls upon the South to dissolve her connection with the North," Carolinian Alfred A. Smith wrote in *De Bow's Review*. The slave South, with its territory, population, and productions had "all the elements for forming a mighty nation." It would be "one of the most powerful nations," "a queen among nations." Southern nationalists argued, "We will be a compact people, made homogenous by a great similarity of interests, and one principle of cohesion above all others — slavery."[54]

In his annual message in 1859, Governor Gist dwelt at length on the rationale for secession. He mentioned specifically northern determination to restrict the entrance of slave states and to prohibit southerners "from carrying our slaves into the common Territories" as cause for southern alienation from the Union. The entire North, he asserted, was "arrayed against us, and pledged to our destruction"; they were waging a "war . . . relentlessly" on southern "institutions" and had "crossed the Rubicon" by encouraging slave rebellion. He predicted, "The election of a Black Republican President will settle the question of our safety in the Union." Recommending southern cooperation on disunion, he reminded Carolinians that the state could "resume her position as a sovereign in the family of nations."

Resolutions and presentments flooded both houses of the state legislature demanding immediate secession, vast appropriations for the defense of the state, withdrawal of the congressional delegation, and a convention of slaveholding states. Others proffered military assistance to Virginia and the border states against abolitionist attacks. As Hamilton confided to Miles, "The Legislature I am sorry to say are wasting a great deal of time in debating Resolutions, but they are nevertheless fully alive to the necessity of placing the State in a proper position of defence if need be." Pope, national Democratic chairman of the house Committee on Federal Relations, admitted that secession was the "rightful remedy" but argued that Carolinians should act only if they had positive indications that the rest of the southern states were prepared for disunion. Simons, another National Democrat, asserted that if a Republican president were elected, he would be chosen on the motto, "Death to the institutions of the South." J. Harleston Read of Prince George Winyaw claimed grandiosely that he was willing to appropriate the whole treasury of the state in preparation for the inevitable war that would follow disunion. Memminger alluded to the inevitability of disunion and to the common resolve of the legislature to form a southern confederacy. He argued that since Virginia had been invaded, it was that state's duty to lead in the secession movement. His resolutions called for a meeting of the slaveholding states to take "united action," for the appointment of a special commission to Virginia, and for an appropriation of $100,000 for "military contingencies."

In the senate, Alexander Mazyck presented a set of resolutions demanding that "slaveholding states" immediately "annul the compact" and form "another Confederacy not hostile to their peculiar rights and property." A. C. Garlington, state senator from Newberry and an ardent secessionist, in a long speech justified immediate disunion. The real problem lay in the fact that the Union was dominated by a "majority" that had produced the "Abolition or Black Republican party." Vindicating "state sovereignty" and South Carolina's leading role in the secession movement, he asked why the slave South should "hesitate" to leave the Union when it had "all the elements of national power and greatness." The senate passed a preamble and resolutions confirming that the state had been ready for secession in 1852 and that it had not dissolved the Union at the time "from consideration of expediency only." Since then, the preamble stated, "assaults upon the institution of slavery" had grown. A resolution informed the rest of the South that the time for "a speedy separation" had come and asked southerners to "inaugurate" the move-ment for nationhood. The house and senate committees met in confer-ence and the senate's preamble passed with Memminger's resolutions. Secessionists commended the legislature's work as evidence of the "har-mony" prevailing in the state on the vital questions of the day. As Mem-minger informed Miles, "all of us are persuaded that in this Union, there is no security and either there must be new terms established or a South-ern Confederacy is the only hope for our safety." Perry, having recovered from his lapse into disunionism, wrote to his wife that he was the only member in the house to vote against a resolution calling for the forma-tion of a southern confederacy. According to one estimate, 50 percent of the senate and 40 percent of the house were for immediate secession; the rest were cooperationists. Legislators from districts with the highest number of slaves supported disunionist proposals more strongly than those from the districts with the lowest percentage of slaves in their population.[55]

Most Carolinian planter politicians rested their hopes for secession on the mission to Virginia. Gist had appointed Memminger as the state's commissioner. Hayne observed that Memminger's reputation as a mod-erate made him an ideal messenger of the "*Carolina view*" without evok-ing fears of the state's penchant for disunion. He felt that Memminger should speak only of the "evils" confronting the slave South and leave the "remedy" to the "proposed conference of the Southern States." Miles, who conferred with Senators R. M. T. Hunter and James Mason of Vir-ginia and secured for Memminger an invitation to address the Virginia General Assembly, advised him, "The sentiment in Virginia is still run-ning strongly in favor of some practical and effectual action. . . . I have no doubt that you can very much aid in giving direction to what may be a vague desire on their part to deal an effective blow at the North. . . . If you can only urge our Carolina view in such a manner as to imbue Virginia with it — (and at present she is in the best condition to be impregnated) — we may soon hope to see the first fruit of your addresses in the sturdy and healthy offspring of whose birth we could be justly so proud — a Southern Confederacy." Boyce, however, warned him that he should not give the impression that South Carolina was trying to lead Virginia into disunion. Memminger assured Miles, "My own opinion and I think the opinion of our State is that the Union cannot be preserved; and that a sectional Government such as we have now is not worthy of preservation." He would frankly present the Carolinian position without appearing to "dictate" to the Virginians. But "the only positive act" that he could recommend would be the meeting of the southern states.[56]

On his arrival in Richmond, Memminger soon ascertained that most Virginian legislators were against any plan that hinted at disunion. Unionist feeling ran high in the predominantly nonslaveholding western section of the state. Virginian governor Letcher proposed a convention of all the states in the Union rather than a southern convention. Memminger wrote that he would now have to ask for a meeting of the southern states as a mere preliminary to this convention but confided that even this proposition had no "direct support." In his address to the legislature, Memminger reiterated his state's desire to meet the rest of the South in convention. "The North and the South stand in hostile array," he asserted. John Brown's raid, Helperism, the exclusion of slavery from the territories, and violations of the fugitive slave law were all indications of this fact. Referring to the Republican Party, he argued that northerners would rule the slave South as its enemy, build up a patronage party in the South, deny slaveholders access to the territories, and completely destroy "southern civilization." To allay suspicions of a Carolinian disunion plot, he concluded, "If our pace be too fast for some, we are content to walk slower. . . . We cannot consent to stand still, but we would gladly make common cause with all."[57]

Memminger conceded the failure of his mission. Hamilton observed that the "Commissioner [was] sneaking back into South Carolina with his tail between his legs." Miles admitted that he was "getting heart-sick of uniting the South in any *practical* and effectual *action*." Simms complained, "The blockhead politicians of Virginia, too selfish to see the right, too timid to pursue it, refused us a conference." As the *Southron* stated, if the rest of the South refused to support South Carolina then it would be "compelled" to act on its own. Benjamin Waldo wrote caustically that the slave South reminded him of an ill person who spurns bitter medicine. However, O'Neall was delighted that Virginia had rebuked the "restless uneasy disunionists" of his state. In March, the Virginia assembly formally rejected all plans for a southern convention. Tennessee also opposed a southern meeting. Memminger's stopover in North Carolina on his return journey also amounted to nothing. Gist complained to Governor Hicks of Maryland of jealousies and differences among the slaveholding states. Hicks rejected the southern convention idea and hoped for "the continuance of the Union in the spirit and to the great ends for which it was formed."[58]

Carolinian secessionists realized that their state and the Lower South would have to make the first move. As Memminger wrote to Rhett, "we farther South will be compelled to act, and to drag after us these divided States." The *Charleston Mercury* opined, the "Slave South — has labored under two fatal errors: First, in relying upon any party of the North as able to protect us; and second, in relying upon the Frontier Southern States — Slave States at convenience — to lead the van of our resistance, and to bear the brunt of the conflict. . . . [T]he Cotton States — must look to themselves alone for defence." The Lower South would form "a nucleus around which several others will rally." To buttress its analysis, the editorial quoted Ruffin, who argued that if the Deep South should secede they would be followed by the "non-seceding and slaveholding" states. D. H. London, a Virginia secessionist, argued, "One thing I can say, I am sure that the *people* of Virginia, will never allow any state of the South, to be trodden down by force."[59]

The response of most lower south states to the southern movement was most reassuring to secessionists. Following South Carolina's lead, the Mississippi legislature passed resolutions in February 1860 calling for a meeting of the southern states in Atlanta. Peter B. Starke, who arrived in Richmond with the Mississippi plan a few days after Memminger's departure, faced the same obstacles as his predecessor. The Florida and Alabama legislatures pronounced that they were ready to cooperate with sister slave states. Lower south unionists, however, opposed the Carolinian plan. Governor Houston, in his message to the Texas legislature, made clear his "unqualified protest against, and dissent from" the South Carolina resolutions, arguing that a southern convention had "no constitutional sanction." He condemned the "doctrines of nullification, secession and disunion" and the "sectional appeals" of "selfish demagogues." Quoting Jackson and Webster on the indestructibility of the Union, Houston recommended that the legislature pass resolutions against the convention and "the abstract right of secession."[60]

Carolinian secessionists worked hard to insure that they could count on the support of other southern states on disunion and avoid the isolation that had dogged them for so long. In October 1860, Gist addressed letters to governors of the southern states asking if they would call for a state convention in the event of Lincoln's election. South Carolina, he wrote, would certainly do so and was prepared to follow any one of them. But Carolinians would secede first if they knew that some other state would join them. Gist received fairly positive responses from Governors A. B. Moore of Alabama, John J. Pettus of Mississippi, M. S. Perry of Florida, and Joseph E. Brown of Georgia. While Moore and Perry expressed the willingness of their states to follow any southern state in secession, Brown and Pettus recommended a southern convention. All four declared that their states would not act alone but evinced a willingness to thwart "Black Republicans." Thomas O. Moore of Louisiana and John W. Ellis of North Carolina sent more discouraging answers. Moore argued that he had no constitutional authority to call a convention but asserted his belief in the "right to secession." Ellis was quite convinced that North Carolinians did not regard Lincoln's election as sufficient cause for secession but assured Gist that his state would resist the "doctrine of coercion" against seceding states. South Carolina, free from sectional and partisan divisions, would have to lead the secession movement.[61]

South Carolina's unique political heritage and long-standing commitment to the politics of slavery and separatism groomed state leaders to play a historic role in the coming of secession and the Civil War. Real and pressing concerns for the safety and perpetuity of slavery inspired the state's road to disunion. Whether it was the protection of slavery in the territories, suspicions of nonslaveholders' and slaves' loyalty, or the threat that Republican ascendancy posed to slavery and slaveholders, slavery rather than vague and undefined republican fears or rhetorical insults to southern honor guided Carolinian planter politicians. As they had long advocated, slavery and its exigencies had been raised to a political principle and were to supersede partisan affiliation and loyalty to the Union. As Preston, a member of South Carolina's seceding delegation at Charleston, proclaimed, "Slavery is our king — slavery is our truth — slavery is our Divine Right."[62] Whether most Carolinians realized it or not, the final vindication of slave society was near at hand.

Secession

Democracy is the principle of abolition.
— DAVID GAVIN, 1858

Give us slavery or give us death.
— EDMUND BRYAN, 1850

Secession, for Carolinian planter politicians, was a long-anticipated response to the election of a president committed to the nonextension and eventual demise of slavery. Southern nationalism rested on the vindication of slavery, and the Republican party mounted the most serious challenge to the progress of slavery. Free labor ideology not only condemned human bondage as a "relic of barbarism" but viewed the sectional controversy as an "irrepressible conflict" between slavery and freedom. The dispute over the extension of slavery laid bare the inherently opposing views of society in the North and South.[1] The defense of slavery and the antidemocratic values of slave society formed the politics and ideology of secession.

South Carolina's statewide plantation economy and politically precocious planter class had made it the perfect breeding ground for southern nationalism. The legacy of Calhoun, nullification, and the first secession crisis: the lack of a party system, an antidemocratic political structure and culture, and the dominance of proslavery thought and separatism gave secessionists a powerful political presence in the state. Secession in South Carolina was not the result of merely a momentary and emotional crisis of fear. It was, rather, the culmination of an influential political ideology of slavery and separatism. The fact that South Carolina became the first southern state to secede was no accident. The vanguard determination of the state's political elite, the lack of organized opposition, an apparent disunionist majority among the citizenry, tactics of intimidation and terror, and the hopeless apathy of outnumbered unionists made the state's secession a relentless juggernaut.[2]

The movement for a southern nation was thus neither a conspiracy of fire-eaters nor a popular, grassroots upsurge for independence.[3] To recognize the proslavery and top-down character of southern nationalism is also to understand the nature of class relations in slave society. In South Carolina, where partisan and sectional rivalries were minimal, slaveholding planters as a class led the secession movement. Based on an unyielding justification of slavery, southern nationalism appealed decisively to all slaveholders and those who participated in the staple economy. The fact that only a tiny section of the state lay outside the realm of the plantation belt, and that nearly a majority of its adult white male population was slaveholding, augmented the state's political unity on disunion. The plain folk of South Carolina were neither dragooned into secession nor were they the leading and avid proponents of southern nationality.[4]

Southern nationality ultimately failed the test of war because military confrontation disrupted power relations within the slave South, giving slaves, the nonplantation-belt yeomanry, and even some white women an opportunity to challenge the regime of planters and slaveholders. The triumph and failure of southern nationalism was a testimony to the success and limits of slaveholders' ability to cast their own class interests as that of their society, section, and the ill-fated southern nation.[5]

Slavery was more than a topical issue in the sectional conflict. It lay at the heart of southern nationalists' understanding of their cause. Slavery as a benevolent and harmonious system that allayed the conflict between capital and labor, as a guarantor of social and political stability, as the engine of economic prosperity, as a result of allegedly natural racial differences, and as a divinely sanctioned institution comprised proslavery dogma in the years preceding the Civil War. Proslavery ideology, or what George Fitzhugh called "southern thought," achieved what no amount of northern criticism could: it created a distinct national identity for the South based on its character as a slave society. Oscar Lieber, writing to his parents in New York, felt that the free North was more alien to him than slave Cuba. If his parents had moved to Cuba, he confessed, "although really a foreign country I would experience less of that national separation having taken place."[6]

Southern nationalism derived its most powerful ideological impetus from proslavery thought. As William Lowndes Yancey stated, "We have settled for ourselves the question that our slave institution, and the institutions resting upon them, form the best governmental policy in the world. That ours is the highest degree of civilization, having the most beneficial effect upon society, both moral and political." James R. Doolittle, Republican senator from Wisconsin, blamed the "Calhoun Revolution" or the defense of "slavery in the abstract" for the southern demand for the extension of slavery. According to Fitzhugh, the sectional "controversy is absolutely narrowed down to a choice between society like our own in the South, and some fanatical, sensual, or infidel form of socialism." In a series of articles entitled "Slavery and Free Labor Defined and Compared," Edmund Ruffin argued that slavery rather than freedom was the natural condition of labor. Once the North used up abundant western lands, its labor system would collapse.[7]

In the years before secession, the proslavery argument grew in scope, adding to its ranks unapologetic propagandists of social subordination. George Fredrick Holmes, who expressed reservations at Fitzhugh's more extravagant claims on behalf of slavery, could still agree that "the question of negro slavery is implicated with all the great social problems of the current age." Reverend George D. Armstrong of Virginia restated the religious defense of slavery, which rested on biblical literalism and a Christian notion of the duties and responsibilities of masters and slaves. In South Carolina, David Ewart's *A Scriptural View of the Moral Relations of African Slavery* was republished with revisions in 1859. As Reverend Iveson Brookes wrote to a northern correspondent in 1860, "The difficulty is that we take the Bible to be our guide and know not whence you will convince us of its [slavery's] sinfulness for we acknowledge no higher law than God's word."[8]

Cotton Is King, the second hefty proslavery anthology, appeared in 1860 and bore the stamp of the political quarrels of the day. In his introduction, editor E. N. Elliot, president of Planters' College, Mississippi, blamed all the troubles facing the slave South, including restrictions on the expansion of slavery, violations of the fugitive slave law, and efforts to incite slave rebellion, on "false doctrines" of slavery. Pertinent political material, the *Dred Scott* decision and justifications of the fugitive slave law were reprinted in the collection. The anthology contained the testimony of northern defenders of slavery such as David Christy and Reverend Charles Hodge of Princeton. James Henry Hammond would popularize Christy's claim that southern staples, especially cotton, were the basis of world economic prosperity, or the "Cotton is King" argument. Elliot included time-tested material such as Hammond's and William Harper's justifications of slavery, Thornton Stringfellow's scriptural defense of slavery, and newer works by Albert Taylor Bledsoe and Dr. Samuel Cartwright. His editorial strategy was to defend slavery in every possible manner, a tactic followed by his contributors. Stringfellow not only repeated the Christian defense of slavery but, on less firm grounds, mounted a "statistical" justification of it. In his "ethnological" defense of slavery, Cartwright, ignoring the debate between proslavery theologians and polygeneticists, argued that both the Bible and "natural history" confirmed "the existence of at least three distinct species of the genus man, differing in their instincts, form, habits, and color." Bledsoe, who repeated the biblical defense of slavery, attempted to reconcile natural rights theory with slavery. He argued that the social contract theorists had erred in thinking that natural liberty was curtailed with the establishment of civil society. Civil law only reinforced natural liberty, which was already based on allegedly natural differences. Only by challenging the universality of natural rights could Bledsoe make it palatable to slave society. He also sought to develop a proslavery reading of the Declaration of Independence, the object of sustained attack by most slavery ideologues. This Aristotelian twist to social contract theory, usually seen as contraposed, continued the proslavery tradition of appropriating and emasculating liberal ideas in the defense of slavery.[9]

According to the proslavery theorists of the 1850s, democracy was the bane of slavery. Slavery, they claimed, had an indispensable role to play in the "progress" of "civilization"; it was to be a bulwark against communism, free lovism, and all the heresies of modernity that challenged traditional social and political relations. The real enemy, to Bledsoe, was abolitionists' devotion to "equality" or, as Elliot termed it, northern "agrarianism." The latter warned northern "merchant princes" and "master manufacturers" that the "Jacobin clubs" and "agrarian doctrines" of the abolitionists would soon vent their rage on them after they had finished with southern slaveholders. According to John Tyler Jr. the sectional conflict was a battle between the "no-property hordes" of the North and the conservative, property-loving, slaveholding South. Free society was based on the "principle of agrarianism," under which rubric he included majority rule, political equality, tolerance, universal suffrage, free public lands, "red republicanism," and the "radical democracy" of "Black Republicans." Similarly, Fitzhugh argued, "We treat the Abolitionists and Socialists as identical, because they are notoriously the same people, employing the same arguments and bent on the same schemes. Abolition is the first step in Socialism; the former proposes to abolish negro slavery, the latter all kinds of slavery — religion, government, marriage, families, property — nay, human nature itself." Bledsoe argued that suffrage should be restricted for the "public good" and condemned the use of the principle of "equality" to determine such questions. He was politic enough to restrict his examples for such a curtailment to foreigners, nonage citizens, free black people, and slaves, but his argument clearly had a wider import. Fitzhugh felt that the establishment of a hereditary aristocracy by reinstituting primogeniture and entail would check the democratic tendencies of the age.[10]

Carolinian planters Alfred Huger and David Gavin also blamed democracy and the cult of egalitarianism for the woes of slaveholders. Ardent admirers of Calhoun's political theories, they gloried in the antidemocratic character of slave societies. Gavin, who bitterly resented the fact that lower-class whites had the right to vote, argued that "[d]emocracy is the principle of abolition" and roundly critiqued self-government and universal suffrage as "the most pernicious humbug of this humbug age." Huger wrote that while northerners, by emancipating slaves, had unleashed "the agrarian tendencies" besetting their society, the slave South was "entirely conservative." Women planters such as Keziah Brevard shared this view. "Oh Father of Mercies," she prayed, "help us all & let some thing be done to check mobocracy. Lord save us from being overpowered by our enemies at the North. . . . Democracy has brought the South *I fear* into a *sad, sad* state."

Huger's and Gavin's strong proslavery, antidemocratic stance undermined their conditional unionism. Gavin wondered whether a republic that allowed democracy to run amuck was worth preserving. In 1856, he declared that the state should leave the Union before paying the fines levied on Preston Brooks for assaulting Charles Sumner. Huger felt that the rise of the Republican Party "tended virtually to dissolve the Union, so far as it is susceptible of dissolution." If he could not have a proslavery Union, Huger was for a "consolidated" southern government, a senate for life, and restricted suffrage. Brevard's fear of secession and war elicited frequent appeals to the Almighty, but her allegiance lay clearly with her "country." The conditional unionism of these planters is best described by Fitzhugh's tongue-in-cheek slogan, "Disunion within the Union."[11]

South Carolina came closest to the proslavery, antidemocratic utopia visualized by slavery ideologues. In his panegyric on the "political annals" of his native state, James De Bow claimed that only property was "the basis of sound representation" and that "[u]niversal suffrage is no suffrage at all; it degenerates into licentiousness." Secessionist Edward Bryan elucidated on a cardinal tenet of the "political philosophy of South Carolina" when he argued that "democratic absolutism" was the new political evil facing the modern world. The answer to this problem, Bryan argued, lay in Calhoun's ideas of state sovereignty and concurrent majority. Gavin's one consolation was that his state did not allow the popular election of the president, governor, and other state offices. One of Benjamin Allston's correspondents, who equated the rise of "unlimited suffrage" with the passing away of the political power of the slave South to the "irresponsible majority" of the free North, wrote, "The power of the south is where it ought to be always, in the hands of the men of property and education. . . . This I may, without flattery to your state pride, say is more than anywhere else that I know of in the whole world, the case in the State of South Carolina." Hammond proudly affirmed, "The Government of So[uth] Ca[rolina] is that of an aristocracy." Like other Carolinian planters, however, he feared that the state's citizens who had the right to vote might one day "break down the Parish Representation and thus crush the Low Country with its Rotten Boroughs and aristocratic Incubi at a single blow."[12]

Carolinian planter politicians made use of and extended the proslavery paradigm to argue for secession. Laurence M. Keitt argued that the genius of slave society was to recognize the value of social inequality versus "inflammatory" appeals to natural rights doctrine. "Extinguish inequality," he argued, "and the universe becomes a 'dead sea.' " In two extended lectures on slavery to Congress, he fleshed out the scriptural justification of slavery and traced the history of the early Christian church, revealing its acceptance of human bondage. "African slavery," he proclaimed, "is the corner-stone of the industrial, social and political fabric of the South; and whatever wars against it, wars against her very existence." In another speech, he developed a racial defense of slavery and spelled out its broader antidemocratic implications. He denigrated the "sentiments" of the revolutionary generation for being contaminated with the ideas of the "French encyclopedists" and the Declaration of Independence. Inequality, he argued, was the norm everywhere in the world and the hallmark of all civilization. "Universal equality was not bestowed by the Almighty, and cannot be created by human law," he chose to remind his antislavery colleagues. He confidently predicted, "The South, with the principle of subordination, gradation, and harmonious inequality pervading her social system, rests upon the law of nature, and may look with confidence to that public opinion which survives passion, prejudice and error." Keitt was asking for the "truths" of slave society to overturn those of the age of revolution and Enlightenment. Calling for secession, he argued that Republicans would foist "impalpable theories of equality" on the slave South.[13]

Other Carolinian politicos used similar antidemocratic arguments to justify the creation of an independent southern nation. Congressman W. W. Boyce characterized the sectional conflict as an "antagonism of classes between the rabble of the North, and the slave-holders of the South. Slavocracy, as they term it, jars upon the notions of the greasy rabble, because according to their conception, it is a kind of aristocracy."

Slave labor and slave society, Leonidas Spratt claimed, were superior to free labor and democratic society, which were prone to such anarchic tendencies as labor riots and women's rights movements. While praising specifically the "natural" relationship of African slavery in the South, he contended that historically societies that possessed "the greatest political inequalities" had revealed "the greatest exhibitions of physical and intellectual strength." Identifying the slave South's demand for nationhood with the cause of reaction throughout the world, he declared that it was similar to that of Spanish slavery and Russian serfdom. For secessionist W. E. Martin the fundamental incompatibility between northern and southern beliefs was evident. "While the present generation of the South are educated into the belief of the humanity and Christianity of slavery, the same generation at the North has been educated — in the Sunday School and Common Schools — that slavery is wrong," he clarified.[14]

In a speech before the Senate, Senator James Chesnut stressed the "conflict of ideas" between the sections. The antislavery men's "creed is the equality of all men and all races naturally, and therefore should be socially and politically." Reverting to the favorite target of proslavery theorists, he asked "by what authority" could the "dogmas of the Declaration of Independence" be made the "basis of the Constitution" or the "principles of the Government." Well educated in the Carolina doctrine, he condemned "a vulgar despotism of mere numbers." Antislavery men advocated "wild ideas" of universal liberty and equality that would push the country into anarchy. "Are not these same ideas of unqualified liberty, fraternity and equality, communism, agrarianism and infidelity, sown sedulously and thick throughout the literature and teachings and preachings of the anti-slavery party of the North?" he asked. Red republicanism in America had merely "blacked its face that's all." For Chesnut, antislavery and proslavery were indicative of a deep ideological divide between free and slave societies, which he described in these terms: "One is absolute theory, excogitated from the brain of the cyclopedists, resting on visions of dreamers, which all history proves to be unsteady, explosive and destructive. Amid eternal confusion, it is ever busy in the endless task of dilapidation and reconstruction." But the southern "view proceeds upon the laws of nature, and the experience of the world. It moves on the accumulation of well tried facts, grouped by generation, and imported into the ever-growing science of human government. It adopts a philosophy which insures steadiness, peace, and advancement." So pleased was Fitzhugh with the senator's oratorical efforts that he bestowed on him "the gown of the philosopher" and "the mantle of the prophet."[15]

The National Democratic politicians of South Carolina shared the proslavery views of states' rights men. In an early speech that was devoted to the advocacy of manufacturing and economic diversification, James L. Orr argued that while African "inferiority" made slavery "more acceptable to the slave and less perplexing to the master," historical "precedents" proved that slavery was the basis of the highest forms of "civilization." Preston Brooks praised slavery for checking the spirit of uncontrolled egalitarianism in the republic: "The institution of slavery, which it is so fashionable now to decry, has been the greatest blessing to this entire country. At the North it has served as the vent for fanaticism, communism, and all those secretions of a morbid sentimentality, which, without this safety-valve, would long since have resulted in a social explosion." Even when characterizing slavery as the "guardianship of an inferior and dependent race," Carolinian planter politicians understood the broader role of racial slavery in shaping the character of their society. As one writer for the *Charleston Courier* put it, slavery "involves all that can distinguish a people, and its ramifications of interest permeate the entire organism of society, and are identified with all the possibilities of progress and perpetuity."[16]

Senator Hammond, who had switched from ardent secessionism to conservative unionism, epitomized the proslavery consensus among the state's political leaders. Significantly, Hammond delivered his well-known proslavery speech in the Senate during the Lecompton controversy. Comparing the two sections, he found the free North to be tottering on the brink of anarchy and the slave South to be vastly superior politically, geographically, economically, and militarily. He claimed that the South alone generated wealth in the country as it dominated world trade — or, "Cotton is King." But the key to southern superiority lay not in cotton but in the "harmony of her political and social institutions." In his oft-quoted words, "In all social systems there must be a class to do the menial duties, to perform the drudgery of life." The South had found a suitable "race" for this purpose: "We use them . . . and call them slaves." He argued that the real cancer in free society lay in the fact that northern lower classes or "mud sills," unlike the southern, had political power and could overthrow government and property "by the quiet process of the ballot-box." Without slaveholders' political presence northern capitalists would be subject to the depredations of their enfranchised working class. Democracy could threaten not only slavery but all property and capital. Instead of being thankful, most northerners viewed his critique of democracy as the worst kind of heresy. According to Stephen Douglas, his position was nothing short of a gross violation of the republican, democratic, and American political creeds.[17]

Far from being irrelevant to politics, proslavery thought inspired Carolinian planter politicians in their battle against northern free soilers. A deep ideological commitment to slavery and to the antidemocratic values to which it gave birth helped create the solid front on secession among the state's planter politicians in 1860.

Carolinian planter politicians' mobilization for secession intensified in 1860 when the election of a Republican president became imminent. The presidential campaign was an extended argument for secession. A "monster meeting" in Charleston ratified the southern ticket of Breckinridge and Lane. Secessionists such as Williams Middleton, R. B. Rhett, and W. E. Martin led the affair, along with National Democrats such as Richard Yeadon and Henry Lesesne. The leading speakers left no doubt as to the course of the state on the election of a Republican president. Rhett took the decidedly low road in his address when he stated that Hamlin had "black blood in him" and that the South should save itself from "the disgrace of having a negro presiding over" it. The *Charleston Mercury* called on the state to resist the "negroism" of the Republicans, and the Newberry *Rising Sun* warned of the consequences of elevating "*a nigger* in principle" to the presidency and "a mullatto [*sic*]" to the vice presidency. Rhett evoked the description of the Republicans as the Brown-Helper party when he pointed out that Lincoln was a "renegade southerner" and Hamlin a "mulatto." Ironically, secessionists laid as much stress on the fact that Lincoln had been a "rail splitter" as his Republican Party managers in the North, obviously with opposite effect. Martin said that Lincoln was known for only two things: one, that he "wishes to revolutionize the South," and two, "that he is a good hand at splitting rails." He argued that splitting rails "is very good in its way, but it is the first time I ever heard of its being a qualification for the President of the United States." The log cabin myth scarcely endeared "Abram Lincoln" to South Carolina's slaveholding aristocracy.[18]

Lincoln's election, Carolinian planter politicians realized, would mark the beginning of the end of slaveholders' national political power, which had flourished in the 1850s under successive Democratic administrations. William Porcher Miles warned that if the slave South were defeated in the presidential contest, it would "allow a sectional fanatical party, whose creed is hatred to the South, the only cement of its heterogeneous mass is hostility to slaveholders," to rule over it. There was a "*reasonable probability*," secessionists asserted, that a southern confederacy would be formed with the election of "an Abolitionist white man as President of the United States, and an Abolitionist colored man as Vice-President of the United States." Boyce felt that Lincoln was nothing but a "northern abolitionist." He even argued that the Republican Party was committed to the idea of "negro equality" and that it would use all the powers and patronage of government to further its aim. Others, quoting from Lincoln's speeches, especially the "House Divided" oration, argued more accurately that he and his party desired the "ultimate extinction of slavery." Slave society could not withstand even a mildly antislavery president, who could effectively challenge the regional mastery of southern planters and slaveholders without ever abolishing slavery. The *South Carolinian* held that the Republican Party was formed around "the idea of Abolitionism" and feared that it might find fertile soil within the slave South. "The chief officer of the Government," B. H. Rutledge argued, would "be vested with all the powers of the Government . . . and to be pledged moreover to carry these [antislavery] doctrines out to their last consummation."[19]

Carolinian leaders' unanimity on secession was evident. All were for Breckinridge or disunion on Lincoln's election. Arthur Simkins, Douglas's erstwhile supporter, quickly changed his tune after Douglas spoke on the illegitimacy of secession and the duty of the federal government to counteract any such movement. Martin Witherspoon Gary, an extreme secessionist, was for secession even if Breckinridge was elected. John Ashmore thought that Breckinridge's election could still save the Union on the slave South's terms, but he was convinced that Lincoln would be elected and prepared for disunion. Williams Middleton recommended that the defeated southern candidate should simply form an alternative government. One by one, Carolinian planter politicians made their views public. Keitt recommended that a state convention be immediately convened on the election of a Republican. Other congressmen such as John McQueen and Milledge Luke Bonham avowed their support for single secession. Boyce advocated the immediate secession of the state if Lincoln were elected and said if the federal government tried to "coerce" the state then the rest of the South would be forced to make "common cause." Prominent National Democrats joined the swelling chorus for secession. Edward McCrady made it clear that "the preservation of the Union as it is, is no longer possible or desirable for ourselves or for mankind." In two public letters, Orr recommended secession on the election of a Republican.[20]

Carolinian planter politicians' open advocacy of secession embarrassed Breckinridge, who tried to fend off charges that he was a disunionist. As Hammond wrote, "My opinion is that So. Ca. should be quiescent as usual in the election and that every blow that she or any of her people strike for B&L, will damage them." He understood that members of the Breckinridge party "*dread* the support of the Mercury and Rhett and want So. Ca. to vote quietly as usual." But South Carolina was the one state that

Breckinridge loyalists could treat as their private rotten borough. Carolinian secessionists proudly pointed to the fact that the Bell and Douglas parties did not exist in their state. Miles argued that "squatter sovereignty" and the Wilmot Proviso were two sides of the same coin and that a southern vote for Douglas was the same as one for Lincoln. He had no regrets on the breakup of the Democratic Party once it had become "subservient to the will of the mobocracy." Southern "union savers," secessionists claimed, were allies of the Republicans insofar as they buttressed the idea that the Union was stronger than slavery.[21]

A few Carolinians deplored the disunionist mentalité of a majority of the state's political leadership. James L. Petigru supported the Bell and Everett ticket and hoped that a fusion between the Bell and Douglas parties would lead to a unionist victory. He hoped that the "virtue" of the rest of the country would redeem his state. He wrote pungently, "If all our country were as lost to respect the difference between right and wrong as South Carolina, it would be time for Hell to enlarge her borders." John Belton O'Neall insisted that "the battle of and for our rights must be in the union and under the aegis of the Constitution." If "the worst happens" and Lincoln is elected, he advised that the state should "*wait*" and "see fully developed the course of his action." B. F. Perry also felt that the election of a president according to the Constitution provided no ground for secession. In a letter that Richard Yeadon published in the *Courier* while expressing his dissent, Perry claimed that Lincoln would be elected by a minority and would head a weak administration checked by a Democratic Senate. At the same time, Perry affirmed that he might be "mistaken in supposing slavery to be out of the reach of the assaults of its foes, and if so I will be as ready as any one to defend it at the sacrifice of the Union itself, as much as I love the Union." Perry's letter provoked long refutations from secessionists. They called him "an unintentional ally and tool of Northern Abolitionists!"[22]

Before election day, every member of the Carolinian congressional delegation would be on the record for immediate secession upon Lincoln's election except Hammond. He rebuked those who abused the South's northern "allies" and predicted that the Republicans would be defeated in 1860 and 1864 and then disappear altogether as a party. He was "buoyant and hopeful" about the future and believed that southern dictation "couched in decent terms and based on reason" would be accepted by the North. He even visualized a reconstruction of the Union with New England and New York left out. In an address to the state, which was suppressed by A. P. Aldrich, he questioned whether Lincoln's election constituted sufficient grounds for secession and recommended that South Carolina let Alabama take the lead. The *Mercury* printed long denunciations of his views, but Perry lauded the fact that he had "given the death blow to disunion and Revolution." Hammond's equivocal unionism was constantly tested. William Henry Seward's "irrepressible conflict" speech had pushed him to a more disunionist position. He declared, "But the true issue is now made. The South is to be Africanized and the elections of 1860 are to decide the question." He formulated resolutions that confirmed that the Republicans were in a "conspiracy" against the slaveholding states and that looked to southern unity on disunion. Hammond was against secession unless being in the Union meant "submitting to gross insult or permanent oppression." He failed to take an active role in the secession movement but insisted, "If there was a fair chance of success I would risk all for a Southern slaveholding confederacy." In his secessionist pamphlet, I. W. Hayne published suitable portions of Hammond's speeches nullifying the effect of his public silence on secession.[23]

Conservative planters such as William Elliot and W. J. Grayson also revealed the limits of conditional unionism in South Carolina. Elliot predicted that only one or two southern states would secede upon Lincoln's election and that they would find the rest of the South "arrayed against their policy." Seeing war as inevitable, he wrote that "the prospects of the country are very black." Later, Grayson would admit to witnessing "the death of the Republic with great sorrow." But he recognized that the causes for disunion were "grave and numerous" and saw the breakup of the country as inevitable. After secession, these men, like many conservatives, would become uncompromising defenders of southern nationality. As the national Democratic paper the *South Carolinian* explained, secessionism rather than unionism was true conservatism: "Every instinct of conservatism prompts us to get away from it [the Union] as soon as possible. To linger is suicide and parricide. It is death to us, our country and its institutions."[24]

Despite the paucity of unionist opposition, Carolinian secessionists inaugurated a massive propaganda campaign for disunion. Robert Gourdin suspected that many quietly supported the Union. Hammond recommended that state leaders should "crack away" and "keep up a racket for the benefit of those less confident" than he was of Breckinridge's victory. In September, some of the wealthiest lowcountry planter families — the Middletons, Aikens, and Lowndes — helped found and finance the 1860 Association at Charleston. Leading Carolinians occupied the offices of the association: W. D. Porter was named president and Robert N. Gourdin headed its executive committee. William Tennant, secretary and treasurer of the association, wrote that "its object is to procure a league of the Cotton States through the publishing of strong and incendiary pam-

phlets, that will be calculated to awake men of the South to a consciousness of their perilous position . . . not least by putting our own gallant
little state, in a position of defence, that will meet the contemplated
emergencies of Lincoln's election." John Townsend, the Edisto Island secessionist planter who owned over 200 slaves, argued that South Carolina
must start the disunion movement. Tennant and Townsend secured the
help of the state's congressmen to distribute the association's pamphlets
among southerners who "hold the true political faith of the South." The
association soon deluged the cotton states and South Carolina with hundreds of secessionist "tracts."[25]

Carolinian planter politicians lived up to their role as the ideological
leaders of secession. Foremost among the association's tracts was Townsend's *The Doom of Slavery in the Union; Its Safety out of It*, which was published along with his 1850 pamphlet, *The South Alone Should Govern the
South, And African Slavery Should be Controlled by Those Only Who are Friendly
to it*. The former was an address to the Edisto Island branch of the association. Townsend graphically detailed the results of a Republican victory if
slaveholders did not secede: "emancipation of their slaves; then poverty,
political equality with their former slaves, insurrection, war of extermination between the two races, and death, or expatriation, to fill up the
picture." Even after all the inculcation in the duties and responsibilities
of masterhood, most Carolinian slaveholders quite sanguinely and regularly predicted the "extermination" of their slaves if they were ever emancipated. The Republican Party, Townsend argued, could achieve its aim
of abolition in various ways, either by directly inciting slave rebellion or by
slowly spreading its "cancerous roots" in the slave South. The North
would soon achieve a sufficient majority in Congress and among the
states to abolish slavery through a constitutional amendment. He quoted
John Tyler Jr., who argued that abolitionists and Republicans agreed on
one goal — "*the ultimate property robbery of the South in respect to both personal
and real estate*." The Republican Party was a "radical democratic party"
that was in favor of "agrarian" enactments such as the Homestead Act.
Townsend added that on Lincoln's election slavery would cease to receive
the protection of the federal government and that the free soil states and
territories surrounding the slave South would act as a haven for every
"disaffected slave." An appendix on the Texas panic drove home the
point. He contended that every unionist of 1860 was an "ABOLITIONIST"
of 1870. A unionist might as well admit "I SUBMIT TO THE EMANCIPATION
OF MY SLAVES."[26] Townsend's pamphlet, the most effective out of all
the tracts churned out by the 1860 Association, was mostly directed at
slaveholders.

Secessionist propaganda revealed the difficulties of accommodating the nonslaveholding yeomanry within a southern nationalist discourse that derived its prime justification from slavery and the ideals of slaveholding. Townsend pointed out that antislavery sentiments had already made incursions into the slave South and that the nonslaveholding populations of the border states were "northern born" and "abolitionist." But he rushed to clarify that on emancipation slaveholders would lose millions of dollars and all southern whites would lose "caste privileges." The second most well-known tract, James De Bow's letter to Gourdin detailing *The Interest in Slavery of the Southern Non-Slaveholder*, tried to allay anxieties about nonslaveholders' loyalty to slave society. De Bow's pamphlet began oddly for a work geared toward nonslaveholders for he spent much time arguing that slaveholding was widespread in the South. He stated that half the populations of the states of South Carolina, Mississippi, and Louisiana were slaveholding and that one-third of the entire population of the South owned slaves. The "poor man" of the South owned between one and five slaves and was an integral part of the "slaveholding interest." Given the centrality of slavery in the construction of a southern national identity, however, De Bow's initial arguments were not odd at all. The "poorest non slaveholder," he argued, would defend slavery, as, with a few exceptions, they were not yet "infected" by northern "isms" and antislavery feeling. The high price of slaves had removed the one potential area of conflict, "slave competition" against white labor in the cities. He claimed that the southern nonslaveholder not only had his "status" as a white man but when his savings would allow could acquire slaves. De Bow's second argument, a southern version of the Horatio Alger rags to riches myth, was hardly an accurate description of slave society on the eve of the Civil War. A slavery-based southern nationalism aggravated the latent contradictions within slave society that would erupt under the stress of war.[27]

Other secessionist propaganda was aimed at establishing the constitutionality of secession. W. D. Porter's rather turgid discourse on state sovereignty was geared to answer Douglas's "coercion" speech. The Union, he insisted, was created by states or "nations" and could be disbanded by them. This further elevation of state to nation was spelled out by Fitzhugh, who argued that the slave South should abandon the doctrine of state sovereignty for "state nationality." John Tyler Jr. criticized majority rule and democracy and reiterated Calhoun's theory of absolute state sovereignty to justify secession. Thomas Hanckel referred to the history of South Carolina as a shining example of state sovereignty in practice.[28]

Carolinian secessionists were not known to rely on arguments alone. With the approach of the presidential elections, time-honored tactics of vigilante violence and intimidation against dissenters became the order of the day. Secessionists such as Rhett and ex-governor James H. Adams formed the "Minute Men for the Defence of Southern Rights" in Columbia on October 7, 1860. Members were provided with arms and sported the nullifiers' blue cockade as a symbol of their defiance. The *Charleston Mercury* reported that companies had been formed in "all principal districts" and that the "leading men" of the state headed these organizations. The black-belt piedmont districts of Kershaw, Abbeville, Richland, and Edgefield had especially strong contingents. While one Carolinian made the fantastical claim that the minute men intended to prevent the inauguration of Lincoln, it is clear that their duties lay nearer home. Along with the vigilance committees, formed in the aftermath of Harpers Ferry, the minute men performed an invaluable service in sustaining the web of conformity in South Carolina in 1860. The Carolinian minute men were a paramilitary force formed to meet "any emergency" and seemed to have specialized in holding secessionist rallies, parading the streets, and threatening those suspected of differing opinions. During the elections for the secession convention, they would threaten Boozer that they would hang him if he dared stand as a cooperationist. At least a few citizens seemed to have been uncomfortable with the terror created by secessionists. For instance, "East Bay," commenting on the formation of the Committee of Twenty in Charleston to prevent unionists from speaking in public, asked, are "we . . . *afraid of ourselves*." There should be no "gag law" in South Carolina, he protested. "A Native Citizen" also deplored the fact that southern unionists were not allowed to speak in the state.[29]

Oddly enough, given the import of the issues, the legislative elections of 1860 do not appear to have been hotly contested except in Charleston. Some candidates gave explicit assurances that they would vote for a secession convention, but others, especially those from the mountain districts, dismissed the question as "premature." The newly elected legislature was decidedly secessionist in cast, with scarcely a Union man present, though cooperationist sentiment had resurfaced in the northern part of the state and in Charleston. Most members had been reelected. As W. G. Simms wrote, "Cooperation is a mere dream. The time for consultation has passed. That of Action has come." Carolinian abandonment of cooperation was not a repudiation of southern unity. Gist would later assert that it was no longer a question of cooperation versus separate action, but one of the "*concurrent action*" of the individual slave states. One writer suggested that secession conventions be in touch with each other via telegraph to ensure "perfect harmony."[30]

Carolinian planter politicians understood their crucial role in precipitating disunion. Gourdin received letters from southern secessionists promising support and asking South Carolina to secede as soon as possible. Spratt claimed that all "the leading men" of the state had received such letters. As the *Mercury* stated, "We have innumerable assurances that the men of action in each and all of the Southern States, earnestly desire South Carolina to exhibit promptitude and decision in this conjuncture. Other States are torn and divided to a greater or lesser extent, by old party issues. South Carolina alone is not." Secretary of Treasury Howell Cobb sent a message through W. H. Trescot that South Carolina should wait until March 4, 1861, the day of Lincoln's inauguration, to secede. Trescot thought that Georgia rather than South Carolina should secede first. But Carolinian secessionists realized that it was "now or never" and that much depended on their acting first and speedily. D. H. Hamilton felt that "So Ca holds the decision of the question in her own hands—if she falters, wavers for one moment—it gives time for compromising and temporizing, and 'Union savers' step in North and South to ask for delay for a few weeks." Miles advised, "I would not delay the secession of South Carolina for a day. It is not on our own account only, but all our best friends in the entire South urge it upon us as the best step calculated to advance the great cause of the South in all their States. They tell us that any delay, under any pretext would demoralize them at home—while it will answer no possible good purpose. . . . We must move instantly or we injure our friends."[31]

The 1860 presidential elections illustrated perfectly the compatibility between the absence of democracy and momentum for secession. It was no coincidence that the leading secessionist state was the only one in the Union to deprive its citizenry of a vote in the presidential elections. Pro forma the legislature cast their votes for Breckinridge. Once the news of Lincoln's election reached the state, the secession movement moved faster and in a more dramatic fashion. "Popular excitement" over secession was stoked by the state's political elite. When George Fitzhugh wrote that the slave South would have to now leave the Union "in despair," Carolinian secessionists replied that they would do so with a "hip! hip! hurrah." In Charleston, Gourdin, foreman of the city's Grand Jury, Judge A. G. Magrath, District Attorney James Conner, and Collector W. J. Colcock resigned from their federal posts. The next day they were feted at a meeting in Institute Hall at which Spratt introduced resolutions asking the assembly to immediately call a convention. According to one observer, all the "respectable citizens of Charleston" were present at this meeting and "persons of note . . . one after the other, in burning phrases counselled immediate secession." Earlier M. L. Bonham and Chesnut had started the ball rolling in Columbia with fire-eating speeches for secession. The minute men of the city rallied against delay and demanded that South Carolina "strike while the iron is hot." One Carolinian reported that the "leading men" made numerous "inflammatory addresses." Edmund Ruffin journeyed to South Carolina where he was serenaded and enlisted to give secessionist speeches. He wrote of the sentiment of Carolina's public men, "No division of opinion. All for immediate secession. Those who hold opposing opinions are cautious in expressing them." In Sumter, a meeting at the court house vowed resistance to Lincoln. In Aiken, a torchlight procession ended with the burning of his effigy and was addressed by Lewis Malone Ayer, a secessionist planter who owned over 100 slaves. On November 10, Chesnut announced his resignation, followed by Hammond, who seems to have been forced into resigning by his colleague's action.[32]

The process of secession proceeded in a hurried manner. Some secessionists were nervous enough to oppose the election of James Simons, head of the state delegation to the Charleston Democratic convention, as Speaker of the state legislature simply because he was reputed to be a moderate. Gist had advised the legislature to stay in session after choosing the presidential electors and to call for a convention immediately upon Lincoln's election. He also recommended the reorganization of the state militia and the arming of all men in the state between the ages of eighteen and forty-five and called for ten thousand volunteers. In the legislature, Henry Lesesne and George Trenholm introduced cooperationist resolutions. Nationals such as Samuel McGowan and B. H. Wilson were also for ensuring southern cooperation. On the other side, Alexander Mazyck in the senate and R. B. Rhett Jr. in the house introduced resolutions looking to immediate secession. Matters were resolved rather quickly when the Charleston delegation met in caucus and decided to support the earliest call for a convention. News of Robert Toombs's resignation from the Senate; the certainty that Alabama, Mississippi, Florida, and Georgia would call for conventions; and the enthusiastic participation of some Georgian delegates to a railroad convention at the secessionist rally in Institute Hall allayed fears of isolation.

Henry Buist of Charleston introduced a convention bill in the house that stipulated the dates for election to the convention as January 8 and its meeting as January 15. Buist's bill passed the senate by a vote of forty-four to one, with only Samuel McAliley of Chester dissenting. A. P. Aldrich introduced an amendment changing the dates for the election and assembling of the convention to December 6 and 20, respectively. His proposal was opposed by two northern upcountry representatives, W. C. Black of York and A. W. Thomson of Union, who felt that they needed more time to "bring the people up to the point" and "to concentrate public opinion" in their districts. John Winsmith of Spartanburg also spoke up for his cooperation resolutions. Brushing aside opposition, John Cunningham asserted that he would rather lose the mountain district of York than lose Alabama by delay. The change in dates was agreed to by a vote of ninety-one to fourteen and the convention bill passed unanimously, 117 to 0 on the second reading and 114 to 0 on the third. The new bill also passed the senate by a unanimous vote of forty-two to 0 with McAliley abstaining. Two state senators from Pickens and Anderson were absent but had voted for the January bill and Wade Hampton was absent but was known to favor secession. W. D. Porter wrote with satisfaction of the "greatest spirit of conciliation and harmony, with a view to united action" and stated that "no one can arrest the current" of secession in South Carolina.[33]

The passage of the convention bill initiated another round of orchestrated celebrations. A. P. Calhoun in his speech to the state agricultural society announced that henceforth historians would be engaged in the task of writing the " 'Decline and Fall' of the Constitution and Government founded in 1787." Secessionists organized another huge rally in Charleston approving of the work of the legislature and asking for "political independence of the present Federal Government" at the "earliest practicable moment." Magrath, Conner, and Colcock were rewarded for their resignations, Magrath being called to the Chair and Conner and Colcock addressing the meeting with secessionist leaders such as Rhett and Spratt. De Bow in his speech referred to the "poison" hidden in the Constitution that had spread steadily until it forced the slave South to act in "self defense." In Columbia, Keitt, Aldrich, and John P. Richardson addressed similar rallies. Loyalty to the Union, Keitt reiterated, was treason to the South.

The haste with which the state's leadership acted aroused some suspicions. According to Greenville representative David Hoke, secessionists wanted "to make a speedy work of the whole matter and that too before two parties can be formed in South Carolina." Petigru wrote that "the South Carolina men show by their precipitancy that they are afraid to trust the second thought of their own people." Carolinian secessionists remained acutely anxious about the popularity of their cause. One writer felt that the state should not wait until December, as the delay might "cool the ardor of our people." R. C. Griffin wrote that "many of the Rhett party are in favor of declaring South Carolina out of the Union, by enacting a law to that effect. — They know that if the people should decide against them, it will be decisive against separate state action for all time to come."[34]

Between the passage of the convention bill and the elections for the convention, state leaders spared no effort to mobilize for secession.

Torchlight processions, parading by minute men, speeches by eminent Carolinians who were present in full force at local gatherings, fireworks, rockets, and serenades rallied the faithful while deterring opposition. A typical request came from John Lee of Leesville to Bonham: "I think that you better appoint some day to address the citizens of our District at the Court House for I assure you they stand in need of some encouragement." From Bluffton, where Rhett had called for secession in the 1840s, came the demand that the convention "*resume at once* the delegated authority of the Sovereign State of South Carolina." Public avowals of secession by men such as William Elliot, Robert W. Barnwell, and F. W. Pickens were given special prominence. Even though Hammond failed to attend many of the secession meetings to which he was invited, he sent suitable exhortations for action.[35]

Secessionists also made a special effort to reach out to groups that had been resistant to disunion. The Charleston mercantile community, predominantly unionist in 1832 and cooperationist in 1850, staged a grand rally to illustrate "their love and devotion to South Carolina." Robert N. Gourdin, a rich Charleston merchant, was one of the leaders of the secession movement. A "secession pole" with the Palmetto flag was raised by the merchants of Hayne and Meeting Streets to inaugurate the "revolution of Southern commerce." Theodore G. Barker assured them, "The Southern Confederacy offers you an ample compensation for your risk — the assurance of free trade with Europe, and free trade with the universal world! With these advantages gained, once free of this Union, with your commerce emancipated, and your Cotton crop to back you, you can control the North and dictate the terms of commercial interchange." Most of these men were the commercial factotums of the planter class and substantial slaveholders themselves. Richard Lathers, a native Carolinian who had established his business in New York, wrote to Henry Gourdin, Memminger, Magrath, Trenholm, and Nelson Mitchell, recommending a southern convention. A "large and important class" of northerners, who suffered under the "financial exactions" of the Republicans, had fought for southern interests and would continue to do so, he assured them. As an "old fellow citizen" he asked them to reconsider secession. In their reply, Magrath and Henry Gourdin argued that an attack on northern capital and property would reveal "the practicable application of those doctrines, which ostensibly were being prepared for our destruction." Why should the slave South share in the "plenitude of agrarian violence and atheistic cruelty" to be unleashed on northern business? They concluded that secession was the only remedy left to the slave South.[36]

Far more worrisome than the Charleston merchants were the strong-

holds of unionism in the mountain districts, which lay outside the plantation belt. The only significant disagreement on the convention bill had
been over the dates of the election and meeting of the convention, as
some legislators from these districts felt they needed more time to prepare their constituents for disunion. In a letter to Hammond, Father
Asbury Mood testified, "As a minister of the Gospel of Peace and Good
Will who can only hold his opinions privately, let me say, that in the Upper
districts of South Carolina at least, the majority are far from believing
that we reap only misfortune and injury in the Union and that prosperity
and blessing is to be had only in South Carolina setting up for herself." At
a Columbia gathering, Orr had touchily "denied the assertion that the
Mountain Districts were lukewarm in this movement." With the exception of Perry, most of the leaders of the upper parts of the state such as
Orr, Farrow, Ashmore, Crook, William K. Easley, Winsmith, and Rev. J. C.
Furman advocated secession and had contributed to the state's monolithic stance on disunion. Greenville's representatives in the assembly,
Hoke and J. M. Sullivan, seemed to be as eager for secession as their
lowcountry counterparts. The press and the local leaders, most of whom
were large slaveholders themselves, were decidedly secessionist. Perry
refrained from launching an active campaign against secession as he had
in 1850. Nevertheless, secessionists deluged these areas with meetings
and pamphlets during this time. At one meeting in Spartanburg, Chesnut, Magrath, and the proslavery divine and Wofford professor, Whitefoord Smith, urged secession. At another, in Greenville, Memminger
used the language of mountain "hunters" to argue the case for a southern confederacy. Chesnut, Orr, Ashmore, and Boyce were especially active in Pickens, Anderson, and Greenville. Ashmore complained that he
was trying his best to negotiate a middle course between Perry's unionist
followers and the "ultra" and "violent" men who rode "roughshod" over
the people. But, he assured Miles, "Throughout summer I have labored
incessantly to get our people up to the right mark."[37]

However, even the northern districts of South Carolina represented, in
the words of one scholar, "the middle ground in the geography of slavery." Nearly one-third of their population were slaves, and by 1860 the
southern halves of these districts were closely tied to the slave and cotton-
growing economy of the piedmont. David Golighty Harris of Spartanburg typifies the attitude of small slaveholding farmers to secession. He
was the owner of five to ten slaves between 1850 and 1860. Despite fears
of war and the future, he ardently identified with the cause of southern
nationalism. Unionist sentiment among the nonslaveholding yeomanry
in the northern reaches of mountain districts, such as the "Dark Corner"
of Greenville, found no effective political leadership or voice in 1860.

Later, some told of hangings and the tarring and feathering of suspected unionists in this area. In December 1860, in the village of Solitude in western Spartanburg a single meeting protested the hasty action of the state. After secession, Harris reported that "a company of men had formed themselves into a Union Milit [*sic*] Co. at Lancaster's Old-field" in January 1861. He was dismayed at the rise of the "submission flag" but concluded complacently that "those men scarcely knew what they were doing." Some Spartanburg unionists also cut down the Palmetto flag raised by the secessionists. Perry wrote that his "Union friends in the Upper part of Greenville District were dissatisfied with the act of secession and disaffected towards the State" and that he addressed 200 to 300 of them to convince them to serve the Confederacy. He worked tirelessly for the southern cause using his clout among small farmers. With his defection, signs of which were apparent earlier, not a single political leader represented this forgotten corner of the state. During the Civil War, the lingering unionism of the Carolina mountain farmers not only led to large-scale desertions from the Confederate Army but also provided a safe haven for escaped Union Army prisoners of war. Ashmore compiled a list of 502 deserters from the mountain districts of the state. The governor was forced to order Confederate troops to suppress disaffection there. But unionists in South Carolina, more than in any other southern state, were hopelessly outnumbered. Resignation and perhaps fear reigned supreme among the mountain unionists on secession.[38]

The election to the secession convention of 1860 was an even more unexciting affair than the elections to the legislature. Simms wrote that men of the "right lineage," such as the Middletons, Heywards, Gadsdens, and Rutledges, should adorn it. One writer argued that all divisions should be forgotten so the world would know that "the Secession Party of 1860 is literally and emphatically the *State* itself." Secessionists made sure that most districts and parishes put up only one ticket for the convention. Local secessionist gatherings simply drew up a single slate of candidates who were elected unopposed. In Charleston, where the elections were more lively, forty-seven names were suggested for twenty-two seats. Secessionists floated a questionnaire among these candidates characterizing them on the basis of their answers as explicit, not so explicit, and those who simply refused to answer on immediate secession. But this system seems to have backfired as the not so explicit candidates and those who refused to answer garnered as many and at times more votes than the explicit candidates. Perhaps the only districts in which two slates were drawn up were the mountain districts of Spartanburg and Greenville. In Spartanburg, the division was based on factional rather than political differences. In Greenville, a cooperationist slate of five headed by Perry was put up merely three days before the election. Two of the five candidates then proceeded to withdraw their names. The only popular test of secession, if its rather uneven contest can be characterized as such, seems to have been made in the old unionist district of Greenville. Results showed that the secessionists won an overwhelming victory there, garnering more than 1,000 votes to Perry's 225. But all five secessionists elected were slaveholders, two did not reside in Greenville, and a majority of the voters in the district had not voted.

It is not surprising that despite the frenzied political atmosphere most citizens did not participate in the Carolina-style elections. Many eligible voters chose to stay away from the polls and voter apathy seems to have dominated the state as a whole. The single-ticket system made the whole exercise of voting a rather meaningless affair. A. C. Spain wrote from Sumter that the Union men in his locality were "dispirited" with the defection of their leaders and planned not to "run an opposing ticket for the Convention." In Newberry not even half the eligible voters cast their ballots and in one place even the formality of opening the polls was dispensed with. As Perry noted, "The Union men thought it was a foregone conclusion that the State would secede, & it was not worth their while to go to the polls." Many, such as Harris, who refused to cast his vote simply because it was too cold to go out, no doubt supported secession. But in the upper districts, R. N. Hemphill of Blackstocks reported, "A goodly number of the Hard shell, Cooperation and Union men refused to attend the polls. Hence the very small vote taken." He repeated the secessionist logic of the day that the slated nominees "must be voted for and no other for fear of divisions &c &c."

While the lack of formal unionist or cooperationist opposition indicates that probably a majority of citizens acquiesced in disunion, South Carolina's secession was not the "landsturm" of the people visualized by Simms and latter-day historians. The average Carolinian citizen followed rather than led the movement for secession in his state. A. P. Aldrich exemplified the secessionist mindset when he wrote, "I do not believe the common people understand it, in fact, I know that they do not understand it; but whoever waited for the common people when a great move was to be made. We must make the move & force them to follow. This is the way of all revolutions & all great achievements, & he who waits until the mind of every body is made up will wait forever & never do anything."[39]

Just as Simms had hoped, the names of the well-known and leading planter families made up the roster of the convention: Middleton, De Saussure, Manning, Calhoun, Manigault, Hayne, Cheves, Hammond, Seabrook, Furman, Chesnut, Barnwell, Rhett, and Richardson. The state's political leaders who had been instrumental in the secession movement of 1860, such as Rhett, Miles, Keitt, Orr, Spratt, Adams, Gregg, Means, Gist, Mazyck, Townsend, and R. N. Gourdin, were also well represented. Some members were veterans of the 1832 and 1852 conventions. The secession convention had the same malapportioned representation as the legislature. Ralph Wooster's study of southern secession conventions reveals that South Carolina's convention was by far the wealthiest body with the highest median property and slaveholding rates. Of the 153 delegates he studied (the convention was composed of 169 delegates), 90.5 percent were slaveowners, 61.5 percent were planters, and 41.4 percent owned more than fifty slaves. Twenty-seven delegates owned a hundred or more slaves. The average number of slaves held by the members was 58.8 and the median, thirty-seven. Reverend J. H. Thornwell only had praise for this "noble body," which was immune to "popular excitement" and the ragtag influence of the populace. In a very literal sense, "the last foray" of aristocracy, the Carolinian slaveholding elite, led the state out of the Union.[40]

South Carolina inaugurated the secession movement by becoming the first southern state to secede from the Union. In his last messages, Gist had assured Carolinians that the rest of the South was no longer "jealous" of the state's leadership. The newly inaugurated governor, Francis W. Pickens, also recommended that the state resume its "sovereignty and independence" and construct a southern confederacy based on "common interest with peoples of homogeneous feelings, united together by all the ties that can bind States in one common destiny." Assurances of southern support encouraged Carolinians to complete the business of secession with dispatch. Commissioners from Alabama and Mississippi, John A. Elmore and Charles E. Hooker, urged immediate secession. Later, Commissioner M. S. Perry of Florida would be on hand to commend the state's secession. An address signed by thirty southern congressmen proclaimed "The argument is exhausted" and urged separate secession by the states. Howell Cobb, who had resigned from Buchanan's cabinet, was invited to take a seat in the convention. A message from some Georgia legislators recommended delay, but Governor Moore sent a dramatic telegram to Elmore that stated, "Tell the Convention to listen to no propositions of compromise or delay."

Carolinian leaders did not need much outside prompting. The convention met behind closed doors in Columbia on December 17 and D. F. Jamison was elected president. A smallpox outbreak forced it to move to Charleston, but not before a resolution declaring the desire of the state to secede passed without dissent. The convention worked, in the words of one of its members, John S. Palmer, "to pull down our government and erect another." On December 20, John Inglis reported the Ordinance of Secession, which passed unanimously by a vote of 169 to 0. On a more ominous note, and revealing the skittishness of the planter elite, the convention passed "An Ordinance to define and punish Treason" prescribing the death penalty for treason against the State of South Carolina. Another ordinance formally excluded all black people from citizenship. Racial slavery was indeed going to be the raison d'être of independent South Carolina. At an official ceremony that evening, anointed by the benedictions of Reverend John Bachman, each member of the convention rose to sign the ordinance in the presence of the legislature and governor, who had been invited for the occasion. Outside the convention hall, church bells peeled and cannonades signaled South Carolina's departure from the American republic. Accounts of the festive atmosphere include the ubiquitous minute men, fireworks, and banners covering city streets. But one observer wrote, "There is no great enthusiasm at the event. Everyone seemed to anticipate it."[41]

According to old Carolinian lore recounted by Pope, on hearing the bells, "Mr. Petigru rushed up and exclaimed: 'Where's the fire?' I said: 'Mr. Petigru, there is no fire; those are the bells ringing in honor of the passage of the Ordinance of Secession.' He turned instantly and said, 'I tell you there is a fire; they have this day set a blazing torch to the temple of constitutional liberty and, please God, we shall have no more peace forever.' " Irked by Petigru's steadfast unionism, Rhett Jr. accused him of being a "monarchist." The redoubtable Petigru replied, "he has no more reason to say so than this, that I am a Union man, and he would prefer monarchy, even under foreign rule, to the Union." Earlier when the *Mercury* had looked around the world to find another shining example of a slaveholding republic, it pointed to "The Trans-Vaal Republic" of South Africa presided over by Dutch slaveholders. And Barker had argued, "The lie which has been written, by Northern construction, upon the margins of our noble Declaration of Independence of '76, must soon be erased. That greater truth, that '*all men* are *not* born free and equal,' written by the finger of God in lines so plain upon the world's history, and so indelibly stamped upon the organization of the negro, must be inscribed boldly upon our banner." The *Charleston Mercury* proclaimed, "Conservative liberty has been vindicated. Mobocratic license has been stricken down." Secessionists such as Gist commended the inauguration of the counterrevolution of slavery.[42]

Reactions to South Carolina's secession varied above and below the Mason-Dixon line. Despite individual and partisan differences, northerners generally condemned the "mad," "rash," and "reckless" action of the state, as did border-state unionists. Henry J. Raymond, editor of the *New York Times*, charged that "South Carolina has never had a particle of sympathy with the fundamental principles which lie at the basis of our Republican institutions." Reverend James W. Hunnicutt, a staunch Virginian unionist who was originally from upcountry Pendleton, had this to say of his native state: "The *honor*, the *imperishable glory*, of *secession* and *inaugurating Civil War* was reserved for South Carolina! Shame on the State, and infamy on the leaders!" Reverend R. J. Breckinridge argued . that secession was a result of "the chronic hatred of South Carolina to the national Union," and that South Carolina had "dictated" disunion to the rest of the southern states. Carolinian secessionists were especially stung by southern criticism and denounced the "phlegmatics" who condemned the "hot haste" and lone action of their state. South Carolina, they pointed out, "gave long notice" that it would secede upon Lincoln's election. Their "timid friends" were responsible for its separate secession. Virginian secessionist D. C. Jarnette felt that the place of his state was with South Carolina, "one of the brightest stars" of the Union.

While great differences in opinion characterized northern, southern, unionist, and disunionist responses to the state's secession, all seemed to agree that it was only natural that South Carolina should take the lead. A sympathetic New Orleans paper explained, "it was requisite that some State should take the initiative; and certainly that position appertained peculiarly to South Carolina, as for years she had been most prominent, emphatic and unconditional in her hostility to and denunciation of the abolition proclivities of the North." Republican newspapers referred back to the "seeds" sowed by Calhoun and nullification to explain the rise of disunionism, one even alluding to the "Calhoun states" of the Lower South. Ruffin wrote, "The people of S.Ca. have been schooled and in training for 30 years in their political doctrines." John Pendleton Kennedy remarked on the "strange insulation of opinion," "exclusive philosophies," and "political sophisms" of South Carolina. He pointed out that the contemporary generation of Carolinian leaders had been taught disunion since childhood.[43]

A sectional divide in the debate over the constitutionality of secession was also evident. Carolinian planter politicians had already established their beliefs in state sovereignty, nullification, and the constitutional right to secession and they alluded to the Carolina doctrines as a self-evident retort to northern criticisms. For if secession was a "constitutional right" then the federal government had no power to "coerce" a state or to hinder the "peaceable" execution of secession. Those southerners who thought of secession as a "revolutionary right" also viewed any effort on the part of the federal government to check secession as "unconstitutional" and "coercive." But for most northerners, secession was a blow not only against the Union, but also against the whole idea of representative government. Francis Lieber, who fashioned a nationalistic interpretation of the Constitution as a rejoinder to secessionist belief in absolute state sovereignty, challenged the idea that secession was a defense of local democracy and decentralization. Having witnessed Carolina-style politics during his fairly long sojourn in that state, he wrote, "It is a fact . . . that almost all, perhaps actually all, the most prominent extremists on the State-Rights side — that is to say, of those statesmen who were most perseveringly bent on coercing the national government into the narrowest circle of helplessness — have been at the same time strongly inclined toward centralization and consolidation of power within their respective States."

The Constitution contained no provisions either for secession or for measures to prevent it. As Petigru wrote, "The success of the project of going out of the Union at will, demonstrates the fallacy of attempting to combine the principle of unity with that of separate independence of the States; and makes the Constitution a mere cobweb." Calhoun's theory of constitutional secession was conceived of as a political device to protect the southern slaveholding minority in a democratic republic and it clearly acted as such in 1860. Carolinian secessionists connected the right to secession with the protection of slavery. As the *Mercury* expressed it, in 1815 New England used "correct" political principles for an "unrighteous cause." Listing all the measures against the expansion of slavery, it implied that the "correct" political principles had been linked to the allegedly righteous cause of slavery.[44]

No other group of Carolinians shed light on the nature of the state's secession more thoughtfully than its clergymen. Smith and Furman had actively participated in the campaign for disunion, while Bachman and others had blessed the work of secession. After secession, these men threw the considerable weight of their combined religious authority behind the cause of an independent slave nation and expounded eloquently on its divinely ordained destiny. On a somber note, Reverend C. C. Pinckney of Charleston explained that disunion was God's visitation on the overweening pride of the American people in their republic. Pride led them to laud the republican principles of their country and disparage the "crumbling monarchies" of Europe. Like the biblical emperor Nebudchadnezzar, the American republic had fallen for the sin of pride. Reverend William O. Prentiss predicted the rise of a great southern nation "phoenix like" from the ashes of the American republic. The "colossal fabric" of this mighty new nation would be created by "three hundred and fifty thousand white men" commanding the labor of "four million African slaves." A writer using the pseudonym "Octogenarian" argued that Republicans' devotion to the Declaration of Independence instead of the "divine truth" was equivalent to Satan's demand for equality with the Almighty.[45]

Foremost among South Carolina's proslavery clergymen who sanctified the creation of a slave nation was Reverend J. H. Thornwell. In a sermon on national sins that he preached on the eve of disunion, he refrained from advising his state on secession, leaving the matter in the hands of Caesar. At the same time, he repeated Calhoun's theory of absolute state sovereignty, which justified secession. Further, he argued that states, like individuals, were capable of committing sins against God and that the nonslaveholding states had "broken faith" with the slaveholding states on slavery. Another "national sin" was the deterioration of representative government. He argued, "Representatives are appointed, not to ascertain what the will of the people actually is, but what it ought to be." Instead, representatives now acted as mere "deputies" of the people who decreed "*Vox populi, vox dei*" (the voice of the people is the voice of God). Thornwell wrote, "If . . . the South is not prepared to see her institutions surrounded by enemies, and wither and decay under these hostile influences, if she means to cherish and protect them, it is her bounden duty to resist the revolution which threatens them with ruin. The triumph of the principles which Mr. Lincoln is pledged to carry out, is the death-knell of slavery." Secession was an eminently conservative measure to stop the destructive effects on slave society of this revolution.

Thornwell's follower and admirer, Reverend Benjamin Morgan Palmer, a native Carolinian who had settled in Louisiana, also argued that the issue of slavery was the "occasion" and "cause" of secession. Palmer's defense of lower south secession was fashioned as a reply to Reverend Breckinridge. Like Thornwell and Palmer, Breckinridge was a conservative Presbyterian minister. An uncle of the southern Democratic presidential nominee, this Breckinridge was a fierce unionist who condemned southern disunionism and northern abolitionism as twin "manifestations" of "the spirit of anarchy." Palmer angrily responded that southern secession had reversed the growth of anarchical tendencies in the country and that political change need not be "disintegrating" but "recuperating." The split between old-line unionist and secessionist Presbyterians was evident. The proslavery Dr. Hodge also condemned secession. In reply, W. J. Grayson justified secession on the grounds that "[t]he North wage war against the social condition of the Southern States." When the national Presbyterian assembly officially came out against secession,

Thornwell led the secession of southern Presbyterians from the church and the formation of the "Presbyterian Church in the Confederate States of America" in 1861. The mission of the new southern church, he argued, would be to enforce the duties of masters and slaves. Thornwell also outlined the mission of the new Confederate government. The American Constitution rested on a "fundamental error," that government was the "offspring of popular will" or the "mere expression of human will." This error had led to "a democratic absolutism." The Confederate nation would realize the supremacy of scriptural authority and reject the expulsion of "Jehovah" from matters of the state. A divinely inspired Christian slave nation would replace the old atheistic, democratic republic.[46]

Secular vindications of secession in South Carolina also stressed the proslavery, antidemocratic nature of the movement. Carolinian planter Gabriel Edward Manigault later wrote that the South had fought for nothing but its "property rights in slaves." The *Mercury*, arguing against proposals for the reconstruction of the Union, held, "The social and political organism of the South is, in all respects, theoretically and practically, different and opposed to that of the North. Southern institutions are essentially conservative. It recognizes distinct order and classes." It pointed out that "[o]ne-third of the whole Southern population do not cast a single vote. They are disenfranchised. They are not recognized as citizens of the several States. They are slaves. In South Carolina one-half of the population of the State are in this category. . . . Southern society is unquestionably of an aristocratic cast." Even as the editorial argued that all whites belong to a "favored class," for its writer, racial slavery was the essential foundation for the South's distinctive conservative order. "The most destructive feature of Northern society, political and social, is radicalism-license. The basis of all Southern organism is conservatism-order. The two systems are in direct antagonism." The union between the slave South and free North was "unnatural and monstrous," in the words of John S. Preston, South Carolina's commissioner to Virginia. Slavery was to the South what "pure democracy of mere numbers" was to the North.[47]

Slavery as it existed, and as the fundament of southern identity — not fears of white slavery, nor fears of political slavery in a nebulous republican cosmology — was the official cause of secession. The secession convention's report authored by a committee headed by C. G. Memminger reiterated that the northern states had specifically violated the Constitution as far as slavery was concerned. Since the Constitution was a "compact" between the states such violations "released" the state from the Union. The report put slavery squarely at the center of the state's grievances, which included violations of the fugitive slave law, efforts to incite "servile insurrection," and, finally, "the election of a man to the high office of President of the United States, whose opinions and purposes are hostile to slavery." The Republican Party, the report pointed out, was not only committed to the nonextension of slavery, but in certain states it had been elected with the votes of free black people, who "by the supreme law of the land, are incapable of becoming citizens; and their votes have been used to inaugurate a new policy, hostile to the South, and destructive of its peace and safety." Secession, the convention argued, was also a suitable check against the spread of democracy. An address to the slaveholding states, prepared by a committee headed by Rhett, announced that the republican experiment inaugurated by the Constitution of 1787 had "failed." The address identified "consolidated democracy" and the "rule of the majority" as the villains of sectional strife. For the free North, "Numbers . . . is the great element of free Government," but for the slave South the whole exercise in constitutional government was to "restrain the majority." Unlike Memminger's report, Rhett's address alluded to "unjust taxation" along with slavery as a cause for secession, apparently with an eye to international favor. But the address justified disunion on the ground that the "rule of a sectional anti-slavery government" would result in "the emancipation of the slaves in the South." It also firmly based a grandiose vision of a southern nation on slavery: "To be one of a great Slaveholding Confederacy, stretching its arms over a territory larger than any power in Europe possesses — with a population four times greater than the whole of the United States when they achieved their independence of the British Empire — with, productions which make our existence more important to the world than that of any other people inhabiting it — with common institutions to defend, and common dangers to encounter — we ask your sympathy and confederation."

South Carolina took the first steps for the formation of a southern nation. On December 31, it called for a meeting of the southern states in Montgomery, Alabama, to draft a provisional constitution for a southern confederacy modeled on the Constitution of the United States. Changes in the U.S. Constitution were recommended with the formation of a permanent government. The convention appointed commissioners to the slave states who urged speedy secession and participation in the proposed southern confederacy. The choice of commissioners was astute: extremists such as Spratt, A. P. Calhoun, and Bonham (later replaced by Armistead Burt) were sent to Florida, Alabama, and Mississippi, states in which secessionist feeling was high; and moderates such as Manning and Orr were sent to Louisiana and Georgia, in which cooperationism was strong. Rhett, Barnwell, Miles, Chesnut, Memminger, Keitt, Boyce, and T. J. Withers were selected as the state's deputies to the Montgomery convention.[48] The counterrevolution of slavery had begun.

Not only did South Carolina lead the Lower South out of the Union during the secession winter of 1860–61, but it was also hardly a coincidence that a military showdown on Carolinian soil precipitated the secession of four upper south states. The secession of the state had given the impetus for lower south secession. By February 1, 1861, Mississippi, Florida, Alabama, Georgia, Louisiana, and Texas had left the Union. There was a dramatic drop in voter turnout in the lower south states between the presidential elections and elections to the secession conventions, and, with the exception of Mississippi and Florida, in these states the convention elections were "remarkably close" and revealed old sectional divisions between yeoman-dominated hill counties and slavery-dominated plantation belts. In none of these states, with the exception of Texas, where voting took place after secession was a *fait accompli*, were the secession ordinances submitted for popular ratification. On February 7, the seceded slave states adopted a provisional constitution for the Confederate States of America.[49]

Slavery was central to the meaning and purpose of the Confederacy. The new slave nation did not turn out to be all that Carolinian secessionists desired. A "secession banner," which hung from the South Carolina Institute Hall after the secession ordinance was signed, showed a resurgent confederacy of all the slave states, including Delaware, Maryland, Missouri, and Kentucky, "built from the ruins" of broken-down free states. Carolinian leaders were also harshly critical of some of the Confederate constitution's features. The three-fifths clause, the African slave trade prohibition, the popular election of the president and vice president, and the absence of a clause prohibiting the entrance of free states elicited lengthy criticisms. Keziah Brevard wrote, "I still fear So. Ca. cannot be pleased — I do not love her disposition to cavil at every move." But the fundamental law of the Confederate nation specifically mentioned and committed it to the perpetuity and expansion of slavery. Though not the perfect slave nation envisioned by Carolinian purists, the Confederacy was a slave nation and fought for its "baptism in blood."[50]

Military confrontation between state and federal authorities was inevitable. In his annual message, President Buchanan repudiated the right to secession, but he squarely blamed the "long-continued and intemperate interference of the Northern people with the question of slavery" for the rise of disunion. He claimed that the federal government was incapable of exercising any further jurisdiction in South Carolina as its chief officers had resigned but he was not willing to give up federal forts within the state. Trescot advised Gist that "the state owes . . . to the President to save him whatever it can in the coming crisis consistently with its honor and interest." As assistant and later acting secretary of state in the days prior to South Carolina's secession, Trescot played an important role in influencing administration policy. Trescot attributed Buchanan's refusal to take decisive action to his unwillingness to do anything that would help Lincoln and to his "secret sympathy" with the South. Buchanan's vacillation reflected the contradictions, engendered by the secession crisis, between his politics and his position as chief executive officer of the federal government. Petigru wrote, "Buchanan's message is out. . . . Like himself, it is a shuffling, insincere and shabby performance. He has receded from one point to another until he has given up all pretension to the respect of anybody. The Secessionists will not be interfered with, at least by him, and his pusillanimity will not conciliate the South, but will greatly disgust those States that are attached to the Union, and lead, perhaps, to a general repudiation of the Constitution as an inefficient and inadequate scheme of government."[51]

Carolinian planter politicians quickly realized that the assertion of independence lay not in arcane constitutional debates but in the establishment of a very basic, physical dominion over the territory of the state. Even before secession Carolinians had been preoccupied with the issue of the federal forts and with erecting defenses for the sea coast and Charleston harbor. Despite all the talk of peaceful secession, they were realistically preparing for war. On December 24, 1860, Governor Pickens issued a proclamation announcing "TO THE WORLD THAT THIS STATE IS, AS SHE HAS THE RIGHT TO BE, A SEPARATE, SOVEREIGN, FREE AND INDEPENDENT STATE; AND, AS SUCH, HAS A RIGHT TO LEVY WAR, CONCLUDE PEACE, NEGOTIATE TREATIES, LEAGUES, OR COVENANTS, AND TO DO ALL ACTS WHATSOEVER THAT RIGHTFULLY APPERTAIN TO A FREE AND INDEPENDENT STATE." But this unequivocal declaration of Carolinian independence was marred by the presence of federal property and troops. Referring to the potential for conflict over the forts, Catherine Gilman exclaimed, "What a volcano we sit over!" The state convention appointed three commissioners, Barnwell, Adams, and Orr, to negotiate the withdrawal of federal forces.

The stalemate over the forts marked the end of cordial relations between Buchanan and Carolinian secessionists. Before any agreement could be reached between the state's commissioners and the administration, Major Robert Anderson of the United States Army moved his regiment from the relatively insecure Fort Moultrie to Fort Sumter on December 26, 1860. Anderson's move was guided both by military logic and a desire to avoid a confrontation with state authorities, who were rearing to occupy the forts. State troops proceeded to occupy Moultrie, Castle Pinckney, the Charleston Arsenal, and Fort Johnson; the other seceding states, learning from the experience of South Carolina, were quick to occupy federal forts and arsenals, gaining in many cases large caches of arms and ammunition. Buchanan made it clear that Anderson had acted independently but, on the prompting of his cabinet, refused to consider South Carolina's demand that he order Anderson back to Moultrie. The state's commissioners accused the president of deliberately deceiving them. In a separate communication, Miles and Keitt repeated this charge and lauded the resignation of the Virginian secretary of war, John B. Floyd, who was already under fire for corruption, ostensibly to protest the president's policy. When Jacob Thompson of Mississippi followed Floyd, southern influence in the administration evaporated. The one southerner in the cabinet was a staunch unionist from Kentucky, the new secretary of war, Joseph Holt. In a special message to Congress, Buchanan now asserted his military authority to defend federal property. Trescot sent a telegram to Miles stating that Holt's appointment and the decision to reinforce Sumter meant "war." The attempt at reinforcement, however, was a distinct failure, as Carolinian guns managed to stop the ship sent, *Star of the West*, from reaching Sumter. Hostilities were averted even though Anderson characterized the firing on the ship as an "act of war." By January 1861 the first shot of the Civil War had already been fired; the first casualty of the war had occurred during the state occupation of Castle Pinckney, when a man was shot to death "by mistake." Both acts reflected the state government's determination to make good on its claim to "eminent domain."[52]

Carolinian leaders had become extremely restless with the continued federal presence at Sumter. As Samuel Wylie Crawford, medical officer at Sumter, wrote, "The Secession of South Carolina is incomplete as long as we remain here. She is now only half out of the Union and her people are stung to the quick that 70 men should keep at bay a whole State in arms." It especially irked secessionists that Anderson, a fellow "southron" and "slaveholder" from Kentucky, commanded the federal garrison at Sumter. Demands to take over the fort forcibly, even at the risk of provoking hostilities before the formation of the southern confederacy, became commonplace. The *Charleston Mercury* argued, "South Carolina must look to herself in this matter and act for and by herself. . . . South Carolina must play her *own* part, directly, unequivocally, upon her own responsibility, if she would maintain herself, her dignity, her great ends. To make her actions subject to that of others, is to strike away her moral weight — to forfeit her position — to make herself a tool, a shuttle cock, a plaything in the hands of others. Alone she must act." To justify this position, Carolinian secessionists argued that Anderson had already committed "an act of invasion" and "hostility" by moving to Sumter. Pickens first sent Magrath and Jamison, members of the newly formed Executive Council, to ask Anderson to surrender the fort. On Anderson's suggestion that such a demand should be addressed to Washington, Pickens sent Hayne with a letter addressed to Buchanan peremptorily demanding the evacuation of the fort.

Senators from the rest of the cotton states hastily interceded, asking Hayne to withhold Pickens's letter and offering to make an "arrangement" with the president to avoid hostilities until the formation of the southern nation. They argued that their states would be forced to share the "evils of war" with South Carolina and that it was only "due from South Carolina to our States — to say nothing of other slaveholding States — that she should, as far as she consistently can with her honor, avoid initiating hostilities between her and the United States or any other Power." Despite their recommendations, Hayne presented Pickens's letter and asserted the state's authority over Sumter. Secretary of War Holt refused to consider evacuation or to bind the government to a pledge against reinforcements. In the meantime, the cotton states' senators were more successful in negotiating a truce over Fort Pickens in Florida. Miles wrote from Montgomery, where a provisional constitution and government for the Confederacy were rapidly created, strongly advising caution. He felt that the state must await the action of the new government, and he assured Pickens, "The *Courage* of South Carolina has been too amply and too habitually proved to require us now to do *anything* merely to demonstrate it further." Carolinian authorities agreed to leave the entire matter to the Confederate government, but Pickens continued to make warlike gestures until General P. G. T. Beauregard assumed command of the Confederate forces on the Carolina coast in March 1861. Petigru remarked, "Things look more favorable since Jeff Davis has superseded Pickens."[53]

Carolinian planter politicians' intransigent attitude in no small measure helped make Sumter the starting point of the Civil War. Their eagerness to precipitate a conflict over Sumter was guided not only by a desire to make real the state's independence, but also, in part, to influence the behavior of the border states. Waddy Thompson reasoned that "if coercion was not attempted and even the border states did not join the southern confederacy — we should lose the advantage of having our border states slaveholding — But if that coercion was attempted the necessities of their position would force those states to unite with us — Thus securing their cooperation in the only event where we should greatly need it." After the lower south states followed South Carolina out of the Union in quick succession, secessionists faced major defeats in the Upper South. Instead, Upper South leaders backed by northern conservatives proposed "compromises" prescribing iron-clad constitutional guarantees for slavery as a way to reconstruct the Union. They hoped to avert disunion by engrafting the slavery agenda of southern nationalists onto the Constitution, an agenda that northerners had decisively rejected by electing a Republican president. At the same time, Upper South "unionists" stated that they would resist federal "coercion" of the seceded states to the point of disunion.

Carolinian secessionists vigorously denounced all plans for compromise and the reconstruction of the Union. State and Confederate authorities realized that only the failure of compromise and a military confrontation would decide the course of the Upper South. Ruffin wished that Anderson would commence hostilities, as it would result in the secession of Virginia and the "waiting states." Roger Pryor assured his Carolina audience, on the eve of the Confederate bombardment of Fort Sumter, that the Old Dominion would send "upon the plains of South Carolina men adequate for any emergency whatsoever." The *Mercury* opined that the Republicans would not start a war as they did not want to lose the border slave states, but that they would "trifle and trick at the risk of bloodshed at the forts." In April 1861, Lincoln informed Pickens that Sumter would be reinforced. After Anderson refused once again to surrender, Confederate forces commenced the bombardment of the fort on April 12. The Confederacy's first shot united the North behind Lincoln's proclamation of war and also resulted in the secession of Virginia, North Carolina, Tennessee, and Arkansas. As Petigru stated, "The Southern Confederacy has indeed proclaimed war, and the Northern States are not slow to take up the gage." After the fall of Sumter, Pickens in his victory speech boasted of the long-held dream of Carolinian secessionists, the humbling of the American flag before "the glorious little State of South Carolina."[54] South Carolina had given the impetus for the secession of both the lower south and the upper south states. Its secessionist planters had fulfilled the historical mission they had been rehearsing for years.

The Counterrevolution
of Slavery

The prevailing ideas entertained by . . . most of the leading statesmen at the
time of the formation of the old Constitution were, that the enslavement of the
African was in violation, of the laws of nature; that it was wrong in principle,
socially, morally and politically. . . . Our new Government is founded upon
exactly the opposite ideas; its foundations are laid, its cornerstone rests, upon
the great truth that the negro is not equal to the white man; that slavery,
subordination to the superior race, is his natural and moral condition. . . .
[O]ur new Government, is the first, in the history of the world, based
upon this great physical, philosophical, and moral truth."
— ALEXANDER STEPHENS,
Vice President of the Confederate States of America, 1861

The counterrevolutionary nature of secession became evident during the
Civil War and the years following it. In the aftermath of the war, George
Fitzhugh gave a perceptive reading of the Carolina-led southern movement of 1860–61. He argued that secession was an overturning of the
Revolution of 1776 and the principles that underlay it; secessionists were
not Whigs but Tories. The American Revolution was "an exceedingly
vulgar, commonplace affair" and the "bombastic absurdity" of its Declaration of Independence, "pompous," "*mal-apropos*," and "silly." "The
Fathers of the Republic most officiously and unwisely rested the splendid
political edifice they had created on powder-cask abstractions," ideas
which had been incorporated in the Republican Party platform in 1860.
The revolution of the "4th of March, '61," he wrote, was the "grandest
explosion the world ever witnessed. The French Revolutions of '89, 1830
and 1848, were mere pop-guns compared to it; as we all see and feel, for
its stunning sound is still ringing in our ears." In contrast, the "doctrine

of the South" drew its inspiration from the Aristotelian, conservative political principle that "in all societies some were formed to command, others to obey, that inequality, not equality, was the necessary condition of man . . . for society can only exist as a series of subordinations." The "Southern Revolution of 1861" was "reactionary and conservative" and a "solemn protest against the doctrines of natural liberty, human equality and the social contracts as taught by Locke and the American sages of 1776, and an equally solemn protest against the doctrines of Adam Smith, Franklin, Say and Tom Paine and the rest of the infidel, political economists, who maintain that the world is too much governed."[1]

For Karl Marx, secession represented not just political reaction nor a protest against free market capitalism but a war against laboring people all over the world. The cause of the black slave, he felt, was inevitably tied to the fate of the working classes. In a letter to Lincoln, he wrote,

> When an oligarchy of 300,000 slave-holders dared to inscribe for the first time in the annals of the world "slavery" on the banner of Armed Revolt, when on the very spots hardly a century ago the idea of one great Democratic Republic had first sprung up, whence the first Declaration of the Rights of Man was issued, and the first im-pulse given to the European Revolution of the eighteenth century; when on those very spots counter-revolution, with systematic thor-oughness, gloried in rescinding "the ideas entertained at the time of the formation of the old constitution," and maintained "slavery to be a beneficent institution," indeed, the only solution to the great problem of "the relation of capital to labor," and cynically pro-claimed property in man "the corner-stone of the new edifice," — then the working classes of Europe understood at once, even before the fanatic partisanship of the upper classes for the Confederate gentry had given its dismal warning, that the slave-holders' rebel-lion was to sound the tocsin for a general holy crusade of property against labour, and that for the man of labour, with their hopes for the future, even their past conquests were at stake in that tremen-dous conflict on the other side of the Atlantic.[2]

Thinkers as diverse as Marx and proslavery ideologues could agree that secession represented the counterrevolution of slavery.

But it was the actions and words of the enslaved that brought out the nature and the import of the issues involved in secession and the war. Behind the familiar story of the dramatic shooting at Fort Sumter, Caro-linian slaves enacted a historical drama of even greater significance, a drama that foreshadowed the events of the Civil War. The main actors in this drama were two Carolinian slaves, mother and son, their names and actions unrecorded by history. In March 1861, the government of South Carolina demanded an explanation for a letter written by a Carolinian slave hired by Major Robert Anderson as his "servant" at Fort Sumter. The letter was addressed to his mother, who lived in Charleston, and it stated that if the state government attacked Sumter then the slaves would rise and "assist" federal troops. The entire affair was considered serious enough to command the attention of no less a personage than D. F. Jamison, president of the secession convention. Despite Anderson's strenuous denials, his servant was "detained" by state authorities, apparently while on a visit to the mainland, and then returned to his Carolinian owner. When Anderson repeatedly asked for the return of his servant, Jamison replied that he could not dispute "the right of the owner" to refuse the services of his slave.

However, the real reason why the slave had not been returned was revealed by Samuel Wylie Crawford, who left a record of the entire incident. He wrote of Jamison's reasoning, "the boy's mother had written things to him at the fort, of preparations in the City that were very improper things to communicate to any one in our garrison, and that the boy's temper, and principles did not seem to be benefitted by a residence in Fort Sumter." The normally calm and cautious Anderson penned an angry rejoinder referring to the "inconveniences" his officers would be subjected to without a "servant" and noted that the master had shown uncharacteristic concern about his slave after "months of neglect" and unconcern about his whereabouts. He cryptically added that the state authorities would "regret" their remark about the bad influence of Sumter on the slave. Anderson, a Kentucky slaveholder who half sympathized with the secessionists, resented the casting of any aspersion on himself and his officers for fostering plans of slave rebellion or involving the slaves of the state in military operations. His "servant" had clearly acted on his own initiative as had his mother.[3]

The slaves' actions provide a glimpse into the future when Carolinian slaves would help cripple the cause their masters fought for, their enslavement. Many would flee to freedom and some would return home triumphantly in Union Army uniforms. Former Carolinian slave Jacob Stroyer recalled that during the Civil War, "the negroes never lost hope, but faithfully supported the Union cause with their prayers." As Armstead Robinson has argued, "A war fought to protect slavery ended in its destruction and slaves whose permanent servitude was to be the Confederacy's triumphant reward helped deny slaveholders the fulfillment of their most cherished dream." Carolinian slaveholders had begun learning that they could hardly rely on the supposedly unquestioned loyalty of their slaves at the time of battle. Keziah Brevard wrote, "My Southern

Sisters & brothers who think their slaves would be on our side in a civil war, will, I fear, find they have been artfully taken in." With the firing on Sumter and the start of the war, she trembled at the thought, "we have enemies in our midst." In 1836, the Carolinian proslavery divine Reverend Iveson Brookes had a prophetic dream, "that in some 20 or 30 years a division of the Northern and Southern States will be produced by the Abolitionists and then a war will exist between Yankees and the slaveholders — that the Army of Yankees will be joined by the N——s who will shew more savage cruelty than the bloodthirsty Indians — and that the Southerners with gratitude for having escaped alive will gladly leave their splendid houses and farms to be occupied by those who once served them." While Carolinian slaves would show considerably more humanity than their erstwhile masters displayed and expected from them on emancipation, the moment of truth envisaged by Brookes would eventually come to South Carolina. J. H. Thornwell, writing in the midst of southern reverses during the Civil War that he explained as God's trial of southern faith and punishment for the sin of pride, lamented at the prospect of defeat, "The civilized world will look coldly upon us, or even jeer us with the taunt that we had deservedly lost our freedom in seeking to perpetuate the slavery of others."[4]

In countless ways, Carolinian slaves would compel the nation to recognize the injustice, the inhumanity, the impropriety, and the inexpediency of their enslavement and help make the war for the Union also a war against southern slavery. "Events themselves," Marx wrote at the beginning of the war, "drive themselves to the promulgation of the decisive slogan — *emancipation of the slaves*."[5] Historians, like contemporaries, have long noted that an overwhelming majority of South Carolinians were for secession. But a majority of South Carolinians had nothing to do with secession or the glorification of human bondage. A majority of South Carolinians in 1860 were slaves.

NOTES

Abbreviations

AH	*Agricultural History*
AHA	American Historical Association
AHR	*American Historical Review*
CWH	*Civil War History*
CG	*Congressional Globe*
DBR	*De Bow's Review*
DU	Perkins Library, Duke University
FHQ	*Florida Historical Quarterly*
GHR	*Georgia Historical Review*
JAH	*Journal of American History*
JEH	*Journal of Economic History*
JER	*Journal of the Early Republic*
JMH	*Journal of Mississippi History*
JNH	*Journal of Negro History*
JSH	*Journal of Southern History*
LC	Library of Congress
LH	*Louisiana History*
MVHR	*Mississippi Valley Historical Review*
NCDAH	North Carolina Department of Archives and History
NCHR	*North Carolina Historical Review*
RAH	*Reviews in American History*
SAQ	*South Atlantic Quarterly*
SCDAH	South Carolina Department of Archives and History
SCHGM	*South Carolina Historical and Genealogical Magazine*
SCHM	*South Carolina Historical Magazine*
SCHS	South Carolina Historical Society
SCL	South Caroliniana Library, University of South Carolina, Columbia
SHC	Southern Historical Collection, University of North Carolina, Chapel Hill
SLM	*Southern Literary Messenger*
SQR	*Southern Quarterly Review*
SWHQ	*South Western Historical Quarterly*
THQ	*Tennessee Historical Quarterly*
WMQ	*William and Mary Quarterly*

1. See for example William W. Freehling, *Prelude to Civil War: The Nullification Controversy in South Carolina, 1816–1836* (New York, 1965); Steven A. Channing, *Crisis of Fear: Secession in South Carolina* (New York, 1970); John Barnwell, *Love of Order: South Carolina's First Secession Crisis* (Chapel Hill, N.C., 1982); Lacy K. Ford Jr., *Origins of Southern Radicalism: The South Carolina Upcountry, 1800–1860* (New York, 1988); Stephanie McCurry, *Masters of Small Worlds: Yeoman Households, Gender Relations, and the Political Culture of the Antebellum South Carolina Low Country* (New York, 1995); William L. Barney, "An Undiagnosed Fever: Political Radicalism in South Carolina," *RAH* 2 (June 1983): 215.

2. James M. Banner Jr., "The Problem of South Carolina," in Eric McKitrick and Stanley Elkins, eds., *The Hofstadter Aegis: A Memorial* (New York, 1974), 60–93; Freehling, *Prelude to Civil War*; Ford, *Origins of Southern Radicalism*, 99–102; Eugene D. Genovese, "South Carolina's Contribution to the Doctrine of Slavery in the Abstract," in David R. Chesnutt and Clyde N. Wilson, eds., *The Meaning of South Carolina History: Essays in Honor of George C. Rogers, Jr.* (Columbia, S.C., 1991), 146–60.

3. Compare this argument with J. Mills Thornton III, *Politics and Power in a Slave Society: Alabama, 1800–1860* (Baton Rouge, La., 1978); Ford, *Origins of Southern Radicalism*; William J. Cooper Jr., *The South and the Politics of Slavery, 1828–1856* (Baton Rouge, La., 1978); Anthony Gene Carey, *Parties, Slavery, and the Union in Antebellum Georgia* (Athens, Ga., 1997); Jonathan M. Atkins, *Parties, Politics, and the Sectional Conflict in Tennessee, 1832–1861* (Knoxville,1997); William G. Shade, *Democratizing the Old Dominion: Virginia and the Second Party System, 1828–1861* (Charlottesville, Va., 1996); Marc W. Kruman, *Parties and Politics in North Carolina, 1836–1865* (Baton Rouge, La., 1983). On Jacksonian democracy and the Second Party System see Daniel Feller, *The Jacksonian Promise: America, 1815–1840* (Baltimore, Md., 1995); Thomas E. Jeffrey, *State Parties and National Politics: North Carolina, 1815–1861* (Athens, Ga., 1989); Harry L. Watson, *Jacksonian Politics and Community Conflict: The Emergence of the Second American Party System in Cumberland County, North Carolina* (Baton Rouge, La., 1981), and *Liberty and Power: The Politics of Jacksonian America* (New York, 1990); Richard P. McCormick, *The Second Party System: Party Formation in the Jacksonian Era* (Chapel Hill, N.C., 1966).

4. Thornton, *Politics and Power*; William J. Cooper Jr., *Liberty and Slavery: Southern Politics to 1860* (New York, 1983); Bradley G. Bond, *Political Culture in the Nineteenth Century South: Mississippi, 1830–1900* (Baton Rouge, La., 1995); Ford, *Origins of Southern Radicalism*, 372.

5. See for example David M. Potter, *The Impending Crisis, 1848–1861* (New York, 1976); Cooper, *The Politics of Slavery*; William W. Freehling, *The Road to Disunion: Secessionists at Bay, 1776–1854* (New York, 1990).

6. Rachel N. Klein, *Unification of a Slave State: The Rise of the Planter Class in the South Carolina Backcountry, 1760–1808* (Chapel Hill, N.C., 1990); J. William Harris, *Plain Folk and Gentry in a Slave Society: White Liberty and Black Slavery in Augusta's Hinterlands* (Middletown, Conn., 1985); Kenneth S. Greenberg, *Masters and Statesmen: The Political Culture of American Slavery* (Baltimore, Md., 1985); Stephanie McCurry, "The Two Faces of Republicanism: Gender and Proslavery Politics in Antebellum South Carolina," *JAH* 78 (Mar. 1992): 1245–64.

7. Steven Hahn, *The Roots of Southern Populism: Yeoman Farmers and the Transformation of the Georgia Upcountry, 1850–1890* (New York, 1983), and "The Yeomanry of the Nonplantation South: Upper Piedmont Georgia, 1850–1860," in

Orville Vernon Burton and Robert C. McMath Jr., eds., *Class, Conflict and Consensus: Antebellum Southern Community Studies* (Westport, Conn., 1982), 29–56; On the southern yeomanry also see Harry L. Watson, "Conflict and Collaboration: yeomen, slaveholders, and politics in the antebellum South," *Social History* 10 (Oct. 1985): 273–98; Eugene D. Genovese, "Yeoman Farmers in a Slaveholders' Democracy," *AH* 49 (Apr. 1975): 331–42; Randolph B. Campbell, "Planters and Plain Folk: The Social Structure of the Antebellum South," in John B. Boles and Evelyn Thomas Nolen, eds., *Interpreting Southern History: Historiographical Essays in Honor of Sanford W. Higginbotham* (Baton Rouge, La., 1987), 48–77; Samuel C. Hyde Jr., ed., *Plain Folk of the South Revisited* (Baton Rouge, La., 1997).

8. Drew Gilpin Faust, *The Creation of Confederate Nationalism: Ideology and Identity in the Civil War South* (Baton Rouge, La., 1988), 32; McCurry, *Masters of Small Worlds.*

9. On republicanism see Daniel T. Rodgers, "Republicanism: The Career of a Concept," *JAH* (June 1992): 11–38; Robert E. Shalhope, "Toward a Republican Synthesis: The Emergence of an Understanding of Republicanism in American Historiography," *WMQ* 29 (Jan. 1972): 49–80, and "Republicanism and Early American Historiography," *WMQ* 39 (Apr. 1982) 334–56. Also see *American Quarterly* 37 (Fall 1985) for the debates on republicanism.

10. Michael F. Holt, *The Political Crisis of the 1850s* (New York, 1978), 243; Michael A. Morrison, *Slavery and the American West: The Eclipse of Manifest Destiny and the Coming of the Civil War* (Chapel Hill, N.C., 1997); James M. McPherson, *What They Fought For, 1861–1865* (Baton Rouge, La., 1994), and *For Cause and Comrades: Why Men Fought the Civil War* (New York, 1997).

11. Eugene Genovese and James Oakes have both described the permanent tension of a slave society caught in the throes of a modern western world. Oakes argues that southern slaveholders' dilemma remained an unsolvable one, as they could neither fully reject nor entirely assimilate the political liberalism of their world. Genovese sees antebellum southern thinkers as attempting to solve this dilemma by developing their own vision of progress and modernity based on slavery and the conservative principles of slave society. James Oakes, *Slavery and Freedom: An Interpretation of the Old South* (New York, 1990); Eugene D. Genovese, *The Slaveholders' Dilemma: Freedom and Progress in Southern Conservative Thought, 1820–1860* (Columbia, Mo., 1992). Also see Drew Gilpin Faust, *Southern Stories: Slaveholders in Peace and War* (Columbia, Mo., 1992), 7–8; Barbara Jeanne Fields, *Slavery and Freedom in the Middle Ground: Maryland During the Nineteenth Century* (New Haven, Conn., 1985); Joseph P. Reidy Jr., *From Slavery to Agrarian Capitalism in the Cotton Plantation South: Central Georgia, 1800–1880* (Chapel Hill, N.C., 1992); James L. Huston, "Property Rights in Slavery and the Coming of the Civil War," *JSH* 65 (1999): 249–86; Douglas R. Egerton, "Markets Without a Market Revolution: Southern Planters and Capitalism," *JER* 16 (Summer 1996): 207–21; John Ashworth, *Slavery, Capitalism and Politics in the Antebellum Republic,* Vol. 1, *Commerce and Compromise, 1820–1850* (Cambridge, Eng., 1995); Mark Smith, *Mastered By the Clock: Time, Slavery and Freedom in the American South* (Chapel Hill, N.C., 1997); Shearer Davis Bowman, *Masters and Lords: Mid-Nineteenth Century U.S. Planters and Prussian Junkers* (New York, 1993); Laurence Shore, *Southern Capitalists: The Ideological Leadership of an Elite, 1832–1885* (Chapel Hill, N.C., 1986); Peter Kolchin, *Unfree Labor: American Slavery and Russian Serfdom* (Cambridge, Mass., 1987); Edward Pessen, "How Different from Each Other Were the Antebellum North and South?" *AHR* 85 (Oct. 1980): 1119–49.

12. See for example Bruce Collins, *White Society in the Antebellum South* (London,

1985); on this issue see also Barbara J. Fields, "Slavery, Race and Ideology in the United States of America," *New Left Review* 181 (1990): 95–118, and "Ideology and Race in American History," in J. Morgan Kousser and James M. McPherson, eds., *Region, Race, and Reconstruction: Essays in Honor of C. Vann Woodward* (New York, 1982), 143–77; George M. Fredrickson, *The Black Image in the White Mind: The Debate on Afro-American Character and Destiny, 1817–1914* (New York, 1971), 68, and *The Arrogance of Race: Historical Perspectives on Slavery, Racism and Social Inequality* (Middletown, Conn., 1988); Alexander Saxton, *The Rise and Fall of the White Republic: Class Politics and Mass Culture in Nineteenth-Century America* (London, 1990).

13. Drew Gilpin Faust, "The Peculiar South Revisited: White Society, Culture, and Politics in the Antebellum Period, 1800–1860," in Boles and Nolen, eds., *Interpreting Southern History*, 78–119; Paul Horton, "Submitting to the 'Shadow of Slavery': The Secession Crisis and Civil War in Alabama's Lawrence County," *CWH* 44 (June 1998): 111–36; Michael P. Johnson, *Toward a Patriarchal Republic: The Secession of Georgia* (Baton Rouge, La., 1977); Christopher Morris, *Becoming Southern: The Evolution of a Way of Life, Warren County and Vicksburg, Mississippi, 1770–1860* (New York, 1995); John Hebron Moore, *The Emergence of the Cotton Kingdom in the Old Southwest: Mississippi, 1770–1860* (Baton Rouge, La., 1989); Samuel C. Hyde Jr., "Mechanisms of Planter Power in Eastern Louisiana's Piney Woods, 1810–1860," *LH* 39 (Winter 1998): 19–44; Randolph B. Campbell, *An Empire for Slavery: The Peculiar Institution in Texas, 1821–1865* (Baton Rouge, La., 1989). For the Upper South see James M. Woods, *Rebellion and Realignment: Arkansas's Road to Secession* (Fayetteville, Ark., 1987); Daniel W. Crofts, *Reluctant Confederates: Upper South Unionists in the Secession Crisis* (Chapel Hill, 1989); Jeffrey, *State Parties and National Politics*, chap. 11.

14. Holt, *The Political Crisis*; Michael F. Holt, *The Rise and Fall of the American Whig Party: Jacksonian Politics and the Onset of the Civil War* (New York, 1999), esp. 981–84; Richard L. McCormick, "Ethno-Cultural Interpretations of Nineteenth Century American Voting Behavior," *Political Science Quarterly* 89 (1974): 351–77; Eric Foner, *Politics and Ideology in the Age of the Civil War* (New York, 1980), 17–19. On including white women in southern political history see Drew Gilpin Faust, *Mothers of Invention: Women of the Slaveholding South in the American Civil War* (Chapel Hill, N.C., 1996); Elizabeth R. Varon, *We Mean to Be Counted: White Women and Politics in Antebellum Virginia* (Chapel Hill, N.C., 1998). On the broadening of nineteenth-century political history see Ronald P. Formisano, "The 'Party Period' Revisited," *JAH* 86 (June 1999): 93–120; Paula Baker, "The Midlife Crisis of the New Political History," *JAH* 86 (June 1999): 158–66.

15. Eric Foner, *Free Soil, Free Labor, Free Men: The Ideology of the Republican Party before the Civil War* (New York, 1970), 4–8; Terry Eagleton, *Ideology: An Introduction* (London, 1991).

16. Avery O. Craven, *The Growth of Southern Nationalism, 1848–1861* (Baton Rouge, La., 1958); Rollin G. Osterweis, *Romanticism and Nationalism in the Old South* (New Haven, Conn., 1949); David M. Potter, *The South and the Sectional Conflict* (Baton Rouge, La., 1968), esp. pt. 1. Potter questions the growth of a full-blown southern nationalism, as does Kenneth M. Stampp, *The Imperiled Union: Essays on the Background of the Civil War* (New York, 1980), 246–69. On southern nationalism also see Faust, *The Creation of Confederate Nationalism*; John McCardell, *The Idea of a Southern Nation: Southern Nationalists and Southern Nationalism, 1830–1960* (New York, 1979).

17. Bertram Wyatt-Brown, *Southern Honor: Ethics and Behavior in the Old South*

(New York, 1984). For a work that combines an emphasis on republicanism with honor see Edward L. Ayers, *Vengeance and Justice: Crime and Punishment in the Nineteenth Century American South* (New York, 1984); also see Kenneth S. Greenberg, *Honor and Slavery: Lies Duels Noses Masks Dressing as a Woman Gifts Strangers Humanitarianism Death Slave Rebellions the Proslavery Argument Baseball Hunting Gambling in the Old South* (Princeton, N.J., 1996).

18. William L. Barney, *The Road to Secession: A New Perspective on the Old South* (New York, 1972), and *The Secessionist Impulse: Alabama and Mississippi in 1860* (Princeton, N.J., 1974); Eugene D. Genovese, *The Political Economy of Slavery: Studies in the Economy and Society of the Slave South* (New York, 1965); John G. Van Deusen, *Economic Bases of Disunion in South Carolina* (New York, 1928); Drew Gilpin Faust, "The Rhetoric and Ritual of Agriculture in Antebellum South Carolina," *JSH* 45 (1979): 541–68; Charles Sellers, "In Search of the Good Overseer: The Failure of the Agricultural Reform Movement in Lowcountry South Carolina, 1821–1834," *JSH* 63 (1997): 753–802.

19. Thornton, *Politics and Power in a Slave Society*; Ford, *Origins of Southern Radicalism*.

20. W. E. Burghardt Du Bois, *Black Reconstruction in America: An Essay Toward a History of the Part Which Black Folk Played in the Attempt to Reconstruct Democracy in America, 1860–1880* (New York, 1935), 13; David Brion Davis, *The Problem of Slavery in the Age of Revolution, 1770–1820* (Ithaca, N.Y., 1975). For the argument that slavery was the basis of revolutionary republicanism see Edmund S. Morgan, *American Slavery, American Freedom: The Ordeal of Colonial Virginia* (New York, 1975); also see Kenneth S. Greenberg, "Revolutionary Ideology and the Proslavery Argument: The Abolition of Slavery in Antebellum South Carolina," *JSH* 42 (1976): 365–84.

21. Compare this argument with Don Higginbotham, "Fomenters of Revolution: Massachusetts and South Carolina," *JER* 14 (Spring 1994): 1–33; David Moltke Hansen, "Protecting Interests, Maintaining Rights, Emulating Ancestors: U.S. Constitutional Bicentennial Reflections on 'The Problem of South Carolina,'" *SCHM* 89 (July 1988): 167–81; Robert M. Weir, "The South Carolinian as Extremist," *SAQ* 74 (Winter 1975): 86–103; Ford, *Origins of Southern Radicalism*; For the argument that secession was a counterrevolution to the elections of 1860 see James M. McPherson, *Battle Cry of Freedom: The Civil War Era* (New York, 1988), 234–75.

22. C. L. R. James, *The Black Jacobins: Toussaint L'Ouverture and the San Domingo Revolution* (New York, 1963); Eugene D. Genovese, *From Rebellion to Revolution: Afro-American Slave Revolts in the Making of the New World* (Baton Rouge, La., 1979); Ira Berlin, Barbara J. Fields, et al., *Slaves No More: Three Essays on Emancipation and the Civil War* (Cambridge, Eng., 1992); Eric Foner, *Reconstruction: America's Unfinished Revolution* (New York, 1988).

Chapter One

1. Peter H. Wood, *Black Majority: Negroes in Colonial South Carolina from 1670 through the Stono Rebellion* (New York, 1974); Rachel N. Klein, *Unification of a Slave State: The Rise of the Planter Class in the South Carolina Backcountry, 1760–1808* (Chapel Hill, N.C., 1990).

2. Duncan J. MacLeod, *Slavery, Race and the American Revolution* (London, 1974); Donald L. Robinson, *Slavery in the Structure of American Politics, 1765–1820* (New York, 1971); Robert A. Olwell, " 'Domestic Enemies': Slavery and Political

Independence in South Carolina, May 1775–March 1776," *JSH* 55 (1989): 21–48, and *Masters, Slaves, and Subjects: The Culture of Power in the South Carolina Low Country 1740–1790* (Ithaca, N.Y., 1998); William W. Freehling, *The Road to Disunion: Seseccionists at Bay, 1776–1854* (New York, 1990); Edmund S. Morgan, *American Slavery, American Freedom: The Ordeal of Colonial Virginia* (New York, 1975). For a book that ignores Carolinian proslavery federalism see Larry E. Tise, *Proslavery: A History of the Defense of Slavery in America, 1701–1840* (Athens, Ga., 1987).

3. William W. Freehling, *Prelude to Civil War: The Nullification Controversy in South Carolina, 1816–1836* (New York: 1965); David Franklin Houston, *A Critical Study of Nullification in South Carolina* (Cambridge, Mass., 1896), 48; Frederic Bancroft, *Calhoun and the South Carolina Nullification Movement* (Baltimore, Md., 1928).

4. Lacy K. Ford Jr., *Origins of Southern Radicalism: The South Carolina Upcountry, 1800–1860* (New York, 1988), chap. 3; Tise, *Proslavery*, 290–91, 323–24, 334–46. Also see Chauncey Samuel Boucher, *The Nullification Controversy in South Carolina* (New York, 1916).

5. John Drayton, *A View of South Carolina As Respects Her Natural and Civil Concerns* (Charleston, S.C., 1802), 2–11; William Gilmore Simms, *The Geography of South Carolina: Being a Companion to the History of that State* (Charleston, S.C., 1848); Klein, *Unification of a Slave State*; William A. Schaper, "Sectionalism and Representation in South Carolina," *Annual Report of the American Historical Association* 1 (1900–1901): 239–438; Peter A. Coclanis, *The Shadow of a Dream: Life and Death in the South Carolina Lowcountry, 1670–1920* (New York, 1989); Joyce E. Chaplin, "Creating a Cotton South in Georgia and South Carolina, 1760–1815," *JSH* 57 (1991): 171–200, and *An Anxious Pursuit: Agricultural Innovation and Modernity in the Lower South, 1730–1815* (Chapel Hill, N.C., 1993).

6. Alfred Glaze Smith Jr., *Economic Readjustment of an Old Cotton State: South Carolina, 1820–1860* (Columbia, S.C., 1958); Tommy W. Rogers, "The Great Population Exodus from South Carolina," *SCHM* 68 (Jan. 1967): 14–21; David Duncan Wallace, *The History of South Carolina* (New York, 1934), 2:496; Blake McNulty, "Uncertain Masters: The South Carolina Elite and Slavery in the Secession Crisis of 1850," in Winfred B. Moore Jr. and Joseph F. Tripp, eds., *Looking South: Chapters in the Story of an American Region* (Westport, Conn., 1989), 82, 86–87; Otto H. Olsen, "Historians and the Extent of Slave Ownership in Southern United States," *CWH* 18 (1972): 111.

7. Julian J. Petty, *The Growth and Distribution of Population in South Carolina* (Columbia, S.C., 1943), 64, 70–71, 76. On free blacks see Marina Wikramanayake, *A World in Shadow: The Free Black in Antebellum South Carolina* (Columbia, S.C., 1973); Larry Koger, *Black Slaveowners: Free Black Slave Masters in South Carolina, 1790–1860* (Jefferson, N.C., 1985); Michael P. Johnson and James L. Roark, *Black Masters: A Free Family of Color in the Old South* (New York, 1984); Bernard E. Powers, *Black Charlestonians: A Social History, 1822–1885* (Fayetteville, Ark., 1994); On Carolinian slavery see Margaret Washington Creel, *"A Peculiar People": Slave Religion and Community-Culture Among the Gullahs* (New York, 1988); Charles Joyner, *Down by the Riverside: A South Carolina Slave Community* (Urbana, Ill., 1984); William A. Dusinberre, *Them Dark Days: Slavery in the Rice Swamps* (New York, 1996); Larry E. Hudson, Jr. *To Have and to Hold: Slave Work and Family Life in Antebellum South Carolina* (Athens, Ga., 1997).

8. Thomas Cooper, ed., *The Statutes at Large of South Carolina* (Columbia, S.C., 1836), 1:184–95; [J. D. B. De Bow], *The Political Annals of South Carolina by a Citizen* (Charleston, S.C., 1854); David Duncan Wallace, "The Constitution of

1790 in South Carolina's Development," in Yates Snowden, *History of South Carolina* (New York, 1920), 1:505–21; Schaper, "Sectionalism and Representation," 369–437; Klein, *Unification of a Slave State*, 147–48, 238–68, 303–5; Patrick Brady, "Political and Civil Life in South Carolina, 1787–1833" (Ph.D. diss., University of California, Santa Barbara, 1971); George Patrick Germany, "The South Carolina Governing Elite, 1820–1860," (Ph.D. diss., University of California, Berkeley, 1972); Ralph A. Wooster, *The People in Power: Courthouse and Statehouse in the Lower South, 1850–1860* (Knoxville, Tenn., 1969), 5–7, 27–28, 40–49, 70–71, 82–117; James M. Banner Jr., "The Problem of South Carolina," in Eric McKitrick and Stanley Elkins, eds., *The Hofstadter Aegis: A Memorial* (New York, 1974), 60–63; Kenneth S. Greenberg, "Representation and the Isolation of South Carolina, 1776–1860," *JAH* 44 (Dec. 1977) 723–43.

9. Fletcher M. Green, *Constitutional Development in the South Atlantic States, 1776–1860: A Study in the Evolution of Democracy* (Chapel Hill, N.C., 1930), 162–203; Charles Sydnor, *The Development of Southern Sectionalism, 1819–1848* (Baton Rouge, La., 1948), 29–59; Wooster, *The People in Power*. The exception of course is Ford, *Origins of Southern Radicalism*.

10. Wooster, *The People in Power*; Chauncey Samuel Boucher, "Sectionalism, Representation, and the Electoral Question in Ante-Bellum South Carolina," *Washington University Studies* 4 (Oct. 1916): 14–39; John Barnwell, *Love of Order: South Carolina's First Secession Crisis* (Chapel Hill, 1982), 8–13, 24–31.

11. L. Glen Inabinet, " 'The July Fourth Incident' of 1816: An Insurrection Plotted by Slaves in Camden, South Carolina," in Herbert A. Johnson, ed., *South Carolina Legal History* (Spartanburg, S.C., 1980), 209–21; George C. Rogers Jr., *The History of Georgetown County, South Carolina* (Columbia, S.C., 1970), 236–37; Freehling, *Prelude to Civil War*, 53–65; Edward A. Pearson, ed., *Designs against Charleston: The Trial Record of the Denmark Vesey Slave Conspiracy of 1822* (Chapel Hill, N.C., 1999); Douglas R. Egerton, *He Shall Go Out Free: The Lives of Denmark Vesey* (Madison, Wis., 1999); John Lofton, *Denmark Vesey's Revolt: The Slave Plot That Lit a Fuse to Fort Sumter* (Kent, Ohio, 1964); William W. Freehling, "Denmark Vesey's Peculiar Reality," in Robert H. Azbug and Stephen E. Maizlish, eds., *New Perspectives on Race and Slavery in America: Essays in Honor of Kenneth M. Stampp* (Lexington, Ky., 1986), 15–47; Richard C. Wade, "The Vesey Plot: A Reconsideration," *JSH* 30 (1964); John Belton O'Neall, *Biographical Sketches of the Bench and Bar of South Carolina* (Charleston, S.C., 1859), 2:320; Governor's Message, Nov. 1824, SCDAH; Alan F. January, "The South Carolina Association: An Agency for Race Control in Antebellum South Carolina," *SCHM* 78 (July 1977): 191–201; Edwin C. Holland, *A Refutation of the Calumnies Circulated against the Southern Western States by a South Carolinian* (Charleston, S.C., 1822), 61. Also see Norrece T. Jones, *Born a Child of Freedom, Yet a Slave: Mechanisms of Control and Strategies of Resistance in Antebellum South Carolina* (Hanover, N.H., 1990).

12. Governor's Messages, Dec. 1825, Jan. 1827 (0010 016 1824 00008 00, 0010 004 1831 00177 00), Nullification—General Assembly Index, SCDAH; Hayne to Gen. Charles F. Mercer, Jan. 13, 1826, Robert Young Hayne Papers, SCL; "South Carolina Opinions of the Colonization Society," *The African Repository and Colonial Journal* 6 (Sept. 1830): 193–209; *Charleston Mercury*, May 17, 30, June 17, July 27, Aug. 17, 1830; William W. Freehling, ed., *The Nullification Era: A Documentary Record* (New York, 1967), 16; Douglas R. Egerton, "Averting a Crisis: The Proslavery Critique of the American Colonization Society," *CWH* 43 (June 1997): 142–56; Stephen Meats and Edwin T. Arnold, eds., *The Writings of Benjamin F. Perry* (Spartanburg, S.C., 1980), 2:347–51; Harper is quoted by George C.

Rogers Jr., *Charleston in the Age of the Pinckneys* (Norman, Okla., 1969), 150. Also see Merton L. Dillon, *Slavery Attacked: Southern Slaves and Their Allies, 1619–1865* (Baton Rouge, La., 1990).

13. For the positive good argument before the 1820s, see Larry Robert Morrison, "The Proslavery Argument in the Early Republic, 1790–1830" (Ph.D. diss., University of Virginia, 1975); Fredrika Teute Schmidt and Barbara Ripel Wilhelm, "Early Proslavery Petitions in Virginia," *WMQ* 30 (1973): 133–46; Tise, *Proslavery*. For the argument that slavery made southern leaders retreat early from the ideals of republicanism see MacLeod, *Slavery, Race and the American Revolution*.

14. William Sumner Jenkins, *Pro-Slavery Thought in the Old South* (Chapel Hill, N.C., 1935), 71–81; [Edward Brown], *Notes on the Origin and Necessity of Slavery* (Charleston, S.C., 1826); Holland, *A Refutation*, 11–13, 45–56; Charles Cotesworth Pinckney, *An Address Delivered in Charleston, before the Agricultural Society of South Carolina* (Charleston, S.C., 1829), 3, 8; *Rev. Dr. Richard Furman's Exposition of the Views of the Baptists Relative to the Colored Population of the United States* (Charleston, S.C., 1823); [Frederick Dalcho], *Practical Considerations Founded on the Scriptures Relative to the Slave Population of South Carolina* (Charleston, S.C., 1823).

15. Sydnor, *The Development of Southern Sectionalism*, 134–56; Cooper, ed., *The Statutes*, 228–29; Freehling, *Prelude to Civil War*, 89–133; Carl J. Vipperman, *William Lowndes and the Transition of Southern Politics, 1782–1822* (Chapel Hill, N.C., 1989); C. Edward Skeen, "Calhoun, Crawford and the Politics of Retrenchment," *SCHM* 73 (July 1972): 141–55; William W. Freehling, ed., *The Nullification Era: A Documentary Record* (New York, 1967), 8–9; Stephen Meats and Edwin T. Arnold, eds., *The Writings of Benjamin F. Perry* (Spartanburg, S.C., 1980), 3:89–94; *Defence of a Liberal Construction of the Powers of Congress* (Philadelphia, Pa., 1832), 3; Edwin L. Green, *George McDuffie* (Columbia, S.C., 1936).

16. Sydnor, *The Development of Southern Sectionalism*, 104–20; Smith, *Economic Readjustment of an Old Cotton State*, 3–19; David Duncan Wallace, *The History of South Carolina* (New York, 1934), 2:418; *Speech of Mr. Lowndes on the Tariff Bill, Delivered in the House of Representatives of the U.S., April 24, 1820* (n.d., n.p.); Theodore D. Jervey, *Robert Y. Hayne and His Times* (New York, 1909), 103–7; Hayne to Warren Davis, Sept. 25, 1827, Robert Young Hayne Papers, SCL; *Memorial of the Sundry Inhabitants of the Upper Counties of the State of South Carolina* (Washington, D.C., 1820); *Memorial of the Inhabitants of St. Luke's Parish, South Carolina* (Washington, D.C., 1824); Charles M. Wiltse, *John C. Calhoun: Nationalist, 1782–1828* (Indianapolis, Ind., 1944), 288–91; *Speech of Mr. Hayne, of South Carolina, against the Tariff Bill; Delivered in the Senate of the United States* (Charleston, S.C., 1824), 33–36; *Speech of Mr. Hamilton on the Tariff Bill, Delivered in the House of Representatives* (Washington, D.C., 1824), 23; *Speech of Mr. Poinsett, of South Carolina on the Tariff Bill, Delivered in the House of Representatives* (Washington, D.C., 1824).

17. Thomas Cooper, *Consolidation: An Account of Parties in the United States, from the Convention of 1787, to the Present Period* (Columbia, S.C., 1824); *Two Essays: 1. On the Foundation of Civil Government; 2. On the Constitution of the United States* (Columbia, S.C., 1826), 47; *On the Proposed Alteration of the Tariff* (Columbia, S.C., 1824), 4–28; Dumas Malone, *The Public Life of Thomas Cooper, 1783–1839* (1926; rpt., Columbia, S.C., 1961), 281–302; Daniel Kilbride, "Slavery and Utilitarianism: Thomas Cooper and the Mind of the Old South," *JSH* 59 (1993): 469–86.

18. *Niles Register*, Sept. 8, 1827, 26–32; *Speech of Mr. McCord at a Meeting of the Inhabitants in the Town Hall of Columbia* (Columbia, S.C., 1827); [William Camp-

bell Preston], *A Letter to the Honorable James Brown, Senator in Congress from the State of Louisiana, on the Tariff by an Inhabitant of the South* (Washington, D.C., 1823).

19. Brutus, *The Crisis: Or Essays on the Usurpations of the Federal Government* (Charleston, S.C., 1827), esp. 7, 9, 12, 26–27, 51, 91–92, 100–110, 115, 124, 130, 139, 149–54; John Stanford Coussons, "Thirty Years with Calhoun, Rhett, and the *Charleston Mercury*: A Chapter in South Carolina Politics" (Ph.D. diss., Louisiana State University, 1971), 19–20.

20. *Memorial of the Inhabitants of Barnwell District* (Washington, D.C., 1827); *Tariff Meeting of the Kershaw District* (n.p., n.d.); *Memorial of the Citizens of Edgefield* (Washington, D.C., 1827); *Memorial of the Inhabitants of Fairfield District* (Washington, D.C., 1827); *Memorial of the Citizens of Orangeburg* (Washington, D.C., 1827); *Memorial of the Agricultural Society of South Carolina* (Washington, D.C., 1828); *Memorial of Citizens of Chesterfield, Marlborough, and Darlington* (Washington, D.C., 1828); *Memorial of the Inhabitants of Newberry District* (Washington, D.C., 1828); *Memorial of the Citizens of Lancaster District* (Washington, D.C., 1828); *Memorial of the Citizens of Laurens District* (Washington, D.C., 1828); *Resolutions and Remonstrances of the Agricultural Society of St. Andrew's Parish* (Washington, D.C., 1827); *Memorial of the Citizens of Columbia* (Washington, D.C., 1827), 4; *Resolutions and Remonstrances of the Agricultural Society of St. John's, Colleton* (Washington, D.C., 1827), 3; *The Memorial and Resolutions Adopted at the Anti-Tariff Meeting Held at Sumter District* (Charleston, S.C., 1827), 11–14; *Niles Register*, June 30, 1827, 294–98.

21. Governor' Message, Nov. 1827, SCDAH; Cooper, ed., *The Statutes of South Carolina*, 1:230–43; Houston, *A Critical Study of Nullification in South Carolina*, v.

22. Wiltse, *John C. Calhoun: Nationalist*, 304–17, 374–78; Clyde N. Wilson and W. Edwin Hemphill, eds., *The Papers of John C. Calhoun, 1825–1829* (Columbia, S.C., 1977), 10:293, 396–97, 399, 411–12, 422; Clyde N. Wilson, ed., *The Papers of John C. Calhoun, 1829–1832* (Columbia, S.C., 1978), 11:210–13, 398–400; James Hamilton to Hammond, June 11, 1831, James Henry Hammond Papers, LC; Gretchen Garst Ewing, "Duff Green, John C. Calhoun, and the Election of 1828," *SCHM* 79 (Apr. 1978): 126–37.

23. On Calhoun, see Irving H. Bartlett, *John C. Calhoun: A Biography* (New York, 1993); John Niven, *John C. Calhoun and the Price of Union* (Baton Rouge, La., 1988); Benjamin F. Perry Diaries, 9, Benjamin F. Perry Papers, SHC.

24. *Speech of Mr. Hamilton, of South Carolina on Mr. Randolph's Motion to Postpone Indefinitely the Tariff Bill* (Washington, D.C., 1828), 9–11; *Speech of Mr. Mitchell of South Carolina, on a Motion to Postpone Indefinitely, the Tariff Bill* (Washington, D.C., 1828); *Camden Journal*, Nov. 8, 22, 1828; Robert V. Remini, "Martin Van Buren and the Tariff of Abominations," *AHR* (1957–58): 903–17; Hayne to Alexander B. MacLeod, Aug. 25, 1835, Robert Young Hayne Papers, SCL.

25. *Charleston Mercury*, July 12, 1828; John B. Edmunds Jr., *Francis W. Pickens and the Politics of Destruction* (Chapel Hill, N.C., 1986), 8; *Preamble and Resolutions, Adopted at the Great Anti-Tariff Meeting* (Columbia, S.C., 1830), 4–13; *A Speech on the Question of the Tariff on the Interests of the South . . . by James Hamilton Jr.* (Charleston, S.C., 1828); Virginia Louise Glenn, "James Hamilton Jr. of South Carolina: A Biography" (Ph.D. diss., University of North Carolina, 1964), 118–19; Wilson and Hemphill, eds., *The Papers of John C. Calhoun*, 10:300–301, 426–28.

26. Wilson and Hemphill, eds., *The Papers of John C. Calhoun*, 10:431–32; T. N. Brevard to Hammond, Oct. 8, 1829, and Robert Y. Hayne to Hammond, Feb. 25, 1830, James Henry Hammond Papers, LC.

27. *The Virginia and Kentucky Resolutions of 1798 and '99* (Washington, D.C.,

1832), 15–20; David B. Mathew et al., eds., *The Papers of James Madison* (Charlottesville, Va., 1991), 17:189–90, 348–49; Adrienne Koch and Harry Ammon, "The Virginia and Kentucky Resolutions: An Episode in Jefferson's and Madison's Defense of Civil Liberties," *WMQ* 5 (1948): 145–76; Jesse T. Carpenter, *The South as a Conscious Minority, 1789–1861: A Study in Political Thought* (New York, 1930), 130–41; *Camden Journal*, July 12, 1828.

28. *Exposition and Protest, Reported by the Special Committee of the House of Representatives, on the Tariff* (Columbia, S.C., 1829), 6. Also see David Scribner, "A Study of the Antecedents, Argument, and Significance of John C. Calhoun's South Carolina Exposition" (Ph.D. diss., University of Houston, 1997), 243–314.

29. *Exposition and Protest*, 7–19; Allen Kaufman, *Capitalism, Slavery, and Republican Values, 1819–1848* (Austin, Tex., 1982), 42–86. Compare Lacy K. Ford Jr., "Republican Ideology in a Slave Society: The Political Economy of John C. Calhoun," *JSH* 54 (1988): 405–24.

30. *Exposition and Protest*, 23–30; *The Virginia and Kentucky Resolutions*, 41–55. For a different argument, see Lacy K. Ford Jr., "Recovering the Republic: Calhoun, South Carolina, and the Concurrent Majority," *SCHM* 89 (July 1988): 146–59.

31. *Important Correspondence on the Subject of State Interposition* (Charleston, S.C., 1832), 14–19, 22–25; Wilson, ed., *The Papers of John C. Calhoun*, 11:605–6; Freehling, *Prelude to Civil War*, 167–70.

32. For discrepancies between Calhoun's draft and the Committee Report, see Hemphill and Wilson, eds., *The Papers of John C. Calhoun*, 10:496–97, 510–13, 522–23; Wilson, ed., *The Papers of John C. Calhoun*, 11:485–97; *Important Correspondence*, 4; Richard E. Ellis, *The Union at Risk: Jacksonian Democracy, States' Rights and the Nullification Crisis* (New York, 1987), esp. 1–12; Merrill Peterson, *The Jefferson Image in the American Mind* (New York, 1960), 51–69; Norman K. Risjord, *The Old Republicans: Southern Conservatism in the Age of Jefferson* (New York, 1965), 272–80; Russel Kirk, *John Randolph of Roanoke* (Indianapolis, Ind., 1978), 118–21.

33. Gordon S. Wood, *The Creation of the American Republic, 1776–1787,* (Chapel Hill, N.C., 1969); Pauline Maier, "The Road Not Taken: Nullification, John C. Calhoun, and the Revolutionary Tradition in South Carolina," *SCHM* 82 (Jan. 1981): 9. For an attempt to draw a link between Calhoun and antifederalists, see David F. Ericson, *The Shaping of American Liberalism: The Debates over Ratification, Nullification and Slavery* (Chicago, 1993), chap. 2; Wilson, ed., *The Papers of John C. Calhoun*, 11:498; *Important Correspondence*, 24.

34. *Exposition and Protest*, 28–31; James Madison to Hamilton, Dec. 13, 1829, James Hamilton Papers, SHC; *Niles Register*, Oct. 16, 1830, 126–28; Drew R. McCoy, *The Last of the Fathers: James Madison and the Republican Legacy* (Cambridge, Eng., 1989), 130–51; Lance Banning, *The Sacred Fire of Liberty: James Madison and the Founding of the Federal Republic* (Ithaca, N.Y., 1995), 387–94; Meats and Arnold, eds., *The Writings*, 2:160–64; *Greenville Mountaineer*, Jan. 17, May 2, 1829; Freehling, ed., *The Nullification Era*, 195–201. For a different view, see Lacy K. Ford Jr., "Inventing the Concurrent Majority: Madison, Calhoun, and the Problem of Majoritarianism in American Political Thought," *JSH* 60 (1994): 19–58.

35. Wiltse, *John C. Calhoun: Nationalist*, 20–38; George C. Rogers Jr., "South Carolina Federalists and the Origins of the Nullification Movement," *SCHM* 71 (Jan. 1971): 17–32; U. B. Phillips, "The South Carolina Federalists, I–II," *AHR* 14 (1908–9): 529–43, 731–43; Gordon S. Wood, *The Radicalism of the American Revolution* (New York, 1992), 268; James M. Banner Jr., *To the Hartford Convention:*

The Federalists and the Origins of Party Politics in Massachusetts, 1789–1815 (New York, 1970).

36. *Exposition and Protest*, 29; *Important Correspondence*, 24–25. For analyses of Calhoun's thought, see J. William Harris, "Last of the Classical Republicans: An Interpretation of John C. Calhoun," *CWH* 30 (1984): 255–67; Robert A. Garson, "Proslavery as Political Theory: The Examples of John C. Calhoun and George Fitzhugh," *SAQ* 84 (Spring 1985): 197–212; William W. Freehling, "Spoilsmen and Interests in the Thought and Career of John C. Calhoun," in John L. Thomas, ed., *John C. Calhoun: A Profile* (New York, 1968), 171–92; Susan Ford Wiltshire, "Jefferson, Calhoun, and the Slavery Debate: The Classics and the Two Minds of the South," *Southern Humanities Review* (special issue): 33–40; Louis Hartz, "South Carolina vs. the United States," in Daniel Aaron, ed., *America in Crisis* (New York, 1952), 73–89; Louis Hartz, *The Liberal Tradition in America* (New York, 1955), 145–200; Richard Hofstadter, *The American Political Tradition and the Men Who Made It* (New York, 1948), 67–91; Lacy K. Ford Jr., "Prophet with Posthumous Honor: John C. Calhoun and the Southern Political Tradition," in Charles W. Eagles, ed., *Is There a Southern Political Tradition?* (Jackson, Miss., 1996), 3–25.

37. *Charleston Mercury*, Nov. 19, 1828; *Journal of the House of Representatives [1829], Columbia S.C.*, SCDAH, 147–48; 0010 004 1829 00117 00, Nullification—General Assembly Index, SCDAH; *Memorial on the Subject of the Late Tariff; Addressed by the General Assembly of the State of Georgia, to the Anti-Tariff States* (n.p., n.d.), 81–83, 86; *Remonstrance to the States in Favor of the Tariff; Adopted by the Legislature of the State of Georgia* (n.p., n.d.); *Resolutions of Virginia on the Powers of the Federal Government* (n.p., n.d.) 77–79; *Lectures on the Restrictive System* (Richmond, Va., 1829); Kaufman, *Capitalism, Slavery and Republican Values*, 92–99; *Camden Journal*, Dec. 13, 1828.

38. *Exposition and Protest*, 39; Meats and Arnold, eds., *The Writings*, 2:83–87; Speech in Support of Jackson, ca. 1828, Langdon Cheves I Papers, SCHS; *Journal of the Senate of South Carolina, 1828*, SCDAH, 194–95, 236–40, 243; *Journal of the House of Representatives of the State of South Carolina, 1828*, SCDAH, 127–29, 154, 181; *Report of the Special Committee to Draft a Declaration on the Resolution of the Senate, Report of the Committee of Conference on the Subjects of Difference between the Two Houses on the Tariff*, 1828-13-01, General Assembly Index, SCDAH; William Elliot to his wife, Nov. 29, Dec. 10, 14, 1828, Elliot-Gonzales Papers, SHC; *Camden Journal*, Jan. 12, 1828.

39. Legaré to his mother, Mar. 8, 1829, Hugh Swinton Legaré Papers, SCL; Rogers, "South Carolina Federalists," 31; Robert V. Remini, *Andrew Jackson and the Course of Freedom, 1822–1832* (New York, 1981), 2:159–60, 175–80, 236; C. C. Cambreling to Van Buren, Sept. 25, 1829, James Hamilton Papers, SHC; John Spencer Bassett, ed., *Correspondence of Andrew Jackson*, 7 vols. (Washington, D.C., 1926–35), 4:241–43.

40. *Charleston Mercury*, Apr. 27, 28, 1830; Wilson, ed., *The Papers*, 11:144, 159–200, 205–10, 220–25, 233–49, 331–37, 342–51, 372–75, 378–79, 382–83, 477, 547, 588–90; Richard J. Calhoun, ed., *Witness to Sorrow: The Antebellum Autobiography of William J. Grayson* (Columbia, S.C., 1990), 128–30; Remini, *Andrew Jackson and the Course of American Freedom*, 160–61, 233–47, 239–44, 291–330, 348–52; John A. Marszalek, *The Petticoat Affair: Manners, Mutiny, and Sex in Andrew Jackson's White House* (New York, 1997); Kirsten E. Wood, " 'One Woman So Dangerous to Public Morals': Gender and Power in the Eaton Affair," *JER* 17 (Summer 1997): 237–75; Bertram Wyatt-Brown, "Andrew Jackson's Honor," ibid., 25–

26; Hayne to Stephen D. Miller, Jan. 26, 1831, Robert Y. Hayne Papers, SCL; Harvey Tolimer Cook, *The Life and Legacy of David Rogerson Williams* (New York, 1961), 242–43, 261–63; John Niven, *Martin Van Buren: The Romantic Age of American Politics* (New York, 1983), 181–200, 247–57; John C. Calhoun to Hammond, May 16, 1831, James Henry Hammond Papers, LC.

41. *Speeches of the Honorable Robert Y. Hayne and the Honorable Daniel Webster Delivered in the Senate of the United States* (Boston, 1830), 9, 23–29, 74–77.

42. *Speeches*, 34–59, 92–96, 105–30; *Charleston Mercury*, Mar. 17, 1830; Thomas D. Clark, ed., *The Grand Tour, 1780–1865* (Columbia, S.C., 1973), 177–78; Jervey, *Robert Y. Hayne*, 214–15, 232–74; Robert V. Remini, *Daniel Webster: The Man and His Time* (New York, 1997), 315–31; Kenneth M. Stampp, *The Imperiled Union: Essays on the Background of the Civil War* (New York, 1980), 30–35; Paul Nagel, *One Nation Indivisible: The Union in American Thought, 1776–1861* (New York, 1964), 39–78.

43. *Charleston Mercury*, Feb. 5, 10, 1830; *Greenville Mountaineer*, Jan. 16, Feb. 27, Mar. 20, 1830.

44. *Speech of Mr. Livingston, of Louisiana, on Mr. Foot's Resolution*, (Charleston, S.C., 1830), 6–21; William B. Hatcher, *Edward Livingston: Jeffersonian Republican and Jacksonian Democrat* (rpt., Gloucester, Mass., 1970), 348–51; Stephen Meats and Edwin T. Arnold, eds., *The Writings of Benjamin F. Perry* (Spartanburg, S.C., 1980), 1:43–51; *A Review of the Article in the Southern Review* (Baltimore, Md., 1830).

45. *An Oration in the First Presbyterian Church* (Charleston, S.C., 1831), 55, 86; *Charleston Courier*, June 9, July 4, 1831; James Hamilton to Miller, July 19, 1831, Stephen D. Miller Papers, SCHS.

46. *Charleston Mercury*, Feb. 3, 24, Mar. 5, July 9, 22, 1831; *An Imaginary Conversation between President Jackson and the Ghost of Jefferson* (Columbia, S.C., 1831); *Journals of the Senate for 1831*, SCDAH, 89–96, 131–53; *House of Representatives Journals*, SCDAH, 107–13; William Elliot to his wife, Dec. 9, 1831, Elliot-Gonzales Papers, SHC; Wilson, ed., *The Papers*, 11:445.

47. Wilson, ed., *The Papers*, 11:228–29, 250–56, 264–79; Calhoun to Hammond, Feb. 16, 1831, James Henry Hammond Papers, LC; *Camden Journal*, June 11, 1831.

48. *Camden Journal*, Dec. 19, 1829; Wilson, ed., *The Papers*, 11:228, 231; *Speech of Warren Davis of South Carolina* (Washington, D.C., 1832); Pickens to Hammond, Dec. 28, 1830, James Henry Hammond Papers, LC; Charles M. Wiltse, *John C. Calhoun: Nullifier, 1829–1839* (Indianapolis, Ind., 1949), 100–103; "Letters on the Nullification Movement in South Carolina, 1830–1834, Including Letters of Thomas Cooper, 1825–1832," *AHR* (July 1901): 744.

49. *Greenville Mountaineer*, Sept. 24, Oct. 1, 1831; Job Johnston to Francis Higgins, Oct. 4, 1831, Francis Bernard Higgins Papers, SCL; *The Journal of the Free Trade Convention* (Philadelphia, Pa., 1831); *Twenty-Second Congress, First Session: Memorial of the Committee of the Free Trade Convention* (n.p., n.d.), 5–7, 51–52, 58–64; *An Exposition of Evidence in Support of the Memorial to Congress* (Boston, 1832), 3–4; *Charleston Mercury*, Nov. 2, 4, 5, 1831.

50. *To the Citizens of the United States: Review of the Address of the Free Trade Convention — No. II By Hamilton 1831* (n.p., n.d.); *Address of the Friends of Domestic Industry, Assembled at New York, Oct. 26, 1831* (Baltimore, Md., 1831); *Predictions on the State of Affairs in the South by Hampden* (n.p., n.d.); *A Common Sense Address to the Citizens of the Southern States July 23, 1828 By Hamilton* (n.p., n.d.); *The Protecting System By Hamilton 1829* (n.p., n.d.); *The New Olive Branch: A Solemn Warning on the*

Banks of the Rubicon 1830–31 (n.p., n.d.), nos. 1 and 7; *A Letter to Col. William Drayton, of South Carolina* (New York, 1831); *Charleston Mercury,* Nov. 15, 1831.

51. *Memorial of the Members of the Legislature of South Carolina* (n.p., n.d.); *Speech of Felix Grundy* (Washington, D.C., 1832); *Speech of Mr. Stewart* (Washington, D.C., 1832); *Speech of Mr. Appleton* (Washington, D.C., 1832), 18; *Speech of Mr. Thomas Bouldin* (Washington, D.C., 1832); *Speech of Mr. Lewis* (Washington, D.C., 1832); *Speech of Henry Clay* (Washington, D.C., 1832); Robert V. Remini, *Henry Clay: Statesman for the Union* (New York, 1991); *Speech of Mr. Ewing* (Washington, D.C., 1832), 20; *Speech of the Honorable Peleg Sprague* (Washington, D.C., 1832), 17; *Speech of Stephen D. Miller* (n.p., n.d.), 34–36; *Charleston Mercury,* Jan. 4, 21, May 9, 1832.

52. *Second Speech of Mr. McDuffie* (Washington, D.C., 1832), 3–4, 20–21; *Remarks of Robert Y. Hayne* (n.p., n.d.), 7; *Political Tract No. 13* (Charleston, S.C., 1832); *Letter of Robert Y. Hayne* (Charleston, S.C., 1832); *Charleston Mercury,* July 30, 1832; *Political Tract No. 12* (Columbia, S.C., 1832), 3; John Felder to Hammond, Mar. 17, May 17, 1832, John C. Calhoun to Hammond, Jan. 15, 1831, and Robert Y. Hayne to Hammond, Dec. 29, 1831, James Henry Hammond Papers, LC; *Political Tract No. 1* (Columbia, S.C., 1832), 13–14; *Political Tract No. 6* (Charleston, S.C., 1832), 3–13.

Chapter Two

1. Richard J. Calhoun, ed., *Witness to Sorrow: The Antebellum Autobiography of William J. Grayson* (Columbia, S.C., 1990), 119; James Brewer Stewart, " 'A Great Talking and Eating Machine': Patriarchy, Mobilization and the Dynamics of Nullification in South Carolina," *CWH* 27 (Sept. 1981): 197–220. For the attempt to link nullification with revivalism, see Stephanie McCurry, *Masters of Small Worlds: Yeoman Households, Gender Relations, and the Political Culture of the Antebellum South Carolina Low Country* (New York, 1995), chap. 4.

2. Hamilton to Calhoun, May 10, 1829, James Hamilton Papers, SHC; Edwin L. Green, *George McDuffie* (Columbia, S.C., 1936), 83–86; Theodore D. Jervey, *Robert Y. Hayne and His Times* (New York, 1909); Meats and Arnold, eds., *The Writings,* 1:256–57, 2:39–46, 47–50, 320–24, 3:160–64, 211–17; Laura White, *Robert Barnwell Rhett: The Father of Secession* (Gloucester, Mass., 1960), 13–14; Henry T. Thompson, *Waddy Thompson* (n.p., 1929), 4–5; John B. Edmunds Jr., *Francis W. Pickens and the Politics of Destruction* (Chapel Hill, 1986), 3–19; Drew Gilpin Faust, *James Henry Hammond and the Old South: A Design for Mastery* (Baton Rouge, La., 1982), 36–57; John Stanford Coussons, "Thirty Years with Calhoun, Rhett, and the *Charleston Mercury*: A Chapter in South Carolina Politics" (Ph.D. diss., Louisiana State University, 1971), 19–20.

3. *Remarks of Mr. Hayne* (Washington, D.C., 1829), 7; Hammond to Robert Y. Hayne, Jan. 27, 1833, James Henry Hammond Papers, LC; *Political Tract No. 10, May 1832* (Columbia, S.C., 1832), 11–12; *Speech of Mr. McDuffie* (Washington, D.C., 1827); *20th Congress 1st Session House of Representatives* (n.p., n.d.), 11–26; *Speech of Mr. McDuffie* (Washington, D.C., 1828); *Charleston Mercury,* Feb. 16, May 3, 1830; *Speech of McDuffie* (Columbia, S.C., 1830), 51–56; Patrick Brady, "Political and Civil Life in South Carolina, 1787–1833" (Ph.D. diss., University of California, Santa Barbara, 1971), 109–12.

4. Margaret L. Coit, *John C. Calhoun: American Portrait* (Cambridge, Mass., 1950), 185; James Petigru Carson, ed., *Life, Letters and Speeches of James Louis Petigru* (Washington, D.C., 1920), 84; *Speech of McDuffie, April 1830,* 8–31; Hemp-

hill and Wilson, eds., *The Papers*, 10:414; *Speech of Mr. McDuffie* (Washington, D.C., 1832); *McDuffie's Second Speech* (n.p., n.d.), 71–72.

5. Fourth of July Oration, 1831, Francis W. Pickens Papers, SCL; *Niles Register*, June 28, 1828, 288; *Address of the Citizens of Richland District* (Columbia, S.C., 1828), 10; Preston to Waddy Thompson, Feb. 14, 1830, William Campbell Preston Papers, SCL; *An Oration Delivered on the 4th of July* (Sumterville, S.C., 1832), 12; *Proceedings of the States Rights Celebration* (Charleston, S.C., 1830), 12, 36; *Charleston Mercury*, Jan. 29, May 29, 1828, Apr. 27, 1832.

6. Drayton to Unknown, June 17, 1828, William Drayton Papers, SCL; *Niles Register*, June 28, 1828, 288, July 26, 1828, 553, Sept. 20, 1828, 58–63; *Proceedings of the States Rights Meeting* (Columbia, S.C., 1830), 46; *Proceedings of States Rights Celebration*, 21, 45–46; *Speech of . . . George McDuffie* (Charleston, S.C., 1831), 27–28; Biographical material, George McDuffie Papers, SCL; *Camden Journal*, Aug. 16, Sept. 27, 1828; Memminger to Franklin Harper Elmore, Mar. 7, 1830, Christopher Gustavus Memminger Papers, SCL; John McCardell, *The Idea of a Southern Nation: Southern Nationalists and Southern Nationalism, 1830–1860* (New York, 1979), 4–7, 28–60.

7. *Charleston Mercury*, June 6, July 23, Aug. 11, 13, 1831; Meats and Arnold, eds., *The Writings*, 1:259, 2:320–24, 3:89–94; "Letters on the Nullification Movement," 741, 745–47; Richard Yeadon to Isaac M. Dwight, June 8, 1831, James Hamilton Papers, SHC; James Hamilton to Miller, Aug. 1, 1830, Stephen D. Miller Papers, SCHS; *Camden Journal*, Jan. 21, Mar. 17, 1832; Virginia Louise Glenn, "James Hamilton Jr. of South Carolina: A Biography" (Ph.D. diss., University of North Carolina, 1964), chap. 9; Hemphill and Wilson, eds., *The Papers*, 10:545; Francis W. Pickens to Hammond, Mar. 13, 1830, James Clark to Hammond, May 11, 1830, James Henry Hammond Papers, LC.

8. *Proceedings of the States Rights Celebration*, 5–7, 24–27; *Proceedings of the States Rights Meeting*, 17–46; O'Neall, *Biographical Sketches*, 1:106–19, 140–41, 270–73, 2:168–70; *Camden Journal*, Oct. 4, 1828; *Greenville Mountaineer*, Sept. 10, 1830; *An Oration Delivered in the First Presbyterian Church* (Charleston, S.C., 1831), 22; Meats and Arnold, eds., *The Writings*, 3:291; *Niles Register*, July 26, 1828, 551–52, Dec. 4, 1830, 244–48; *Speech of . . . William Smith* (Camden, S.C., 1831); *Charleston Mercury*, July 16, 1828; *Speech of Mr. Blair* (Washington, D.C., 1830); *An Account of the Celebration of the Fifty-Fifth Anniversary*, 82–86; *Greenville Mountaineer*, Sept. 10, 1830; Williams to Stephen D. Miller, Sept. 7, Oct. 25, 1828, Aug. 11, Sept. 4, Oct. 10, 1830, David Rogerson Williams Papers, SCL; *Camden Journal*, Oct. 25, 1828; *A Looking Glass for Nullifiers* (n.p., n.d.).

9. *Camden Journal*, Sept. 27, Nov. 29, 1828; Job Johnston to Miller, Aug. 20, 1828, Thos. Harrison to Miller, Sept. 6, 1828, Pinckney to Miller, Aug. 23, 1828, R. B. Smith to Miller, July 10, 1830, J. H. Witherspoon to Miller, Nov. 26, 1830, Stephen D. Miller Papers, SCHS; Williams to Stephen D. Miller, Oct. 10, 1830, David Rogerson Williams Papers, SCL; William Elliot to his wife, Nov. 24, 1828, Elliot-Gonzales Papers, SHC; Francis W. Pickens to Hammond, June 26, 1830, James Henry Hammond Papers, LC; Perry Diaries, 15, Benjamin F. Perry Papers, SHC; *Proceedings and the Resolutions and Address Adopted by the State Rights Party* (Charleston, S.C., 1830).

10. Meats and Arnold, eds., *The Writings*, 2:300–302, 381–89, 3:127–32, 158–64; *Oration on the Absolute Necessity of the Union* (Charleston, S.C., 1829); William W. Freehling, *Prelude to Civil War: The Nullification Controversy in South Carolina, 1816–1836* (New York, 1965), 181; Lyon G. Tyler, "James Louis Petigru: Freedom's Champion in a Slave Society," *SCHM* 83 (Oct. 1982): 272–86; William H.

Pease and Jane H. Pease, *James Louis Petigru: Southern Conservative, Southern Dissenter* (Athens, Ga., 1995); Laylon Jordan, "Schemes of Usefulness: Christopher Gustavus Memminger," in Michael O'Brien and David Moltke-Hansen, eds., *Intellectual Life in Antebellum Charleston* (Knoxville, Tenn., 1986), 211–29; Barbara L. Bellows, *Benevolence among Slaveholders: Assisting the Poor in Charleston, S.C., 1670–1860* (Baton Rouge, La., 1993), 45–53; A. E. Keir Nash, "Negro Rights, Unionism and Greatness on the South Carolina Court of Appeals: The Extraordinary Chief Justice John Belton O'Neall," *South Carolina Law Review* 21 (1909): 141–90; James Hemphill to William Hemphill, July 26, 1833, Hemphill Family Papers, DU; Herbert Everett Putnam, *Joel Roberts Poinsett: A Political Biography* (Washington, D.C., 1935); J. Fred Rippy, *Joel R. Poinsett: Versatile American* (Durham, N.C., 1935), 220; Frederika Bremer, *The Homes of the New World: Impressions of America* (New York, 1853), 1:287–88.

11. *Charleston Mercury*, Jan. 15, 16, 1828; Meats and Arnold, eds., *The Writings*, 2:177–81, 375–80; Archie Vernon Huff Jr., *Langdon Cheves of South Carolina* (Columbia, S.C., 1977); *Charleston Courier*, Oct. 6, 1830; Michael O'Brien, *A Character of Hugh Legaré* (Knoxville, Tenn., 1980), 180; William Gilmore Simms, *The History of South Carolina* (rpt., Columbia, S.C., 1927), 166.

12. *Review of a Late Pamphlet* (Charleston, S.C., 1828); *Greenville Mountaineer*, Jan. 31, Feb. 21, 1829; *Niles Register*, July 26, 1828, 551–56.

13. *The Question of the Tariff* (Charleston, S.C., 1827), 5, 9–10, 35; *Charleston Courier*, July 18, 19, 1828, July 10, 19, 1830; *Greenville Mountaineer*, June 25, July 23, 30, 1830; W. B.[?] to Robert Witherspoon, Dec. 11, 1831, Witherspoon Family Papers, SCL; *An Account of the Celebration*, 68–69, 87–88; *The Calhoun Doctrine* (Charleston, S.C., 1831), 5–6, 10; *Signs of the Times* (Columbia, S.C., 1831), 5, 11–12, 25; *Proceedings of a General Meeting* (Columbia, S.C., 1832), 4–6, 11–15; *Camden Journal* June 18, Oct. 15, 1831.

14. *An Address to a Public Meeting* (Columbia, S.C., 1831), 33–38; Lacy K. Ford Jr., *Origins of Southern Radicalism: The South Carolina Upcountry, 1800–1860* (New York, 1988), 126; MP, Aug. 1831, newspaper cutting, letter extract, Oct. 29, 1830, Thomas Sumter Papers, SCL; Meats and Arnold, eds., *The Writings*, 3:303; Anne King Gregorie, *History of Sumter County, South Carolina* (Sumter, S.C., 1954), 147–49; *Proceedings of the States Rights Meeting*, 6; *The Report . . . Union and State Rights Party* (n.p., n.d.), 9; *Charleston Daily Courier*, Mar. 29, June 26, Aug. 3, 7, 11, 24, Sept. 13, 1830; *Charleston Mercury*, June 8, 9, Aug. 5, 23, 1831.

15. *Charleston Courier*, June 30, Sept. 25, 1830, July 28, Aug. 8, 1831; *Charleston Mercury*, Sept. 14, Oct. 8, 1831. Compare with Freehling, *Prelude to Civil War*, 368–69.

16. Jane H. Pease and William H. Pease, "The Economics and Politics of Charleston's Nullification Crisis," *JSH* 47 (1981): 335–62; *Charleston Courier*, Sept. 8, 1829, Sept. 24, Oct. 14, 16, Dec. 15, 16, 1830, Sept. 7, 1831; *Charleston Mercury*, Aug. 30, Oct. 14, 15, 1830, Sept. 7, 26, 27, 1831, Sept. 5, 7, 1832; *Speech of Thomas S. Grimké* (Charleston, S.C., 1829); Stephen Elliot to William Elliot, July 27, 1830, Elliot-Gonzales Papers, SHC; Walter J. Fraser Jr., *Charleston! Charleston!: The History of a Southern City* (Columbia, S.C., 1989), 187–213; John Radford, "Race, Residence and Ideology: Charleston, South Carolina in the Mid-Nineteenth Century," *Journal of Historical Geography* 2 (1976): 329–46; George C. Rogers Jr., *Charleston in the Age of the Pinckneys* (Norman, Okla., 1969).

17. John N. Barrillon to John T. Seibels, Sept. 5, 1830, Seibels Family Papers, SCL; Lillian Kibler, *Benjamin F. Perry: South Carolina Unionist* (Durham, N.C., 1946), 31, 92–95; Meats and Arnold, eds., *The Writings*, 1:296–98; Speech against

the Convention, 1830, Benjamin F. Perry Papers, SHC; *Greenville Mountaineer*, June 11, 25, July 9, 23, 30, Aug. 6, 27, Sept. 10, 1830; James Hamilton to Thompson, June 8, 1832, Waddy Thompson Papers, SCL; Archie Vernon Huff Jr., *Greenville: The History of the City and County in the South Carolina Piedmont* (Columbia, S.C., 1995), 102–6; James Wylie Gettys, "Mobilization for Secession in Greenville District" (M.A. thesis, University of South Carolina, 1967), 16–18; William Joseph MacArthur, "Antebellum Politics in an Up Country District: National, State and Local Issues in Spartanburg County, South Carolina, 1850–1860" (M.A. thesis, University of South Carolina, 1966), 7–9; J. Mauldin Lesesne, "The Nullification Controversy in an Upcountry District," *Proceedings of the South Carolina Historical Association* (1939): 13–24; Benjamin F. Whitner to Hammond, Sept. 11, 1830, James Henry Hammond Papers, LC.

18. *Greenville Mountaineer*, Apr. 3, June 4, June 11, 25, 1830; *Charleston Mercury*, May 15, 1830; Brady, "Political and Civil Life," 56–67; Meats and Arnold, *The Writings*, 3:108–13.

19. *The Tariff* (Charleston, S.C., 1830); *The American System Exemplified* (Sumterville, S.C., 1830); *To the People* (Charleston, S.C., 1830); *The Quintessence of Long Speeches* (Charleston, S.C., 1830); *Charleston Mercury*, May 17, June 7, 26, July 26, Aug. 17, 20, 1830; James Hamilton to Hammond, Jan. 10, 1831, Stephen D. Miller to Hammond, Jan. 20, 1831, James Clark to Hammond, Dec. 19, 1831, James Henry Hammond Papers, LC; *Senate Journals, Nov. 22, 1830–Dec. 18, 1830*, SCDAH, 47, 56, 66, 120–23; *The Debate in the South Carolina Legislature* (Columbia, S.C., 1831), 4–5, 9–12, 17, 36–37, 144, 197; *Journals of the House of Representatives, Nov. 22, 1830–Dec. 18, 1830*, SCDAH, 40, 200–208; Meats and Arnold, eds., *The Writings*, 2:382; *Greenville Mountaineer*, June 18, 1831.

20. *Political Tract No. 1* (Columbia, S.C., 1831); *Political Tract No. 3, Part 2* (Charleston, S.C., 1831); *Political Tract No. 3* (Charleston, S.C., 1831); *The Genuine Book of Nullification* (Charleston, S.C., 1831); *Charleston Mercury*, June 4, 13, 14, Aug. 26, 1831; *Political Tract No. 6* (Columbia, S.C., 1832); *Political Tract No. 7* (Charleston, S.C., 1832); *Political Tract No. 8* (Columbia, S.C., 1832); *Political Tract No. 9* (Columbia, S.C., 1832); *An Oration Delivered in the City of Charleston* (Charleston, S.C., 1832); *Political Tract No. 12: Address of the State Rights and Free Trade Association* (n.p., n.d.), 4; *Charleston Courier*, July 6, 1832; *Camden Journal*, July 14, 23, 1832; *Address to the People* (Charleston, S.C., 1832), 9–10; Hammond to Gentlemen, Sept. 12, 1832, I. W. Hayne to Hammond, Aug. 21 [1832], James Henry Hammond Papers, LC.

21. James Hemphill to Miller, Mar. 24, 1832, Stephen D. Miller Papers, SCHS; Meats and Arnolds, eds., *The Writings*, 1:259–60; *Occasional Reviews No. 1* (Charleston, S.C., 1832), 11–15; *Occasional Reviews No. 2* (Charleston, S.C., 1832), 14–15; *Camden Journal*, May 5, 12, 19, Sept. 22, 1832; Robert Witherspoon to his son, June 7, 1832, Witherspoon Family Papers, SCL; *Greenville Mountaineer*, June 23, Aug. 11, Sept. 15, 1832; *An Oration . . . before the Union and State Rights Party* (Charleston, S.C., 1832), 10–13; *Address to the People*, 15; *Constitutional Arguments* (Charleston, S.C., 1832), 15–19; Carson, ed., *Life, Letters and Speeches*, 91–96.

22. Miller to Rob. E. [Yates], May 9, 1832, Yates to Miller, June 26, 1832, James Hemphill to Miller, Apr. 29, 1832, Stephen D. Miller Papers, SCHS; James Clark to Hammond, Sept. 11, 1832, James Henry Hammond Papers, LC; Wilson, ed., *The Papers*, 11:658, 660–62.

23. *The Crisis; or Nullification Unmasked* (n.p., n.d.), 15; *Charleston Courier*, Aug. 4, 7, 21, 31, Sept. 17, 24, Oct. 3, 1832; *Greenville Mountaineer*, Sept. 1, 22, Nov. 3, 1832; *Camden Journal*, Oct. 6, Dec. 8, 1832; Perry Diaries, 47, Benjamin F. Perry

Papers, SHC; John N. Barrillon to John Seibels, Aug. 29, 1832, Seibels Family Papers, SCL; Chauncey Samuel Boucher, "Sectionalism, Representation, and the Electoral Question in Antebellum South Carolina," *Washington University Studies* 4 (Oct. 1916): 7–12.

24. Jack Kenny Williams, "The Code of Honor in Antebellum South Carolina," *SCHM* 54 (July 1953): 113–28; Faust, *James Henry Hammond*, 50–53; Lesesne, "The Nullification Controversy," 18–19; Gregorie, *History of Sumter County*, 150–51; William J. Grayson, *James Louis Petigru: A Biographical Sketch* (New York, 1866), 108–9; Rebecca Rutledge to Lt. Edward Rutledge, Sept. 6, Oct. 5, 10, 1832, Rutledge Family Papers, SCL; Carson, ed., *Life, Letters and Speeches*, 101; James Clark to Hammond, Sept. 11, 1832, James Henry Hammond Papers, LC.

25. See election returns in *Columbia Hive*, Oct. 20, 1832; *Charleston Courier*, Oct. 11, 12, 13, 15, 16, 17, 20, 1832; *Charleston Mercury*, Sept. 5, Oct. 11, 12, 13, 15, 16, 17, 1832; Chauncey Samuel Boucher, *The Nullification Controversy in South Carolina* (New York, 1916), 203; Freehling, *Prelude to Civil War*, 254–55, 365–69; George C. Rogers Jr., *The History of Georgetown County, South Carolina* (Columbia, S.C., 1970), 242–43; Ford, *Origins of Southern Radicalism*, 137–39; J. P. Ochenkowski, "The Origins of Nullification in South Carolina," *SCHM* 83 (Apr. 1982): 121–53; Paul Bergeron, "The Nullification Controversy Revisited," *THQ* 35 (Fall 1976): 263–75; McCurry, *Masters of Small Worlds*, 271–75.

26. Hamilton to Patrick Noble, Oct. 9, 1832, James Hamilton Papers, SCL; *Journals of the Senate, Oct. 22–26, 1832*, SCDAH, 10–14; *Journals of the House of Representatives, Oct. 22–26, 1832*, SCDAH, 8–17; *Charleston Mercury*, Nov. 13, 1832; *Greenville Mountaineer*, Nov. 3, 1832.

27. *To the People of South Carolina* (n.p., n.d.); Union party circulars, Nov. 2, 1832, Feb. 21, 1833, Benjamin F. Perry Papers, SCDAH; David Johnson to O'Neall, Oct. 15, 1832, John Belton O'Neall Papers, SCL; Committee of Correspondence to Robert Witherspoon, Nov. 2, 1832, Witherspoon Family Papers, SCL; James Harrison to William R. Hemphill, Nov. 10, 1832, Hemphill Family Papers, DU; Meats and Arnold, eds., *The Writings*, 1:168–71.

28. Schaper, "Sectionalism and Representation," 439–47; *Journals of the Conventions of the People of South Carolina Held in 1832, 1833, and 1852* (Columbia, S.C., 1860), 17–18, 20.

29. *Journals of the Conventions*, 11, 27–77; Wm. C. Clifton to Hammond, Nov. 21, 1832, A. P. Butler to Hammond, Nov. 20, 1832, James Henry Hammond Papers, LC; *The Governor's Message*, Oct. 22, 1832, James Hamilton Papers, SCL; *Hints, Suggestions, and Contributions* (Columbia, S.C., 1832).

30. *Reports and Resolutions of 1832* (n.p., n.d.) 4–5; Thomas Cooper, ed., *The Statutes at Large* (Columbia, S.C., 1836), 1:371–76; *Journals of the Senate, Nov. 26–Dec. 20, 1832*, 78, 84, 90, 105, 124, 133–37; *Journals of the House of Representatives, Nov. 26, 1832–Dec. 20, 1832*, SCDAH, 70, 91, 120–21, 153; 0010 004 1832 00025 00, Nullification — General Assembly Index, SCDAH.

31. Compare this argument with William H. Denney, "South Carolina's Conception of the Union in 1832," *SCHM* 78 (July 1977): 171–83.

32. *Hampden and His Times* (n.p., n.d.) 227, 242–49; *Strictures on Nullification* (Boston, 1832), 28–30, 33–37, 46–52, 67–69; *Letter on the Relations* (n.p., n.d.); Robert J. Walker, "Nullification and Secession," *Continental Monthly*, Feb. 1863, 179–94; Richard B. Latner, "The Nullification Crisis and Republican Subversion," *JSH* 43 (1977): 19–38.

33. Michael Paul Rogin, *Fathers and Children: Andrew Jackson and the Subjugation of the American Indian* (New York, 1975); James Taylor Carson, "State Rights and

Indian Removal in Mississippi: 1817–1835," *JMH* 62 (Feb. 1995): 25–42; Robert V. Remini, *The Legacy of Andrew Jackson: Essays on Democracy, Indian Removal and Slavery* (Baton Rouge, La., 1988); *Executive Message from the President* (Washington, D.C., 1832), 8–10; Richard E. Ellis, *The Union at Risk: Jacksonian Democracy, States' Rights and the Nullification Crisis* (New York, 1987), 46–51, 81–83.

34. Charles Sellers, ed., *Andrew Jackson, Nullification, and the State-Rights Tradition* (Chicago, 1963), 36–38; Charles Petigru to Legaré, Dec. 21, 1832, Hugh Swinton Legaré Papers, SCL; Robert V. Remini, *Andrew Jackson and the Course of American Democracy, 1833–1845* (New York, 1984), 3:17–23; Ellis, *The Union at Risk*, 83–88; Major L. Wilson, " 'Liberty and Union': An Analysis of Three Concepts in the Nullification Controversy," *JSH* 33 (1967): 331–55; *President Jackson's Proclamation* (n.p., n.d.), 4–14, 16–20.

35. Remini, *The Legacy*; John M. McFaul, "Expediency vs. Morality: Jacksonian Politics and Slavery," *JAH* 62 (1975–76): 24–39; Leonard L. Richards, "The Jacksonians and Slavery," in Lewis Perry and Michael Fellman, eds., *Antislavery Reconsidered: New Perspectives on the Abolitionists* (Baton Rouge, La., 1979), 99–118; Richard H. Brown, "The Missouri Crisis, Slavery, and the Politics of Jacksonianism," *SAQ* 65 (1966): 55–72; Charles G. Sellers, *The Market Revolution: Jacksonian America, 1815–1846* (New York, 1991), 326–31; Daniel Feller, *The Jacksonian Promise: America, 1815–1840* (Baltimore, Md., 1995); Harry L. Watson, *Liberty and Power: The Politics of Jacksonian America* (New York, 1990); Sean Wilentz, "On Class and Politics in Jacksonian America," *RAH* (Dec. 1982): 45–63.

36. A. P. Butler to Hammond, Dec. 18, 1832, Hammond to Robert Y. Hayne, Dec. 20, 1832, Jan. 8, 1833, Hayne to Hammond, Dec. 21, 1832, Printed Circulars, Dec. 20, 26, 1832, Jan. 30, 1833, James Henry Hammond Papers, LC; Hamilton to William Campbell Preston, Dec. 28, 1832, James Hamilton Papers, SCL; Perry Diaries, Jan. 13, 30, 1833, Benjamin F. Perry Papers, SHC; William Campbell Preston to Miller, Dec. 24, 1832, P. E. Pearson to Miller, Dec. 26, 1832, Charles W. Miller to Stephen Miller, Jan. 2, 1833, Stephen D. Miller Papers, SCL; *Journals of the Senate, 1832*, 149–63; *Journals of the House of Representatives, 1832*, 181–87; *Documents Accompanying the President's Message, Jan. 1833* (n.p., n.d.), 111; "Letters on the Nullification Movement," 752–60, 764; Pickens to Daniel Wallace, Jan. 17, 1833, Francis W. Pickens Papers, DU.

37. William Campbell Preston to Hammond, Dec. 31, 1832, Jan. 14, 1833, James Henry Hammond Papers, LC; *Nullification Considered and Defended* (Charleston, S.C., 1833), 7–9; *Remarks on the Ordinance* (Charleston, S.C., 1833), 5–12, 32–48, 64–67; *Charleston Mercury*, Jan. 5, 29, 1833; Perry Diaries, Jan. 30, July 3, 1833, Benjamin F. Perry Papers, SHC.

38. *Address of the Washington Society* (Charleston, S.C., 1832), 3–8; Robert Witherspoon to his son, Dec. 1, 1832, Witherspoon Family Papers, SCL; Perry Diaries, Nov. 28, 1832, Benjamin F. Perry Papers, SHC; *Greenville Mountaineer*, Feb. 9, 1830; *Camden Journal*, Dec. 8, 22, 1832; *Charleston Courier*, Dec. 1, 7, 8, 1832; *Charleston Mercury*, Nov. 28, Dec. 3, 7, 1832; Petigru to Hugh Swinton Legaré, Dec. 21, 1832, James Louis Petigru Papers, SCL; *The Report*, 4–9.

39. *Greenville Mountaineer*, Jan. 19, Feb. 9, 1833; Poinsett to George Ticknor, Jan. 9, 1833, R. Cunningham to Poinsett, Mar. 5, 1833, Joel R. Poinsett Papers, SCL; John Spencer Bassett, ed., *Correspondence of Andrew Jackson*, 7 vols. (Washington, D.C., 1926–35), 4:481–82, 486–88, 491–92, 501–2, 5:6–10, 13–14, 16–17, 21–22; Freehling, ed., *The Nullification Era*, 170–71; Putnam, *Joel Roberts Poinsett*, 117, 129–31; Rippy, *Joel R. Poinsett*, 136; Meats and Arnold, eds., *The Writings*,

1:172–73; Catherine Gilman to Mrs. A. M. White, Jan. 15, 1833, Catherine H. Gilman Papers, SCHS; Rebecca Rutledge to Lt. Rutledge, Jan. 30, 1833, Rutledge Papers, SCL.

40. Bassett, ed., *Correspondence of Andrew Jackson*, 4:485–86, 493–94, 5:5–6, 11–12, 14–15; Freehling, ed., *The Nullification Era*, 175–77; Meats and Arnold, eds., *The Writings*, 1:173–75, 260–61, 2:354–57; *Documents Accompanying the President's Message* (n.p., n.d.), 92–99; *State of the Union Message* (n.p., n.d.).

41. *State Papers on Nullification* (Boston, 1834), 101, 104–8, 112–30, 132–59, 163–66, 168–71, 203–9, 212–15, 244–67, 283–86, 287–92, 378–81; *Governor's Message . . . New Jersey* (n.p., n.d.); *Report . . . Delaware* (n.p., n.d.); Ellis, *The Union at Risk*, chap. 7; Freehling, ed., *The Nullification Era*, 200.

42. Bassett, ed., *Correspondence of Andrew Jackson*, 5:11; *State Papers on Nullification*, 200–202, 218–25, 228–31, 238–39, 269–80, 287–92; *Niles Register*, Dec. 1, 1832, 221; *Speech of Wensley Hobby* (Augusta, Ga., 1832); *Charleston Mercury*, Jan. 1, 1833; *Journals of the Convention*, 87–109; Ellis, *The Union at Risk*, chaps. 5, 6; Lucie Robertson Bridgeforth, "Mississippi's Response to Nullification, 1833," *JMH* 45 (Feb. 1983): 1–22; Paul Bergeron, "Tennessee's Response to the Nullification Crisis," *JSH* 39 (1973): 23–44; Jonathan M. Atkins, *Parties, Politics, and the Sectional Conflict in Tennessee, 1832–1861* (Knoxville, Tenn., 1997), 26–32; Thomas E. Jeffrey, *State Parties and National Politics: North Carolina, 1815–1861* (Athens, Ga., 1989), 39–40; Harry L. Watson, *Jacksonian Politics and Community Conflict: The Emergence of the Second American Party System in Cumberland County, North Carolina* (Baton Rouge, La., 1981), 153–54; E. Merton Coulter, "The Nullification Movement in Georgia," *GHQ* 5 (Mar. 1921): 3–39; Anthony Gene Carey, *Parties, Slavery, and the Union in Antebellum Georgia* (Athens, Ga., 1997), 24–32; William J. Cooper Jr., *The South and the Politics of Slavery 1828–1856* (Baton Rouge, La., 1978), 43–48.

43. Petigru to Hugh Swinton Legaré, Feb. 6, 1833, James Louis Petigru Papers, SCL; William Campbell Preston to Hammond, Dec. 31, 1832, James Henry Hammond Papers, LC; Clyde N. Wilson, ed., *The Papers of John C. Calhoun, 1833–1835* (Columbia, S.C., 1979), 12:8–9; Rebecca Rutledge to Lt. Edward Rutledge, Jan. 30, 1833, Rutledge Family Papers, SCL; *Consolidation Part 2* (Columbia, S.C., 1834), 3, 35–37; Hammond to Robert Y. Hayne, Jan. 10, 1833, James Henry Hammond Papers, LC; Richard Hofstadter, *The Idea of a Party System: The Rise of Legitimate Opposition in the United States, 1780–1840* (Berkeley, Calif., 1969); Marc Kruman, "The Second Party System and the Transformation of Revolutionary Republicanism," *JER* 12 (Winter 1992): 509–37.

44. *A Discourse Delivered in the Presbyterian Church* (Pendleton, S.C., 1833), 14; *Niles Register*, Feb. 2, 1833, 380–84; Meats and Arnold, eds., *The Writings*, 2:320–24.

45. Wilson, ed., *The Papers*, 12:18–26, 29–36, 40–42, 96–101, 137–40; Robert V. Remini, *Henry Clay: Statesman for the Union* (New York, 1991), 425–35; Peter B. Knupfer, *The Union As It Is: Constitutional Unionism and Sectional Compromise, 1787–1861* (Chapel Hill, N.C., 1991), 111–14; Merrill D. Peterson, *Olive Branch and Sword: The Compromise of 1833* (Baton Rouge, La., 1982); Ellis, *Union at Risk*, 160–76; Hammond to Robert Y. Hayne, Feb. 7, 1833, James Henry Hammond Papers, LC.

46. *Speeches of John C. Calhoun and Daniel Webster* (Boston, 1833), 13–19, 33–38, 43–44, 48–52, 74–89; Wilson, ed, *The Papers*, 12:101–36; Robert V. Remini, *Daniel Webster: The Man and His Time* (New York, 1997), 377–82; David F. Ericson,

The Shaping of American Liberalism: The Debates over Ratification, Nullification, and Slavery (Chicago, 1993), chaps. 5, 6, and "The Nullification Crisis, Republicanism and the Force Bill Debate," *JSH* 61 (1995): 249–70.

47. Wilson, ed., *The Papers*, 12:15–17, 37–39; Perry Diaries, Mar. 6[?], 1833, Benjamin F. Perry Papers, SHC.

48. *Journals of the Convention*, 83–89, 100–104, 106–10, 112–15, 120–33; *Speeches Delivered in the Convention* (Charleston, S.C., 1833), 12–27, 29–35, 38–42, 47–62; White, *Robert Barnwell Rhett*, 33; Robert Y. Hayne to Hammond, Mar. 6, 1833, J. B. Earle to Volunteers (printed letter), Mar. 27, 1833, James Henry Hammond Papers, LC.

49. *Camden Journal*, Apr. 6, 20, 1833; *Speeches Delivered in the Convention*, 42–46, 63–68; Meats and Arnold, eds., *The Writings*, 1:176–82; *Journals of the Convention*, 110–12, 124; Hammond to M. C. M. Hammond, Mar. 27, 1833, James Henry Hammond Papers, LC.

50. *Speeches Delivered in the Convention*, 69–74; *Charleston Mercury*, Nov. 22, 28, 1833; *Camden Journal*, Aug. 24, 1833; Meats and Arnold, eds., *The Writings*, 1:181; *Oration of the Principal Duties of Americans* (Charleston, S.C., 1833), 19–23, 34–36; *Journals of the Senate, Nov. 25, 1833–Dec. 19, 1833*, SCDAH, 55, 78, 90–91, 100–101, 110–12; *Journals of the House of Representatives, Nov. 25, 1833–Dec. 19, 1833*, SCDAH, 39, 78–80.

51. *Greenville Mountaineer*, Feb. 9, 1833, Mar. 1, Oct. 18, 1834; *Camden Journal*, Aug. 24, Oct. 5, Dec. 21, 1833, Jan 18, Feb. 1, 8, 15, Mar. 1, 8, 15, 23, Apr. 5, 1834; *State Rights and Free Trade Evening Post*, Jan. 16, 30, Mar. 4, 1834; Perry Diaries, Feb. 8, 1834, Benjamin F. Perry Papers, SHC; Jacob Frederick Schirmer Diaries (ca. 1833), SCHS; James Petigru to Hugh Swinton Legaré, Apr. 24, 1834, James Hamilton Papers, SHC; Lesesne, "The Nullification Controversy," 23; Gettys, "Mobilization for Secession," chap. 3; Jean Martin Flynn, *The Militia in Antebellum South Carolina Society* (Spartanburg, S.C., 1991), 128–38.

52. *The Book of Allegiance* (Columbia, S.C., 1834), 1–69, 93–123, 209–82; Richard Yeadon to Isaac M. Dwight, Mar. 31, 1834, Hamilton to Waddy Thompson, May 23, 1834, James Hamilton Papers, SHC; O'Neall, *Biographical Sketches*, 1:281; *Charleston Mercury*, June 10, 11, July 24, 1834; *Camden Journal*, June 21, 1834; Robert Y. Hayne to Thompson, Jan. 24, 1834, Waddy Thompson Papers, SCL.

53. *Charleston Mercury*, Oct. 7, 8, 10, Nov. 27, Dec. 10, 1834; *Greenville Mountaineer*, Oct. 25, Nov. 4, 1834; *Charleston Courier*, Oct. 16, Nov. 6, Dec. 11, 1834; D. J. Rogers to W. R. Hemphill, Nov. 10, 1834, Hemphill Family Papers, DU; Meats and Arnold, eds., *The Writings*, 2:162.

54. General Assembly Petitions, 1834-1-01, SCDAH; Grayson, *James Louis Petigru*, 131; Petigru to Hugh Swinton Legaré, Aug. 1, Nov. 29, 1834, James Louis Petigru Papers, SCL; *Camden Journal*, Aug. 16, 1834; Wilson, ed., *The Papers*, 12:175, 331–32, 362–63, 377–78; James Petigru to Hugh Swinton Legaré, Dec. 15, 1834, James Hamilton Papers, SHC; *Camden Journal*, Dec. 20, 25, 1834; *Charleston Mercury*, Dec. 12, 1834; W. R. Hill to Gen. T. F. Jones, Jan. 18, 1835, Jones, Watts, and Davis Family Papers, SCL; Meats and Arnold, eds., *The Writings*, 1:262; I. W. Hayne to Hammond, Dec. 8, [1834], James Henry Hammond Papers, LC; Perry Diaries, Dec. 16, 1834, Benjamin F. Perry Papers, SHC; *An Address Delivered at the Celebration of the 54th Anniversary of the Battle of Cowpens* (Greenville, S.C., 1835), 10–12.

55. Joe Wilkins, "Window on Freedom: South Carolina's Response to British West Indian Slave Emancipation, 1833–1834," *SCHM* 85 (Apr. 1984): 135–44; Meats and Arnold, eds., *The Writings*, 2:177–81, 3:278–80, 291–95; *Greenville*

Mountaineer, Nov. 8, 1834; *The South Vindicated from the Treason and Fanaticism of the Northern Abolitionists* (Philadelphia, Pa., 1836); John W. Higham, "The Changing Loyalties of William Gilmore Simms," *JSH* 42 (1943): 210–23; Austin L. Venable, "William L. Yancey's Transition from Unionism to State Rights," *JSH* 10 (1944): 331–42; O'Neall, *Biographical Sketches,* 1:182, 2:36; William Sumner Jenkins, *Pro-Slavery Thought in the Old South* (Chapel Hill, N.C., 1935), 171.

56. Frank Otto Gatell, ed., "Postmaster Huger and the Incendiary Publications," *SCHM* 64 (July 1963): 193–201; William W. Freehling, *The Road to Disunion: Secessionists at Bay, 1776–1854* (New York, 1990), 290–92; Calhoun, ed., *Witness to Sorrow,* 1–10.

57. Meats and Arnold, eds., *The Writings,* 3:127–32, 204–8; Kibler, *Benjamin F. Perry,* 347–52; Grayson, *James Louis Petigru;* Lesesne, "The Nullification Controversy," 13–24; Gettys, "Mobilization for Secession"; Bird M. Pierson to Gen. T. F. Jones, Jan. 3, 1835, Jones, Watts, and Davis Family Papers, SCL.

58. Petigru to Hugh Swinton Legaré, July 15, 1833, James L. Petigru Papers, SCL; *Camden Journal,* June 15, Aug. 3, 1833; Perry Diaries, July 29, 1833, Benjamin F. Perry Papers, SHC; *An Oration Delivered in the Independent or Congregational Church* (Charleston, S.C., 1833), 41–44. Hammond is quoted by Faust, *James Henry Hammond,* 147; *Charleston Mercury,* Apr. 26, Aug. 10, 1833, Feb. 22, 1834; *A Dissertation on the Relative Duties between the Different Classes and Conditions of Society* (Columbia, S.C., 1836); *Sermon upon the Subject of Slavery by Samuel Dunwoody* (Columbia, S.C., 1837); *An Eulogium on the Public Services and Character of Robert J. Turnbull* (Charleston, S.C., 1834), 30. McDuffie is quoted by Jenkins, *Pro-Slavery Thought,* 78.

Chapter Three

1. David M. Potter, *The Impending Crisis* (New York, 1976), chap. 1; Eric Foner, *Free Soil, Free Labor, Free Men: The Ideology of the Republican Party Before the Civil War* (New York, 1970).

2. Michael F. Holt, *The Political Crisis of the 1850s* (New York, 1978); Michael A. Morrison, *Slavery and the American West: The Eclipse of Manifest Destiny and the Coming of the Civil War* (Chapel Hill, N.C., 1997).

3. George C. Rable, "Slavery, Politics, and the South: The Gag Rule as a Case Study," *Capitol Studies* 3 (1975): 69–87; William W. Freehling, *The Road to Disunion: Secessionists at Bay, 1776–1854* (New York, 1990), 308–52; William Lee Miller, *Arguing about Slavery: The Great Battle in the United States Congress* (New York, 1996); Clyde N. Wilson, ed., *The Papers of John C. Calhoun, 1835–1837* (Columbia, S.C., 1980), 13:394, and *The Papers of John C. Calhoun, 1837–1839* (Columbia, S.C., 1981), 14:31–32, 36–41, 45–51, 54–55, 56–76, 80–100.

4. *Address of Honorable R. Barnwell Rhett* (n.p., n.d.); *Southern State Rights, Free Trade and Anti-Abolition Tract No. 1* (Charleston, S.C., 1844); Elmore to R. B. Rhett, Aug. 22, 1846, Franklin Harper Elmore Papers, LC; Rhett to Burt, Sept. 9, 1844, Armistead Burt Papers, DU; John P. Richardson to Rhett, Jan. 21, May 17, 1842, "The Address of Mr. Calhoun to His Friends and Supporters," Dec. 21, 1843, Robert Barnwell Rhett Papers, SHC; *Charleston Mercury,* July 9, 10, Aug. 4, 1846; John Barnwell, ed., "Hamlet to Hotspur: Letters of Robert Woodward Barnwell to Robert Barnwell Rhett," *SCHM* 77 (Oct. 1976): 240–41, 245–46, 251–53; J. Franklin Jameson, ed., "Calhoun Correspondence," *Annual Report of the AHA for the Year 1899* 2 (1900): 538–44, 547–49, 552–57, 559–60, 562–70, 571–73, 592–94, 636–37; Clyde N. Wilson, ed., *The Papers of John C. Calhoun, 1844* (Co-

lumbia, S.C., 1988), 18:534; ibid. (Columbia, S.C., 1990), 19:254–55, 430–31, 472–73, 525–27, 552–53, 661–62; ibid. (Columbia, S.C., 1991), 20:489–90, 584; Richard K. Cralle, ed., *The Works of John C. Calhoun* (New York, 1874), 5:246–311; Chauncey S. Boucher, "The Annexation of Texas and the Bluffton Movement in South Carolina," *MVHR* 4 (June 1919): 3–33; Laura White, *Robert Barnwell Rhett: The Father of Secession* (Gloucester, Mass., 1960), 68–84; Carol Bleser, ed., *Secret and Sacred: The Diaries of James Henry Hammond, a Southern Slaveholder* (New York, 1988), 120–28, 132–33, 138–39.

5. Jameson, ed., "Calhoun Correspondence," 559; Calhoun to McDuffie, Dec. 4, 1843, George McDuffie Papers, SCL; Frederick Merk, *Slavery and the Annexation of Texas* (New York, 1972), and *Fruits of Propaganda in the Tyler Administration* (Cambridge, Mass., 1971); Freehling, *The Road to Disunion*, pt. 4; Oliver P. Chitwood, *John Tyler: Champion of the Old South* (New York, 1939); Claude H. Hall, *Abel Parker Upshur: Conservative Virginian, 1790–1844* (Madison, Wis., 1964); John H. Shroeder, "Annexation or Independence: The Texas Issue in American Politics, 1836–1845," *SWHQ* 89 (1985): 137–64; David E. Narrett, "A Choice of Destiny: Immigration Policy, Slavery, and the Annexation of Texas," *SWHQ* 100 (Jan. 1997): 271–302; Edward P. Crapol, "John Tyler and the Pursuit of National Destiny," *JER* 17 (Fall 1997): 467–91; Michael A. Morrison, "Martin Van Buren, the Democracy, and the Partisan Politics of Texas Annexation," *JSH* 61 (1995): 695–724; Herman V. Ames, ed., *State Documents on Federal Relations: The State and the United States* (rpt., New York, 1970), 224–32.

6. Jameson, ed., "Calhoun Correspondence," 634; Cralle, ed., *The Works*, 5:330–47; Wilson, ed., *The Papers*, 17:354–57, 381–83, 511–12, 545–49, 579, 18:273–78, 348–51, 19:571–78; Merk, *Slavery and the Annexation of Texas*, 81, 85–92, 138–40; Charles G. Sellers, *James K. Polk: Continentalist, 1843–1846* (Princeton, N.J., 1966), 205–8; Thomas B. Alexander, *Sectional Stress and Party Strength: A Study of Roll-Call Voting Patterns in the United States House of Representatives, 1836–1860* (Nashville, Tenn., 1967), 51–54; Joel H. Silbey, *The Shrine of Party: Congressional Voting Behavior, 1841–1852* (Pittsburgh, Pa., 1967), 60–62; Chaplain W. Morrison, *Democratic Politics and Sectionalism: The Wilmot Proviso Controversy* (Chapel Hill, N.C., 1967), 5–9; Michael F. Holt, *The Rise and Fall of the American Whig Party: Jacksonian Politics and the Onset of the Civil War* (New York, 1999), 168–83, 218–22; Arthur C. Cole, *The Whig Party in the South* (Washington, D.C., 1913), 109–18; Michael A. Morrison, "Westward the Curse of Empire: Texas Annexation and the American Whig Party," *JER* 10 (Summer 1990): 221–49; Elizabeth Perry to Perry, Dec. 1, 1844, Benjamin F. Perry Papers, SCL; James Henry Hammond to Burt, Feb. 11, Mar. 18, 1845, Armistead Burt Papers, DU; Bleser, ed., *Secret and Sacred*, 144.

7. Clyde N. Wilson, ed., *The Papers of John C. Calhoun, 1845* (Columbia, S.C., 1993), 21:444, 528–29; Cralle, ed., *The Works*, 4:258–90; *CG*, appendix, 29th Cong., 1st sess., 165–67, 184–89, 264–65, 502–6; Duff Green to Calhoun, Feb. 22, 1846, John C. Calhoun Papers, Clemson University; *Charleston Mercury*, Jan. 3, 8, 12, 13, Feb. 3, 9, 16, 17, 27, Mar. 5, 7, 20, Apr. 8, 9, 16, 20, 27, 1846; John C. Calhoun to Hammond, Jan. 22, 1846, James H. Hammond Papers, LC; Chauncey S. Boucher and Robert P. Brooks, eds., "Correspondence Addressed to John C. Calhoun, 1837–1849," *Annual Report of the AHA for the Year 1929* (1930): 325–27; Allan Nevins, ed., *Polk: The Diary of a President, 1845–1849, Covering the Mexican War, the Acquisition of Oregon, and the Conquest of California and the Southwest* (New York, 1929), 34–35, 56–57, 72–73; Sellers, *James K. Polk*, 357–72, 388–90, 409–15; Frederick Merk, *The Oregon Question: Essays in Anglo-American Diplomacy*

and Politics (Cambridge, Mass., 1967); Reginald C. Stuart, *United States Expansionism and British North America, 1775–1871* (Chapel Hill, N.C., 1988), chap. 4; Edwin A. Miles, " 'Fifty-Forty or Fight': An American Political Legend," *MVHR* 44 (1957): 291–309; Morrison, *Democratic Politics*, 11–13.

8. Hammond to M. C. M. Hammond, Feb. 26, 1847, Hammond to W. G. Simms, Mar. 21, 1847, James Henry Hammond Papers, LC; Jameson, ed., "Calhoun Correspondence," 633–34, 637, 653, 694–96, 698–99, 737–39, 741–42; Cralle, ed., *The Works*, 4:303–39, 362–82, 396–424; Wilson, ed., *The Papers*, 20:305, 320–21, 21:389–90, 461, 539; Clyde N. Wilson and Shirley Bright Cook, eds., *The Papers of John C. Calhoun, 1846* (Columbia, S.C., 1996), 23:92–95, 98–103, 111–13, 172, and *The Papers of John C. Calhoun, 1846–1847* (Columbia, S.C., 1998), 24:115–33, 615–16, 637–39, 642–45, 647–48, 666–68; *CG*, 29th Cong., 1st sess., appendix, 932–34, 30th Cong., 1st sess., 53–55, appendix, 590–91; *Camden Journal*, Jan. 19, 1848; Boucher and Brooks, eds., "Correspondence," 282–84, 377–78, 429–30; Calhoun to R. F. W. Allston, July 19, 1846, Elwood Fisher to Calhoun, 1847, John A. Campbell to Calhoun, Mar. 1, 1848, Waddy Thompson to Calhoun, Oct. 22, Dec. 18, 1847, John C. Calhoun Papers, Clemson University; *Charleston Mercury*, May 16, 19, 21, 22, 24, 25, June 9, 20, July 1, Dec. 14, 1846, July 10, Sept. 28, 1847; Henry T. Thompson, *Waddy Thompson* (n.p., 1929), 29; Ernest M. Lander, "General Waddy Thompson, a Friend of Mexico during the Mexican War," *SCHM* 78 (Jan. 1977): 32–42; McDuffie to Burt, Jan 13, [1848], George McDuffie Papers, DU; *Georgetown Winyaw Observer*, July 19, 1846; J. Abner to Burt, July 23, 1846, Armistead Burt Papers, DU. Also see Ernest McPherson Lander Jr., *Reluctant Imperialists: Calhoun, the South Carolinians and the Mexican War* (Baton Rouge, La., 1980); John H. Schroeder, *Mr. Polk's War: American Opposition and Dissent, 1846–1848* (Madison, Wis., 1973); Thomas R. Hietala, *Manifest Design: Anxious Aggrandizement in Late Jacksonian America* (Ithaca, N.Y., 1985), chap. 5; Reginald Horseman, *Race and Manifest Destiny: The Origins of American Racial Anglo-Saxonism* (Cambridge, Mass., 1981); John B. Edmunds Jr., *Francis W. Pickens and the Politics of Destruction* (Chapel Hill, N.C., 1986), 101–5; Jon L. Wakelyn, *The Politics of a Literary Man: William Gilmore Simms* (Westport, Conn., 1973) 100; Drew Gilpin Faust, *James Henry Hammond and the Old South: A Design for Mastery* (Baton Rouge, La., 1982), 285–86.

9. Cralle, ed., *The Works*, 4:323; Wilson and Cook, eds., *The Papers*, 24:43, 67, 69; W. F. DeSaussure to Hammond, Mar. 13, 1847, James Henry Hammond Papers, LC; Waddy Thompson to Calhoun, Dec. 18, 1847, George M. Thatcher to Calhoun, Jan. 5, 1848, John C. Calhoun Papers, Clemson University; *Charleston Mercury*, Feb. 17, 1847; Cole, *The Whig Party*, 118–23; John D. P. Fuller, "The Slavery Question and the Movement to Acquire Mexico, 1846–1848," *MVHR* 21 (June 1934): 31–48.

10. William J. Cooper Jr., *The South and the Politics of Slavery, 1828–1856* (Baton Rouge, 1978), 103–18, 287–89; Sellers, *James K. Polk*, 318–20.

11. DeSaussure to Hammond, Mar. 13, 1847, James Henry Hammond Papers, LC; Jameson, ed., "Calhoun Correspondence," 700–701, 703–5, 709–10, 714–16; Calhoun to Elmore, Dec. 10, 1846, Franklin Harper Elmore Papers, LC; Nevins, ed., *Polk*, 181–83; *Charleston Mercury*, Aug. 13, 14, Dec. 14, 1846, Jan. 7, 13, 1847; Eric Foner, "The Wilmot Proviso Revisited," *JAH* 56 (1969): 262–79; Richard R. Stenberg, "The Motivation of the Wilmot Proviso," *MVHR* 18 (1932): 535–41; Morrison, *Democratic Politics*, 13–24; Cooper, *The South and the Politics of Slavery*, 234–42; Alexander, *Sectional Stress*, 57–60; Cole, *The Whig Party*, 123–24.

12. *CG*, 29th Cong., 2nd sess., 178–80, 30th Cong., 1st sess., 1075; *Charleston*

Mercury, Jan. 19, 1847; *Camden Journal*, Aug. 2, 9, 1848; R. F. Simpson to Perry, Aug. 1, 1848, Benjamin F. Perry Papers, SCDAH; Nevins, ed., *Polk*, 186–87, 338; Paul H. Bergeron, *The Presidency of James K. Polk* (Lawrence, Kans., 1987), 201–11; Potter, *The Impending Crisis*, 64–70, 72–73, 76; R. Alton Lee, "Slavery and the Oregon Territorial Issue: Prelude to the Compromise of 1850," *Pacific Northwest Quarterly* 64 (July 1973): 112–19; Morrison, *Democratic Politics*, 32–34; Diary, Mar. 4, 1847, William P. Hill Papers, SHC.

13. Calhoun to Andrew Pickens Calhoun, Feb. 23, 1848, John C. Calhoun Papers, NCDAH; Nevins, ed., *Polk*, 177; Mary C. Simms Oliphant et al., eds., *The Letters of William Gilmore Simms*, vol. 2 (Columbia, S.C., 1953), 2:278, 288–89, 332–33, 353; Armistead Burt to Perry, July 20, 1848, R. F. Simpson to Perry, Aug. 1, 1848, Benjamin F. Perry Papers, SCDAH; Potter, *The Impending Crisis*, 73–75; Silbey, *The Shrine*, 92–93; Cole, *The Whig Party*, 125–26; Holt, *The Rise and Fall of the American Whig Party*, 252–53, 335–37.

14. *CG*, 29th Cong., 2nd sess., appendix, 314–18; Potter, *The Impending Crisis*, chap. 3; Robert R. Russel, "Constitutional Doctrines with Regard to Slavery in the Territories," *JSH* 32 (1966): 466–86; Foner, *Free Soil*, 83–87; Eric Foner, "Politics and Prejudice: The Free Soil Party and the Negro," *JNH* 50 (Oct. 1965): 239–56; Richard H. Sewell, *Ballots for Freedom: Antislavery Politics in the United States, 1837–1860* (New York, 1976), chap. 8; Frederick J. Blue, *The Free Soilers: Third Party Politics, 1848–1854* (Urbana, Ill., 1973).

15. *Charleston Mercury*, Feb. 5, 6, 1847; Ames, ed., *State Documents*, 244; *Speech of the Honorable Robert Barnwell Rhett* (Washington, D.C., 1847), 3–14; *CG*, 29th Cong., 2nd sess., appendix, 116–19, 30th Cong., 1st sess., appendix, 655–59; Cralle, ed., *The Works*, 4:339–49; Wilson and Cook, eds., *The Papers*, 24:169–76, 182–91; "Slavery in the Territories," *Commercial Review of the South and the West* 7 (July 1849): 62–73.

16. On this issue, also see Arthur Bestor, "State Sovereignty and Slavery: A Reinterpretation of Proslavery Constitutional Doctrine, 1846–1860," *Journal of the Illinois State Historical Society* 54 (1961): 117–80, and "The American Civil War as a Constitutional Crisis," *AHR* 69 (1963–64): 327–52.

17. *Speech of Mr. J. A. Woodward* (Washington, D.C., 1848), 3–6, 9, 10–12; *CG*, 30th Cong., 1st sess., appendix, 848–52; Bestor, "State Sovereignty and Slavery," 127–30, 140–67.

18. Hammond to W. G. Simms, June 20, 1848, Hammond to M. C. M. Hammond, June 9, 1848, James Henry Hammond Papers, LC; Faust, *James Henry Hammond*, 293–94.

19. *Charleston Mercury*, Apr. 13, May 31, July 2, 1847, Apr. 20, 1848; Boucher and Brooks, eds., "Correspondence," 373–74; *Huntsville Democrat*, Aug. 18, 1847; Ames, ed., *State Documents*, 3–7; Thelma Jennings, *The Nashville Convention: Southern Movement for Unity* (Memphis, Tenn., 1980), 3–14; Henry T. Shanks, *The Secession Movement in Virginia, 1847–1861* (Richmond, Va., 1934), 14–15, 22–23; Clarence Phillips Denman, *The Secession Movement in Alabama* (Montgomery, Ala., 1933), 2–9; Joseph Carlyle Sitterson, *The Secession Movement in North Carolina* (Chapel Hill, N.C., 1939), 40–42; Cleo Hearon, "Mississippi and the Compromise of 1850," *Publications of the Mississippi Historical Society* 14 (1913): 27; *Commercial Review of the South and West* 3 (May 1847): 421.

20. *Charleston Mercury*, Feb. 25, Mar. 11, 13, Aug. 9, 18, 19, 21, 1847; Calhoun to Henry Conner, Aug. 25, 1847, John C. Calhoun Papers, SCL; I. W. Hayne to Hammond, Aug. 25, 1847, James Henry Hammond Papers, LC; Henry Conner to Burt, Aug. 4, 1847; Armistead Burt Papers, DU; Henry W. Peronneau to Calhoun,

Sept. 29, 1847, John C. Calhoun Papers, Clemson University; Jameson, ed., "Calhoun Correspondence," 723–75; Wilson and Cook, eds., *The Papers*, 24:642–45; 0010 016 ND00 00751 00, 0010 016 ND00 00752 00, 0010 004 1847 00080 00, 0010 004 1847 00087 00, 0010 004 1847 00083 00, 0010 004 1848 00006 00, 0010 004 ND00 00937 00, 0010 016 ND00 00219 00, 0010 016 1848 00024 00, General Assembly Index — Wilmot Proviso, SCDAH; *Journal of the Senate* (Columbia, S.C., 1847), 30–32, 131, 176–77; *Journal of the House of Representatives* (Columbia, S.C., 1847), 10, 52, 55, 121, 207; *Journal of the House of Representatives* (Columbia, S.C., 1848), 59–60, 95–97, 107–8, 122; *Resolutions of the Legislature of South Carolina*, 30th Cong., 1st sess., miscellaneous no. 51 (n.d.).

21. M. M. Noah to M. C. Mordecai, Oct. 21, 1846, Franklin Harper Elmore Papers, LC; Wilson and Cook, eds., *The Papers*, 24:404–5, 424–26, 470–71, 487–92, 504–5, 509–13, 530–33, 538–39, 559–60, 574–77, 632–34; Calhoun to Armistead Burt, Sept. 21, 1847, John C. Calhoun Papers, NCDAH; *Charleston Mercury*, Feb. 9, 20, Mar. 17, 1847; W. G. Simms to Hammond, July 14, 1847, I. W. Hayne to Hammond, Aug. 25, 1847, James Henry Hammond Papers, LC; Howard C. Perkins, "A Neglected Phase in the Movement for Southern Unity," *JSH* 12 (1946): 153–203.

22. Henry W. Peronneau et al. to Calhoun, Sept. 25, 1847, L. M. Keitt to Calhoun, Oct. 1, 1847, Henry Conner to Calhoun, Aug. 8, Aug. 23, 1847, John C. Calhoun Papers, Clemson University; John C. Calhoun to Henry W. Peronneau, Sept. 28, 1847, in *Washington Union*, May 8, 1851; R. B. Rhett to Elmore, Dec. 8, 1847, Franklin Harper Elmore Papers, SCL; printed letters, Mar. 1847, n.d., Benjamin F. Perry Papers, SCDAH; Boucher and Brooks, eds., "Correspondence," 370–72, 374–75, 389–90, 391–93, 395–98, 399–406, 413–15; *Charleston Mercury*, Mar. 10, 23, 1847; Cralle, ed., *The Works*, 4:382–96; Wilson and Cook, eds., *The Papers*, 24:248–59; printed letters, Mar., Aug. 2, 1847, A. P. Aldrich to Hammond, Aug. 26, 1847, D. F. Jamison to Hammond, Oct. 4, 1847, James Henry Hammond Papers, LC.

23. *Charleston Mercury*, July 22, Aug. 9, 10, 11, 12, 14, 17, 18, 19, 27, 28, Sept. 30, Oct. 4, 9, 14, 19, 22, Nov. 16, 1847, Feb. 22, May 4, Sept. 7, 8, 11, 12, Oct. 14, Nov. 21, 30, 1848, May 30, July 12, 1849; *Camden Journal*, Aug. 30, Sept. 28, 1848; MS Wilmot Proviso, Franklin Harper Elmore Papers, LC; 0010 004 ND00 00938 00, General Assembly Index — Wilmot Proviso, SCDAH; Wilson and Cook, eds., *The Papers*, 24:565–71; Philip May Hamer, *The Secession Movement in South Carolina, 1847–1852* (Allentown, Pa., 1918), 11–14, 25; I. W. Hayne to Hammond, Aug. 25, 1847, James Henry Hammond Papers, LC. Also see Major L. Wilson, "The Controversy over Slavery Expansion and the Concept of the Safety Valve: Ideological Confusion in the 1850s," *Mississippi Quarterly* 24 (1971): 135–53; William L. Barney, *The Road to Secession: A New Perspective on the Old South* (New York, 1972).

24. B. F. Perry to Calhoun, Sept. 15, 1847, John C. Calhoun Papers, Clemson University; "Journal Extracts, 1832–63," 91–94, Benjamin F. Perry Papers, SCDAH; Kibler, *Benjamin F. Perry*, 220–22; Boucher and Brooks, "Correspondence," 486; *Charleston Mercury*, Oct. 9, 1847, Feb. 5, Nov. 21, 30, 1848; Oliphant et al., eds., *The Letters*, 2:294–96, 298, 312, 354; Hamer, *The Secession Movement*, 24–25; Chauncey Samuel Boucher, "The Secession and Cooperation Movements in South Carolina, 1848 to 1852," *Washington University Studies* 5 (Apr. 1918): 71–72.

25. Nevins, ed., *Polk*, 210–11; Jameson, ed., "Calhoun Correspondence," 727–28; James Clark to Hammond, July 24, 1847, Hammond to I. W. Hayne, June 4,

1847, Hammond to W. G. Simms, Apr. 1, 5, 19, Nov. 1, 1847, June 20, 1848, James Henry Hammond Papers, LC; Bleser, ed., *Secret and Sacred*, 183; *Charleston Mercury*, May 13, 1847; Joseph G. Rayback, "The Presidential Ambitions of John C. Calhoun, 1844–1848," *JSH* 14 (1948): 331–56.

26. John C. Calhoun to Elmore, Dec. 22, 1847, Franklin Harper Elmore Papers, LC; *Charleston Mercury*, Dec. 30, 31, 1847, Jan. 6, 17, Feb. 2, 11, 1848; *CG*, 30th Cong. 1st sess., appendix, 655–59, 848–52; Richard Cralle to Calhoun, Apr. 18, 1847, John C. Calhoun Papers, Clemson University; Calhoun to Henry W. Conner, Apr. 4, 1848, John C. Calhoun Papers, SCL; *Charleston Mercury*, May 5, 20, 26, 30, June 1, 2, 1848; *Camden Journal*, June 7, 1848; Milo Milton Quaife, *The Doctrine of Non-Intervention with Slavery in the Territories* (Chicago, 1910); Morrison, *Democratic Politics*, 87–92; Potter, *The Impending Crisis*, 57–59, 71–72; Cooper, *The South and the Politics of Slavery*, 253–57; William Carl Klunder, "Lewis Cass and Slavery Expansion: 'The Father of Popular Sovereignty' and Ideological Infanticide," *CWH* 32 (Dec. 1986): 293–99.

27. B. F. Whitner to Hammond, July 11, 1848, James Gadsden to Hammond, Sept. 15, 1848, James Henry Hammond Papers, LC; *Charleston Mercury*, June 28, July 3, Aug. 15, Oct. 14, 1848; Sewell, *Ballots*, chap. 7; Joseph G. Rayback, *Free Soil: The Election of 1848* (Lexington, Ky., 1970); Blue, *The Free Soilers*.

28. Wilson and Cook, eds., *The Papers*, 24:298, 327, 350, 357–58, 372, 409–10, 430–31, 463; Beverly Tucker to Hammond, Oct. 13, 1847, June 12, Sept. 20, 1848, Hammond to W. G. Simms, May 29, June 20, July 26, 28, Sept. 7, 22, 1848, Hammond to M. C. M. Hammond, June 12, Sept. 10, 12, 18, Nov. 15, 1848, W. G. Simms to Hammond, June 15, Aug. 29, Sept. 14, 1848, M. C. Keith and A. G. Magrath to Hammond, Aug. 10, 1848, Hammond to M. C. Keith and A. G. Magrath, Aug. 14, 1848, Hammond to A. B. Holt and the Committee, Oct. 10, 1848, James Gadsden to Hammond, Aug. 4, 1848, 1848, L. M. Ayer to Hammond, July 16, 1848, I. W. Hayne to Hammond, Aug. 13, 1848, "Looking One Way and Rowing the Other," Sept. 21, 1848, James M. Walker to Hammond, Aug. 22, 1848, James Henry Hammond Papers, LC; Calhoun to Henry W. Conner, Apr. 20, 1848, John C. Calhoun Papers, SCL; Bleser, ed., *Secret and Sacred*, 189–91; *Camden Journal*, Mar. 29, Aug. 9, 23, 1848; Petigru to his daughter, Susan, Sept. 11, 1848, James Louis Petigru Papers, LC; Thomas W. Bacot to his daughter, July 22, 1848, Bacot-Huger Collection, SCHS; Paul Quattlebaum to Burt, Armistead Burt Papers, DU; Calhoun to Lesesne, July 15, 1848, Joseph W. Lesesne Papers, SHC; Boucher and Brooks, eds., "Correspondence," 374–75, 376–77, 413–15, 450–54, 463–65; *Charleston Mercury*, June 10, 16, 21, 24, July 3, 18, 19, 20, 21, 22, Aug. 3, 5, 11, 21, 26, Sept. 4, 5, 14, 16, 20, 23, 25, 29, Oct. 2, 6, 9, 16, 1848; Cole, *The Whig Party*, 126–34; Cooper, *The South and the Politics of Slavery*, 244–53; Holt, *The Rise and Fall of the American Whig Party*, 268–70, 285–88, 313–14, 356–60; Jon L. Wakelyn, "Party Issues and Political Strategy of the Charleston Taylor Democrats," *SCHM* 17 (Apr. 1972): 72–86; Hamer, *The Secession Movement*, 21.

29. Abraham Watkins Venable Scrapbook, DU; Calhoun to Wilson Lumpkin, Sept. 1, 1848, John C. Calhoun Papers, LC; Calhoun to Conner, Oct. 18, 1848, John C. Calhoun Papers, CLS; *Charleston Mercury*, Aug. 21, 1848, Jan. 20, 1849; Herman V. Ames, "John C. Calhoun and the Secession Movement of 1850," *Proceedings of the American Antiquarian Society* 28 (1918): 23; Charles Wiltse, *John C. Calhoun: Sectionalist* (Indianapolis, Ind., 1951), 378–88; Melvin Johnson White, *The Secession Movement in the United States, 1847–1852* (New Orleans, La., 1910), 28–31.

30. Ulrich B. Phillips, ed., "The Correspondence of Robert Toombs, Alexan-

der H. Stephens, and Howell Cobb," in *Annual Report of the AHA for the Year 1911* (Washington, D.C., 1913), 139–42, 145; Hammond to M. C. M. Hammond, Jan. 26, 1849, John C. Calhoun to Hammond, Feb. 14, 1849, James Henry Hammond Papers, LC; *Charleston Mercury*, Jan. 22, 1849; Jameson, ed., "Calhoun Correspondence," 761–62; Calhoun to Henry W. Conner, Feb. 2, 1849, John C. Calhoun Papers, CLS; John C. Calhoun to Starke, Apr. 5, 1849, William Pinckney Starke Papers, SCL; Potter, *The Impending Crisis*, 84–86; Holt, *The Rise and Fall of the American Whig Party*, 385–87.

31. *The Address of Southern Delegates* (n.p., n.d.), 1–15; John Niven, *John C. Calhoun and the Price of Union* (Baton Rouge, 1988), 325; *Charleston Mercury*, Jan. 31, 1849.

32. *Address to the People of the United States* (n.p., n.d.), 1–8; Daniel Walker Howe, *The Political Culture of American Whigs* (Chicago, 1979), 238–62; Thomas Brown, *Politics and Statesmanship: Essays on the American Whig Party* (New York, 1985), chaps. 6, 7, 8; Cole, *The Whig Party*, chap. 5; Charles Grier Sellers Jr., "Who Were the Southern Whigs?" *AHR* 59 (1953–54): 335–46.

33. Tucker to Hammond, Jan. 30, 1849, Calhoun to Hammond, Feb. 14, 1849, James Henry Hammond Papers, LC; Ames, ed., *State Documents*, 250–52; Jennings, *The Nashville Convention*, 17–24, 27–33; Freehling, *The Road to Disunion*, 462–72; White, *The Secession Movement*, 32–40; Ames, "John C. Calhoun," 30; Shanks, *The Secession Movement in Virginia*, 24–28; Richard Harrison Shryock, *Georgia and the Union in 1850* (Durham, N.C., 1926), 182–98; Herbert J. Doherty, "Florida and the Crisis of 1850," *JSH* 19 (1953): 36–37; John Meador, "Florida and the Compromise of 1850," *Florida Historical Quarterly* 39 (1960–61): 17; Charles M. Harvey, "Missouri from 1849 to 1860," *Missouri Historical Review* 92 (Jan. 1998): 119–20; St. George L. Sioussat, "Tennessee, the Compromise of 1850, and the Nashville Convention," *MVHR* 2 (Dec. 1915): 315–16; Sitterson, *The Secession Movement in North Carolina*, 46–52.

34. Phillips, ed., "Correspondence," 159, 163–64; Nevins, ed., *Polk*, 358–60, 364–68, 370–71; Thomas H. Benton, *Thirty Years' View; or, a History of the Working of the American Government for Thirty Years, from 1820 to 1850* (New York, 1856), 2: 696–700, 712–13, 732–36; Wilson and Cook, eds., *The Papers*, 24:195–210; John C. Calhoun, *To the People of the Southern States* (n.p., n.d.); Samuel Treat to Calhoun, June 17, 1849, John C. Calhoun Papers, Clemson University; Brooks and Boucher, eds., "Correspondence," 505–6, 512–13, 515–18, 521–22; *Camden Journal*, July 18, Aug. 8, 1849; *Charleston Mercury*, July 16, 17, 18, 1849; Randolph Campbell, "Texas and the Nashville Convention of 1850," *SWHQ* 76 (July 1972): 2–3; Harvey, "Missouri from 1849 to 1860," 119–23; Benjamin C. Merkel, "The Slavery Issue and the Political Decline of Thomas Hart Benton, 1846–1856," *Missouri Historical Review* 38 (1944): 388–407.

35. *Camden Journal*, Aug. 30, Sept. 28, 1848, Jan. 24, 31, Feb. 21, May 9, 1849; *Charleston Mercury*, Aug. 21, Sept. 15, Nov. 21, 29, Dec. 11, 16, 1848, Feb. 26, Mar. 8, 16, 17, 22, May 1, 4, 1849; Whitemarsh Seabrook to Calhoun, Feb. 5, 1849, Henry W. Conner to Calhoun, Feb. 12, 1849, John C. Calhoun Papers, Clemson University; Calhoun to Henry W. Conner, Feb. 2, 1849, John C. Calhoun Papers, CLS; Hammond to M. C. M. Hammond, Nov. 16, 1849, James Henry Hammond Papers, LC; Oliphant et al., eds., *The Letters*, 2:482–83; "Journal Extracts, 1832–63," 106, Benjamin F. Perry Papers, SCDAH; Boucher, "Secession and Cooperation in South Carolina," 77–81.

36. Blake McNulty, "Uncertain Masters: The South Carolina Elite and Slavery in the Secession Crisis of 1850," in Winfred B. Moore Jr. and Joseph F. Tripp, eds.,

Looking South: Chapters in the Story of an American Region (Westport, Conn., 1989), 79–94; Steven A. Channing, *Crisis of Fear: Secession in South Carolina* (New York, 1970), 36; Russel B. Nye, *Fettered Freedom: Civil Liberties and the Slavery Controversy, 1830–1860* (East Lansing, Mich., 1949), 148–49; Archie Vernon Huff Jr., *Greenville: The History of the City and County in the South Carolina Piedmont* (Columbia, S.C., 1995), 128–29; Clement Eaton, *The Freedom-of-Thought Struggle in the Old South* (Durham, N.C., 1940); Franklin Harper Elmore to Seabrook, May 30, 1849, Whitemarsh Benjamin Seabrook Papers, LC; *Charleston Mercury*, Aug. 9, 13, 16, 1849, Oct. 15, 1850; Wilson, ed., *The Papers*, 18:473–74; *CG*, 31st Cong., 1st sess., 136, 30th Cong., 2nd sess., 317; William Joseph MacArthur, "Antebellum Politics in an Upcountry District: National, State and Local Issues in Spartanburg County, South Carolina, 1850–1860" (M.A. thesis, University of South Carolina, 1966), 22–23.

37. Beverly Tucker to Hammond, Dec. 27, 1849, James Chesnut to Hammond, Mar. 15, 1849, James Henry Hammond Papers, LC; L. M. Keitt to Calhoun, Jan. 14, 1849, John H. Means to Calhoun, Mar. 28 [1849], Calhoun to John H. Means, Apr. 13, 1849, Henry W. Conner to Calhoun, Feb. 12, 1849, R. B. Rhett to Calhoun, July 19, 1849, John C. Calhoun Papers, Clemson University; Elmer Don Herd Jr., "Chapters from the Life of a Southern Chevalier: Laurence Massillon Keitt's Congressional Years, 1853–1860" (M.A. thesis, University of South Carolina, 1958), iii–iv; Eric H. Walther, *The Fire-Eaters* (Baton Rouge, La., 1992), chaps. 5, 8; Meats and Arnold, eds., *The Writings*, 2:1–6, 3:97–102; John Barnwell, *Love of Order: South Carolina's First Secession Crisis* (Chapel Hill, N.C., 1982), 81–82; Hamer, *The Secession Movement*, 36–37; *Charleston Mercury*, May 14, 15, 16, 17, 1849.

38. Franklin Harper Elmore to Seabrook, May 30, 1849, Whitemarsh Benjamin Seabrook Papers, LC; Jameson, ed., "Calhoun Correspondence," 1195–1202; Avery O. Craven, *The Growth of Southern Nationalism, 1848–1861* (Baton Rouge, La., 1958), 14–25; John McCardell, *The Idea of a Southern Nation: Southern Nationalists and Southern Nationalism, 1830–1860* (New York, 1979), 72–76.

39. *Black River Watchman*, July 13, 1850; *National Era*, June 12, 1851; Franklin Harper Elmore to Calhoun, Aug. 6, 1849, Judge Anderson Hutchinson to Calhoun, Oct. 5, 1849, John C. Calhoun Papers, Clemson University; Jameson, ed., "Calhoun Correspondence," 1204–7; Daniel Wallace to Seabrook, June 8, Oct. 20, Nov. 7, 1849, Whitemarsh Benjamin Seabrook Papers, LC; *Charleston Mercury*, Nov. 26, Dec. 1, 1849; Ames, ed., *State Documents*, 14–18; Ames, "John C. Calhoun," 32–35; Hearon, "Mississippi and the Compromise of 1850," 39–68; Jennings, *The Nashville Convention*, 25–27, 35–40; White, *The Secession Movement*, 61–64.

40. *Charleston Mercury*, Nov. 14, 15, 28, Dec. 10, 1849, Feb. 25, 28, 1850; Calhoun to Hammond, Dec. 7, 1849, James Henry Hammond Papers, LC; 0010 011 1849 00027 00, 0010 004 1849 00100 00, 0010 004 1849 00093 00, General Assembly Index, Wilmot Proviso, SCDAH; *Reports and Resolutions* (Columbia, S.C., 1849), 312–14.

41. Allston to his wife, Adele, Dec. 16, 1849, Robert F. W. Allston Papers, SCHS; *Charleston Mercury*, Dec. 17, 18, 20, 27, 28, 1849, Jan. 25, 1850; *Camden Journal*, Feb. 1, 1850; Abraham Watkins Venable Scrapbook, DU; Jameson, ed., "Calhoun Correspondence," 771; Cooper, *The South and the Politics of Slavery*, 276–80; Allan Nevins, *Ordeal of the Union: Fruits of Manifest Destiny, 1847–1852* (rpt., New York, 1992), 1:240–47, 250–64; K. Jack Bauer, *Zachary Taylor: Soldier, Planter, Statesman of the Old Southwest* (Baton Rouge, La., 1985), 269–72, 289–303.

42. Ames, ed., *State Documents*, 243; Potter, *The Impending Crisis*, 89–96; Nevins, *Ordeal of the Union*, 1:216, 220–21; William O. Lynch, "Anti-Slavery Tendencies of the Democratic Party in the Northwest, 1848–50," *MVHR* 11 (Dec. 1924): 319–31; *Charleston Mercury*, Dec. 27, 1848; Jameson, ed., "Calhoun Correspondence," 776, 780.

43. *CG*, 31st Cong., 1st sess., pt. 1, 244–47; Robert Remini, *Henry Clay: Statesman for the Union* (New York, 1991), chap. 40; Knupfer, *The Union as It Is*, chap. 5; Howe, *The Political Culture*, 132–35, 147–48; *Charleston Mercury*, Feb. 12, 13, 20, 21, 1850; *Camden Journal*, Feb. 5, 1850; Bleser, ed., *Secret and Sacred*, 197–98.

44. John C. Calhoun to Hammond, Feb. 16, 1850, Jan. 4, 1850, "Resolutions Dictated to Joseph A. Scoville by John C. Calhoun a Few Days before His Death," James Henry Hammond Papers, LC; Calhoun to John Raven Mathews, Jan. 10, 1850, John C. Calhoun Papers, SCL; Calhoun to Thomas G. Clemson, Feb. 6, 1850, John C. Calhoun Papers, Clemson University; *Speeches of Honorable John C. Calhoun and Honorable Daniel Webster* (New York, 1850), 2–12.

45. *Speeches of Honorable John C. Calhoun and Honorable Daniel Webster*, 13–32; Calhoun to Thomas G. Clemson, Mar. 10, 1850, John C. Calhoun Papers, Clemson University; Calhoun to Henry W. Conner, Mar. 18, 1850, John C. Calhoun Papers, SCL; *Charleston Mercury*, Mar. 11, 14, 1850; Herbert Darling Foster, "Webster's Seventh of Mar. Speech and the Secession Movement, 1850," *AHR* 27 (1921–22): 245–70; Major L. Wilson, "Of Time and the Union: Webster and His Critics in the Crisis of 1850," *CWH* 14 (1968): 287–306; Robert V. Remini, *Daniel Webster: The Man and His Time* (New York, 1997), 669–81; Brown, *Politics and Statesmanship*, chap. 3; Maurice G. Baxter, *One and Inseparable: Daniel Webster and the Union* (Cambridge, Mass., 1984), chap. 25.

46. *CG*, 31st Cong., 1st sess., pt. 1, appendix, 260–69; Frederic Bancroft, *The Life of William H. Seward* (New York, 1900), 1:242–68; John M. Taylor, *William Henry Seward: Lincoln's Right Hand* (New York, 1991), 83–86; Hammond to W. B. Hodgson, Apr. 2, 1850, James Henry Hammond Papers, DU.

47. Hammond to John C. Calhoun, Mar. 6, 1850, James Henry Hammond Papers, LC; *Thoughts Suited to the Present Crisis* (Columbia, S.C., 1850), 4–33; Bremer, *The Homes of the New World*, 2:298–99, 304–5; "Journal Extracts, 1832–1863," 132–36, 143, Benjamin F. Perry Papers, SCDAH; Perry Diaries, June 10, 1850, Benjamin F. Perry Papers, SHC; Irving H. Bartlett, *John C. Calhoun: A Biography* (New York, 1993), 378; Alfred Huger to Gourdin, Apr. 20, 1850, Robert N. Gourdin Papers, DU.

48. John P. Thomas, ed., *The Carolina Tribute to Calhoun* (Columbia, S.C., 1857), 72–82; James Blount Miller Scrapbook, 3–4, SCL; *Reports and Resolutions* (Columbia, S.C., 1850), 152–55, 232–37; James Hamilton to Hammond, Mar. 31, 1850, W. G. Simms to Hammond, Apr. 4, 1850, Henry W. Conner to Hammond, Apr. 6, 9, 26, 1850, Hammond to T. L. Hutchinson, Apr. 8, 1850, W. H. Gist to Hammond, Apr. 20, 1850, James Henry Hammond Papers, LC; Bleser, ed., *Secret and Sacred*, 199–200; Langdon Cheves to Whitemarsh Seabrook, Apr. 9, 1850, Cheves Family Papers, SCL; Barnwell, *Love of Order*, 98–100; *Obituary Addresses* (Washington, D.C., 1850), 130–59; *An Oration on the Life, Character and Services of John Caldwell Calhoun* (Charleston, S.C., 1850), 35–59; Faust, *James Henry Hammond*, 297–301; White, *Robert Barnwell Rhett*, 33–35, 114–15.

49. Richard K. Cralle, ed., *The Works of John C. Calhoun: A Disquisition on Government and a Discourse on the Constitution and Government of the United States* (Charleston, S.C., 1851), 1:12–35, 46, 47–51, 236, 270, 301–2, 377–95; Huger to D. B. Huger, Sept. 16, 1853, Huger to Marshall Hall, Dec. 21, 1853, Alfred Huger

Letterbook, DU; George Fitzhugh, "The Politics and Economics of Aristotle and Mr. Calhoun," *De Bow's Review* 23 (Aug. 1857): 163–72; Niven, *John C. Calhoun*, 329–33; Eugene D. Genovese, *The Southern Tradition: The Achievement and Limitations of an American Conservatism* (Cambridge, Mass., 1994), 45–53, 60–61; Robert A. Garson, "Proslavery as Political Theory: The Examples of John C. Calhoun and George Fitzhugh," *SAQ* 84 (Spring 1985): 197–212; James Clarke, "Calhoun and the Concept of 'Reactionary Enlightenment': An Examination of the *Disquisition on Government*" (Ph.D. diss., University of Keele, 1982).

50. Cralle, ed., *The Works*, 1:54–59; J. William Harris, "Last of the Classical Republicans: An Interpretation of John C. Calhoun," *CWH* 30 (1984): 255–67; Gillis J. Harp, "Taylor, Calhoun, and the Decline of a Theory of Political Disharmony," *Journal of the History of Ideas* 46 (1985): 107–20; Richard Hofstadter, *The American Political Tradition and the Men Who Made It* (New York, 1948), 67–91; Louis Hartz, *The Liberal Tradition in America* (New York, 1955), 145–200; Lacy K. Ford Jr., "Prophet with Posthumous Honor: John C. Calhoun and the Southern Political Tradition," in Charles W. Eagles, ed., *Is There a Southern Political Tradition?* (Jackson, Miss., 1996), 3–25.

51. Wilson, ed., *The Papers*, 13:384–97, 14:84–85; Cralle, ed., *The Works*, 4:450–54, 505–12; Jameson, ed., "Calhoun Correspondence," 749–58; "The Oregon Bill: Remarks on the South Carolina Doctrine in Regard to Territories," *American Review* 2 (Aug. 1848): 111–19; *Charleston Mercury*, Aug. 26, 1847.

52. On the proslavery argument, see Eugene D. Genovese, *The Slaveholders' Dilemma: Freedom and Progress in Southern Conservative Thought, 1820–1860* (Columbia, Mo., 1992), and "South Carolina's Contribution to the Doctrine of Slavery in the Abstract," in David R. Chesnutt and Clyde N. Wilson, eds., *The Meaning of South Carolina History: Essays in Honor of George C. Rogers Jr.* (Columbia, S.C., 1991), 146–60; William Sumner Jenkins, *Pro-Slavery Thought in the Old South* (Chapel Hill, N.C., 1935); Drew Gilpin Faust, ed., *The Ideology of Slavery: Proslavery Thought in the Antebellum South, 1830–1860* (Baton Rouge, La., 1981), introduction; Michael Wayne, "An Old South Morality Play: Reconsidering the Social Underpinnings of the Proslavery Ideology," *JAH* 77 (Dec. 1990): 838–63; Gaines M. Foster, "Guilt over Slavery: An Historiographical Analysis," *JSH* 56 (1990): 665–94; Peter Kolchin, "In Defense of Servitude: American Proslavery and Russian Proserfdom Arguments, 1760–1860," *AHR* 85 (Oct. 1980): 809–27; Bertram Wyatt-Brown, "Modernizing Southern Slavery: The Proslavery Argument Reinterpreted," in J. Morgan Kousser and James M. McPherson, eds., *Region, Race, and Reconstruction: Essays in Honor of C. Vann Woodward* (New York, 1982), 27–49.

53. Thomas Cooper, "Slavery," *Southern Literary Journal* 1 (Nov. 1835): 189; "Harper's Memoir on Slavery," in *The Pro-Slavery Argument as Maintained by the Most Distinguished Writers of the Southern States* (Charleston, S.C., 1852), 6–19; "Hammond's Letters on Slavery," in ibid., 109–10; "The Morals of Slavery," in ibid., 247–60; Clyde N. Wilson, ed., *Selections from the Letters and Speeches of the Hon. James H. Hammond, of South Carolina* (Spartanburg, S.C., 1978); *Speech of Mr. J. A. Woodward*, 6; *Charleston Mercury*, Apr. 7, 1852. For a different view, see Kenneth S. Greenberg, "Revolutionary Ideology and the Proslavery Argument: The Abolition of Slavery in Antebellum South Carolina," *JSH* 42 (1976): 365–84.

54. *Charleston Mercury*, Mar. 11, 12, 14, 17, 1848; "Hammond's Letters," 104–6; *Speech of Mr. J. A. Woodward*, 10–11; *Speech of the Honorable Langdon Cheves*, 17–19; Wilson, ed., *The Papers*, 13:66; Wilson, ed., *Selections*, 15–49; L.S.M., "Justice and Fraternity," *SQR* 15 (July 1849): 356–74; L.S.M., "The Right to Labor," *SQR* 16 (Oct. 1849): 138–60; L.S.M., "Negro and White Slavery—Wherein Do They

Differ?," *SQR* 20 (July 1851): 119–20. On McCord, see Manisha Sinha, "Louisa Susanna McCord: Spokeswoman of the Master Class in Antebellum South Carolina," in Susan Ostrov Weisser and Jennifer Fleischner, eds., *Feminist Nightmares, Women at Odds: Feminism and the Problem of Sisterhood* (New York, 1994), 62–87; Elizabeth Fox-Genovese, *Within the Plantation Household: Black and White Women of the Old South* (Chapel Hill, N.C., 1988), 281–82; Richard C. Lounsbury, ed., *Louisa McCord: Selected Writings* (Charlottesville, Va., 1997), 1–15; On this issue, also see James Oakes, *Slavery and Freedom: An Interpretation of the Old South* (New York, 1990); James L. Huston, "Property Rights in Slavery and the Coming of the Civil War," *JSH* 65 (1999): 249–86.

55. *Address of Lawrence M. Keitt* (Columbia, S.C., 1851), 7–10; Wilson, ed., *Selections*, 41–45; *The Political Annals*, 28; Beverly Tucker to Hammond, Apr. 14, 21, 1848, "Occasional Meditations," Mar., 1852, Trescot to Hammond, Feb. 16, 1850, James Henry Hammond Papers, LC; Robert Nicholas Olsberg, "A Government of Class and Race: William Henry Trescot and the South Carolina Chivalry, 1850–1865" (Ph.D. diss., University of South Carolina, 1972).

56. "The Morals," 248; L.S.M., "Enfranchisement of Woman," *SQR* (Apr. 1852): 322–41; L.S.M., "Woman and Her Needs," *DBR* 13 (1852): 267–91; Sinha, "Louisa Susanna McCord," 72.

57. On this issue, see Wilfred Carsel, "The Slaveholders' Indictment of Northern Wage Slavery," *JSH* 6 (1940): 504–20; Eugene D. Genovese, *The World the Slaveholders Made: Two Essays in Interpretation* (New York, 1969), pt. 2; [D. F. Jamison], "British and American Slavery," *SQR* 24 (Oct. 1853): 369–411; "Harper's Memoir," 19–34, 84–87; *The Hireling and the Slave* (Charleston, S.C., 1854), v–xii, 49; William H. Trescot, *The Position and Course of the South* (Charleston, S.C., 1850), 10–11.

58. John B. Adger and John L. Girardeau, eds., *The Collected Writings of James Henley Thornwell* (Richmond, Va., 1873), 4:405–6; *Domestic Slavery Considered as a Scriptural Institution* (New York, 1845), 148–54; *A Defence of the South* (Hamburg, S.C., 1850), 30–34; Iveson Brookes to James Edeton[?], Apr. 10, 1854, Iveson L. Brookes Papers, SCL; *National Sins: A Call to Repentance* (Charleston, S.C., 1849), 17–18; *God the Refuge of His People* (Columbia, S.C., 1850), 10–11; *The Committing of Our Cause to God* (Charleston, S.C., 1850), 6–9. Also see Eugene D. Genovese, *"Slavery Ordained of God": The Southern Slaveholders' View of Biblical History and Modern Politics* (Gettysburg, Pa., 1985); Donald G. Mathews, *Slavery and Methodism: A Chapter in American Morality* (Princeton, N.J., 1965); Eugene D. Genovese and Elizabeth Fox-Genovese, "The Religious Ideals of Southern Slave Society," *GHQ* 70 (Spring 1986): 1–16, and "The Divine Sanction of Social Order: Religious Foundations of the Southern Slaveholders' World View," *Journal of the American Academy of Religion* 55 (Summer 1987): 211–33.

59. Adger and Girardeau, eds., *The Collected Writings*, 384, 403, 542–43; "Hammond's Letters," 109; *A Defence*, 8–9, 19–23; John Bachman, *The Doctrine of the Unity of the Human Race* (Charleston, S.C., 1850); *The Rights and Duties of Masters* (Charleston, S.C., 1850), 11; *The Commercial Review of the South and West* 9 (July 1850): 9–10, 10 (Feb. 1851): 113–32; Faust, ed., *The Ideology of Slavery*, 206–38; L.S.M., "Diversity of the Races: Its Bearing upon Negro Slavery" *SQR* (Apr. 1851): 392–419; L.S.M., "Negro Mania," *DBR* (May 1852): 507–24; John B. Adger, *Christian Mission and African Colonization* (Columbia, S.C., 1857), 18; H. Shelton Smith, *In His Image, But . . . : Racism in Southern Religion, 1780–1910* (Durham, N.C., 1972), 134–35; Thomas Virgil Peterson, *Ham and Japheth: The Mythic World of Whites in the Antebellum South* (Metuchen, N.J., 1978); William Stanton, *The*

Leopard's Spots: Scientific Attitudes toward Race in America, 1815–1859 (Chicago, 1960); George M. Fredrickson, *The Black Image in the White Mind: The Debate on Afro-American Character and Destiny, 1817–1914* (New York, 1971), chaps. 2, 3.

60. *The Rights and Duties; The Committing of Our Cause,* 15–16; *The Religious Instruction of the Colored Population* (Charleston, S.C., 1847); *The Christian Doctrine of Human Rights and Slavery* (Columbia, S.C., 1849), 12–18; *Charleston Mercury,* June 3, 1852; David Ewart, *A Scriptural View of the Moral Relations of African Slavery* (Columbia, S.C., 1849); Rev. H. N. McTyeire et al., *Duties of Masters to Servants* (Charleston, S.C., 1851); Jack P. Maddex Jr., " 'The Southern Apostasy' Revisited: The Significance of Proslavery Christianity," *Marxist Perspectives* 2 (Fall 1979): 132–41; William W. Freehling, "James Henley Thornwell's Mysterious Antislavery Moment," *JSH* 57 (1991): 383–406; James Oscar Farmer Jr., *The Metaphysical Confederacy: James Henley Thornwell and the Synthesis of Southern Values* (Macon, Ga., 1986).

Chapter Four

1. Michael F. Holt, *The Political Crisis of the 1850s* (New York, 1978), chap. 8; William W. Freehling, *The Road to Disunion: Secessionists at Bay, 1776–1854* (New York, 1990); Thelma Jennings, *The Nashville Convention: Southern Movement for Unity* (Memphis, Tenn., 1980).

2. John Barnwell, *Love of Order: South Carolina's First Secession Crisis* (Chapel Hill, N.C., 1982); Philip May Hamer, *The Secession Movement in South Carolina, 1847–1852* (Allentown, Pa., 1918).

3. Jennings, *The Nashville Convention,* 57–134; William J. Cooper Jr., *The South and the Politics of Slavery, 1828–1856* (Baton Rouge, La., 1978), 292–95; Jonathan M. Atkins, *Parties, Politics, and the Sectional Conflict in Tennessee, 1832–1861* (Knoxville, Tenn., 1997), 167–68; Farrar Newberry, "The Nashville Convention and Southern Sentiment in 1850," *SAQ* 11 (1912): 259–73; Melvin Johnson White, *The Secession Movement in the United States, 1847–1852* (New Orleans, La., 1910), 64–72; Randolph Campbell, "Texas and the Nashville Convention of 1850," *SWHQ* 76 (July 1972): 6–11; James Kimmins Greer, "Louisiana Politics, 1845–1861," *Louisiana Historical Quarterly* 12 (Oct. 1929): 570–81; Joseph Carlyle Sitterson, *The Secession Movement in North Carolina* (Chapel Hill, 1939), chap. 4; Herbert J. Doherty, "Florida and the Crisis of 1850," *JSH* 19 (1953): 38–42; *Charleston Mercury,* Mar. 21, 27, Apr. 1, 2, 3, 4, 8, 9, 11, 13, 16, 18, 19, 20, 23, 26, 27, 29, May 10, 17, 18, 21, 29, June 1, 1850; B. C. Yancey to Chairman of Committee of Electoral Delegates, Apr. 20, 1850, Benjamin Cudsworth Yancey Papers, SHC.

4. "Journal Extracts, 1832–1863," 138, Benjamin F. Perry Papers, SCDAH; Carol Bleser, ed., *Secret and Sacred: The Diaries of James Henry Hammond, a Southern Slaveholder* (New York, 1988), 202; Hammond to W. B. Hodgson, Apr. 2, 1850, James Henry Hammond Papers, DU; Robert Tucker, "James H. Hammond and the Southern Convention," *Proceedings of the South Carolina Historical Association* (1960): 9–10; Mary C. Simms Oliphant et al., eds., *The Letters of William Gilmore Simms,* vol. 2 (Columbia, S.C., 1953), 2:575, 3:8–9, 24, 43; "Southern Convention," *SQR* (Sept. 1850): 208–32; "Nashville Convention," Robert F. W. Allston Papers, SCHS; *Camden Journal,* June 28, 1850; St. George L. Sioussant, "Tennessee, the Compromise of 1850, and the Nashville Convention," *MVHR* 2 (Dec. 1915): 331–37; Hammond to W. G. Simms, June 27, 1850, James Henry Hammond Papers, LC.

5. *Resolutions and Address Adopted by the Southern Convention* (Columbia, S.C., 1850), 3–23.

6. *Charleston Mercury*, June 13, 15, 18, 21, 24, July 20, 1850; Hammond to W. G. Simms, June 16, 1850, James Clark to Hammond, July 1, 1850, James Henry Hammond Papers, LC; Laura White, *Robert Barnwell Rhett: The Father of Secession* (Gloucester, Mass., 1960), 109–10.

7. Don E. Fehrenbacher, *The South and Three Sectional Crises* (Baton Rouge, La., 1980), 40–44, 69; Robert R. Russel, "What Was the Compromise of 1850?," *JSH* 22 (1956): 292–309; Holman Hamilton, *Prologue to Conflict: The Crisis and Compromise of 1850* (Lexington, Ky., 1964); Mark J. Stegmaier, "Zachary Taylor versus the South," *CWH* 33 (1987): 217–41; Elbert B. Smith, *The Presidencies of Zachary Taylor and Millard Fillmore* (Lawrence, Kans., 1988), 165–69, 183–84; David M. Potter, *The Impending Crisis, 1848–1861* (New York, 1976), chap. 5; Freehling, *The Road to Disunion*, chap. 28; Thomas B. Alexander, *Sectional Stress and Party Strength: A Study of the Roll-Call Voting Patterns in the United States House of Representatives, 1836–1860* (Nashville, Tenn., 1967), chap. 8; Joel H. Silbey, *The Shrine of Party: Congressional Voting Behavior, 1841–1852* (Pittsburgh, Pa., 1967), chap. 8.

8. *CG*, 31st Cong., 1st sess., pt. 1, 941, pt. 2, 1471, 1189; *Speech of Daniel Wallace . . . on the Slavery Question* (Washington, D.C., 1850), 3, 5–6, 8–13; *Speech of Mr. Butler . . . on the Compromise Bill* (n.p., n.d.), 1–7, 15–16; *Speech of the Honorable I. E. Holmes* (Washington, D.C., 1850), 3–4, 7; *Speech of A. P. Butler . . . on . . . Fugitive Slaves* (Washington, D.C., 1850), 3–8; A. P. Butler to Hammond, July 23, 1850, B. F. Whitner to Hammond, Mar. 2, 1850, James Henry Hammond Papers, LC; John Springs to Dr. Baxter, July 22, 1850, Springs Family Papers, SHC; Armistead Burt to Perry, Jan. 16, 1850, Benjamin F. Perry Papers, SCDAH; D. Wallace to John Bomar, Aug. 12, 1850, Edward Earle Bomar Papers, DU; Edward Noble to Burt, Feb. 25, 1850, Armistead Burt Papers, DU; *An Oration . . . by W. Alston Pringle* (Charleston, S.C., 1850); Samuel to W. D. McDowell, Aug. 4, 1850, Witherspoon-McDowell Papers, DU; *Proceedings of the United States Senate on the Fugitive Slave Bill* (n.p., n.d.), 1–13, 22–57; *Charleston Mercury*, Feb. 28, Mar. 2, 4, 9, May 21, June 19, 26, 27, 28, Aug. 21, Sept. 11, 1850; *Camden Journal*, May 3, 31, June 14, 28, 1850; Oliphant et al., eds., *The Letters*, 3:8; John Barnwell, ed., " 'In the Hands of the Compromisers': Letters of Robert W. Barnwell to James H. Hammond," *CWH* 29 (1983): 159.

9. *CG*, 31st Cong., 2nd sess., 579, appendix, 298–99, 414–16; *CG*, 32nd Cong., 1st sess., appendix, 42–65; Bleser, ed., *Secret and Sacred*, 230; *Charleston Mercury*, June 1, 3, July 4, 1850, Jan. 11, Feb. 20, 24, 25, 26, Mar. 4, 1851; *Camden Journal*, Oct. 8, 1850, June 20, 1851; *Speech of Mr. Butler . . . on the Resolution . . . by Mr. Foote* (n.p., n.d.); *The Compromise Measures . . . R. Barnwell Rhett* (Washington, D.C., 1851).

10. Richard Yeadon to Perry, Oct. 19, 1850, Benjamin F. Perry Papers, SCDAH; Poinsett to Col. J. J. Albert, June 26, 1850, Joel R. Poinsett Papers, SCL; Elizabeth Perry to Perry, Dec. 14, 17, 1850, Benjamin Perry Papers, SCL; Perry Diaries, June 4, 10, 23, Aug. 4, 1850, Perry Papers, SHC.

11. Seabrook to Col. T. U. Leland, Sept. 18, 1850, Whitemarsh Benjamin Seabrook Papers, LC; *Charleston Mercury*, Aug. 23, Sept. 5, 7, 17, 24, 25, 26, 30, Oct. 1, 4, 5, 8, 9, 10, 12, 15, 17, 19, 21, 22, 24, 30, Nov. 1, 8, 11, 16, 1850; *Camden Journal*, Sept. 17, 27, Oct. 12, Nov. 5, 8, 22, 1850; Hammond to S. L. Ray and Others, Aug. 12, 1850, Hammond to W. H. Trescot, Aug. 25, 1850, Hammond to Wm. Sloan and Others, Sept. 20, 1850, Hammond to S. Rouche and Others, Sept. 29, 1850, J. J. Seibels to Hammond, Sept. 19, 1850, James Henry Hammond Papers, LC.

12. [Muscoe R. H. Garnett], *The Union Past and Future* (Charleston, S.C., 1850), 3–49; [E. N. Derby], *Reality vs. Fiction* (Boston, 1850), 3–15.

13. Peter Della Torre, *Is Southern Civilization Worth Preserving?* (Charleston, S.C., 1851), 5–12; [John Townsend], *The Southern States, Their Present Peril and Their Certain Remedy* (Charleston, S.C., 1850), 5–11, 16–18; *The Rights of the Slave States by a Citizen of Alabama* (n.p., n.d.), 32–43; William H. Trescot, *The Position and Course of the South* (Charleston, S.C., 1850), 20; "The Prospect Before Us," *SQR* (Apr. 1851): 537; Edward B. Bryan, *The Rightful Remedy Addressed to the Slaveholders of the South* (Charleston, S.C., 1850), 3, 77–78.

14. Trescot, *The Position*, 6–11, 17; *The Southern States*, 20–21; J.A.C., "Slavery throughout the World," *SQR* (Apr. 1851): 305–9; Bryan, *The Rightful Remedy*, 5–53, 112–16, 147; Della Torre, *Is Southern Civilization Worth Preserving?*, 20, 31–38.

15. "Southern Convention," 204; Della Torre, *Is Southern Civilization Worth Preserving?*, 30; *Commercial Review of the South and the West* 9 (July 1850): 121–24.

16. Brookes to William Hearth, Mar. 21, 1849, Jno. Bauskett to Brookes, Apr. 19, 1851, Iveson L. Brookes Papers, SHC; Mitchell Snay, *Gospel of Disunion: Religion and Separatism in the Antebellum South* (Cambridge, Eng., 1993); Clarence C. Goen, "Scenario for Secession: Denominational Schisms and the Coming of the Civil War," in *Varieties of Southern Religious Experience* (Baton Rouge, La., 1988), 11–21; Richard J. Carwardine, *Evangelicals and Politics in Antebellum America* (New Haven, Conn., 1993), 159–74; *A Defence of the South* (Hamburg, S.C., 1850), 1–2, 4–8, 35–41, 45–48; *God the Refuge of His People* (Columbia, S.C., 1850), 9–10, 19–21; John B. Adger to Thornwell, Sept. 30, 1850, James Henley Thornwell Papers, SCL; B. M. Palmer, ed., *The Life and Letters of James Henley Thornwell* (Richmond, Va., 1875), 477.

17. *The Rights and Duties of Masters* (Charleston, S.C., 1850), 7–9; Adger and Girardeau, eds., *The Collected Writings*, 396; Palmer, ed., *The Life and Letters*, 574–78; James Oscar Farmer Jr., *The Metaphysical Confederacy: James Henley Thornwell and the Synthesis of Southern Values* (Macon, Ga., 1986).

18. Daniel Walker Hollis, "James H. Thornwell and the South Carolina College," *Proceedings of the South Carolina Historical Association* (1953): 17–36; *Speech of . . . I. E. Holmes*, 4; *CG*, 29th Cong., 2nd sess., appendix, 177; Bryan, *The Rightful Remedy*, 7–8.

19. Bryan, *The Rightful Remedy*, 150–52; undated clipping, Abraham Watkins Venable Scrapbook, DU; Barnwell, ed., "In the Hands of the Compromisers," 167.

20. Jennings, *Nashville Convention*, 188–91; Bleser, ed., *Secret and Sacred*, 204–6, 208–10, 213–16; Hammond to W. G. Simms, Sept. 30, 1850, A. P. Aldrich to Hammond, Oct. 10, 1850, I. W. Hayne to Hammond, Oct. 15, 1850, Hammond to Whitemarsh Seabrook, Oct. 18, 1850, Whitemarsh Seabrook to Hammond, Oct. 23, 1850, M. L. Bonham to Hammond, Nov. 3, 1850, Maxcy Gregg to Hammond, Nov. 4, 1850, James Henry Hammond Papers, LC; Oliphant et al., eds., *The Letters*, 3:88; Tucker, "James H. Hammond," 11–14.

21. *Speech of the Honorable Langdon Cheves* (Columbia, S.C., 1850), 3–5, 7–15, 17–18; *Charleston Mercury*, Nov. 15, 22, 1850; Archie Vernon Huff Jr., *Langdon Cheves of South Carolina* (Columbia, S.C., 1977), 214, 228–30; *Resolutions and Address Adopted by the Southern Convention*, 24–27; Jennings, *The Nashville Convention*, 193–97; Atkins, *Parties, Politics and the Sectional Conflict*, 170–71.

22. Jennings, *The Nashville Convention*, 175–86; White, *The Secession Movement*, 78–80; "Journal Extracts," 148, 158, 161, Benjamin F. Perry Papers, SCDAH; A. P. Butler to Seabrook, Oct. 22, 1850, Whitemarsh Benjamin Seabrook Papers,

LC; Robert Barnwell to Hammond, July 25, Aug. 14, Sept. 9, 28, 1850, James Henry Hammond Papers, LC; Barnwell, ed., "In the Hands of the Compromisers," 165–67.

23. Seabrook to Col. T. U. Leland, Sept. 18, 21, 1850, Seabrook to the Governors of Alabama, Mississippi, and Virginia, Sept. 20, 1850, Governor Towns to Seabrook, Sept. 25, 1850, John A. Quitman to Seabrook, Sept. 29, 1850, Seabrook to Governor Towns, Oct. 8, 1850, John A. Quitman to R. B. Rhett, Nov. 30, 1850, Whitemarsh Benjamin Seabrook Papers, LC; *Charleston Mercury*, Sept. 13, Oct. 3, 4, 1850; Hamer, *The Secession Movement*, 67–71; "Speech of the Honorable R. B. Rhett Delivered at a Mass Meeting in Macon, Georgia 22 August, 1850," Robert Barnwell Rhett Papers, SHC.

24. White, *The Secession Movement*, chap. 6; Freehling, *The Road to Disunion*, 523–28; Cooper, *The South and the Politics of Slavery*, 304–10; Arthur C. Cole, *The Whig Party in the South* (Washington, D.C., 1913), chap. 6; Holt, *The Rise and Fall of the American Whig Party*, 607–16; Marc W. Kruman, *Parties and Politics in North Carolina, 1836–1865* (Baton Rouge, 1983), 133.

25. Ames, ed., *State Documents*, 271–72; *Charleston Courier*, Dec. 17, 1850; Richard Henry Shryock, *Georgia and the Union in 1850* (Durham, N.C., 1926), 303–63; John T. Hubbell, "Three Georgia Unionists and the Compromise of 1850," *GHQ* 51 (1967): 307–23; Anthony Gene Carey, *Parties, Slavery, and the Union in Antebellum Georgia* (Athens, Ga., 1997), 160–73; Arthur C. Cole, "The South and the Right to Secession in the Early Fifties," *MVHR* 1 (1914): 376–99.

26. Ames, ed., *State Documents*, 35–36; White, *The Secession Movement*, 94–95, 110–12; J. Mills Thornton III, *Politics and Power in a Slave Society: Alabama, 1800–1860* (Baton Rouge, La., 1978), chap. 4; Cleo Hearon, "Mississippi and the Compromise of 1850," *Publications of the Mississippi Historical Society* 14 (1913): 27.

27. *Charleston Mercury*, Dec. 5, 1850; John Blount Miller Scrapbook, SCL; Carson, ed., *Life, Letters and Speeches*, 283, 285–86; William H. Pease and Jane H. Pease, *James Louis Petigru: Southern Conservative, Southern Dissenter* (Athens, Ga., 1995), 153; Lieber to [?], Jan. 18, 1850, Lieber to H. W. Hilliard, Aug. 11, 1850, Francis Lieber Papers, SCL; Meats and Arnold, eds., *The Writings*, 3:40–42, 381–86; *Camden Journal*, Nov. 5, 1850; "Journal Extracts, 1832–63," 165, Joel R. Poinsett to Perry, Dec. 16, 1850, Edmund Webb to Perry, Dec. 23, 1850, Richard Yeadon to Perry, Jan. 6, Oct. 19, 20, 1850, James O'Hanlon to Perry, Jan. 27, 1851, James Petigru to Perry, Nov. 18, 1850, Benjamin F. Perry Papers, SCDAH; Elizabeth to Benjamin Perry, Dec. 3, 5, 14, 17, 1850, Benjamin F. Perry Papers, SCL; Phillips, ed., "Correspondence," 217.

28. *Letter to His Excellency Whitemarsh B. Seabrook* (Charleston, S.C., 1850), 3–10, 20–22; *The Union, Past and Future* (Charleston, S.C., 1850), 1–4, 7; Meats and Arnold, eds., *The Writings*, 2:295–99; *To the Honorable W. J. Grayson* (n.p., n.d.); *Reasons for the Dissolution of the Union* (Charleston, S.C., 1850), 16; *Charleston Mercury*, Oct. 22, 26, Nov. 14, 18, 1850.

29. *Camden Journal*, Nov. 1, 1850; *Journal of the House of Representatives of . . . South Carolina* (Columbia, S.C., 1850), 59; Whitemarsh Seabrook to Millard Fillmore, Nov. 29, 1850, Daniel Webster to Whitemarsh Seabrook, Dec. 7, 1850, Beaufort Taylor Watts Papers, SCL; John H. Means to Rhett, July 30, 1850, Robert Barnwell Rhett Papers, SHC; *Charleston Mercury*, Oct. 30, Nov. 28, Dec. 10, 1850; E. W. Rhett to Rhett, Nov. 7, [1850], Robert Barnwell Rhett Papers, SCHS; Diary, Oct. 11, 13, 15, 16, 1851, Mathew J. Williams Papers, DU; D. F. Jamison to Hammond, Dec. 9, 1850, James Henry Hammond Papers, LC; Francis W. Pickens to Perry, Oct. 30, 1850, Benjamin F. Perry Papers, SCDAH; James L. Petigru to

Corwin, Nov. 16, 1850, Thomas Corwin Papers, LC; Chauncey Samuel Boucher, "The Secession and Cooperation Movements in South Carolina, 1848 to 1852," *Washington University Studies* 5 (April 1918): 106–7.

30. Oliphant et al., eds., *The Letters*, 3:76–77; John Blount Miller Scrapbook, SCL; Virginia Louise Glenn, "James Hamilton Jr. of South Carolina: A Biography" (Ph.D. diss., University of North Carolina, 1964), 400–407; Hammond to W. H. Gist, Dec. 2, 1850, Hammond to W. G. Simms, Dec. 23, 1850, L. M. Ayer to Hammond, Dec. 18, 1850, A. P. Aldrich to Hammond, Jan. 3, 7, 1851, Paul Quattlebaum to Hammond, Jan. 28, 1851, A. H. Brisbane to Hammond, Feb. 25, 1851, James Jones to Hammond, Feb. 27, 1851, James Henry Hammond Papers, LC; Bleser, ed., *Secret and Sacred*, 216–20.

31. *Charleston Mercury*, Dec. 14, 18, 1850; John S. Palmer to Major Edward Manigault, Sept. 15, 1851, in Louise P. Towles, ed., *A World Turned Upside Down: The Palmers of South Santee, 1818–1881* (Columbia, S.C., 1996), 171; *Journal of the Senate . . . of . . . South Carolina* (Columbia, S.C., 1850), 153, 159–62; *Journal of the House*, 46–48, 51, 56–57, 72, 103–4, 165–68, 188–210, 276; *Camden Journal*, Dec. 6, 13, 1850; 0010 016 1850 00015 00, 0010 016 1850 00014 00, 0010 016 1850 00016 00, 0010 016 1850 00017 00, General Assembly Index—Secession, SCDAH; *Speech of the Hon. B. F. Perry* (Charleston, S.C., 1851), 3–17, 29–39; Paul Quattlebaum to Hammond, Dec. 17, 20, 1850, James Jones to Hammond, Feb. 19, 1851, James Henry Hammond Papers, LC; *Reports and Resolutions of the General Assembly*, 54; *Acts of the General Assembly . . . Passed in Dec. 1850* (Columbia, S.C., 1850), 55–59; Edward McCrady to Louisa McCrady, Nov. 26, 1850, McCrady Family Papers, SCL; Bleser, ed., *Secret and Sacred*, 207–13; Hamer, *The Secession Movement*, 77–84; Boucher, "Secession and Cooperation," 111–14.

32. *Charleston Mercury*, Jan. 8, 10, 13, 14, 20, 21, 22, 28, Feb. 1, 4, 5, 13, 14, 19, 21, 27, Apr. 21, 29, 30, May 1, 2, Aug. 11, 1851; *Camden Journal*, Jan. 21, 31, Feb. 4, 28, June 3, 17, July 15, Sept. 30, 1851; *Southern Patriot*, Feb. 28, Mar. 28, May 9, 23, Sept. 5, 1851; Catherine H. Lewis, *Horry County, South Carolina 1730–1993* (Columbia, S.C., 1998), 27–28; John T. Seibels to Jacob Seibels, Jan. 1851, Seibels Family Papers, SCL; A. P. Aldrich to Hammond, Jan. 25, 1851, John N. Russell to Hammond, Feb. 10, 1851, Hammond to W. G. Simms, Feb. 14, 1851, James Henry Hammond Papers, LC; A. C. Garlington to Simpson, Jan. 21, 1851, William Dunlap Simpson Papers, SCL; John Springs to Dr. Baxter, Feb. 14, 1851, Springs Family Papers, SHC; J. M. Rutland to Perry, Mar. 17, 1851, James L. Petigru to Perry, Apr. 1, 1851, Benjamin F. Perry Papers, SHC; Stephen R. Mallory to Col. Jm. English, Mar. 6, 1851, Means-English-Doby Papers, SCL; Barnwell to Orr, Aug. 26, 1851, Orr-Patterson Papers, SHC; D. H. Hamilton to Burt, Sept. 11, 1851, Armistead Burt Papers, DU; H. A. Houses[?] to Whitstone, Oct. 19, 1851, Nathan C. Whitstone Papers, DU; Barnwell, *Love of Order*, 145–46.

33. *Charleston Mercury*, Apr. 30, 1851; B. F. Whitner to Hammond, May 2, 1851, Beverly Tucker to Hammond, Mar. 26, July 17, 1850, Feb. 4, Apr. 19, June 6, 1851, James Henry Hammond Papers, LC; Francis Lieber to Perry, Mar. 12, 1851, Benjamin F. Perry Papers, SCDAH; Palmer, *The Life and Letters*, 477; John Quitman to Seabrook, June 26, 1851, Seabrook to John Quitman, July 12, 1851, Whitemarsh Benjamin Seabrook Papers, LC; [Beverly Tucker], "South Carolina: Her Present Attitude and Future Action," *SQR* 20 (Oct. 1851): 273–98.

34. *Camden Journal*, Mar. 18, Apr. 18, June 20, May 9, 13, 1851; *Charleston Mercury*, Jan. 11, 22, Feb. 20, 24, 25, Mar. 4, 10, Apr. 1, May 6, 7, 9, 19, Dec. 19, 22, 23, 27, 1851; *Charleston Courier*, Apr. 29, May 1, 7, 1851; *Tract for the Times No. 1* (n.p., n.d.), 1–4; Nathaniel W. Stephenson, "Southern Nationalism in South

Carolina in 1851," *AHR* 36 (Jan. 1931): 320; Bremer, *The Homes of the New World*, 2:494–96; *Proceedings of the Meeting of the Delegates from the Southern Rights Associations of South Carolina* (Columbia, S.C., 1851), 3–7, 12–22; "Circular from the Central Committee to Presidents of the Southern Rights Association in So. Carolina," May 26, 1851, Benjamin C. Yancey Papers, SHC; Maxcy Gregg to Hammond, May 27, 1851, James Henry Hammond Papers, LC.

35. *Proceedings of the Meeting*, 8–12, 22–23; *Letter of W. W. Boyce to the Honorable John P. Richardson* (n.p., n.d.); Langdon Cheves to David McCord, Aug. 15, 1851, Cheves Family Papers, SCL; Meats and Arnold, eds., *The Writings*, 2:27, 41–42, 50, 86, 3:139; A. P. Aldrich to Hammond, May 16, 1851, James Henry Hammond Papers, LC; *Charleston Mercury*, May 17, 19, 24, 27, 28, 30, 1851; James Blount Miller Scrapbook, SCL; *Charleston Courier*, May 17, 23, 24, 1851; Roger P. Leemhuis, *James L. Orr and the Sectional Conflict* (Washington, D.C., 1979), 24–27; speech manuscript, James L. Orr Papers, SCL.

36. James Blount Miller Scrapbook, SCL; *Southern Patriot*, Mar. 14, Apr. 18, 1851; Palmer, *The Life and Letters*, 578–80; *Charleston Mercury*, Dec. 2, 5, 1851.

37. Newspaper clipping, *Charleston Mercury*, Apr., 1851, A. P. Aldrich to Hammond, May 16, 20, 1851, James Henry Hammond Papers, LC; Bleser, ed., *Secret and Sacred*, 231; Drew Gilpin Faust, *James Henry Hammond and the Old South: A Design for Mastery* (Baton Rouge, 1982), 332–35.

38. Seabrook to A. P. Butler, May 12, 1851, A. P. Butler to Seabrook, May 19, June 20, 1851, Whitemarsh Benjamin Seabrook Papers, LC; John T. Seibels to Jacob Seibels, June 25, 1851, Seibels Family Papers, SCL; Bleser, ed., *Secret and Sacred*, 235–36; W. J. Grayson to Perry, Feb. 17, 1851, Benjamin F. Perry Papers, SCDAH; *Southern Patriot*, Apr. 28, 1851; Meats and Arnold, eds., *The Writings*, 3:97–102; John B. Edmunds Jr., *Francis W. Pickens and the Politics of Destruction* (Chapel Hill, N.C., 1986), 120–22.

39. Jacob Frederick Schirmer Diaries, July, 1851, SCHS; James Blount Miller Scrapbook, SCL; J. K. Bennett to Faber, May 20, 1851, John Christopher Faber Papers, SCL; [R. Dewar Bacot] to Dr. H.H.B.[?], Oct. 13, 1850, Bacot-Huger Papers, SCHS; Barnwell, *Love of Order*, 157–73; Oliphant et al., eds., *The Letters*, 3:90; "Separate Secession," *SQR* 20 (Oct. 1851): 298–316.

40. James E. Harvey to Corwin, Apr. 5, May 28, 1851, Thomas Corwin Papers, LC; Henry D. Capers, *The Life and Times of C. G. Memminger* (Richmond, 1893), 200–204; A. P. Aldrich to Hammond, May 16, 1851, James Henry Hammond Papers, LC; Robert Witherspoon to his nephew, June 4, 1851, Witherspoon Family Papers, SCL; William Joseph MacArthur, "Antebellum Politics in an Upcountry District: National, State and Local Issues in Spartanburg County, South Carolina, 1850–1860" (M.A. thesis, University of South Carolina, 1966), 23–38; Lillian Kibler, *Benjamin F. Perry: South Carolina Unionist* (Durham, N.C., 1946), 245–64; James Wylie Gettys, "Mobilization for Secession in Greenville District" (M.A. thesis, University of South Carolina, 1967), 6–9, 18–24; Stephenson, "Southern Nationalism," 327–32.

41. Abraham Watkins Venable Scrapbook, DU; W. J. Grayson to Corwin, Apr. 12, 16, 1851, Thomas Corwin Papers, LC; Henry Sumner to Wade Hampton, Sept. 9, 1851, Job Johnston Papers, DU; John Blount Miller Scrapbook, SCL; A. P. Aldrich to Hammond, May 16, 1851, James Henry Hammond Papers, LC; *Southern Patriot*, Apr. 28, May 30, June 13, July 11, 18, Aug. 6, 22, 1851; *Camden Journal*, Aug. 1, 8, Sept. 19, 23, 30, Oct. 3, 10, 1851; *Charleston Mercury*, June 23, 24, July 30, 1851; *Southern Rights Documents Cooperation . . . July 29th, 1851* (n.p., n.d.).

42. Keitt to Sue Sparks, July 11, 1851, Lawrence Massillon Keitt Papers, DU;

Tracts for the People No. 1 (n.p., n.d.); *Tracts for the People No. 2* (n.p., n.d.); *Tracts for the People No. 3* (n.p., n.d.); *Tracts for the People No. 4* (n.p., n.d.); *Tracts for the People No. 8* (Charleston, S.C., 1851), 15–16; *Tract No. 1* (n.p., 1851), 13–16; *Charleston Mercury*, Sept. 20, Oct. 9, 10, 1851; *Meeting and Address of the Southern Rights Association . . . South Carolina College* (n.p., n.d.), 14–15; *Letter of . . . J. K. Paulding* (Charleston, S.C., 1851); *An Oration upon the Policy of Separate State Secession* (Charleston, S.C., 1851), 9–11; A. P. Aldrich to Hammond, July 6, 1851, James Henry Hammond Papers, LC.

43. *An Address . . . by Lewis Malone Ayer* (Charleston, S.C., 1851), 7–9, 16–18; *Separate Secession Practically Discussed . . . by Rutledge* (Edgefield, S.C., 1851), 3–7, 11–12, 16–19, 21–26, 30–33; *Speech of Honorable F. W. Pickens* (Edgefield, S.C., 1851), 5–10; *Charleston Mercury*, June 19, Aug. 7, 12, 13, 14, Sept. 11, 15, 1851; M. Lyles to James Chesnut, July 1, 1851, Chesnut-Miller-Manning Papers, SCHS; Bennett to Faber, Sept. 4, 17, Oct. 17, 1851, John Christopher Faber Papers, SCL.

44. A. G. Magrath to Yancey, Mar. 24, 1851, Benjamin Cudworth Yancey Papers, SHC; John Springs to Dr. Baxter, Aug. 22, 25, Sept. 2, 5, 1851, Springs Family Papers, SHC; *Southern Rights and Cooperation Documents: The "Rutledge" Pamphlets Reviewed* (n.p., n.d.); *An Address . . . by W. A. Owens* (Charleston, S.C., 1851), 20–35; *The Letters of Agricola* (Greenville, S.C., 1852), 4–13; *Southern Patriot*, May 16, 1851; Oliphant et al., eds., *The Letters*, 3:98–99, 107–8,123, 227; John Blount Miller Scrapbook, SCL; *Southern Rights and Cooperation Documents No. 2* (n.p., n.d.); *Southern Rights and Cooperation Documents No. 3* (n.p., n.d.); *Southern Rights and Cooperation Documents No. 4* (Charleston, S.C., 1851); *Southern Rights Documents Speech of the Honorable J. L. Orr* (n.p., n.d.); *Southern Rights and Cooperation Documents No. 6* (Charleston, S.C., 1851), 4–8, 13–15; *Southern Rights and Cooperation Documents No. 7* (Charleston, S.C., 1851), 7–15; F. I. Moses to James Chesnut, Sept. 30, 1851, Chesnut-Miller-Manning Papers, SCHS; Elliot to his wife, Sept. 1, 1850, Elliot-Gonzales Papers, SHC.

45. *An Address . . . by Lewis Malone Ayer*, 10; *Charleston Mercury*, Aug. 9, Sept. 22, 1851; Boucher, "Secession and Co-operation," 124; Donald H. Breese, "James L. Orr, Calhoun and the Cooperationist Tradition in South Carolina," *SCHM* 80 (Oct. 1979): 273–85; John S. Palmer to Major Edward Manigault in Towles, ed., *A World Turned Upside Down*, 170–71.

46. John Blount Miller Scrapbook, SCL; *Southern Patriot*, May 16, 1851; *Speech of Winchester Graham* (n.p., n.d.), 2–10, 16; Elizabeth Perry to her aunt, Apr. 9, 1851; Benjamin F. Perry Papers, SCL; Hamer, *The Secession Movement*, 117–24; Blake McNulty, "Uncertain Masters: The South Carolina Elite and Slavery in the Secession Crisis of 1850," in Winfred B. Moore Jr. and Joseph F. Tripp, eds., *Looking South: Chapters in the Story of an American Region* (Westport, Conn., 1989), 79–94; Christopher G. Memminger to Hammond, Apr. 28, 1849, James Henry Hammond Papers, LC.

47. [Brutus], *An Address to the Citizens of South Carolina* (n.p., n.d.), 1–4; Blake McNulty, "William Henry Brisbane: South Carolina Slaveholder and Abolitionist," in Walter J. Fraser Jr. and Winfred B. Moore Jr., eds., *The Southern Enigma: Essays on Race, Class and Folk Culture* (Westport, Conn., 1983), 119–41.

48. MacArthur, "Antebellum Politics," 21–22, 41–42; "Speech of Benjamin F. Perry at the Anti-Secession Meeting at Spartanburg, Sept. 20, 1851," Benjamin F. Perry Papers, SHC; *Southern Patriot*, May 23, 30, June 13, 20, July 18, Aug. 1, Nov. 6, 27, Dec. 11, 1851, Jan. 1, 8, 1852; *An Address on Secession . . . by Francis Lieber* (New York, 1865), 4–10.

49. McNulty, "Uncertain Masters,"; Laurence Shore, *Southern Capitalists: The Ideological Leadership of an Elite, 1832–1885* (Chapel Hill, 1986), 48.

50. *Southern Patriot*, Oct. 23, 30, Nov. 6, 1851; *Camden Journal*, Oct. 17, 21, 1851; *Charleston Mercury*, Oct. 14, 16, 29, Dec. 2, 1851; Barnwell, *Love of Order*, 181, 198–99; Boucher, "Secession and Cooperation," 128–29; Hamer, *The Secession Movement*, 123–24; Lacy K. Ford Jr., *Origins of Southern Radicalism: The South Carolina Upcountry, 1800–1860* (New York, 1988), 204–9.

51. "Address on Occasion of the Caucus of the Members of the Legislature of South Carolina held at Carolina Hall, Columbia, S.C., 28th Nov., 1851," Allston to his wife, undated, Robert F. W. Allston Papers, SCHS; *Camden Journal*, Oct. 24, Dec. 2, 1851; *Charleston Mercury*, Oct. 17, 18, 25, Nov. 7, 10, 26, 27, 29, Dec. 1, 2, 5, 1851, Jan. 12, 14, 1852; *Southern Patriot*, Nov. 27, 1851; Francis Lieber to Perry, undated, Benjamin F. Perry Papers, SCDAH; *Speech of O. M. Dantzler* (Columbia, S.C., 1851), 17–20; Bleser, ed., *Secret and Sacred*, 231–32, 239–42; Owens to Hammond, Aug. 20, Sept. 3, 1851, H. R. Spain to Hammond, Aug. 25, 1851, W. D. Porter et al. to Hammond, Aug. 25, 1851, Hammond to W. D. Porter et al., Sept. 1, 1851, John Cunningham to Hammond, Nov. 10, 1851, Maxcy Gregg to Hammond, Nov. 14, 16, 1851, Apr. 2, 1852, James Jones to Hammond, Oct. 26, Nov. 16, 1851, Edmund Ruffin to Hammond, Nov. 11, 13, 1851, I. W. Hayne to Hammond, Nov. 9, 1851, APA to Gentlemen, Nov. 18, 1851, A. P. Aldrich to Hammond, Nov. 10, 11, 14, 26, 28, Apr. 20, 1852, Hammond to W. G. Simms, Nov. 21, 1851, Apr. 27, 1852, James Henry Hammond Papers, LC.

52. Thomas Thomason to his wife, Dec. 2, 1851, Thomas Thomason Papers, DU; L. M. Ayer to Hammond, Dec. 1, 1851, A. P. Aldrich to Hammond, Dec. 9, 1851, James Henry Hammond Papers, LC; *Journal of the Senate . . . 1851* (n.p., n.d.), 172–73; *Journal of the House of Representatives* (Columbia, S.C., 1851), 54, 68–69, 78–79, 102–9, 118–20; *Acts of the General Assembly* (Columbia, S.C., 1851), 110; *Southern Patriot*, Jan. 8, Feb. 12, Apr. 8, 1852; *Charleston Mercury*, Apr. 8, 12, 13, 16, 1852; J. N. Whitner to Perry, Oct. 11, 1851, Rasborough to Perry, Apr. 26, 1852, Benjamin F. Perry Papers, SCDAH.

53. *Journal of the State Convention of South Carolina; Together with the Resolution and Ordinance* (Columbia, S.C., 1852), 9–10, 14–19, 23–26; A. P. Aldrich to Hammond, Apr. 28, May 3, 1852, James Henry Hammond Papers, LC; Meats and Arnold, eds., *The Writings*, 1:27–35.

54. *Charleston Mercury*, May 1, 3, 4, 5, 10, 12, 13, 17, 1852; *Southern Patriot*, May 13, 20, 1852; *Speech . . . by William F. Huston* (n.p., n.d.), 1–4; White, *Robert Barnwell Rhett*, 132–33; Faust, *James Henry Hammond*, 335; Bleser, ed., *Secret and Sacred*, 256–58.

55. *Speech . . . by Huston* 12–13; *Charleston Mercury*, May 31, June 7, 11, 14, 15, 17, 19, 26, 28, July 3, 13, 28, Aug. 13, Oct. 25, Nov. 4, Dec. 18, 1852; *Southern Patriot*, June 17, July 8, 24, 1852; Laura White, "The National Democrats in South Carolina, 1852 to 1860," *SAQ* 28 (Oct. 1929): 370–89; Meats and Arnold, eds., *The Writings*, 2:225–32.

56. *Judgements . . . by James H. Thornwell* (Columbia, S.C., 1854), 17–18; Bryan, *The Rightful Remedy*; "Occasional Meditations," Mar. 1852, James Henry Hammond Papers, LC; *Charleston Mercury*, Apr. 7, June 3, 1852; *Address of Lawrence M. Keitt*, 7–10; *The Pro-Slavery Argument* (Charleston, S.C., 1852); Jeannette Reid Tandy, "Pro-Slavery Propaganda in American Fiction of the Fifties," *SAQ* 21 (1922): 41–50; L.S.M., "Uncle Tom's Cabin," *SQR* 23 (Jan. 1853): 81–120; [Louisa S. McCord], "Stowe's Key to Uncle Tom's Cabin," *SQR* 24 (July 1853):

214–54; *Slavery in the Southern States by a Carolinian* (Cambridge, Mass., 1852), 10–13, 31–32, 47–51; Thomas D. Clark, ed., *South Carolina: The Grand Tour, 1780–1865* (Columbia, S.C., 1973), 279.

Chapter Five

1. W. E. Burghardt Du Bois, *The Suppression of the African Slave Trade to the United States of America, 1638–1870* (rpt., New York, 1969); Ronald Takaki, *A Pro-Slavery Crusade: The Agitation to Reopen the African Slave Trade* (New York, 1971). See, for example, William J. Cooper Jr., *Liberty and Slavery: Southern Politics to 1860* (New York, 1983); Lacy K. Ford Jr., *Origins of Southern Radicalism: The South Carolina Upcountry, 1800–1860* (New York, 1988), 259, 261; Philip D. Curtin, *The Atlantic Slave Trade: A Census* (Madison, Wis., 1969); James A. Rawley, *The Trans-Atlantic Slave Trade* (New York, 1981).

2. David M. Potter, *The Impending Crisis, 1848–1861* (New York, 1976), 395–404; Barton J. Bernstein, "Southern Politics and Attempts to Reopen the African Slave Trade," *JNH* 51 (1966): 16–35.

3. Ronald Takaki, "The Movement to Reopen the African Slave Trade in South Carolina," *SCHM* 66 (Jan. 1965): 38–54; Harold S. Schultz, *Nationalism and Sectionalism in South Carolina, 1852–1860: A Study of the Movement for Southern Independence* (Durham, N.C., 1950); Laura White, "The National Democrats in South Carolina, 1852 to 1860," *SAQ* 28 (Oct. 1929): 370–77.

4. Takaki, *A Pro-Slavery Crusade*, 1–2, 13–14, 19; Schultz, *Nationalism and Sectionalism*, 130; Bernstein, "Southern Politics," 17; *Southern Standard*, Oct. 5, 1853; *Charleston Mercury*, May 29, June 24, 1854.

5. *Charleston Mercury*, Mar. 7, 8, 21, 23, May 29, June 24, 1854; *Charleston Daily Courier*, Oct. 8, 1853, Feb. 9, 16, 21, 22, Mar. 2, 16, 17, 18, May 17, 26, 1854; *CG*, 33rd Cong., 1st sess., appendix, 232–34, 371–75, 723–52, 463–68; Chauncey Samuel Boucher, "South Carolina and the South on the Eve of Secession, 1852 to 1860," *Washington University Studies* 4 (Apr. 1919): 97–100; Bernstein, "Southern Politics," 20; Takaki, *A Pro-Slavery Crusade*, 10–21; Gerald W. Wolff, *The Kansas-Nebraska Bill: Party, Section, and the Coming of the Civil War* (New York, 1977).

6. *Charleston Mercury*, Oct. 24, 27, 31, Nov. 4, 8, 1854; *Southern Standard*, Nov. 9, 1854.

7. *Charleston Mercury*, Feb. 11, June 24, Oct. 17, 1853, Oct. 31, Dec. 4, 1854, Jan. 18, 20, 23, Mar. 12, 27, 29, 30, 31, Apr. 2, 16, 17, 18, 23, 25, 28, 1855, Aug. 26, 1856, Mar. 5, 1857, Feb. 26, 1858, Jan. 24, Feb. 16, Mar. 10, Apr. 21, 1859; *Southern Standard*, Oct. 28, Nov. 7, 1853; *The Black River Watchman*, Apr. 27, 1855; *Charleston Daily Courier*, Oct. 5, 1854, Mar. 10, 1855, Jan. 22, 1859; W. H. Trescot to E. M. Seabrook, Feb. 3, 1859, Whitemarsh B. Seabrook Papers, LC; Gavin Wright, *The Political Economy of the Cotton South: Households, Markets, and Wealth in the Nineteenth Century* (New York, 1978), chap. 2; Alfred Glaze Smith Jr., *Economic Readjustment of an Old Cotton State: South Carolina, 1820–1860* (Columbia, S.C., 1958), 58–130; Roger P. Leemhuis, *James L. Orr and the Sectional Conflict* (Washington, D.C., 1979), 44; Robert E. May, *The Southern Dream for a Caribbean Empire, 1854–1861* (Baton Rouge, La., 1973).

8. Takaki, *A Pro-Slavery Crusade*, 70–82; *Charleston Mercury*, June 20, 28, July 7, 17, 21, Sept. 13, 1854; *Camden Weekly Journal*, June 20, 1854; *Southern Standard*, July 3, 10, Sept. 20, 1854; William Sumner Jenkins, *Pro-Slavery Thought in the Old South* (Chapel Hill, N.C., 1935), 95–106, 146–48.

9. *Camden Weekly Journal*, Oct. 10, 1854: *Abbeville Banner*, Oct. 12, 1854, quoted

in *Southern Standard*, Oct. 17, 1854; William W. Boddie, *History of Williamsburg* (Columbia, S.C., 1923), 315–16; 0010 015 1854 00022 00, 0010 004 1854 00010 00, General Assembly Index — African Slave Trade, SCDAH; *Charleston Mercury*, Nov. 8, Dec. 7, 1854.

10. *Southern Patriot*, Oct. 12, 26, Nov. 2, 1854; *Charleston Mercury*, Dec. 7, 1854; Lillian Kibler, *Benjamin F. Perry: South Carolina Unionist* (Durham, N.C., 1946), 282.

11. *CG*, 34th Cong., 1st sess., appendix, 118–22, 442–46; *Charleston Mercury*, Feb. 22, Mar. 12, 14, 15, 19, 20, 28, Apr. 11, 18, 19, June 5, 1856; *Charleston Daily Courier*, Feb. 25, Mar. 15, 1856; *The Southron*, Apr. 30, July 2, 1856; speech by Martin Witherspoon Gary, Apr. 3, 1856, Martin Witherspoon Gary Papers, SCL; Schultz, *Nationalism and Sectionalism*, 106–11; Boucher, "South Carolina," 98–99. On the Kansas wars, see Gunja SenGupta, *For God and Mammon: Evangelicals and Entrepreneurs, Masters and Slaves in Territorial Kansas, 1854–1860* (Athens, Ga., 1996); Thomas Goodrich, *War to the Knife: Bleeding Kansas, 1854–1861* (Mechanicsburg, Pa., 1998); Manisha Sinha, "The Caning of Charles Sumner and the Struggle for a Non-Racial Democracy in the Age of the Civil War," paper presented at the OAH conference, San Francisco, Calif., Apr. 1997; Huger to Wade Hampton, Dec. 17, 1856, Alfred Huger Letterbook, DU.

12. *Charleston Daily Courier*, Aug. 16, Nov. 6, 7, 1855; *Camden Weekly Journal*, Aug. 21, 1855; Oscar Lieber to Francis Lieber, Apr. 24, 1858, Francis Lieber Papers, SCL; *Charleston Mercury*, July 13, Aug. 7, 25, 1855, May 28, June 2, July 3, 9, 14, 23, 28, Aug. 3, 7, 25, Nov. 19, Dec. 4, 1855, Jan. 16, 26, 30, Feb. 15, Apr. 4, May 10, 20, Oct. 15, 16, 21, 22, 23, 29, Nov. 7, 1856; *Black River Watchman*, June 2, Oct. 3, Nov. 7, 14, 1855, Jan. 23, Dec. 3, 1856; speech, Mar. 1856, Martin Witherspoon Gary Papers, SCL; James L. Orr to John L. Manning, Sept. 22, 1856, Chesnut-Miller-Manning Papers, SCHS; Francis W. Pickens to Burt, Aug. 8, 1856, Armistead Burt Papers, DU; Tyler Anbinder, *Nativism and Slavery: The Northern Know Nothings and the Politics of the 1850s* (New York, 1992); W. Darrell Overdyke, *The Know-Nothing Party in the South* (Baton Rouge, La., 1950); James Marchio, "Nativism in the Old South: Know-Nothingism in Antebellum South Carolina," *Southern Historian* 8 (Spring 1987): 39–53.

13. Meats and Arnold, eds., *The Writings*, 1:6; *Southern Standard*, Jan. 27, 1854; *Southern Patriot*, Jan. 5, 1854; *Black River Watchman*, Dec. 29, 1854; Takaki, *A Pro-Slavery Crusade*, 12; *Message No. 1 of His Excellency Jas. H. Adams, Governor of South Carolina* (Columbia, S.C., 1856), 7, 9–11.

14. *Charleston Mercury*, Nov. 26, 1856; Bernstein, "Southern Politics," 22; *Black River Watchman*, Dec. 17, 1856; Robert N. Gourdin to Miles, Nov. 28, 1856, William Porcher Miles Papers, SHC; Preston to Thompson, undated fragment, "Letters Wm. C. Preston to Gen. Waddy Thompson, 1823–1860, W.P.A. Statewide Historical Project, Copied by Mrs. Ellen Shealy, Columbia, S.C., 1937," William Campbell Preston Papers, SCL.

15. *Journal of the House of Representatives of the State of South Carolina* (Columbia, S.C., 1856), 52–55, 163–65, 168; 0010 016 1856 00029 00, 0010 004 1856 00099 00, 0010 0116 1856 00030 00, 0010 004 1856 00098 00, General Assembly Index — African Slave Trade, SCDAH; Edward McCrady to Louisa McCrady, Nov. 28, 1856, McCrady Family Papers, SCL; *Journal of the Senate of South Carolina* (Columbia, S.C., 1856), 79; Schultz, *Nationalism and Sectionalism*, 131–32.

16. *Report of the Special Committee of the House of Representatives of South Carolina* (Charleston, S.C., 1857), 3–6, 8–9, 13–16, 18–47, 54; *Report of Special Committee* (n.p., n.d.), 1–16.

17. *Charleston Mercury*, Dec. 12, 1857; *Journal of the Senate of South Carolina* (Columbia, S.C., 1857), 37, 68, 89; Schultz, *Nationalism and Sectionalism*, 143.

18. Leonidas Spratt to Pettigrew, [Dec. 1853], Victor C. Bellinger to Pettigrew, Feb. 8, 1854, James Conner to Pettigrew, Dec. 5, 1856, James Orr to Pettigrew, Apr. 20, 1857, Oct. 30, 1857, Jan. 18, 1858, James Farrow to Pettigrew, Sept. 24, 1857, Samuel Earle to Pettigrew, Nov. 18, 1857, Saml. McCord to Pettigrew, Dec. 4, 1857, James Johnston Pettigrew Papers, NCDAH; newspaper clipping, *Carolina Times*, Dec. 22, 1857, James Johnston Pettigrew Scrapbook, NCDAH; *Report of the Minority of the Special Committee* (Charleston, S.C., 1858), 3–40; "A Sketch of J. J. Pettigrew's Life by William S. Pettigrew," Pettigrew Family Papers, SHC; Clyde N. Wilson, *Carolina Cavalier: The Life and Mind of James Johnston Pettigrew* (Athens, Ga., 1990), 76, 98–99, 107–8.

19. *Charleston Mercury*, Dec. 19, 21, 25, 1857, Jan. 11, 1858; *Charleston Daily Courier*, Aug. 28, Dec. 16, 1857; S. G. Barker to Pettigrew, Dec. 5, 1857, James Johnston Pettigrew Papers, NCDAH; newspaper clippings, *Columbia South Carolinian*, Dec. 6, 1857, *Winnsboro Register*, Dec. 17, 1857, *Carolina Spartan*, June 14, 1858, James Johnston Pettigrew Scrapbook, NCDAH.

20. Wilson, *Carolina Cavalier*, 96–97; *Charleston Mercury*, Aug. 23, Dec. 6, 1858; J. H. Adams to Hammond, Aug. 23, Sept. 22, 1858, Hammond to M. C. M. Hammond, Nov. 28, 1858, James Henry Hammond Papers, LC; W. W. Boyce to John L. Manning, Mar. 16, 1858, Chesnut-Miller-Manning Papers, SCHS; Harold Schultz, "Movement to Revive the Foreign Slave Trade, 1853–1861" (M.A. thesis, Duke University, 1960), 45–46.

21. Schultz, *Nationalism and Sectionalism*, 143, 159–64, 183–84, and "Movement to Revive," 38–54; Takaki, *A Pro-Slavery Crusade*, 194–98; William A. Dusinberre, *Them Dark Days: Slavery in the Rice Swamps* (New York, 1996); Wright, *The Political Economy*, 150–54; John Ashworth, *Slavery, Capitalism and Politics in the Antebellum Republic*, vol. 1, *Commerce and Compromise, 1820–1850* (Cambridge, Eng., 1995), 264–79; Laurence Shore, *Southern Capitalists: The Ideological Leadership of an Elite, 1832–1885* (Chapel Hill, 1986), 49–60; Lacy K. Ford Jr., "Republics and Democracy: The Parameters of Political Citizenship in Antebellum South Carolina," in David R. Chesnutt and Clyde N. Wilson, eds., *The Meaning of South Carolina History: Essays in Honor of George C. Rogers Jr.* (Columbia, S.C., 1991), 130–31, 134–38.

22. Julian J. Petty, *The Growth and Distribution of Population in South Carolina* (Columbia, S.C., 1943), 77–84; Robert Nicholas Olsberg, "A Government of Class and Race: William Henry Trescot and the South Carolina Chivalry, 1850–1865" (Ph.D. diss., University of South Carolina, 1972), 36–42; Christopher Silver, "A New Look at Old South Urbanization: The Irish Worker at Charleston, South Carolina, 1840–1860," *South Atlantic Urban Studies* 3 (1979): 141–72.

23. *Charleston Mercury*, Nov. 4, 1854, July 28, 1858; [Bryan], *Report of the Special Committee*, 53–54; [Pettigrew], *Report of the Minority*, 20–21; *An Appeal to the State Rights Party of South Carolina* (Columbia, S.C., 1858), 3–7; *De Bow's Review* 24 (June 1858): 487; [Edward B. Bryan], *Letters to the Southern People* (Charleston, S.C., 1858), 31–37.

24. *CG*, 36th Cong., 1st sess., 224–27, 2269–70; W. H. Trescot to Miles, Feb. 8, 1859, William Porcher Miles Papers, SCHS; J. Holt Merchant Jr., "Lawrence M. Keitt: South Carolina Fire Eater" (Ph.D. diss., University of Virginia, 1976), 246–52; Eric H. Walther, *The Fire-Eaters* (Baton Rouge, La., 1992), 284–85.

25. *Charleston Mercury*, June 4, June 25, 1857, Mar. 22, June 12, 1858; John

Stanford Coussons, "Thirty Years with Calhoun, Rhett, and the *Charleston Mercury*: A Chapter in South Carolina Politics" (Ph.D. diss., Louisiana State University, 1971); Laua White, *Robert Barnwell Rhett: The Father of Secession* (Gloucester, Mass., 1960), 140–41; Robert Barnwell Rhett Jr. to Hammond, July 26, 1858, James Henry Hammond Papers, LC.

26. Laura A. White, "The South in the 1850s as Seen by British Consuls," *JSH* 1 (1935): 40; *Charleston Mercury*, Mar. 13, 31, Apr. 1, 2, 16, May 9, 12, June 27, Sept. 1, Oct. 26, 30, 31, Nov. 2, 9, 13, 21, 23, 24, Dec. 10, 11, 12, 1857, Feb. 5, 22, Mar. 8, 9, 22, 17, Apr. 5, 7, 12, May 1, 3, 7, 20, 22, 24, June 12, 28, July 7, 15, 24, 28, 31, Aug. 3, 7, 11, 13, 1858; *Camden Weekly Journal*, Apr. 13, May 4, 1858; *Charleston Courier*, Jan. 29, Mar. 10, 1858. *CG*, 35th Cong., 1st sess., appendix, 68–71, 197–98; *Black River Watchman*, Jan. 13, 1858; *Address on Reopening the Slave Trade by C. W. Miller* (Columbia, S.C., 1857), 3–10; [Bryan], *Letters to the Southern People*, 39–41.

27. *Charleston Mercury*, Sept. 3, 6, 7, 8, 9, 29, Oct. 1, 1859; *Charleston Daily Courier*, Sept. 29, 1859.

28. *Speech of Honorable James H. Hammond Delivered at Barnwell Court House Oct. 29, 1858* (Washington, D.C., 1858), 7–11; *Charleston Mercury*, Aug. 2, Nov. 2, 10, 17, 18, 1858; *Charleston Daily Courier*, Aug. 5, 6, Nov. 3, 1858; Frank G. Ruffin to Hammond, Apr. 24, 1858, R. B. Rhett Jr. to Hammond, Aug. 2, 1858, John Cunningham to Hammond, Aug. 2, Oct. 9, 1858, Hammond to W. G. Simms, Aug. 13, 1858, J. H. Adams to Hammond, Sept. 22, Oct. 8, 1858, Maxcy Gregg to A. P. Aldrich, etc., Oct. 23, 1858, W. P. Miles to Hammond, Nov. 15, 1858, Hammond to M. C. M. Hammond, Nov. 28, 1858, W. H. Trescot to Hammond, July 27, Dec. 5, 1858, James Henry Hammond Papers, LC; Mary C. Simms Oliphant et al., eds., *The Letters of William Gilmore Simms*, vol. 4 (Columbia, S.C., 1955), 4:92; Lawrence T. McDonnell, "Struggle against Suicide: James Henry Hammond and the Secession of South Carolina," *Southern Studies* 22 (Summer 1983): 109–37; Jon L. Wakelyn, "The Changing Loyalties of James Henry Hammond: A Reconsideration," *SCHM* 75 (Jan. 1974): 1–13.

29. *De Bow's Review* 21 (Aug. 1856): 177–81, 23 (Sept. 1857): 226–38, 303–19, 24 (Oct. 1857): 440; 25 (Oct. 1858): 379–95; Robert F. Durden, "J. D. B. De Bow: Convolutions of a Slavery Expansionist," *JSH* 17 (1951): 441–61; Ottis Clark Skipper, *J. D. B. De Bow: Magazinist of the Old South* (Athens, Ga., 1958), 96–98.

30. William Kauffman Scarborough, ed., *The Diary of Edmund Ruffin*, vol. 1 (Baton Rouge, La., 1972), 1:186–88, 325; *Charleston Mercury*, July 14, 1859; Walther, *The Fire-Eaters*, 171.

31. *Charleston Mercury*, Feb. 19, 1857; Schultz, "Movement to Revive," 23–42; *De Bow's Review* 22 (May 1857): 447–62, 23 (June 1857): 570–83; George Fitzhugh, *Sociology for the South, or the Failure of Free Society* (New York, [1854]), chap. 26, and *Cannibals All! or, Slaves without Masters*, ed. C. Vann Woodward (rpt., Cambridge, Eng., 1960), 79, 201–2; Eugene D. Genovese, *The World the Slaveholders Made: Two Essays in Interpretation* (New York, 1969), pt. 2; Edward Pollard, *Black Diamonds Gathered in the Darkey Homes of the South* (rpt., New York, 1968), 55–58, 65–69; Takaki, *A Pro-Slavery Crusade*, 96–102; Stanford M. Lyman, ed., *Selected Writings of Henry Hughes: Antebellum Southerner, Slavocrat, Sociologist* (Jackson, Miss., 1985), 18–61, 73–143, 146–48, 167–82; Douglas Ambrose, *Henry Hughes and Proslavery Thought in the Old South* (Baton Rouge, La., 1996), 145–80.

32. *Speech upon the Foreign Slave Trade* (Columbia, S.C., 1858), 7–8; *Black River*

Watchman, Aug. 26, 1857; Charleston Mercury, Aug. 28, 1857; Bryan, Report of the Special Committee, 5; [Bryan], Letters, 7; "Southern Convention at Knoxville," DBR 23 (Sept. 1857): 317.

33. L. W. Spratt, "Report on the Slave Trade," DBR 24 (June 1858): 473–91; The Foreign Slave Trade (Charleston, S.C., 1858), 26–30. Compare Ford, "Republics and Democracy," 136.

34. Schultz, "Movement to Revive," 26–28; Earl W. Fornell, "Agitation in Texas for Reopening the Slave Trade," SWHQ 40 (Oct. 1956): 245–58; Takaki, A Pro-Slavery Crusade, 177; The New Orleans Delta is quoted in Charleston Mercury, Jan. 1, 1857.

35. Stella Herron, "The African Apprentice Bill," Proceedings of the Mississippi Valley Historical Association 8 (1914–15): 135–45; James Paisley Hendrix, "The Efforts to Reopen the African Slave Trade in Louisiana," Louisiana History 10 (Spring 1969): 99–111; Scarborough, ed. The Diary, 1:164–65; Charleston Mercury, Feb. 25, 1858; Sumter Watchman, Mar. 10, 1858; W. J. Carnathan, "The Proposal to Reopen the African Slave Trade in the South," SAQ 25 (Oct. 1926): 424; Randolph Campbell, An Empire for Slavery: The Peculiar Institution in Texas, 1821–1865 (Baton Rouge, La., 1989), 214–15; Fornell, "Agitation in Texas," 251.

36. De Bow's Review 25 (Nov. 1858): 491–506; Hendrix, "Efforts to Reopen," 118–19; The Natchez Free Trader is quoted in Charleston Daily Courier, Jan. 25, 1859.

37. Fornell, "Agitation in Texas," 254–59; Robert G. Harper, An Argument against the Policy of Re-opening the African Slave Trade (Atlanta, Ga., 1858), 3–5, 9–33, 61–70.

38. Harvey Wish, "The Revival of the African Slave Trade in the United States, 1856–1860," MVHR 27 (Mar. 1941): 581, 588; Bernstein, "Southern Politics," 32–34.

39. Vicki Vaughn Johnson, The Men and Vision of the Southern Commercial Conventions, 1845–1871 (Columbia, Mo., 1992); Robert Royal Russel, Economic Aspects of Southern Nationalism, 1840–1861, rev. ed. (New York, 1960), chap. 5; John McCardell, The Idea of a Southern Nation: Southern Nationalists and Southern Nationalism, 1830–1860 (New York, 1979), 96–132; J. H. Easterby, "The Charleston Commercial Convention of 1854," SAQ 25 (Apr. 1926): 181–97; Herbert Wender, Southern Commercial Conventions, 1837–1859 (Baltimore, Md., 1930), 62; Southern Standard, Jan. 16, 1855.

40. Jones is quoted by Takaki, A Pro-Slavery Crusade, 110; Wender, Southern Commercial Convenions, 170–85; De Bow's Review 22 (Jan. 1857): 89–94, 102, 23 (Feb. 1857): 216–24; Proceedings of the Southern Commercial Convention at Savannah (n.p., n.d.); Schultz, "Movement to Revive," 14–19.

41. [Bryan], Letters, 48–63, 73–89; Charleston Daily Courier, June 8, 15, 20, July 24, 29, 30, Dec. 4, 1857; Charleston Mercury, Jan. 5, May 1, June 8, 17, 19, Aug. 15, 1857; Charleston Weekly Standard, Dec. 29, 1857; W. H. Trescot to Miles, May 30, 1858, Feb. 8, 1859, William Porcher Miles Papers, SHC; Oliphant et al., eds., The Letters, 4:64–65.

42. De Bow's Review 23 (Sept. 1857): 226–38, 303–39, 24 (Oct. 1857): 440; Charleston Mercury, Sept. 29, 1857; Bruno Gujer, "Free Trade and Slavery: Calhoun's Defense of Southern Interests against British Interference, 1811–1848" (Ph.D. diss., University of Zurich, 1971).

43. W. D. Porter to Hammond, Nov. 3, 1858, James Henry Hammond Papers, LC; Journal of the House of Representatives of the State of South Carolina (Columbia, S.C., 1858), 129, 204–5; 0010 016 1858 00019 00, General Assembly Index—

African Slave Trade, SCDAH; *Journal of the Senate of South Carolina* (Columbia, S.C., 1858), 32, 109–10, 119–20, 200; *Charleston Daily Courier*, Nov. 23, 29, 30, 1858; *Reports and Resolutions of the General Assembly* (Columbia, S.C., 1858), 436.

44. Diary, May 10, 11, 14, 1858, David Wyatt Aiken Papers, SCL; *De Bow's Review* 24 (June 1858), 473–91, 574–605; *Sumter Watchman*, July 7, 1858; *Charleston Mercury*, May 14, 19, 1858, July 1, 1859 (the *Richmond Enquirer* is quoted on June 2, 1858).

45. "Late Southern Convention at Montgomery," *DBR* 24 (June 1858): 584–85, 598–99.

46. *Charleston Mercury*, Dec. 7, 1854, Aug. 11 1858; Mazyck, *Report,* 10–15; *De Bow's Review* 26 (Jan. 1859): 23–28, 51–66, 27 (Feb. 1859): 144–47, 27 (Oct. 1859): 382–87.

47. *De Bow's Review* 25 (Dec. 1858): 626–53, 27 (July 1859): 94–103, 27 (Aug. 1859): 205–20, 27 (Sept. 1859): 360–65, 27 (Oct. 1859): 468–71; *Charleston Mercury*, May 27, 1859; *Charleston Daily Courier*, May 19, 1859; Takaki, *A Pro-Slavery Crusade,* 152–53; Foote is quoted by Wish, "Movement," 587; James Farrow to Pettigrew, May 13, 23, 1859, James Johnston Pettigrew Papers, NCDAH.

48. Du Bois, *The Suppression of the African Slave Trade,* 173–78.

Chapter Six

1. David M. Potter, *The Impending Crisis, 1848–1861* (New York, 1976), chap. 15; Jack K. Williams, "The Southern Movement to Reopen the African Slave Trade, 1854–1860: A Factor in Secession," *Proceedings of the South Carolina Historical Association* (1960): 21–31.

2. On the Confederacy, see Emory M. Thomas, *The Confederate Nation, 1861–1865* (New York, 1979); William C. Davis, *"A Government of Our Own": The Making of the Confederacy* (New York, 1994).

3. *Charleston Daily Courier*, Aug. 30, 31, Sept. 15, 1858; *Sumter Watchman*, Sept. 1, 1858; James Hamilton to Hammond, Sept. 10, 1858, James Henry Hammond Papers, LC; Francis Lieber to Wade Hampton, Sept. 15, 1858, Francis Lieber Papers, SCL; Huger to [?], Sept. 1, 1858, Alfred Huger Letterbook, DU; *Charleston Mercury*, Sept. 1, 2, 8, 1858.

4. *Charleston Mercury*, Sept. 4, 7, 15, 1858; *Charleston Daily Courier*, Aug. 30, Sept. 1, 1858; Tom Henderson Wells, *The Slave Ship Wanderer* (Athens, Ga., 1967), 50.

5. *Charleston Daily Courier*, Sept. 7, 9, 10, 11, 1858; *Charleston Mercury*, Sept. 15, 1858.

6. *Charleston Daily Courier*, Sept. 4, 16, 17, Nov. 24, 1858; *Charleston Mercury*, Sept. 18, 1858.

7. James Hamilton to Hammond, Sept. 10, 24, 1858, James Henry Hammond Papers, LC; George to Krilla, Aug. 30, 1858, George A. Gordon Papers, DU; James Buchanan to Rhett, Robert Barnwell Rhett Papers, SCHS; *Charleston Daily Courier*, Nov. 24, 1858.

8. *Charleston Daily Courier*, Dec. 7, 11, 1858; Isaac W. Hayne, *Argument before the United States Circuit Court* (New York, 1859), 4–6, 10–12, 18–20, 22–24; Oscar Lieber to his parents, Dec. 11, 1858, Francis Lieber Papers, SCL.

9. *Charleston Mercury*, Sept. 10, 13, 14, 15, 18, 20, 21, 23, 25, 27, 28, 29, 30, Oct. 5, 7, 8, 9, 11, 12, 14, 15, 16, 17, 23, Dec. 7, 1858; Frederick A. Porcher to John S. Palmer, Oct. 19, 1858, in Towles, ed., *A World Turned Upside Down,* 225.

10. *Charleston Mercury*, Jan. 5, Feb. 16, 1859; Van Tromp, *The Pirates of the Echo* (Charleston, S.C., 1859); *Charleston Daily Courier*, Nov. 23, 29, 30, 1859.

11. *Charleston Mercury*, July 1, 2, 3, 4, 6, 7, 8, 9, 1857, June 7, Aug. 31, Sept. 6, 7, 11, Oct. 23, 1858; John Cunningham to Hammond, Jan. 15, 1859, Edward Bryan to Hammond, James Henry Hammond Papers, LC; *Charleston Daily Courier*, Sept. 4, Nov. 10, 1858; W. E. B. Du Bois, "The Enforcement of the Slave Trade Laws," in *Annual Report of the AHA for the Year 1891* (Washington, D.C., 1892), 172–73; *The Charleston Courier and the Slave Trade* (n.p., n.d.), 1–3, 12–14.

12. *Report of the Trials in the Echo Cases, in Federal Court, Charleston, South Carolina* (Columbia, S.C., 1859), 8–12, 14–20, 61–67, 73, 76–81, 96–113; *Argument of Mr. Bellinger* (Columbia, S.C., 1859), 9–12, 40–41; *Charleston Daily Courier*, Apr. 14, 15, 18, 1859; *Charleston Mercury*, Jan. 19, Apr. 8, 13, 14, 15, 16, 18, 20, 1859; Ronald Takaki, *A Pro-Slavery Crusade: The Agitation to Reopen the African Slave Trade* (New York, 1971), 215–18; Wells, *Wanderer*, 50–51.

13. *Charleston Mercury*, Jan. 13, 20, 21, Apr. 19, May 25, Oct. 26, 1859; *Charleston Daily Courier*, Jan. 21, 1859; Wells, *Wanderer*, 51; *Camden Weekly Journal*, Feb. 15, 1859.

14. Printed circular, James Henry Hammond Papers, LC; "A Slave Trader's Letterbook," *North American Review* 143 (Nov. 1886): 447–56; *Charleston Daily Courier*, June 1, 7, 8, 1858.

15. *The Reply of C. A. L. Lamar, of Savannah, Georgia, to the Letter of Howell Cobb, Secretary of Treasury of the United States* (Charleston, S.C., 1858), 8–10; *Charleston Mercury*, June 3, 9, 1858.

16. *Charleston Mercury*, June 14, Aug. 2, Dec. 22, 1858; Wells, *Wanderer*, 1–34; John Randolph Spears, *The American Slave-Trade* (New York, 1900), 197–201.

17. Spears, *American Slave-Trade*, 208–9; Wells, *Wanderer*, 86–87; Harvey Wish, "The Revival of the African Slave Trade in the United States, 1856–1860," *MVHR* 27 (Mar. 1941): 582–85; *Charleston Mercury*, Mar. 28, 1859; Scarborough, ed., *The Diary*, 1:299–300; "Speech of Mr. Spratt of South Carolina," *De Bow's Review* 28 (Aug. 1859): 212.

18. *Charleston Daily Courier*, Jan. 6, Feb. 15, 1859; Wells, *Wanderer*, 46; James Hemphill to W. R. Hemphill, Oct. 17, 1859, Hemphill Family Papers, DU.

19. John B. Adger, *A Review of Reports to the Legislature of South Carolina, on the Revival of the Slave Trade* (Columbia, S.C., 1858), 1–7, 12–16, 35–36, and *Christian Mission and African Colonization* (Columbia, S.C., 1857), 18–52.

20. Palmer, *The Life and Letters*, 422–23; Adger and Girardeau, eds., *The Collected Writings*, 472–78; *Letters of the Late Bishop John England to the Honorable John Forsyth* (Baltimore, Md., 1844), 16–18; R. Frank Saunders Jr. and George A. Rogers, "Bishop John England of Charleston: Catholic Spokesman and Southern Intellectual, 1820–1842," *JER* 13 (Fall 1993): 318–20; *Southern Episcopalian* 5 (Mar. 1859): 654–60.

21. Rev. J. Leighton Wilson, *The British Squadron on the Coast of Africa* (London, 1850), and *The Foreign Slave Trade* (n.p., 1859), 5–20.

22. *Notice of the Reverend John B. Adger's Article on the Slave Trade* (Charleston, S.C., 1858), 3–6, 14–16, 23–27; *Charleston Mercury*, July 11, 1854, Apr. 8, 1859; Miller, *Address on Reopening the Slave Trade*, 3–5; Takaki, *A Pro-Slavery Crusade*, chap. 6; Iveson L. Brookes, *A Defence of the South against the Reproaches and Inchroachments of the North* (Hamburg, S.C., 1850), 42–43.

23. Petigru to John Belton O'Neall, Jan. 1, 1859, James L. Petigru Papers, SCL; Lieber to Wade Hampton, Sept. 15, 1858, Francis Lieber Papers, SCL; Huger to Evan Edwards, Aug. 9, 1858, Huger to James Conner, Dec. 7, 1858, Alfred Huger Letterbook, DU; Preston is quoted in W. E. Burghardt Du Bois, *The Suppression of*

the *African Slave Trade to the United States of America, 1638–1870* (rpt., New York, 1969), 174.

24. Hammond to W. G. Simms, Mar. 10, Apr. 22, July 30, 1859, James Henry Hammond Papers, LC.

25. *Charleston Daily Courier*, Jan. 3, 4, 8, June 23, Nov. 17, 1859; *Charleston Mercury*, Jan. 1, 3, 5, 1859; undated fragment by Oscar Lieber, Francis Lieber Papers, SCL.; James H. Adams to James Chesnut Jr., Jan. 14, 1859, Chesnut-Miller-Manning Papers, SCHS; *The Wanderer Case; The Speech of Hon. Henry R. Jackson of Savannah, Georgia* (Atlanta, Ga., [1891]), 22–63; "A Slave Trader's Letterbook," 456–57; I. W. Hayne to W. P. Miles, Mar. 10, 22, 24, Apr. 2, 1859, James Conner to James Buchanan and W. P. Miles, Mar. 28, 1859, James Buchanan to James Conner, Mar. 31, 1859, James Conner to W. P. Miles, Apr. 2, 1859, I. W. Hayne to Jacob Thompson, Apr. 5, 1859, William Porcher Miles Papers, SHC; Takaki, *A Pro-Slavery Crusade*, 209–11; Wells, *Wanderer*, 37–38, 53–57.

26. "Charge of Mr. Justice Wayne of the Supreme Court of the United States Given on the Fourteenth Day of November, 1859, to the Grand Jury of the Sixth Circuit Court of the United States, for the Southern District of Georgia" and "Circuit Court of the United States. In Admiralty. The United States of America, by Information, versus the Schooner Wanderer, and Cargo," in Paul Finkelman, ed., *The African Slave Trade and American Courts: The Pamphlet Literature* (New York, 1988), 2:1–29, 203–396; *Charleston Daily Courier*, May 30, June 20, Oct. 22, 1860; "A Slave Trader's Letter Book," 460; Wells, *Wanderer*, 57–59, 63–83.

27. *Charleston Daily Courier*, Jan. 18, Feb. 14, Mar. 25, May 14, 19, 26, 1859; *Charleston Mercury*, Jan. 17, 18, 1859; A. G. Magrath to Hammond, Jan. 21, 1859, James Henry Hammond Papers, LC; Wells, *Wanderer*, 49–50.

28. *The Slave Trade Not Declared Piracy by the Act of 1820: The United States versus William C. Corrie Presentment for Piracy Opinion of the Honorable A. G. Magrath* (Columbia, S.C., 1860), 14–26; Wells, *Wanderer*, 59–62; A. G. Magrath to Hammond, May 30, 1860, James Henry Hammond Papers, LC; *Charleston Daily Courier*, Apr. 19, 1860; *Charleston Mercury*, Apr. 19, 1860.

29. *De Bow's Review* 28 (Sept. 1859): 365; *CG*, 36th Cong., 1st sess., 224–27, 2269–70; W. H. Trescot to Miles, May 12, 1860, D. H. Hamilton to Miles, May 29, 1860, William Porcher Miles Papers, SHC; W. D. Porter to Hammond, Nov. 3, 1858, A. G. Magrath to Hammond, Jan. 21, 1859, I. W. Hayne to Hammond, Mar. 29, 1859, James Henry Hammond Papers, LC.

30. *CG*, 34th Cong., 1st sess., appendix, 107, 444–46, 34th Cong., 3rd sess., 123–26; *The Responsibility of the North in Relation to Slavery* (Cambridge, Eng., 1856); Takaki, *A Pro-Slavery Crusade*, 6–8.

31. *Speech of Emerson Etheridge of Tennessee* (Washington, D.C., 1857), 3–12; *Charleston Weekly Standard*, Jan. 6, 1857.

32. *CG*, 35th Cong., 2nd sess., 349, 1051–52; Wells, *Wanderer*, 37; *Charleston Mercury*, Mar. 19, 1859; Eric Foner, *Free Soil, Free Labor, Free Men: The Ideology of the Republican Party before the Civil War* (New York, 1970), 117; Henry Wilson, *History of the Rise and Fall of the Slave Power in America* (Boston, 1884), vol. 2, chap. 48.

33. *CG*, 35th Cong., 2nd sess., 1053–57, 36th Cong., 1st sess., 1137–39; *Charleston Mercury*, Jan. 29, 1859; Edmund Ruffin, *African Colonization Unveiled* (n.p., n.d.); *The Regina Coeli Correspondence* (Baltimore, Md., 1858); *Remarks on the Colonization of the Western Coast of Africa*, 3–13; *Camden Weekly Journal*, Feb. 15, 1859; "A Slave Trader's Letterbook," 460.

34. *CG*, 36th Cong., 1st sess., 1245, 36th Cong., 2nd sess., 182; Wilson, *Rise and*

Fall, 2:617–23; *The Suppression of the Slave Trade: Speech of . . . Henry Wilson* (Washington, D.C., 1860); *Charleston Daily Courier*, Aug. 24, Dec. 29, 1859, Aug. 21, 1860; Harral E. Landry, "Slavery and the Slave Trade in Atlantic Diplomacy, 1850–1861," *JSH* 27 (1961): 196–205.

35. *CG*, 36th Cong., 1st sess., 2303–9, 2956–57, 2638–44; Harold Schultz, "Movement to Revive the Foreign Slave Trade, 1853–1861" (M.A. thesis, Duke University, 1960), 58; Wish, "The Revival of the African Slave Trade," 579–80; Williams, "The Southern Movement," 28; Warren S. Howard, *American Slavers and the Federal Law, 1837–1862* (Berkeley, Calif., 1963).

36. *Charleston Mercury*, Mar. 9, 10, 31, Apr. 21, June 14, 1859; *Charleston Daily Courier*, Sept. 29, 1859; undated cutting from *Yorkville Enquirer*, Milledge Luke Bonham Papers, SCL.

37. *The Southron*, Mar. 9, 1859; *Charleston Mercury*, Apr. 9, 12, May 11, Oct. 12, 15, 25, 26, Nov. 5, 1859; *Charleston Daily Courier*, Oct. 21, 22, 25, 29, 1859; *Sumter Watchman*, Oct. 18, 1859.

38. *Journal of the Senate of South Carolina* (Columbia, S.C., 1859), 5; *Journal of the House of Representatives of South Carolina* (Columbia, S.C., 1859), 32; *The Southron*, Mar. 14, 21, 1860; *Speech of Hon. Wade Hampton on the Constitutionality of the Slave Trade Laws* (Columbia, S.C., 1860); 0010 016 NDOO 00745 00, 0010 004 1859 00009 00, African Slave Trade—General Assembly Index, SCDAH; *Charleston Daily Courier*, Dec. 9, 12, 1859; *Charleston Mercury*, Dec. 12, 1859; Harold S. Schultz, *Nationalism and Sectionalism in South Carolina, 1852–1860: A Study of the Movement for Southern Independence* (Durham, N.C., 1950), 183–85.

39. Rufus Clark, *The African Slave Trade* (Boston, 1860), 7–16, 31–78, 86–102; *Proceedings of the Republican National Convention* (Albany, N.Y., 1860), 81; James A. Rawley, "Captain Nathaniel Gordon, the Only American Executed for Violating the Slave Trade Laws," *CWH* 39 (Summer 1993): 216–24.

40. *Charleston Mercury*, Feb. 20, June 5, Aug. 25, 1860; W. H. Gist to Hammond, Feb. 16, 1859, James Henry Hammond Papers, LC; W. H. Trescot to Miles, Feb. 8, 1859, William Porcher Miles Papers, SHC; Oscar Lieber to his mother, Nov. 3, 1860, Francis Lieber Papers, SCL; *Charleston Daily Courier*, Nov. 21, 1860.

41. *Sumter Watchman*, July 19, 1859; *Charleston Daily Courier*, Apr. 27, 29, May 2, 1860; Roy Franklin Nichols, *The Disruption of American Democracy* (New York, 1948), 293, 298–301; Takaki, *A Pro-Slavery Crusade*, 227–30; Wish, "The Revival of the African Slave Trade," 587; Earl W. Fornell, "Agitation in Texas for Reopening the Slave Trade," *SWHQ* 40 (Oct. 1956): 254–56; *Speech of Hon. W. L. Yancey, Delivered in the Democratic State Convention, of the State of Alabama* (Montgomery, Ala., 1860), 17–18.

42. Henry J. Raymond, *Disunion and Slavery: A Series of Letters to W. L. Yancey, of Alabama* (n.p., n.d.), 10–19. Also see *Disunion and Its Results to the South. A Letter from a Resident of Washington to a Friend in South Carolina* (n.p., n.d.), 2–3.

43. *Charleston Daily Courier*, Feb. 9, 11, 15, 1861; *Charleston Mercury*, Feb. 13, 15, 1861; Takaki, *A Pro-Slavery Crusade*, 233–36; Schultz, "Movement to Revive," 64–68; Potter, *The Impending Crisis*, 503–11; Daniel W. Crofts, *Reluctant Confederates: Upper South Unionists in the Secession Crisis* (Chapel Hill, N.C., 1989); editorial letter by G.W.B., *SLM* 32 (Jan. 1861): 71–76.

44. "Despatch from the British Consul at Charleston to Lord John Russell, 1860," *AHR* (July 1913): 783–87; Takaki, *A Pro-Slavery Crusade*, 232–33; Arney Robinson Childs, ed., *The Private Journal of William Henry Ravenel, 1859–1887* (Columbia, S.C., 1947), 57–59; Howard Jones, *Union in Peril: The Crisis over British Intervention in the Civil War* (Chapel Hill, N.C., 1992).

45. *Charleston Daily Courier*, Feb. 12, 19, Mar. 16, Apr. 1, 4, 1861; *Charleston Mercury*, Feb. 13, Mar. 15, 1861; Schultz, "Movement to Revive," 68; Hammond to J. D. Ashmore, Apr. 8, 1861, James Henry Hammond Papers, LC; John F. Marszalek, ed., *The Diary of Miss Emma Holmes, 1861–1866* (Baton Rouge, La., 1979), 21; *Journal of the Convention of the People of South Carolina, Held in 1860, 1861 and 1862, Together with the Ordinances, Reports, Resolutions, etc.* (Columbia, S.C., 1862), 207, 214–15, 236–64, 539; Takaki, *A Pro-Slavery Crusade*, 237–39; A. L. Hull, ed., "The Making of the Confederate Constitution," *Publications of the Southern History Association* 9 (Sept. 1905): 288; Davis, *"A Government of Our Own,"* 224–61, 295–96.

46. "The Philosophy of Secession: A Protest from South Carolina against a Decision of the Southern Congress," *Living Age*, 3rd ser. (Mar. 1861): 801–10; "Slave Trade in Southern Congress," *SLM* 32 (June 1861): 409–20; "The African Slave Trade," *SLM* 33 (Aug. 1861): 105–13.

47. *The African Slave Trade and the Secret Purpose of the Insurgents to Revive It* (Philadelphia, Pa., 1863), 7–23; *The Rebuke of Secession Doctrines by Southern Statesmen* (Philadelphia, Pa., 1863), 13–16; Du Bois, *The Suppression of the African Slave Trade*, 196; Bell Irvin Wiley, *Southern Negroes, 1861–1865* (New Haven, Conn., 1938), 85–86.

Chapter Seven

1. See, for example, Michael F. Holt, *The Political Crisis of the 1850s* (New York, 1978), and *The Rise and Fall of the American Whig Party: Jacksonian Politics and the Onset of the Civil War* (New York, 1999); William J. Cooper, *Liberty and Slavery: Southern Politics to 1860* (New York, 1983); Michael A. Morrison, *Slavery and the American West: The Eclipse of Manifest Destiny and the Coming of the Civil War* (Chapel Hill, 1997); J. Mills Thornton III, *Politics and Power in a Slave Society: Alabama, 1800–1860* (Baton Rouge, 1978); Lacy K. Ford Jr., *Origins of Southern Radicalism: The South Carolina Upcountry, 1800–1860* (New York, 1988); Anthony Gene Carey, *Parties, Slavery, and the Union in Antebellum Georgia* (Athens, Ga., 1997); Jonathan M. Atkins, *Parties, Politics, and the Sectional Conflict in Tennessee, 1832–1861* (Knoxville, Tenn., 1997); William G. Shade, *Democratizing the Old Dominion: Virginia and the Second Party System, 1828–1861* (Charlottesville, Va., 1996); Marc W. Kruman, *Parties and Politics in North Carolina, 1836–1865* (Baton Rouge, 1983).

2. David M. Potter, *The Impending Crisis, 1848–1861* (New York, 1976), chap. 17; William J. Cooper Jr., "The Politics of Slavery Affirmed: The South and the Secession Crisis," in Walter J. Fraser Jr. and Winfred B. Moore Jr., *The Southern Enigma: Essays on Race, Class and Folk Culture* (Westport, Conn., 1983), 199–215; William L. Barney, *The Secessionist Impulse: Alabama and Mississippi in 1860* (Princeton, N.J., 1974); Paul Horton, "Submitting to the 'Shadow of Slavery': The Secession Crisis and Civil War in Alabama's Lawrence County" *CWH* 44 (June 1998): 111–36; Michael P. Johnson, *Toward a Patriarchal Republic: The Secession of Georgia* (Baton Rouge, La., 1977); Donald A. DeBats, *Elites and Masses: Political Structure, Communication, and Behavior in Antebellum Georgia* (New York, 1990); Randolph Campbell, *An Empire for Slavery: The Peculiar Institution in Texas, 1821–1865* (Baton Rouge, La., 1989), 209–30; James M. Woods, *Rebellion and Realignment: Arkansas's Road to Secession* (Fayetteville, Ark., 1987); Daniel W. Crofts, *Reluctant Confederates: Upper South Unionists in the Secession Crisis* (Chapel Hill, N.C., 1989); Barbara Jeanne Fields, *Slavery and Freedom in the Middle Ground: Maryland during the Nineteenth Century* (New Haven, Conn., 1985).

3. Laura White, "The National Democrats in South Carolina, 1852 to 1860," *SAQ* 28 (Oct. 1929): 370–89; Harold S. Schultz, *Nationalism and Sectionalism in South Carolina, 1852–1860: A Study of the Movement for Southern Independence* (Durham, N.C., 1950), 83–103; Joel H. Silbey, *The Partisan Imperative: The Dynamics of American Politics before the Civil War* (New York, 1985), 120–26.

4. *Black River Watchman*, June 2, Sept. 12, Oct. 3, Nov. 7, 1855, Jan. 23, 1856; *Charleston Mercury*, Mar. 15, 26, May 28, June 2, July 3, 9, 13, 14, 28, Aug. 7, 1855, Mar. 4, 29, Apr. 4, May 10, 1856; *Camden Weekly Journal*, June 12, Aug. 21, 1855; Preston Brooks to Orr, Nov. 10, 1855, Orr-Patterson Papers, SHC; *Proceedings of the Democratic State Convention of South Carolina* (Columbia, S.C., 1856), 3–28; *Charleston Daily Courier*, May 9, 27, 1856; Chauncey Samuel Boucher, "South Carolina and the South on the Eve of Secession, 1852 to 1860," *Washington University Studies* 4 (Apr. 1919): 109–13.

5. J. Holt Merchant Jr., "Lawrence M. Keitt: South Carolina Fire Eater" (Ph.D. diss., University of Virginia, 1976), 87–89; *Black River Watchman*, Nov. 14, 1855; *Charleston Mercury*, Nov. 19, 1855, Jan. 26, 30, Feb. 15, May 10, 20, June 2, 1856; *Camden Weekly Journal*, June 12, 1855; *Sumter Watchman*, Dec. 3, 1856; *Charleston Daily Courier*, Nov. 25, 1857.

6. James Orr to John L. Manning, Sept. 22, 1856, Chesnut-Miller-Manning Papers, SCHS: F. W. Pickens to Burt, Aug. 8, 1856, Armistead Burt Papers, DU; newspaper clipping from the *Liberator*, Oct. 24, 1856, Preston Smith Brooks Papers, SCL; Bacon to Arthur, June 11, 1855, Pierce Mason Butler Papers, SCL; A. P. Butler to Thompson, Aug. 20, 1856, Waddy Thompson Papers, SCL; Huger to Allen S. Izard, Aug. 6, 1856, Huger to J. J. McCarter, Oct. 4, 1856, Huger to T. B. Huger, Sept. 16, Oct. 16 1856, Alfred Huger Letterbook, DU; Hiram Power to H. Gourdin, Oct. 23, 1856, William Porcher Miles Papers, SHC.

7. Meats and Arnold, eds, *The Writings*, 381–86; *Charleston Daily Courier*, Apr. 6, 8, 9, 14, 15, 16, 17, 1857. Also see *De Bow's Review* 25 (Aug. 1858): 128–44.

8. *A Series of Articles on the Value of the Union to the South* (Charleston, S.C., 1855); *Camden Weekly Journal*, June 12, 1855; *Charleston Mercury*, Jan. 26, 30, Feb. 15, May 10, 20, June 2, 7, 9, Nov. 10, 1856; *Sumter Watchman*, Dec. 3, 1856; Schultz, *Nationalism and Sectionalism*, 104, 125–310; Boucher, "South Carolina and the South," 116; G. Bailey to Miles, Oct. 13, 1856, William Porcher Miles Papers, SHC; Perry quoted by Kenneth M. Stampp, *America in 1857: A Nation on the Brink* (New York, 1990), 10; "A firm friend of the Union" to W. R. Hemphill, Oct. 29, 1856, S. Corley to W. R. Hemphill, Nov. 3, 24, 1856, Hemphill Family Papers, DU.

9. Stampp, *America in 1857*, 330; *Charleston Mercury*, June 7, 9, 1856; F. W. Pickens to Perry, June 27, 1857, Benjamin F. Perry Papers, SCDAH.

10. *De Bow's Review* 25 (Nov. 1858): 547, 22 (June 1857): 583–90; *Charleston Mercury*, Nov. 10, 1856, Jan. 6, 12, Feb. 21, 24, Mar. 23, Apr. 2, 20, 23, 1857; Keitt to Sue, June 8, 1856, Lawrence [Laurence] Massillon Keitt Papers, DU; *Sumter Watchman*, June 3, 1857.

11. *Charleston Mercury*, May 11, June 3, 1857; I. W. Hayne to Hammond, Jan. 24, 1858, W. H. Trescot to Hammond, Mar. 20, 1858, James Henry Hammond Papers, LC; W. H. Trescot to Miles, Dec. 29, 1856, W. G. Simms to Miles, Dec. 20, 1857, William Porcher Miles Papers, SHC; "Review of 'The North and South,'" *SQR* 27 (Jan. 1855).

12. *Charleston Mercury*, Mar. 3, 13, 18, 19, 31, Apr. 1, 16, 20, 21, May 9, 12, 21, June 10, 27, July 20, 25, 28, 30, Aug. 1, 3, 21, Sept. 1, 5, Oct. 26, 30, 31, Nov. 9, 13, 21, 23, 24, Dec. 10, 11, 12, 1857; *Sumter Watchman*, June 17, 1857, Jan. 13, 20,

1858; D. F. Jamison to Hammond, Feb. 22, 1858, John Cunningham to Hammond, Nov. 13, 1859, James Henry Hammond Papers, LC.

13. *Charleston Mercury,* Dec. 28, 29, 30, 31, 1857, Feb. 5, 22, Mar. 2, 9, 17, 24, Apr. 5, 7, 12, May 1, 3, 7, 1858; *Charleston Daily Courier,* Feb. 8, Mar. 27, Apr. 16, 1858; John Cunningham to Hammond, June 20, 1857, Jan. 25, 26, 1858, L. M. Keitt to Hammond, Dec. 18, 1857, B. F. Perry to Hammond, Jan. 8, Mar. 7, 1858, Robert Barnwell to Hammond, Jan. 18, 1858, W. H. Trescot to Hammond, Mar. 20, 1858, Hammond to W. G. Simms, Dec. 19, 1857, Jan. 20, Feb. 7, 1858, James Henry Hammond Papers, LC; A. G. Magrath to Miles, Feb. 18, 1858, William Porcher Miles Papers, SHC; Oliphant et al., eds., *The Letters,* 4:16–31, 34; John N. Davis to Bonham, Jan. 20, 1858, Milledge Luke Bonham Papers, SCL; W. W. Boyce to J. L. Manning, Mar. 16, 1858, Chesnut-Miller-Manning Papers, SCHS.

14. *CG,* 35th Cong., 1st sess., appendix, 509–11; *Charleston Daily Courier,* June 30, 1858; newspaper clippings, Milledge Luke Bonham Papers, SCL; *Charleston Mercury,* Aug. 9, 14, 20, Nov. 19, 1858.

15. *Charleston Mercury,* Mar. 5, 22, 29, Apr. 1, 5, May 16, 18, 19, 20, June 6, Aug. 2, 18, 22, 24, Sept. 14, 15, 16, Oct. 11, 1859; *Sumter Watchman,* July 19, 1859; John A. Calhoun to Hammond, Mar. 26, 1858, James Henry Hammond Papers, LC.

16. *Appeal to the State Rights Party of South Carolina* (Columbia, S.C., 1858), v–viii, 1–7, 12–24; *Charleston Daily Courier,* Dec. 9, 14, 1859; *Charleston Mercury,* Aug. 23, Dec. 7, 1858; Maxcy Gregg to Rhett, Sept. 14, 1858, Robert Barnwell Rhett Papers, SCHS.

17. Newspaper clipping from *Charleston Mercury,* Sept. 23, 1858, William Lowndes Yancey Papers, SCL; Scarborough, ed., *The Diary,* 1:222–23.

18. *CG,* 36th Cong., 1st sess., 1613; *Charleston Mercury,* Mar. 10, 1860; Potter, *The Impending Crisis,* 403–4; Robert W. Johannsen, "Stephen A. Douglas, Popular Sovereignty and the Territories," *The Historian* 22 (Aug. 1960): 378–95; Arthur Bestor, "State Sovereignty and Slavery: A Reinterpretation of Proslavery Constitutional Doctrine, 1846–1860," *Journal of the Illinois State Historical Society* 54 (1961): 117–80.

19. *Charleston Daily Courier,* Aug. 19, Dec. 9, 1859; John Ashmore to Hammond, Jan. 16, 1859, James Orr to Hammond, Sept. 27, 1859, James Henry Hammond Papers, LC; Lillian Kibler, *Benjamin F. Perry: South Carolina Unionist* (Durham, N.C., 1946), 295; Oliphant et al., eds., *The Letters,* 4:105.

20. *Charleston Mercury,* Sept. 3, 6, 7, 8, 9, 29, 1859; *Charleston Daily Courier,* Sept. 29, 1859; *Sumter Watchman,* Apr. 21, 1858, Sept. 20, 1859.

21. J. H. Hammond to Miles, Nov. 5, 1858, William Porcher Miles Papers, SHC; Hammond to M. C. M. Hammond, Dec. 11, 1858, W. D. Porter to Hammond, [Oct. 1, 1859], John Cunningham to Hammond, Apr. 18, 1859, Hammond to W. G. Simms, Apr. 22, July 30, 1859, Apr. 3, 1860, W. H. Trescot to Hammond, Aug, 9, Oct. 25, 1859, James Henry Hammond Papers, LC; *CG,* 36th Cong., 1st sess., 1613.

22. *CG,* 35th Cong., 1st sess., appendix, 69; *Charleston Mercury,* July 7, 1859, May 7, 1860; Jean H. Baker, *Affairs of Party: The Political Culture of Northern Democrats in the Mid-Nineteenth Century* (Ithaca, N.Y., 1983); *Charleston Daily Courier,* July 6, 1859, May 10, 28, 30, June 6, 16, 1860; Steven A. Channing, *Crisis of Fear: Secession in South Carolina* (New York, 1970), 211–13; Donald E. Reynolds, *Editors Make War: Southern Newspapers in the Secession Crisis* (Nashville, Tenn., 1966), 49; James L. Petigru to Perry, Oct. 8, 1860, Benjamin F. Perry Papers, SHC.

23. *Charleston Daily Courier,* Jan. 22, July 6, 1859; White, *Robert Barnwell Rhett,* 154–55, 163; *Speech of Hon. W. L. Yancey, Delivered in the Democratic State Convention, of the State of Alabama* (Montgomery, Ala., 1860), 5–31; Percy Lee Rainwater, *Mississippi: Storm Center of Secession, 1856–1861* (New York, 1969), 98; *Charleston Mercury,* May 16, 18, 19, 20, July 14, Sept. 14, 15, 16, Oct. 11, 13, Nov. 9, 29, 30, Dec. 1, 2, 3, 5, 9, 12, 24, 1859, Jan. 11, 14, 16, 19, Feb. 21, 27, 29, Mar. 2, 3, 13, 15, Apr. 3, 13, 16, 21, 23, 24, 25, 26, 1860; *The Southron,* Feb. 13, 1860; James Orr to Hammond, Sept. 27, 1859, Hammond to W. G. Simms, Apr. 3, 1860, Hammond to M. C. M. Hammond, Apr. 22, 1860, James Henry Hammond Papers, LC.

24. *Charleston Daily Courier,* Apr. 5, 16, 18, 1860; *Sumter Watchman,* Mar. 7, 1860; W. H. Trescot to Miles, Feb. 22, 1860, R. B. Rhett Jr. to Miles, Mar. 28, 1860, William Porcher Miles Papers, SHC; John Cunningham to Bonham, Sept. 26, 1860, Milledge Luke Bonham Papers, SCL; John Cunningham to Hammond, Nov. 13, 1858, Apr. 18, Oct. 14, 1859, I. W. Hayne to Hammond, Apr. 15, 1860, W. H. Gist to Hammond, Feb. 16, 1859, John C. Hope to Hammond, Mar. 10, 1860, James Henry Hammond Papers, LC; F. Sumter to James Chesnut, Aug. 30, 1859, Chesnut-Miller-Manning Papers, SCHS; Schultz, *Nationalism and Sectionalism,* 210–14.

25. *Charleston Daily Courier,* Dec. 9, 1859; *Charleston Mercury,* Dec. 24, 1859, Feb. 14, 1860; W. D. Porter to Hammond, Apr. 12, 1860, James Henry Hammond Papers, LC.

26. *Charleston Daily Courier,* Feb. 9, 23, Mar. 18, Apr. 17, 18, 19, 1860; *Proceedings of the Democratic State Convention of South Carolina* (Columbia, S.C., 1860), 3–19; Charles Edward Cauthen, *South Carolina Goes to War, 1860–1865* (Chapel Hill, N.C., 1950), 15–16; Roger P. Leemhuis, *James L. Orr and the Sectional Conflict* (Washington, D.C., 1979), 65–67; John Ashmore to James L. Orr, Orr-Patterson Papers, SHC; Perry to Elizabeth Perry, Apr. 17, 1860, Benjamin F. Perry Papers, SCL; *Charleston Mercury,* Feb. 24, Apr. 19, 23, 1860.

27. W. H. Trescot to Hammond, Apr. 15, 28, 1860, Paul Quattlebaum to Hammond, Apr. 18, 1860, John B. O'Neall to Hammond, Mar. 17, 1860, Hammond to W. G. Simms, Apr. 8, 1860, I. W. Hayne to Hammond, Apr. 15, 1860, A. L. Hammond to Hammond, Mar. 28, 1860, James Henry Hammond Papers, LC; Edward Noble to Pickens, Aug. 10, 1859, Francis W. Pickens Papers, DU; Susanna Keitts to her father, Sunday, 26, [1860], Susanna Keitts to A. D. Banks, Mar. 1, 1860, Lawrence Massillon Keitts Papers, DU; telegram, R. B. Rhett Jr. to Miles, Apr. 17, 1860, John Cunningham to Miles, Apr. 5, 1860, D. M. Hamilton to Miles, Apr. 4, 1860, Alfred Huger to Miles, Apr. 4, 1860, R. N. Gourdin to Miles, Apr. 4, 1860, William Porcher Miles Papers, SHC; M. R. H. Garnett to John L. Manning, Mar. 21, 1860, Chesnut-Miller-Manning Papers, SCHS.

28. E. G. Mason, "A Visit to South Carolina in 1860," *Atlantic,* Feb. 1884, 241–47; Diary, Apr. 23, 1860, Thomas Porcher Ravenel Papers, SCHS; Walter J. Fraser Jr., *Charleston! Charleston!: The History of a Southern City* (Columbia, S.C., 1989), 228–42; Michael P. Johnson, "Planters and Patriarchy: Charleston, S.C., 1800–1860," *JSH* 46 (Feb. 1980): 44–70; John Radford, "The Charleston Planters in 1860," *SCHM* 77 (Oct. 1976): 227–35; Michael O'Brien and David Moltke-Hansen, eds., *Intellectual Life in Antebellum Charleston* (Knoxville, Tenn., 1986); Robert W. Johannsen, *Stephen A. Douglas* (New York, 1973), 732–48; *Charleston Daily Courier,* Apr. 9, 1860.

29. William B. Hesseltine, ed., *Three against Lincoln: Murat Halstead Reports the Caucuses of 1860* (Baton Rouge, La., 1960), 3–40; *Charleston Daily Courier,* Apr. 21, 23, 24, 25, 26, 1860; John Taylor to John L. Manning, [1860], Chesnut-Miller-

Manning Papers, SCHS; *Official Proceedings of the Democratic National Convention* (1860): 10–25; D. H. Hamilton to Miles, Apr. 26, 1860, William Porcher Miles Papers, SHC; Austin L. Venable, "The Conflict between the Douglas and Yancey Forces in the Charleston Convention," *JSH* 8 (1942): 231–41.

30. Hesseltine, ed., *Three against Lincoln*, 44–57; *Charleston Daily Courier*, Apr. 27, 28, 29, 30, 1860; *Official Proceedings*, 31–40; *Speech of the Honorable William L. Yancey of Alabama* (n.p., n.d.), 1–16; *Charleston Mercury*, Apr. 30, 1860.

31. *Official Proceedings*, 50–71; *Charleston Daily Courier*, May 1, 2, 19, 1860; Hesseltine, ed., *Three against Lincoln*, 86–87.

32. *Charleston Mercury*, May 1, 2, 3, 1860; Diary, Thomas Porcher Ravenel Papers, SCHS; Edmund Ruffin to Hammond, May 4, 21, 1860, James Henry Hammond Papers, LC.

33. A. G. Magrath to Hammond, May 2, 1860, James Henry Hammond Papers, LC; Hesseltine, ed., *Three against Lincoln*, 88–117; *Charleston Daily Courier*, May 2, 3, 4, 1860; *Proceedings of the Delegates Who Withdrew from the National Democratic Convention* (n.p., n.d.); *Official Proceedings*, 78–90; Mason, "A Visit," 249–50.

34. *Charleston Daily Courier*, May 12, 19, 1860; *Speech of B. F. Perry of South Carolina, in the National Democratic Convention* (n.p., n.d.); Perry to Elizabeth Perry, Apr. 29, 1860, Benjamin F. Perry Papers, SCL; Meats and Arnold, eds., *The Writings*, 136–39, 376–400; Rosser H. Taylor, ed., "Letters Dealing with the Secession Movement in South Carolina," *Bulletin of Furman University* 16 (Dec. 1934): 8–9; Leemhuis, *James L. Orr*, 69–70.

35. "Address to the National Democracy," MS, James Henry Hammond Papers, LC; Roy F. Nichols, *The Disruption of American Democracy* (New York, 1948), 309–10; R. N. Gourdin to Miles, May 12, 1860, William Porcher Miles Papers, SHC; *Charleston Mercury*, May 12, 21, 1860.

36. *Charleston Mercury*, May 5, 8, 16, 21, 22, 26, 30, 1860; *Charleston Daily Courier*, May 21, 23, 28, 19, 31, 1860.

37. *Proceedings of the State Democratic Convention* (Columbia, S.C., 1860), 3–100; *Charleston Daily Courier*, June 1, 2, 4, 5, 1860; *Charleston Mercury*, June 4, 5, 6, 13, 14, 1860; Cauthen, *South Carolina*, 21–25; W. H. Trescot to Miles, May 8, 1860, Alfred Huger to Miles, June 1, 1860, William Porcher Miles Papers, SHC; Scarborough, ed., *The Diary*, 1:423–25; I. W. Hayne to Hammond, June 3, 1860, Jas. Gillian to Hammond, June 4, 1860, James Henry Hammond Papers, LC.

38. Scarborough, ed., *The Diary*, 1:430, 432, 438; D. F. Jamison to John Jenkins, June 8, 1860, David Flavel Jamison Papers, DU; Oliphant et al., eds., *The Letters*, 4:221, 226–27; *Charleston Daily Courier*, June 13, 15, 1860; *Charleston Mercury*, June 9, 13, 1860; Hesseltine, ed., *Three against Lincoln*, 178–84.

39. *Official Proceedings*, 93–185; *Charleston Daily Courier*, June 21, 22, 23, 25, 28, 1860; Hesseltine, ed., *Three against Lincoln*, 185–264; [Democratic National Committee], *To the Democracy of the United States* (n.p., n.d.), 1–16; Nichols, *The Disruption*, 312–20.

40. *Charleston Mercury*, June 19, 30, July 2, 3, 6, 1860; *Charleston Daily Courier*, June 19, 1860; Hesseltine, ed., *Three against Lincoln*, 265–78; Hammond to W. G. Simms, July 10, 1860, James Henry Hammond Papers, LC.

41. Ollinger Crenshaw, *The Slave States in the Presidential Election of 1860* (Baltimore, Md., 1945), chaps. 1–3; Potter, *The Impending Crisis*, chap. 16.

42. *Charleston Mercury*, Oct. 19, 20, 25, 27, 29, 31, Nov. 1, 2, 3, 4, 8, 14, 22, 26, 1859; *Charleston Daily Courier*, Oct. 21, 22, 24, 31, Nov. 15, 16, Dec. 2, 3, 5, 7, 9, 12, 1859; *Sumter Watchman*, Nov. 8, 1859; W. H. Trescot to Hammond, Oct. 25, Dec. 30, 1859, James Henry Hammond Papers, LC; Armstead L. Robinson, "In

the Shadow of Old John Brown: Insurrection Anxiety and Confederate Mobiliza-
tion, 1861–1863," *JNH* 65 (Fall 1980): 279; Channing, *Crisis of Fear*, 82–93; Paul
Finkelman, ed., *His Soul Goes Marching On: Responses to John Brown and the Harpers
Ferry Raid* (Charlottesville, Va., 1995).

43. *Charleston Mercury*, Dec. 5, 13, 1859; *CG*, 36th Cong., 1st sess., 36–37;
Alfred Huger to Miles, Nov. 28, 1859, D. H. Hamilton to Miles, Dec. 9, 1859,
William Porcher Miles Papers, SHC; Hammond to M. C. M. Hammond, "Confi-
dential Drafts—Amendments to United States Constitution," James Henry Ham-
mond Papers, LC; J. H. Hammond to Watts, Dec. 6, 1859, Beaufort Taylor Watts
Papers, SCL; F. W. Pickens to Perry, Nov. 21, 1859, Benjamin F. Perry Papers,
SCDAH; F. W. Pickens to Bonham, Dec. 31, 1859, Milledge Luke Bonham Papers,
SCL; Potter, *The Impending Crisis*, 383.

44. Harvey Wish, "The Slave Insurrection Panic of 1856," *JSH* 5 (1939): 206–
22; C. Vann Woodward, *The Burden of Southern History* (Baton Rouge, La., 1960),
62–68.

45. *CG*, 36th Cong., 1st sess., 533, 594–95, 644–45; Jack J. Cardoso, "Southern
Reaction to Helper's *The Impending Crisis*," *CWH* 16 (Mar. 1969): 5–17; Hinton
Rowan Helper, *The Impending Crisis of the South: How to Meet It*, ed. George M.
Fredrickson (rpt., Cambridge, 1968), introduction; *Charleston Mercury*, Dec. 6,
1859, Jan. 23, 1860; W. H. Trescot to Hammond, Dec. 30, 1859, James Henry
Hammond Papers, LC; *CG*, 36th Cong., 1st sess., 533, 644–45; Taylor, ed., "Let-
ters Dealing with the Secession Movement," 7.

46. W. H. Gist to Miles, Dec. 20, 1859, W. H. Trescot to Miles, May 2, 1858,
Alfred Huger to Miles, Dec. 12, 1859, William Porcher Miles Papers, SHC; Scarborough, ed., *The Diary*, 1:382; Merchant, "Lawrence M. Keitt," 166–72; Sue to
Alex, undated, Lawrence Massillon Keitt Papers, DU; Keitt to Dr. Keitt, Dec. 9,
1859, Ellison Summerfield Keitt Papers, SCL; Ollinger Crenshaw, "The Speakership Contest of 1859–1869: John Sherman's Election a Cause of Disruption?,"
MVHR 29 (Dec. 1942): 329, 333–34.

47. *Speech of Hon. Milledge L. Bonham of South Carolina, on the Election of Speaker.
Delivered in the House of Representatives, Dec. 16, 1859* (n.p., n.d.), Milledge Luke
Bonham Papers, SCL; *CG*, 36th Cong., 1st sess., 165–67, 308–12; *Speech of Hon.
Lawrence Keitt of South Carolina, on the Organization of the House* (Washington, D.C.,
1860), 3, 10–15; *Charleston Mercury*, Feb. 1, 3, 6, 1860.

48. *Charleston Mercury*, Oct. 31, Nov. 1, 2, 30, Dec. 5, 10, 1859; Laura A. White,
"The South in the 1850s as Seen by British Consuls," *JSH* 1 (1935): 44–45; John
Hammond Moore, *Columbia and Richland County: A South Carolina Community,
1740–1990* (Columbia, S.C., 1993), 151–52; Brookes to Dr. P. Church, Mar. 7,
1860, Iveson L. Brookes Papers, SCL; *Sumter Watchman*, Nov. 1, 1859; Allan Nevins, *The Emergence of Lincoln: Prologue to Civil War, 1859–1861* (New York, 1950),
2:110; Channing, *Crisis of Fear*, chap. 1; Boucher, "South Carolina and the
South," 130–31; David Gavin Diary, Dec. 2, 17, 1859, David Gavin Papers, SHC;
Charleston Daily Courier, Nov. 24, 29, Dec. 9, 1859, Jan. 18, 1860; W. Duncan to
Hammond, [Dec. 2, 1859], James Henry Hammond Papers, LC; Diary, Jan. 3, 4,
1860, Thomas Porcher Ravenel Papers, SCHS.

49. James Wylie Gettys, "Mobilization for Secession in Greenville District"
(M.A. thesis, University of South Carolina, 1967), 26–27, 51; A. B. Crook to
Perry, Dec. 4, 1859, Benjamin F. Perry Papers, SCDAH; Channing, *Crisis of Fear*,
104–5; *Sumter Watchman*, Jan. 17, Feb. 29, 1860; D. M. Hamilton to Miles, Jan. 23,
Feb. 2, 1860, William Porcher Miles Papers, SHC.

50. *Charleston Mercury*, Oct. 25, 26, 27, 1859.

51. *Journal of the House of Representatives of South Carolina* (Columbia, S.C., 1859), 83; *Charleston Daily Courier*, Nov. 30, 1859; *Journal of the Senate of South Carolina* (Columbia, S.C., 1860), 20; Scarborough, ed., *The Diary*, 1:506; Channing, *Crisis of Fear*, 52–55; 0010 004 NDOO 03201 00 (1859), General Assembly Index — Secession, SCDAH; Michael P. Johnson and James L. Roark, eds., *No Chariot Let Down: Charleston's Free People of Color on the Eve of the Civil War* (Chapel Hill, N.C., 1984); Marina Wikramanayake, *A World in Shadow The Free Black in Antebellum South Carolina* (Columbia, S.C., 1973), chap. 9.

52. Moore, ed., *A Plantation Mistress*, 32, 39, 81, 83, 97, 110–11; Mary Milling to James S. Milling, Nov. 23, 1860, James S. Milling Papers, SHC; *Charleston Mercury*, Oct. 13, 23, Nov. 15, 1860; Allan MacFarlane to Gourdin, Oct. 18, 1860, Robert N. Gourdin Papers, DU; Channing, *Crisis of Fear*, 264–73; *Charleston Daily Courier*, Aug. 22, 1860; William Joseph MacArthur, "Antebellum Politics in an Upcountry District: National State and Local Issues in Spartanburg County, South Carolina, 1850–1860" (M.A. thesis, University of South Carolina 1966), 74; James J. Palmer to John S. Palmer, Oct. 5, 1860 in Towles, ed., *A World Turned Upside Down*, 270; L. M. Keitt to Hammond, Sept. 10, 1860, James Henry Hammond Papers, LC; Orr quoted by Crenshaw, *The Slave States*, 99; Reynolds, *Editors Make War*, chap. 5; Armstead Louis Robinson, "Day of Jubilo: Civil War and the Demise of Slavery in the Mississippi Valley, 1861–1865" (Ph.D. diss., University of Rochester, 1977), chap. 1.

53. *Charleston Daily Courier*, Nov. 30, 1859; *Journal of the Senate of the State of South Carolina* (Columbia, S.C., 1860), 15; *Journal of the House of Representatives for the Called Session of November, 1860* (n.p., n.d.), 20–21; Ira Berlin, *Slaves without Masters: The Free Negro in the Antebellum South* (New York, 1974), chap. 11; Petigru to Edward Everett, Oct. 28, 1860, James Louis Petigru Papers, LC; Childs, ed., *The Private Journal*, 34.

54. *Charleston Mercury*, Mar. 17, May 13, Sept. 2, 6, Nov. 5, 8, 19, 1858; 0010 016 NDOO 00757 00 (1858), General Assembly Index — Secession, SCDAH; *Charleston Daily Courier*, June 29, 1858; *Camden Weekly Journal*, July 26, 1859; MS dated July 4, 1859, Martin Witherspoon Gary Papers, SCL; *De Bow's Review* 23 (Nov. 1857): 473, 24 (Apr. 1858): 269–74, 26 (May 1859): 575–78.

55. *Charleston Daily Courier*, Nov. 30, Dec. 6, 7, 9, 14, 19, 23, 1859; *Charleston Mercury*, Dec. 6, 13, 24, 28, 1859, Feb. 14, 1860; 0010 016 NDOO 00598 00 (1859), 0010 003 NDOO 63590 00 (1859), 0010 004 1859 00146 00 (1859), General Assembly Index — Secession, SCDAH; *Journal of the House of Representatives . . . 1859*, 83; D. H. Hamilton to Miles, Dec. 9, 1859, C. G. Memminger to Miles, Dec. 27, 1859, William Porcher Miles Papers, SHC; *Journal of the Senate of South Carolina* (Columbia, S.C., 1859), 43, 48, 136, 168; *Journal of the Senate of South Carolina* (Columbia, S.C., 1860), 20; *Reports and Resolutions of the General Assembly* (Columbia, S.C., 1859), 574, 578–79; Perry to Elizabeth Perry, Dec. 16, 1859; Benjamin F. Perry Papers, SCL; Boucher, "South Carolina and the South," 132–33; Schultz, *Nationalism and Sectionalism*, 191–99.

56. *Charleston Daily Courier*, Mar. 2, 1860; H. B. Sexton to Col. A. B. Springs, Feb. 15, 1860, Springs Family Papers, SHC; C. G. Memminger to Miles, Dec. 27, 1859, Jan. 3, 1860, I. W. Hayne to Miles, Jan. 5, 1860, William Porcher Miles Papers, SHC; W. P. Miles to Memminger, Jan. 10, 1860, W. W. Boyce to Memminger, Jan. 4, 1860, Christopher G. Memminger Papers, SHC; Laylon Jordan, "Between Two Worlds: Christopher G. Memminger of Charleston and the Old South in Mid-Passage, 1830–1861," *Proceedings of the South Carolina Historical Association* (1981): 56–76; Henry D. Capers, *The Life and Times of C. G. Memminger*

(Richmond, Va., 1893), 241–42; Ollinger Crenshaw, "Christopher G. Memminger's Mission to Virginia, 1860," *JSH* 8 (1942): 334–49.

57. Henry T. Shanks, *The Secession Movement in Virginia, 1847–1861* (Richmond, Va., 1934), 92–99; C. G. Memminger to Miles, Jan. 16, 1860, William Porcher Miles Papers, SHC; *The Mission of South Carolina to Virginia* (n.p., n.d.), 3–33.

58. C. G. Memminger to Miles, Jan. 24, Feb. 9, 1860, D. H. Hamilton to Miles, Feb. 2, 1860, William Porcher Miles Papers, SHC; W. P. Miles to Memminger, Jan. 15, 18, Feb. 3, 1860, Memminger to W. H. Gist, Feb. 13, 1860, W. H. Gist to Memminger, Jan. 30, 1860, W. H. Thomas to Memminger, Jan. 7, 1860, Christopher G. Memminger Papers, SHC; Oliphant et al., eds., *The Letters*, 4:228; *The Southron*, Mar. 21, 1860; W. E. Martin to Bonham, Dec. 27, 1859, Benjamin Waldo to Bonham, Jan. 12, 1860, Milledge Luke Bonham Papers, SCL; John B. O'Neall to Hammond, Mar. 17, 1860, James Henry Hammond Papers, LC; *Charleston Daily Courier*, Feb. 18, Mar. 9, 19, 1860.

59. C. G. Memminger to R. B. Rhett, Jan. 28, 1860, quoted by Shanks, *The Secession Movement*, 98; *Charleston Mercury*, Mar. 10, 1860; D. H. London to Memminger, Jan. 18, 1860, Christopher G. Memminger Papers, SHC.

60. Robert W. Dubay, "Mississippi and the Proposed Atlanta Convention of 1860," *Southern Quarterly* 5 (Apr. 1967): 347–62; Dwight Lowell Dumond, *The Secession Movement, 1860–1861* (New York, 1931), 26–34; *Charleston Daily Courier*, Feb. 6, 1860.

61. Gist to Thomas O. Moore, Oct. 5, 1860, A. B. Moore to Gist, Oct. 25, 1860, John J. Pettus to Gist, Oct. 26, 1860, Joseph E. Brown to Gist, Oct. 31, 1860, M. S. Perry to Gist, Nov. 9, 1860, Thomas O. Moore to Gist, Oct. 26, 1860, John W. Ellis to Gist, Oct. 18, 1860, William Henry Gist Papers, SCL; Allston to Benjamin Allston, Oct. 6, 1860, Robert F. W. Allston Papers, SCHS.

62. *Charleston Daily Courier*, June 4, 1860.

Chapter Eight

1. Eric Foner, *Free Soil, Free Labor, Free Men: The Ideology of the Republican Party before the Civil War* (New York, 1970), and *Politics and Ideology in the Age of the Civil War* (New York, 1980), 3–53.

2. Steven A. Channing, *Crisis of Fear: Secession in South Carolina* (New York, 1970); Harold S. Schultz, *Nationalism and Sectionalism in South Carolina, 1852–1860: A Study of the Movement for Southern Independence* (Durham, N.C., 1950); Charles Edward Cauthen, "South Carolina's Decision to Lead the Secession Movement," *NCHR* 18 (Oct. 1941): 360–72.

3. William J. Donnelly, "Conspiracy or Popular Movement: The Historiography of Southern Support for Secession," *NCHR* 42 (Winter 1965): 70–84; Eric H. Walther, *The Fire-Eaters* (Baton Rouge, La., 1992); David S. Heidler, *Pulling the Temple Down: The Fire-Eaters and the Destruction of the Union* (Mechanicsburg, Pa., 1994).

4. For a different view, see Lacy K. Ford Jr., *Origins of Southern Radicalism: The South Carolina Upcountry, 1800–1860* (New York, 1988), chap. 10; Stephanie McCurry, *Masters of Small Worlds: Yeoman Households, Gender Relations, and the Political Culture of the Antebellum South Carolina Low Country* (New York, 1995), chap. 8.

5. Armstead L. Robinson, "Day of Jubilo: Civil War and the Demise of Slavery in the Mississippi Valley, 1861–1865" (Ph.D. diss., University of Rochester, 1977);

Ira Berlin, Barbara J. Fields, et al., eds., *Freedom: A Documentary History of Emancipation, 1861–1867: The Destruction of Slavery*, ser. 1, vol. 1 (Cambridge, Eng., 1985), 1–56; Eric Foner, "The South's Inner Civil War," *American Heritage* 40 (Mar. 1989): 46–56; Paul D. Escott, "Southern Yeomen and the Confederacy," *SAQ* 77 (Spring 1978): 146–58; Stephen E. Ambrose, "Yeoman Discontent in the Confederacy," *CWH* 8 (Sept. 1962): 259–68; Georgia Lee Tatum, *Disloyalty in the Confederacy* (Chapel Hill, N.C., 1934); George C. Rable, *Civil Wars: Women in the Crisis of Southern Nationalism* (Urbana, Ill., 1989); Drew Gilpin Faust, *Mothers of Invention: Women of the Slaveholding South in the American Civil War* (Chapel Hill, N.C., 1996).

6. Oscar Lieber to his parents, Dec. 11, 1858, Francis Lieber Papers, SCL.

7. *Charleston Mercury*, June 21, 22, 24, July 1, 4, 14, 1860; *The Calhoun Revolution: Its Basis and Progress. Speech of Hon. J. R. Doolittle of Wisconsin* (n.p., n.d.), 1–5, 11–13; *De Bow's Review* 21 (July 1856): 90–95, 23 (Oct. 1857): 339, 28 (Feb. 1860): 132–39.

8. [George Frederick Holmes], "Slavery and Freedom," *SQR* 29 (Apr. 1856): 62–95; George D. Armstrong, *The Christian Doctrine of Slavery* (New York, 1857), and *A Discussion on Slaveholding* (Philadelphia, Pa., 1858); David Ewart, *A Scriptural View of the Moral Relations of African Slavery* (Charleston, S.C., 1859); Brookes to Dr. P. Church, Mar. 7, 1860, Dr. P. Church to Brookes, Mar. 17, 1860, Iveson L. Brookes Papers, SCL.

9. E. N. Elliot, ed., *Cotton Is King and Pro-Slavery Arguments* (Augusta, Ga., 1860), iv–xi, 271–336, 461–546, 716; J. W. Cooke, "Albert Taylor Bledsoe: An American Philosopher and Theologian of Liberty," *Southern Humanities Review* 8 (Spring 1974): 215–28.

10. Elliot, ed., *Cotton Is King*, 322–23, 897–98; Fitzhugh, *Sociology for the South*, 291; *De Bow's Review* 22 (Feb. 1857): 113–32, 28 (Jan. 1860): 1–7, 28 (May 1860): 523–31, 29 (July 1860): 62–69.

11. Diary, Feb. 9, July 23, Nov. 3, 4, 1856, May 1, 1857, Apr. 12, 1858, June 12, 1860, David Gavin Papers, SHC; Huger to Daniel Ravenel, Oct. 21, 1856, Huger to Mr. Wickham, June 2, 1858, Huger to R. N. Gourdin, Jan. 23, 1859, Alfred Huger Letterbook, DU; Huger to W. P. Miles, Sept. 30, 1858, Dec. 12, 1859, June 1, 1860, William Porcher Miles Papers, SHC; Alfred Huger to F. W. Pickens, Dec. 27, 1860, Francis Wilkinson Pickens and Milledge Luke Bonham Papers, LC; Moore, ed., *A Plantation Mistress*, 76.

12. *The Political Annals of South Carolina*, 28; [Edward B. Bryan], "Political Philosophy of South Carolina," *SQR* 23 (Jan. 1853): 120–40, 26 (Oct. 1854): 471–503; David Gavin Diary, Nov. 3, 4, 1856, SHC; Wm. P. C. [?] to Bob [Benjamin Allston], May 27, 1860, Henry F. Thompson to Benjamin Allston, Sept. 17, 1860, Robert F. W. Allston Papers, SCHS; Bleser, ed., *Secret and Sacred*, 220–21.

13. *Charleston Daily Courier*, Nov. 23, 1852; *CG*, 35th Cong., 1st sess., appendix, 404–9, 35th Cong., 2nd sess., appendix, 270–75; *Speech of the Honorable Lawrence Keitt, of South Carolina* (Washington, D.C., 1860), 4–8; *Charleston Mercury*, July 20, 1860.

14. *Black River Watchman*, Nov. 14, 1855; *A Series of Articles on the Value of the Union to the South* (Charleston, S.C., 1855), 1–33; *Charleston Daily Courier*, July 11, 1860. Also see Peter Kolchin, *Unfree Labor: American Slavery and Russian Serfdom* (Cambridge, Mass., 1987).

15. *CG*, 36th Cong., 1st sess., 1613–19; *Charleston Daily Courier*, Apr. 18, 1860; *De Bow's Review* 29 (Aug. 1860): 176, 178.

16. *Black River Watchman*, Dec. 1, 1854; Roger P. Leemhuis, *James L. Orr and the Sectional Conflict* (Washington, D.C., 1979), 35–37; *CG*, 33rd Cong., 1st sess., appendix, 374; *Charleston Daily Courier*, Apr. 18, May 10, 1855, June 4, 1860.

17. *CG*, 35th Cong., 1st sess., appendix, 68–71, 197–98; *Charleston Mercury*, Mar. 8, 1858; Fredrickson, *The Arrogance of Race*, chap. 1.

18. *Charleston Daily Courier*, July 11, 1860; *Charleston Mercury*, July 10, 1860.

19. *Charleston Daily Courier*, July 12, Aug. 8, 1860; *Charleston Mercury*, July 27, 30, Aug. 6, Oct. 11, 13, 18, 29, Nov. 3, 6, 1860; Reynolds, *Editors Make War*, 58; Dwight L. Dumond, ed., *Southern Editorials on Secession* (New York, 1931), 153–57; *Charleston Daily Courier*, July 11, 1860; Robert W. Johannsen, *Lincoln, the South, and Slavery: The Political Dimension* (Baton Rouge, La., 1991), chap. 4.

20. Reynolds, *Editors Make War*, 67; newspaper clipping from *Yorkville Enquirer*, 1860, Martin Witherspoon Gary Papers, SCL; John A. Ashmore to Hammond, July 10, Aug. 10, 1860, W. P. Miles to Hammond, Aug. 5, 1860, James Henry Hammond Papers, LC; *De Bow's Review* 28 (Jan. 1860): 17–20; A. G. Baskin to Manning, Oct. 27, 1860, John L. Manning Papers, SCHS; *Charleston Mercury*, July 20, Aug. 10, Sept. 25, Oct. 20, 30, 1860; *Charleston Daily Courier*, Aug. 8, Sept. 1, 11, 22, 29, 1860; Leemhuis, *James L. Orr*, 70–71; Charles Edward Cauthen, *South Carolina Goes to War, 1860–1865* (Chapel Hill, 1950), 34, 50–51; Channing, *Crisis of Fear*, 235–38, 267–68.

21. J. H. Hammond to Miles, July 16, 1860, William Porcher Miles Papers, SHC; *Charleston Mercury*, Aug. 2, 4, 1860; *Charleston Daily Courier*, July 11, 1860.

22. James L. Petigru to Perry, Oct. 8, 1860, speech of Benjamin F. Perry at Anderson Court House, Oct. 10, 1860, Benjamin F. Perry Papers, SHC; Carson, ed., *Life, Letters and Speeches*, 356–57; John B. O'Neall to Hammond, Feb. 13, June 7, Sept. 22, 1860, James Henry Hammond Papers, LC; *Charleston Daily Courier*, Aug. 20, 24, 27, 1860; *Charleston Mercury*, Aug. 21, 22, 1860.

23. R. B. Rhett Jr. to Hammond, July 26, Aug. 2, 1858, John Cunningham to Hammond, Oct. 9, 1858, Apr. 18, 1859, July 30, 1860, Maxcy Gregg to A. P. Aldrich, etc., Oct. 23, 1858, Hammond to M. C. M. Hammond, Nov. 28, 1858, Aug. 30, 1860, W. H. Trescot to Hammond, Aug. 15, 1858, May 12, 1860, W. P. Miles to Hammond, Nov. 15, 1858, Aug, 9, Oct. 25, 1859, Hammond to W. G. Simms, Dec. 19, 1857, July 3, Jan. 20, Feb. 7, 1858, Apr. 22, July 30, 1859, Apr. 3, Sept. 23, Oct. 23, 1860, W. D. Porter to Hammond, [Oct. 1, 1859], Henry Lesesne to Hammond, May 12, 1860, L. M. Keitt to Hammond, Aug. 4, Oct. 23, 1860, I. W. Hayne to Hammond, Sept. 15, 1860, Hammond to I. W. Hayne, Sept. 19, 1860, speech (undated MS), Hammond to A. P. Aldrich, etc., Nov. 8, 1860, James Henry Hammond Papers, LC; J. H. Hammond to Miles, Nov. 5, 23, 1858; William Porcher Miles Papers, SHC; *Charleston Mercury*, Aug. 2, 3, Nov. 10, 17, 1858, Feb. 21, 25, 1859; Benjamin F. Perry Diary, Aug. 29, 1858, Benjamin F. Perry Papers, SHC; George to Krilla, July 27, 1858, George A. Gordon Papers, DU; *Speech of the Honorable James H. Hammond* (Washington, D.C., 1860); Bleser, ed., *Secret and Sacred*, 274–78; Oliphant et al., eds, *The Letters*, 4:84–85, 87; *Tract No. 3: To the People of the South* (Charleston, S.C., 1860). Also see Lawrence T. McDonnell, "Struggle against Suicide: James Henry Hammond and the Secession of South Carolina," *Southern Studies* 22 (Summer 1983): 109–37; Jon L. Wakelyn, "The Changing Loyalties of James Henry Hammond: A Reconsideration," *SCHM* 75 (Jan. 1974): 1–13; Drew Gilpin Faust, *James Henry Hammond and the Old South: A Design for Mastery* (Baton Rouge, La., 1982), 356–60.

24. William Elliot to Ralph Elliot, Sept. 26, 1860, Elliot-Gonzales Papers, SHC; Lewis Pinckney Jones, "William Elliot, South Carolina Nonconformist," *JSH* 17

(1951): 361–81; Calhoun, ed., *Witness to Sorrow*, 182–92; Dumond, ed., *Southern Editorials*, 289.

25. R. N. Gourdin to Miles, Aug. 20, 1860, William Porcher Miles Papers, SHC; J. H. Hammond to Bonham, Oct. 3, 1860, William Tennant to Bonham, Oct. 10, 1860, John Townsend to Bonham, Oct. 16, 1860, Milledge Luke Bonham Papers, SCL; *Tract No. 3*, 24; *Charleston Mercury*, Oct. 19, 1860. Also see Jon L. Wakelyn, ed., *Southern Pamphlets on Secession, November 1860–April 1861* (Chapel Hill, N.C., 1996), introduction.

26. [John Townsend], *The Doom of Slavery in the Union; and Its Safety Out of It* (Charleston, S.C., 1860); *Charleston Mercury*, Oct. 20, 1860; *Charleston Daily Courier*, Apr. 6, Dec. 4, 1860; Hammond to W. G. Simms, Oct. 23, 1860, James Henry Hammond Papers, LC.

27. [Townsend], *The Doom of Slavery*, 12–13; *Tract No. 5: The Interest in Slavery of the Southern Non-Slaveholder* (Charleston, S.C., 1860); *Charleston Mercury*, Oct. 31, 1860.

28. *Tract No. 2: Mr Douglas and the Doctrine of Coercion* (n.p., n.d.); *De Bow's Review* 28 (Apr. 1860): 367–92, 29 (Sept. 1860): 302–20, 29 (Nov. 1860): 561–69, 631–38.

29. G. D. Tillman to Hammond, Oct. 9, 1860, James Henry Hammond Papers, LC; Thomas Ravenel Diary, Nov. 14, 1860, Thomas Porcher Ravenel Papers, SCHS; Childs, ed., *The Private Journal of Henry William Ravenel*, 31; Channing, *Crisis of Fear*, 269–73; *Charleston Mercury*, Oct. 15, 1860; *Charleston Daily Courier*, Nov. 5, 17, 19, 20, 1860.

30. Cauthen, *South Carolina Goes to War*, 50–61, and "South Carolina's Decision," 300–72; Emily Bellinger Reynolds and Joan Reynolds Faunt, eds., *Biographical Directory of the Senate of the State of South Carolina, 1776–1964* (Columbia, S.C., 1964), 57–58; Walter B. Edgar, ed., *Biographical Directory of the South Carolina House of Representatives* (Columbia, S.C., 1974), 1:378–85; Oliphant et al., eds., *The Letters*, 4:245, 249, 253, 256, 260–62; *Charleston Daily Courier*, Nov. 6, 1860.

31. W. C. Daniels to Gourdin, Dec. 9, 19, 1860, John W. Pratt to Gourdin, Dec. 12, 1860, John M. Richardson to Gourdin, Dec. 14, 1860, A. R. Lawton to Gourdin, Dec. 16, 1860, D. H. Hamilton to Gourdin, Nov. 26, 1860, W. P. Miles to Gourdin, Dec. 10, 1860, Robert N. Gourdin Papers, DU; Dr. J. P. Logan to Thornwell, Dec. 7, 1860, James Henley Thornwell Papers, SCL; J. F. Wadell to Bonham, Nov. 19, 1860, Milledge Luke Bonham Papers, SCL; Spratt quoted by Cauthen, *South Carolina Goes to War*, 53; *Charleston Mercury*, Oct. 18, 29, Nov. 3, 6, 1860; Trescot to R. B. Rhett, Nov. 1, 1860, William Henry Trescot Papers, LC; Trescot to Miles, Nov. 8, 1860, L. M. Keitt to Miles, Oct. 30, 1860, William Porcher Miles Papers, SHC.

32. On the presidency and secession, see Thomas B. Alexander, "The Civil War as Institutional Fulfillment," *JSH* 47 (Feb. 1981): 3–32; *Charleston Mercury*, Nov. 8, 9, 1860; *Charleston Daily Courier*, Nov. 7, 10, 13, 1860; McCarter Journal, Oct.–Nov. 1860, LC; J. N. Claxton to Mr. Jones, Nov. 10, 1860, Milledge Luke Bonham Papers, SCL; Jacob Frederick Schirmer Diaries, Nov. 1860, SCHS; "Recollections of Louisa Rebecca Hayne McCord," 40, Louisa McCord Smythe Papers, SCL; Scarborough, ed., *The Diary*, 1:483–99; Childs, ed., *The Private Journal of Henry William Ravenel*, 32; James Chesnut to Hammond, Nov. 10, 1860, Hammond to M. C. M. Hammond, Nov. 12, 1860, James Henry Hammond Papers, LC.

33. W. H. Gist to James Simons, Nov. 7, 1860, "How the War Started" (undated MS), William Henry Gist Papers, SCL; *Charleston Daily Courier*, Nov. 6, 7, 9, 10, 12, 13, 15, 1860; Ralph A. Wooster, *The People in Power: Courthouse and Statehouse in the*

Lower South, 1850–1860 (Knoxville, Tenn., 1969), 36; *Journal of the Senate . . .* *1860*, 21; *Journal of the Senate of the State of South Carolina for the Called Session of November, 1860* (n.p., n.d.), 9–10, 18–20; *Journal of the House of Representatives for the Called Session of November, 1860* (n.p., n.d.), 18–21, 30–39; "How South Carolina Seceded, by the Private Secretary of Governor Pickens of South Carolina," *Nickell Magazine*, Dec. 1897, 345–49; *Charleston Mercury*, Nov. 10, 1860; W. D. Porter to Hammond, Nov. 11, 1860, James Henry Hammond Papers, LC.

34. *Charleston Daily Courier*, Nov. 15, 21, 1860; Taylor, ed., "Letters Dealing with the Secession Movement," 10; Carson, ed., *Life, Letters and Speeches*, 361; Anonymous [A. Turnbull?] to the editor of the *Mercury*, Nov. 10, 1860, Robert Barnwell Rhett Papers, SHC; R. C. Griffin to D. L. Dalton, Nov. 6, 1860, Milledge Luke Bonham Papers, SCL.

35. *Charleston Daily Courier*, Nov. 16, 19, 20, Dec. 3, 1860; Jn. N. Lee to Bonham, Nov. 15, 1860, Milledge Luke Bonham Papers, SCL; Hemphill et al. to Hammond. Nov. 20, 1860, Hammond to Mitchell et al., Nov. 22, 1860, Hammond to R. F. Simpson, Nov. 22, 1860, James Henry Hammond Papers, LC.

36. *Charleston Daily Courier*, Nov. 19, 1860; Lathers to Henry Gourdin et al., Nov. 28, 1860, A. G. Magrath and Henry Gourdin to Lathers, Dec. 8, 1860, newspaper clipping from *New York Herald*, Dec. 16, 1860, Richard Lathers Papers, LC; Alvan F. Sanborn, ed., *Reminiscences of Richard Lathers: Sixty Years of a Busy Life in South Carolina, Massachusetts and New York* (New York, 1907), 74–91, 116–19; James Gibbes to Pickens, Jan. 6, 1861, Francis Wilkinson Pickens and Milledge Luke Bonham Papers, LC. Also see Ronald L. F. Davis, "The Southern Merchant: A Perennial Source of Discontent," in Walter J. Fraser Jr. and Winfred B. Moore Jr., eds., *The Southern Enigma: Essays on Race, Class and Folk Culture* (Westport, Conn., 1983), 131–41; Philip S. Foner, *Business and Slavery: The New York Merchants and the Irrepressible Conflict* (Chapel Hill, N.C., 1941).

37. Fr. Asbury Mood to Hammond, Nov. 2, 1860, James Henry Hammond Papers, LC; *Charleston Daily Courier*, Nov. 16, 23, 1860; Archie Vernon Huff Jr., *Greenville: The History of the City and County in the South Carolina Piedmont* (Columbia, S.C., 1995), 132–34; Taylor, ed., "Letters Dealing with the Secession Movement," 9–12; Lillian Kibler, *Benjamin F. Perry: South Carolina Unionist* (Durham, N.C., 1946), 337–52; John D. Ashmore to Miles, Nov. 20, 1860, William Porcher Miles Papers, SHC.

38. Philip N. Racine, ed., *Piedmont Farmer: The Journals of David Golightly Harris, 1855–1870* (Knoxville, Tenn., 1990), 2–4, 16, 161–63, 165–66, 168, 171–73; William Joseph MacArthur, "Antebellum Politics in an Upcountry District: National, State and Local Issues in Spartanburg County, South Carolina, 1850–1860" (M.A. thesis, University of South Carolina, 1966), 62–81; James Wylie Gettys, "Mobilization for Secession in Greenville District" (M.A. thesis, University of South Carolina, 1967); *A History of Spartanburg County, Compiled by Spartanburg Unit of the Writers' Program of the W.P.A. in the State of South Carolina* (rpt., Spartanburg, S.C., 1976), 125–26, 134–35; speech at a public meeting in Greenville, May 20, 1861, Benjamin F. Perry Papers, SHC; James T. Otten, "Disloyalty in the Upper Districts of South Carolina during the Civil War," *SCHM* 75 (Apr. 1974): 95–110; Huff, *Greenville*, 142; Tatum, *Disloyalty in the Confederacy*, 135–42. Also see John Inscoe, *Mountain Masters: Slavery and the Sectional Crisis in Western North Carolina* (Knoxville, Tenn., 1989); Michael K. Honey, "The War within the Confederacy: White Unionists of North Carolina," *Prologue* 18 (Summer 1986): 75–93; Philip Shaw Paludan, *Victims: A True Story of the Civil War* (Knoxville, Tenn., 1981); Ted R. Worley, "The Arkansas Peace Society of 1861: A Study in Mountain

Unionism," *JSH* 4 (1958): 445–56; Hugh C. Bailey, "Disaffection in the Alabama Hill Country 1860," *JSH* 4 (1958): 183–93; David C. Hsiung, *Two Worlds in the Tennessee Mountains: Exploring the Origins of Appalachian Stereotypes* (Lexington, Ky., 1997); Robert Tracy McKenzie, *One South or Many?: Plantation Belt and Upcountry in Civil War-Era Tennessee* (Cambridge, Eng., 1994).

39. Oliphant et al., eds., *The Letters*, 4:263, 267–69; *Acts of the General Assembly of the State of South Carolina, Passed in November and December, 1860 and January 1861* (Columbia, S.C., 1861), 859–60; *Charleston Mercury*, Nov. 13, 14, 15, Dec. 3, 1860; *Charleston Daily Courier*, Nov. 20, 21, 23, 26, 28, 29, 30, Dec. 1, 4, 5, 6, 1860; Perry quoted by Huff, *Greenville*, 134; A. C. Spain to Fraser, Oct. 8, 1860, Thomas Boone Fraser Papers, SCL; John S. Palmer to James J. Palmer, Nov. 16, 1860 in Towles, ed., *A World Turned Upside Down*, 272; Cauthen, *South Carolina Goes to War*, 63–67; Racine, ed., *Piedmont Farmer*, 165; R. N. Hemphill to W. R. Hemphill, Dec. 14, 1860, Hemphill Family Papers, DU; Aldrich quoted by Channing, *Crisis of Fear*, 282.

40. *Charleston Daily Courier*, Dec. 10, 12, 1860; *Journal of the Convention of the People of South Carolina Held in 1860, 1861 and 1862* (Columbia, S.C., 1862), 5–7; Laura A. White, "The Fate of Calhoun's Sovereign Convention in South Carolina," *AHR* 34 (1928–29): 757–71; Ralph A. Wooster, *The Secession Conventions of the South* (Princeton, N.J., 1962), chap. 2, and "An Analysis of the Membership of the Secession Conventions in the Lower South," *JSH* 24 (1958): 360–68; John Amasa May and Joan Reynolds Faunt, *South Carolina Secedes* (Columbia, S.C., 1960); J. H. Thornwell, *The State of the Country* (Columbia, S.C., 1861), 3–5; "How South Carolina Seceded," 349–50; Chalmers Gaston Davidson, *The Last Foray: The South Carolina Planters of 1860: A Sociological Study* (Columbia, S.C., 1971).

41. *Charleston Daily Courier*, Dec. 8, 18, 19, 21, 25, 1860; *Journal of the Senate . . . 1860*, 20–23; Lieber to H. W. Hilliard, Nov. 28, 1860, Francis Lieber Papers, SCL; Howell Cobb, "Letter . . . to the People of Georgia," in Wakelyn, ed., *Southern Pamphlets*, 88–100; *Journal of the Convention*, 3–17, 22–23, 26–27, 42–49, 73, 81, 477–79; John S. Palmer to Esther Simons Palmer, Dec. 19, 1860 in Towles, ed., *A World Turned Upside Down*, 279–300; Bonham to W. H. Gist, Dec. 3, 1860, W. H. Gist to Bonham, Dec. 6, 1860, E. S. Shorter to Bonham, Dec. 13, 1860, W. P. Miles to Bonham, Dec. 19, 1860, Milledge Luke Bonham Papers, SCL; "How South Carolina Seceded," 346–51; *Journal of the House . . . 1860*, 278; Jacob Frederick Schirmer Diaries, Dec. 20, 1860, SCHS; "Recollections of Louisa Rebecca Hayne McCord," 41, Louisa McCord Smythe Papers, SCL; Childs, ed., *The Private Journal of Henry William Ravenel*, 43–44; Elizabeth W. Allston Pringle, *Chronicles of Chicora Wood* (New York, 1922), 173; Samuel Crawford Diary, Dec. 19, [20], 1860, Samuel Wylie Crawford Papers, LC.

42. Carson, ed., *Life, Letters and Speeches*, 364, 382; *Charleston Mercury*, Aug. 28, Dec. 21, 22, 1860; Lacy K. Ford Jr., "James Louis Petigru: The Last South Carolina Federalist," in Michael O'Brien and David Moltke-Hansen, eds., *Intellectual Life in Antebellum Charleston* (Knoxville, Tenn., 1986), 152–85; Scarborough, ed., *The Diary*, 1:511–13; *Charleston Daily Courier*, Nov. 19, 1860. Also see George M. Frederickson, *White Supremacy: A Comparative Study in American and South African History* (New York, 1981), chap. 4.

43. *Disunion and Slavery* (n.p., n.d.), 9, 13, 19; Howard Cecil Perkins, ed., *Northern Editorials on Secession* (Gloucester, Mass., 1946), 1:97–98, 104–5, 107–9, 158–201; *The Conspiracy Unveiled* (Philadelphia, Pa., 1863), 92–94; *Charleston Daily Courier*, Dec. 24, 1860; *Charleston Mercury*, Jan. 28, 1861; *Speech of the Honorable D. C. Jarnette, of Virginia* (n.p., n.d.), 6–7; Dumond, ed., *Southern Editorials,*

357–60, 375–77, 391–92; Carson, ed., *Life, Letters and Speeches*, 375; Scarborough, ed., *The Diary*, 1:580; Albert Taylor Bledsoe, *Secession and the South* (n.p., n.d.); Dr. R. J. Breckinridge, "Discourse Delivered on the Day of National Humiliation, January 4, 1861, at Lexington, Kentucky," in Wakelyn, ed., *Southern Pamphlets*, 247–61; John P. Kennedy, *The Border States: Their Power and Duty in the Present Disordered Condition of the Country* (Philadelphia, Pa., 1861), 3–38.

44. Dumond, ed., *Southern Editorials*, 386–91, 483–86; Perkins, ed., *Northern Editorials*, 1:158–99, 331–82, 2:922–56; Robert J. Walker, "Nullification and Secession," *Continental Monthly*, Feb. 1863, 179–94; Judah P. Benjamin, "The Right to Secession," in Wakelyn, ed., *Southern Pamphlets*, 101–14; Francis Lieber, *What Is Our Constitution — League, Pact or Government?* (New York, 1861), 34; Carson, ed., *Life, Letters and Speeches*, 372; *Charleston Mercury*, Dec. 31, 1860, Jan. 9, 1861. Also see Alexander H. Stephens, *A Constitutional View of the Late War between the States; Its Causes, Character, Conduct and Results*, 2 vols. (Philadelphia, Pa., 1868, 1870); Jesse T. Carpenter, *The South as a Conscious Minority, 1789–1861: A Study in Political Thought* (New York, 1930). For an anachronistic justification of southern views on the constitutionality of secession, see Mark E. Brandon, *Free in the World: American Slavery and Constitutional Failure* (Princeton, N.J., 1998).

45. *Nebudchadnezzar's Fault and Fall* (Charleston, S.C., 1861), 5–10; *A Sermon Preached at St. Peter's Church . . . by the Reverend William O. Prentiss* (Charleston, S.C., 1860), 3–12; *The Origin and End of the Irrepressible Conflict by Octogenerian* (n.p., [1861]), 6–7.

46. Adger and Girardeau, eds., *The Collected Writings*, 4:439–66, 510–56; Thornwell, *The State of the Country*, 6–9, 24–29; David B. Chesebrough, ed., *"God Ordained This War": Sermons on the Sectional Crisis, 1830–1865* (Columbia, S.C., 1991), 193–220; B. M. Palmer, *A Vindication of Secession and the South from the Strictures of Reverend R. J. Breckinridge* (Columbia, S.C., 1861), 4–17; [W. J. Grayson], *Reply to Professor Hodge, on the "State of the Country"* (Charleston, S.C., 1861), 4; Palmer, *The Life and Letters*, 481–90, 494–95, 499–512; James Oscar Farmer Jr., *The Metaphysical Confederacy: James Henley Thornwell and the Synthesis of Southern Values* (Macon, Ga., 1986), 238–86.

47. Gabriel Manigault Autobiography, MS, transcribed by the W.P.A., South Carolina, 315–19, Gabriel Edward Manigault Papers, SCL; *Charleston Mercury*, Jan. 18, 1861. Also see "Admission of Northern States into the Southern Confederation," Mar. 25, 26, 27, 28, 1861; *Address Delivered before the Virginia State Convention* (Richmond, Va., 1861), 43–64.

48. *Journal of the Convention*, 21, 39, 41–12, 92–93, 124–34, 143, 150, 153–54, 156, 171–73, 461–76, 480–83; *Journal of the Senate . . . 1860*, 24–25; *Charleston Mercury*, Dec. 24, 1860; Armand J. Gerson, "The Inception of the Montgomery Convention," *Annual Report of the AHA* (1910): 179–87; William C. Davis, *A Government of Our Own: The Making of the Confederacy* (New York, 1994), 11–12.

49. David M. Potter, *The Impending Crisis, 1848–1861* (New York, 1976), 492–504; Paul Horton, "Submitting to the 'Shadow of Slavery': The Secession Crisis and Civil War in Alabama's Lawrence County," *CWH* 44 (June 1998): 111–36; Michael P. Johnson, *Toward a Patriarchal Republic: The Secession of Georgia* (Baton Rouge, La., 1977); Seymour Martin Lipset, *Political Man: The Social Bases of Politics* (New York, 1960), chap. 11; Peyton McCrary, Clark Miller, and Dale Baum, "Class and Party in the Secession Crisis: Voting Behavior in the Deep South, 1856–1861," *Journal of Interdisciplinary History* 8 (Winter 1978): 429–57. For a different view, see Ralph A. Wooster, "The Secession of the Lower South: An Examination of Changing Interpretations," *CWH* 7 (June 1961): 117–27;

Roy R. Doyon and Thomas W. Hodler, "Secessionist Sentiment and Slavery: A Geographic Analysis," *GHQ* 73 (Summer 1989): 323–48; David Y. Thomas, "Southern Non-Slaveholders in the Election of 1860," *Political Science Quarterly* 26 (1911): 222–37.

50. May and Faunt, eds., *South Carolina Secedes*, illustration facing p. 80; Moore, ed., *A Plantation Mistress*, 110; Steven A. Channing, "Slavery and Confederate Nationalism," in Walter J. Fraser Jr. and Winfred B. Moore Jr., eds., *From the Old South to the New: Essays on the Transitional South* (Westport, Conn., 1981), 219–25; Drew Gilpin Faust, *The Creation of Confederate Nationalism: Ideology and Identity in the Civil War South* (Baton Rouge, La., 1988).

51. *Charleston Daily Courier*, Dec. 5, 10, 11, 12, 15, 19, 22, 24, 28, 1860; Trescot to W. H. Gist, Dec. 14, 1860, Trescot to James Chesnut, Dec. 16, 1860, "Memorandum of Views Submitted to General Cass and the President," [1860], William Henry Trescot Papers, SCL; Gaillard Hunt, ed., "Narrative and Letter of William Henry Trescot Concerning the Negotiations between South Carolina and President Buchanan in December, 1860," *AHR* (Apr. 1908): 528–53; John McQueen, W. P. Miles, M. L. Bonham, W. W. Boyce, and L. M. Keitt to James Buchanan, Dec. 10, 1860, William Porcher Miles Papers, SHC; *Charleston Mercury*, Dec. 19, 1860; [James Buchanan], *Mr. Buchanan's Administration on the Eve of the Rebellion* (rpt., New York, 1970), 108–230; Carson, ed., *Life, Letters and Speeches*, 363.

52. *Charleston Daily Courier*, Dec. 5, 11, 23, 25, 28, 31, 1860, Jan. 8, 10, 1861; "C. G." to "children," Dec. 16, 24, 30, 1860, Catherine H. Gilman Papers, SCHS; *Journal of the Convention*, 53–59, 63–67, 70, 90–91, 107, 110–11, 115, 121–22; Hunt, ed., "Narrative and Letter of William Henry Trescot," 542–48; *Charleston Mercury*, Dec. 13, 18, 19, 21, 27, 1860; telegram, W. H. Trescot to Miles, Dec. 31, 1860, William Porcher Miles Papers, SHC; Towles, ed., *A World Turned Upside Down*, 285–86. Also see Philip G. Auchampaugh, *James Buchanan and His Cabinet on the Eve of Secession* (Lancaster, Pa., 1926).

53. *Charleston Daily Courier*, Jan. 8, 10, 24, Feb. 4, 11, Mar. 4, 1861; *Charleston Mercury*, Jan. 3, 10, 11, 17, 19, 21, 30, Feb. 5, 9, 16, 1861; Childs, ed., *The Private Journal of Henry William Ravenel*, 49, 53–54; Jefferson Davis, "Remarks on the Special Message on Affairs in South Carolina, Jan. 10, 1861," in Wakelyn, ed., *Southern Pamphlets*, 115–26; Crawford to "brother," Jan. 12, 1861, Gov. Pickens to Jefferson Davis, Jan. 23, 1861, A. B. Longstreet to Gov. Pickens, Feb. 3, 1861, Samuel Wylie Crawford Papers, LC; Richard De Treville to Pickens, Jan. 9, 1861, I. W. Hayne to Pickens, Jan. 16, 22, 1861, G. B. Lamar to Pickens, Jan. 17, 1861, Francis Wilkinson Pickens and Milledge Luke Bonham Papers, LC; Miles to Gov. Pickens, Feb. 9, 1861, William Porcher Miles Papers, LC; W. P. Miles to M. L. Bonham, Dec. 23, 1860, Orr-Patterson Papers, SHC; Carson, ed., *Life, Letters and Speeches*, 365–66, 368, 374. Also see Samuel Wylie Crawford, *The Genesis of the Civil War: The Story of Sumter, 1860–1861* (New York, 1887); Cauthen, *South Carolina Goes to War*, chaps. 7–8.

54. Thompson to Richard Yeadon, undated, Waddy Thompson Papers, SCL; *Charleston Mercury*, Jan. 17, 23, 31, Feb. 2, 8, 11, Mar. 12, 17, 18, 22, 25, Apr. 4, 6, 9, 10, 13, 1861; *Charleston Daily Courier*, Jan. 29, 31, Feb. 1, 8, 9, 11, Mar. 13, 14, 21, Apr. 8, 10, 11, 12, 15, 16, 17, 19, 1861; Towles, ed., *A World Turned Upside Down*, 294–96; Marszalek, ed., *The Diary of Miss Emma Holmes*, 22–33; Scarborough, ed, *The Diary*, 1:582–606; Carson, ed., *Life, Letters and Speeches*, 380–81. Also see Peter B. Knupfer, *The Union as It Is: Constitutional Unionism and Sectional Compromise, 1787–1861* (Chapel Hill, 1991), 208–11; Robert Gray Gunderson, *Old Gentlemen's Convention: The Washington Peace Conference of 1861* (Madison, Wis.,

1961); Kenneth M. Stampp, *And the War Came: The North and the Secession Crisis, 1860–1861* (Baton Rouge, La., 1950); David M. Potter, *Lincoln and His Party in the Secession Crisis* (New Haven, Conn., 1942); George Harmon Knowles, ed., *The Crisis of the Union* (Baton Rouge, La., 1965); Harold M. Hyman, "The Narrow Escape from a 'Compromise of 1860': Secession and the Constitution," in Hyman and Leonard W. Levy, eds., *Freedom and Reform: Essays in Honor of Henry Steele Commager* (New York, 1967), 149–66; John V. Mering, "The Slave-States Constitutional Unionists and the Politics of Consensus," *JSH* 43 (1977): 395–410; Daniel W. Crofts, *Reluctant Confederates: Upper South Unionists in the Secession Crisis* (Chapel Hill, N.C., 1989); Richard N. Current, *Lincoln and the First Shot* (New York, 1963); Brian Holden Reid, "The Crisis at Fort Sumter in 1861 Reconsidered," *History* 77 (Feb. 1992): 3–32.

Epilogue

1. *De Bow's Review* 4 (July–Aug. 1867): 36–47.

2. Karl Marx and Friedrich Engels, *Selected Works in Three Volumes* (Moscow, 1969), 2:22; Richard Enmale, ed., *The Civil War in the United States* (New York, 1937). For critical assessments of Marx's views, see Gerald Runkle, "Karl Marx and the American Civil War," *Comparative Studies in Society and History* 6 (Jan. 1964): 111–19; Eugene D. Genovese, *In Red and Black: Marxian Explorations in Southern and Afro-American History* (New York, 1968), chap. 15.

3. Fort Sumter Diary, Mar. 1, 4, 19, 1861, Samuel Wylie Crawford Papers, LC.

4. Jacob Stroyer, *My Life in the South* (Salem, Mass., 1898), 99; Armstead L. Robinson, "Day of Jubilo: Civil War and the Demise of Slavery in the Mississippi Valley, 1861–1865" (Ph.D. diss., University of Rochester, 1977), 571; Ira Berlin, Barbara J. Fields, et al., *Slaves No More: Three Essays in Emancipation and the Civil War* (Cambridge, Eng., 1992); Joel Williamson, *After Slavery: The Negro in South Carolina during Reconstruction* (Chapel Hill, N.C., 1965), chap. 1; Winthrop D. Jordan, *Tumult and Silence at Second Creek: An Inquiry into a Civil War Conspiracy* (Baton Rouge, La., 1993); Herbert Aptheker, "Notes on Slave Conspiracies in Confederate Mississippi," *JNH* 29 (Jan. 1944): 75–79; Harvey Wish, "Slave Disloyalty under the Confederacy," *JNH* 23 (Oct. 1938): 435–50; Paul D. Escott, "The Context of Freedom: Georgia's Slaves during the Civil War," *GHQ* 58 (Spring 1974): 79–104; Leon F. Litwack, *Been in the Storm So Long: The Aftermath of Slavery* (New York, 1979); Moore, ed., *A Plantation Mistress*, 87, 114; Brookes to Sarah Brookes, Feb. 25, 1836, Iveson L. Brookes Papers, DU; Palmer, *The Life and Letters*, 582. Also see Eugene D. Genovese, *A Consuming Fire: The Fall of the Confederacy in the Mind of the White Christian South* (Athens, Ga., 1998).

5. Enmale, ed., *The Civil War in the United States*, 82.

BIBLIOGRAPHY
OF PRIMARY SOURCES

Manuscripts

CHAPEL HILL, NORTH CAROLINA
Southern Historical Collection, University of North Carolina Library
   Iveson L. Brookes Papers
   Elliot-Gonzales Papers
   David Gavin Diary
   James Hamilton Papers
   William P. Hill Diary
   Samuel Cram Jackson Diary
   Alexander Lawton Papers
   Christopher G. Memminger Papers
   William Porcher Miles Papers
   James S. Milling Papers
   Orr-Patterson Papers
   Benjamin F. Perry Papers
   Pettigrew Family Papers
   Robert Barnwell Rhett Papers
   Springs Family Papers
   Witherspoon-McDowell Family Papers
   Benjamin Cudworth Yancey Papers

CHARLESTON, SOUTH CAROLINA
South Carolina Historical Society
   Robert F. W. Allston Papers
   Bacot-Huger Collection
   Chesnut-Miller-Manning Papers
   Langdon Cheves Papers
   Fraser Collection
   Catherine H. Gilman Papers
   Stephen D. Miller Papers
   Thomas Porcher Ravenel Collection
   Robert Barnwell Rhett Collection
   Jacob Frederick Schirmer Diaries

COLUMBIA, SOUTH CAROLINA
South Caroliniana Library, University of South Carolina
   David Wyatt Aiken Papers
   Lewis Malone Ayer Papers

Albert Taylor Bledsoe Papers
Milledge Luke Bonham Papers
Bradley Family Papers
William Waters Boyce Papers
Iveson L. Brookes Papers
Preston Smith Brooks Papers
Pierce Mason Butler Papers
Langdon Cheves Papers
Cheves Family Papers
William Drayton Papers
Stephen Elliot Papers
Franklin Harper Elmore Papers
John Christopher Faber Papers
Thomas Boone Fraser Papers
Martin Witherspoon Gary Papers
William Henry Gist Papers
Maxcy Gregg Papers
James Hamilton Papers
William Harper Papers
Robert Young Hayne Papers
Francis Bernard Higgins Papers
David Flavel Jamison Papers
Jones, Watts and Davis Family Papers
Ellison Summerfield Keitt Papers
Hugh Swinton Legaré Papers
Lide, Coker, Stout Family Papers
Francis Lieber Papers
William Pinckney McBee Papers
McCrady Family Papers
George McDuffie Papers
Gabriel Edward Manigault Papers
Manigault Family Papers
John Laurence Manning Papers
Virgil Maxcy Papers
Means-English-Doby Papers
Christopher Gustavus Memminger Papers
Williams Middleton Papers
Middleton Family Papers
James Blount Miller Scrapbook
Stephen Decatur Miller Papers
John Belton O'Neall Papers
James L. Orr Papers
Benjamin Franklin Perry Papers
James Louis Petigru Papers
Francis Wilkinson Pickens Papers
Joel Roberts Poinsett Papers
Francis Peyre Porcher Papers
William Campbell Preston Papers
James Henry Rion Papers
Rutledge Family Papers
Whitemarsh Benjamin Seabrook Papers

Seibels Family Papers
James Simons Papers
William Dunlap Simpson Papers
Louisa McCord Smythe Papers
Thomas Sumter Papers
Waddy Thompson Papers
James Henley Thornwell Papers
William Henry Trescot Papers
Beaufort Taylor Watts Papers
David Rogerson Williams Papers
Witherspoon Family Papers
William Lowndes Yancey Papers

DURHAM, NORTH CAROLINA
Perkins Library, Duke University
Anonymous Diary
William Blanding Journal
Edward Earle Bomar Papers
Iveson L. Brookes Papers
Oze Reed Broyles Papers
Armistead Burt Papers
Ellison Capers Papers
John Fox Papers
George A. Gordon Papers
Robert N. Gourdin Papers
James Henry Hammond Papers
Hemphill Family Papers
Alfred Huger Letterbook
David Flavel Jamison Papers
Job Johnston Papers
Lawrence Massilon Keitt Papers
George McDuffie Papers
Stephen D. Miller Papers
Hugh Swinton Legaré Papers
James L. Orr Papers
Francis Wilkinson Pickens Papers
Robert Barnwell Rhett Papers
John Simpson Papers
Thomas Thomason Papers
Abraham Watkins Venable Scrapbook
Nathan C. Whitstone Papers
Mathew J. Williams Papers
George M. Witherspoon Papers

RALEIGH, NORTH CAROLINA
North Carolina Department of Archives and History
James Johnston Pettigrew Papers

WASHINGTON, D.C.
Library of Congress
Langdon Cheves Letters
Thomas Corwin Papers

Samuel Wylie Crawford Papers
Franklin Harper Elmore Papers
Edward Frost Papers
James Henry Hammond Papers
Richard Lathers Papers
Hugh S. Legaré Papers
McCarter Journal
William Porcher Miles Letter (typed)
James Louis Petigru Papers
Francis Wilkinson Pickens–Milledge Luke Bonham Papers
Joel Roberts Poinsett Papers
Whitemarsh Benjamin Seabrook Papers
Waddy Thompson Papers
William Henry Trescot Papers

Newspapers and Journals

Camden Journal/Camden Weekly Journal
Charleston Courier/Charleston Daily Courier
Charleston Mercury
Commercial Review of the South and West
De Bow's Review
Greenville Mountaineer
Niles Register
Southern Quarterly Review
Southern Literary Messenger
Southern Standard
Southern Patriot
The Southron
Sumter Watchman/Black River Watchman
States Rights and Free Trade Evening Post

Official Documents

Acts of the General Assembly of the State of South Carolina. Published annually.
     Columbia, S.C., 1828–60.
Ames, Herbert V. ed. State Documents on Federal Relations: The States and the United
     States. Reprint. New York, 1970.
Congressional Globe
Documents Accompanying the President's Message, Jan. 1833. N.p.
Executive Message of the President of the United States . . . Dec. 4, 1832. Washington,
     D.C., 1832.
Exposition and Protest, Reported by the Special Committee of the House of Representatives
     on the Tariff; Read and Ordered to Be Printed, Dec. 19th 1828. Columbia, S.C.,
     1829.
General Assembly Index. Miscellaneous Documents — African Slave Trade,
     Nullification, State Rights, Secession, Wilmot Proviso.
Governor's Messages, 1824–1860. South Carolina Department of Archives and
     History, Columbia.
Governor's Message Communicating Certain Documents from South Carolina and New
     Jersey. N.p., n.d.

Journal of the Convention of the People of South Carolina Held in 1832, 1833 and
    1852. Columbia, S.C., 1860.
Journal of the Convention of the People of South Carolina Held in 1860, 1861 and 1862,
    Together with the Ordinances, Reports and Resolutions, Etc. Columbia, S.C., 1862.
Journal of the House of Representatives of the State of South Carolina. Annual and
    Special Sessions. Columbia, S.C., 1828–60.
Journal of the Senate of the State of South Carolina. Annual and Special Sessions.
    Columbia, S.C., 1828–60.
Journal of the State Convention of South Carolina, Together with the Resolutions and
    Ordinance. Columbia, S.C., 1852.
Message No. 1 of His Excellency J. H. Adams, Governor of South Carolina, to the Senate
    and the House of Representatives, at the Session of 1856, with Accompanying
    Documents. Columbia, S.C., 1856.
President Jackson's Proclamation against the Nullification Ordinance of South Carolina,
    Dec. 11, 1832. N.p.
Report of a Special Committee of the Senate, of South Carolina, on the Resolutions
    Submitted by Mr. Ramsay, on the Subject of State Rights. Columbia, S.C., 1827.
Report of Special Committee on So Much of Governor Adams's Message as Relates to the
    Slave Trade [by Alexander Mazyck]. N.p., n.d.
Report of the Committee of the State of Delaware on the Ordinance of the State of South
    Carolina. N.p., n.d.
Report of the Committee on Federal Relations on So Much of the Governor's Message as
    Relates to the Tariff. N.p., n.d.
Report of the Minority of the Special Committee of Seven, to Whom It Was Referred So
    Much of Gov. Adam's Message, No. 1, as Relates to Slavery and the Slave Trade [by
    J. Johnston Pettigrew]. Charleston, S.C., 1858.
Report of the Special Committee of the House of Representatives of South Carolina, on So
    Much of the Message of His Excellency Gov. Jas. H. Adams, as Relates to the Slave
    Trade [by Edward B. Bryan]. Columbia, S.C., 1857.
Reports and Resolutions of the General Assembly of the State of South Carolina. Annual
    Sessions. Columbia, S.C., 1828–60.
[Resolutions of the] Legislature of the State of South Carolina in the House of
    Representatives, Dec. 15, 1825. N.p., n.d.
State of the Union: Message from the President of the United States . . . Jan. 16, 1833. N.p.
State Papers on Nullification. Boston, 1834.

Published Works

Address Delivered at the Celebration of the 54th Anniversary of the Battle of Cowpens . . .
    Jan. 17, 1835, by B. F. Perry. Greenville, S.C., 1835.
Address Delivered before the Virginia State Convention. Richmond, Va., 1861.
Address of Hon. R. Barnwell Rhett to His Constituents. N.p., n.d.
Address of Lawrence M. Keitt . . . Dec. 15, 1851. Columbia, S.C., 1851.
Address of the Citizens of Richland District to the Citizens of South Carolina. Columbia,
    S.C., 1828.
Address of the Friends of Domestic Industry, Assembled at New York, Oct. 26, 1831.
    Baltimore, Md., 1831.
Address of the State Rights and Free Trade Association to the People of Darlington District,
    Darlington Courthouse, South Carolina, Aug. 28th, 1832. N.p.
Address of the Washington Society to the People of South Carolina. Charleston,
    S.C., 1832.

Address on Reopening the Slave Trade by C. W. Miller, Esq., of South Carolina, to the Citizens of Barnwell at Wylde-Moore, Aug. 29, 1857. Columbia, S.C., 1857.

An Address on Secession Delivered in South Carolina in the Year 1851 by Francis Lieber. New York, 1865.

Address on the Question of Separate State Secession, to the People of Barnwell District, by Lewis Malone Ayer, Jr. Charleston, S.C., 1851.

Address to a Public Meeting, of the Citizens of Union District by William Harper. Columbia, S.C., 1831.

Address to the People of Barnwell District on Separate State Secession, by W. A. Owens. Charleston 1851.

Address to the People of St. Helena Parish by the Honorable William Elliot. Charleston, S.C., 1832.

Adger, John B. *The Christian Doctrine of Human Rights and Slavery, in Two Articles from the Southern Presbyterian Review.* Columbia, S.C., 1849.

——. *Christian Mission and African Colonization.* Columbia, S.C., 1857.

——. *A Review of Reports to the Legislature of South Carolina, on the Revival of the Slave Trade (from the April Number of the Southern Presbyterian Review).* Columbia, S.C., 1858.

Adger, John B., and John L. Girardeau, eds. *The Collected Writings of James Henley Thornwell.* Vol. 4. Richmond, Va., 1873.

African Slave Trade and the Secret Purpose of the Insurgents to Revive It, The. Philadelphia, Pa., 1863.

American System Exemplified . . . by a Citizen of Sumter District, The. Sumterville, S.C., 1830.

Appeal to the State Rights Party of South Carolina: In Several Letters on the Present Condition of Public Affairs. Columbia, S.C., 1858.

Argument before the United States Circuit Court, by Isaac W. Hayne, Esq., on the Motion to Discharge the Crew of the Echo . . . Dec. 1858. New York, 1859.

Argument of Mr. Bellinger in the Echo Case in Federal Court, Charleston, S.C., April 1859. Columbia, S.C., 1859.

Armstrong, George D. *The Christian Doctrine of Slavery.* New York, 1857.

Bachman, John. *The Doctrine of the Unity of the Human Race Examined on the Principles of Science.* Charleston, S.C., 1850.

Ball, Charles. *Fifty Years in Chains.* Lewistown, Pa., 1836.

Barnwell, John, ed. "Hamlet to Hotspur: Letters of Robert Woodward Barnwell to Robert Barnwell Rhett." *South Carolina Historical Magazine* 77 (Oct. 1976): 236–56.

——. " 'In the Hands of the Compromisers': Letters of Robert W. Barnwell to James H. Hammond." *Civil War History* 29 (June 1983): 154–68.

Bassett, John Spencer, ed. *Correspondence of Andrew Jackson.* Vols. 4–5. Washington, D.C., 1929, 1931.

Benton, Thomas Hart. *Thirty Years' View; Or a History of the Working of the American Government.* Vol. 2. New York, 1856.

Berlin, Ira, et al., eds. *Free at Last: A Documentary History of Slavery, Freedom, and the Civil War.* New York, 1993.

Berlin, Ira, Barbara J. Fields, et al., eds. *Freedom A Documentary History of Emancipation, 1861–1867: The Black Military Experience.* Ser. 2. Cambridge, Eng., 1982.

——. *Freedom: A Documentary History of Emancipation, 1861–1867: The Destruction of Slavery.* Ser. 1, vol. 1. Cambridge, Eng., 1985.

Berrien, John M. *Address to the People of the United States.* N.p., n.d.

Bledsoe, Albert Taylor. *Secession and the South from the Southern Presbyterian Review.* N.p., n.d.

Bleser, Carol, ed. *Secret and Sacred: The Diaries of James Henry Hammond, a Southern Slaveholder.* New York, 1988.

Book of Allegiance, The. Columbia, S.C., 1834.

Boucher, Chauncey S., and Robert P. Brooks, eds. "Correspondence Addressed to John C. Calhoun, 1837–1849." *Annual Report of the AHA for the Year 1929* (1930).

Bremer, Frederika. *The Homes of the New World: Impressions of the New World.* 2 vols. New York, 1853.

British Squadron on the Coast of Africa by the Rev. J. Leighton Wilson, The. London, 1850.

Brookes, Iveson L. *A Defense of the South: Against the Reproaches and Inchroachments of the North.* Hamburg, S.C., 1851.

[Brown, Edward]. *Notes on the Origins and Necessity of Slavery.* Charleston, S.C., 1826.

Brutus [Robert Turnbull]. *The Crisis, or Essays in the Usurpations of the Federal Government.* Charleston, S.C., 1827.

Brutus [William Henry Brisbane]. *An Address to the Citizens of South Carolina.* N.p., n.d.

Bryan, Edward B. *Letters to the Southern People Concerning the Acts of Congress and the Treaties with Great Britain in Relation to the African Slave Trade.* Charleston, S.C., 1858.

——. *The Rightful Remedy Addressed to the Slaveholders of the South.* Charleston, S.C., 1850.

[Buchanan, James]. *Mr. Buchanan's Administration on the Eve of the Rebellion.* Reprint. New York, 1970.

Buckingham, J. S. *The Slave States of America.* 2 Vols. London, 1842.

Buxton, Thomas Fowell. *The African Slave Trade and Its Remedy.* London, 1840.

[Calhoun, John C.] *The Address of Southern Delegates in Congress, to Their Constituents.* N.p., n.d.

——. *To the People of the Southern States.* N.p., n.d.

Calhoun, Richard J., ed. *Witness to Sorrow: The Antebellum Autobiography of William J. Grayson.* Columbia, S.C., 1990.

Calhoun Doctrine on State Nullification . . . by a Democratic Republican, The. Charleston, S.C., 1831.

Calhoun Revolution, The: Its Basis and Progress. Speech of Hon. J. R. Doolittle of Wisconsin . . . Dec. 14, 1859. N.p.

[Carey, Mathew]. *A Common Sense Address to the Citizens of the Southern States July 23, 1828, by Hamilton.* N.p.

——. *The New Olive Branch: A Solemn Warning on the Banks of the Rubicon, 1830–31.* N.p.

——. *Predictions on the State of Affairs in the South by Hampden.* N.p., n.d.

——. *The Protecting System by Hamilton, 1829.* N.p.

——. *To the Citizens of the United States: Review of the Address of the Free Trade Convention — No. II by Hamilton, 1831.* N.p.

Carson, James Petigru, ed. *Life, Letters and Speeches of James Louis Petigru: The Union Man of South Carolina.* Washington, D.C., 1920.

Charleston Courier and the Slave Trade by Las Casas, The. N.p., n.d.

Chesebrough, David B., ed. *"God Ordained This War": Sermons on the Sectional Crisis.* Columbia, S.C., 1991.

[Cheves, Langdon]. *Occasional Reviews No. I and No. II*. Charleston, S.C., 1832.

Childs, Arney Robinson, ed. *The Private Journal of Henry William Ravenel, 1859–1887*. Columbia, S.C., 1947.

———. *Rice Planter and Sportsman: Recollections of J. Motte Alston, 1821–1909*. Columbia, S.C., 1953.

Clark, Rufus. *The African Slave Trade*. Boston, 1860.

Clark, Thomas D., ed. *The Grand Tour, 1780–1865*. Columbia, S.C., 1973.

Committing of Our Cause to God, The: A Sermon . . . by Reverend Ferdinand Jacobs. Charleston, S.C., 1850.

Conspiracy Unveiled, The. The South Sacrificed; or, the Horrors of Secession by Rev. James W. Hunnicutt. Philadelphia, Pa., 1863.

Constitutional Arguments Indicating the Rights and Policy of the Southern States by Charles Stevens. Charleston, S.C., 1832.

Cooper, Thomas. *Consolidation: An Account of Parties in the United States, from the Convention of 1787, to the Present Period*. Columbia, S.C., 1824.

———. *Consolidation, Part 2: An Account of Parties in the United States Being Strictures on an Article in the North American Review*. Columbia, S.C., 1834.

———. *Hints, Suggestions, and Contributions toward the Labors of a Convention*. Columbia, S.C., 1832.

———. *On the Proposed Alteration of the Tariff, Submitted to the Consideration of the Members of South Carolina, in the Ensuing Congress of 1823–24*. Columbia, S.C., 1824.

———. "Slavery." *Southern Literary Journal* 1 (Nov. 1835): 188–93.

———. *Two Essays: 1. On the Foundation of the Civil Government: 2. On the Constitution of the United States*. Columbia, S.C., 1826.

———, ed. *The Statutes at Large of South Carolina*. Vol. 1. Columbia, S.C., 1836.

Cralle, Richard K., ed. *The Works of John C. Calhoun*. Vol. 1, Charleston, S.C., 1851; Vols. 4, 5, New York, 1870, 1874.

Crawford, Samuel Wylie. *The Genesis of the Civil War: The Story of Sumter, 1860–1861*. New York, 1887.

Crisis or Nullification Unmasked by an Exposition Sep. 1832, The. N.p.

[Cruger, Lewis C.] *The Genuine Book of Nullification: Being a True—Not an Apocryphal—History . . . to Which Are Added the Opinions of a Distinguished Statesman, on State Rights Doctrine by Hampden [F. W. Pickens]*. Charleston, S.C., 1831.

Dalcho, Frederick. *Practical Considerations Founded on the Scriptures Relative to the Slave Population of South Carolina*. Charleston, S.C., 1823.

Debate in the South Carolina Legislature in Dec. 1830, The. Columbia, S.C., 1831.

[De Bow, J. D. B.] *The Political Annals of South Carolina by a Citizen*. Charleston, S.C., 1854.

Defence of a Liberal Construction of the Powers of Congress, as Regards Internal Improvements, etc. . . . Written by George McDuffie, in the Year 1821, over the Signature "One of the People" to Which Are Prefixed an Encomiastic Advertisement of the Work by Major (now Governor) Hamilton, and a Preface. Philadelphia, Pa., 1832.

[Derby, E. N.] *Reality vs. Fiction: A Review of the Pamphlet Published at Charleston . . .* . Boston, 1950.

[DeSaussure, Henry W.] *A Series of Numbers Addresses to the Public . . . .* Columbia, S.C., 1822.

"Despatch from the British Consul at Charleston to Lord John Russell, 1860." *AHR* (July 1913): 783–87.

Discourse Delivered in the Presbyterian Church . . . by Richard B. Cater, A. Pendleton, S.C., 1833.

Discussion on Slaveholding, A: Three Letters to a Conservative by George D. Armstrong. . . . Philadelphia, Pa., 1858.

Dissertation on the Relative Duties between the Different Classes and Conditions of Society . . . by the Rev. James Lowry, A. Columbia, S.C., 1836.

Disunion and Its Results to the South. A Letter from a Resident of Washington to a Friend in South Carolina. N.p., n.d.

Domestic Slavery Considered as a Scriptural Institution: In a Correspondence between the Reverend Richard Fuller, of Beaufort, South Carolina and the Reverend Francis Wayland. . . . New York, 1845.

Donnan, Elizabeth, ed. *Documents Illustrative of the History of the Slave Trade to America: The Border Colonies and the Southern Colonies.* Vol. 4. Washington, D.C., 1935.

Doubleday, Abner. *Reminiscences of Forts Sumter and Moultrie in 1860–'61.* New York, 1876.

Drago, Edmund L., ed. *Broke by the War: Letters of a Slave Trader.* Columbia, S.C., 1991.

Drayton, John. *A View of South Carolina as Respects Her Natural and Civil Concerns.* Charleston, S.C., 1802.

[Drayton, William]. *The South Vindicated from the Treason and Fanaticism of the Northern Abolitionists.* Philadelphia, Pa., 1836.

Dumond, Dwight L., ed. *Southern Editorials on Secession.* New York, 1931.

Elliot, E. N. *Cotton Is King and Pro-Slavery Arguments.* Augusta, Ga., 1860.

Ellison, Thomas. *Slavery and Secession in America: Historical and Economical.* London, [1861].

Eulogium on the Public Services and Character of Robert J. Turnbull . . . by James Hamilton. Charleston, S.C., 1834.

Ewart, David. *A Scriptural View of the Moral Relations of African Slavery.* Columbia, S.C., 1849.

Exposition of Evidence in Support of the Memorial to Congress [Free Trade Convention]. Boston, 1832.

Faust, Drew Gilpin, ed. *The Ideology of Slavery: Proslavery Thought in the Antebellum South.* Baton Rouge, La., 1981.

Featherstonehaugh, G. W. *Excursion through the Slave States.* New York, 1844.

Finkelman, Paul, ed. *The African Slave Trade and American Courts: The Pamphlet Literature.* Vol. 2. New York, 1988.

Fitzhugh, George. *Cannibals All!: Or, Slaves without Masters.* edited by C. Vann Woodward. Reprint. Cambridge, 1960.

———. *Sociology for the South, or the Failure of Free Society.* New York, [1854].

Foote, Henry S. *Casket of Reminiscences.* Washington, D.C., 1874.

Foner, Eric, ed. *Nat Turner.* Englewood Cliffs, N.J., 1971.

Foreign Slave Trade, The: The Source of Political Power, of Material Progress, of Social Integrity, and of the Social Emancipation of the South by L. W. Spratt. Charleston, S.C., 1858.

Freehling, William W., ed. *The Nullification Era: A Documentary Record.* New York, 1967.

Furman, Richard. *Exposition of the Views of the Baptists Relative to the Colored Population of the United States.* Charleston, S.C., 1832.

[Garnett, Muscoe R. H.] *The Union Past and Future: How It Works and How to Save It by a Citizen of Virginia.* Charleston, S.C., 1850.

God the Refuge of His People. A Sermon . . . Delivered by Whitefoord Smith. Columbia, S.C., 1850.

Grayson, William John. *The Hireling and the Slave.* Charleston, S.C., 1854.

———. *James Louis Petigru: A Biographical Sketch.* New York, 1866.

———. *Letter to His Excellency Whitemarsh B. Seabrook Governor of the State of South Carolina on the Dissolution of the Union.* Charleston, S.C., 1850.

———. *Reply to Professor Hodge, on the "State of the Country."* Charleston, S.C., 1861.

———. *The Union, Past and Future: How It Works and How to Save It.* Charleston, S.C., 1850.

Hall, Capt. Basil. *Travels in North America, in the Years 1827 and 1828.* 2 vols. Philadelphia, Pa., 1829.

[Hamilton, James]. *An Account of the Late Intended Insurrection among a Portion of the Blacks . . . .* Charleston, S.C., 1822.

Hampden and His Times. N.p., n.d.

Harper, Robert G. *An Argument against the Policy of Re-opening the African Slave Trade.* Atlanta, Ga., 1858.

Helper, Hinton Rowan. *The Impending Crisis of the South.* New York, 1857.

Hesseltine, William B., ed. *Three against Lincoln: Murat Halstead Reports the Caucuses of 1860.* Baton Rouge, La., 1960.

Hewatt, Alexander. *An Historical Account of the Rise and Progress of the Colonies of South Carolina and Georgia.* 2 vols. London, 1779.

Holland, Edwin C. *A Refutation of the Calumnies Circulated against the Southern Western States by a South Carolinian.* Charleston, S.C., 1822.

"How South Carolina Seceded by the Private Secretary of Governor Pickens of South Carolina." *Nickell Magazine,* Dec. 1897, 345–49.

Hughes, Henry. *Treatise on Sociology: Theoretical and Practical.* Philadelphia, Pa., 1854.

Hull, A. L., ed. "The Making of the Confederate Constitution." *Publications of the Southern Historical Association* 9 (Sept. 1905): 272–92.

Hundley, Daniel R. *Social Relations in Our Southern States.* New York, 1860.

Hunt, Gaillard, ed. "Narrative and Letter of William Henry Trescot Concerning the Negotiations between South Carolina and President Buchanan in December, 1860." *American Historical Review* 11 (April 1908): 528–53.

Imaginary Conversation between President Jackson and the Ghost of Jefferson, An. Columbia, S.C., 1831.

Important Correspondence on the Subject of State Interposition, between His Excellency Governor Hamilton and Honorable John C. Calhoun, Vice President of the United States (Copied from the Pendleton Messenger of 15th Sep., 1832). Charleston, S.C., 1832.

Jameson, J. Franklin, ed., "Calhoun Correspondence." *Annual Report of the AHA for the Year 1899, Vol. II* (1900).

Johnson, Michael P., and James L. Roark, eds. *No Chariot Let Down: Charleston's Free People of Color on the Eve of the Civil War.* Chapel Hill, N.C., 1984.

Journal of the Free Trade Convention, Held in Philadelphia, from Sep. 30 to Oct. 7, 1831; and Their Address to the People of the United States: To Which Is Added a Sketch of the Debates in the Convention. Philadelphia, Pa., 1831.

Judgements: A Call to Repentance: a Sermon . . . by James H. Thornwell. Columbia, S.C.,1854.

Kennedy, John P. *The Border States: Their Power and Duty in the Present Disordered Condition of the Country.* Philadelphia, Pa., 1861.

Kennedy, Lionel H., and Thomas Parker. *An Official Report of the Trials of Sundry Negroes*. Charleston, S.C., 1822.

Lectures on the Restrictive System, Delivered to the Senior Politics Class of William and Mary College by Thomas R. Dew, Professor of History, Metaphysics and Political Law. Richmond, Va., 1829.

Leiber, Francis. *What Is Our Constitution — League, Pact or Government?* New York, 1861.

Letter of W. W. Boyce to the Honorable John P. Richardson, President of the Convention of Southern Rights Associations of South Carolina. N.p., n.d.

Letter on the Relations of the States and General Government, Dec. 1832. N.p.

Letter to Col. William Drayton, of South Carolina . . . by Gullian C. Verplanck, One of the Representatives in Congress from the State of New York. New York, 1831.

Letter to the Honorable John C. Calhoun, Vice President of the United States, Robert Y. Hayne, Senator of the United States, and James Hamilton, Jr., Governor of the State of South Carolina by Thomas S. Grimké. Charleston, S.C., 1832.

Letters of Agricola, The; By Honorable William Elliot. Greenville, S.C., 1852.

Letters of the Late Bishop John England to the Honorable John Forsyth on the Subject of Domestic Slavery. Baltimore, Md., 1844.

Looking Glass for Nullifiers Consistency in Full Perfection, A. N.p., n.d.

Lyell, Sir Charles. *A Second Visit to the United States of North America*. 2 vols. New York, 1849.

Lyman, Stanford M., ed. *Selected Writings of Henry Hughes: Antebellum Southerner, Slavocrat, Sociologist*. Jackson, Miss., 1985.

McDuffie's Second Speech . . . May, 1830. Columbia, S.C., 1830.

Mackay, Charles. *Life and Liberty in America, or Sketches of a Tour in the United States and Canada, in 1857–1858*. 2 vols. London, 1859.

McKitrick, Eric, ed. *Slavery Defended: The Views of the Old South*. Englewood Cliffs, N.J., 1963.

McTyeire, Rev. H. N., Rev. C. F. Sturgis, and Rev. A. T. Holmes. *Duties of Masters to Servants: Three Premium Essays*. Charleston, S.C., 1851.

[Magrath, A. G.] *To the Honorable W. J. Grayson Dated 25 October 1850 from "One of the People."* N.p.

Marszalek, John F., ed. *The Diary of Miss Emma Holmes, 1861–1866*. Baton Rouge, La., 1979.

Martineau, Harriet. *Society in America*. 2 vols. New York, 1837.

Mason, E. G. "A Visit to South Carolina in 1860." *Atlantic*, Feb. 1884, 247–48.

Mathew, David B., et al., eds. *The Papers of James Madison*. Vol. 17. Charlottesville, Va., 1991.

Meats, Stephen, and Edwin T. Arnold, eds. *The Writings of Benjamin F. Perry*. 3 vols. Spartanburg, S.C., 1980.

Meeting and Address of the Southern Rights Association. N.p., n.d.

Memorial and Resolutions Adopted at the Anti-Tariff Meeting, Held at Sumter District . . . 3rd of September, 1827. Charleston, S.C., 1827.

Memorial of the Agricultural Society of South Carolina . . . Jan. 9, 1828. Washington, D.C., 1828.

Memorial of the Citizens of Chesterfield, Marlborough, and Darlington . . . Feb. 4, 1828. Washington, D.C., 1828.

Memorial of the Citizens of Columbia . . . Dec. 18, 1827. Washington, D.C., 1827.

Memorial of the Citizens of Edgefield, against the Woollens Bill, Dec. 27, 1827. Washington, D.C., 1827.

Memorial of the Citizens of Lancaster District . . . Jan. 15, 1828. Washington, D.C.,
1828.

Memorial of the Citizens of Laurens District . . . Jan. 22, 1828. Washington, D.C.,
1828.

Memorial of the Citizens of Orangeburg . . . Dec. 24, 1827. Washington, D.C., 1827.

*Memorial of the Committee of the Free Trade Convention, Held at Philadelphia in Sep. and
Oct., 1831, Remonstrating against the Existing Tariff of Duties.* N.p.

Memorial of the Inhabitants of Barnwell District . . . Dec. 24, 1827. Washington, D.C.,
1827.

Memorial of the Inhabitants of Fairfield District . . . Dec. 14, 1827. Washington, D.C.,
1827.

Memorial of the Inhabitants of Newberry District . . . Feb. 25, 1828. Washington, D.C.,
1828.

Memorial of the Inhabitants of St. Luke's Parish . . . April 5, 1824. Washington, D.C.,
1824.

*Memorial of the Members of the Legislature of South Carolina, Opposed to Nullification,
Jan. 23, 1832.* N.p.

*Memorial of the Sundry Inhabitants of the Upper Counties of the State of South Carolina,
Nov. 28, 1820.* Washington, D.C., 1820.

*Memorial on the Subject of the Late Tariff; Addressed by the General Assembly of the State of
Georgia, to the Anti-Tariff States.* N.p., n.d.

Meriwether, Robert L., ed. "Preston S. Brooks on the Caning of Charles
Sumner." *South Carolina Historical and Genealogical Magazine* 52 (1951): 1–4.

Mills, Robert. *Atlas of the State of South Carolina.* Baltimore, Md., 1825.

———. *Statistics of South Carolina Including a View of Its Natural, Civil and Military
History, General and Particular.* Charleston, S.C., 1826.

Mission of South Carolina to Virginia, The (from De Bow's Review). N.p., n.d.

*Mr. McDuffie's Second Speech against the Prohibitory System; Delivered in the House of
Representatives, May 1830.* N.p.

Moore, John Hammond, ed. *A Plantation Mistress on the Eve of the Civil War: The
Dairy of Keziah Goodwyn Hopkins Brevard, 1860–1861.* Columbia, S.C., 1993.

National Sins: A Call to Repentence. A Sermon . . . by the Reverend Whitefoord Smith.
Charleston, S.C., 1849.

Nebudchadnezzar's Fault and Fall: A Sermon . . . by Rev. C. C. Pinckney. Charleston,
S.C., 1861.

Notice of the Reverend John B. Adger's Article on the Slave Trade. Charleston, S.C.,
1858.

Nevins, Allan, ed. *The Diary of John Quincy Adams, 1794–1845: American Political,
Social and Intellectual Life from Washington to Polk.* New York, 1929.

———. *Polk: The Diary of a President, 1845–1849, Covering the Mexican War, the
Acquisition of Oregon, and the Conquest of California and the Southwest.* New York,
1929.

Nullification Considered and Defended . . . by Thomas Blackwood. Charleston, S.C.,
1833.

*Obituary Addresses Delivered on the Occasion of the Death of the Honorable John C.
Calhoun.* Washington, D.C., 1850.

O'Connor, Mary D., ed. *The Life and Letters of M. P. O'Connor.* New York, 1893.

Oliphant, Mary C. Simms, et. al., eds. *The Letters of William Gilmore Simms.* 5 vols.
Columbia, S.C., 1952–56.

*Official Proceedings of the Democratic National Convention, Held in 1860, at Charleston
and Baltimore.* N.p., 1860.

Olmsted, Frederick Law. *A Journey in the Backcountry.* New York, 1860.

———. *A Journey in the Seaboard States in the Years 1853–1854, with Remarks on Their Economy.* 2 vols. New York, 1856.

O'Neall, John Belton. *Biographical Sketches of the Bench and Bar of South Carolina.* 2 vols. Charleston, S.C., 1859.

———. *The Negro Law of South Carolina.* Columbia, S.C., 1848.

Oration Delivered before the Fourth of July Association . . . by W. Alston Pringle. Charleston, S.C., 1850.

Oration Delivered by Appointment before the Union and State Rights Party, on the 4th of July 1832 . . . by James H. Smith Esq. Charleston, S.C., 1832.

Oration Delivered in the City of Charleston, before the State Rights and Free Trade Party . . . by Robert J. Turnbull. Charleston, S.C., 1832.

Oration Delivered in the First Presbyterian Church, Charleston, on Monday, July 4, 1831 by the Honorable William Drayton. Charleston, S.C., 1831.

Oration Delivered in the Independent or Congregational Church, Charleston, before the State Rights and Free Trade Party . . . by the Honorable Robert Y. Hayne. Charleston, S.C., 1831.

Oration Delivered in the Independent or Congregational Church . . . by Henry L. Pinckney. Charleston, S.C., 1833.

Oration Delivered in the Presbyterian Church in Columbia, on the 4th of July, 1831, by Isaac William Hayne, Esq. Columbia, S.C., 1831.

Oration Delivered on the 4th of July, 1832, at Sumter Court House, by John Hemphill, Esq. Sumterville, S.C., 1832.

Oration of the Absolute Necessity of the Union . . . Delivered 4th of July, 1809, by Thomas S. Grimké and Speech of Thomas S. Grimké Delivered in Dec., 1828 . . . Both Dedicated to the People of South Carolina. Charleston, S.C., 1829.

Oration of the Principal Duties of Americans . . . by Thomas S. Grimké with the Farewell Address of William Drayton. Charleston, S.C., 1833.

Oration on the Life, Character and Services of John Caldwell Calhoun. Charleston, S.C., 1850.

Oration upon the Policy of Separate State Secession . . . by D. H. Hamilton. Charleston, S.C., 1851.

"Oregon Bill, The: Remarks on the South Carolina Doctrine in Regard to Territories." *American Review* 2 (Aug. 1848): 111–19.

Origin and End of the Irrepressible Conflict by Octogenerian, The. N.p., [1861].

Orr, James L. *Speech to the Convention of Southern Rights Associations, Held in Charleston, May, 1851.* Charleston, S.C., 1851.

Palmer, B. M. *The Life and Letters of James Henley Thornwell.* Richmond, Va., 1875.

———. *A Vindication of Secession and the South from the Strictures of Reverend R. J. Breckinridge.* Columbia, S.C., 1861.

Pearson, Edward A., ed. *Designs against Charleston: The Trial Record of the Denmark Vesey Conspiracy of 1822.* Chapel Hill, N.C., 1999.

Pease, Jane H., and William H. Pease, eds. "Walker's Appeal Comes to Charleston: A Note and Documents." *Journal of Negro History* 59 (1974): 289–92.

Perkins, Howard Cecil, ed. *Northern Editorials on Secession.* 2 vols. Gloucester, Mass., 1946.

Perry, Benjamin F. *Reminiscences of Public Men with Speeches and Addresses.* Philadelphia, Pa., 1883.

Phillips, Ulrich B., ed. "The Correspondence of Robert Toombs, Alexander H. Stephens, and Howell Cobb." *Annual Report of the AHA for the Year 1911.* Washington, D.C., 1913.

Pinckney, Charles Cotesworth. *An Address Delivered in Charleston, before the Agricultural Society of South Carolina . . . on Tuesday the 18th August, 1829.* Charleston, S.C., 1829.

Political Tract No. 1: The Question, by Gracchus, "The Bane and Antidote Before Us." Columbia, S.C., 1831.

Political Tract No. 3, Dec. 1831: A Catechism on the Tariff . . . Published by the State Rights and Free Trade Association. Charleston, S.C., 1831.

Political Tract No. 3, Part 2, Sep. 1831: A Catechism on the Tariff . . . Published by the State Rights and Free Trade Association. Charleston, S.C., 1831.

Political Tract, New Series, No. 1, Jan. 1, 1832: Address by the State Rights and Free Trade Association to the People of South Carolina. Columbia, S.C., 1832.

Political Tract No. 6, Feb. 1832: The Prospect before Us, or Strictures on the Late Message of the President of the United States . . . to Which Is Subjoined the Late Address of Gov. Hamilton, before the State Rights and Free Trade Association. Charleston, S.C., 1832.

Political Tract No. 7, March 1832: Proceedings of the State Rights and Free Trade Convention, Held in Charleston (South Carolina) on the 22d and 25th Feb., 1832. Charleston, S.C., 1832.

Political Tract No. 8, April 1, 1832: Free Trade and the American System; A Dialogue between a Merchant and a Planter. Columbia, S.C., 1832.

Political Tract No. 9, May 1, 1832: Dialogue between a Merchant and a Planter, Part II. Columbia, S.C., 1832.

Political Tract No. 10, May, 1832: Judge Harper's Speech before the Charleston State Rights and Free Trade Association . . . April 1, 1832, Explaining and Enforcing the Remedy of Nullification. Columbia, S.C., 1832.

Political Tract No. 10, June 1832: A View of the Remedies Proposed for the Existing Evils. Columbia, S.C., 1832.

Political Tract No. 12, July 1, 1832: An Appeal to the People on the Question What Shall We Do Next? Columbia, S.C., 1832.

Political Tract No. 13, Aug., 1832: The Last Day's Debate on the Tariff in the Senate of the United States. Charleston, S.C., 1832.

Pollard, Edward. *Black Diamonds Gathered in the Darkey Homes of the South.* Reprint. New York, 1968.

Preamble and Resolutions, Adopted at the Great Anti-Tariff Meeting, of the People of Abbeville District, on Thursday, 25th Sep. 1828. Columbia, S.C., 1830.

[Pressley, Benjamin C.] *Reasons for the Dissolution of the Union, Being a Reply to the Letter of the Honorable W. J. Grayson, and to His Answer to One of the People.* Charleston, S.C., 1850.

[Preston, William Campbell]. *A Letter to the Honorable James Brown, Senator in Congress from the State of Louisiana, on the Tariff by an Inhabitant of the South.* Washington, D.C., 1823.

[Pringle, Edward J.] *Slavery in the Southern States by a Carolinian.* Cambridge, Mass., 1852.

Proceedings and the Resolutions and Address Adopted by the State Rights Party in Charleston . . . 9th Sep., 1830. Charleston, S.C., 1830.

Proceedings of a General Meeting Held at the Chester Courthouse, Nov. 18, 1831. Columbia, S.C., 1832.

Proceedings of the Delegates Who Withdrew from the National Democratic Convention at Charleston, in April, 1860. N.p.

Proceedings of the Democratic State Convention of South Carolina. Columbia, S.C., 1856.

Proceedings of the Democratic State Convention of South Carolina. Columbia, S.C., 1860.

Proceedings of the Meeting of Delegates from the Southern Rights Associations of South Carolina. Columbia, S.C., 1851.

Proceedings of the Republican National Convention Held at Chicago, May 16, 17, and 18, 1860. Albany, N.Y., 1860.

Proceedings of the Southern Commercial Convention at Savannah. N.p., n.d.

Proceedings of the State Democratic Convention Held at Columbia, South Carolina, May 30–31, 1860. Columbia, S.C., 1860.

Proceedings of the State Rights Celebration at Charleston. Charleston, S.C., 1830.

Proceedings of the United States Senate on the Fugitive Slave Bill, the Abolition of the Slave Trade in the District of Columbia, and the Imprisonment of Colored Seamen in the Southern Ports. N.p., n.d.

Pro-Slavery Argument as Maintained by the Most Distinguished Scholars of the South, The. Charleston, S,C, 1852.

Question of the Tariff Discussed, The. Columbia, S.C., 1827.

Quintessence of Long Speeches Arranged as a Political Catechism by a Lady [Maria Pinckney] for Her God-Daughter, The. Charleston, S.C., 1830.

Racine, Philip N., ed. *Piedmont Farmer: The Journals of David Golighty Harris, 1855–1870*. Knoxville, Tenn., 1990.

Ramsay, David. *A Sketch of the Soil, Climate, Weather and Diseases of South Carolina*. Charleston, S.C., 1796.

Raymond, Henry J. *Disunion and Slavery: A Series of Letters to W. L. Yancey, of Alabama*. N.p., n.d.

Rawick, George P., ed. *The American Slave: A Composite Autobiography: South Carolina Narratives*. Vols. 2, 3. Westport, Conn., 1972.

Rebuke of Secession Doctrines by Southern Statesmen, The. Philadelphia, Pa., 1863.

Regina Coeli Correspondence between the Honorable James Henry Hammond and John H. B. Latrobe, Esq., President of the American Colonization Society, The. Baltimore, Md., 1858.

Religious Instruction of the Colored Population, The: A Sermon Preached by Rev. John B. Adger. Charleston, S.C., 1847.

Remarks of Mr. Hayne, of South Carolina on the Presentation of the Protest of That State against the Tariff . . . Feb. 10, 1829. Washington, D.C., 1829.

Remarks of Robert Y. Hayne, of South Carolina, on the Third Reading of the Tariff Bill [1832]. N.p., n.d.

Remarks on the Ordinance of Nullification . . . by a South Carolinian. Charleston, S.C., 1833.

Remonstrance to the States in Favor of the Tariff; Adopted by the Legislature of Georgia. N.p., n.d.

Reply of C. A. L. Lamar, of Savannah, Georgia, to the Letter of Howell Cobb, Secretary of Treasury of the United States, Refusing a Clearance to the Ship Richard Cobden. Charleston, S.C., 1858.

Report of the Committee of the Convention of the Union and State Rights Party . . . 10th Dec. 1832, with Their Remonstrance and Protest. N.p.

Report of the Trials in the Echo Cases, in Federal Court, Charleston, South Carolina, April, 1859; Together with the Arguments of Counsel and Charge of the Court. Columbia, S.C., 1859.

Resolutions and Address Adopted by the Southern Convention Held at Nashville, Tennessee, June 3d to 12th, Inclusive, 1850: Together with a Preamble and Resolutions, Adopted November 18th, 1850. Columbia, S.C., 1850.

Resolutions and Remonstrances of the Agricultural Society of St. Andrew's Parish . . . Dec. 14, 1827. Washington, D.C., 1827.

Resolutions and Remonstrances of the Agricultural Society of St. John's, Colleton . . . Dec. 14, 1827. Washington, D.C., 1827.

Resolutions of Virginia on the Powers of the Federal Government. N.p., n.d.

Responsibility of the North in Relation to Slavery, The. Cambridge, Mass., 1856.

Review of a Late Pamphlet, under the Signature of "Brutus" by Hamilton, First Published in the Charleston Courier. Charleston, S.C., 1828.

Review of the Article in the Southern Review, for 1830, on the Several Speeches Made during the Debate on Mr. Foot's Resolution . . . by Lucius Falkland. Baltimore, Md., 1830.

Rights and Duties of Masters, The: A Sermon . . . by Reverend J. H. Thornwell. Charleston, S.C., 1850.

Ripley, C. Peter, ed. *Witness for Freedom: African American Voices on Race, Slavery, and Emancipation.* Chapel Hill, N.C., 1993.

Ruffin, Edmund. *African Colonization Unveiled.* N.p., n.d.

Scarborough, William Kauffman, ed. *The Diary of Edmund Ruffin.* Vol. 1. Baton Rouge, La., 1972.

Second Speech of Mr. McDuffie . . . June, 1832. Washington 1832.

Sellers, Charles, ed. *Andrew Jackson, Nullification and the State-Rights Tradition.* Chicago, 1963.

Separate Secession Practically Discussed in the Edgefield Advertiser by Rutledge. Edgefield, S.C., 1851.

Series of Articles on the Value of the Union to the South, Lately Published in the Charleston Standard by L. W. Spratt, One of the Editors. Charleston, S.C., 1855.

Sermon Preached at St. Peter's Church, Charleston by the Reverend William O. Prentiss. Charleston, S.C., 1860.

Signs of the Times; Reflections on Nullification by a Citizen of Abbeville. Columbia, S.C., 1831.

Simms, William Gilmore. *The Geography of South Carolina: Being a Companion to the History of That State.* Charleston, S.C., 1848.

———. *The History of South Carolina.* Rev. ed. Columbia, S.C., 1927.

Sketch of the Theory of Protecting and Prohibitory Duties, with a Few Practical Applications to the Present State of the Union. Charleston, S.C., 1828.

Slave Trade Declared Not Piracy by the Act of 1820, The: The United States versus William C. Corrie Presentment for Piracy Opinion of the Honorable A. G. Magrath. Columbia, S.C., 1860.

"Slave Traders' Letterbook, A." *North American Review* 143 (Nov. 1886).

Southern Episcopalian 5 (Mar. 1859): 654–60.

Southern Rights and Cooperation Documents. N.p., n.d.

Southern Rights and Cooperation Documents No. 2: Remarks of the Honorable R. W. Barnwell. N.p., n.d.

Southern Rights and Cooperation Documents No. 3: Letter from the Honorable Armistead Burt. N.p., n.d.

Southern Rights and Cooperation Documents No. 4: Speech of the Honorable A. P. Butler. Charleston, S.C., 1851.

Southern Rights and Cooperation Documents No. 6: Proceedings of the Great Cooperation and Anti-Secession Meeting. Charleston, S.C., 1851.

Southern Rights and Cooperation Documents No. 7: Speech of Mr. Memminger. Charleston, S.C., 1851.

Southern Rights Documents: Cooperation Meeting Held in Charleston, S.C., July 29th, 1851. N.p.

Southern Rights Documents: Speech of the Honorable J. L. Orr. N.p., n.d.

Speech Delivered before the Combahee Troop, 3d July, 1852 by William Huston. N.p., n.d.

Speeches Delivered in the Convention of the State of South Carolina. Charleston, S.C., 1833.

Speeches of John C. Calhoun and Daniel Webster . . . on the Enforcing Bill. Boston, 1933.

Speeches of the Honorable John C. Calhoun and Honorable Daniel Webster on the Subject of Slavery. New York, 1850.

Speeches of the Honorable Robert Y. Hayne and the Honorable Daniel Webster . . . with a Sketch of the Preceding Debate on the Resolution of Mr. Foot Respecting the Sale, &c, of Public Lands. Boston, 1830.

Speech of A. P. Butler, of South Carolina, on the Bill Providing for the Surrender of Fugitive Slaves. Washington, D.C., 1850.

Speech of B. F. Perry of South Carolina, in the National Democratic Convention at Charleston, S.C. N.p., n.d.

Speech of Daniel Wallace (of South Carolina) on the Slavery Question . . . April 8, 1850. Washington, D.C., 1850.

Speech of Emerson Etheridge of Tennessee. The Revival of the African Slave Trade and the President's Message . . . Feb. 21, 1857. Washington, D.C., 1857.

Speech of Henry Clay, in Defence of the American System, against the British Colonial System . . . Feb. 2d, 3d and 6th, 1832. Washington, D.C., 1832.

Speech of Honorable F. W. Pickens . . . July 7, 1851. Edgefield, S.C., 1851.

Speech of Hon. Lawrence M. Keitt of South Carolina, on the Organization of the House . . . Jan. 25, 1860. Washington, D.C., 1860.

Speech of Hon. M. L. Bonham of South Carolina, on the Election of Speaker . . . Dec. 16, 1859. N.p.

Speech of Hon. W. L. Yancey, Delivered in the Democratic State Convention, of the State of Alabama. Montgomery, Ala., 1860.

Speech of Hon. Wade Hampton on the Constitutionality of the Slave Trade Laws . . . Dec 10th 1859. Columbia, S.C., 1860.

Speech of Mr. Appleton, of Massachusetts, in Reply to Mr. McDuffie . . . 30th of May, 1832. Washington, D.C., 1832.

Speech of Mr. Blair, of South Carolina . . . May 1830 to Which Is Annexed an Address to His Constituents. Washington, D.C., 1830.

Speech of Mr. Butler, of South Carolina, on the Compromise Bill . . . July 9, 1850. N.p.

Speech of Mr. Butler . . . Reaffirming the Compromise Measures. N.p., n.d.

Speech of Mr. Calhoun of South Carolina in Senate March 13, 1840. N.p.

Speech of Mr. Ewing, of Ohio . . . Feb. 17 and 20, 1832. Washington, D.C., 1832.

Speech of Mr. Hamilton, of South Carolina on Mr. Randolph's Motion . . . 19 April, 1828. Washington, D.C., 1828.

Speech of Mr. Hamilton on the Tariff Bill . . . April 6th, 1824. Washington, D.C., 1824.

Speech of Mr. Hayne, of South Carolina, against the Tariff Bill . . . April 1824. Charleston, S.C., 1824.

Speech of Mr. J. A. Woodward of South Carolina, on the Relations between the United States and Their Territorial Districts . . . July 3, 1848. Washington, D.C., 1847.

Speech of Mr. Lewis, of Alabama . . . June 15, 1832. Washington, D.C., 1832.

Speech of Mr. Livingstone, of Louisiana, on Mr. Foot's Resolution . . . Feb. 20, 1830. Charleston, S.C., 1830.

Speech of Mr. Lowndes on the Tariff Bill . . . April 24, 1820. N.p., n.d.

Speech of Mr. McCord at a Meeting of the Inhabitants in the Town Hall of Columbia . . . 2nd July, 1827. Columbia, S.C., 1827.

Speech of Mr. McDuffie, of South Carolina . . . Feb. 7, 1827. Washington, D.C., 1827.

Speech of Mr. McDuffie . . . April, 1828. Washington, D.C., 1828.

Speech of Mr. McDuffie . . . April 1830. Columbia, S.C., 1830.

Speech of Mr. McDuffie of South Carolina, on the Bill Proposing a Reduction of the Duties on Imports . . . May 28, 1832. Washington, D.C., 1832.

Speech of Mr. Mitchell of South Carolina, on a Motion to Postpone Indefinitely, the Tariff Bill . . . April 15, 1828. Washington, D.C., 1828.

Speech of Mr. Poinsett, of South Carolina on the Tariff Bill . . . April 8, 1824. Washington, D.C., 1824.

Speech of Mr. Stewart, of Pennsylvania . . . June 5, 1832. Washington, D.C., 1832.

Speech of Mr. Thomas T. Bouldin of Virginia . . . June, 1832. Washington, D.C., 1832.

Speech of O. M. Dantzler, Esq. . . . Oct. 24, 1851. Columbia, S.C., 1851.

Speech of R. Barnwell Rhett on the Resolution Submitted by Mr. Foot . . . Dec. 15th and 16th 1851. Washington, D.C., 1851.

Speech of the Hon. Benjamin F. Perry of Greenville District. Charleston, S.C., 1851.

Speech of the Honorable D. C. Jarnette . . . Jan. 10, 1861. N.p., n.d.

Speech of the Honorable Felix Grundy (of Tennessee) . . . on Mr. Clay's Resolution. Washington, D.C., 1832.

Speech of the Honorable George McDuffie, at a Public Dinner Given to Him by the Citizens of Charleston . . . May 19, 1831. Charleston, S.C., 1831.

Speech of the Honorable I. E. Holmes . . . Sep. 3, 1850. Washington, D.C., 1850.

Speech of the Honorable James Henry Hammond of South Carolina, on the Relation of States . . . May 21, 1860. Washington, D.C., 1860.

Speech of the Honorable John C. Calhoun . . . Aug. 5, 1842. Washington, D.C., 1842.

Speech of the Honorable Langdon Cheves, Delivered before the Delegates of the Nashville Convention. Columbia, S.C., 1850.

Speech of the Honorable Peleg Sprague (of Maine) . . . on Clay's Resolution in Relation to the Tariff. Washington, D.C., 1832.

Speech of the Honorable Robert Barnwell Rhett . . . on the Oregon Territory Bill. Washington, D.C., 1847.

Speech of the Honorable Stephen D. Miller (of South Carolina) . . . on Mr. Clay's Resolution in Relation to the Tariff. N.p.

Speech of the Honorable William L. Yancey of Alabama, Delivered in the National Democratic Convention . . . with the Protest of the Alabama Delegation. N.p., n.d.

Speech of the Honorable William Smith Delivered on Monday, Aug. 1, 1831 at a Meeting of the Citizens of Spartanburg District, Against the Doctrine of Nullification. Camden, S.C., 1831.

Speech of Winchester Graham on the Compromise Measures. N.p., n.d.

Speech on the Question of the Tariff, on the Interests of the South, and the Constitutional Means of Redressing Its Evils . . . by James Hamilton Jr. at a Public Dinner Given to Him by His Constituents of Colleton District. Charleston, S.C., 1828.

Speech upon the Foreign Slave Trade, before the Legislature of South Carolina, Esq. of Charleston. Columbia, S.C., 1858.

Starobin, Robert S., ed. *Denmark Vesey: The Slave Conspiracy of 1822.* Englewood Cliffs, N.J., 1970.

Statement of So Much of the Proceedings of the National Democratic Convention at Charleston, April, 1860, as Lead to the Withdrawal of the Delegates from Certain States. N.p., n.d.

Stephens, Alexander H. *A Constitutional View of the Late War between the States; Its Causes, Character, Conduct and Results.* 2 vols. Philadelphia, Pa., 1868, 1870.

Stirling, James. *Letters from the Slave States.* London, 1857.

Stoney, Samuel Gaillard, ed. "The Poinsett-Campbell Correspondence." *South Carolina Historical Magazine* 42 (Oct. 1941): 149–68.

Strictures on Nullification. N.p., n.d.

Stringfellow, Thornton. *Brief Examination of the Institution of Slavery.* Washington, D.C., 1850.

Stroyer, Jacob. *My Life in the South.* Salem, Mass., 1898.

Suppression of the African Slave Trade, The: Speech of Honorable Henry Wilson, of Massachusetts . . . May 21, 1860. Washington, D.C., 1860.

Tariff, The: Its True Character and Effects Practically Illustrated. Charleston, S.C., 1830.

Tariff Meeting of the Kershaw District. N.p., n.d.

Taylor, Rosser H., ed. "Letters Dealing with the Secession Movement in South Carolina." *Bulletin of Furman University* 16 (Dec. 1935).

Thomas, John P., ed. *The Carolina Tribute to Calhoun.* Columbia, S.C., 1857.

Thornwell, J. H. *The State of the Country: An Article Republished from the Southern Presbyterian Review.* Columbia, S.C., 1861.

Thoughts Suited to the Present Crisis . . . by James H. Thornwell. Columbia, S.C., 1850.

To the Democracy of the United States. N.p., n.d.

To the People. An Address in 5 Numbers . . . Union and State Rights Party. Charleston, S.C., 1830.

To the People of South Carolina . . . Union, State Rights and Jackson Party Oct, 25, 1832. N.p.

Towles, Louis P., ed. *A World Turned Upside Down: The Palmers of South Santee, 1818–1881.* Columbia, S.C., 1996.

Townsend, John. *The Doom of Slavery in the Union: And Its Safety Out of It.* Charleston, S.C., 1860.

———. *The South Alone Should Govern the South and African Slavery by Those Friendly to It.* Charleston, S.C., 1850.

———. *The Southern States, Their Present Peril and Their Certain Destiny: Why Do They Not Right Themselves? And So Fulfill Their Glorious Destiny.* Charleston, S.C., 1850.

Tracts for the Times, No. 1. N.p., n.d.

Tracts for the People, No. 1: South Carolina in 1832. N.p., n.d.

Tracts for the People, No. 2: South Carolina in 1850. N.p., n.d.

Tracts for the People, No. 3: State Secession. N.p., n.d.

Tracts for the People, No. 4: Allegiance. N.p., n.d.

Tracts for the People, No. 8: Behind and Before, What Is to Be Done? Charleston, S.C., 1851.

Tract No. 1: Containing the Resolutions of the Nashville Convention. N.p., 1851.

Tract No. 2: Mr. Douglas and the Doctrine of Coercion. N.p. [1860].

Tract No. 3: To the People of the South. Charleston, S.C., 1860.

Tract No. 5: The Interest in Slavery of the Southern Nonslaveholder. Charleston, S.C., 1860.

Trescot, William Henry. *The Position and Course of the South.* Charleston, S.C., 1850.

Trollope, Mrs. [Francis Milton]. *Domestic Manners of the Americans.* London, 1832.

Virginia and Kentucky Resolutions of 1798 and '99 . . . Calhoun's Address, Resolutions of the Several States in Relation to State Rights with Other Documents in Support of the Jeffersonian Doctrines of '98. Washington, D.C., 1832.

Wakelyn, Jon L., ed. *Southern Pamphlets on Secession, November 1860–April 1861.* Chapel Hill, N.C., 1996.

Walker, Robert J. "Nullification and Secession." *Continental Monthly,* Feb. 1863, 179–94.

Walker's Appeal in Four Articles by David Walker and an Address to the Slaves of the United States of America by Henry Highland Garnet. Reprint. New York, 1969.

Wanderer Case, The: The Speech of Hon. Henry R. Jackson of Savannah, Georgia. Atlanta, Ga., [1891].

Wilson, Clyde N., ed. *Selections from the Letters and Speeches of James H. Hammond of South Carolina.* Spartanburg, S.C., 1978.

———. *The Papers of John C. Calhoun.* Vols. 11–21. Columbia, S.C., 1978–93.

Wilson, Clyde N., and Shirley Bright Cook, eds. *The Papers of John C. Calhoun.* Vols. 22–24. Columbia, S.C., 1995–98.

Wilson, Clyde N., and W. Edwin Hemphill, eds. *The Papers of John C. Calhoun.* Vol. 10. Columbia, S.C., 1977.

Wilson, Henry. *History of the Rise and Fall of the Slave Power in America.* 3 vols. Boston, 1872–77.

Wilson, Rev. J. Leighton. *The Foreign Slave Trade: Can It Be Revived without Violating the Most Sacred Principles of Honor, Humanity and Religion? From the Southern Presbyterian Review.* N.p., 1859.

INDEX

Abbeville Banner, 127
Abbeville district, 20, 31, 34, 45, 58, 80, 130, 235
Abolition movement, 15, 31, 50, 59, 67, 79, 99, 134, 147, 258; literature mailing issue, 59–60; proslavery rhetoric on, 64, 66, 67, 73, 77–78, 81, 88–89, 92, 129, 224, 225; and nonextensionism, 69–70; vigilantism against, 79–80, 211–15; South Carolinians linked with, 80, 117; John Brown's raid and, 188, 207–8, 210, 213, 235; secessionist charges against, 191, 193, 224, 229, 231, 233–34
Adams, Charles F., 75
Adams, James H., 97, 113–14, 167, 184, 190, 235, 243, 251; and revival of African slave trade movement, 127, 130–31, 134, 135–36, 138, 173
Adams, John Quincy, 19, 26, 32
Adger, John B., 92, 103, 165–66
African Americans, 50, 70, 80, 83. *See also* Free blacks; Slavery; Slaves
African contract labor, 150
African Labor Supply Association, 140, 150
African Methodist Episcopal Church, 15
African slave trade revival movement, 1, 125–52, 153–86; economics of, 7, 128; arguments for, 127–29, 131, 132–33, 137, 144, 155, 178; and need for new slaves, 133, 135, 137, 141; arguments against, 133–34, 138, 140–42, 143, 180; sectional division over, 135, 173–78; support for, 136; spread of, 142–43; U.S.

constitutional power over, 149, 173; and Vicksburg convention, 149–51; and judicial nullification, 153, 170, 171, 173; Confederate ban on, 154, 183–85, 250; and *Echo* case, 155–58; and federal suppression, 158, 176, 178; smuggling activity of, 164; religious opposition to, 164–66, 180; moral condemnation of, 173–74; dissipation of, 181–86
African squadron, 126, 146–47, 175, 176
Agrarianism, 224, 233
Aiken, David, 148, 174
Aiken, William, 72
Aiken family, 232
Alabama, 53, 67, 71, 78, 83, 98, 143, 144, 145; platform, 75; and first secession crisis, 105, 107; secession by, 183, 250; disavowal of Democratic convention by, 196, 197, 200, 201; and secession movement, 220, 237, 238, 243, 249
Aldrich, Alfred P., 113, 115, 120–21, 205, 215, 231, 242
Alien and Sedition Acts, 21
All Saints Parish, 36
Allston, Benjamin, 225
Allston, R. F. W., 72, 104, 113, 159, 189
American Colonization Society, 80, 158, 166, 175–76, 177
American Revolution, 7, 140, 255
American system, 16, 31, 55
Amis des Noirs, 15
Anderson, Robert, 251–52, 253, 254, 257
Anderson district, 57, 73, 198

Anti-expansionists. *See* Non-
extentionists
Aristocracy, 34, 35, 90, 141, 225, 226,
243
Aristotle, 4, 87, 88, 90, 224, 256
Arkansas, 202, 203, 206
Armstrong, George D., 223
Ashmore, John, 195, 203, 209, 230,
240–41
Association of 1860, 232–33
Atchison, David, 67, 79
Avery, W. W., 201
Ayer, Lewis Malone, 76, 113, 115–16,
237

Bachman, John, 92, 244, 246
Bacot, Thomas W., 76
Bagby, George W., 183
Baltimore convention, 203, 206–7
Baptist church, 103, 166
Barker, Theodore G., 239, 244
Barksdale, Ethelbert, 182
Barnburner Democrats, 69, 75
Barnwell, Robert W., 73, 86, 97, 99,
104, 105, 109, 192; and secession,
51, 110, 111, 113, 116, 120, 121,
239, 250–51
Barnwell family, 242
Barnwell district, 36, 45, 73, 79–80,
114, 115, 120
Barrett, J. M., 80
Barrillon, John, 44
Bay, Judge, 58
Bayly, Thomas, 77
Beaufort, 45, 52, 204
Beauregard, P. G. T., 253
Bell, John, 207, 231
Bellinger, Edmund, 113, 127, 160–61
Benjamin, Judah P., 177, 185
Benton, Thomas, 69, 76, 79, 85, 96
Berrien, John M., 53, 67, 77, 78, 108
Bible, 15–16, 89, 91–92, 102, 103,
155, 165–66, 214, 224, 226, 246
Black, Jeremiah, 168, 170
Black, W. C., 237
Black belt, 46, 118, 120, 235
Blackstone, William, 24
Blair, James, 38, 44
Bledsoe, Albert Taylor, 223–24
Bluffton movement, 65
Bonham, Milledge Luke, 127, 136,

178, 192; and secession, 80, 230,
236, 239, 249; on southern nation-
alism, 210
Boozer, Lemuel, 202, 235
Border states, 52, 96, 99, 183, 187–
88, 234, 245, 250, 253, 254
Boyce, W. W., 111, 113, 134, 138, 171,
189, 210, 226; and slave trade
revival, 174, 178; moderation advo-
cacy of, 192, 195; and secession,
218, 230, 240, 250
Branch, John, 53
Breckinridge, John, 148, 207, 229–32,
236
Breckinridge, R. J., 245, 247
Brevard, Keziah, 214, 225, 250,
257–58
Brevard, T. N., 21
Brisbane, William H. ("Brutus"), 117
British West Indies, 59
Brookes, Iveson, 91–92, 102–3, 166,
211, 223
Brooks, Preston S., 174, 189; assault
on Sumner by, 130, 209, 225; on
slavery, 228; prophetic dream of,
258
Brown, Albert Gallatin, 175, 177, 194
Brown, Governor, 71
Brown, James, 79
Brown, John, 188, 207–8, 210–13,
215, 218, 229
Brown, John L., 79
Brown, Joseph E., 220
Bryan, Edward, 101–3, 113, 123, 162,
225; and slave trade revival, 37,
127, 132–34, 136, 140–41, 146–48,
179
Buchanan, James, 164, 168, 175, 176,
177, 189–90, 192, 200, 243; and
secession, 250–51, 252, 253
Buist, Henry, 237
Bunch, Robert, 137, 183, 211
Burt, Armistead, 34, 65, 68, 76, 89,
112, 189, 205, 249
Butler, Andrew Pickens, 26, 73, 76,
80, 99, 100, 127, 173; and nullifica-
tion, 34, 42; and conventions, 105,
121, 189; as cooperationist, 112,
113, 122
Butler, Benjamin F., 182, 201
Butler, P. M., 48

Butler, William, 76
Butler family, 14
Bynum, Turner, 44

Calhoun, Andrew P., 127, 148, 193,
  205, 238, 249
Calhoun, John A., 127
Calhoun, John C., 16, 17, 61, 67, 70,
  76; and Jackson, 19, 26, 27, 29, 30,
  32, 202; adroitness of, 19; state
  interposition theory of, 19, 43, 56;
  as vice president, 19; presidential
  ambitions of, 19–20, 30–31, 57,
  65–66, 71, 74, 76–77; as antitariff
  leader, 20–23; proslavery leadership by, 22–23, 64, 77–78, 87–88;
  secession justification by, 23,
  80–81, 86, 87, 246; state sovereignty doctrine, 23–24, 49, 58, 63,
  70–71, 87, 96, 190, 225, 247; and
  Webster-Hayne debate, 28; planter
  politician leadership by, 34, 64, 72,
  105; U.S. Senate seat of, 49, 109;
  and Clay tariff, 55, 57; and test
  oath, 59; political power of, 61; and
  Texas, 65–66; and Mexican War,
  66–67; and southern movement,
  67–68, 70–71, 77–79, 82, 93; and
  Oregon, 68–69, 88; and resolutions
  of 1847, 70; political legacy of, 77,
  86–90, 93, 98–99, 103, 116–18,
  127, 139, 147, 151, 159, 170, 188–
  89, 193, 200, 202, 215, 221, 223,
  225, 234, 245–47; and Benton,
  79, 85; on Compromise of 1850,
  84–85; deathbed pronouncement
  on slavery, 84–85, 96; death of,
  85–86; political writings by, 86;
  concurrent majority theory of,
  86–87, 189, 225; political thought
  of, 87–88; evocations of, 116–17;
  unionist backlash against, 118;
  and slave trade, 159. See also
  Nullification
Calhoun family, 14, 242
California statehood, 82–83, 84, 98,
  99, 105
Camden Weekly Journal, 21, 39, 60,
  127, 137, 155, 178–79, 215
Campbell, John Archibald, 98, 101–2
Capers, William, 112

Capitalism, 90
Carey, Matthew, 31
Cartwright, Samuel, 223–24
Cass, Lewis, 74, 76, 146
Castle Pinckney, 52, 54, 252
Catholic Church, 165
Central America, 125, 156, 162
Central Southern Rights Association
  of South Carolina, 111
Central State Committee of Safety
  and Vigilance, 81, 82
Charleston, S.C., 40, 79, 135, 141,
  213; antitariff meeting, 35; unionist and nullifier division in, 39–40,
  44; election of 1832, 44, 45; federal
  troops in, 48, 52, 251–52; nullifier
  meeting, 54; support for Calhoun
  in, 72–73; and first secession crisis,
  110, 114, 116, 117, 119; Kansas association of, 130; Echo case in, 154–
  57; proslavery ideology in, 200;
  secessionist activity in, 236, 241,
  243; unionist and secessionist division in, 239
Charleston Arsenal, 252
Charleston Chamber of Commerce,
  18
Charleston City Gazette, 39
Charleston convention, 144, 198–
  202, 237
Charleston Courier, 36, 39–40, 100,
  114, 190; on slave trade movement,
  134, 137, 139, 146, 159–60, 184;
  on Echo case, 155–56; on Wanderer
  case, 169, 171; on squatter sovereignty, 196; on Democratic convention, 200; on slavery, 228; and
  Perry, 231
Charleston Evening News, 114, 159,
  163, 190
Charleston Mercury, 34, 40–41, 67,
  72, 75, 126, 127, 166, 203, 208,
  229, 235, 248; as official nullifier/
  secessionist organ, 17–18; and
  Colleton, 20; on Hayne-Webster
  debate, 29; on Wilmot Proviso, 73;
  and Calhoun, 74, 88; and Nashville
  convention, 98; and secession, 115,
  219, 236, 244, 246; on slave trade
  movement, 129, 131, 134, 136–37,
  146, 149, 159–60, 163, 178–79,

184; on *Echo* case, 157–58, 161; and Democratic politics, 191, 193, 195, 197, 199–201; and Lecompton, 192–93; "Slaveholder" articles, 213; and Hammond, 230–32; and Sumter, 252–54

Chartism, 88

Cheraw, S.C., 117, 193

Cheraw Gazette, 155

Chesnut, James, 113, 134, 138, 167, 171, 208; and slave trade revival, 176–77, 184; and slave code proposal, 195, 196; proslavery argument by, 227; and secession, 236, 237, 240, 250

Chesnut family, 242

Chester district, 45, 57, 73

Chesterfield district, 44, 45, 47, 73, 204; test oath opposition in, 57; and first secession vote, 110, 119

Cheves, Langdon, 26, 37–38, 85–86, 89, 109, 121; and Nashville convention, 97, 104–5; and single secession, 111

Cheves family, 242

Christ Church Parish, 45, 179, 204, 447

Christy, David, 223

Civil War, 12, 63, 154, 173, 184–85, 215–18; sectional crises leading to, 1; S.C. principles and, 19, 220; upper South unionism during, 188; desertions by unionists during, 241; first shot of, 252, 254; and former slaves in Union Army, 257–58. *See also* Confederacy; Expansion of slavery; Proslavery ideology; Secession

Clarendon district, 44–45, 47

Clark, James, 43–44, 74

Clark, Rufus, 180

Clay, Cassius, 78

Clay, Clement C., 55, 175, 176, 177

Clay, Henry, 32, 75, 76, 85; on American system, 16, 31; and nullification, 49; and tariff bill compromise, 54–55, 56, 57; gradual abolition of slavery proposal of, 78; and Compromise of 1850, 83, 98–99; and Nashville conventions, 96

Clayton, John, 69, 126

Clemens, Jeremiah, 83, 106

Clergy: slavery justifications by, 64, 91–92, 102–3, 112, 223–24, 226; as critics of slave trade revival, 164–66, 180; secession justifications by, 246–48; on Civil War reversals, 258

Clingman, Thomas L., 83, 175

Clotilde (slaver ship), 164

Clowney, William, 58

Cobb, Howell, 79, 83, 106, 162–63, 168, 236, 243

Colcock, C. J., 48

Colcock, W. F., 113–14, 162, 236, 238

College of Charleston, 158

Colleton District, 34, 35, 44, 45

Colleton letters, 20

Colonization, 15, 19, 38, 80. *See also* American Colonization Society

Colquitt, Walter, 67, 106

Columbia, S.C. 34, 35, 43, 47, 52, 81, 236–37, 238, 243

Columbia *Carolina Times*, 159

Columbia convention, 199, 204

Columbia memorial, 17, 18

Columbia *South Carolinian*, 155, 159, 230, 232

Columbia Telescope, 36

Commander, J. M., 75

Commercial Review of the South and West. See *De Bow's Review*

Committee of Judiciary, 175

Committee of Twenty One, 121

Committee on Federal Relations, 41, 132, 147, 179–80, 216

Committee on the Colored Population, 129, 132

Compendium (Helper), 209

Compromise of 1850, 1, 83–85, 95, 96–100, 103, 105, 107, 111, 113, 115, 151

Concurrent majority theory, 86–87, 118, 189, 225, 246

Confederacy, 1, 9, 57, 243, 248, 249; and first secession crisis, 112; and prohibition of foreign slave trade, 154, 183–85; slavery as central to, 250; provisional constitution and government of, 250, 254; as counterrevolutionary, 255–56. *See also* Civil War

Congress, Confederate, 183, 184, 185
Congress, U.S., 70, 99–100, 104, 149,
    192, 195; tariff debates in, 19–20,
    31–32; nullifier speeches in, 34, 35;
    and Calhoun's Senate seat, 49, 109;
    Texas annexation vote by, 66; Cal-
    houn resolution on role of, 70;
    and slavery in territories, 71, 194;
    Compromise of 1850 vote by, 99;
    Brooks's assault on Sumner in, 130,
    209, 225; and African slave trade,
    149, 157, 158, 171, 173–79; and
    slavery, 158, 167, 194–97; and
    House speakership controversy,
    208–10; pre-secession atmosphere
    in, 209–10; proslavery speeches in,
    226, 228; and secession resolu-
    tions, 237
Conner, Henry W., 55, 67, 72–73
Conner, James, 156–57, 160, 168,
    170–71, 236, 238
Conscience Whigs, 75
Conservativism, 7, 9, 16, 24, 87, 91,
    120, 122–23, 224–25, 244, 248,
    255, 256
Constitution, Confederate, 154, 183–
    85, 253; critics of, 250
Constitution, U.S., 21, 117, 227, 231;
    and slavery, 9, 98, 100, 104, 128,
    148–50, 157, 161, 177, 179, 181,
    254; and nullification, 23, 49,
    55–56; and states' rights, 24; Cal-
    houn cites, 24, 86–87; and seces-
    sionists, 25, 63, 106, 189–91, 231,
    238, 245–46, 248–49, 251, 254;
    tariff debate and, 26, 32; and
    Hayne-Webster debate, 28, 29; and
    expansion of slavery, 70, 71; and
    African slave trade, 128, 148–49,
    150, 157–58, 171, 177; and com-
    merce power, 157; interpretation
    of by Douglas, 181
Constitutional Democrats, 202, 206
Constitutionalism, 10
Constitutional Union Party, 106, 207
Cooper, Thomas, 17, 18, 22, 34, 37,
    54; on Declaration of Indepen-
    dence, 88–89; influence of, 103
Cooperation Party, 113–17, 118–22,
    242
Cooswatchie, S.C., 36

Co-property doctrine, 123, 127
Corley, Simeon, 190
Corrie, William, 163–64, 169–72
Corwin, Thomas, 114
Cotton, 10–12, 183, 223; boom of
    1850s, 11–12, 128; tariff issue and,
    16, 31, 35, 44
Cotton Is King (Elliot), 223
Couper, Hamilton, 168–69
Cralle, R. K., 81
Crawford, Samuel Wylie, 252, 257
Crawford, William H., 16
Crittenden, John J., 96
Crook, A. B., 212, 240
Cuba, 126, 159, 163, 222; proposed
    annexation of, 128, 130, 146, 176
Cunningham, John, 130, 134, 159,
    179, 190, 192, 198, 238
Cunningham, Richard, 40
Cushing, Caleb, 200

Dalcho, Frederick, 15–16
Dallas, George M., 74
Dantzler, D. M., 179–80
Dantzler, O. M., 120, 127, 132
Dargan, George, 113
Darlington district, 44, 45, 47, 73
Davis, Benjamin, 163
Davis, Jefferson, 67, 106, 167, 194,
    203, 253; and slave trade, 144, 176,
    177, 185
Davis, John, 68
Davis, Warren, 25, 34, 58
Deas, J. S., 18
De Bow, James D. B., 71–72, 90, 92,
    102, 238; and slave trade revival,
    126, 139, 146, 150; proslavery argu-
    ments of, 139, 234; on suffrage,
    225
De Bow's Review, 71–72, 139, 143, 215
Declaration of Independence: Cal-
    houn on, 88–89; proslavery read-
    ing of, 224; proslavery attacks on,
    226, 227, 244, 247, 255
Deep South, 95, 96, 125, 142
Defence of the South, A (Brooks), 103
Delaware, 52, 77, 83, 96, 149, 250
Della Torre, Peter, 73, 101–2, 112
Delony, Edward, 143
Democracy: rejection in S.C. of, 2–3,
    9, 10, 13–14, 26–27, 60–61, 123,

225–26, 236; proslavery discourse against, 5, 7, 88–89, 148, 224–27, 228, 234; Calhoun argues against, 22–23, 24, 34, 87, 88; Hayne-Webster debate on, 27–28; nullifier discourse on, 35. *See also* Jacksonian democracy; Majority rule; Representation
Democratic Party, 26, 50, 68, 99, 231, 232; as southern-northern alliance, 50; and Texas annexation, 65, 66; and extension of slavery, 69; and Wilmot Proviso, 71; and Cass candidacy, 74, 76; and 1848 presidential election, 74–76; southern members of, 75, 79, 106, 190–95, 216; southern state conventions, 78, 182, 197; unionists in, 79; post-1850 southern resurgence of, 122, 123; in S.C., 122, 188–89, 193, 196–98, 227; as proslavery, 123, 190–91; and slave trade revival, 125–38, 143, 148, 150, 160; and Kansas debate, 130; and secession, 134, 230; and *Wanderer* case, 171; differences over slavery in, 174, 180, 188–201; Charleston convention, 181–82, 193, 196–200, 202–3, 206, 237; national vs. states' rights factions in, 188; and planter politicians, 188, 191, 200, 229; sectionalism of, 188, 193–95; national convention, 197–203, 206–7; Cincinnati popular sovereignty platform of, 200–201; breakup of, 200–203, 207; Baltimore convention, 203, 206–7; Richmond convention, 203–4, 206–7; and speakership controversy, 209; and Breckinridge candidacy, 229; and slaveholders, 229–30
Democratic republicanism, 50
Denmark Vesey conspiracy, 15, 207, 213
DeSaussure, Henry W., 25
DeSaussure, W. F., 67–68, 72
DeSaussure family, 242
Deseret, Utah, 98, 106
De Treville, Richard, 160–61
Dew, Thomas R., 15, 26, 31
Dickinson, Daniel S., 74

Dickson, Richard, 163
Discourse on the Constitution and Government of the United States, A (Calhoun), 86–87
Disquisition on Government, A (Calhoun), 86
District of Columbia, 73, 76–77, 78, 82, 83, 98, 99
Disunion. *See* Secession
Dolphin (U.S.S.), 154, 156, 160
Domestic slave trade, 106, 165
Doolittle, James R., 223
Dorrism, 88
Douglas, Stephen A., 99, 181, 203, 206, 209, 228, 230, 231; and illegal slave trade, 164, 182; southern Democratic opposition to, 192–201 passim, 234; presidential candidacy of, 206
Drayton, William Henry, 31, 36–38, 57, 59
Dred Scott decision, 69, 137, 156–57, 190–91, 194–95, 199, 223
Dubignon family, 164, 168
Du Bois, W. E. B., 7, 125, 151
Dudley, C. W., 113
Dueling, 38, 44, 169
Dwight, Timothy, 25

E. A. Rawlins (slaver ship), 163–64
Easley, William K., 240
"East Bay" (pen name), 235
Eaton, John, 27
Eaton, Peggy, 27
Echo case, 154–62, 167–68, 171, 172, 174–75, 177, 180
"Edgefield" (pen name), 158
Edgefield Advertiser, 159, 196
Edgefield district, 34, 36, 44, 45, 73, 79, 120, 164, 167, 168, 198, 235
Egalitarianism, 25, 88, 91, 226, 228; and secession, 255–56. *See* Democracy
1828 Exposition (Calhoun), 21–23, 25, 26
1860 Association, 232–33
Election of 1832, 44–46
Election of 1834, 58
Election of 1848, 74–76
Election of 1856, 189–90

Election of 1860, 181–82, 195, 196, 235; Democratic politics in, 197–207; as precipitating secession, 229, 236. *See also* Democratic Party; Republican Party

Elections of 1850–51, 107, 119–20

Elliot, E. N., 223

Elliot, J. H., 165

Elliot, William, 26, 116, 232, 239

Ellis, John W., 220

Elmore, Franklin Harper, 65, 72, 80, 81, 86, 97

Elmore, John A., 243

Emancipation, 15, 19, 59, 129, 146, 214, 233; Calhoun on, 78; Seward on, 85; Townsend on, 233–34; Marx on, 258

England, Bishop John, 165

English, Thomas R., 42

English compromise bill (1858), 192

Etheridge, Emerson, 173–74

Evans, D. R., 18

Evans, Josiah J., 122, 134

Everett, Edward, 207, 231

Ewart, David, 223

Ewing, Senator, 31

Expansion of slavery, 1, 7, 63–77, 88, 96, 123, 163, 174, 175, 187, 201, 218, 221, 223; Northwest Ordinance on, 28; state sovereignty and, 63; annexation of Texas and, 65–66; Oregon and, 66, 69–70, 79, 88; nonextension principle and, 69–70; sectional divisions over, 69–70, 83, 123, 126; Taylor and, 82–83; first secession movement and, 93, 105, 106; African slave trade movement and, 125–33, 135, 136, 137, 141, 153; Kansas wars and, 129–30, 137, 141–42, 173, 191–93, 201; filibustering and, 162; as secession issue, 187, 200–201, 249; as northern-southern issue, 192, 201; southern demands for, 194–97, 206–7. *See also* Compromise of 1850; Popular sovereignty; Wilmot Proviso

Fairfield district, 44, 45, 73, 74, 79, 110, 120

Farnum (seaman), 168–69

Farrow, James, 138, 151, 171–72, 199, 240

Faust, Drew, 4

Federalism, 9, 10, 24, 25, 28, 35

Federalist paper No. 10 (Madison), 25

Felder, John M., 32

Filibustering, 162

Fillmore, Millard, 76, 99, 108, 114

Filmer, Sir Robert, 39

Fire-eaters, 97, 154, 167, 182, 194, 201, 204, 236

First secession crisis, 1, 64, 93, 95–124, 221; agenda of, 104–5; factions, 109–20

Fitzhugh, George, 87, 126, 140–41, 149, 227; "southern thought" of, 222, 223, 224, 225, 236; and "state nationality," 234; on secession, 255–56

Florida, 27, 67, 71, 75, 78, 105, 150, 161, 177, 253; withdrawal of from Democratic convention, 202; and secession movement, 220, 237, 243, 249; secession by, 250

Floyd, John, 53, 78

Floyd, John B., 78, 252

Foote, Henry S., 83, 99, 106, 143, 150–51

Force Bill. *See* Wilkins Act of 1833

Ford, Timothy, 25

Fort Hill Address (Calhoun), 23, 30

Fort Hill plantation, 44

Fort Johnson, 252

Fort Moultrie, 251, 252

Fort Pickens, 253

Fort Sumter, 157, 188, 251–54, 256–58

Franklin, Benjamin, 256

Free blacks, 6, 15, 80, 83, 213, 214

Free labor, 90–91

Free Soil Party, 64, 75, 83, 88, 189

Free trade. *See* Tariff controversy

Free Trade Convention (1831), 31

Fremont, John C., 130, 190

French Revolutions, 255

Fugitive slave laws, 73, 78, 83, 84, 98, 99–100, 106, 107, 179, 218, 223, 249

Fuller, Richard, 91

Furman, J. C., 240, 246

Furman, Richard, 15–16
Furman family, 242

Gadsden, C. P., 165
Gadsden, James, 75, 76
Gadsden family, 241
Gag Rule, 64
Gaillard, Franklin, 205
Ganahl, George, 168–69
Garlington, A. C., 193, 205, 217
Garnett, Muscoe R. H., 101, 200
Garrisonian abolitionism, 15
Gary, Martin Witherspoon, 215, 230
Gavin, David, 212, 225
Gender inequality, 5, 90, 227
Georgetown, S.C., 45, 52, 130, 213
Georgia, 16, 50–51, 53, 67, 71, 75, 78, 83; secession movement in, 105, 220, 237, 243, 249–50; and slave trade revival, 143, 144; and *Wanderer* case, 163–64, 168–69, 170; secession by, 183, 250; and Southern Address, 203
Georgia Assembly, 26
Georgia convention, 105, 106–7, 110
Gibson, Samuel R., 47–48
Gidding, Joshua, 83
Gilman, Catherine, 251
Girardeau, J. R., 18
Gist, W. H., 111, 113, 181, 198, 209, 213–20, 235, 237, 243, 251
Glover, T. W., 18
Gordon, George A., 156–57
Goulden, W. B., 144–45, 182
Gourdin, Henry, 72, 239
Gourdin, Robert N., 200, 203, 232, 234, 235–36, 239, 243
Gray, Henry D., 67
Gray, Peter W., 143
Grayson, William J., 34, 41, 60, 91, 107–8, 113, 232, 247
Great Britain, 146–47, 176, 183, 211
Greeley, Horace, 140
Green, Duff, 19, 65, 72
Greenville district, 12, 34, 43, 44, 45, 47, 79, 80; unionism in, 51, 52, 59, 212, 240–41; test oath opposition in, 57, 58; anti-Wilmot Proviso meetings, 74; and first secession crisis, 111, 114, 119; and secession, 240–42

Greenville Mountaineer, 29, 38, 41, 57, 114
Greenville Republican, 38
Gregg, Maxcy, 97, 111, 113, 120–21, 127, 158, 160, 193, 243; "Appeal to the State Rights Party of South Carolina, An," 158, 193
Gregory XVI, Pope, 165
Grier, R. C., 80
Griffin, R. C., 238
Grimké, Thomas S., 38, 40, 58
Grow, Galusha, 209

Habeas corpus writ, 155–56, 157
Haitian revolution, 14–15
Hale, John P., 173
Halstead, Murat, 201–2, 206
Ham, curse of, 92, 103
Hamburg meeting, 114
Hamilton, D. H., 115, 154, 156, 168, 172, 216, 218, 236; changes view of slave trade, 154; on unionism of yeomanry, 212–13
Hamilton, James, Jr. ("Sugar Jimmy"), 23, 27, 34, 38, 41, 85, 116; and Vesey conspiracy, 15; and nullification doctrine, 20; and nullification, 36–37, 47–48, 54; on single secession, 108, 110
Hamlin, Hannibal, 207, 229
Hammond, James Henry, 34, 37, 43, 44, 51, 54, 57, 59, 60, 65, 71, 74–76, 79, 80, 86, 110, 112, 122, 175, 181, 200, 205, 207, 223, 240; and Mexican territory, 66–67; on southern Whigs, 77; and Seward, 85, 232; proslavery arguments of, 89, 90, 92, 208, 228; defense of aristocracy by, 90, 226; and Nashville convention, 97–98, 104; and Rhetts, 100, 137, 184; and secession, 105, 109, 111, 113, 139, 230–32, 239; and southern congress elections, 120; on democracy, 123; and James H. Adams defeat, 134; and slave trade revival, 138–39, 167, 176–77; and *Wanderer* case, 171–72; and Kansas, 192; and slave code proposal, 195; and Lecompton, 196; and Charleston convention, 198; and Richmond conven-

tion, 204; resignation from Senate by, 237

Hammond, M. C. M., 127, 132

Hammond family, 242

Hampton, Wade, 72, 109, 180, 238

Hampton family, 14

Hanckel, Thomas, 234

Harper, Robert G., 143

Harper, William, 31, 34, 37, 39, 58; as nullification theorist, 15; and nullification crisis, 48, 56; slavery justification by, 89–91, 123, 223

Harpers Ferry raid, 188, 207–8, 210, 213, 218, 235

Harris, David Golighty, 240–42

Hartford convention, 10, 25, 28, 36

Harvey, James, 114

Hayne, Isaac W., 42, 59, 72, 97, 157, 204–5, 217, 232, 253

Hayne, Robert Y., 20, 21, 32, 35, 36, 73, 76, 120; and Vesey conspiracy, 15; and debate with Webster, 27–29; on tyrannical majority, 34; and nullification, 48, 51–52; as governor, 49, 58; slavery defense by, 74; and single vs. joint secession, 116

Hayne family, 242

Hayne-Webster debate (1830), 27–29

Helper, Hinton Rowan, 209–10, 212, 215, 218, 229

Hemphill, James, 165

Hemphill, John, 35

Hemphill, R. N., 242

Hemphill, William, 38

Henry, Robert, 112

Heyward, Nathaniel, 72

Heyward family, 241

Hicks, Governor, 219

Hill, William R., 42, 59, 82

Hilliard, Henry W., 83, 106, 143, 148

Hodge, Charles, 223, 247

Hoke, David, 238, 240

Holland, Edwin C., 15

Holmes, George Frederick, 223

Holmes, I. E., 73, 76, 103

Holt, Joseph, 252–53

Holt, J. S., 151

Homestead Act, 174, 233

Honor, 6–7, 64, 74, 81, 96

Hooker, Charles E., 243

Horry district, 44, 45, 47, 51, 57, 110, 115, 119

House of Representatives. *See* Congress, U.S.

Houston, David Franklin, 19

Houston, Sam, 69, 79, 99, 143, 219

Huger, Alfred, 47, 167; on mailing abolitionist literature, 59–60; anti-democratic outlook of, 87, 225; on Brooks's assault on Sumner, 130; and disunion, 190, 208; and Democratic conventions, 199, 205; and speakership controversy, 210

Huger, Daniel E., 38, 42, 47, 57, 59

Hughes, Henry, 126, 140, 142, 150

Humphreys, John, 150

Hunnicutt, James W., 245

Hunter, John L., 41

Hunter, R. M. T., 175, 217

Huston, William, 122

Impending Crisis, The (Helper), 209, 212

Inglis, John, 244

Internal improvements, 16, 30, 65

Interstate slave trade, 106, 165

Jackson, Andrew, 28, 30, 56, 76, 193, 219; and Calhoun, 19, 26, 27, 29, 30, 32, 202; nullification opposition by, 27, 29–30, 32, 49–55, 57; and states' rights, 29; and S.C. unionists, 29, 37. *See also* Jacksonian democracy

Jackson, Henry R., 168–69

Jacksonian democracy, 2, 14, 26, 27, 29, 38, 87, 187; nature of, 50–51; death of, 207

Jacobs, Ferdinand, 91

Jamison, D. F., 73, 97, 108, 113, 192, 205–6, 243, 253, 257

Jarnette, D. C., 245

Jefferson, Thomas, 17, 20–21, 24, 27, 30, 88, 89, 91, 102, 148

Jeffersonian republicanism, 4, 25, 53

Johnson, David, 68, 72, 79, 113

Johnson, John, 163

Johnson, Judge, 58

Joint Committee on the Military, 213

Jones, Charles Colcock, 144–45

Jones, James, 120

Journal of Commerce, 137
Judicial nullification, 73, 153–86
Judiciary Act of 1789, 20, 49

Kansas, conflict over, 126–30, 137,
    141–42, 173, 191–93, 201; and
    Lecompton constitution, 191–92
Kansas-Nebraska Act, 127, 139, 174,
    188, 189
Keitt, Laurence M., 73, 109, 123, 128,
    209–10, 214, 252; and secession,
    80, 113–14, 115, 138, 230, 238,
    243, 250; and social inequality, 90,
    226; and slave trade revival, 127,
    136, 174, 178; and Kansas, 173,
    192; and Democratic state conven-
    tion, 189; and Calhoun monument,
    215
Keitt, Susanna, 200, 209–10
Kennedy, John Pendleton, 245
Kentucky, 78–79, 96, 149, 250
Kentucky Resolutions (1798, 1799),
    21, 28, 29
Kershaw district, 45, 47, 59, 79, 204,
    235
Kilgore, David, 176
King, Preston, 68, 69
King, William R., 106
Klein, Rachel, 13
Know Nothing movement, 130
Knoxville convention (1857), 146
Knoxville *Southern Citizen,* 142
Kossuth, Louis, 122

Lafitte and Co., 162, 163
Lamar, Charles A. L., 155, 162–64,
    167–69, 176
Lancaster district, 44, 45, 47–48, 51,
    119; test oath opposition in, 57,
    58–59; cooperationists in, 114
Lane, Joseph, 207, 229
Lathers, Richard, 239
Laurens district, 36, 45, 73, 79, 120
Lecompton constitution, 191–96,
    200, 228
Lee, John, 239
Legaré, Hugh Swinton, 26–27, 38,
    40, 59
Leigh, Benjamin Watkins, 53, 56
Lesesne, Henry, 107, 229, 237
Letcher, John O., 218

Lewis, Dixon, 53, 67
Lexington district, 44, 45, 202
Liberalism, 5, 25
Liberia, 166, 175–76
Liberty: Calhoun on, 87; proslavery
    views of, 88–89, 91, 224, 256
Liberty Party, 75
Lieber, Francis, 107, 110, 117, 157,
    246; on slave trade by, 154,
    166–67
Lieber, Oscar, 157, 167, 181, 222
Lincoln, Abraham, 7, 28, 50, 172,
    180, 256; and presidency, 182, 188,
    207, 214, 219–20, 232–33, 236,
    245; southern attacks on, 229–31,
    233, 235, 237, 247; and secession
    crisis, 251; proclamation of war by,
    254
Litchfield Law School, 25
Livingston, Edward, 29
Locke, John, 256
London, D. H., 219
Louisiana, 29, 53, 67, 96, 142–43,
    145, 234; secession by, 183, 250;
    withdrawal from Democratic
    convention, 202; and Southern
    Address, 203; and secession move-
    ment, 249–50
Lovejoy, Joseph P., 179
Lowcountry, 9–12, 25, 44, 47, 57, 79,
    107, 109, 114, 115, 119–20, 127
Lower South, 95, 97, 106, 145, 149,
    151–52; judicial nullification in,
    154–55; secession movement in,
    187, 219, 221, 249–50, 254
Lowndes, Charles T., 72
Lowndes, Rawlins, 158
Lowndes, William, 16, 26
Lowndes family, 14, 232
Loyalty oath. *See* Test oath
Lynchings, 211, 212

McAliley, Samuel, 237–38
McClernand, John A., 209
McCord, David J., 17
McCord, Louisa, 89, 90, 92, 114
McCrady, Edward, 58, 121, 132, 230
McCready v. Hunt, 58
McDaniel, James, 58
McDaniel v. McMeekin, 58
McDonald, Charles, 67, 104, 106

McDuffie, George, 16, 17, 32, 34, 35, 48, 55, 60, 65
McGhee, Capt., 163
McGimsey, J. W. P., 144
McGowan, Samuel, 189, 237
McKendree church, 97
McLane, Louis, 52
Macon, Nathaniel, 53
McQueen, John, 80, 113, 174, 189, 192–93, 230
Madison, James, 21, 25, 49, 56
Maffite, Lt., 154
Magrath, Andrew G., 76, 162, 173, 192, 202, 239, 253; judicial nullification by, 153, 170, 171, 173; and *Echo* case, 156, 157, 160; and *Wanderer* case, 169–72, 181–82; and secession, 172, 236, 238, 240
Majority rule, 10; and Calhoun, 22–26, 85, 87; and Jackson, 27, 50; nullifier discourse on, 34; unionist support for, 39; proslavery opposition to, 224, 234. *See also* Concurrent majority theory; Democracy
Mallory, Stephen R., 177
Mangum, Willie P., 83
Manigault, Gabriel Edward, 72, 127, 135, 184, 248
Manigault family, 14, 242
Manning, John L., 72, 137, 249
Manning, Richard I., 43
Manning family, 14, 242
Marion district, 45, 119
Marlboro district, 44, 45
Martin, W. D., 36
Martin, W. E., 193, 204–5, 227, 229
Martineau, Harriet, 59, 90
Marx, Karl, 256, 258
Maryland, 53, 96, 149, 250
Mason, E. G., 200
Mason, James, 67, 84, 176–77, 208, 217
Mason, John Y., 55
Maysville veto, 30
Mazyck, Alexander, 136, 147–49; and slave trade revival, 127, 132–33, 134, 179, 180; and *Echo* case, 158–59; and Confederate Constitution, 184; and secession, 190, 216–17, 237, 243
Meagher, Timothy, 164

Means, John H., 74, 80, 109, 113, 120, 121, 204, 243
Mechanics, 6
Memminger, Christopher G., 36, 38, 52, 74, 109; and secession, 116–17, 216–19, 240, 250; as Pierce supporter, 122; and Brown execution, 208; and southern convention, 239; and secession convention report, 248–49
Methodist church, 103
Mexican antislavery laws, 70, 83
Mexican War, 66–67, 69, 75
Middle Passage, 154
Middleton, Henry, 47
Middleton, John Izard, 127, 132, 184, 190, 205
Middleton, N. R., 72
Middleton, Williams, 229–30
Middleton family, 14, 232, 241–42
Miles, William Porcher, 89, 123, 138, 172, 181; and secession, 80, 191, 198, 209, 216–18, 236, 240, 243, 250; and slave trade revival, 127, 136; and Kansas, 192; and election of 1860, 229, 231; and Sumter, 252–53
Militia, 57–58
Militia Act of 1833, 57
Milledgeville convention, 53
Miller, C. W., 127, 137
Miller, Stephen D., 18, 19, 31, 43, 48; as U.S. Senate candidate, 37–38; and test oath, 57
Minority veto. *See* Nullification
Minute Men for the Defence of Southern Rights, 235–37, 239
Mississippi, 53, 67, 71, 83, 97, 152, 197, 234; and first secession crisis, 105, 106, 107; secession by, 183, 250; and Democratic convention, 202, 206; and secession movement, 219–20, 237, 243, 249
Mississippi platform, 81–82
Missouri, 67, 78, 79, 96, 149, 250
Missouri Compromise, 68, 69, 98, 127, 148, 172, 197
Missouri crisis, 10, 14, 15–16, 24
Missouri line. *See* Missouri Compromise
Mitchell, Nelson, 239

Monarchism, 34, 39
Monroe, James, 27, 148
Montgomery convention, 148–49, 178, 250
Mood, Asbury, 240
Moore, A. B., 144, 220, 243
Moore, Thomas O., 220
Moses, F. I., 208
Mountain unionists. *See* Greenville district; Yeoman farmers

Nashville conventions, 96–98, 103–6, 109
Natchez Free Trader, 143
National Era (periodical), 88
Nationalism. *See* Southern nationalism
Nativism, 130, 196
Natural rights, 88, 224, 226, 256
Negro Seamen's Act, 15
Newberry district, 45, 114, 214, 242
New Mexico, 82, 83, 98, 106, 145
New Orleans Courier, 126
New Orleans Delta, 142
New York, 53
New York resolutions, 180
New York Times, 182, 245
New York Yacht Club, 163, 169
Niagara, U.S.S., 157–58, 174
Nixon, Henry G., 36
Nonextentionists, 64, 67, 69–70, 75
Nonslaveholders: increase in numbers of, 128, 135; southern loyalty of questioned, 210, 212; secessionist propaganda on, 234. *See also* Yeoman farmers
North Carolina, 53, 67, 78, 83, 96, 149, 219, 220
Northwest Ordinance, 28, 68, 70
Nott, Josiah, 92
Nuckolls, W. T., 32
Nullification, 1, 2, 33–61, 103, 116, 159, 221; crisis, 1, 9, 51–54; economics of, 7, 19; significance of, 9–10; and slavery linked, 9–10, 12, 14, 19, 25, 64; Calhoun leadership of, 10, 15, 19–26, 30, 32–37, 43–44, 47–50, 53–56, 59, 64–77, 80–86, 96, 131; and Negro Seamen's Act, 15; Turnbull propaganda for, 17–18; theory development, 19,

21–25; Calhoun articulates doctrine of, 20–25, 26, 86; and secession, 23; and traditional states' rights, 24; Jackson opposes, 27, 29–30, 32, 49–55, 57; first public debate over, 27–32; discourse of, 34–37; unionist opposition to, 38–39, 117; and election of 1832 victories, 44, 45–47; and test oath controversy, 48, 49, 51, 57–59; legislation enacting, 48–49; national response to, 49–56; radical vs. moderate, 56; new ordinance of, 57; political aftermath of, 59; Grayson and, 108, *See also* Judicial nullification
Nullification convention, 47–49, 56–57
Nullifiers. *See* Nullification

O'Connor, Michael, 199
O'Neall, John Belton, 38, 58, 60, 100, 200, 218, 231
Opposition Party, 207
Orangeburg district, 45, 73, 79, 120, 130, 211
Orangeburg *Southron*, 155, 179, 198, 218
Ordinance of Secession (1860), 244
Oregon question, 66, 69, 70, 79, 88
Orr, James L., 76, 112–13, 122, 128, 214; and slave trade revival, 133, 138, 174; and defeat of James H. Adams, 134; and *Wanderer* case, 171; and Democratic convention, 189, 198–99, 203; and House speakership, 190; slavery justification by, 228; and secession, 230, 240, 243, 249, 251
Ostend manifesto, 128, 174
Owens, W. A., 80, 113, 116

Pacheo, Antonio, 89
Paine, Tom, 256
Pakenham, Richard, 65
Palmer, Benjamin Morgan, 247
Palmer, John S., 117, 244
Palmetto state. *See* South Carolina
Parish system, 13, 226
Patriot (periodical), 117–18
Paulding, J. K., 115

Payne, Henry B., 201

Pee Dee Times, 155

Pendleton district, 12, 34, 44, 45, 110, 119

Pendleton Messenger, 114

Pennington, William, 210

Pennsylvania, 53, 59

Perkins, John, 185

Perry, Benjamin F., 16, 20, 34, 37–41, 44, 58, 100, 107, 109, 110, 190, 191, 208, 212; and postnullification, 51, 56, 60, 74; confederacy predicted by, 59; and support for southern states convention, 79; on Calhoun, 85; and southern nationalism, 114; and secession, 117, 217, 240–41; and presidential electors, 121–22; opposition to slave trade revival, 129, 132; and Kansas, 192; and Democratic convention, 199, 202–3; and election of 1860, 231–32; and Hammond, 232

Perry, M. S., 220, 243

Personal liberty laws, 78

Petigru, James, 35, 38, 40, 52, 54, 100, 211; and test oath case, 58; on Calhoun, 59; unionism of, 60, 107, 196–97, 231, 245; and secession, 108, 114, 238, 244, 246, 251; on illegal slave trade, 166; on Douglas, 196–97; on feared slave uprisings, 215; and start of Civil War, 253, 254

Pettigrew, J. Johnston, 133–34, 138, 165, 199, 204

Pettus, John J., 220

Pickens, Francis W., 30, 34–35, 37, 67, 189, 208; and nullification origination, 20; and Nashville convention, 97; and Butler, 113; and S.C. convention, 121; and secession, 191, 239; on proposed slave code, 194–95; as governor, 243; declaration of S.C. independence by, 251; and Sumter, 253–54

Pickens district, 44, 57, 238

Piedmont district, 44, 120, 135, 240

Pierce, Franklin, 122

Pike, Albert J., 145

Pinckney, Charles Cotesworth, 15, 136, 246

Pinckney, Henry L., 34, 40, 42, 60

Pinckney family, 14

Piracy Act of 1820, 146, 148, 153, 156, 157, 159; nullification of, 170, 171

Plantation belt, 10, 11, 44, 95–96, 118–19

Plantation economy, 9–14, 16, 46; 1850s revival of, 128

Planter politicians, 2–6, 64, 88, 130, 229; southernism leadership by, 1, 2, 9, 60–64, 68, 70, 73–74, 80–81, 88, 93, 95–97, 108, 122–23, 187, 188, 208, 217–35 passim, 242–43, 245, 254; ideology of, 4, 89; power of, 6, 9, 13, 19, 80–82, 93, 95–97; as counterrevolutionaries, 7, 255–58; antidemocratic world of, 9–14, 26–27, 123, 196, 225; as elite ruling class, 10, 12, 13–14, 22–23, 46; nullification support by, 10, 17, 19, 31–34, 46, 60; and perceived threats to slavery, 14–15; as anti-tariff, 22; and Jacksonian reforms, 26–27; Calhoun leadership of, 34, 64, 72, 105; unionist rhetoric against, 39–40; convention control by, 47; and expansion of slavery, 68, 70, 128–30, 138, 172–73; and Wilmot's Proviso, 72; and election of 1848, 75; and southern movement, 79, 251; and vigilance and safety committees, 79–80; and Compromise of 1850, 99; and southern unity strategy, 105–6; cooperationist-separatist division among, 120; support for slave trade revival by, 125, 128, 135–37, 181; and illegal slave trade, 172–73; political unity of, 188; and Democratic party, 188, 191, 200, 229; and proposed slave code, 196; vulnerability of, 207; precautions against slave uprisings by, 214–15; slavery's perpetuation as primary force behind, 220; as secession movement leaders, 222; and national power, 229–30; and secession convention, 243; and federal fort takeover, 251–52, 253

Planter's College, 223

Poindexter, George, 53
Poinsett, Joel R., 16, 38, 52, 60, 85, 100; unionism of, 107, 114, 117
Polk, James K., 66, 67, 68, 69, 74, 79
Pollard, Edward, 126, 140
Pope, J. D., 199, 204, 216, 244
Pope, William, 41
Popular sovereignty, 74–75, 192, 194, 195–96, 200, 201, 231
Porcher, Frederick A. ("F. A. P.," "P. A. F."), 158
Porter, W. D., 147, 172, 199, 232, 234, 238
Prentiss, William O., 246
Presbyterian Church in the Confederate States of America, 247–48
Preston, John S., 113, 203, 205, 220, 248
Preston, William Campbell, 17, 21, 34, 35, 51, 54; on slave trade revival, 131–32, 167
Prince George Winyaw Parish, 44, 129, 198
Prince William's Parish, 44
Pringle, James, 40
Property: representation based on, 4, 13, 225; slaves as, 71, 89, 129–30, 135, 165, 178; proslavery defense of, 89, 224
Proslavery Argument, The (Hammond, Harper, Simms), 123
Proslavery ideology, 14, 17, 87–93, 222–29; planter politicians' leadership in, 1, 2, 68, 70, 73–74, 88, 122–23, 187, 208, 228; as reactionary, 5; and gender inequality, 5, 90; pamphlet writers, 15, 101, 103; Christian defenders of, 15–16, 64, 91–92, 102–3, 112, 223–24, 226; biblical citations for, 15–16, 89, 91–92, 102, 103, 155, 224, 226; nullifier discourse and, 35, 51, 64; unionist converts to, 59; based on southern identity, 63–64, 93, 210, 222–23; Calhoun's contributions to, 65–66, 77–78, 87–88; and secession movement, 100–103, 220, 226, 246, 247; on slave trade revival, 128–29, 131, 136, 140, 151; as nativist, 130, 196; dogma of, 165, 222–29; as counterrevolutionary,

255–58. See also Expansion of slavery
Proudhon, Pierre-Joseph, 89
Pryor, Roger A., 148, 178, 254

Quattlebaum, Paul, 198–200
Quitman, John, 67, 106, 110, 126

Racism, 5, 67, 88, 89–90, 92, 128, 139
Rainey, Dr., 157
Ramsay, John, 19
Randolph, John, 16, 24
Ravenel, Henry, 215
Ravenel, Thomas, 200, 202
Raymond, Daniel, 22
Raymond, Henry J., 182, 245
Read, J. Harleston, 72, 129, 216
Reconstruction, 14, 78
Report against the Alien and Sedition Acts (Madison), 21, 25
Representation: property-based, 4, 13, 225; Calhoun and, 22–23; upcountry complaints about, 41, 43–44, 47–48; in S.C. secession convention, 243–44; secession as blow against, 246; Thornwell and, 247
Republicanism, 3–5, 9, 10, 25, 123; nullification as subversion of, 49
Republican Party, 161, 215, 245; southern view of, 149–51, 172, 178, 182, 188–203 passim, 208–10, 214, 216–20, 225, 226, 229–33, 236, 239, 245, 247, 249, 254–55; and illegal slave trade, 173, 174, 178, 180; and Democratic Party, 188, 189, 201; as challenge to slavery, 188, 221, 224; 1860 presidential ticket, 207; and speakership controversy, 209–10
Revolutions of 1848, 88, 255. See also Egalitarianism
Rhett, Edmund, 108, 111, 167, 180, 198, 204
Rhett, R. B., Jr., 137, 167, 179, 197, 204–5, 237, 244
Rhett, Robert Barnwell, 70, 73, 76, 80, 106, 196, 219, 230; and Bluffton movement, 65; as secession leader, 80, 116, 136, 138–39, 190,

193–94, 197, 235, 238–39, 243; eulogy for Calhoun, 86; as Nashville convention delegate, 97–98; on Fugitive Slave Act, 99–100; bellicosity of, 108; Senate seat of, 109, 122, 134; and single secession, 113–14, 116, 197; and southern congress, 119; and slave trade revival, 126–27, 130–31, 137, 148, 167, 179, 183–84; secessionist agenda of, 130–31; and Democratic state conventions, 189, 204–5; and Richmond convention, 203; and speakership controversy, 210; and public safety plan, 212; and Breckinridge, 229; secession address, 249; and southern convention, 250. *See also* Smith, Robert Barnwell

Rhett family, 14, 242

Rhode Island, 88

Rice plantations, 12

Richard Cobden (slaver ship), 162–63

Richardson, F. D., 127, 130, 132, 155–56

Richardson, John P., 42, 43, 59, 109, 111, 121, 238

Richardson, John S., 37, 38, 57, 58

Richardson family, 14, 242.

Richland district, 44, 45, 79, 180, 235

Richmond convention, 203–7

Richmond Enquirer, 53, 139, 148

Rising Sun (Newberry), 229

Ritchie, Thomas, 53

Robinson, Armstead, 257

Rocky Creek Baptist Church, 164

Rogers, James, 58

Ruffin, Edmund, 120, 126, 139, 164, 194, 213, 254; and secession, 205–6, 219, 237, 245; and speakership controversy, 209; proslavery articles of, 223

Runnels, Hardin R., 143

Russell, John, 109

Rutledge, B. H., 230

Rutledge, John, 72, 158

Rutledge, Rebecca, 52, 54

Rutledge family, 14, 241

Safety committees, 212

St. Andrew's Parish, 18, 44

St. Bartholomew's Parish, 44, 115

St. George Dorchester Parish, 45, 47, 204

St. Helena's Parish, 36

St. James's Goose Creek Parish, 45, 47, 115, 120

St. John's Berkeley Parish, 44, 115, 130, 212

St. John's Colleton Parish, 18, 115, 130

St. Mathew's Parish, 115, 179

St. Michael's Parish, 40, 134

St. Paul, Henry, 142

St. Paul's Agricultural Society, 18

St. Paul's Parish, 44, 204

St. Philip's Parish, 40, 134

St. Stephen's Parish, 44, 79, 115, 204

Say, Jean-Baptiste, 256

Scott, A. L., 145

Scott, Winfield, 52

Seabrook, Whitemarsh, 15, 18, 19, 34, 41, 72; as governor, 79, 81–82, 85, 100, 105–6, 108; and secession, 113–14; and S.C. convention, 121

Seabrook family, 242

Secession, 1–3, 7, 68, 86, 187–253; S.C. leadership in, 1, 2, 100, 187–90, 198, 219–21, 229–30, 243–46, 249–50, 254; first crisis of, 1, 64, 93, 95–124, 221; as demise of Second Party System, 2, 187; early support for, 17–18; Calhoun justifies, 23–24, 49, 80–81, 86, 87, 246; Hartford convention and, 25, 28; nullifier threat of, 33, 48, 49–50, 51; former unionist leaders support, 59, 60; planter politicians lead, 60–61, 80–81, 187, 217–18; justifications for, 63, 190, 216, 226–27, 246–48; as constitutional right, 63, 190, 245–46; Fairfield resolutions and, 74; politics of, 79, 256; and party rivalries, 95, 191; joint vs. individual state, 96, 103–4, 108–22, 197, 230; propaganda for, 100–101, 103, 115, 215–16, 232–34, 240; ideology of, 102, 193; clergy supporters of, 102–3, 112, 246–48; and slave trade revival, 129–31, 136, 139–41, 142, 150, 151–52, 178–79, 181–86; and election of Republican president, 130–

31, 149, 150, 151, 172, 178, 182,
188, 189, 190, 199, 210, 214, 216,
219–20, 221, 229–33, 236, 237,
245, 249; and slavery, 154, 178–81,
183, 246, 247; and vigilante violence, 188, 234–35, 241; and sectional differences, 191, 193–94;
from Democratic national convention, 202–3; and Harpers Ferry
raid, 207–8; out-of-state support
for, 235–37; mobilization for, 239;
unanimous S.C. vote on, 244; slavery as official cause of, 248–49;
commissioners, 249–50; states following S.C., 250, 254; and occupation of federal facilities, 252; counterrevolutionary nature of, 255–58;
Marxist view of, 256

Secession conventions, 181, 183, 235,
237–39, 241–44, 248–49, 250

Secessionist party, 193–94

Second Party System, 2, 187

Seddon, James, 67

Select Committee of Twenty One, 48,
111

Senate. *See* Congress, U.S.

Separatism, 2–3, 6, 43, 79, 113–22

Seward, William Henry, 82, 85, 167,
174–75, 192, 232

Sharkey, William, 82, 97, 104, 106

Sherman, John, 209–10

Shorter, Eli, 182

Simkins, Arthur, 196, 200, 202, 230

Simms, William Gilmore, 38, 59,
67, 69, 76, 90, 192, 195, 207; and
secession, 74, 116, 218, 235, 241–
42; on slavery, 89, 123; and Nashville convention, 97; on compromises, 99; on California, 105; on
single secession, 108, 116; and withdrawal of African squadron, 146;
and southern nationality, 191; and
Richmond convention, 206

Simons, James, 116, 199, 202, 216,
237

Slave code, 194–97, 199, 201

Slaveholders. *See* Planter politicians

Slave rebellion, fears of, 15, 80, 100,
211–14, 223, 249, 257

Slavery: political significance of, 2–5,
7, 9–13; and nullification, 9–10, 12,

14, 19, 25, 64; and tariff, 14, 16–19,
32; states' rights and, 24, 56; unionist moderates on, 38–39, 59; and
Jacksonian democracy, 50–51; and
Republican Party, 188; economics
of, 194–97, 199, 201; S.C. commitment to, 220; counterrevolution of,
244, 250, 255–58; as official cause
of secession, 248–49; as central to
Confederacy, 250; Marxist view of,
256, 258. *See also* Expansion of slavery; Slaves

Slaves, 6; as majority in S.C., 9, 12, 46,
213, 258; as property, 71, 89, 129–
30, 135, 165, 178; and former masters, 256–58

Slave trade. *See* African slave trade
revival movement; District of
Columbia; Domestic slave trade;
Interstate slave trade

Slave Trade Acts, 172

Slave trade meetings, 179

Slave traders. *See* African slave trade
revival movement

Slidell, John, 126–27, 167, 173, 177,
206

Smith, Adam, 256

Smith, Alfred A., 215

Smith, Junius, 80

Smith, Robert Barnwell, 34, 36–8,
56, 58–59. *See also* Rhett, Robert
Barnwell

Smith, Whitefoord, 91, 103, 240, 246

Smith, William, 16, 19, 20, 30

Smith family, 14, 41

Sneed, William, 147

Social contract theory, 224, 256

Soule, Pierre, 67, 96

South Africa, 244

South Carolina, 1–32, 105, 219; secession by, 1, 221, 248, 254 (*see also*
Secession); antebellum politics,
1–6, 9–10, 13–15; exceptionalism,
2, 11, 53–54, 80, 96; proslavery politics, 9–10; slave economy, 9–11, 16,
46, 128; geographical division,
10–11; 1820–1860 population,
12; absence of two-party system in,
14, 60–61; and national vs. states
rights, 16; tariff opposition, 17;
separatist politics, 34, 110–11; leg-

islative politics, 41–42; test oath controversy, 48, 49, 51, 57–59; legislative nullification actions, 48–49; judicial nullification by, 73, 153–54, 170, 171; and southern nationalism, 74, 96, 105–6, 110, 121–22; southern movement in, 81; and death of Calhoun, 85–86; and first secession crisis, 95–124; single vs. joint secessionist debate in, 96, 103–4, 108–9, 112, 114–16; Nashville convention delegation, 97–98; cardinal political beliefs, 123; and slave trade revival, 125–52; white population growth in, 135; and Confederate Constitution, 184; withdrawal of from Democratic convention, 202; expulsion of northerners from, 211–12; as first seceding state, 221, 243; as proslavery utopia, 225–26; leaders on secession, 230–32; legislative elections of 1860, 235; federal fort stalemate, 251–52. *See also* Calhoun, John C.; Nullification; Planter politicians

South Carolina Association, 15, 80, 213

South Carolina College, 17, 103, 107, 115, 118, 126

South Carolina convention, 109–10, 121–22

South Carolina Exposition and Protest (Calhoun), 21–23, 25, 26

South Carolina State Rights and Free Trade Party, 36

Southern Address, 203, 206

Southern commercial conventions, 144–48

Southern congress, 109, 113, 119–20

Southern convention, 42–43, 76, 78, 79, 81–82, 218–20, 239, 249–50

Southern Episcopalian, 165–66, 179

Southern Guardian, 155

Southern Literary Messenger, 183

Southern Methodist Episcopalian Church, 166

Southern movement, 64, 77–79, 81–82, 93; divisions over secession in, 96–98; ideological unity of, 103–5. *See also* First secession crisis

Southern nationalism, 2, 5, 18, 19, 63–93, 125, 138; nullification and, 36, 38; slavery and, 63–64, 87–93, 101, 102, 105, 178, 187, 210, 221–23, 234; S.C. unity on, 74, 96, 105–6, 110, 121–22; Calhoun's death and, 85–86; basis of, 87–89, 93; progress to 1850 of, 93; and yeomanry, 95, 234; and single vs. joint secession, 104, 115; unionist opponents of, 106–7; and Georgia platform, 110–11; S.C. separatists and, 115–16; slave trade and, 142, 151–52, 153, 178, 182–83; and border states, 187–88; Upper South resistance to, 187–88; and House speakership, 210; triumph and failure of, 222; and S.C. Ordinance of Secession, 244. *See also* Confederacy; Expansion of slavery; Secession

Southern Nationalist Party, 109

Southern Patriot, 114, 129

Southern Presbyterian Review, 112

Southern Press, 73, 103–5

Southern Quarterly Review, 111

Southern Rights Associations, 100, 111, 114, 115

Southern Rights Party, 106

Southern Standard, 114, 126, 131, 133

Southern Times, 34

Spain, A. C., 242

Spartan, 114, 122

Spartanburg district, 12, 44, 45, 47, 51, 117; unionist societies, 51, 52, 241; test oath opposition, 57; and southern convention, 79; and first secession vote, 110, 119, 120; cooperationists, 114; slave rebellion fears, 214; and secession, 240, 241

Speakership controversy, 208–10

Spratt, William Leonidas, 162, 164, 167, 179, 184; and slave trade revival, 126–27, 133–37, 140–41, 144–45, 147–51, 185; and *Echo* case, 155–57, 160–61; and secession, 190, 236, 238, 243, 249; on slavery, 227

Spruance, Peleg, 69

Squatter sovereignty. *See* Popular sovereignty

Starke, Peter B., 219

Star of the West (ship), 252
State interposition, 19, 27, 42, 43, 54, 56
State Rights and Free Trade Associations, 36
State Rights and Free Trade Evening Post, 51
State Rights and Free Trade Party, 32, 47
State sovereignty, 1, 23–24, 49, 58, 63, 70–71, 84, 87, 96, 123, 190, 225, 234, 247
States' rights, 10, 16, 17, 19, 21, 32, 71, 149; and absolute state sovereignty, 23–24, 56; and Hayne-Webster debate, 28, 29; Jacksonian view of, 29; and nullification, 37, 53; unionist advocates of, 38; and Democratic Party, 188, 189
State veto. *See* Nullification
Stephens, Alexander, 77, 83, 106, 144
Stono rebellion (1739), 213
Stowe, Harriet Beecher, 123
Stringfellow, Thornton, 223–24
Stroyer, Jacob, 257
Suffrage, 13, 87, 224, 225–26, 236, 242, 248
Sullivan, J. M., 240
Sullivan's Island, 52
Sumner, Charles, 130, 209, 225
Sumter, Thomas, 39
Sumter district, 18, 31, 45, 79, 130, 204, 237; and first secession vote, 110; cooperationists in, 114
Sydney letters (Pickens), 20

Takaki, Ronald, 125, 128
Tariff bill (1824), 16
Tariff controversy, 10, 14–20, 26–38; nullifiers on, 34–38; and nullification ordinance, 48–49; and Jackson, 50, 54–55; and nullification, 53; and Clay compromise, 54–55, 56, 57
Tariff of 1828, 20, 48–49
Tariff of 1832, 32, 48
Tariff of 1842, 65
Tarpley, Collin S., 82
Taylor, Colonel, 39
Taylor, John, 38–39
Taylor, J. W., 142

Taylor, Zachary, 75–77, 82–83, 99, 202
Tazewell, Littleton Waller, 53, 67
Tennant, William, 232–33
Tennessee, 53, 78, 96, 142, 144, 150, 218–19
Territories, slavery in. *See* Expansion of slavery
Test oath (nullification ordinance), 48, 49, 51, 57–59
Texas, 71, 96, 98, 105, 142, 143, 145, 219; annexation of, 65–66, 84; and 1860 Democratic convention, 202, 206; slave panic of 1860, 214, 233; secession by, 250
Thompson, Jacob, 252
Thompson, Waddy, 34–35, 41, 67, 253–54
Thomson, A. W., 237
Thornwell, James Henley, 85, 103, 110, 112, 247; Christian proslavery ideology of, 91, 92; conservativism of, 92, 123; opposition to slave trade revival by, 165; and *Wanderer* case, 171; and secession convention, 243; secession justification by, 247–48; on South's Civil War reversals, 258
Toombs, Robert, 71, 77, 83, 106, 144, 176–77, 237
Towns, Governor, 105
Townsend, Edward C., 160–61
Townsend, John, 101–2, 127, 205, 233–34, 243
Tradewell, James, 193
Treaty of Guadalupe Hidalgo, 69
Trenholm, George, 237, 239
Trescot, William Henry, 91, 101–2, 138–39, 146, 172, 191, 198, 199, 208, 209, 236, 251, 252; and slave trade revival, 181; and Kansas, 192; and federal slave code, 195
Troup, George M., 53, 55
Trowbridge, N. C., 163, 168
Troy, D. S., 149
Tucker, Beverly, 75, 78, 90, 97, 110
Turnbull, Robert J. ("Brutus"), 15, 17–18, 20, 34–35, 48, 74, 145
Turner, Nat, 15, 207
Tyler, John, 54–55, 65, 66, 147
Tyler, John, Jr., 224, 233–34

INDEX

Uncle Tom's Cabin (Stowe), 123
Union, 44, 49, 84, 86; and Jackson, 50, 79; and secession, 246
Union and State Rights Party, 52
Union Army, 251–52, 257–58
Union Convention (1832), 39
Union district, 57, 58, 120
Unionists, 29, 31, 33, 35; on slavery, 38–39; against nullification, 38–41; and nullification crisis, 45, 51–52, 54, 57; in hill country, 49, 60, 95, 240, 241; test oath opposition by, 57–59; and secession movements, 59, 60, 100, 106–7, 114, 121, 183, 188, 196–97, 225, 231–32, 235, 239, 240–41, 242, 245; postnullification attitudes of, 59–60; anti-Wilmot Proviso meetings, 74; as Democratic Party adherents, 79, 202; and Nashville convention, 96; and first secession crisis, 106–8; and cooperationists, 114; and oppositional politics, 118–19; and slave trade revival, 129, 143, 150–51, 166–67; and smuggling of slaves, 166; in western Virginia, 218; conditional, 225; and 1860 presidential election, 231; reactions to S.C. secession, 245
Union Party, 38–43, 47; beliefs of, 38–39; during nullification, 42, 43, 59–60; and election of 1832, 44, 45; resistance to test oath, 58–59; response to first secessionist crisis, 106–7
United States Telegraph, 19
Upcountry, 13; opposition to nullification, 41; complaints about representation, 41, 43–44; unionist voters, 44, 240; separatist vote, 120
Upper South, 97, 105, 142, 148, 149, 182, 183; resistance to southern nationalism, 187–88, 202, 203; state secession in, 250; secession compromises, 254
Upshur, Abel P., 53–54, 65
Utah, 98, 106

Van Buren, Martin, 20, 27, 30–31, 50, 53, 55, 65, 75
Venable, Abraham Watkins, 67

Verplanck, Gullian, 31, 54–55
Verplanck Act, 54–55
Vesey, Denmark, 15, 207, 213
Vicksburg convention (1859), 149–51, 171–72, 180
Vigilantism, 79, 188, 211–15, 234–35, 241
Virginia, 9, 16, 26, 53, 54, 67, 75, 206; resolution against Wilmot Proviso, 71, 78; and first secession crisis, 105, 107; and slave trade revival, 145, 148, 149, 183; and Southern Address, 203; resistance to S.C. secession, 217–18; secession by, 254
Virginia Resolutions and Report of 1798 and 1800, 21, 25, 28, 29, 56
Voting rights. *See* Suffrage

Waldo, Benjamin, 205, 218
Walker, Leroy Pope, 182, 201
Wallace, Daniel, 82, 113
Wallace, W. L., 211
Walterborough speech (Hamilton), 20
Walton, Thomas, 149
Wanderer case, 162–65, 167–71, 174, 180, 181–82
Wayland, Francis, 91
Wayne, James M., 157, 160–61, 168, 170–71
Webster, Daniel, 32, 219; and debate with Hayne, 27–29; nullification opposition by, 49, 50, 55–56; and Calhoun, 84–85
Webster-Ashburton Treaty (1842), 126, 133, 146–48, 173, 177
Whig Party, 65, 66, 67, 69, 71; and Z. Taylor candidacy, 75–76; and southern politics, 77, 79, 82–83, 96–99, 106, 123, 131
Whitner, Benjamin F., 41, 75, 110
Wigfall, Louis T., 126, 139–40, 182
Wilkins, William, 55
Wilkins Act of 1833 (Force Act), 55, 57, 65, 193
Williams, David Rogerson, 37–38
Williamsburg district, 44–45, 129, 211–12
Wilmot, David, 68–69

Wilmot Proviso, 64, 68, 71–74, 76, 78, 82, 83, 84, 93, 231
Wilson, B. H., 198–99, 237
Wilson, Henry, 172, 174–76
Wilson, J. Leighton, 166
Wilson, John, 15, 26
Winsmith, John, 237–38, 240
Winyaw Intelligencer, 38
Wise, Henry, 209
Withers, T. J., 113, 211, 250
Witherspoon, Robert, 42
Women's rights, 5, 90, 227
Wood, Gordon, 25
Woodward, J. A., 70, 71, 89
Woollens bill (1827), 18, 19
Wooster, Ralph, 13, 243
Wyllys, Harold, 212

Yale University, 25
Yancey, William Lowndes, 59, 67, 75, 97, 106, 222–23; and secession, 107, 194; and slave trade revival, 126, 139, 148–49, 178, 182–83; and slave code proposal, 197; and Charleston convention, 201–3; and Baltimore convention, 206–7
Yates, Robert E., 43
Yeadon, Richard, 36, 59, 100, 107, 132, 159, 190, 192, 229, 231
Yeoman farmers, 5, 6, 9, 41, 43–44, 53, 117; as minority, 10; unionism of, 40, 60, 95, 110, 212–13, 240, 241; opposition to test oath by, 57–58; secession views of, 97, 234, 240–41; and opposition to slave trade revival, 135
York district, 44, 45, 79, 114, 120, 195
Yorkville Enquirer, 155, 179
Yorkville Pioneer, 38–39
Yulee, David, 67, 177